OTHER NORTH SHORE BOOKS
BY JOSEPH E. GARLAND

LONE VOYAGER
The Life of Howard Blackburn

THAT GREAT PATTILLO
The Life of James William Pattillo

THE GLOUCESTER GUIDE
A Stroll through Place and Time

GUNS OFF GLOUCESTER
Cape Ann in the American Revolution

DOWN TO THE SEA
The Fishing Schooners of Gloucester

ADVENTURE
Queen of the Windjammers

THE EASTERN YACHT CLUB
A History from 1870 to 1985

GLOUCESTER ON THE WIND
A Photographic History of America's Greatest Fishing Port
in the Days of Sail: 1870 to 1938

BEATING TO WINDWARD
A voyage in the *Gloucester Daily Times* through the stormy
years from 1967 to 1973

BEAM REACH
Further voyaging in the *Gloucester Daily Times* with other
miscellaneous musings from 1951 to 1997

THE NORTH SHORE
A Social History of Summers Among the Noteworthy,
Fashionable, Rich, Eccentric and Ordinary on Boston's Gold
Coast, 1823–1929

Eastern Point

*A Nautical, Rustical and More or Less
Sociable Chronicle of Gloucester's Outer
Shield and Inner Sanctum, 1606–1990*

Eastern Point

JOSEPH E. GARLAND

Commonwealth Editions

Beverly, Massachusetts

First published by William L. Bauhan,
Dublin, New Hampshire, 1971, 1973.

Library of Congress Catologing-in-Publication Data
Garland, Joseph E.
  Eastern Point : a nautical, rustical and more or less
sociable chronicle of Gloucester's outer shield and inner
sanctum, 1606–1990 / by Joseph E. Garland
      p.   cm.
  Includes biobliographical references and index.
  ISBN 1-889833-07-X (cloth : alk. paper)
  1. Eastern Point (Mass. : Cape)--History.
2. Gloucester Region (Mass.)--History. I. Title
F74.G5G313 1999
974.4'5--dc21   99-22392
                                                                CIP

Frontispiece: Niles Pond about 1900
(Martha Rogers Harvey photo)

Designed by Joyce C. Weston.

Published and distributed by Commonwealth Editions,
an imprint of Memoirs Unlimited, Inc.,
21 Lothrop Street, Beverly, Mass. 01915.
Printed in the United States of America.

CONTENTS

In memoriam

J. G. and M. C. G.

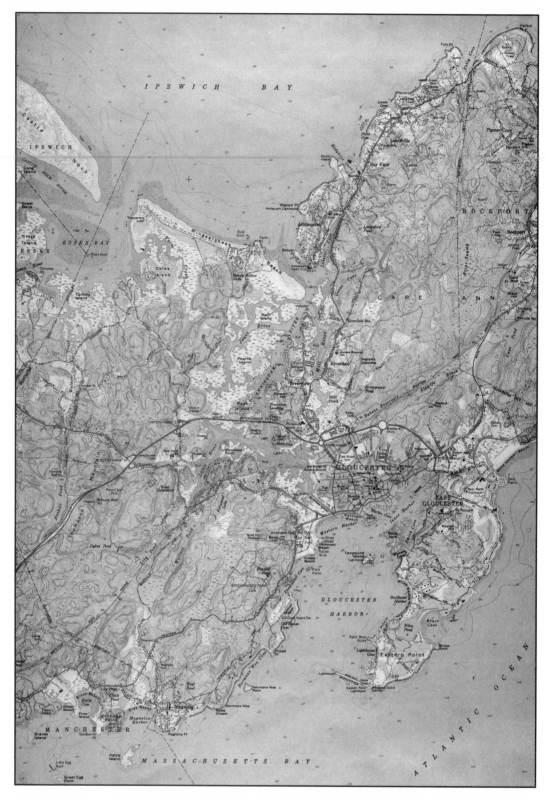

Eastern Point makes Gloucester Harbor.

PREFACE TO THE FIRST EDITION

How FANTASTIC TO FANCY THAT our subject should have shaped the destiny of the nation! And how delightfully true! If you want verification, ask the local historian (myself) and he will tell you with solemn pedantry that the jut of ledge called Eastern Point (by which was meant in the old times the whole of East Gloucester, Bass Rocks and Rocky Neck) *made* Gloucester *the* port from which to catch the cod (staple of the Bay Colony, fuel of the political engine) and, ergo, altered the course of empire.

Therefore, because we are diffident about such patent claims to fame and glory, and shamelessly self-centered, it was the more surprising that out of our umbilical preoccupation a book should emerge. It develops that all the while it was putting Gloucester on the map this modest peninsula of something less than three square miles has been making its own history, a curiosity, an intricacy of joy, terror, love, hate, villainy, suspense, humor, heroism, the poetic, the whimsical, the beautiful and the bizarre.

Not unexpectedly, the sea-laved contours of the Point have lured countless hapless craft and cracked their bones, even as they have warned away or sheltered their sisters without number. In nearly four hundred years of settlement, it hasn't yet been really subdued by the hand or soul of man, for it is more of sea than land. May it remain so. Over its centuries it has harbored a most uncommon fleet of human vessels from the seas of life, whose commonality is their surrender to it. May it continue to.

To the discriminating observer the Point is an islandlike laboratory, the more curious due to the success of successive owners in sequestering their sanctum from indiscriminate trespass. The historic curbs on public access are ideologically if not legally moot, but I dare say this jealous watch by a dynasty of landholders has preserved the environment (including now a wildlife sanctuary) rather more happily than would have been the event had its fate resided in the consciences of speculators and politicians.

Unhappily, no island (let alone a pinpoint twenty miles from Boston) is an island any longer when trespassed by those pervasive vandals, the offshore winds and tides of poison and pollution. And we are in double jeopardy: this precious place exists precariously in a society desperate for virtue, haunted by crisis, taut with frustration, torn by violence. It is a resort of privilege, and like privilege everywhere and always, it remains inviolate by sufferance of the whole.

So we wonder: can an exurban retreat, even as seabound as Eastern Point, protect itself forever behind its ramparts, its ledges and legalities, when all around, the trumpets are sounding? Can a society? The answer is no in either case, not without wide and drastic cures, granted time . . . a luxury which is in shorter supply by the minute.

The world is still decorated with points and pockets like ours. But they are shrinking. Their natural defenses are under unnatural siege. The future of the beautiful places is dark.

Should the reading of this light chronicle sharpen somewhat the old saw that past is porlogue, and hone the edge of your conviction that the future of all the Eastern Points deserves to be spared the fate of epilogue, any slight purpose to which it pretends will have been served.

And now I make special acknowledgment to the memory of the late Winifred Kay Shepard, who lived over seventy of her summers on Eastern Point and knew it as no one else; she first unlocked its past for me, and without her inspiration and memories this work would not have been undertaken. And how much would have been missed without the astounding power of recall, reaching back ninety years, of the late James C. Walen, who died last month at the age of ninety-eight! Nor can I forget the exhortation of our late poet Charles Olson to write Gloucester history "still celebratable. . . . As *a Garland,* an Eastern Pointer, you bridge the gap between Reverend Bentley's Diary—and Babson—to the Present. So you have an opportunity??" I am glad that I did.

Finally, to my good friend and fellow Pointer Donald F. Monell, whose counsel and assistance have been with me from start to finish, and to my neighbors in the Association of Eastern Point Residents for their backing, my thanks.

J. E. G.

"Black Bess," Eastern Point
September 1970

PREFACE TO THE SECOND EDITION

Closing in on thirty years since the first appearance of *Eastern Point* and fifty years since its 1950 cut-off, and with the millenium dead ahead, and my seventy-fifth birthday in the rearview mirror, it seemed that the time might be ripe for correction, expansion and some judicious updating.

The result follows, thanks to Webster Bull, publisher in 1998 of *The North Shore,* a somewhat condensed version of the two-volume regional history to which *Eastern Point* gave rise. His Commonwealth Editions took it on when Gordon Baird and fourteen other neighbors in our Association of Eastern Point Residents pledged the means to prime the pump for the production of what has turned out to be not a smaller but a very much bigger book about a very small place that's as small as ever.

There were numerous corrections to be taken care of, then folders of more material and illustrations gathered over three decades since the first time around, finally the knotty matter of updating.

Fortuitously, a near epidemic of generational departures made 1950 an appropriate terminus for the first edition, and in 1969, the year I began it, the midcentury was just far enough astern to avoid most of the entanglements with one's contemporaries in such a work as this—a dilemma a neighborly writer of mild temperament and only ten years' residence sought to avoid.

The pace of life has unnecessarily if inevitably quickened in thirty years, perforce pushing me more than I'd prefer to bring matters to 1990, too close for comfort. Not wishing merely to avoid offending my *contemporary* contemporaries equally by omission or commission, it occurred to me that by combining the roles of chronicler, essayist and memoirist I might personalize the sequel enough to be forgiven idiosyncracies and, God forbid, outright inaccuracies—and be damned more or less equally by all, if that be my fate.

Most of us Pointers today are year-rounders, enchanted by the springs and autumns, and the rises and falls, by turns fascinated and frustrated in the windy embrace or clutch of a winter that is noticeably milder and briefer than elsewhere on the coast, and we care more about our environment than ever because we have to. We socialize less, drink less, smoke less, rely less if at all on domestic help, perhaps take ourselves more seriously than our predecessors, may even on occasion work harder, and are infinitely more afflicted with road rage.

Are we less interesting? I am not sure, but I suspect so. It is more challenging to be interesting, not to mention informative, when communication has been digitalized, when more and more of us are talking and fewer and fewer listening. But who knows? Nostalgia tends to be for days one never knew.

To Helen, who put up with all the *Sturm und Drang* of it with her usual serenity, and to whom I was betrothed in 1945, I avow again my gratitude for the second chance. After thirty-three years of incommunicado, we were married in 1981 on the sun porch of "Black Bess," surely by foreordination:

> (1) She acquired her house on the Hudson in New York in 1959 from the late George Fraser, brother of our neighbor Sarah Fraser Robbins, the year I got "Black Bess" here. Coincidence?
> (2) Her late aunt Mollie Williams Bryan, a granddaughter of Mrs. Raymond, mistress of "The Ramparts," summered up the road. Coincidence?
> (3) My great, great, great, great-grandmother Rogers sold the largest portion of the Eastern Point farm, including the lot we inhabit, to Major Addison Plumer of Gloucester, with whom Helen shares direct descent from the Plumer settlers of Newbury. He sold to J. P. Cushing, who sold it to my great, great-grandfather Niles.
> Coincidence? Destiny!

I would express my warm appreciation to Webster Bull and to his wife Katie (who coped endlessly with "just a couple more" illustrations) for being so tolerant of a volume that has expanded before their very eyes like over-yeasted bread dough.

And my gratitude to Gordon and Joe Ann Hart Baird, Richard and Winnie Bell, Dorothy A. Brown, George and Judith Carter, Theodore and Janice Charles, William and Susan Copeland, Robert and Jan Crandall, Jochen and Ute Haller von Hallerstein, John Haley, Frederick and Harriet Holdsworth, Daniel and Jenifer McDougall, Sarah Fraser Robbins, Roger Saunders, Kenneth P. Weiss, and Linda and the late Edward P. Williams for providing the yeast.

J. E. G.

"Black Bess," Eastern Point
February 1999

Eastern Point

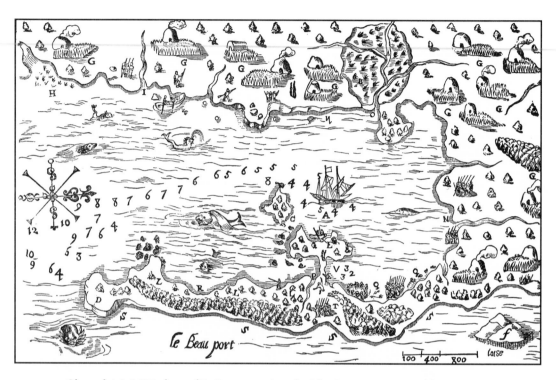

Le Beau port

Champlain's 1606 chart of Le Beauport ringed with wigwams recreates his encounter with the natives near Rocky Neck. The central wooded area of Eastern Point is described as "a tongue of plain ground, where there are saffrons, nut-trees and vines." (Pringle's History of Gloucester*)*

~1~
DISCOVERED

They were the discoverers. They swept in from the endless Western Ocean around this Eastern Point, this arm of wild-grown ledge that makes the bay of Gloucester.

In a thousand fleets since, the men have dropped their port astern, outward bound back round the Point for the sea and the fish.

But these were the first.

It was a sweet serene summer day, yes, and the forest scent seduced them in, wafted to their shallop on the soft westerly; and, as Pastor Higginson would, they glided through drifts of blossoms "sometymes scattered abroad, sometymes joyned in sheets 9 or 10 yards long," tide-borne from the marshes.[1]

They came up on the seething shore, and the slow swells lifted them by the arm's fierce fist, white-knuckled with surf. Heaving their lead ahead across the shoals, yards aback, they tacked into the still waters of the unfound bay, three-quarters ringed with wilderness.

And they waded ashore, these unknowns, up the bleached beach, and they filled their bellies and their barrels with the ice water that gushed from the deep of the forest to meet the tide. Above them soared the curious crying gulls. At their feet, "ripe strawberries and gooseberries, and sweet single roses."

And they sailed off, into time.

Or they drove down on this sheer and sea-smashed coast in a curved galley with dragon head, riding reckless on the bucking back of the easterly gale, flicked from nowhere to nowhere.

There, in the lightning flash, the cursing helmsman discovered the black, white-plumed Back Shore and bore off. Fearful, they leapt to their sheets and braces, and to their sweeps, and the sea god who carried them there kept them off, and they swung on with the screecher. The unspoken wisdom in them steered them clear of those guardian monsters, the dog-toothed rocks and the snarling breakers.

In the flat-whipped water of the Point's lee they anchored (the splash of the first anchor), and their tired dragon fetched up against his tether, and settled back.

Whoever they were, these wanderers, they left no mark and they made no record, and the stern cape of rock and tree and marsh and sea remained the unbothered place of the few Native Americans who could survive it.

Until the Christian year 1605, July 16. On this day the Frenchman Samuel de Champlain came cruising from the eastward in his barque and chanced on the headland that he called *Cap aux Iles* for the three islands offshore.

Champlain didn't follow around the Point to investigate its lee, but continued on his coasting voyage. He must have made note of it, however, for late the next summer he returned this way.

The French settlement had moved from the St. Croix River in Quebec to Port Royal in Acadia, or Nova Scotia, and Champlain took another expedition to the westward. One day the last week of September they fetched *Cap aux Iles,* and that night they anchored their barque just inside Eastern Point.

Next morning they sailed up the harbor in the lee of the Point and again anchored, in the stream broad off Rocky Neck, where Champlain and his men went ashore in their boat. Here on this neck of Eastern Point, at the end of September 1606, occurred the first documented landing of Europeans at Cape Ann.

Here it all begins, in the words of the Chevalier de Champlain:

> We saw some good ripe grapes, Brazil nuts, gourds and some roots which the savages cultivate. They gave us some of these in exchange for little trifles we had given them. They had already gathered their harvest. We saw 200 savages in the place, the chief of which, Quiouhamenec, came to us with a cousin named Cohonepec, for whom we made good cheer. Onemechin, a Saco chief, also came to see us, to whom we gave a coat, which he soon gave away to another because it did not fit him.
>
> We also saw a savage who had been wounded in the heel, while running toward the bark, and had lost so much blood that he fainted. Many others came around him, singing some time before they would touch him; then, making certain gestures with their hands and feet, they moved his head, and, upon their blowing upon him, he came to himself. Our surgeon dressed his wound and he went gaily away; "but two hours after, he came again," adds L. Escarbot, "the most jocund in the world, having put about his head the binding cloth wherewith his heel was wrapped, for to seem the more gallant."
>
> The next day, as some of our men were caulking my shallop, the Sieur de Poutrincourt saw in the woods a number of savages who came with the intention of making us some trouble. They were

going to a little brook which is upon the narrow part of a bank which leads to the mainland, where our people wash their linen. [This must be the brook that flows under the road to the Point, into Wonson's Cove.]

As I was walking along this bank they perceived me, and to put a good face on the matter, because they saw that I had discovered them, they began to shout and prepare for dancing. Then they came towards me with their bows, arrows, quivers and other arms, and, as there was a meadow between them and me, I made signs to them that they should dance again, whereupon they formed a circle and put all their arms in the center of it.

They had hardly commenced to dance when they saw the Sieur de Poutrincourt within the wood, with eight arquebusiers, which astonished them. They stopped dancing, and retired from one side and the other, with apprehension that we should do them some harm. We said no more to them, however, and only made some demonstrations of rejoicing. Then we returned to our boat in order to put to sea and get away from them. They wanted us to stay one day, saying that more than 2000 men would come to see us, but not willing to lose time we would not longer delay. I believe that they wanted to surprise us.

They have some cultivated land and are clearing it up all the time. See how they do it! They cut the trees at the height of three feet from the ground; then they burn the branches upon the trunk and sow their corn between the cut wood; and in the course of time they take away the roots. There are also meadows there sufficient for nourishing a number of cattle.

This port is a very good one, having sufficient water for vessels, and affording shelter behind some islands. It is in the latitude of 42 degrees, and we have named it Le Beau Port.[2]

Champlain sketched a map showing wigwams and Indian settlements and clearings and corn patches planted along the western shore from Muscle Point around the head of the harbor to the marshes behind Little Good Harbor. Eastern Point itself, by which until 150 years ago the entire peninsula was designated, he showed as barren of any habitation, and he called it a "tongue of plain ground, where there are saffrons, nut-trees and vines."

The explorer published his account in Paris in 1613, but it was not translated into English until 1870. It rings authentic.

These were doubtless Massachuset Indians and accomplished trap fishermen, which suggests that Ten Pound and Five Pound Islands in Gloucester Harbor took these curious names not from the amounts the settlers paid the savages for them (after all, the town in 1701 gave Samuel English, an Indian, seven pounds to settle his claim to the whole of Cape Ann), but from the rather more plausible circumstance that a clever crew of Massachuset weir men could stake twice as many "pound" nets out from the large island as the small to catch whatever wandering mackerel might be schooling along the shore.

When the Dorchester Company had its first abortive go at fishing from the stage on the western shore of the harbor in 1623, the Englishmen must have had the wilderness to themselves. Champlain's encounter provides the only evidence of the aboriginal presence on Cape Ann, and the presumed disappearance of the Indian during the intervening seventeen years can be attributed to the plague that (beginning in 1614) decimated the original proprietors of the land just as the first friction with the new settlers on the coast of Massachusetts Bay was coming to the fore.

The most plausible theory holds this pestilence to have been a communicable disease of childhood introduced from England—chicken pox, measles or scarlet fever perhaps. The settlers were immune, but for the Indians it was death, and within a few months their tribe between the capes of the bay decreased from 100,000 to 5,000. Thus was all their best land opened up to the Europeans, who conquered for the first—and only—time by unintentional corruption.

A few corn patches gone to brush, charred tree stumps, piles of clam shells, burial mounds and a sparse scattering of half-starved aboriginal Americans were all that remained. But a vision of the past sometimes hibernates and survives like a lost echo, and strange things were attributed to the ghosts of the dispossessed. How else explain this odd conversation that the Englishman John Josselyn remembered engaging in while he was on the Maine coast in June 1639?

> At this time we had some neighboring Gentlemen in our house, who came to welcome me into the Countrey; where amongst variety of discourse they told me of a young Lyon not long before kill'd at Piscataway by an Indian; of a Sea-Serpent or Snake, that lay quoiled up like a Cable upon a Rock at Cape-Ann: a Boat passing by with English aboard, and two Indians, they would have shot the Serpent but the Indians disswaded them, saying, that if he were not kill'd out-right, they would be all in danger of their lives.[3]

Edmund Garrett, strolling about the Point three centuries later, thought that Brace Rock itself must have been the mammoth throne where Josselyn's monster took the sun: "I can imagine his shaggy head reposing on the great green backed rock that first shoulders off the surges, and his crimson mottled 'quoils' luxuriously coiled by the dazzling bouquets of foam that break on the purple and sienna ramparts of his lair."[4]

But we are not done with Josselyn. He went on to introduce another of his guests that day, and one can imagine that the setting for this grotesque tale might have been broad off Brace Cove:

> The next story was told by Mr. Foxwell, now living in the province of Main, who having been to the Eastward in a Shallop,

as far as Cape-Ann . . . in his return was overtaken by the night, and fearing to land upon the barbarous shore, he put off a little further to Sea; about midnight they were wakened with a loud voice from shore, calling upon Foxwell, Foxwell come ashore, two or three times: upon the Sands they saw a great fire, and Men and Women hand in hand dancing round about it in a ring. After an hour or two they vanished, and as soon as the day appeared, Foxwell puts into a small Cove, it being about three quarters flood, and traces along the shore, where he found the footing of Men, Women and Children shod with shoes; and an infinite number of brand-ends thrown up by the water, but neither Indian nor English could he meet with on the shore, nor in the woods.[5]

The Dorchester Company's pitiful attempt to plant a plantation on the barren bosom of Cape Ann collapsed in despair and bankruptcy in 1626. Roger Conant led his followers to Naumkeag and created Salem. The virgin Gloucester forest and the sea-beaten shores resumed their dialogue in solitude, rid of their Indians and abandoned by their settlers.

But the white man returned, and in 1642 the General Court of the Massachusetts Bay Colony incorporated the Town of Gloucester. The Reverend Richard Blynman arrived with various of his flock from Plymouth, Massachusetts, and the first grants of land on Cape Ann were assigned.

Their foothold was at the Green, where Route 128 now regains the earth after its leap across the Annisquam River. It was a hard trek to get to what soon was called Eastern Point, that entire promontory beginning from the Little Good Harbor marshes, southward into the sea.

Once there, what good was it? All the Back Shore was bold and breakered, a shield against the tumult of the wild Atlantic. On the harbor side, quiet as a cradle, an anchorage for a king's fleet . . . in anything less than a whole gale. But this sheltered shore of the Point, outward from the Rocky Neck of Peter Mud to its tip, was remote from the Harbor Village by land, defiant of the farmer and useless to the mariner. Two miles of ledge and beach, and no safe place to berth a vessel against the turbulence that surged through the outer Bay when the northeast storms sent seas crashing over Dog Rocks and Round Rock Shoal to pile up on the mainland shore and bounce back in against the Point, like a rocking pan of water.

What good was such a storm-battered, beautiful hump of rock and beach and brush, except to make a harbor?

Brace Rock, Eastern Point, *oil by Fitz Hugh Lane, 1863.*
Bemo Ledge in the foreground, low tide. (Private collection)

~2~
GRANTED

Pristine its beaches, charming the sweep from harbor to pond to sea, rough and rusty its ledges, and delicious to the eye its azured sky overhead and its surprise glimpses of the coastline and the blue Atlantic. Yet fish was what the settlers were after—fish, freedom and fortune. All that Eastern Point offered was a breathtaking view, angling for tautogs and the chance to start some game—and all were free for the taking.

In fact, the Point may not have been considered worth the granting in the initial subdivision of 1642; it is known only that three of the eighty-two proprietors before 1650 owned some portion of the peninsula then or soon thereafter.

William Addes was one. He was among the first eight selectmen in 1642. A trader, at some time before he moved on from Cape Ann in 1659 he sold a lot on the Point.

Robert Elwell was a less footloose forefather, a respected goodman who removed to the Point from his homestead in the Harbor Village and settled up in back of Cripple Cove (a curious redundancy, a *cripple* being a *cove*) by the town landing. He too was a selectman.

The third was William Stevens, master shipbuilder, first citizen of upright character and unbending integrity who would go to jail for his defiance of the King's commissioners, selectman, town clerk and representative to the General Court. The town thought so well of Stevens that it granted him five hundred acres between Chebacco and Annisquam River, six more near the Green and another eight at the Cut, where he resided. In spite of his esteemed position, he struck more than one run of bad luck and died a poor man.

Only fragments of information about Stevens have survived, and these in the pages of John Babson's *History of Gloucester*. Here and there, two pieces of the jigsaw puzzle of the past seem to fit. So it is with the exact location of the early grants and the identity of the grantees. The evidence strongly implies that in addition to the lands that have been positively linked to William Stevens, he was the original grantee of all of Eastern Point lying below the body of fresh water referred to as early as 1704 variously as the "Great Pond" and "Brases Pond," and now known as Niles Pond.

The greater part of the rest of modern-day Eastern Point, bounded by the farm wall that tumbles jaggedly southeast from the north end of Niles Beach to the Back Shore (along with some of the Great Pasture beyond the wall that extended all the way up to Bass Rocks), was granted to Joseph Allen, a blacksmith who was encouraged to settle in Gloucester in 1674 with the enticement of lands and common right.

Allen was only twenty-one, but he was a go-getter. He established himself and was elected selectman and representative and captain of the militia. When he died in 1724 he was the greatest landholder in Gloucester, and his estate included 220 acres on Eastern Point valued at 880 pounds.

Farther back in the main trunk of the peninsula, which in time was differentiated from the Point as East Gloucester, Babson locates a handful of early settlers or their sons.

Joseph Gardner and Elisha Curney both were born in 1672; the latter presumably found a good little fishing hump of rocky bottom in eight fathoms, three-quarters of a mile off Bass Rocks, identified in an early chart as Curney's Ledge. Then there were John Hammons and Samuel Witham and Benjamin Averill, whose land adjoined that of Samuel Ingersol, the builder of several small vessels, likely at Smith Cove. And William Sargent II, mariner and owner of a coasting sloop, John Smith and Abraham Robinson, all neighbors along the shore in the area of the town landing, behind the Square.

Old Robinson was the son of Abraham (the first settler) and in 1668 was granted this plot on which he died around 1740, reportedly at the splendid age of 102. He had a son whom he named Andrew, born in 1679, and when that interesting would-be adventurer and Indian fighter reached twenty-one his father gave him a nearby lot of land. Here Captain Andrew Robinson built his "great house." A dozen years later, in 1713, he launched from his shipyard below the square the peculiar vessel to which—whether for her hull or rig, or merely through some onomatopoeical inspiration of the moment—he gave the everlasting name "scooner."

Captain Schooner Robinson's daughter Hannah was wooed and won in 1738 by Captain James Pearson, said to have settled in Gloucester from Bristol, England. His land lay between Joseph Allen's at Grape Vine Cove and that of Samuel Pearce, shipwright, in the area of Wonson's Point on the harbor. Pearce settled from Duxbury, Massachusetts, and his eldest son, David, accumulated in Gloucester one of the great mercantile fortunes of his time.

Cape Ann in these early colonial days before 1700 was timbered over large areas with a majestic virgin forest, said to have been superior to the mainland growth. Allen Chamberlain in his history of Pigeon Cove surmises that it was intermixed with greater variety, now practically disappeared, including red spruce and possibly fir among the softwoods, and rock maple, buttonwood, hickory, aspen, black birch and basswood among the hardwoods.

Initial restrictions on the cutting of wood gave way under the pressure of demand, and much of the finest stock fell to the builders of Salem and Boston. In January 1667, the town voted to permit cordwood to be cut "from the eastern side of Brace's Cove to Little Good Harbor, forty poles from the sea side up into the woods; and from Little Good Harbor, round the head of the cape, to Plum Cove." Since a pole was a rod, the width of the permissible cut was 660 feet.[1]

Incidentally, this is one of the earliest references to what should properly be called Brace Cove, variously identified as Bracy's and Brase's in contemporary documents. Viewed as a proper name, the etymology leads to a dead end; but rid yourself of that mental set, and the derivation is surpassingly direct: a brace, from the Middle English and Old French, was an arm. Brace is an obsolete word for an arm of the sea, an inlet—a perfect figure of speech in the case of this stunning cove whose waters are so nearly embraced by the lethal, pincerlike arms of Brace Rock and Bemo Ledge.

The mystery of Bemo remains as defiant and fascinating as the ledge and the jagged, sea-dashed rocks that hold its secret. A bristling arm, or a jaw, if you will, studded with teeth for crunching ships, the ledge seems to have its name all to itself. Did it crush a hapless craft named Bemo when the New World was really new? Is it the sailor's shortening of *bemoan*, the lament of the breakers. Or of *beam on*, how the stricken vessel lies, cast up on its beam ends?

We may infer from the 1667 vote permitting the cutting of wood along the shore east of the cove that the trees were protected westerly to the end of Eastern Point. A venerable grove of oaks stood here, for generations the mariner's daymark. Sixty years earlier Champlain marked on his map a stand of thick woods extending almost out to the Point's outermost tip.

With their usual succinctness the settlers called the undulating upland of several hundred acres above the Back Shore the Great Pasture, common land, mostly, to which local people were assigned "cow rights." The town's prerogative to regulate timbering eventually went by the board, and the moors were cleared extensively, probably in the eighteenth century. (When the tenth hole of the Bass Rocks Golf Club was being laid out eighty or ninety years ago, the crew excavated several large stumps, thought to be cedar, whose ability to resist decay suggests they could have been quite ancient.)

No man-made sea wall reinforced the thread of strand between Niles Pond and Brace Cove. The two were separated by a thin dune of sand. One can postulate that this intimate isthmus is a barrier reef raised up from the ceaseless scrubbing of the cove's bottom by the easterly breaking swells. Nathaniel Shaler, in his *Geology of Cape Ann*, observes that Brace Beach was built up by the erosion of loose moraine against the softer rock bed of the cove's bottom, to which was added detritus resulting from the smashing of waves and stones against the Back Shore ledges, carried into the cove by the coastal current.

If Brace Cove at a time more distant actually extended into the depression now filled so charmingly by the little lake and its marshes, then the sands carried forward by the seas funnelling in between the arms would have piled up, steeper and steeper, helped by the wind, until they made a sand bar, a barrier reef and then a dune. Once sealed off, the springs that feed the pond took over, and it was but a matter of time before the fresh water replaced the captive ocean.

Long ere this conjectured process commenced, when the postglacial sea was a fathom deeper and higher, the entire peninsula was undoubtedly an island, and the tide coursed through what are now the marshes between the head of the harbor and the back channel of Little Good Harbor. Rocky Neck was a scraggly island then, and so too must have been all of Eastern Point beyond the pond; there would have been no pond then, no cove, and the seas would have swept through into the harbor between the ledges to the north and south, making it no difficult matter to surmise that the causeway over which the road now winds betwixt pond and harbor was raised as a bar by much the same process that created the pond itself.

Wild and remote, Eastern Point slumbered on, unscathed by the hand of man. The brush was aflutter with game. The migratory birds and waterfowl chirped and crooned and trilled and whistled and honked in the woods and thickets and meadows and coves. Life swarmed through the sands and rocks of its tidelands in seawater of such primeval purity that the bottom could be clearly seen under four fathoms.

For the hunter, the berry picker, the nut gatherer, the shell fisherman and the naturalist, it was paradise.

Rarely did events bring Eastern Point to the notice of colonial chroniclers. In 1671 it got in the way of a tornado, as related by an early historian:

> A whirlwind at Cape Ann passed through the neck of land that makes one side of the harbor, towards the main sea. Its space or breadth was about 40 feet from the sea to the harbor; but it went with such violence, that it bore away whatever it met in the way. Both small and great trees, and the boughs of trees that on each side hung over that glade, were broken off, and carried away therewith. A great rock, that stood up in the harbor as it passed along, was scarce able to withstand the fury of it, without being turned over.[2]

And in 1704 it was the scene of a manhunt.

A pirate by the very piratical name of Captain John Quelch of the brigantine *Charles* had been annoying the coast that spring, and the governor's commissioners got up a bunch to go after him at Cape Ann, and perhaps Eastern Point, where he was said to be hiding with his crew. But when they got to Gloucester they found their quarry had slipped off in a cohort's vessel on the ninth of June.

Major Stephen Sewall commandeered a fishing shallop and a pinnace, and with forty-two stout men started out after the pirates at sunset. They had to row through the calms, but they caught up and captured them at the Isles of Shoals, with forty-five ounces and seven pennyweight of gold.

Standing for Salem, Major Sewall put a patrol of his men ashore on Eastern Point, with orders to rouse the Cape Ann people after two of Quelch's gang (William Jones and Peter Roach, by name) had mislaid themselves and been left behind by their fleeing leader.

The search was cut short when the two, "being strangers and destitute of all Succours," surrendered and were hied off to Salem jail to join the rest. Captain Quelch was tried and hung. Whatever befell his cutthroats, they doubtless deserved.

If any date can be said to mark the first tentative penetration of the civilizing influences of man into Eastern Point, that was March 20, 1704, the day the town of Gloucester decided the time had come to lay out a road around from the head of the harbor skirting the inside shore "and so along to the pasture of William Stevens, deceased, on Eastern Point."

The Point's dwindling grove of landmark oaks beyond Ten Pound Island, from Fort Point at the entrance to the inner harbor, in a watercolor by Captain John Gorham Low of Gloucester, about 1815. (Cape Ann Historical Association)

~3~
SETTLED

Shipwright william stevens placed a portion of his extensive lands (which we are reasonably sure included all of Eastern Point below the Great Pond) in trust with his sons James and Isaac for the benefit of Philippa, his wife, whom he predeceased.

Philippa died in 1681. Isaac's fate is unknown. But James was probably a shipbuilder like his late father, and he was elected a deacon, selectman, representative to the General Court and officer of the militia—the criteria of success in times when there was room for but few at the top.

The first member of the family whose ownership of the Point land can be indisputably established was Samuel Stevens, son of James. Deeds establish Samuel as the proprietor of all that lay below the pond in 1697, seven years after the death of his father. The conclusion is that the land passed from William, the first settler, to Philippa to James to Samuel.

Samuel Stevens was born in 1665. A merchant, and like his father and grandfather a selectman (in 1705 and 1727) and representative (for six one-year terms between 1721 and 1732), he lived on Front (now Main) Street between Hancock and Centre.

At the time of his father's death Samuel was thirty-two and had been married for four years to Mary Ellery. Between 1704, the year the town extended the road to his pasture, and 1707 he acquired seven parcels of about five acres each, lying generally between the pond and the harbor. These he integrated with the family holdings south of the pond, apparently with the aim of building a house and barn and farming his estate, either on his own or by tenancy.

Two lots he bought from Captain Joseph Allen, the blacksmith who owned nearly all the land north of the pond, then five acres apiece from brothers William and Nathaniel Sargent, George Giddings and John Prince. This was during a period when the town was on another round of ceding citizens small grants of the common land up to eight acres. There is no evidence that these grantees lived on their properties.

His seventh block of five acres Samuel bought from Captain William

Card in 1707. Card was married to Hannah Coit, widow of Job Coit, another grandson of Shipwright Stevens; hence this lot may have been part of the old man's Point estate.

An eighth acquisition was made in 1722 when Samuel purchased from his cousin Nathaniel Coit, the late Job's brother, a tract described as already lying within the Stevens farm. Nathaniel was an absentee owner who had inherited the land from John Fitch, his stepfather, who had married his widowed mother Mary, daughter of Shipwright Stevens. Thus Samuel brought these last two lots back into the immediate family fold, from which they had strayed no great distance.

At about this time he mortgaged it all to his brother-in-law from Newport, Captain Benjamin Ellery, who (after removing there from Gloucester) made his way until he was a deputy in the Rhode Island Assembly, a county judge and the wealthy, if absent, owner of extensive lands on Cape Ann. In July 1722, Samuel repaid in full his debt of 317 pounds to the man who was the grandfather of William Ellery, signer of the Declaration of Independence, and great-great-grandsire of the Unitarian divine William Ellery Channing (of whom his physician-brother Walter remarked when asked which doctor was which: "He preaches and I practice").

Some fifteen families—a start, at least, toward a community—were scattered by 1728 from the head of the harbor to as far out on the Point as what people called "Longe Beach," being Niles Beach, from which a cart track ambled across the upland to Grape Vine Cove.

As early as 1722 Samuel Stevens was the owner of a going farm on Eastern Point; the inference that he had erected the first human habitation of record there is given substance in a 1744 paper concerning financial dealings between Samuel and his sons John and William wherein the farm was estimated to consist of about 200 acres (closer to 250, actually), including "buildings, stock of cattle, sheep, swine, horses and other creatures," all to the value of 500 pounds. It is a virtual certainty that the farmhouse was built on the historic ground that would be occupied by it and its successor for nearly two centuries, where the pond and the harbor are closest, on the slight neck beyond the end of the Longe Beach.

Samuel Stevens died in 1756, ending a marriage of sixty-three years, and his widow Mary within two more accepted the proposal of Elder Edmund Grover of Sandy Bay, whose own wife had expired the previous year. Mary Stevens was eighty-one when she plighted her troth for the second time; she lived but a few months, and Elder Grover followed his second wife to the grave three years after.

John and William Stevens were middle-aged when their father died in 1756, and they continued to manage the family farm jointly until the sixth of July 1765, when they entered into an indenture of partition. The portions are impossible to locate precisely after two hundred years, for they are described in widely differing terms in a succession of deeds. The clearest delineation of John's division is found in an old deed:

Beginning at the sea on Brace's Cove so called, running westerly along the fence to the pond, and on the southerly Side of said pond to a stone wall about 20 rods to the southward of a small swamp, thence along said wall to a meadow, thence to a small maple tree or where the same formerly stood [sic!], thence to a ditch and thence along the ditch and brook to the sea, thence all round by the sea to a fence on a sea wall the first mentioned bound . . .[1]

Broadly speaking, this brother's birthright consisted of the entire outer Point, from the wall midway on the dike between the pond and Brace Cove clockwise all the way around the shore to a brook draining into the harbor. which was likely Indian Spring that empties midway along Wharf Beach; then it must have crooked east and northeast to the pond and along its south shore back to the starting point between the two bodies of water.

William took the balance of the estate—everything west of the pond and above Indian Spring, including the northern half of Wharf Beach, Black Bess Point, the farm buildings and the pond itself, to the Allen land, the bound here being marked by a wall that ran partway from the pond's northwest shore toward the harbor. William granted John a right of way through his land.

This Colonel John Stevens was fifty-eight at the time of the partition of his father's lands. He lived on Middle Street. His first wife, Rachel, was the granddaughter of Blacksmith Allen, whose son Joseph was heir to the Allen grant north of the pond. After her death John Stevens married in 1754 Mrs. Elizabeth Gorham, widow of Colonel John Gorham of Barnstable, Massachusetts, my great, great, great, great, great-grandfather, who died of smallpox in London about 1750 while trying to get reimbursed the expenses he incurred helping to finance the Crown expedition against Cape Breton in 1745.

Colonel Stevens was a merchant and a member of Gloucester's Committee of Safety during the Revolution, and he lived almost long enough to see his country independent. After he died on April 13, 1779, at seventy-two, they engraved on his tombstone that in his character were united "the firm patriot, the useful citizen, the exemplary Christian, the affectionate husband, the tender parent, social friend—an honest man."[2]

William Stevens was six years Colonel John's junior when he came into his share of the family farm—the working end of it—and he was already at sea financially, having attempted to combine an agricultural and maritime career without much luck at either. He had married another granddaughter of Blacksmith Allen, Elizabeth, sister of his brother John's first wife Rachel, and owned a house in town where they probably lived. He was the fourth generation of his family to follow in the tradition of public service: selectman three times and representative for seven one-year terms. Such eminence entitled him to commission John Singleton Copley to paint his wife, in a plum-colored satin dress, seated in a green armchair.

Captain Will Stevens had not owned his 100-acre portion four months when he increased it by half again, in October 1765, with the purchase of a pasture of about fifty acres north of Brace Cove for 200 pounds from his wife's brother, William Allen, a Blacksmith Allen heir. Its borders ran from about midway between Brace and Grape Vine Coves on the Back Shore northwesterly through the Great Pasture to a high rock, thence southwesterly to the north shore of the pond, following this easterly to Brace Cove and along the seashore to the start.

That north boundary, marked now by a stone wall that intersects the part of the Great Pasture known by latter-day fishermen as the Seine Field where they dry their nets, survives today as the official border of Eastern Point.

To the north of this fifty-acre pasture acquired by Captain Stevens was the land of Thomas Marshall. Mr. Marshall's star was on the rise. While stitching away as a tailor in Boston, he looked up from his bench one day and fell in love with Blacksmith Allen's daughter Lucy, who had that moment entered his shop to be measured for a riding habit. He married her and apparently her share of her father's estate. At his apogee he was Colonel Marshall, patriot, commanding officer of the Fourth Massachusetts Regiment at Valley Forge. He and Lucy were painted by Copley.

When he died at fifty-four in 1767, only two years after the partition with his brother, Captain William Stevens left the Eastern Point farm of 150 acres, valued at 800 pounds, his house in town, three schooners and a flock of debts.

His son John, known as John Jr. to keep him straight from Colonel John, was administrator of his father's estate, so sadly encumbered by the widespread depression in America that the radicals were blaming on the stupid cupidity of Britain's colonial policies. In less than a year these debts forced the heir to mortgage his patrimony to John Matchett of Boston, a merchant. This must be the same Captain John Matchett, member of the radical North End Caucus, destined to be amongst the patriot bully boys who would put his shoulder to the wheel of events that culminated in the confrontation of March 5, 1770—the Boston Massacre.

Among the assets of the Stevens farm were a dwelling house and barn, outbuildings, two fish houses and flakes (the outdoor racks for drying salt fish). Nothing of wharves or landings from this early period remains. As there was nowhere beyond Rocky Neck sheltered enough for a large vessel to land any quantity of fish, the Stevens family or their tenant would appear to have been carrying on a catch-as-catch-can salt-fishing operation from small boats that kept close inshore and could be stranded and unloaded at the Long Beach we now know as Niles Beach. There the flake yards and storehouses and perhaps a smokehouse may well have been located.

Such an adjunctive setup for the Stevens farm was in the tradition of the locale, which to this day has remained a breeder of shore fishermen. In those times two men could row out, hand-line a doryload of haddock a couple of miles off the Point, return, dress their fare, row out again, catch another trip, row home and dress for the second time, all between sunup and sundown. And one veteran recalls the men filling their dories with haddock over a ledge off Ten Pound Island.

But it took more than fish to pay debts. When young John Stevens mortgaged the Point farm to Matchett for 621 pounds in April 1768, he gave him his bond for double that and his promise to pay the whole off in two years.

So he lost the family farm on the cold thirteenth of January 1770, three months before the note came due. Matchett took it for 754 pounds.

Poor Junior John. It went from bad to worse for him, and in the end all the debts he had inherited from his father and his own mismanagement caught up with him. To avoid jail he fled Gloucester in one of the vessels of his wealthy and powerful father-in-law, Winthrop Sargent.

John Stevens was put ashore on the microscopic island of St. Eustatius in the West Indies. Some years later, after the news of his death reached Gloucester, his widow, who had been Judith Sargent, became the second wife of her father's old friend, the Reverend John Murray, founder of Universalism in America.

Daniel Rogers (1734–1800), oil by John Singleton Copley, 1767.
(Museum of Fine Arts, Boston)

~4~

A VERY ROUGH FARM

Gloucester suffered intensely in the Revolution. Those of her sons who weren't in the field were off privateering on raiders such as the *General Stark,* a new ship of 400 tons, mounting eighteen guns, built and fitted out chiefly by David Pearce, who owned land by the Point road beyond Rocky Neck. Captain James Pearson, whose father's pasture adjoined Pearce's, was her sailing master.

The families of the men gone to war were doubly deprived, since the able-bodied absent ones neither fished nor farmed, and there wasn't work enough to support many of those who remained, for the British controlled the seas. Gloucester was only just getting established in the fishing industry, which verged on the marginal at best, when the war laid her prostrate. The town was reduced to borrowing money to import corn and grain for the poor.

Apprehensive about the threat of smallpox, the townsmen voted on October 18, 1773, to negotiate with Captain John Matchett, owner of the Stevens place on Eastern Point, to buy or rent it for a pesthouse for the isolation of the sick, but no action was taken until 1777, when a hospital was put up in West Parish; the pox swept through next year.

These frustrations and privations on the home front whetted the combativeness of Gloucester people, and they gave better than they bore whenever the chance presented to have a crack at the British.

Oft told is the proud tale of their famous fall-in with the short-tempered Captain Linzee during August 1775, when his harassments of the town in his sloop-of-war *Falcon* terminated at the hands of the aroused Gloucester home guard with the loss of his two prizes, two of his barges, thirty of his men captured and three killed before he withdrew around Eastern Point, gnashing his teeth, and stood back out to sea.

Not so familiar in local lore are the exploits of John Manley. Washington gave him command of the schooner *Lee,* with the interesting rank of captain in the army, when he was fitting out a small fleet to operate against the British transports in the fall of 1775.

On the twenty-eighth of November, Captain Manley and the lads of the

Lee captured the brigantine *Nancy,* bound from London for Boston, and brought her triumphantly around Eastern Point into Gloucester. *Nancy* was an ordnance ship, and her cargo of 2,000 muskets, thirty-one tons of musket shot, 3,000 round shot, numerous barrels of powder and a thirteen-inch mortar were landed and immediately carted to Cambridge, where they were received with rejoicing by the hard-pressed siegers of Boston, who pronounced the mortar the finest ever seen in America and christened it *The Congress.*

Congress in the spring of 1777 conferred on Manley the grade of captain in the Continental Navy, and he took command of the new frigate *Hancock* and sailed from Boston in company with the frigate *Boston,* Captain Hector McNeill, and a mosquito fleet of privateers.

It was probably during this cruise that Eastern Point had the honor to be the scene of an engagement, as it were, of the American Revolution.

Captain Manley had captured a British brig carrying a cargo of oats, bacon, porter and other articles and put a prize crew aboard to bring her to port. However, it was their bad luck to fall in with the British frigate *Milford,* which chased them into Brace Cove, where the Yanks drove their prize onto the rocks and jumped ashore.

This engagement had been seen from the Point, and Captain Joseph Foster, the same whose militia had repelled the invasion of the *Falcon,* mustered his men and marched them over to Brace's to guard the prize and relieve it of its cargo.

Biding his time until the dead of night, when Yankee activity aboard his wrecked prize appeared to have been suspended until daybreak, the commander of the *Milford* sent a boat into the cove. The English sailors boarded the brig, torched her and slipped back to their frigate. Thus were the spoils spoiled. There is no record of a shot having been exchanged, but it was a hostile encounter no less for that.

Suffering in Gloucester was never more severe than during the winter of 1779-80. The town's own privateer *General Stark* from mid-December to the twentieth of March was icebound in the harbor, which froze enough for walking from Dolliver's Neck across to Black Bess on Eastern Point.

Black Bess. A bizarre name for a hump of harbor rock. But regard this gull and shag-haunted ledge outcropping at half tide, and you will make out the blotched back of a plodding nag, neck stretched, head straining forward toward the sea in weary flight from some timeless pursuer.

Is this not unmistakably Black Bess, the mare that bore Dick Turpin on that wild ride from London to York, immortalized by Harrison Ainsworth in his Gothic romance *Rookwood?*

Turpin was a butcher's boy born in 1706 who fell into the bad company of smugglers and deer thieves. He pulled off a string of notorious robberies and was traced by means of a horse he had stolen; but he escaped on her and settled in Yorkshire, where he changed his name to Palmer and his occupation to horse trader. Black Bess was the name of the horse that carried him to a new life.

But they caught up with Dick and convicted him of horse stealing. He confessed to his crimes and was executed in 1739. The fame of Dick Turpin in his brief and naughty lifetime, and of the mare he stole, was surely carried around the globe wherever English was spoken. Which explains why some sailor or settler, gazing idly over at the peculiar ledge as his vessel beat into Gloucester Harbor at about half tide, called it "Black Bess" then and there.

> *Bold Turpin vunce, on Hounslow Heath,*
> *His bold mare Bess bestrode.*
> —*Charles Dickens,* The Pickwick Papers

Old Colonel John Stevens lived not quite long enough to witness the independence he had labored for. He died in April 1779. After five years, on February 24, 1784, his executor sold his broad, largely undeveloped tract that encompassed almost all of outer Eastern Point below the pond to John Rust, a Gloucester mariner, for 300 pounds. It remained in the Rust family, of which nothing more can be learned, for forty-four years, and the high ground of it was known for generations after as Rust's Pasture.

Six years after John's piece of the Point was sold out of the family, the farm next to it that his nephew had lost on foreclosure was bought back in.

The purchaser was Daniel Rogers, a leading merchant and shipowner of Gloucester, who was married to a Stevens. The seller was John Matchett, who had foreclosed on young John Stevens Jr. and taken his farm twenty years before. The date was April 24, 1790. (One infers that Matchett had moved to Gloucester, handier to his lands, just before or during the late war, for John Babson in his *History of Gloucester* remarks that at the close of the Revolution owners of mansions "in the best style of their time" on Middle Street included "Capt. John Matchet.")

Rogers added fifty more acres to the farm in January 1793, with the purchase for sixty pounds of the open land to the northwest of the Brace Cove pasture. It was bounded by the line of his farm running between the pond and the harbor, nearly the entire length of Niles Beach and the Pearce and Pearson lands on the north. This acquisition completed the northern border of the Eastern Point of today.

This fifty-acre addition to the Eastern Point farm, described as "a pasture, a field and a mowing ground all joining each other," had been the property of John Sayward, mariner, who bought it the year previous from Samuel Sayward, trader, who was probably his father. Samuel got it in 1772 from Captain John Low, who inherited it from Blacksmith Allen. Thus were the 100 acres of the Allen grant of pasture above the pond reunited under Daniel Rogers. They expanded the farm to about 250 acres, including the pond. The right of way through the farm that William Stevens had allowed his brother John at the time of partition remained in force, permitting the Rusts access to their land at the end of the Point.

Daniel Rogers was my great, great, great, great-grandfather, an ancestry shared with a veritable population owing to the fecundity of his two marriages, which produced twenty-one children. His father was the

Reverend John Rogers of Kittery, Maine, and his elder brother, also the Reverend John Rogers, came up to Gloucester from Kittery to be the first minister of the Fourth Parish in 1744. In eight or ten years, when Daniel was about nineteen, his father packed him off to Gloucester under his brother's eye, as an apprentice to, of all people, Colonel John Stevens.

Colonel Stevens had a little granddaughter, Rachel Ellery, who "required considerable tending, of which a large share fell to the lot of the new member of the family; but he contrived, by pinching and pricking the little one, to rid himself of this employment; and, having other cause of discontent, soon ran away from his disagreeable home. He was next apprenticed to Nathaniel Allen, another merchant of the town, with whom he served his time."[1]

Dan Rogers went into business for himself when he reached twenty-one in 1755, and he was an immediate and brilliant success. In four years he married Elizabeth Gorham, one of the trio of beautiful daughters of the widowed Mrs. Elizabeth Gorham, who was none other than the second wife of the widowered Colonel Stevens. His stepfather-in-law welcomed the prodigal apprentice who had made good back to his hearth with open arms. This was attested to by the Reverend Samuel Chandler, a frequent visitor to his parishioners on the Point, who entered in his diary for November 6, 1759: "I visited at Eastern Point, further end; married Daniel Rogers and Elizabeth Gorham"—no doubt in the farmhouse.[2]

Elizabeth Rogers had six children by her husband, and both had their portraits by John Singleton Copley. His shows a gloriously brocaded, amiable yet shrewd looking burgher of thirty-four, sans wig, who has evidently dined well and often. Hers has been described as of "a graceful and lovely young lady dressed in a rich blue satin. She is apparently coming from the garden with a fancy basket on her arm and in her hand a hat. Her costume is painted in an exceedingly graceful manner . . . It is said that Copley took great delight in painting this picture . . . But she was delicately organized, and died after a short married life."[3]

The beautiful Betsey Rogers expired in 1769, and the next year Daniel returned to Colonel Stevens's family for her successor, the very same Rachel Ellery whom he had pinched and pricked to be rid of when he was a lowly apprentice to the colonel. Rachel was now twenty, sixteen years younger than her husband, whose brother, the Reverend John, was married to her aunt, further adding to the confusion in the family.

Rachel's dowry is said to have been a vessel loaded and manned for the West Indies. She too was painted by Copley. More sturdily organized than her predecessor, the second Mrs. Rogers produced for her husband fifteen children and lived to eighty-three.

Daniel Rogers entertained with a grand conviviality at his handsome home on Middle Street, and at the outbreak of the Revolution he owned seven Grand Bank fishing schooners and half-shares in three others jointly with Joseph Allen. His business suffered by the war, but with peace it was more prosperous than ever until he had sixteen vessels in the fisheries and foreign commerce. He served a term each as selectman and representative to the General Court and in 1788 was one of the three delegates from Cape Ann to the state convention to ratify the federal Constitution.

Among the most peripatetic divines of this time in Essex County was the enthusiastic shepherd and scholarly bon vivant who ministered to the East Church in Salem, the Reverend William Bentley. In June 1791, a little more than a year after Daniel Rogers acquired his country seat on Eastern Point, Dr. Bentley visited Gloucester to attend a conference of his brethren. As luck would have it, this tireless diarist improved the occasion by accepting the hospitality of Daniel Rogers, first at his town house in Middle Street, next day on a tour of his Point farm for a picnic:

> June 14 (1791) . . . After dinner we were introduced to drink Tea at Mr. Rogers, the first merchant in the place, who has a numerous family, & preserves unusual vivacity, while above sixty years of age. [He was fifty-seven.] In the evening we were conducted to a Mr. Sergeants' at whose house Music was prepared for the evening. There was a considerable number of gentlemen & Ladies & very handsome entertainment. The instrumental & vocal music were well performed. We have nothing like it in Essex. The Conviviality is remarkable. The pieces were of different classes. At eleven we retired. The hospitality of Capt Rogers secured me at his house, and the expectation of a chearful day to succeed, made a succession of very pleasurable emotions. He has a fine wife, & gay children, who contributed their full share to the entertainment, & the pleasure.

> June 15. This morning it was agreed to go to Eastern Point, which makes the entrance to the Harbour, above a mile below the Town. . . . About half a mile without the Fort Hill is "Tenpound Island," not containing an acre of ground, & between which & Eastern point there is a communication at the lowest tides, & many difficult rocks. Below on eastern point is a Ledge called Black Bess, & nearer the point Dog Rocks. Without the Point about one mile, eastward is Brace's Cove. It has a Bluff head on the western side, which is a large & lofty rock. It has a Ledge on the eastern side & Rocks without it. It has often proved fatal to mariners, & the Cove has been mistaken for the entrance into Cape Ann Harbour. The Cove is clear after you are within the eastern Ledge. It enters almost half a mile, & by a narrow Beach is separated from a Pond, which extends almost across the eastern point, which is joined to the main by this beach formed by the sea, a few rods wide, & by the road not much wider on the side towards Cape Ann Harbour. From Brace's Rock the lights at Thatcher's Islands are in full view, above a league's distance.

> The Farm of Eastern point, purchased last year by Daniel Rogers, who was with us, is very rough. There is a delightful grove

of Oaks, &c. within the point, to which company resorts and enjoys a fine air in the warmest weather. The Farm is very rough, affords pasture, but there was no tillage land beyond the Pond towards the Point. About 200 acres lay towards the point, & the rest, amounting to 300 acres was sold together for 320 pounds. The tenant pays an annual rent of 27 pounds. The House is on the road by the pond, after you have passed it going to eastern Point, not a mile from the Grove . . .

Our party consisted of above 60 persons of both sexes. With Col Pearce in a skif we caught several dozen of perch, & after two we dined in a friendly manner. Another party in a sloop larger than our own furnished us with Cod from the Bay, & after dinner till Tea parties were engaged in Walking, dancing, singing, & Quoiting, & Swinging & every amusement we could imagine. The Poets story of Twandillo was realized. There was but one instrument of Music with us, which was a fiddle brought by its owner to pick up a few coppers. To see him play with it upon his head, under his arm, &c., furnished a pleasure which the happiness of ignorance may innocently occasion.

> Hark,—his tortured catgut squeals
> He tickles every string, to every note
> He bends his pliant neck
>   —The fond yielding Maid
> Is tweedled into Love.

We set out about ten in the morning, and arrived before nine in the evening safe at the same wharf. And what deserves notice, not a single accident, not an angry word, occasioned the least interruption to so large a party. The principal Gentlemen were in this party, Daniel Rogers, Esqr, his two sons John & Charles, Capts Soames, Tucker, Sergeant, Beach, Col. Pearce, Major Pearson, Master Harkin, Mr. Parsons, &c. . . . I lodged at Esqr Rogers, who collected his family & finished the scene by an act of devotion.

June 16. . . . While we were on eastern point, another party, with whom was the Revd. Mr. Murray went into the Bay after Cod & continued off the point all day. . . .[4]

Three years passed, and Dr. Bentley was again the guest of Daniel Rogers. This time he found even more reason to complain about the roughness of Eastern Point. It was March 6, 1793:

After dinner we went with Mr Rogers to see his farm of 300 acres at eastern Point. Mr Rowe, the Attorney & Son in Law of Mr Rogers accompanied us. The road was horrible, & my young companion after travelling across the neck to view the Thatcher's Island lights accompanied me into the Town on foot, both of us dreading to ride back through such dangerous passes. In the evening there was an assembly, at which my young companion attended. He gave me a very humorous account. They had six candles, 12 ladies, 7 gentlemen, a black fiddler for 2s, & a fifer for 1s 6. Both sexes partook of the grog provided on the occasion.[5]

In the closing decade of the century Squire Rogers reportedly presented each of his twenty-one children a house upon his or her marriage, and a porringer to each new grandchild. So records (with possibly a pardonable tinge of pride) another of his descendants, Elliott C. Rogers of Gloucester. The formidable captain of commerce, he writes, "was rather temperamental, however, and in one instance he was feeling so displeased with one of his daughters that he did not send her a porringer when a new baby arrived. The daughter was not lacking in resourcefulness: when her father presently had occasion to call at her home, she saw him coming and quickly instructed the nurse to be heating the baby's food in a tin cup over the coals as grandfather entered the house. Soon thereafter the baby received his silver porringer.[6]

Daniel Rogers gave more than porringers to his grandchildren—for example, a tall clock that has been passed down through six generations of my family, truly a grandfather's clock in every respect. The case is a towering and fiercely Victorian edifice of solid oak. Inside the waist door a small pen-and-inked panel depicts the Rogers house on Middle Street, with this undated legend: "This clock wore out its original case some 40 years ago. It was given by my great-grandfather Daniel Rogers, to my father, as a token of regard for the fourth Daniel named after him. The clock was made about 1700 and stood for many decades in Rogers Homestead on Middle Street— (*signed*) Daniel N. Rogers (D.R. ye 5th)."

How the Rogers clock "wore out" its original case is one of those family mysteries, or secrets.

One other legacy skipped two or three generations of rightful beneficiaries before it attained a rather exponential fulfillment, through no fault of the old gentleman farmer of Eastern Point. It seems that on the thirteenth of February 1798, the French privateer *La Vengeur* seized the Gloucester schooner *Esther* and her cargo on the high seas while bound for Bilboa in another of those depredations that nearly brought America into conflict with Bonaparte. The French condemned ship and cargo.

For a century the French spoliation claims were the subject of amongst the most dogged negotiations in the annals of human tenacity. At long last, on May 27, 1902—104 years after the fact—Congress settled the matter and appropriated $6,022.14 in compensation for the seizure of the *Esther*, to be distributed among the 139 living descendants of the long late Daniel Rogers, her owner.

On January 6, 1800, the Reverend Bentley noted in his diary. "We hear of the death of D. Rogers Esqr the principal Merchant in Cape Ann. He died suddenly. He had a good estate & many children."[7]

The brig Persia *and the ship* Howard, *Salem vessels fated for the Back Shore of Eastern Point, portrayed in their halcyon days. (Peabody Essex Museum)*

~5~

SHIPWRECK SHORE

The first shipwreck on eastern Point of which any detail has been preserved unhappily reflects no great credit on the natives. On the other hand, since even circumstantial evidence was lacking at the time, the blame for its sequel had best be put on human weakness and cupidity and the natural wants of poor people in the realm of earthly, if seaborne, goods.

The night of February 28, 1807, was black and blowy. A heavy southeast gale drove the seas high on the Back Shore ledges, sending spray sweeping through the brush. The storm carried the roar of the surf far inland, but of course not any hint of this was reaching the straining senses of the lookout on board the ship *Howard*, barely two hours' run from her home port of Salem, within two or three leagues of completing her long voyage from Calcutta with a $100,000 cargo consisting mainly of the finest East Indian baled cotton goods.

Captain Bray, a Marbleheader, had assured himself that he was keeping his offing, for he had no wish, so close to his snug hearth once again, to pile up on the rocks of Cape Ann. But no light marked Eastern Point, no visible night mark nor buoy, and the captain, or his helmsman, had miscalculated.

The lookout's scream stuck in his throat, and the *Howard* hurtled into Grape Vine Cove.

She was a big ship, but she broke her back, and stove. The seas hammered her against the rocks while the terrified crew clung to the deck. And then the *Howard* broke clean in two. A lunging wave flicked Captain Bray, his mate and two foreign sailors overboard. The survivors lashed themselves to the quarterdeck and were washed ashore and dashed on the pebbles.

Bruised and bleeding, sopping, frozen, they straggled over the moors of the Point until they stumbled on a house on the harbor side, where a poor woman took them in and no doubt saved them from freezing to death. Charles Thacher was one of that crew, later a Boston merchant, and every year until she passed away he sent their benefactress a barrel of flour.

Howard's cargo was strewn along the Back Shore, and one version of what happened next reported:

> The floating goods were the cause of no little strife among the inhabitants, who as the bales were washed open, seized the loose ends and struggled to obtain possession of as much of the cloth as they could sever by tearing, and in the heat of the encounter sometimes using their knives to the detriment of the contestants' fingers and hands, giving to the scene the appearance of a bloody fight. The combat became so animated that the hope of saving any considerable portion of the cargo was given up, and the goods were abandoned to the wreckers. Such at least is the tradition.[1]

This, certainly, was the gist of the first report to reach Salem. Dr. Bentley remarked on March 4, four days after the stunning disaster, that it "has not given a higher opinion of Cape Ann than we have been taught to hold of Cape Cod. The disposition to pilfer was not easily restrained even by guards, and if we cannot prevent thefts at fires in our best towns, we cannot preserve our goods scattered on the shore when the storm is over. Much must be allowed for description, but after many deductions, pilfering is a sad vice when it has any excuse for it or any temptation to it. The Law must have a lash to it & the soldier only can execute it."[2]

William Gray of Salem owned about thirty vessels, of which the *Howard* was one. He posted a guard over the goods that were finally rescued, and what now transpired was recalled as follows a half a century later.[3]

One night this sentry spotted a dark figure skulking about with a large bag slung over his shoulder. He hollered for help and gave chase. After a long pursuit that carried them over several acres of pasture, the guards collared the suspect, who proved to be a rogue from over town named Jack Low.

When the surrender of his plunder was demanded, Low cursed his luck, threw his bag to the ground and again took to his heels. The watchmen dumped it out, and to their disgust it was filled with hay. By the time they got back to the cache they were guarding, they were at a loss to know how much had been expropriated by the clever Jack's cohorts while he had been playing the wild goose.

What remained of the *Howard*'s cargo was securely stored, finally, in Gloucester, and a string of teams started out with it for Salem one bright starlit evening.

In the Manchester woods, according to this account, this caravan was brought up short by a tree lying across the road. The drivers walked forward to remove it, and of course when they returned to their teams, the last wagon in the train was empty, and loot and thieves had melted into the forest.

Then, Gloucester vindicated! On March 17 Dr. Bentley got the word from Henry Phelps, the Gloucester postmaster, that sufficient evidence had been obtained that the charges respecting the pilfering of the Shipwreck cargo belonging to the Ship Howard lately were false. That the principal articles of value missing instead of being plundered were concealed in the piles on shore by the persons employed to collect the remains in hopes that being sold on the spot they might profit from the concealed articles, & that the truckmen had been discovered as privy to such secret villainy. The truckmen here are the lowest class of our citizens, generally foreigners, upon low wages, & nothing is regarded in the choice of them but their strength. The most aggravated charges were at first brought against the inhabitants.[4]

The retrospective view was taken by the *Advertiser* from what one concludes was a doleful accumulation of experience:

It cannot be denied that the time has been, and not back in the dark ages either, when a shipwreck was looked upon as a regular Godsend by a numerous class on Cape Ann. Large ships with valuable cargoes have been driven ashore on Eastern Point, and the islands the other side, and the people of our town were by no means slow in availing themselves of the facilities thus offered them to lay in a stock of the good things or substantials of life, whichever might come on shore. Indeed, they would have been sorry to lose the portion of their income thus derived, and looked upon it as much a matter of course as the fishermen look forward to the reception of the bounty.[5]

Enough of wrecks and rascals. Redemption was at hand. The opportunity to clean the slate with the cloth of patriotism arose during the third year of the War of 1812 with Britain. In midsummer 1814

a Portsmouth schooner, laden with flour, was chased by one of the enemy's cruisers into Gloucester Harbor, and run ashore somewhere on Eastern Point. Some men were sent from the cruiser in a boat to take possession of the schooner; but Col. Appleton, then commanding the Gloucester regiment of militia, had by this time arrived at the spot with the artillery company, who used their guns with such effect, that the enemy were driven off, and the schooner was saved.[6]

The war's end brought sighs of relief all round and a hiatus of political euphoria diagnosed by the uncritical as the Era of Good Feelings. Still, for all the acrimony that seethed beneath the smiles, an earthy pride of nation pervaded the land. On Cape Ann this newfound spirit of brotherhood was expressed every Fourth of July with a chowder party at Eastern Point, usually in the stately grove behind Wharf Beach.

These rejoicings were cherished in the memories of the merrymakers, and the earliest of record was brought to mind in his autumn years by

"Webfoot," the pen name of Captain William D. Phelps, a Gloucester merchant skipper born about 1804, famous in the California and China trade and unhappily transplanted to inland Lexington, where he died in 1876. Captain Phelps lamented that he had toured the world but never found the match for these celebrations in the days of his youth before the regrettable restrictions on the free run of the Point:

The sloop *Randolph,* commanded by Capt. Epes Procter, and the sloop *Swallow,* Capt. Tom Millett, were the only regular packets from Gloucester to Boston in 1815 and thereabouts. The first named stood A No. 1 both as regards vessel and captain, and was the largest. The *Swallow* was of lesser size, a dull craft and of a generally untidy appearance. The captains of both vessels were men of heavy weight and portly appearance; it was said they could alter the trim of their crafts a foot either way, by moving themselves from stem to stern; and as fat men are proverbially jolly, so both skippers stood high in public favor.

For some days previous to the 4th the *Randolph* was always chartered for the occasion. The vessel was well cleaned inside and out, the ballast levelled, and a plank platform laid fore and aft, for the accommodation of the passengers. Sometimes the *Swallow* was also put on service when the company was too large for one vessel; but the *Randolph* and her more genial captain always had the preference. . . .

At an early hour on the eventful day, the *Randolph* was at the end of Sargent's wharf, ready to receive her freight, and by 9 A.M. was generally under way, her decks, cabin and hold pretty well stowed with living humanity, while dozens of us youngsters were hanging on the ratlines, or perched on the bowsprit. The quarterdeck was occupied by captains and mates who had seen service, but now were loafing around Commodore Epes, who did not need their support, as he always had his own way on his own quarterdeck. We always seemed to have to beat out of the Harbor; but with a brisk breeze this was quite agreeable to the passengers, especially the younger, as it afforded opportunities for flirting and much merriment. A boat had been sent out early with experienced fishermen outside of the Point, to get the desired fish, and was sure to be at the landing when the sloop anchored, with the fish cleaned and ready for the pot and pan. And now came the landing of the passengers, which was another exciting and jolly incident. The ladies must be landed dry-shod on the rocks, and the gentlemen were very careful of their polished boots, but as the landing was effected under charge of men experienced in boats, there were no mishaps. The gathering in the shade of the noble trees was soon effected, where lemonade, coffee and cakes were in circulation, and where with song and frolic the time was rapidly used up.

The presiding genius in concocting the chowder was our noble Capt. Epes Procter—he was verily a great man, physically and mentally, and so was Daniel Webster; both knew how to make famous chowders, and in that knowledge was no small portion of their greatness. The great event of the day was at length announced— "Chowder is ready!"—and of course everybody was ready for it, and everybody there was soon satisfied that it was the best one ever concocted by mortal hands. A fry always accompanies a chowder at Eastern Point, which with many niceties prepared by the ladies for small stowage, made up a feast which picnic parties of the present day would find it hard to beat.

After a proper discussion of the good things at the table, the party separated and rambled in groups as their fancies dictated. Some were very intent on geological pursuits; botany and berries were attended to by others. On the outside points of rock facing the broad bay would be seen a pair seated listening to "what the wild waves were saying"; other pairs might be seen examining the beach in the interests of conchology—"they gathered shells upon the shore." But the principal and central groups were the old sea-dogs of the party. They were averse to parbuckling over the rocks, and at the present time were not given to scientific pursuits. Forming a circle around a fresh tub of lemonade, with which, in the absence of the ladies, a few bottles of Old Jamaica had been mingled, good punch was ladled out by liberal hands, good cigars were smoked, and songs and sentiment abounded. Naval and national songs were in the ascendant, and found ready chorus, "the fun grew fast and furious," and thus "the minutes winged their way with pleasure" until the hoarse shout from the Commodore of "all aboard," summoned the revellers to the boats.

The embarkation was conducted in good order, but not so dry-footed as in the morning—the gentlemen were not so careful of their glossy boots, and the ladies would get their feet wet. Whether this was owing to the rocks being more slippery than in the morning, or whether it was caused by the absence of ice from the lemonade or the presence of Old Jamaica in it, your deponent will not undertake to say.

Again on board and homeward bound, the ladies took charge of the quarterdeck; the majority of the gents were closely examining the planks of the hold, perhaps studying the grain of the wood or selecting a plank for the next political platform. The wharf was reached in good season, and all separated well satisfied.[7]

Jollity and Old Jamaica neither churned butter nor laid eggs, and after the death of her efficient and commanding husband in 1800 the Widow Rogers, from the vantage of the great house on Middle Street, relied wholly on a succession of tenants to maintain the solvency of the Eastern Point farm.

The most notable of these (being the only one of whom we have record) was Thomas Hillier, an Englishman wise in the ways of the soil who had emigrated to Boston in 1802 when he was thirty-two, shifted down to Marblehead, thence farther on to Ipswich around 1805, thence up to West Gloucester, thence out to Eastern Point about 1810. In 1812 he purchased a small home on Mt. Pleasant Avenue, up on the high land, built in 1754. In time, he extended his acreage across the Great Pasture to the Back Shore.

By 1821, and probably before that, Hillier was renting the Eastern Point farm from Mrs. Rogers for $140 a year. He continued at least through 1831 and seems to have lived in the farmhouse in preference to his own home, which was over a mile away.

On May 8, 1826, Hillier wrote his son Daniel in Maine:

> Ben is pretty much engaged with the sheep and lambs. Have got about 80 and expect 20 more. The little field is broke up and I shall finish planting it 9th May at 12 o'clock. The potatoe field is not quite finished ploughing. The grass looks very promising but the hill field will be nothing. But for want of hay cannot do what in March we expected.
>
> We have had in April some white weather—frost and snow—so as to make good sledding out of the woods and very cold—freezing the water pail very hard and the manure in the barn—and wind very high and extreme cold. . . .[8]

Thomas Hillier lived almost to ninety and was remembered for his adherence to the old English customs. He dressed the country squire, in the frock of the British farmer. Sunday he wore to church an immaculate white coat that brushed his heels, a tall beaver hat and hobnail shoes; the combination made this excellent yeoman a figure of some distinction in the neighborhood.

Squire Hillier was a good and faithful Methodist, and he was rewarded for his virtue according to the peculiar laws of his adopted country. He and the other trustees of the Methodist Church on Prospect Street that people called "Old Sloop" for some surely worthy purpose had seen fit to borrow money from the Reverend Jacob Sanborn, which belonged to two orphans of whom the minister was guardian.

Through the workings of some legal irony, in order to prevent his claim on the loan from being invalidated, the clergyman found himself in the uncomfortable position of being forced to have his trustees Thomas Hillier and Nathaniel Witham arrested for debt. These two pillars were confined in Salem jail for a fortnight; all that saved the third, Amos Story, from joining them was the interesting fact that as keeper of the light on Ten Pound Island he was exempt from arrest.

After the death of his first wife, Farmer Hillier took for his second the Widow Pamelia Oakes. She is said to have been the daughter of Henry Sayward, the one-handed sailor who relished the reputation far and wide of being as able aloft to haul out a weather earing as the liveliest of the young fellows.

On the twenty-ninth of March 1828, the *Gloucester Telegraph* issued a historic exhortation to mariners:

> We have received a communication respecting the decayed state of the trees on Eastern Point, which have so long served as a guide for the many vessels sailing up or down the Bay, and those coming from sea. The writer informs us that there is now standing only seventeen of those venerable oaks, which have withstood the "peltings of the pityless storm." He recommends that some persons interested should draw up a petition to Congress, asking aid from Government to erect a monument, instead of again planting trees, as the former would be more durable, and be discerned at a greater distance than the latter. It is well known that the materials for such a purpose are already within a few rods of the spot, where a monument would most probably be erected. Those who are concerned in navigation will do well to think of this subject, as it is for their benefit that a monument is needed.

For many years the government had tried to preserve this invaluable daymark at the end of the Point in an early, if unsuccessful, attempt at conservation. As late as 1870, long after a lighthouse had been built, an old-timer with a long memory recalled that when he was a boy, around 1820, he had been told that the ancient oaks were preserved by order of the U.S. government and not even the owner could lay an axe on them. If so, the grove could assuredly have been sacred since the town's 1667 vote allowing woodcutting east of Brace Cove only, and even earlier. Tree by tree, it had fallen to time and the fierce elements, all efforts at reforestation notwithstanding.

Eight months after the *Telegraph* laid its proposition before the public, the Rust land below the pond, which included all of the Point that wasn't owned by the Widow Rogers, was offered at auction by Jacob Rust of Boston, administrator of the estate of the Boston merchant and late owner Jacob Parsons Rust. The buyer that October 25, 1828, was Gorham Burnham of Gloucester, a smart young bachelor of twenty-nine who took it with a bid of $420.

Clever speculation, if that's what it was, because in nine months—on July 24, 1829—Burnham sold to the United States of America one acre and six poles (square rods) at the extreme outer tip of his new property, together with all rocks and ledges and "the reserved way through the land adjoining my premises belonging to the estate of Daniel Rogers deceased, thence to continue in a way to be two rods wide through my land to the conveyed premises."[9] He further conceded a convenient landing place with a suitable passageway to the cove near the same.

The government paid Burnham $100 for his acre and without wasting any time that fall of 1829 built an unlighted stone monument as far out on the ledge as it could be safely and securely placed.

This Burnham was a hustler. He started blacksmithing on Dr. Coffin's wharf up in Gloucester, and in 1822 when he was only twenty-three, he invented the first successful bait mill for grinding up chum aboard the mackerel hookers; it consisted of knives projecting out of two wooden cylinders that revolved by each other. This portable piece of deck equipment took on so well that one year, besides his anchor forging and other metal work, Burnham made and sold $1,600 worth at $10 apiece.

Gorham Burnham married Sally Baldwin of Salem, and one of their daughters, Frances, married the East Gloucester patriarch George Marble Wonson. Thomas Hillier, in his agricultural pursuits at the Eastern Point farm, was indebted to Burnham at about this time in the amount of $6.23 for shoeing horses and oxen, mending a fork, ironing a plough and the purchase of sundry hinges and nails—so says an old bill.

The erection of the day beacon at Eastern Point was nine months too late to avert the most celebrated shipwreck in the Point's history, though it was certainly spurred by it. The hanging of a lantern could hardly have made any difference anyway.

The brig *Persia*, Captain Thissell, Nathaniel B. Seward, mate, both of Beverly, bound from Trieste for Salem with a cargo mostly of rags, was caught—even as the *Howard* had been so close to home—in a violent southeasterly during the night of March 5, 1829. It was snowing thickly. Visibility was zero, and there were no aids to navigation in the area. She cut too close to the Point, and without warning or a moment's opportunity to alter course *Persia* smashed up on the foaming ledge five hundred yards to the southwest of Brace Rock. It was surmised afterwards that she must have broken up very quickly.

This was Thursday. Not until Saturday, after the storm had passed, was the tragedy on this isolated shore discovered. The *Gloucester Telegraph* reported the sketchy details:

> From a watch found in the pocket of the steward, it may be supposed that the brig was wrecked about 11 o'clock, as the watch had stopped at half past 11. The long boat came ashore nearly whole which may lead to the conjecture that the crew left the vessel in it—marks were visible on it where the gripes had been cut. Nine bodies were found; among these the captain, mate, cook and steward were recognized, and taken to their friends.
>
> The remaining five bodies were decently interred on Tuesday, from the Rev. Mr. Jones' Meeting house and attended to the grave by a large number of seamen and others. From the marks on the bodies, perhaps some of the seamen may be known.
>
> One had the letter "I" in the inside of the left arm, about 25 years old—another an "L" on his stockings, dark complexion, a large scar on the right cheek—about 5 feet 4 inches high, 30 years old. From his dress we supposed him the 2nd mate or a passenger— 4 doubloons were taken from his pocket—2 appeared to be broth-

ers, from their resemblance to each other—the 5th had two characters indented on the right arm, representing a man and woman, under which were the initials of "O.E." and "K.B."

We are thus particular, supposing that their friends may recollect these marks. The above doubloons and other articles, are deposited, for the rightful claimants.

Much of the cargo has been saved, and with the spars, rigging and wreck sold for about $700. The cables and anchors are to be raised and carried to Salem. A large portion of the rags and junk was purchased by Salem people and shipped to that place. It is supposed that there were 13 persons on board of the brig, but no others have yet been found.[10]

One report had it that the schooner *Mariner* was stationed offshore at the time, for the purpose of aiding vessels in distress. They saw the *Persia* bearing down on the coast and gave chase to warn her, but the ill-fated brig outsailed the *Mariner* in the heavy gale and soon disappeared into the murk.

The editor of the *Telegraph*, William E. P. Rogers, found a bag of silver dollars at the scene of the wreck. It was tied up in a peculiar fashion, and thereby he tracked down the owner's next of kin. Captain Thissell, it developed, had been unable to find a proper string in his hurry to embark on his voyage, and his wife, equal to the emergency, had volunteered, "Father, take one of my garters."

The folks in the Rogers farmhouse, probably the Hilliers, heard the cries of the shipwrecked men carried across the Point above the howl of the easterly, but they paid them no mind, thinking it was the sheep. So tradition has it in my family.

John Kimball Rogers, great-grandson of Daniel Rogers and my great-grandfather, was eight at the time and never forgot the sight of the corpses laid out in the churchyard.

Two more of the crew were found in a few days, their bodies so wedged in between the rocks that it took six men with ropes to extricate them.

The *Salem Courier* informed its readers that the *Persia*'s rags were sold at auction, as "to leave them on the Point was to have them certainly stolen"; it followed this with a lecture on the evil of plundering.[11]

Shades of the *Howard*. The *Gloucester Telegraph* reprinted the Salem paper's insinuations, bristling editorially at this "unmerited compliment to our people" and rejoining, "that our inhabitants are more dishonest than our neighbors in cases similar to the above, we doubt."[12]

The agent for the owners hired Point folk to "fish up" the *Persia*'s sodden rags for a fifty-fifty cut of what little they were worth, and that closed the book on the worst shipwreck in Cape Ann history.

*Sketch of the old Eastern Point Lighthouse by E. R. Morse in 1875 shows the covered walk to the keeper's cottage. (*Frank Leslie's Illustrated Newspaper, *March 27, 1875)*

~6~

LIGHTHOUSE

The ghastly wreck of the Persia in March 1829 on the unmarked backside of Eastern Point profoundly affected the people of the district. Who knew how many vessels had gone up or lives been lost there before the keeping of records? There was no more menacing nor deceitful lee between outer Cape Cod and Sable Island. Before the year was up a petition was going the rounds begging Congress to place a light on the recently erected monument at the end of the Point.

In due course a bill was filed. The appropriation was at first opposed by President Andrew Jackson but finally carried in late 1830 or early 1831. Old Hickory's initial hostility to spending federal funds for a lighthouse on Gloucester's Eastern Point conceivably issued from his creed that in politics you reward your friends and punish your enemies—that is, if it was related to the 1828 election that yielded him 77 of the 530 votes cast on Cape Ann.

The prospect of a manned lighthouse operated by the federal government at the tip of Eastern Point and the sensible assumption that a road would have to be built thereto, and maintained, through the intervening private lands may not have been unrelated to a sudden burst of real estate activity that now occurred: the entire Point changed hands within the span of two weeks.

Two months after the lighthouse petition went into circulation, on February 24, 1830, Gorham Burnham sold the outer Point to George Clark, Jr., of Gloucester—identified for posterity only as "laborer"—for $800. In his sixteen months of proprietorship of the picturesque but seemingly useless seashore for which he paid $420, Burnham got rid of one acre and six poles of rock to the United States for $100 and the rest of it to Mr. Clark for eight times that, clearing $480 less his taxes, or 112 percent on his investment.

A mere fortnight later Mrs. Rachel Rogers and thirteen other heirs of Daniel Rogers sold the rest of the Point, the Eastern Point farm, to Addison Plumer of Gloucester for $2,800, for which he gave his note at 6 percent. The Widow Rogers was feeble, four days short of her eightieth birthday, and the transaction relieved her numerous children of a type of unpleasantly divided family responsibility for real property that usually winds up dividing the family rather more than the responsibility.

Major Plumer, as he desired to be addressed, was forty-five upon his acquisition of the Point farm, and he had but five years to live. He was the son of David Plummer (with twin m's), a merchant in town whose politics during the Revolution "were not entirely agreeable to his townsmen; and in order to shield himself from the suspicion of cherishing Tory principles, he was obliged to make a public declaration of his sympathy with the popular cause."[1] Compounding the irregularity of his principles, the old man was a Universalist as well.

Three of Major Plumer's cousins (sons of his uncle, Dr. Samuel Plummer) were the victims or instruments of tragedy: David was lost in a shipwreck on Plum Island; John was knocked overboard and drowned a spit off Eastern Point by the jibe of the main boom of a yacht he was taking to the West Indies for sale; and Samuel, Jr., fled Gloucester for thirty years after the pregnant body of a female slave belonging to his father, with whom he was studying medicine, was discovered in a pasture, the doctor's bloody sword wedged in a crevice nearby.

A solitary glimpse of Addison Plumer the young man, during the War of 1812, has come down. He was twenty-eight and captain of Gloucester's artillery company assigned to the defense of the town, and this of course required target practice.

On the eighth of May 1813, Captain Plumer mustered his men at the Gunhouse at the head of Pleasant Street and paraded them to the Cut, dragging their nine-pounder for range firing. Eight rounds were lobbed out over the harbor at Shag Rock off Ten Pound Island and also at the extreme tip of Eastern Point, and it is proudly related that a couple came quite close.

Well satisfied with the nearness of their misses, Captain Add marched his lads back to the Gunhouse where they fell out for a collation of crackers and cheese washed down with rounds of grog, which likely were right on target. Subsequently he was advanced to major, if not for his marksmanship then for his comradeship.

Plumer retained Thomas Hillier as tenant after acquiring the Eastern Point farm. With the matter of a lighthouse before Congress, and the government's right of way to it through his farm already secured, the new owner reserved to himself some significantly specific prerogatives in a power of attorney he assigned to Hillier two months later.

The document was signed on May 19, 1830, and Plumer referred to the power invested in him "in my right as owner of the Farm occupied by him the aforesaid Thomas Hilliard and especially to prevent trespasses from persons taking ballast, stone or sand, seaweed, kaile or drift wood, spoil from wrecks, etc., and prevent teams passing through other than on the road laid out to Russes [Rust's] lands . . ."[2]

The sixteenth of that September the first great fire of Gloucester crackled up Front Street and consumed twenty homes and forty stores and

outbuildings before it was heroically halted by the short-handed fire department and its four ancient hand engines, a volunteer force of gentlemen hustled up from Boston and three hundred spirited females. More than half of
the business district was wiped out, and the total loss exceeded $150,000,
most of it uninsured.

But Gloucester's maritime progress was not to be deterred by any such
shoreside setbacks. The town was on the move. In 1828 it fitted out 165
schooners in the cod fishery, forty-five coasting and commercial schooners,
fourteen sloops, seven brigs, five ships and a single barque—with a population of but 7,500 on all of Cape Ann. Its vessels ranged from the West Indies
to the East, and that year alone twenty-nine foreign arrivals rounded
Eastern Point, and the Gloucester Customs collected $127,000 in duties.

Up in the harbor, Five Pound Island served for hauling boats, and Ten
Pound had been marked by a lighthouse since 1821. The town spilled down
to the waterfront, as it has ever since. A ropewalk and a grain-grinding
windmill were prominent landmarks on Pavilion Beach, and the old redoubt
still dominated Fort Point. Rocky Neck was a pasture, still an island off
Eastern Point except at low water.

The fishing schooners were almost exclusively pinkies, hardly a square
stern in the fleet. The shore fishery was at its peak, providing work for 800
men. But the frontiersmen of the Atlantic were adventuring farther to the
eastward every season; the Bank fishery was being resumed with more vigor
than ever after the late hostilities; the shoals of Georges were just beginning
to be recognized as a cornucopia (so it seemed then) of cod, haddock and
halibut; and the mackerel jiggers were commencing the annual summer
cruises to the Bay of St. Lawrence that would swell to fleets of 300
schooners from this port alone.

So it's understandable, if quixotic, that an attempt at whaling, traditionally
the hunting province of Nantucket and New Bedford, should have been
revived at this time in Gloucester, notwithstanding David Pearce's rather
middling postrevolutionary effort. In 1833 the ship *Mount Wollaston*, 325
tons, Captain David L. Abrams, was being fitted out for her maiden try at
whaling when, Glosta being Glosta, a prelude to the prey, albeit putrefying,
was provided the public, as announced in the *Telegraph* of July 27.

A Whale—One of these mighty inhabitants of the deep was
towed from George's Bank into our harbor a few days since, and is
now being cut up and tried out on Eastern Point. It is about 50 feet
long and 10 feet through, but in consequence of the length of time
since his decease, will not yield so much oil as a whale of this size
usually does. Our citizens who have never seen one of these sea
monsters had better avail themselves of this opportunity to gratify
their curiosity. We can assure them, (we speak from experience)
that a *real whale* is worth seeing.

A year passed, and the Gloucester whalers had just returned seventy-

Captain James W. Pattillo. (Author's collection)

five days out from the South Atlantic islands of Tristan da Cunha, in a disappointing maiden voyage of fifteen months with a mere 1,600 barrels of oil and 13,000 pounds of bone. For all that, the owners were in the midst of readying their second voyage when what should come wandering into the innermost recesses of the harbor one morning but a second whale, this time very much alive and announcing himself to the public by surfacing and blowing a lazy cloud of vapor into the June sunlight off Five Pound Island, a few rods from the establishment of Giles and Wonson.

So it must have been the crew of the *Mount Wollaston,* taunted by the presence almost in their berth of the huge prey they had sailed halfway around the world for with such indifferent success, who leaped in their whaleboat, eager for vindication in the bosom of their home port.

The men pulled with strong strokes across the few feet of open water, swinging their oars to the lusty shouts of the steerer. Harpooner poised taut and tense in the bow, weapon at the ready, they bore down on the basking quarry. Now they were almost against him, and the spear sang and thudded into the expanse of glistening back.

Suddenly the quiet balm of the June morning was rent by the fierce and frenzied thrashing of the wounded leviathan. He whipped the water into a churn of spray flecked with the red of his blood and bore off with a thunderous smash of his tail whence he came. The line zipped through the chocks, and when it fetched up, off they dashed, whale and boat at a steaming clip, through Gloucester Harbor at the utmost hazard to themselves and the fleet.

Out the length of the harbor the furious whale towed his shouting entourage at breakneck speed—Gloucester fishermen on a regular Nantucket sleigh ride, their boat careening and plunging in the boiling wake of their steed. But when they found themselves outside of Eastern Point after a few incredibly short moments, headed for the open Atlantic, their velocity undiminished and with no means at hand of dispatching their victim (who seemed to take on strength as he entered his mother waters), they held a quick conference and voted one and all to cut the line.

This was immediately tended to. The prey sounded and was off in a maelstrom of bubbles and froth, taking with him one harpoon and a length of severed manila. His pursuers drifted to a stop and then dejectedly rowed back into the harbor, reflecting on the irony of the encounter and the leers it would provoke on their return.

Whaling aside, Gloucester was but in the prelude to its greatness. The wharves still clustered around Harbor and Vincent Coves, and there were only three of any importance on the entire peninsula of Eastern Point— where Ben Parsons, John Wonson and the firm of Giles and Wonson serviced their small fleets and spread the salt fish to dry in the sun on wood frames called flakes near the town landing behind the Square.

Giant Jim Pattillo, a young Nova Scotia fishing skipper of Scots ancestry whose thundering fists and obstreperous nature while in drink got him into enough trouble in Canadian waters, found his way to Gloucester, where he secured a site skippering Giles and Wonson's schooner *Nautilus* on his vow that not a drop should touch his lips—on this trip anyway. From my biography *That Great Pattillo,* the following inconsequentially abbreviated excerpt hints at the more raucous side of waterfront life below what is now East Gloucester Square in 1834.

That great Pattillo from Nova Scotia with the wild reputation was as good as his word and mild as milk from start to finish. Not a drop of spirits touched his lips during the whole trip, so that when *Nautilus* wore around Rocky Neck and groaned all heavy with salt fish to her berth, he was dry as a sponge. The Fourth of July was a couple of weeks away, and all the fishermen were home or on the way for the holiday. Happy times were in order, but Jim swore to himself that he would hold to his good behavior; damned if he didn't like what he saw of Cape Ann and her people, and he was bound to make good here.

Others had different plans for him, however.

While he was off on his first trip out of Gloucester there had been some powerful talk from his old countrymen along the waterfront about Jim Pattillo's gigantic strength and his monumental bouts with fist and bottle—more of the same that had scared his mates into a shore mutiny before they ever sailed with him.

So the men of Giles and Wonson thought it would be great fun to see the newcomer in action, and they had their eyes peeled for the *Nautilus* to round the Point. It occurred to these schemers that the Novie might be the means of silencing a noisy bantam rooster named Percy Mathews, a fisherman from Blue Hill, Maine. There had been a difficulty between him and the owners with the result that he went over to Ben Parsons's wharf across the slip and had been crowing loud and long how he would flog them or any of their gang that crossed his path.

Jim had no more than walked ashore when the men gathered round and pointed out Mathews to him across the way. Take the rooster on, they urged, and stop his noise. But thinking of all the trouble his fists had brought him, even to fleeing from his homeland, he shook his head and pushed them off and would have none of their troublemaking, as he said—good, bad or indifferent.

Two of the Giles and Wonson skippers, Job Rowe and Stephen Rich, were the ringleaders in this affair. When they saw it was useless to push their man or pull him, they resolved to get to the windward of him. There was more than one way to shape a course. They would bide their time.

The Fourth of July in this fifty-eighth year of the United States held a promise of boisterous political goings-on. It was all owing to Old Hickory.

The Common Man had swept President Andrew Jackson and his Democrats to such a swamping victory over Henry Clay in 1832 that it demolished the tottering National Republican Party. The hoary hero of the War of 1812, with his ramrod principles and spoils system, his strongman view of the Presidency and hatred of the Federalists, had amputated the tentacles of the monopolistic Bank of the United States by vetoing its recharter and now was squeezing the blood of government deposits from the body. These battles with privilege entrenched the old general's popularity with the common men, none more so than the Gloucester fishermen; and they drove his political enemies to regroup under the shield of a revived Whig Party early in 1834.

Faced with this new threat to Jacksonism the Democrats of Cape Ann in the days preceding the national birthday laid plans to whomp the Whigs with bombast in absentia at a mass gathering in the bucolic seaside environment of Eastern Point, the favorite locale for the celebration of the Fourth as long as anyone could remember. It would be a gala, a circus, a display of numerical and oratorical strength that would set the Whigs to rout. All the Democratic politicians would be there, the rum would flow, and the attraction of the day, as touted by the *Gloucester Telegraph,* would be a fish dinner "consisting of halibut, codfish, haddock, hake, cunners, lobsters, etc. etc., which will be stewed, boiled, fried, baked, roasted, chowdered, hashed, minced, etc., and be on the table at precisely one o'clock. Salutes will be fired and the bells rung, morning, noon and night, in honor of the day." Tickets were on sale at Giles and Wonson, from whose premises the affair would radiate.

It was here that the conspiracy of Captains Rich and Rowe to test the mettle of Jim Pattillo was to unfold.

Church bells a-ringing and a resounding twenty-four-gun salute by a detachment of the Gloucester Artillery Company roused the sun and raised the curtain on a grand and glorious Fourth of July. By mid-morning the crowds were gathering from all about the Cape and the North Shore, arriving by boat, carriage, wagon, horse and foot. Some inspected the wharves and schooners, sniffed the fish drying acrid on the flakes in the rising heat or stood idly by under the trees kibitzing on the preparations. The old men with their pipes and whiskers talked politics and slapped gnarled hands on thin thighs and pined for the good old days. The ladies snapped open their parasols as the sun mounted overhead. Lovers strolled over the rocks and along the beach. Others picked wildflowers and berries in the upland meadows, and the youngsters played merry, high-pitched games across the fields.

As the morning wore on the dignitaries and politicians staged their arrivals—the Honorable Robert Rantoul, Jr., handsome young Gloucester lawyer and the main speaker of the day who would be a national figure of promise in Congress; Jonathan Cutler, Theophilus Herrick and John Wonson, Representatives in the Legislature; General John Webber, Addison Winter and jovial Dr. John Moriarty, all three hundred and fifty pounds of him.

Over in Giles and Wonson's cooper shop Job Rowe was cooking up the chowder that was to be the mainstay of the fish dinner. But he kept one eye on the door, and when the big Pattillo lounged past, hands in pockets and pipe in mouth, Captain Rowe called Jim inside, informed him with a wink that he was one of his lads, and gave him two long drinks from his black bottle.

At this moment Captain Steve Rich dropped in to observe the progress of the chowder. The plotters fell to talking about this and that and before long worked round to the subject of strong men they knew of. Rich approached Jim and felt the muscle in his bulging arm:

"Jim, you must be a mighty strong man yourself, I'd say."

"Well, I suppose I am," acknowledged the object of this innocent observation with some diffidence, taking another swig offered from the black bottle.

"How much d'you spose you could lift, Jimmy?" Captain Rowe inquired. He threw a panful of onions in the chowder.

"Lift? Oh, I don't know exactly, Cap." Jim cogitated the matter. "I can say this: from the time I was fifteen in the Provinces I never hired a horse to take a barrel of flour from any store or wharf up to my mother's. I carried 'em on my shoulders. Now that's about all I can do—and I can do that easily."

Rich glanced slyly at Rowe:

"That's pretty good, but I know little men that come to your chin, Jimmy, what could take up barrels from the ground like winking and put 'em on their shoulders."

The fogbell of Eastern Point Lighthouse from an 1875 sketch by E. R. Morse. (Frank Leslie's Illustrated Newspaper, March 27, 1875)

Our friend flushed and took the hook.

"Skip," said he, "if you can produce such a man, large or small, as can bring a barrel of flour up from the ground and put it on his shoulder as you say, I'll pay for it—but if he fails, by God, then he and you can go to the devil together and it belongs to me!"

The wager was accepted and off went Captain Rich for Percy Mathews, in high glee and spreading the word of the contest.

The best barrel of flour in their store, value eight dollars, weight two hundred pounds, was rolled out and a ring was formed in the sun over by the flake yard, the people coming on the run from all over to see the fun.

Mathews peeled back his sleeves, cocky as you please, and took hold of the barrel with slow deliberation, commenting that if it contained pork or beef or fish or something that had weight in it the effort would be worth his while, but flour was nothing in his hands.

Then he straightened up, flexed his arms and looked at the great barrel lying in the dust. Beads of perspiration appeared on his face, but he still did not offer to lift this object of his contempt.

"Haw!" whinnied a voice from the crowd. "I could whittle a better man out of a piece o' pine!"

This set up a laugh, and someone else chimed in:

"A piece o' pine! Why I could go over to the graveyard and dig up a better man!"

A roar of laughter this time, and a few catcalls. Mathews glared around him and looked uncomfortable, but still did not touch the barrel.

Jim was beside himself with mirth. "All right boys, don't be too hard on the poor jack! Give him time! Give him enough time and he can shoulder the barrel—if his mother makes the flour into bannock cakes so he can eat 'em. That's how he'll shoulder it!"

Such a fanciful jibe raised a howl of delight, and the crowd whistled and jeered and made all manner of fun of Rich for wasting their time with his blowhard. Captain Steve put on a mock show of embarrassment, but the humiliated Mathews danced up and down and shook his fist at Jim:

"Yer a bag o' wind. You can't do it yerself!"

"What! What was that?"

Mathews suddenly grinned.

"A gallon of rum says you can't shoulder that barrel yerself!"

"Stand clear!" roared Jim. With a leap he sprang to the barrel, caught hold of it by the chimes, hove it up on his shoulder, strode over to the shop with it and knocked in both heads on the rock that served as a doorstep, sending up a cloud of flour that drifted down like snow.

All dusted with white, he made for Mathews, who was retreating into the crowd, knocked aside five or six spectators that stood in his channel, plucked him up by the neck of his shirt and the slack of his britches and tossed him off the wharf into the mud.

The gallon of rum he won was passed around amongst his admirers and lasted until chowder time.

During the dinner and after it and all through the hot afternoon and into the evening, the oratory rolled forth like the thunder of the twenty-four-gun salutes that periodically marked the progress of the day. Each speech was accompanied by a toast, and there were fifty-one of them by actual count, ranging from down with the Whigs, the Bank and the monied aristocracy to up with Old Hickory and the Democrats, the fishermen and the Fourth of July.

As for Jim Pattillo, he was a Jacksonian by principle and a son of Gloucester by adoption from that day on.

Commerce, in and out of Gloucester and coastwise, increased rapidly during the 1820s, and with it the hazards of piloting. An economy-minded, agriculturally oriented federal government had been inexcusably

The clockwork of the Eastern Point Lighthouse bell as sketched by E. R. Morse. (Frank Leslie's Illustrated Newspaper, March 27, 1875)

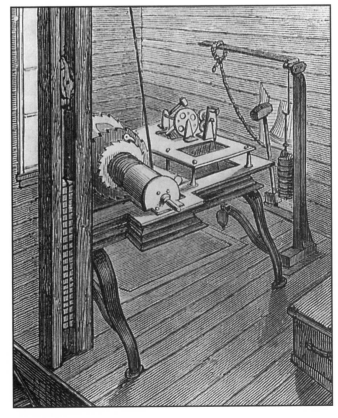

laggard in adorning a dangerous coast with the most rudimentary aids to navigation. The twin lights on Thacher's Island were lit in 1771; Baker's Island, marking the entrance to Salem and Beverly Harbors, was illuminated in 1798. A vessel could not fetch one from the other at night or in the thick without running up on Eastern Point, whose mass obscured the line of sight between them.

Coming out of the eastward, bound home for Salem, the masters of the *Howard* and the *Persia* made the same costly miscalculation: having presumably picked up Thacher's, both believed they would safely clear Eastern Point.

One edition after another of the pilot's bible, Blunt's *American Coast Pilot,* appended these words of warning to its directions for the approaches to Gloucester Harbor: "In sailing from Cape Ann lights [Thacher's] to Cape Ann harbour, you will first open Braces Cove, before you come up with the harbour, which will, when open, bear N.N.W. which you must avoid. Cape Ann harbour lies one mile farther to the westward, and when you open bears N.N.E."

Cape Ann harbour lies one mile farther to the westward—the voice of grim experience. And yet, there the day monument had been built on the acre purchased for the purpose by the government, so far out on the extreme tip of Eastern Point that when a lantern was hung in the top of it the beams would be blanketed to the eastward by the mass of the Back Shore. Inevitably the light must be invisible from the deck of a vessel making for the harbor from that quarter, after fetching Thacher's, unless its master kept to a most conservative offing—a haphazard reliance under conditions of darkness, tide, wind, storm, snow, rain, unfamiliarity with the coast and even calms, as we shall see.

That "False Point," as wary mariners dubbed it, created by the north shore of Brace Cove in contrast against the unobstructed glimpse across the pond to the harbor and made the more illusory by the false promise of a lighthouse that is obscured from view, would take a terrible toll of craft trying to round into Gloucester a mile too soon.

They had built the day monument 300 yards too far to the west along the shore. But there it was. There is no evidence that the danger compounded by this miscalculation was appreciated at the time. A remedy (and a poor one) was not undertaken for another fifty years.

Congress passed and President Jackson signed a bill authorizing a lighthouse on Eastern Point. On August 26, 1831, Samuel Friend contracted with the government "to alter the monument on the eastern point of Gloucester, Mass." into a lighthouse, equip it with the necessary apparatus and build a cottage for the keeper, all for $2,450. He appears merely to have adapted the obelisk put together two years earlier of rubble stone from the area.

According to information supplied by lighthouse historian Richard W. Updike:

The 1831 lighthouse was a fixed (nonrevolving) light of ten lamps with twelve-inch reflectors. Under optimum conditions, the light could be seen eleven miles. The tower was thirty feet in height. The lantern was only six feet in diameter, leaving the keeper without enough room to stand comfortably when trimming the lamps.

Because the posts of the lantern were imbedded only twelve inches in the wall of the tower, the lantern shook so violently in gales as to sometimes break the panes. Ten years after the tower's completion, the soapstone deck leaked in every direction, causing the inside walls to be covered with ice in winter and green mould in the summer. The leaks caused all of the woodwork to decay, including the staircase and the window casings.

Samuel Wonson, first keeper of Eastern Point Lighthouse, and his wife Lydia. (Carolyn Wonson Pattillo)

The Eastern Point Light was illuminated for the first time on the night of January 1, 1832, by its first keeper, Samuel Wonson. His salary was $400 a year, and his employer was the Fifth Auditor of the Treasury of the United States.

Keeper Wonson was fifty-eight when he and his wife Lydia packed up and moved out to this wind-shaken aerie on the last lonely ledge of the Point. One assumes he had retired from fishing. Several of his sons (he had nine, and three daughters) followed the sea, and one of them, John Fletcher Wonson, already was a fisherman of daring and some renown. Samuel himself was the first of thirteen children by the two marriages of his father, who had shifted from Sandy Bay to Eastern Point below Rocky Neck around the turn of the century and whose descendants are tolerably numerous.

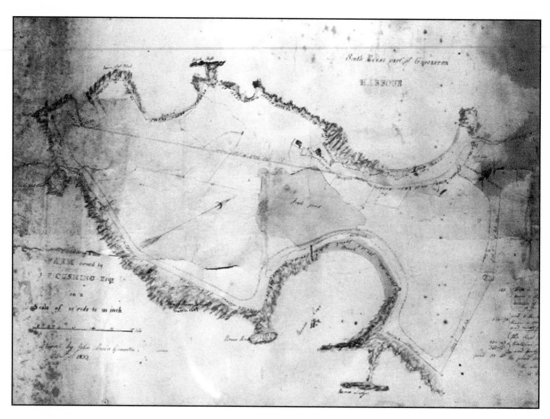

John Mason's 1833 survey of the Cushing farm is the earliest known accurate map of Eastern Point.
(Cape Ann Historical Association)

~7~
KU-SHING

On THE THIRTY-FIRST OF OCTOBER, 1833, John Perkins Cushing, Esquire, of Boston purchased the Eastern Point farm from Addison Plumer for $3,100, and the entire outer Point, excepting the lighthouse reservation, from George Clark for $1,075.

Cushing paid cash and in one stroke became the owner of the whole of Eastern Point as presently bounded, consisting of some 448 acres including the freshwater pond, the beaches and the ledges, for the sum of $4,175.

The new owner of Eastern Point was said to be the richest man in New England. He had grand visions and left little doubt that he could afford them. He reserved his grandest, his most imaginative, his most sweeping, for the Point: he intended transforming this uncut gem of the ocean into the most glittering seaside estate in America.

Cushing had the luck to be born in Boston in 1787 and the colossal luck to be the nephew of Colonel Thomas Handasyd Perkins, one of the great merchants in the Hub of the Universe. Jack was smart as a whip, too, and while yet a young fellow he was hired as a clerk into the firm of his uncles, J. & T. H. Perkins Company, just then moving into the China trade.

When he had reached sixteen in 1803, the uncles sent their nephew in the custody of Ephraim Bumstead, their senior apprentice, on a voyage to Canton to learn how to deal with the mysteries of the East at a profit.

Years later Colonel Perkins recollected that Jack "wrote a fine hand, was a very steady lad, and had a great taste for going abroad"—adding as an afterthought that "he was well repaid for his undertaking by the result."[1]

A female relative, however, reminisced in a somewhat dissenting vein that Jack was a boy of literary and artistic leanings who possessed no desire whatsoever to become a merchant. Whether pushed or drawn to China, there would be no argument that he was indeed well repaid.

Hardly had the two young Bostonians touched the soil of Canton when Bumstead fell sorely ill; he embarked for home alone, and died at sea. This foul turn of fate left a raw youth of sixteen with the preposterous responsibility of promoting the mercantile interests of his uncles on the shore of the strangest of all lands, halfway around the world from Boston.

The foul was fated to turn fair. When the stale tidings of fresh disaster reached him, Colonel Perkins prepared to take ship for China, was delayed, and before he could set sail received further word from his nephew reflecting such unexpected maturity and competence that he concluded, for the time, to give him his rein.

Jack Cushing was more than precocious. In an astoundingly short time he proved a commercial genius. Of course his naturally sharp wits received an occasional avuncular honing from Colonel Perkins in the form of such bland admonitions as this, from an 1806 letter of instructions: "It is y'r duty to warn the Chinese against the wiles of our Countrymen. . . . "[2]

Next year he returned to the States after four years in China, for a brief visit in Boston. He was twenty. And then he spent the next twenty in China, a full partner in the family firm. Cushing engaged, among other diverse activities, in the opium trade, and made fast the bonds of friendship with his equally brilliant cousin, the dashing and adventurous, handsome and contumacious, nautical Cellini of Boston, Captain Robert Bennet Forbes, known to friend and foe as Black Ben.

Black Ben harbored strong affection for his kinsman, and long after "Ku-Shing," as the Cantonese called Jack, returned finally and triumphantly to his native city with his fortune and his retinue of Chinese servants, Forbes wrote of him:

> While in China he lived for about 25 years almost a hermit, hardly known outside of his factory, except by the chosen few who enjoyed his intimacy, and by his good friend Houqua, but studying commerce in its broadest sense, as well as its minutest details. Returning home with well earned wealth, he lived hospitably in the midst of his family and of a small circle of intimates. Scorning words and pretensions from the very bottom of his heart, he was the truest and staunchest of friends; hating notoriety, he could always be absolutely counted upon for every good work which did not involve publicity.[3]

When the expatriate returned for good in August 1831, he was forty-four and the possessor of a fortune estimated at $7 million, said to be the largest of his generation in New England. And he was free with it. He had not been back in Boston two months when he gave $5,000 to the Massachusetts General Hospital, as he had earlier pressed an equal amount on the Massachusetts Humane Society, among his other charities.

Wanting a Western wife after twenty-five years of oriental hermitry, Cushing brushed aside Boston's other belles who "beset him like bumblebees about a lump of sugar" and married Mary Gardiner, daughter of the Reverend John Sylvester John Gardiner, late rector of Trinity Church and a founder of the Boston Athenaeum. Then to the wonderment and admiration of Boston, Cushing built an opulent town house on Summer Street, the elm-shaded retreat of retired shipowners, and ensconced therein his Far Eastern menage behind an inscrutable wall of Chinese porcelain, surrounded by the astonishing souvenirs of his mysterious past.

John Perkins Cushing now took the next step in his repatriation, as revealed by Thomas Niles, who succeeded him in the property:

> Upon his return from China with the great fortune which he had there accumulated, Mr. Cushing had proposed to make a seaside estate which should surpass in beauty of situation and in completeness of detail any other in the United States. For this, after careful examination of a great part of the coast of New England, he had finally selected Eastern Point as best adapted to his purpose.[4]

Uncle Tom Perkins some twelve or thirteen years earlier had discovered the cooling summer easterlies and the restorative privacies of Nahant and built a hotel there that coincided with its connection to Boston by steamer. The returned China hand would have been beguiled by a visit to the breezy Perkins seat, suspended in the ocean by a thread of sand from Lynn. Off in the haze to the eastward, Eastern Point lay waiting, insular and unspoiled—so far, and yet so near—by water.

Cushing made his decision and his offers and bought and integrated the Plumer and Clark lands in October 1833. Then he engaged John Mason of Gloucester, tavernkeeper, carpenter and surveyor, to make the first accurate map of Eastern Point in existence. And then he had a heavy stone wall built between his new property and that to the north of him, three-quarters of a mile from shore to shore. Most of the Cushing Wall remains today, marking the boundary between the Point and the rest of East Gloucester.

There was no steamer from Boston, as to Nahant, and the road was awful. The same fall Cushing laid the keel for a seventy-ton, sixty-foot schooner yacht at the Whitmore and Holbrook yard up the Mystic River at Medford; cousin Ben Forbes, home between voyages, supervised her construction. A way to the Point? Why not?

Sylph hit the water in the spring of 1834, and probably the cousins cruised her that summer, anchoring off Cushing's new estate at Gloucester. The following spring Captain Forbes was elected commodore of the Boat Club, the pioneer yacht club in Boston. This fact and his connection with her put a sort of official stamp on *Sylph*'s victory on the third of August, 1835, over the schooner *Wave,* owned by John C. Stevens, the future founding commodore of the New York Yacht Club. Historian Samuel Eliot Morison called it the first recorded American yacht race. Black Ben told how the match came off:

> We arrived, (with Messrs. Cushing, S. Cabot, R. D. Shepherd and others aboard) at Woods Hole in good time when Governor Swain of Naushon came aboard and offered to pilot us through Lone Rock passage where the tide rushes through like a mill race. Our pilot, Sylvanus Dagett, said it would not be safe but Mr.

John Perkins Cushing's fast schooner Sylph *beats out Boston Bay. (Peabody Essex Museum)*

Cushing concluded to try it. The breeze was fresh and all went well until we had got by Lone Rock when the tide caught her and she went on the ledge opposite the Lone Rock. At the moment I saw the cutter *Hamilton*, Captain W.A. Howard, in the sound, bound west. I fired a gun and lowered our flag and Howard instantly came and anchored as near as was safe. Our ballast was taken out and finally the *Sylph* was floated. Captain Howard hove her out and smoothed the broken false keel and the copper. While she was on the rock with one end out of the water and the other submerged, Mr. Cushing proposed to sell her by auction and she was knocked off to me for about one fourth of her cost.[5]

What a dirge the wily mariner must have keened over the "wreck" to get his equally wily cousin to part with her! The race occurred on the return passage, *Sylph* now belonging to Captain Forbes:

As we opened out Holmes Hole, we saw the *Wave* at anchor and immediately hauled up for her and, passing near, I jumped on board. Commodore John C. Stevens and his guests were at breakfast; I invited him to a trial of speed to Newport and we were soon under way, running down towards West Chop, and while in smooth water the *Wave* gained rapidly but when we got nearly up to Tarpaulin Cove the Sea became rough and it soon became apparent that the *Sylph* was gaining. I had remained on board the *Wave* and watched every movement of both boats; it soon became certain that the *Sylph* was gaining and Commodore Stevens concluded to bear away and wait in Tarpaulin Cove for better weather.[6]

And now *Sylph* was challenged. Thomas Handasyd Perkins, Jr., back from London, where he had been representing his father's interests, was persuaded by another Boat Club member, Captain Philip Dumaresq, to buy a sleek thirty-ton schooner he had seen in Baltimore, the *Dream*.

Shortarm Perkins, as he was known (his right arm was slightly shorter than his left), was an excellent athlete and small boat sailor. He and Dumaresq offered to race his cousins Cushing and Forbes in *Sylph* to a buoy outside Boston Harbor; the first boat around was to drive a boathook into the spar, the loser to retrieve it.

Dream rounded first and Shortarm drove his gaff into the buoy. When *Sylph* sailed in she didn't have it, and for years after, whenever Perkins ran across Forbes in the street he'd yell at him:

"Ben, ahoy! Where's my boathook?"

Sylph was a pilot boat in Boston Harbor for a couple of years, and then Forbes sold her to the Sandy Hook pilots. A blizzard took her, with all hands, in the winter of 1851 off Barnegat, New Jersey.

For reasons that are not clear (its isolation may have been among them), Cushing abandoned his grand design of making Eastern Point his summer estate. One chronicler recollected abruptly that "he made some improvements on the property, and intended to make it his residence, but for some reason changed his mind."[7]

Thomas Niles, who should have known, claimed that "the reasons which induced Mr. Cushing to abandon his project concerning Eastern Point were wholly personal, and are believed to have been chiefly disagreements with the town officers of Gloucester, concerning assessment and taxation of his property. He abandoned it with regret; and what he thought the position capable of and what he had planned concerning it may be inferred from what he subsequently executed on the magnificent estate created by him at Watertown."[8]

It's hard to believe that Cushing and the Gloucester assessors couldn't come to satisfactory terms, whatever their civic cupidity, for it is related that at Watertown, once, the assessors came to talk about his taxes. "What is the entire amount to be raised?" he asked. They named the sum needed by the town. "You can charge the whole amount to me," replied Cushing.[9]

Around 1836 Cushing made an arrangement with Gardner Greenleaf of Roxbury, a mason to whom he gave a bond for a deed; that is, he promised to sell the Point to Greenleaf at an agreed price when and if he saw the color of his money. All that can be learned of the man is that he occupied the farmhouse off and on until the Point was bought by Thomas Niles.

And so westward turned the fancy of the China merchant, as already mentioned, and he purchased from the same R. D. Shepherd who had sailed on *Sylph* against *Wave* a two hundred-acre tract on a broad height where Watertown, West Cambridge and Waltham conjoined.

Cushing sent architects as far off as Washington for ideas, and his ships around the world for materials, and he built what long was regarded by many as the most beautiful mansion in America. He called it "Belmont," from which that town took its name when it incorporated in 1859, three years before his death. He was its largest taxpayer.

It was a concentric house, a house within a house, designed to keep cool in summer and warm in winter. It had fifty fireplaces of Italian marble, finished in mahogany, oak and ebony. The gardens were unmatched anywhere on the continent, they said, interlaced with oriental trees and shrubs and exotic flora, with numerous greenhouses and conservatories and a regiment of gardeners. Every week during the summer he opened his grounds to the public, and thousands came to wonder at New England's most lavish horticultural display of the age.

John Cushing reserved to himself such a retiring side of his nature that it is doubtful if there is a likeness of him in existence. Yet, behind his walls, he indulged in a subtle flamboyance; on these occasions, he was the Yankee comprador, the benign American mandarin, and it is delightful to picture him, engrossed in his favorite hospitality, entertaining hordes of boys and girls from Boston. The children's supper parties of Mr. Ku-Shing were unbearably exciting with volleys of Chinese firecrackers, pony rides, haystacks to play in, fire-balloons, dancing on the lawn led by the famous Signor Papanti, flights of strange music and the bizarre processions and costumes of the mysterious land where the host had made his fortune. Leaving "Belmont" after one surpassingly thrilling fete in 1840, the children shouted "Hurrah for Cushing forever!"

Such was the splendor that might have been Eastern Point's.

Gardner Greenleaf's principal occupation on the Point, aside from farming, was quarrying. He began cutting the ledge on the small headland between the last two coves before the new lighthouse, probably in 1836. His first object was to build a solid fill wharf at the south end of the beach handy to the works so that cut stone could be taken on by lighter, schooner or sloop; it cost him more than $3,000, by his own account, and it gave the strand its name—Wharf Beach.

The granite was of good quality, and some of it is in the foundation of the first Boston Custom House, completed in 1847 in the neoclassical style, which serves as the base of the present tower piled on it in 1915. Along with the Torrey Pit at Sandy Bay, the Point quarry also supplied stone for Fort Warren on Georges Island in Boston Harbor, and it is said to have provided the granite for various other buildings in Boston.

Among Greenleaf's first workers at "Quarry Point" was Benjamin Haskell, who was apprenticed to Nathaniel Webster in 1833 at the age of sixteen to learn blacksmithing. In four years he was a journeyman, and Greenleaf hired him to sharpen the tools of the workmen at the pit. The Eastern Point quarry reportedly yielded Greenleaf $20,000 from the first year of cutting.

About noontime on the twenty-eighth of November, 1837, the Stevens farmhouse, which had stood by the road between the pond and the harbor for perhaps 100 years, caught fire.

The flames burst out through a flue and moved so fast through the two-and-a-half-story, gambrel-roofed place with the end chimneys that two female relatives of Mr. Greenleaf and others in the house had to flee for their lives. A thousand bushels of potatoes in the cellar and a store of other produce from the farm were baked beyond eating, and the loss was figured at around $4,000.

As soon as the smoke was spotted across the harbor, they rang the alarm, and *Hydraulion* was on her way. She was the pride of Gloucester, the first suction pumper bought after the big fire of 1830. The men flew out of the engine house on Church Street with her for the long haul to Eastern Point. Meanwhile, old *Cataract* was roused by the fire company at East Gloucester, which had been organized only five years and had to make do with this clattery bucket tub whose better days were astern of it.

They got *Cataract* on the move, thumping and rattling over the hill and upland recently bought by Isaac Patch, following the road past Wonson's Field and along the sandy beach, joined by the barking dogs and shouting boys and the citizens puffing onward at their own pace, and eventually by *Hydraulion* and company. Of course, when they all came up short at this distant homestead there was nothing much to see through the clouds of smoke but snapping embers in the cellar hole and the former occupants standing about in the yard, weeping or cursing according to their sex.

All in good time—for the old place was insured for $2,500—a new farmhouse rose on the site of the old.

These were the days when Gloucester's tide was on the flood, and the intimacy with which her sons lived and died by the sea bred in all who had to do with fishing an almost casual fatalism. The sentinel Point was her cradle, her shield and her graveyard.

One gusty day in the middle of December 1838, the schooner *Martha*, a new vessel, was sailing around Eastern Point from Essex. Among those on board was her owner, Adoniram Boyd. Off Brace Cove a squall struck her. The newspaper reported the "Melancholy Event":

> A small schooner belonging to this town (West Parish) was out, on board of which were four persons, Mr. Boyd and three others. Nothing was heard of her until a few days since, when she was discovered ashore on the outer side of Eastern Point. She was capsized in the squall, and the probability is that every soul that was on board has perished. Mr. B., we understand, who was a very worthy man, has left a wife and family of eight children.[10]

Eastern Point. When not the stage, the backdrop:

> Schooner *Sevo* was run down in the night [in 1839], by steamer *Huntress*, off Thacher's Island, and sank almost immediately. Capt.

Pelatiah Barker, Jr., of Portland, succeeded in climbing on board the steamer. Winthrop Sargent, a lad of twelve years, crawled out to the end of the bowsprit, and as the vessel was going down, grasped a splitting table which floated by, and by his cries attracted the attention of those on board the steamer, who rescued him with much difficulty. The steamer pursued her course, and the sails of the vessel drifting ashore near Brace's Cove, it was thought all hands were lost.

On the return trip of the steamer, young Sargent was brought home, and at two o'clock in the morning, was landed at Eastern Point, and, lad though he was, commenced his lonely journey of walking to town. He reached his father's house at about four o'clock, and knowing that he slept in a bedroom on the lower floor, tapped on the window.

His father immediately awoke and exclaimed, "Who is there?" "It's your boy Winthrop," was the reply. Mr. Sargent at first thought it must be the ghost of the lad, as he had given him up as drowned; but young Winthrop had no idea of being taken for a ghost, and soon gave evidence that he was alive and well, which caused great rejoicing in the family. There were four men lost in this vessel. . . .[11]

Eastern Point. Always there to be reckoned with.

"If the wind be to the eastward," advised the ninth edition of Blunt's *American Coast Pilot,* "you may anchor in a bay that makes between Ten pound island and Eastern point, the latter bearing S. by E. and Ten pound island bearing N. Here you may anchor in 4 fathoms water, on muddy bottom. This is a good harbour against easterly winds, but if the wind be S.W. you are exposed to it in which case you may clear away Ten pound island, leaving said island on your starboard hand, and steer into the harbour, as above directed, and come to near Five pound island."

Saturday the fourteenth of December, 1839, had been a mild and unpretentious day, and quite a fleet of vessels had set sail from Down East ports for the westward. Sunday morning, however, the glass fell, a gale came up out of the southeast and sixty of these coasters ducked in around the Point to anchor, as Blunt directed, in the outer harbor where they had every reason to suppose they would be secure.

Instead of blowing by and going on its way, the gale rose, full on the harbor from the open sea. It piled in the swells, setting Dog Bar in a rage; a rocking, surging undertow caromed from the west shore to the Point and back; it shoved the vessels forward, bows on their cables with every swell, then yanked them back on the bounce. Everything was obscured in a splatting mixture of rain and snow.

By nightfall twenty-two vessels had been wrenched from their moorings and were smashing against the western ledges in the mountainous surf. When Monday morning dawned, thirty-two more lay at their anchors dismasted, or had disappeared out to sea. Many crews were taken off during the fury of the storm by rescue boats manned by heroic Gloucestermen. Twelve bodies were recovered from the rocks. Another eight were known to be dead, and it was thought the toll might go as high as forty; but there was no way of knowing for sure because most of the vessels were strangers.

Luckily for the Gloucester fleet, nearly all were home during the seasonal lull in the fisheries, safe at their berths in the inner harbor.

Two days after Christmas, another mighty storm struck the coast. But this time only a few ships were caught beyond Ten Pound Island. Five drove ashore; four were wrecked and the fifth was got off. A sixth held to her anchor when the crew grabbed axes and chopped away her masts. The other two or three rode it out.

Gloucester people shook their heads. Had the craft seeking shelter in that first storm in the outer harbor taken the precaution of sliding inside Ten Pound Island to the inner anchorage that could hold five hundred sail, which Blunt described as "safe against all winds that blow," the losses, they believed, would probably have been reduced by more than half.

It was the most destructive storm in Gloucester's history, but her own fleet suffered little by it, and it doesn't seem to have occurred to anyone that a breakwater from the end of Eastern Point might have saved two or three dozen vessels and as many lives.

Sarah McClennen Niles (1800–1830) and Thomas Niles (1797–1872), painted by Roches, 1829. (Private collection)

~8~
THE COMING OF
THOMAS NILES

TEN YEARS AND EIGHT MONTHS had elapsed since Ku-shing wedded the domains of Eastern Point behind his wall—but, decree as he might, no stately pleasure-dome arose nor "gardens bright with sinuous rills." His vision of a jeweled pendant upon the sea cracked if not shattered, John Perkins Cushing threw his energy and his treasure into the creation of "Belmont" on the inland hills. With mingled regret and relief, the China merchant on July 15, 1844, sold his Gloucester estate and some small real estate in Boston in the bargain to Thomas Niles of Boston for $5,000—400 acres of mainly undeveloped farm, pasture, woods and brush, a pond, ledges and beaches, house, barn, quarry and wharf—at $12 an acre, more or less.

My great-great-grandfather was born in a house on Milk Street in Boston on March 6, 1797, the son of Ebenezer Niles, descendent of a Welsh settler, and Mary Jenkins. Nothing is known of his youth except that he was "an old sailor of the War of 1812, one of the captives of the Dartmoor prison, where he lingered for twice a twelvemonth a patriotic sufferer, sharing the dangers of Shortland's Massacre."[1]

The English prison was crammed with 6,000 American prisoners, among them young Niles, when the Treaty of Ghent was ratified in February 1815; but their release was delayed, and they grew restive and insubordinate to the verge of mutiny. On the sixth of April Captain T. G. Shortland, the commandant, ordered his soldiers to fire into the Yankees. Five were killed and thirty-five wounded, and "Shortland's Massacre" stirred up a storm in America.

Some time after his release and return home Niles and a brother operated a livery stable on School Street in Boston, formerly the barn and stable with a large yard and garden on the Washington Street side of the house of the surgeon John Warren, a founder of the Massachusetts General Hospital and Harvard Medical School.[2] Family tradition has it that Grandsir Niles supplied the equipage for the triumphal visit to the city of Marie Joseph

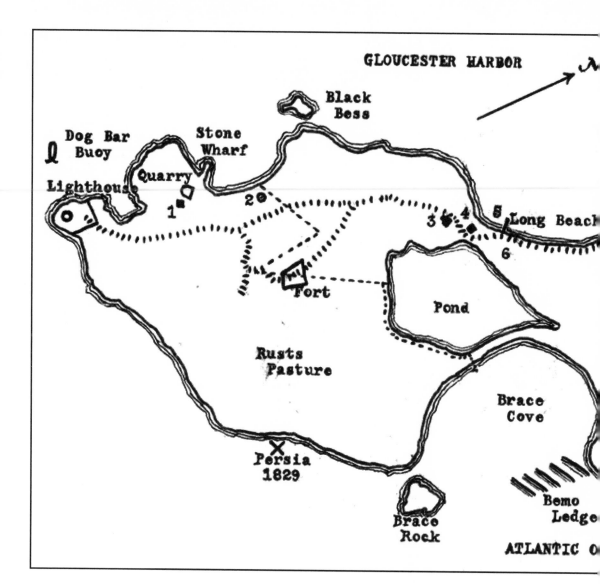

GLOUCESTER HARBOR

Paul Yves Roch Gilbert du Motier, Marquis de Lafayette, the aging hero of the Revolution, for the start of his grand tour as guest of the nation he helped create.

None of his men were to mount the box that day in August 1824. No sir. Tom Niles himself preempted the coachman, behind a dashing team of white horses, and conducted the great man through rounds of entertainment and parades punctuated with the clamor of bells, artillery salutes and rockets. A lady spectator recalled Lafayette "with his coat thrown back, his ugly, benevolent, kind, old French face, with the high reddish-brown wig, and the small, beaming eyes."[3] Perhaps back to this unforgettable event harked the lifelong partiality of Liveryman Niles for fast white horses.

The Niles stable (evidently operated by his brother William after his move to the Point and the nucleus of later shops and offices that would be known as the Niles Block) was one of the most popular in Boston, accord-

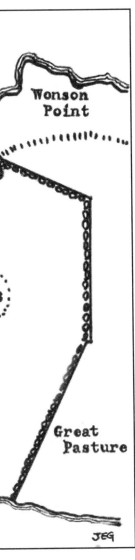

Wonson
Point

Great
Pasture

JEG

ing to a reminiscent account. "The entrance was a passage a little lower than the present avenue to Court square. This stable had a great reputation for its large party sleighs on evening rides about the middle of this century, when snowstorms were more severe and the street railroads did not destroy all opportunities for sleighing by carting off the snow as soon as it fell. Many a party has gone to Brighton or Lexington in one of these great sleighs."[4]

As for the appearance of the new owner of Eastern Point, his only known portrait, painted in 1829, shows a young man of thirty-two in the high-collared style of the day, whose handsome and clean-shaven features suggest a certain wryness of temperament.

A companion portrait depicts the firm but warm face of his first wife, Sarah McClennen, at the age of twenty-nine. Great-great grandmother was nineteen when they wed. She died the year after she was painted, following the birth of their seventh child. Eleven months later he married her youngest sister, Maria Victoria McClennen, and she was nineteen too. Maria had given him four more children when he retired from active business in Boston at the age of forty-seven and transplanted this already substantial family to a wholly different way of life at Eastern Point.

Tradition has it that like Noah, Niles herded the clan aboard his boat, sailed down from Boston and herded them ashore at his estate. Whether he came bearing dove and olive branch would soon be a matter for some discussion among his neighbors.

His boat was a smart sailer and much admired— so much so that a property owner on Rocky Neck, thinking to unload a liability on the city bumkin while he was in a land-buying frame of mind, offered him the entire eastern half of the Neck in exchange for the yacht, which was valued at some $500. Niles wanted no part of such a sharp bargain. Four years later Cyrus Story did, and bought the half-Neck for just that—$500.

"I designed to make it my home, and I did so," wrote Thomas Niles, looking back. "And I believed that I should be able here to pass the remainder of my days (being then well advanced into middle life) on an estate unsurpassed for beauty of situation, though then sterile and unimproved, engaged in the congenial pursuit of improving it and rendering it fertile, and believing that on my death my children would inherit in it a sure fortune by its steady enhancement in value, if I should not earlier have disposed of it to such advantage as to realize to them that fortune during my life."[5]

(Facing page) Author's map of Eastern Point in Niles era, showing 1. barn, 2. Indian Spring, 3. main barn, 4. farmhouse, 5. farm and ice wharf, 6. ice houses, 7. lifesaving station, 8. Hill of Rocks, 9. main gate. The old Cushing wall, dividing the Niles and Patch lands runs roughly up and down at right. The old farm road runs from Wonson Point out to the lighthouse with a branch to the fort. The finer dotted line shows the outer boundary of the old Eastern Point farm.

Early photo of Niles farm shows barn (left) and farmhouse. (Author's collection)

Niles was not behind the times. The gilding of what Samuel Eliot Morison calls the "Gold Coast" from Beverly Cove to Eastern Point started when four Boston merchants and a retired Salem shipmaster acquired most of the Beverly Farms shore between 1844 and 1846 and Richard Henry Dana built the first summer estate in Manchester.

Each party to these seaside transactions, naturally, knew he was giving the other a close shave. One native who sold a Boston man 100 acres on the water for $6,000 was so guilt-stricken, according to Morison, that he threw in a yoke of oxen to ease his conscience. And Gloucester people must have thought Niles as daft as Cushing before him.

Daft as a fox. Exactly two months after he took title to the Eastern Point farm the prominent citizens of Gloucester held a public rally pushing to connect Cape Ann with the Eastern Railroad to Boston. Three more years, and the first train steamed along the Gloucester Branch into the depot. From that day on, Cape Ann was a summer resort.

Others besides Niles were consulting the crystal ball. George H. Rogers, a Gloucester merchant of a speculative turn of mind, was buying up the common or "cow" rights of local people to the harbor pasture in the Bass Rocks area, and Isaac Patch, a smart farmer who foresaw the day when the Great Pasture would be more than a grazing ground, was enlarging his holdings; of him we shall relate more later.

The train would really open up Cape Ann to the "off-islander," although of course the Squam River had been breached before the penetration of the rails by those outriders of the leisure class whose backbones were sturdy enough to stand the roads.

Among these was the family of Joseph Kidder, a Boston druggist. The year before Thomas Niles bought the Cushing farm, in 1843, the Kidders persuaded Mrs. Judith Wonson, then only twenty-three, to put them up in her home, and thus they became the first summer boarders of record in East Gloucester. The Kidders brought their friends, and their friends brought their friends, and so was ushered in the era of Victorian summers, destined for nostalgia and conceived (or, more properly, born) in the Wonson homestead, on whose site, in another generation or two, it would burst into full flower with the blossoming forth of the famous Hawthorne Inn.

Within a season of the Kidders' pioneering visit, Mrs. Mary Wonson opened her house to summer guests, up on the hill across the road from Judith; she called it The Fairview, and the old place is still putting them up. It was Judith's establishment that evoked long memories from Editor George Procter:

> There was no market in those days, and the only grocery was the outfitting store of Giles & Wonson, in the square. But there were ducks and chickens raised on the place, together with fresh vegetables, apples, pears and currants from the garden. John Bray, with his well known butcher's cart, with its choice assortment of meats, supplied the demands in this line. A cow supplied butter and cream. Lobsters and fish were plentiful, and the catching of the cunners furnished a never-ending pleasure in front of the rocks near the house. Then there was bathing and sailing, going over to the harbor, roaming the shores of the Niles property, all of which furnished most congenial amusement.
>
> The cooking was done by an open fire on the hearth, and there was one of the old style brick ovens which turned out delicious brown bread and beans, Indian pudding, pies and berry cakes. Later on came the Yankee baker, a tin oven placed in front of the open fire. There was an orchard of apple trees where the inn now stands, surrounded by a white fence, with a row of currant bushes inside the fence. There were no currant worms at that time and the fruit was large and delicious. A brook flowed through the meadow, and wild roses grew in profusion about the rocks in front of the house.[6]

Thomas Niles looked to four sources for the improvement of his farm:

1. By working the granite quarries opened by Mr. Greenleaf.
2. By clearing the land of boulders and surface rock, smoothing its slopes, bringing portions of it into cultivation, and gradually fitting the whole for subdivision into lots for gentlemen's sea-side residences,—in the mean while farming on it.

3. By the building of ice-houses, and the cutting and sale of ice from the fresh water pond on the estate.

4. By the gradual growth of the town itself, and the extension of its commerce, which would result in the settling of the upper portion of the Point, the building of wharves and storehouses along its western shore, and the transfer of part of the business of the town to that side of the harbor.[7]

After a period of indecision he decided to suspend the quarry operation indefinitely. It would have been profitable, he believed, and he kept in the back of his mind reopening it as a source of residential building material when the time was ripe to subdivide the farm into smaller estates. But in view of his other plans Niles concluded to put neither the capital nor the time into it.

His second object was to clear and improve the Point, ultimately for speculation, in the meantime for agriculture, and he wasted no time at it. The next summer Thomas Hillier, former tenant of the Eastern Point Farm, now seventy-five and proprietor of his own lands up beyond Patch's, wrote his son in Maine of hometown doings. Remarking in some wonder that Gloucester was filled with Bostonians for the season and that city people were discovering the seaboard, he continued:

> Just returned from the old farm tyred enough with a cow. Mr. Niles very kind. No charge. Patch loses his 50 cents. The old home looked very natural. Great alterations there. Fields green and handsome. Beautiful rye in shock. Many trees set out. Green look. Corn in Rusts Pasture. Great field taken in from the corner of the old barn straight to the crab tree. The great swamp cleared most up. Nearly 3 cord of wood cut and hauled home. Mr. Niles has asked me to come and see him. Very pleasant . . .[8]

Chalk one up for Farmer Niles. In a neighborly gesture he had waived the customary charge for pasturage a landowner could levy when a foreign bossy got into his field. Hillier's cow had strayed clear across the Patch land onto the Niles Farm, doing Patch out of what he might have collected. Either that, or Patch bet Hillier that Niles would charge him and lost the wager.

The new owner moved into the farmhouse that had been rebuilt after the fire of 1837, added onto it for his still expanding family and lived there year round for a decade. Until the Gloucester Branch was opened in 1847, he traveled to Boston on business when necessary (he owned the Niles Block next to Boston City Hall) in the jouncing confines of the Gloucester, Salem and Boston mail coach.

Of his first twenty years of work, Thomas Niles wrote in review:

> Excluding beaches, rocky shores, and the pond, the area of the estate was 336 acres. During this time I cleared and brought into cultivation about 100 acres, removing altogether from these 100 acres between 3000 and 4000 tons of boulders and surface stones.

I constructed three miles of smooth and solid roads over the estate, and planted their borders with poplars and elms. I planted more woodland, and cultivated carefully the young plantations already growing.

I enlarged and almost rebuilt the farmhouse, which I took for my own residence; built three large barns for storing hay and farm products, built also a cattle barn and a corn barn, carriage and harness house, tool house, shed, wash and bath houses, and dairy room. I planted two orchards with apple, pear, plum and quince trees; and I set out great numbers of ornamental trees, elms, silver poplars, walnuts and willows, of which more than 1000 have now fifteen years' growth.

Some estimate of the value of these improvements may be gathered from the fact that I have $13,500 insured upon the farm buildings and farming stock and utensils. I also built a wooden pier, on spiles, at the southwestern end of the long sandy beach, for the common use of the farm, and also for shipment of ice.

I built also six ice-houses; and to secure the pond from the sea, and preserve it for icecutting and for ornament, I constructed on its sea side towards Brace's Cove, a stone wall four hundred feet long, five feet high and three and a half feet wide.[9]

During these twenty years from 1844 to 1863, he estimated, he spent at least $2,000 annually improving the ground. Said he: "Land which was strewn with boulders so thickly as to be useless even for pasturage, and which showed all kinds of unevenness of surface, I cleared and smoothed and converted into fertile slopes covered with excellent haying grass, at a cost in many cases in labor and money of $500 to the acre."[10]

Drawing by Sarah Rogers of the ice house and wharf at the Niles farm, with Ten Pound Island Lighthouse beyond. (Author's collection)

Probably most of the ice Niles cut from the pond was loaded from his icehouses across the road into the holds of schooners docking at his wooden pier, and thence to Boston. From there, who knows where? Mayhap as far as the Far East, for Boston's international trade in ice from nearby ponds and lakes was booming under the reign of the Ice King, Frederic Tudor. Sixty-five thousand crudely insulated tons were shipped all over the world in 1846—a profitable statistic of which the Point's new owner obviously was aware.

Time has eroded the Niles mark on Eastern Point but not erased it. His road beds remain. Some of the trees he planted, and many of their progeny, flourish. He believed that, but for his riprapping, the Pond that took his name would have been recaptured by Brace Cove, for he found it "in danger of destruction by encroachment of the sea."[11] He may have been right; his seawall stands, in any case.

Four thousand tons is a mountain of boulders, and their removal by oxen a heroically Stonehengian project. But where did he put them all?

His oldest and mightiest barn was fifty yards beyond the farmhouse, across the road. The second barn stood back of the stone wharf at the edge of the quarry; with the Lighthouse it dominates the end of the Point in a Fitz Hugh Lane painting done from up in the harbor—a striking, white, cupolaed landmark visible for miles. When two mighty elms at the fork of the lighthouse road and today's Aileen Terrace died and were felled in 1975, each stump revealed about 125 rings, dating them to around 1850.

No trace remains of the earthly structures of Thomas Niles with one exception: the stubs of the double row of spiles supporting the pier he built across the road from his icehouses at the southern end of his beach. They are there yet, marching into the harbor at low water, and they are liable to continue so—if nobody pulls them up—for their next 125 years.

In late September 1848 the *Gloucester Telegraph* ran the following item:

> The two greatest sailing matches ever known in this country came off in this bay and harbor on Wednesday afternoon and Thursday morning. The prize on Wednesday afternoon was the best anchoring ground. Between 3 and 4 o'clock that afternoon the vessels began to make their appearance off the Point, coming in with a fair breeze from the south. From the time mentioned til long after dark, there was one continual string of schooners coming into the harbor, and at dark it was estimated there were 500 vessels inside of Eastern Point! At times there were from 100 to 150 vessels under sail between the Fort and the Point; and they would come into the harbor four and six abreast—even when it would be supposed that there was scarcely room for another vessel to anchor. It was certainly one of the most magnificent views of the kind we ever witnessed.[12]

Probably the mackerel fleet. Next morning at daylight, Thursday, they were making sail and by eleven the last had rounded the Point for the eastward. But Friday morning the wind came ahead, from the east, and by noon three hundred of them were back at anchor in the harbor to await a favorable shift of wind.

The Eastern Point Lighthouse after sixteen years had turned out to be a miserable, carelessly designed, cramped, leaking, decaying affair, the shame of the keeper and a disgrace to the government. Finally the Fifth Auditor of the Treasury (the Lighthouse Board was four years in the future) was persuaded, and on September 20, 1848, contracted with Winslow Lewis to rebuild and modernize it for $2,550.

Captain Lewis was a striking figure, a Cape Codder who retired from the sea to take up as a chandler ashore. In 1807 his experiments with an improved lantern led to a contract to equip all forty-nine existing lighthouses, which established him in the rewarding business of supplying them with sperm oil and from there into their actual construction. By 1848, two years before his death, he had survived forty years of wheeling and dealing with generations of bureaucrats and politicians, accusations of finagling, chicanery and graft, and most of his enemies; he was the leading lighthouse builder in the United States and a bona fide pioneer in the betterment of aids to navigation.

Captain Lewis was seventy-eight when he arrived at Eastern Point to supervise the job and proudly told one and all that this was his 125th lighthouse, which may have been a slight exaggeration. He was not long at it.

Less than four weeks after the contract was signed, on October 16, the workmen were tearing down the old structure, and a temporary lamp was placed on Keeper Wonson's cottage. In nine more days the new lighthouse was almost finished. Another five and it was all but done.

This second beacon was built on the foundation of the old; it was hard brick laid in cement. The height of the lamp was thirty-four feet. Every trace of wood had been eliminated from the tower. A circular staircase of finished stone led to the lantern room, whose window sashes and frames were of wrought iron and much larger than formerly. The nonrevolving lantern gave out a red beam (it would be called the Ruby Light); it was glazed with the finest French plate glass encircling eleven whale oil lamps and 15-inch reflectors.

On the evening of November 3, 1848, at seven o'clock, Captain Lewis's latest light was lit for the first time, a mere eighteen days after his men began razing its predecessor. For the first thirty minutes the ruby rays of the new Eastern Point Light were directed up the harbor toward town. It was manifestly superior to the old, "strong as that from Ten Pound Island, although a mile and a half more distant."[13]

Ernest L. Blatchford's photograph from about 1900 looks south along the dirt road toward the Niles farmhouse. (Cape Ann Historical Association, Gordon W. Thomas collection)

~9~
AN OPEN AND SHUT CASE

IF THERE WERE NEIGHBORS THAT first summer after the Boston man Niles bought the Eastern Point farm who, like Thomas Hillier, found him "very kind and very pleasant," others did not.

For two hundred years, give or take a few, Gloucester people had been hiking, riding or coming by water to the Point, tramping over it, gunning, fishing, berrying, nutting, gathering ye rosebuds, sparking and chowdering without any particular let or hindrance from its dynasties of owners as long as the rights and privacies of the proprietors were held in reasonable regard.

Then this all changed. In the fall of 1847, when he had been three years on the land, Mr. Niles brought three fishermen before Justice of the Peace William Ferson and charged them with trespass.

On the twenty-seventh of September, he alleged, Thomas Jefferson Rowe and his son, William, and Benjamin Brazier had "with force and arms broke and entered the plaintiff's close . . . and then and there with force as aforesaid, his grass and corn of the value of $10 then and there growing, beat down and consumed, and then and there with force as aforesaid, threw down three rods of the plaintiff's fence of the value of $5 and other enormities then and there did against the peace."[1]

Nor was this the first time. Back in 1845, on the first of October, the same three had entered his land and "his grass, corn and herbage there growing of the value of five dollars trod down and consumed and destroyed" and perpetrated other enormities to the tune of twenty dollars' damage.[2]

Justice Ferson found the three local fishermen guilty, and they appealed to the Massachusetts Supreme Judicial Court. Their case was continued for nearly two years, but when it came to hearing in September 1849, they failed to show up in Salem. The Court upheld Justice Ferson's judgment by reason of default and awarded Niles $1.50 damages and costs of $49.68.

A small matter, no doubt.

The Rowes were among Gloucester's sturdiest fishing families. Thomas

Jefferson, the elder, was one of the first to risk the winter fishery on Georges Bank. At the time of his run-in with Mr. Niles, he was fifty. In his old age he forsook the schooners for dory shore fishing, which he followed into his eighties. In the evening of his life he gave as much fun as he took, telling the fortunes of his neighbors.

A close kin of Jeff's was John Rowe, a fisherman of about the same age. Johnny always claimed to have invented the trawl, that he made up and set the first one ever tried—across the mouth of Brace Cove in 1820. If so, he was nineteen years ahead of the record book. When he passed on at nearly ninety, it was written that "he was quite an ingenious man, and used to say that he never made a figure or letter in any school whatever—that he never saw a shoe made til he made one himself, and never saw house built til he built one himself. He never used liquors or tobacco in any form, and gave up the use of coffee and tea in early life."[3]

While Niles was having his row with the Rowes, Captain Stephen Dodd of Rockport took him to court in September 1848 for refusing to pay a debt of $60. This case, too, went to the highest court in the state, which persuaded the disputants to submit it to arbitration. The referees thought Niles should pay $50 and costs, and the court so ordered.

Was there a contentious streak in Mr. Niles?

To get back and forth to the lighthouse a person had to go by water or traverse the government's right of way through the Niles farm. Roger William Wonson enjoyed telling his grandchildren how he hiked out there to help his Grandpa Wonson tend the light as a boy of twelve or so. More than once he was attacked by the Niles dog. So the lad took to carrying a gun with him. One day he was stopped by Mr. Niles, wanting to know what he was doing with that gun. Replied Roger smartly:

"Well, sir, I aim to shoot a dog if I have to."

There was no further trouble among boy, dog and man.[4]

After eighteen years on the job Samuel Wonson retired as the first Keeper of the Eastern Point Light and was replaced on October 1, 1849, by another of the Rowes named James. Keeper Wonson died the next September at seventy-seven.

The first sign of the big trouble was a small notice in the *Gloucester Telegraph*:

FIFTY DOLLARS REWARD

The above reward will be paid for such evidence, as will lead to the conviction of the man or men who, on the evening of the 26th inst., DESTROYED THE GATE at the entrance of the premises of the subscriber.

THOMAS NILES

Gloucester, August 28th, 1850

He ran this notice twice a week for four months, evidently without results.

But the case of the gate was by no means shut. Two and a half years passed, and in June 1853 Niles entered an action of tort in the Court of Common Pleas alleging that his neighbor, Isaac Patch, had (at an unspecified time) taken down, carried away and converted to his own use a gate and stone wall belonging to the plaintiff, and that, furthermore, Patch had entered his land and carted off sand and seaweed, damaging him in all to the extent of $1,000.

One of the intriguing aspects of this suit is that it followed right on the heels of an interesting acknowledgment by Mr. Patch on May 13, notarized and recorded at the Registry of Deeds, that back in 1840 when Gardner Greenleaf was working the farm for Cushing, he (Patch) had, for the consideration of one dollar, quit claim and released all right and title to the beaches on the Eastern Point farm and any rights of way he had across it, and any other interest he may have had in it.

The court continued the suit until September, when Patch applied to have it removed to the State Supreme Court, where it was docketed for November.

Isaac Patch was a large, ruddy, sociable man from Hamilton, four years the junior of Thomas Niles but hardly any less combative when aroused. Leaving Hamilton, he had settled in Rockport, the home of his mother's family, the Pooles, and he and his brothers Levi and William farmed there and sold produce around the Cape. Among his good customers was Captain Samuel Giles of the fishing firm of Giles & Wonson in East Gloucester, who one day braced the young farmer while dickering with him for a load of vegetables, as follows: "Young man, it seems to me that the proper place for you to reside is here in East Gloucester. You can raise all the vegetables you want, can furnish milk and ice, also ballast to the fishing fleet, and you will be right here with us and it will save the long haul from Rockport which is now quite a burden. If you think favorably of this, and there is every reason for you to think so, I can put you in the way of getting some land which will give you a start."[5]

Patch turned this proposition around in his head, talked it over with his judicious wife Eliza, regarded the growing Giles & Wonson fleet and its needs and the increase in business on the Eastern Point side of the harbor, and in 1835 he purchased his first tract—66 acres on the western side of the Point from the foot of the Mount Pleasant Hill to the Cushing farm at the north end of the beach, including some land of Captain Giles.

Farmer Patch built up his herd and sold milk and produce to the neighborhood. He put an icehouse above Wonson's Cove and cut ice from his wee pond on the hill for local use and for the fleet, and then he added ballast to his line, as Captain Giles had suggested, carrying fine smooth stones from the High Popples Beach across the Point to the wharves by oxcart. He built his homestead on what inevitably was called Patch's Hill. It remains a dignified and spacious old country house with touches of columned and corniced elegance.

Some time along around 1848 or 1850 Patch picked up another 130

Isaac Patch
(1801–1886).
(Isaac Patch III)

acres right across the top of the Niles farm to the Back Shore. In all probability, it was this acquisition that brought these two strong-willed men into conflict.

While his suit was pending that summer of 1853, Niles thought, he would move to improve his public relations by making it known that visitors were welcome to the Point—by invitation. So he gave a party. Well, that was the impression of the guests, anyway.

It was on a Thursday in August, and a large throng accepted his invitation to visit the farm. Some were Gloucester people, some were boarders at the Pavilion (the large frame hotel with the bold balconies on the present site of the Tavern), and some were dismissed in the public print as "strangers" (gate-crashers, likely)—a breed frowned upon by the host.

They arrived by carriage and by boat, and by one in the afternoon a gala and cheerful concourse was milling around the big tent pitched back of the stone wharf. Some strolled out to the rocks to view the passing vessels, some visited down to the lighthouse, and then the call went out, and one and all assayed the chowder, baked clams, roasted corn, fried fish and lesser goodies. An oven of flat stones had been laid out on the beach, a good hot fire torched off, then the ashes swept away, the clams spread on the rocks, and over them a thick steaming blanket of seaweed nuggeted with ears of golden corn.

After the eaters had pronounced themselves well et, a speech or two of gratitude was tendered Mr. Niles, to which he replied with graciousness. Procter's Band tuned up, the guests added voice for some old favorites and danced away the hours until the day was done, when all turned homeward in the finest kind of spirits, declaring their host not a bad sort after all.

Well, next week the newspaper apologized that it had certainly not intended to give readers the impression that this was Mr. Niles's affair. The party had been gotten up at the Pavilion by an ad hoc arrangements committee of which the owner of the Point farm was merely a member. He had generously offered the use of his property, and the *Telegraph* had supposed that those in attendance understood they would be assessed for the expenses.[6]

That November Gardner Greenleaf conveyed to Thomas Niles for one dollar Isaac Patch's old release to him of any rights of way he may have reserved over the Eastern Point farm. The same month Niles's trespass suit against his neighbor came before the Supreme Court term and was put over for another year.

Maria Victoria McClennen, second wife of Thomas Niles and youngest sister of his first, had died in September 1851, at thirty-nine, having borne seven children (three of them at Eastern Point), and in December 1853 he took his third, Rhoda Barry Porter, daughter of Captain Benjamin Porter of Danversport. (Captain Porter's litigious son-in-law, not unexpectedly, offered in the course of time to take *him* before the Supreme Court over some forgotten difference between them, but the matter seems to have been settled on the way.)

Meanwhile, the case of *Niles v. Patch* kept returning to haunt the court, and in November 1854 it had wormed its way back to the top of the judicial backlog. It was a jury trial, and his peers concluded that the arguments of Mr. Niles were inconclusive and found for his neighbor. The plaintiff—all his ire returning over the loss of suit, gate, wall, sand and seaweed—asked the court to set aside the verdict as being "against the evidence" and grant him a new trial.

The hearing on his exceptions was continued to next spring, when a crowd of Point people was summoned to Salem to testify. The upshot was that the Supreme Court overruled his appeal and ordered Niles to reimburse Patch the $130.50 it had cost to repel the accusations of trespass and gate stealing.

Defeat was missing from the vocabulary of a veteran of Dartmoor. Damn custom and commonage! This was his land, his close, his privacy, and no one should set foot on it for any purpose whatever except by his express invitation or on business with the lighthouse. No, he would not be put down.

In November 1856, three and a half years after he mounted his legal campaign against Isaac Patch, Thomas Niles was back before the Supreme Judicial Court of Massachusetts praying for a review of his case. The weary judges put him off for another year.

Niles was a methodical strategist. While waiting next summer for his appeal to come to trial he wrote a certain letter of inquiry to Boston, and as soon as he had received the reply he anticipated, he went over to the *Gloucester Telegraph* and inserted a notice, complaining to Editor John S. E. Rogers as he did so that he had been annoyed day and night for years by trespassers who left his gates open for his cattle to stray, picked his fruit and robbed his cranberry meadow, and he had had enough:

PUBLIC NOTICE

The Proprietor of the Eastern Point Farm calls the attention of citizens and strangers to the following statement.

For fourteen years he has consented that the public may pass through his premises to the Eastern Point Light House. He regrets to add that the courtesy has been perverted by many, and that his grounds are made public by Fishing, Gunning, Pic Nic and Berrying Parties, added to which the patrons of the Light House Keeper, until it can no longer be borne without serious inconvenience and damage to himself, and oblige him in future to forbid all persons from passing on or over his road or premises unless having direct and official business with the Government.

The annexed letter from the Collector of Boston, will show the relative position of the citizens and the Government.

THOMAS NILES

Gloucester, Sept. 4th, 1857.

Boston Custom House
Aug. 28, 1857

Dear Sir—I have your favor of Aug. 27th. I find upon inquiry that the United States have merely a permissive right over your premises, and that for the benefit of the official who has charge of the light.

I have notified Mr. Norwood of the Regulations in the respect to the converting his Light House dwelling into a house of entertainment, and have demanded an explanation.

You have a right of action against every person who passes over your land to go to the Light House, except the person is officially connected with the Light House, or has legitimate business there.

All persons not included in the original permissive right are trespassing, and as such are liable to you in damages.

I will endeavor to take such steps as will redress you. When at Boston, I would be glad to see you.

Very faithfully, your ob't servant,

ARTHUR W. AUSTIN

To drive the point home, Niles ran this notice every week for the rest of the year.

When the litigants again appeared before the Supreme Court in December, as scheduled, they brought crowds of partisans, some unwilling; that is, 150 were subpoenaed as witnesses. The courthouse at Salem was packed to the doors, and the trial created great excitement in Gloucester. Beyond these lean tidbits the newspapers passed along only one further item: the most unusual participant was a very large gate (presumably *the* gate) that had been lugged up from Eastern Point and propped in the entry as a "dumb witness."

The arguments and testimony must have been bitter and drawn out. It took the jurors twelve hours of wrangling to reach a verdict, and this time it was for Thomas Niles. They reversed the earlier judgment for Patch and awarded Mr. Niles a legal victory with faint praises—$2.50 damages.

Now Ike Patch did the howling. He fired back with a bill of exceptions, and the patient Court (probably hoping he would drop it) put the case over for another sixteen months.

Editor Rogers thought matters had come to a pretty pass between Thomas Niles and his adopted town and offered some comment to his readers on the impact he had made since buying the Point fourteen years earlier:

> He was a stranger to our citizens, being known to only a few of them. Not wishing to have his crops trampled upon, he forbid trespassers from passing over his land, and soon after from passing along the shore. This aroused the indignation of those who had heretofore considered the beaches and rocks around the Point as common property, and a petty warfare was commenced. Persons were driven off, and prosecutions succeeded.
>
> One thing led to another, til about the whole population on Eastern Point became united in opposition to Mr. Niles, and many things were done on both sides which have since been matters of regret. Mr. Niles claimed the beach and road up to the gateway near Wonson's Point, and Mr. Patch who owned property bounded on the road beyond the gateway, was prosecuted for trespassing, and the case, besides increasing the feeling of opposition to Mr. Niles in our community, has occupied considerable of the time of the Supreme Court, and we believe has not yet been decided.[7]

Nevertheless, Thomas Niles had won the third round. His right to bar his land and his road and his beaches and ledges and cranberry meadows to the general public had been affirmed by the bench. So the Gloucester selectmen discontinued the road to the lighthouse as a town way.

Public opinion against the owner of the Eastern Point farm was outraged. But how would you have decided, esteemed reader, in *Re Niles v. Patch?*

The steam ferry Little Giant *crosses the inner harbor past the British steamer* Petunia *en route from East Gloucester to Duncan's Point around 1900. (Ernest Blatchford photo, Gordon Thomas collection)*

~10~
THE FOUR-CENT FERRY

While farmer Niles had his back to his wall defending his privacy, the rest of Eastern Point was surrendering its to the four-cent ferry.

It started with the Gloucester Branch, that day in November 1847, when the steam locomotive clickety-clacked across the new bridge over Squam River, blurting smoke and cinders out of its cracker-barrel stack. That was the first inroad.

In one leap the rails put the stagecoach out of business and brought Cape Ann within an hour's swaying ride of Boston, where before the trip had consumed the worst part of a day.

One lesser leap was all that was required to shortcut the two more miles of wretched road that separated Gloucester Center (the Harbor Village) from the Point, which was yielding to the press of the waterfront around the head of the harbor, but remained a place apart. Inevitably one revolution in transportation opened the eyes of some smart entrepreneur to the potentialities of another.

Captain John W. Wonson of Eastern Point was the man for it, and he had a strong back besides. In October 1849 he inaugurated this second revolution by the expedient of rowing a dory, as often as passengers appeared, between Duncan's Point at the entrance to Harbor Cove and the old town landing behind the square in the section that people were now calling East Gloucester, contraposed to the Eastern Point farm. This tranquil passage was secured exclusively to the ferryman until 1860 by a charter from the Great and General Court of Masachusetts, which required of him merely that he schedule a minimum of six round trips a day at a maximum fare of four cents each way.

Captain Wonson had sized up the state of commerce correctly. Business was so brisk that he added two rowboats in the spring of 1850. In July 1856 James Davis, Jr., launched for him the first steamboat ever built on Cape Ann, the ferry *East Gloucester*. After two years, when Captain Wonson was ferrying 160 passengers a day, he sold out to Israel Gill.

Progress in transportation tends to be of the leapfrog sort, and hardly had the ferry put the land route in disgrace when a stagecoach was licensed to operate regularly between East Gloucester Square and the town. Then in 1859 a local company chartered the steamer *Mystic* to make the first scheduled runs between Gloucester and Boston.

As late as 1868 the "omnibus" stage persisted in competing with the ferry for the traffic between East Gloucester and over town, and it survives in anecdote. That June, "when a very fat lady got in last week a passenger grumbled 'Omnibuses were not made for elephants.' To which she retorted with a twinkle 'Sir, omnibuses are like Noah's Ark, intended for all kinds of beasts.' A burst of applause from the other passengers, and soon somebody got out, but it wasn't the fat lady."[1]

But it was the ferry, which took only four minutes (at a penny a minute) to steam across the harbor, that ended the innocence of the Eastern Point of yore.

By 1858 East Gloucester had 1,000 residents and 130 homes. It was a community in its own right, and people were content to let *Eastern Point* apply henceforth to the end of the peninsula beyond the stone wall and gate of Mr. Niles.

East Gloucester was a pleasant district of country and sea, with a good school or two and snug clapboard houses strung along the harbor road, bunched in the village around the Square. The ladies of the East Gloucester Sewing Circle raised half of the $2,000 it cost to build the new Baptist Chapel. The volunteer firemen boasted one of the smartest tubs in town. Procter and Perkins ran large nurseries, Collins and Clark were blacksmiths, Henry Wonson had opened a Union Store and Isaac Patch had his big farm and ice and ballast business.

The be-all and end-all of all this was fishing. East Gloucester, and Rocky Neck, with the only open shore left, were caught up in the fever. Samuel Wonson and Sons, successors to Giles & Wonson, were said to be the biggest fishing firm in the whole country. They hired hundreds of hands ashore and afloat and sent a fleet of close to fifty of the old square-stern vessels and a few of the clipper schooners that were becoming popular off to the banks from Georges to Grand, hand-lining for cod, haddock and halibut and jigging for the mackerel east as far as Labrador in the summer and fall. The fleets of John F. Wonson and William Parsons 2nd added to the restless energy that had awakened this side of the harbor. Back of the prickle of spars, acres of salt fish dried in the pungent flake yards.

All kinds of Yankee operations were summoned into being to serve the needs of a town in the world trade of salt fish. To ship fish, for instance, required butts, and every butt must have its bung. That was the business of Joseph Wonson, whose product was in such demand by the spring of 1858 that at last he lost patience with the unreliability of his power source, succumbed to the Industrial Revolution and installed a small steam engine in place of the windmill that had cranked around the machinery of his bung factory, when it was so moved. A visitor was entranced with his little engine

... so very small "it is certainly a curiosity to see it in motion ... has the power of four men and takes but a shillingsworth of fuel a day to operate ... the cheapest power on Cape Ann ... all progressive men should come and look it over."

Rocky Neck, not so many years past a mere sheep pasture, had been linked to the main by a causeway built up on the bar. The census of 1859 credited this insular hamlet with 22 houses and 143 very individualistic residents. Dodd & Tarr owned the north end of the neck and had a store, warehouses and a wharf for their fish business which took out regularly from fifteen schooners; they had just the location for it and were planning to build a large marine railway.

The "omnibus" pauses in East Gloucester Square. (James B. Benham collection)

By road, it was another mile from East Gloucester Square around Smith Cove, over the bar and out to the end of Rocky Neck. But by water it was 300 yards, and once again Captain Wonson saw his opportunity and made the tip of the neck a stop for his ferry (being right on route anyway) on demand of passengers or freight.

Not that the isolation of the old Eastern Point dating back to colonial times was so easily breached by the four-cent ferries and the omnibuses. The quaint ways of the backwash clung on with a wonderful tenacity, and even today East Gloucester remains a special haven for the odd and the eccentric.

Suffice it to mention one particular rustic sport, strikingly like an earthy Brueghel scene. Customarily each Christmas morning in East Gloucester the men strung a rope across one of their streets between two trees, about twenty feet high, from which they hung a fat turkey in a bag (presumably already plucked). Upon paying his ten cents to the pot, each contestant in turn was blindfolded, armed with a long staff, led off a rod or two, spun around a few times and told to go at it. If he could hit the gobbler with his stick, it was his Christmas dinner.

Great work for the crowd, baiting, dodging and buffing the blind ones

who lurched about the neighborhood swinging at trees, hitching posts, gates, fences, houses, horses and whatever stood in their aimless way. One turkey generally lasted the day before it met up with a winner.

Although the Coast Survey had been created by Congress in 1807, the government failed to begin a systematic charting until 1843. At midcentury, in spite of an explosion of commerce, aids to navigation remained primitive and haphazard, and except for the scattering of lighthouses, next to worthless in anything less than broad daylight.

Nothing warned the mariner off the Back Shore of Cape Ann between the Twin Lights and the partially obscured light on Eastern Point. Even the Londoner, the ledge a cable's length east of Thacher's Island awash at low water, was not marked until around 1855 when they placed an iron spindle on it.

And it seems unbelievable that the ledge southwest by south from the tip of the Point, in the way of passing vessels and with only 7 feet over it at slack tide, should have remained undetected and unmarked until January

1855, when Captain Webber, one of the Gloucester pilots, chanced to be sounding in the area and found it; it was promptly named Webber Rock and given a spar buoy.

The hulking rock of Norman's Woe lurked off the western entrance to the harbor, unwarned of. A black spar buoy was moored on Round Rock Shoal, at the edge of the entering channel. A white spar buoy bobbed astride of Dog Bar that jutted across from the Point, about halfway along it. Prairie Ledge outside Freshwater Cove and those southwest of Ten Pound Island also were buoyed. But none of these markers betrayed their presence by light or sound. On the other hand, Halfway Rock, broad off Salem and Beverly Harbors and bare now of any traces of the hand of man, sprouted a fifteen-foot stone monument that raised a spindle another fifteen feet, topped off with a copper ball two feet across.

For what small comfort it afforded mariners, the lighthouse board in 1857 installed an automatic fog bell at the Eastern Point Station, driven by a handwound clockwork. Simultaneously, it modernized the Ruby Light with a fourth-order Fresnel lens that was supposed to extend its visibility from eleven to thirteen nautical miles.

Perhaps it was this evidence of bureaucratic interest in Gloucester that encouraged a group of citizens a month or so later to get up a petition to Congress to build a breakwater between Rocky Neck and Ten Pound Island over the bar between the two. The average there at low water was barely two feet, they reasoned, and there was never sufficient depth at any tide to admit a vessel drawing eight feet, though the apparent passage had often been mistaken—with unfortunate results—for a channel.

A breakwater there, the petitioners argued, would secure the inner harbor from the disastrous undertow raised up by onshore storms. One may speculate that if they had succeeded in their halfway measure, Congress could never have been persuaded to put the breakwater where it finally did fifty years later, out from Eastern Point across Dog Bar.

The irascible Grandsir Niles.
(Author's collection)

~11~
I DID NOT LIKE
HIS CONDUC

A SPARK OF LIGHT IN THE DARKNESS
beyond the window of the lighthouse keeper's cottage, where she was, caught Mrs. Nancy Montgomery's eye. She turned to look closer. It was a flame—the size of a hat—on the roof of Mr. Niles's lower barn across the cove, behind the quarry. She called to Keeper Norwood, her brother-in-law. Lem ran outside and clanged the fog bell furiously.

It was twenty minutes to eleven, the evening of February 11, 1858; Aunt Charlotte, the keeper's wife, remembered because she glanced at the lighthouse clock, a government timepiece that was unfailingly accurate. Five minutes later they were astonished to see a second red glow flare into the night sky, but they couldn't tell if it was the Niles farmhouse or the other big barn across the road from it.

Both barns were on fire all right, within minutes, and close to a third of a mile apart.

Many of the townspeople were at a levee that evening, and it took longer than usual to muster the hand-tub companies. The ruts had frozen, which made it hard going over the road. In no time at all the two fires were roaring skyward.

Niles was in Boston on business, but his wife, their two-year-old daughter Rhoda, an aged aunt, three farm hands and Mary Mansfield, the servant woman, were asleep in the house. At the cry of fire, they tumbled from their beds into one of the coldest nights of the winter. The house was in no real danger because the frosty air was still. The flames crackled straight up through the main barn across the road, and Mary's first thought, as she said later, was "to try and save the poor dumb beasts."

> Dressed, or rather undressed, as she was, and she had even less than the ordinary night apparel of a female, she rushed out, in that terrible winter night, and endeavored to get from the barn the horses, oxen and cows. But the fire had progressed too far, and a sheet of living flame barred all ingress or egress at the doors. Thus

Sarah Rogers drawing of the Niles farmhouse. (Author's collection)

prevented from fulfilling the dictates of kindly pity, the sense of duty to her employer prompted her to try and save some little of the property which the fire was fast devouring. From the barn she went to the carriage house adjoining. There all alone she struggled, succeeded in drawing out one valuable carriage, and was in the act of removing another, when the flames, which had been all the while raging around her, at last actually reached her person, and, blistering her almost from head to foot, drove her, despairingly, from her work of love and duty.[1]

The barns and sheds burned to the ground; in the larger were lost two horses, two yoke of oxen, three cows, a dozen pigs, harness, carriages, wagons and about twenty tons of hay. Total loss $5,000, partly insured. The fires burned themselves out. When the firemen arrived there was nothing to do but warm themselves by the embers. A few days later the owner took out a card of thanks in the newspaper and expressed regrets that due to his absence no one had offered them the hospitality of his house and some warm refreshments.

When Farmer Niles returned from Boston to find his barns and everything in them gone, he was greatly agitated, to put it mildly. Only a month back somebody had unhung and carried off his gate again, and he had posted a $50 reward in the paper for evidence that would lead to the punishment of "the villains."

Considering his unpopularity and the circumstances, most people figured the fires had been set. "It would appear," observed the *Telegraph*, "that some of the enemies of Mr. Niles are determined to give him no peace."[2]

The selectmen posted an unprecedented reward of $1,000, to which Niles added $500 of his own, for information that would bring about the conviction of the arsonists.

Action followed with surprising swiftness. Ten days after the fires a secret jury was impaneled in Salem to inquire into their cause under an act of the General Court passed only three years earlier, providing for summary fire inquests. The undisclosed evidence pointed to one Daniel Ross, an ex-hired hand on the Niles farm. Ross was arrested in the last week of February and held in Salem jail, unable to raise $5,000 bail. A few days later Ross's former boss, Robert Marshall, was arrested; he had been Niles's tenant farmer until shortly before the fires, when he and Ross had moved out of the house. He was freed on bail. Both were charged with arson.

As if some Puck had been loosed on Eastern Point to gall the peevish squire, Mary Mansfield was hailed into police court on a charge of assaulting with a pistol two men who had tried to pass through the farmhouse gate on their way to the lighthouse on business. Miss Mansfield pleaded innocent.

This singular confrontation before the Niles front door was alleged to have occurred on the twenty-seventh of February, the day after Daniel Ross's arrest. It was not Mary's first court appearance; immediately after their employer won his case against Isaac Patch she was fined two dollars for attacking Ross at the farm.

The Niles family had left the Point temporarily after the fires, and her master had put Mary in charge of the premises, with instructions to keep the gate locked. On the afternoon of the twenty-seventh, Albert Hale and his daughter, of Rockport, and Nehemiah Knowlton were headed for the lighthouse in a wagon to dicker with Keeper Norwood about buying some old iron he had lying around, and a cow. At the gate before the Niles house Knowlton got out, found it locked and walked up to the door, where he was met by Mary Mansfield, who inquired what he wanted.

To get through to the lighthouse on business.

She couldn't allow that, said she. She had orders from Mr. Niles not to let anyone pass.

Knowlton returned to the gate, tried various of his own keys, and after none would fit, spun around at the sound of a high-pitched oath from the lady, who had gone into the house and was back on the steps with a pistol.

"If you offer to go through that gate," Miss Mansfield was quoted as declaring firmly, "I'll blow your brains out. It is my master's bidding, and I'll do it as long as there is a drop of blood in my body."

She was about twenty-five feet off, and she pointed the gun at Mr. Knowlton's head. She looked very wild and mad to the thunderstruck travelers.

By what authority did she stop him thus? Knowlton managed to ask.

"By the authority of Governor Banks," she replied emphatically. Congressman Nathaniel P. Banks was governor-elect of Massachusetts, and this doorstep mandamus—whatever its basis—had the desired effect.

The three left the wagon at the gate and continued on foot. On the way to the lighthouse they met the Norwoods, and two ladies and two schoolteachers who were visiting with them, and all nine walked back to the gate, apparently with the intention of remonstrating with its inhospitable keeper.

"There comes that gray-headed son of a bitch," they were shocked to hear Miss Mansfield direct at Mr. Knowlton as he approached. She then accused him of attempting to break the gate down, which he denied.

Is the pistol loaded? he asked.

It is, said she, and capped too, and she would shoot him if he tried to open the gate. Mary followed this with an abusive volley at Aunt Charlotte, who refrained from returning the fire, probably wisely.

Keeper Norwood, when all this came out in court, testified that he "hadn't had much difficulty with Mr. Niles," and that the collector in Boston, his superior, had assured him that his family and that of his wife had the right to pass through to and from the lighthouse.

Justice Joshua Trask found probable cause and released Miss Mansfield in $400 bond for arraignment before the Court of Common Pleas, but no further record can be found, and the case must have been dropped.[3]

A fortnight after this extraordinary encounter the public hearing on the arson charges against Robert Marshall and Daniel Ross was conducted by Justice Trask in the Town Hall. Nothing else had been talked of in Gloucester, and the hall was packed.

Thomas Niles was the first witness, and he said merely, as to Ross, that "his labor was satisfactory, but his disposition was not."

The prosecution's star witness, Thomas H. Payne of West Cambridge, was sworn. A lad of seventeen, he too had recently quit work for Farmer Niles.

He and Ross had certainly been on the outs with Mr. Niles, no doubt of that. They had complained about his meanness, Payne admitted, "spoken of ridiculous things" about him, "damned him some," talked "pretty hard" against him and written bad words about him on the side of the barn.

One day Ross went down to the lighthouse, Payne testified, and coming back told him he'd thought of a pretty good joke on the old man: set fire to his barns—"that would gall Mr. Niles more than anything." And Ross had worked up a few other "good capers" that might frighten the owner off his farm such as shaving the tails of his horses, tying a string across the road to trip his mare and (one they carried out jointly) hiding the dog in the corn barn for the fun of hearing Mary Mansfield whistle for it in vain. But Payne denied that he had dug holes in the beach to upset Mr. Niles's horse and break his carriage.

Right after the fires, the boy told the court, Ross admitted to him that he and another fellow had set them and that his partner had gone to sea. Ross warned him to keep it quiet, as he had confided in him as a friend, and he was the only other to know.

Neither of them got along with Mary Mansfield, Payne conceded, and Ross had even tried to get a warrant for her arrest to "bother the trial" and had worked on Payne (who had to admit that he "liked to plague her") to testify against Mary before she took the stand against them.

It was when Ross told him that he, Payne, was suspected that he thought he had better testify against his friend before his friend took after him, the witness said. Thus did Tom Payne weave his web of incrimination around the defendant.

The prosecution spun tighter. Niles and Marshall had hassled over the ownership of the property in the barns, a dispute that the week before the fires had been resolved by referees entirely in Mr. Niles's favor. On the Saturday previous to the fires Marshall and Ross moved out of the farmhouse. On Tuesday Marshall was notified of the referee's decision against him. Thursday night the barns burned.

Ross did not take the stand in his own defense, but Marshall did in his. He stated that he had quit Niles five days before the fires to work at Patch's ice pond, and that he and his wife and two children had moved off the farm into a two-room house. The evening of the fires Ross had come for supper and the night. They then retired to the same bed, in the kitchen, because the children were sick and sleeping with his wife. They were awakened, Marshall declared, by the alarm of fire, dressed and hurried over to the farm.

As a matter of fact, said Robert Marshall in some agitation, he thought Mr. Niles himself was accessory to the burning of his barns. Whereupon he fainted into the arms of a bystander.

When the uproar subsided and the witness had revived, he continued that he had heard others, including Mr. Patch, state that they suspected Mr. Niles. In fact, he had suspected for some time that the Niles barns might burn "because everybody spoke against him." He denied under cross-examination that he and Ross had agreed before the fact to occupy the same bed that night for an alibi.

When this sensational hearing was resumed in five days, Marshall retracted his insinuations about Niles's involvement and those he attributed to neighbors, including Mr. Patch, who had confronted him with the newspaper account of his testimony and demanded that he sign an affidavit that he had lied. Why he had lied he could not tell. He had suffered four or five fainting spells before; perhaps "being unconscious makes me tell lies."

Mrs. Marshall took the stand. She knew her husband and Ross were abed at the time of the alarm because she heard them breathing, she said. As for young Payne: "I saw Payne on the day of the inquest. He said he did not know anything at all about the fire. He was sorry the house and all in it had not burned up. He wished to G___ Niles had been in it, he would not have pulled him out. He said he thought Mr. Niles was as deep in the mud as anyone; Niles told him going to town that he expected his buildings would be burned before he got back."

Before the inquest, Mrs. Marshall admitted, she told Constable Lane that her husband was innocent, that she'd swear to it, and if it came to that, "I could swear the legs off an iron pot, as the old saying goes."

Payne was recalled. He quoted Marshall as telling him before the fires that if they wanted to do anything to Niles they could take a boat over to the Point any time—and afterwards that Ross had a spite against his employer and that public opinion held that Niles had torched them off himself.

Faced with such a flood of accusation and denial and such a drought of evidence, Justice Trask was unable to resolve the guilt or innocence of the defendents; but they were most certainly guilty, he declared, if Payne—on whose credibility he was not called upon to pass—were to be believed. So he found probable cause and ordered them held in $5,000 each for the criminal term of the Court of Common Pleas. Marshall was again bailed, and Ross was jailed again for want of it.[4]

Farmer Niles had acted injudiciously, in the mildly expressed opinion of Editor Rogers, when he got Collector Austin at Boston to draw a virtual *cordon sanitaire* around the lighthouse. The embargo had been so complete as to put the Norwoods in an intolerable situation; they were practically prisoners of Mr. Niles on the government reservation at the end of his property.

The events of the winter, and the fires of public animosity they rekindled, must have so unsettled Thomas Niles and so raised his choler that he now forsook his better judgment altogether.

Early in June Keeper Norwood was summarily fired by the collector and replaced by Robert Poole, Jr., who was transferred over from the Baker's Island Light.

Within a few hours an angry petition was circulating around Gloucester charging that Norwood had been canned wholly due to personal malice, for

Drawing of Niles barn by Sarah Rogers. (Author's collection)

there was no doubt in anyone's mind who was responsible for his downfall; it attested to his competence and demanded that he be put back on the job at once. Though Lem and Aunt Charlotte were well known and loved in Gloucester, job security did not exist in government service, and the outcry had no immediate effect. Soon people were muttering that the new keeper was letting the fog bell at Eastern Point run down during thick weather.

Unquestionably Niles had connections in high places, probably more through his Boston than his Cape Ann associations; to be linked with him locally, as a matter of fact, had become more harmful politically than otherwise. The prosecutor in the celebrated arson case was Otis P. Lord of Salem, a conservative Whig. Niles, too, was a Whig high enough in county party councils to be elected in 1850 one of the two vice presidents of the district convention in Salem; as a mossback he perhaps did not retain much influence with the emerging Republicans, though it is interesting to note that their leader was Governor Banks, whose name had been so unexpectedly invoked by Mary Mansfield at the gate.

Otis Lord that November of 1858 ran for Congress as an American, or Conservative Independent, against both the American Republican and Democratic candidates, and lost.

This was hard for the local conservatives to take. John Rogers of the *Telegraph,* a staunch Whig, wrote with an edge of bitterness that Keeper Norwood's removal so powerfully affected the campaign on Cape Ann that "men who would otherways have voted the American ticket at the November election, would not look at a ticket with Otis P. Lord's name upon it, and the Democratic ticket in this town received a much larger vote than it otherwise would in consequence of Mr. Lord's connection with Mr. Niles."[5]

The two incendiary suspects were brought to trial before the Court of Common Pleas (soon to be reformed into the Superior court system) in

Lawrence that same November. The jury was hung, reportedly eleven to one for conviction, and a new trial was scheduled for January in Salem. Marshall continued free on bail.

But poor Ross, still unable to raise the $5,000 bond, remained behind bars at Salem, where he had now languished for almost a year on suspicion of a crime that had not yet, as the *Cape Ann Weekly Advertiser* indignantly editorialized, been proven against him.

Further noting that the young Nova Scotian was utterly illiterate until the summer preceding the fires, when a visiting "collegian" undertook to give him a few lessons in Gloucester, the *Advertiser* on January 7, 1859, published an elegy said to have been composed by the prisoner entirely without assistance. This was some six weeks before the new trial.

THE LAIT. DANIEL. M. ROSS
It was on the twenty forth of september
*   as you Shal under stand*
on that verry day my boys
*   i saw this very land*

My hart was glad Rejoicing
*   when first I did it see*
but now i am filled with sorow
*   all in america*

i first landed in boston
*   but short time there did stay*
when i hired with a farmar
*   in north america*

i hired with this farmar
*   for the term of one year*
but i had not been long with him
*   unto he proved sovere*

i did not like his Conduc
*   as you shal understand*

i Served him for foar months
*   before i did disband*
then i hired with two farmars
*   that had latley took his farm*

i served them for eight months
*   and well wee did a gree*
but mark my sad misfortun
*   in north america*

i served my time all on this farm
my waiges did instore
then forto seek my fortun
i started once more

i did not travel fur to i hired again
it was with a joley ice Cuter
abe williams was his name
he lived down in Gloucester
near to the Regin main

it was on the twentry sixth of febuary
O mark that Cruel day
when i was taken prisner
and sent to Salem jail

there lying and condoling
my triel to wait on
for four months i lay for triel
before it did Comeon

but mark my sad misfortun
my triel was a jurned
for four months more i lay pauling
my mind it was most gon

it was on the forth of november
my triel did comeon
for three days it did continu
before it did a jurn

the jurey on my triel
it is true did not a gree
so i am back in prison
to wait my distinee

now my story is mos Ended
now friends come pity me
and think on my sad misfortun
in north a merica

Painting of the Niles farmhouse by William Niles, 1870s. (Private collection)

~12~
FARMER NILES BELEAGUERED

SAD INDEED WAS YOUNG ROSS'S "misfortun in north a merica." He and Marshall, hired hand and tenant farmer accused of the spite-burning of Thomas Niles's barns on Eastern Point, were tried for the second time in Salem at the end of February 1859, and this jury found them guilty.

The public was in an uproar—at any rate, the newspapers were. The *Salem Gazette* remarked mildly enough that circumstances had pointed at the pair from the beginning. But the *Salem Advocate* reported that the verdict outraged the community and astonished all the members of the bar present at the trial, including the successful prosecutor himself.

The *Gloucester Telegraph*, reviewing the deterioration of Mr. Niles's relations with the public, found his fellow citizens to be almost unanimously sympathetic to the defendants. Everyone at the trial on both sides had believed this jury would be as hung as its predecessor was in November. Consequently, its finding of guilty took all by surprise. Rumors that the jurors were divided down the middle when they left the courtroom and continued at loggerheads for a day and a half before the last holdout gave in prompted the *Telegraph* to ask soberly whether threats had found their way into the jury room.

This remarkable impugnment of the Court of Common Pleas was picked up and amplified to full cry by the *Cape Ann Weekly Advertiser*, the *Telegraph*'s infant competitor of sixteen months, which seems to have been an even more intimate party to the jury's supposedly secret deliberations:

> The conviction is almost universal here that the verdict has been obtained by some unfair means, and that some, if not all of the jurymen have given a verdict contrary to their deliberate judgments. That one of them was induced by what he considered threats, to violate his firm Convictions, we do know; and the five jurymen who stood out for acquittal from the time the case was given them on Tuesday evening til the next forenoon, must give some good rea-

son for their change at that time, or the community will suspect them of being influenced by considerations which no honest man would heed.

The *Advertiser* proposed darkly that Mr. Niles had the whole trial in his pocket from the start; that having made up his mind that Marshall and Ross, who had given him a hard time on the farm, were guilty, everything to indicate the contrary had been "carefully excluded throughout"; that the two had been denied counsel at the initial inquest which had been conducted by smart out-of-town lawyers specially imported for the purpose; while at this trial the presiding justice, prosecuting attorney and *all* the jurymen were "intimate friends of Mr. Niles and unquestionably designated by him."

An extraordinary accusation!

Moreover, asked the *Advertiser,* why had not the prosecution made the slightest effort to trace a man alleged to have been met by several people coming away from the fires that night and acting very suspiciously? "We can think of no reason in the world for this neglect, but the determination to exclude every other hypothesis, except that Marshall and Ross were the guilty parties."

The newspaper predicted that the trial would weaken public confidence in juries and in justice generally in Essex County. It thought the Fire Inquest Act of 1854 should be amended by the General Court to guarantee counsel to witnesses. And it demanded a third trial for Marshall and Ross, to which end the feeling was said to be so strong in Gloucester that more than $400 had been subscribed already to defray their legal fees if one were granted.

Thus spoke the *Advertiser,*[1] and so much a part of the common talk had the case become around Cape Ann that a patent medicine advertisement pitched:

> The verdict in this case has caused great dissatisfaction throughout our community, but had the subject for the jury been the merits of MCLEAN'S STRENGTHENING CORDIAL AND BLOOD PURIFIER, the result would have been very different, and both jury and people would have been unanimous in its favor, the evidence not being circumstantial but positive. . . . Sold by dealers in medicine everywhere.[2]

Arguing for a new trial a few days later, counsel for the convicted pair, C. P. Thompson and B. F. Hallett, contended that the jury had rendered a false verdict and that one member in particular, though believing them innocent, had voted guilty "for the sole purpose of avoiding some supposed or threatened evil consequences which might arise to himself from a refusal on his part to render said verdict."[3]

Judge Aiken declined to admit in evidence the juror's affidavit to this effect, on the grounds that he could not bring a charge of improper conduct against himself and there was no evidence of improper influence having penetrated the jury room. He refused a new trial, and the defense prepared to take its exceptions up to the Massachusetts Supreme Court.

While the lawyers wrangled in Salem, seventeen bundles of hay disappeared from Mr. Niles's new barn near the quarry (he had rebuilt both barns), a further harassment that a Boston newspaper (so far afield had passions been excited by the trial) attributed to "some fiend in human Shape."[4]

A month after this celebrated trial, in mid-April, there issued from Boston a twenty-page pamphlet, *Trial of Marshall and Ross for Barn-Burning: A Brief Exposure of a Systematic Attempt to Mislead the Public Mind, and to Create a False Sympathy in Behalf of Convicted Incendiaries,* by "A Looker-on in Vienna." Disclaiming any professional connection with the affair, the whimsically anonymous author in some heat defended the government's case, the last jury verdict and most especially the admittedly eccentric character of the dauntless Mary Mansfield in the face of what he viewed as the scurrilous campaign of the *Gloucester Telegraph, Boston Traveller and Journal* and *Salem Advocate* to manufacture a hostile public sentiment out of whole cloth.

One of the newspapers was quoted by "Looker-on" as calling testimony for the prosecution "such as no honest party could use, or ought to use. . . . Payne acknowledged himself to be a scamp, a conspirator to burning, and Miss Mansfield showed herself to be what a regard to delicacy forbids me to name . . . testimony coming from the vilest of the vile, unworthy to be listened to on the trial of a mad dog."

"Arrant nonsense and flagitious perversion of the truth!" snorted the outraged "Looker-on in Vienna." And from a lengthy defense of Payne's credibility, he or she took up the cudgels in behalf of Miss Mansfield with this disarming preface:

> Undoubtedly, this woman has peculiarities and eccentricities of character, which, for aught I know, may have exhibited themselves, occasionally, in an unbecoming and improper use of that "little member," which we have high authority for saying, "*no man,*" and *à fortiori,* no WOMAN, "hath tamed," or "can tame."[5] Nor will she, perhaps, be likely to be very soon accounted "better than the mighty," on the ground that she "*is slow to anger*"—or "better than he that taketh a city," because she "*ruleth her spirit.*" But to question the intentional truth of her statements, under oath, during a protracted examination of several hours . . . (is a) monstrous absurdity.

The *Gloucester Telegraph* remained unmoved by the cogency of *A Brief Exposure* and advised dryly that if the circular was produced by a friend of Mr. Niles it did him more disservice than otherwise.

Isaac Patch had waited six years for this midsummer day of reckoning toward the end of July 1859. It was in June 1853 that his neighbor Niles had taken him to court for gate-crashing, trespassing and sand-and-sea-weed-stealing. Patch had won the first round and been reaffirmed in the second. It had dragged on and on. Niles had appealed again; the verdict was overturned and Niles took the third round. Patch appealed, and on it dragged. Now, finally, his exceptions had come before the full bench of the Massachusetts Supreme Court.

The wheels of justice ground and came to a halt. The court overrode Patch's exceptions and declared finally and irrevocably that Thomas Niles was the winner, the absolute monarch of his land, right down to the harbor's mean low-water mark. He had gained his object, the long-term security of his investment that depended upon legal guarantees of waterfront privacy to himself, his heirs and future owners of Eastern Point.

The court directed Isaac Patch to pay his victorious neighbor the sum of $2.50 damages, to return the costs that in the first case Niles had paid him and to remunerate him for his court costs in the two subsequent litigations.

Damages of $2.50, costs of $985.80. Niles had sued him for $1,000 at the outset.

It was a year of ironies . . . for Isaac Patch and Daniel Ross . . . and for the schooner *Prudence* of Bangor, Maine.

This ill-named vessel was beating down from Boston for home, fighting for every inch against a northeast storm. It was the devil's hour, two in the morning, December 4, 1859. The helmsman braced against the canting deck and strove with his weather wheel, straining his pelted eyes through the swirl of snow; but of course he could see nothing beyond the shuddering foot of his jib, beyond the foreboom, and Captain Nickerson sensibly ordered his schooner about, to run for Gloucester Harbor and a safe anchorage for the night.

After a few minutes, running with the gale, the lookout cried out, a light! Must be Eastern Point. Haul in them sheets and put your helm over . . . we'll haul by the light, yelled the skipper.

But no, it was not the lighthouse at all; it was the masthead light of the steamer *Menemon* of Sanborn, Maine, lying at anchor where she had taken refuge on the Pancake Ground in the harbor, off Niles Beach. (The sandy-bottomed stretch of harbor off the Eastern Point shore from Niles Beach to the breakwater is traditionally known locally as the Pancake Ground for its ability to hold an anchor, hence a good anchorage.) What they saw from the deck of the onrushing schooner was her light, beckoning around the False Point from clear across Brace Cove and Niles Pond.

Prudence struck on the outside of Brace Rock. Some whimsy of the deep, some further irony, held her there, and Captain Nickerson and his men had the presence of mind and the crazy luck in the breakers and the snow and the blackness to swing her main boom over to the great rock and crawl along this slender bridge to the ledge. One of them was nearly flipped off by a sea on the way, but he clung to the spar like life itself. They huddled on the lee side of the rock and listened to the storm smashing their schooner to pieces on the sea face of it. In two hours *Prudence* was driftwood, whacking about in the surf at their feet.

At daybreak, the tide having ebbed, they waded ashore and stumbled on a warm house somewhere, perhaps at Mr. Niles's, who may have forgiven them their trespasses under the circumstances. Nothing was saved, and the mixed cargo of the *Prudence* was strewn from Brace's to the lighthouse. Across Cape Ann that same night the schooner *Magellan Cloud* drove ashore and broke up at Squam Point, and the British schooner *Victoria* came to the same end at Lanesville. Not a man was lost from any of the three.

After sixteen years of battling his rocks and rills and neighbors, Thomas Niles in June of the following year, 1860, put his saltwater estate up for sale. He advertised (not locally, but probably in Boston) that it was under good cultivation as a farm, and for a summer residence unequaled on the Atlantic coast.

For about five years he had been spending eight months at Eastern Point and four at his winter seat in Brighton, a small country town of vistas, fertile fields and spacious estates just west of Boston. He was sixty-three. Grave troubles threatened the Union, and the future was never more uncertain. He had many heirs, and his offer to sell may have been a half-serious market test to see what interest his property might arouse, improved as it was, and secured by his court victory over Isaac Patch.

Taxes were hardly driving Mr. Niles off the farm any more than they would have John Cushing (who was the biggest taxpayer in Belmont when he died). The tax bill against the Niles farm in 1855 was $211.50 and fell to $153 in 1858, the rate and the assessment having been reduced.

Circumstantial evidence in the reconstruction of events can be as unreliable in the writing of history as in a prosecution for arson, and there is no justification for inferring that, simply because Farmer Niles placed his estate on the market even as the Massachusetts Supreme Court was pondering the merits of a third trial for Marshall and Ross, by the coincidence of these events they were connected.

They did, however, coincide. Moreover, at the end of June the court sustained the exceptions to their conviction and granted them a new trial (was it a third chance to prove their innocence, or a third for the state to prove their guilt?). New evidence was said to have been brought forward, having to do with the habits of a watchdog belonging, one supposes, to Niles. The *Telegraph,* for reasons it did not elaborate, thought it unlikely they would again be brought to the bar, and this appears to have been the case. There is nothing in the record to indicate that government or Niles pushed the matter further.

If, indeed, the sad misfortune of "The Lait Daniel. M. Ross" was finally ended, and he walked out of Salem Jail a free man and twenty-eight months older, guilty or innocent he had paid for having crossed the path of Thomas Niles.

Anyway, no one bought the Eastern Point farm, and suddenly the mood changed. A more permissive spirit seemed to exude from Squire Niles once again. Parties were made welcome, or at least were not summarily kicked off the beach. Some days after the Supreme Court decision the yachts *Rob Roy* and *Sea Breeze* landed excursions of ladies and gentlemen on the Point for a Fourth of July chowder as of old, and the *Right Bower,* Captain Low, repaired to Black Bess for another.

The *Rob Roy* was owned by Arthur Caswell, assistant editor of the *Cape Ann Weekly Advertiser;* it was probably George Procter, the editor, who frequently shipped with him on summer afternoon sails, who recalled a long time afterwards that Mr. Niles ("as I recollect him, a man of fine presence, courteous and gentlemanly in his deportment who had great faith in the future of the fine property in which he had invested his money") permitted them to land at the quarry wharf, cook chowder and roam as they pleased, "only requesting that we would be careful to extinguish our fires and leave the premises as we found them."[6] These dispensations may not have disinclined the *Advertiser* from treating their grantor less harshly in its pages.

And then (would these wonders never cease?), Lem Norwood was reinstated as keeper of the lighthouse, two years after his abrupt dismissal following the famous standoff at the gate. But he lived less than a year before he fell dead of a heart attack on duty at only forty-nine.

A friend remembered the Norwoods, "a wide-awake, energetic woman . . . a man of good repute and greatly esteemed." One autumn evening they had a party at the lighthouse. "We went over in Jack Wonson's Eastern Point express wagon, which at that time was used to convey passengers between Gloucester proper and East Gloucester. There were several young ladies from Rockport, relatives of Mrs. Norwood's, and we had a good time. A bountiful supper was served, and all went merry." One of the guests fiddled while the rest danced.

Aunt Charlotte was kept on as keeper after Lem's death and until Benjamin Cross succeeded to the post late in 1861. Continuing the recollection: "It is said that when the lighthouse department came under the supervision of the United States naval department, the young naval officer who came around for inspection thought he had caught a tartar when he set out to criticize Aunt Charlotte's care of the light. She had a peculiar shrill voice, and when excited she would pitch it on a high key which sent it home to her hearers in no unmistakable manner, and it was quite apt to carry conviction with it."[7]

That black twelfth of April 1861, the Rebels fired on Fort Sumter, and in four days the vanguard of Cape Ann boys marched down to the depot behind the Gloucester Cornet Band, all in such a rush that only thirty-nine of Company G of the Massachusetts Eighth Infantry were around town to respond to the call, as some were off fishing.

The war was far away, but in the first two months of 1862 alone Gloucester lost 19 schooners and 156 men, 120 of whom were taken to the bottom in 15 vessels by one awful gale on Georges Bank the twenty-fourth of February.

The war seemed far away when the sea took such as this in one night, more than a company of infantry. And though Gloucester's boys marched off, not one was killed on the battlefield the whole first year of it.

Eastern Point slumbered. Whether he could not hire enough help or for some other reason, Farmer Niles in October 1862 put about everything but the buildings up for auction, advertising a farm horse, two yoke of working oxen, four cows, one pig, two farm carts, two hay trucks, an express wagon, a harness, a carryall, ploughs, rakes, hay cutter, roller, harrow, grindstone, forks, scythes, a hay press, ice cutting tools, snow plows and scrapers— along with fifty tons of English hay, ten tons of oat straw, five tons of Rowen, two tons of salt hay, a quantity of manure, 5,000 feet of white pine boards, 3,000 pickets and a lapstreak pleasure boat with a new sail.

One week later, as the shadows of the Civil War fell longer on the land, he appears to have changed his mind and offered the whole works for rent (puffing his land by a fourth and his pond by a third):[8]

> To Rent. The Eastern Point Farm in Gloucester, and immediate possession given from one to five years—comprising 500 acres, including a freshwater pond of 40 acres in the center. On the premises are 3 large barns and a cattle barn nearly new, of the capacity of 250 tons hay and 40 head cattle, carriage house, tool house and shed, together with a large farm house and out buildings in excellent repair; there is also an ice house, new, of the capacity of 1200 tons; and wharf adjoining, within a few rods of the pond, which may be extended as the demand is yearly increasing. This farm possesses an advantage over every inland farm, from the inexhaustible supply of sea manure thrown annually upon its beaches. The stock of the farm, tools and furniture of the house can be purchased if the lessee desires. The population of Gloucester being over 10,000, makes the demand good for all the produce of the farm. Undoubted guarantees will be required for the full performance of the lease.
>
> THOMAS NILES, Brighton

Dress parade at Eastern Point fort during the Civil War. (Cape Ann Historical Association)

~13~

FORT NO-NAME

THE GLOUCESTER SCHOONER *Cadet* rounded Eastern Point on the twenty-fourth of June, 1863, home from Georges Bank with a short trip of fish and a deckload of bad news.

Two days earlier she had barely escaped destruction, slipping away through the fog that had scaled just enough for her scared crew to witness the depradations of a black and very inimical privateer, like a wolf in the sheep, amongst the other Gloucestermen anchored nearby.

Confederate Lieutenant Reed, U.S. Naval Academy Class of 1860, a prize crew and one deck gun had been transferred to the barque *Tacony* after her capture by the prize brig *Clarence*, which in her turn had been taken by the cause of it all, the South's steam sloop *Florida*. Young Reed went after the Gloucester Georges fleet. When his grim day's work was done, marauding in the fog, he had burned and sunk (after taking off their crews) the schooners *Marengo, Ripple, Elizabeth Ann, Rufus Choate, Ada* and *Wanderer.*

Cadet brought the war home to Gloucester with a bang that no number of boys hustled off to the front could match. Reb raiders were on the coast, six of the fleet had been sunk and no vessel would be safe. The cry went up—the whole town lay defenseless before an attack from the sea. An emergency meeting was called; a frantic wire was sent to Secretary of the Navy Gideon Welles demanding the protection of a battle cruiser; delegations were posted to the governor and the commodore of the Boston Navy Yard.

Welles reacted surprisingly fast by ordering the immediate commissioning of three swift schooners, and *Tacony* was soon captured. The army was equally solicitous in calming the nightmares (and political agitation) of the coast and called on its Corps of Engineers to supply the balm.

Arguing as early as 1703 that "we are a frontier town by sea and much exposed to the danger of the inroads of any foreign enemy," the selectmen had vainly begged the colonial government to fortify Ten Pound Island or the neck that formed the west shore of Harbor Cove. The following year a watch house, at least, to raise the alarm against Indians or pirates was erected on this neck, which finally, as war with France loomed, was actually fortified by the Colony in 1743, long known as Fort Point.

After the War of 1812, in 1826, Brigadier General John C. Barnard and Lieutenant Colonel Joseph C. Totten urged the army's chief engineer, Major General Alexander Macomb, that Gloucester was an important link in the chain of coastal defense and should be fortified, noting that its position commanding navigation in Massachusetts Bay was of much greater significance than its commerce alone at that time warranted.

Ten years passed, and in 1836 Colonel Totten again emphasized the strategic location of Gloucester in a report to Secretary of War Lewis Cass, and he proposed that a 100-gun fort be erected there, with a peacetime garrison of 50 men and a siege complement of 500, to cost $200,000. Without doubt he had in mind Eastern Point. In 1840 he was back, pushing his plan with Secretary of War J. R. Poinsett.

By 1851 the War Department, at least, had been won over by the persistent Totten, and Secretary C. M. Conrad recommended to Congress that it approve the project. The hundred guns would cost an additional $93,274, and he also asked for $10,000 to repair the old 1812 fort at Stage Head on the western shore and set it up for a garrison of eighty, and fifteen guns. Congress took no action.

Twelve more years, and North and South were at war. Colonel Totten, now chief engineer of the army, advised Governor John A. Andrew that he had ordered a study of defensive positions at Gloucester with a view to their repair and possible extension. On April 7, 1863, General Totten, just promoted, instructed Lieutenant Colonel Barton S. Alexander (who, under his direction, had built the great lighthouse on Minot's Ledge after the original was destroyed by a storm in 1851) to recommend a system of temporary defense works for the coasts of Connecticut and Massachusetts.

Colonel Alexander spent two days surveying Gloucester in May and was in the act of preparing his report to General Totten when the *Tacony* struck and the town cried for help. Immediately, Major C. E. Blunt was ordered to take possession of the high ground of Eastern Point in the name of the Secretary of War and to set about surveying and laying out the site of a temporary ten-gun fieldwork, and make it snappy.

Almost at the same time, on June 29, Alexander forwarded his advisory to General Totten. He wanted not one, but two forts on Eastern Point: the main work on the heights to command the approaches to Gloucester and to hold the enemy from shelling the harbor; and a smaller battery on the southwest ground of Quarry Point, which he considered the best position on the east side of the harbor for defending its entrance.

Major Blunt's survey commandeered for the army a plot of 53 1/4 acres, in the approximate shape of a parallelogram, including all of Quarry Point, the stone wharf, Niles's new barn next to the quarry and the best part of the owner's cleared farmland on the hill.

As these heights were the joy of the engineers, they were the pride of

Thomas Niles. Here was the commanding ground of Eastern Point, magnificent for the defense of Gloucester and the eastern sweep of Massachusetts Bay, delightful for its panoramic view, the very heart of the man's investment.

Worse still, it was the portion of his farm from which Mr. Niles had removed most boulders and been most profligate with his manure and seed, and it was just this spring planted to six or eight acres of corn, squash and potatoes, which the engineers asked him to level, to his exceeding irritation. Not the kind of tenant for the farm he had advertised for. Mr. Niles was not pleased, but he bit his lip, for a Dartmoor veteran was nothing if not a good patriot.

The road to the lighthouse at this time, after passing between the Niles farmhouse and the big barn by the pond, cut in slightly from its present course near the harbor and followed Elm Avenue, on to the Ruby Light, some 200 or 250 feet inland of today's route along the shore. A farm lane, now Fort Hill Avenue, cut off in a southeasterly direction from the lighthouse road until it attained the high ground, where it bent southwest through the site chosen for the fort and then looped to the west and rejoined the road to the light behind the stone wharf.

Early in July the army assigned ten casemate 32-pounders, mounted on carriages, to the Gloucester defenses. They arrived from New York aboard the schooner *Euphemia* on July 20, when the plans were altered to place seven of them at Eastern Point and the remaining three in the old fort at the stage, where work was promptly started to make ready for them. Colonel Alexander's suggestion of a small emplacement on Quarry Point was rejected.

Even as the guns were being lashed aboard the *Euphemia* in New York, a deckload of lumber arrived at Eastern Point, somewhat short, however, of its intended destination, Neponset. It happened in a dripping thick fog the afternoon of July 13; the schooner *Boston Packet* of Hampden, Maine, seeing nothing beyond, confidently put in around the False Point and drove up on Bemo Ledge. The men got off, her deckload went by the board, and she went to pieces.

Major Blunt's plan of a redoubt in the shape of a parallelogram about 150 feet by 300 feet called for a thick earthwork cut through by seven embrasures for the guns, each piece to be housed in a casemate, its carriage free to swing on a traverse track; this arrangement would materially increase their range and field of fire.

The job started and ran head on into a labor shortage. Thousands of yards of dirt had to be moved, requiring a big crew, and local men were reluctant to sweat the day long in the midsummer heat for the $1.25 the government was paying. So on July 24 the town voted to add a daily bonus of fifty cents, which had the desired effect. About thirty men showed up, and the works got under way in earnest.

By early September most of the embankment was raised; one of the three powder magazines was built, and the cannon were ready to be moved into place.

The two guns at the northern end of the fort enfiladed the whole interior of the harbor. The three on the longest side, facing west southwest, raked the entrance. The embrasure at the southeastern corner ranged out to sea, while the one looking to the eastward covered the entire Back Shore and its offing. With their overlapping sectors the guns of the Eastern Point fort swept every square foot of Gloucester Harbor and its approaches.

The three magazines, supposed to be shellproof, were built of timber and earthed over. Likewise the long bombproof quarters of the gun crews, thrown up inside and against the northern earthwork. A well was dug inside the fort, handy to the dugout. The farm road was relocated around the east side of the work, as Mr. Niles would not be needing it for a while.

It took three and a half months to turn Farmer Niles's vegetable garden into a fort which, though not yet quite finished, was ready for action. The Eleventh Unattached Company of Heavy Artillery, under Captain Thomas Herbert, was ordered to Gloucester.

Winter was in the air when the first advance detachment arrived on November 10, 1863, and on the sixteenth the rest of the company of 150 men filed off the train at the Gloucester depot, into the cold and rain. They formed ranks behind Cilmore's Full Military Band and marched up Prospect and down Pleasant to Front Street, and back along Front and down Spring. And then for the long hike around the head of the harbor, through East Gloucester, past the wharves and flake yards and schooners and the knots of cheering citizens. Slogging along in the mud by Rocky Neck, up Patch's Hill and past Wonson's Point, through Mr. Niles's gate and over his beach, tramping past his front door and up the road to the raw earthwork, an uninviting camp, slipping and sliding in the sleek mud, soaking and cursing it all, but glad to be on this windy point and not at Chattanooga. Cold and wet, the men of the Eleventh rolled into their bare but bombproof quarters that evening without supper.

What a shame the people of the town didn't think to provide some hot food for these brave lads sent to its defense, rued the newspaper. "It is not too much to say that finer specimens of soldiers cannot be found anywhere."[1]

The Eleventh had occupied Mr. Niles's high ground for not much more than a week when the walls of their bombproof barracks cracked and sagged ominously under the enormous weight of rainsoaked earth overhead. The men mustered outside pell-mell. A fine storm was sweeping across the Point, and they tried to squeeze into the magazines but were ordered back out and told to pitch their tents in the gale. A gang of laborers was put to work clearing some of the mud from the bombproof roof in an effort to save the barrack from total collapse.

Then Thanksgiving arrived, and with it two horsemen bearing bottled cheer. The better for discipline, if the worse for morale, the commandant did not smile on these hospitable overtures and ordered a squad to drum the pair out of camp. "Captain Herbert would not tolerate the outrage," approved the newspaper. "Hence the rogue's march."[2]

To drive home that this was a respectable outfit, the captain saw to it that next Sunday his men were prominently in attendance at the Baptist and Catholic churches in Gloucester.

Driving home also was Mr. A. J. Rowe, home to the fort from town one pitch-black night in December with half a dozen of the Eleventh when he veered too close to the ditch at the entrance and upset. No one was more than bruised, but his carriage was demolished.

The living quarters, mudproofless as they proved to be, appear to have remained unlived in, because Clough and Wheeler in short order received a contract for new buildings, the main one to be a barrack eighty feet long, with a fifty-foot attached kitchen and mess hall. It was finished early in January 1864, and the artillerymen gratefully struck their tents and moved in.

The bitter, damp weather blowing in off the sea brought on such a cacophony of hacking and coughing and sniffling that plans were pushed for a post hospital, which the same contractor completed the beginning of February for $650. Both were frame buildings, the barrack fifty yards beyond the north embankment and the infirmary another fifty beyond that, on the farm road. Grouped nearby were stable, guardhouse, sutlery and officers' quarters with seven plastered rooms and a kitchen ell.

By February Mr. Neal Wing was instructing the fort's fifteen-piece band on the advantages of starting and finishing all together, and they were stepping out on morning and evening parade. One of the musicians, "having been home on a furlough, on account of indisposition, a story of his death was circulated. Judge of his surprise on returning to duty to find the members of the band discussing the question of a dirge for his funeral, and the company preparing to drill with reversed arms, in preparation for the same occasion."[3]

The sole combat engaged in by the gunners of Eastern Point in the twenty-month life of their fort was against an enemy more to be feared than any the Confederacy could send against Gloucester: fire.

Six below zero it was, and a gale out of the northwest. Early in the morning of the eighteenth of February, 1864, the shout went up that fire had burst from the rear of a tailor shop on the water side of Front Street, back of Harbor Cove. Driven by the screeching wind, the flames jumped from one wooden block to the next and leaped across the street to engulf the other side.

The desperate alarm was carried all around the Cape and as far as Salem: get here as fast as you can—we're burning up.

The illumination of the black sky and the crackling across the harbor roused the Eleventh from their cots at Eastern Point. Sixty of them, nearly half the company, double-timed over the frozen road with a rattling wagon-ful of buckets, and quite possibly some gunpowder.

Over town the inferno had swallowed block after block, up Front Street almost to the Customs House. At this point, Chief Pettingell had no other way out: he ordered buildings blown up in its path, hoping to rob it of what it fed on. The Babson Block and the house of Captain Parsons were detonated, then the home of my great-grandfather, Dr. Joseph Garland, on Pleasant Street.

And then, at the height of it, when it was touch and go because the Gloucester tubs simply couldn't pump water (and beer and whisky and whatever wouldn't freeze in the lines) fast enough, they rolled up Salem's pride, her sparking, bellowing, shrieking, shining steamer, sent down to Gloucester on the flatcar.

The *Salem Steamer* poured a perfect torrent of water on the Customs House and saved it, and they blew up Captain Low's across Front Street from it, and the sixty soldiers from the Point fell into bucket brigade formation in the front line of the garden and handed water up the stairs to soak the roof of the Mansfield house next door, and saved that.

All these efforts—the men pumping their hearts out at the tubs, the Eleventh Unattached Brigade of Buckets, the trumpeting *Salem Steamer*—stopped the fire in the Mansfield garden, or maybe it just tired of the game and quit.

It was the Eleventh's one skirmish in the defense of Gloucester, and they fought heroically. As for the town, it might have fared better had a Rebel cruiser steamed in and shelled at will. Fifteen acres and 103 buildings were reduced to ashes.

It began to occur to people, as they recovered from the shock of the fire, that their proud fort rated a name—particularly since the work at the stage had just been designated Fort Conant after Roger Conant, Cape Ann's first governor in 1625, and Major Blunt wanted the town to pick one for its main defense, which he had built. Someone suggested "Fort Rantoul," after the late Congressman Robert Rantoul, Jr., who had practiced law in Gloucester; someone else, "Fort Parran," honoring Alexander Parran of Gloucester, who left his right arm on the battlefield of Bunker Hill; a third proposed "Fort Robinson," for Captain Andrew Robinson, who launched the first schooner up the road. And in May "Fort Allen" was advanced in memory of Lieutenant Colonel David Allen, Jr., the selectman who had raised Gloucester's second company, just killed that month in the Battle of the Wilderness.

But Gloucester never got around to doing anything about it, and the "Eastern Point fort" it remained until its dissolution.

> *Thousands at his bidding speed,*
> *And post o'er land and ocean without rest;*
> *They also serve who only stand and wait.*[4]

President Lincoln brought to the war the coordination he had for so long been seeking when in April he appointed Ulysses S. Grant his General-in-

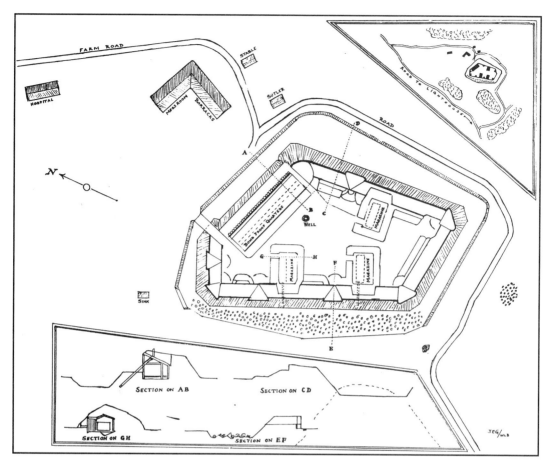

Labels visible in plan: FARM ROAD, STABLE, HOSPITAL, MESS ROOM, BARRACKS, SUTLER, ROAD TO LIGHTHOUSE, ROAD, N, BOMB PROOF QUARTER, WELL, MAGAZINE, SINK, A, B, C, D, E, F, G, H, SECTION ON AB, SECTION ON CD, SECTION ON GH, SECTION ON EF, JEG/WLB

chief. And while Milton's thousands at Grant's bidding sped, on Eastern Point the sturdy garrison continued to stand and wait.

The enemy had their troubles elsewhere, and to relieve the tedium of their scenic but isolated post, the noncommissioned officers and the band early that month mounted a combined "military and civic ball" in the Town Hall, after which the enlisted men trooped to town and put on a show at the hall to raise money for a library at the fort.

Family tradition insists that the younger daughters of Grandsire Niles, locked in their bedrooms by their father on the nights of the officers' dances, defenestrated themselves by the knotted bedsheet route to join their waiting swains in the starlight.

Spring came, and the thaw, and the road was such a muck that the man from the *Telegraph* apologized "we haven't had the courage" to inspect the improvements at the fort. For several weeks a detail of the Eleventh had been at the spar yard of John J. Somes shaping the loftiest flagstaff Cape Ann had ever seen or ever would—a timber 112 feet long by official measure.

This Olympian spar, far outreaching the main stick of any Gloucester schooner, must have been floated across the harbor to Wharf Beach and conducted from there up the hill, for it surely could never have made the bends overland. On the twentieth of April, with the proper application of the rigger's art, block and tackle and a little trigonometry, they upended this toothpick and planted it inside their fort.

May Day was to be the great celebration, and were there ever such firsts of May as on Eastern Point, the fresh verdance of the spring drifting down to the sparkling sea all round?

The garrison planned a field day, with two foot races, climbing the greased pole and the greasy pig contest in the forenoon. To colors at noon while the band played and Old Glory mounted its new staff. Then in the afternoon sack races and a dress parade and a mock dress parade, winding up with a dance in the evening.

But it was not in the cards. The day before their gala the Eleventh received marching orders for the South and departed Gloucester, perhaps not too happily on the 1:40 train, to the tunes of their band. A crowd of grateful citizens saw them off, and the *Telegraph* wished them luck:

> They seemed in good spirits. They have been at considerable private expense in fitting up their quarters in a tasteful and convenient manner, but fortunes of war require that they should leave their pleasant quarters for more active scenes, and like loyal soldiers, they make no complaint.

Lieutenant Bragdon was in command of the fort during the eleven days it was unmanned until the arrival on May 11 of Beverly's Company E of the Eighth Massachusetts Regiment under Captain F. E. Porter. A few weeks later they were joined by a Lynn company under Captain Bacheller, which remained at the post until early July, apparently for training, then departed to take over the fort at Marblehead.

A welcome break in the drone of garrison life was looked for on the twenty-seventh of July, the day scheduled for an inspection of the post by Governor Andrew and his staff. The Commonwealth's dynamic war leader, whose militia were the first to respond to President Lincoln's first appeal for troops and who had long since taken the part of abolition and full citizenship for the black man, was to visit Gloucester aboard the new 153-foot steamer *Regulator* on her maiden run in service between Gloucester and Boston.

It turned out that the tide was too low for the *Regulator* to land at the stone wharf, so the big guns up on the hill roared out a salute, and Captain Porter was rowed to the steamer for a collation with His Excellency, who was afterwards landed in town for a visit with friends before entraining back to Boston.

This Captain Porter was a great recruiter. About forty of his ninety-day men from Beverly reenlisted for another hundred, and he filled out his new company with sixty more recruits from that town, mustering the old out and the new in at the fort on August 6. But when November rolled around he had had enough of it and declined command of the new company at the Point, the sixth running that he had raised since the war.

His successor was Captain Leonard G. Dennis, a combat veteran who kept his command neat and the discipline tight. As always, the draft operated along lines that defied ordinary civilian logic: it was observed that most of the men at the Point garrison "count upon the quotas of Gloucester, and thus relieve a large number of our citizens from the rigors of the conscription."[5]

The week before Christmas in this fourth year of the Civil War it was as if a false star hung over the False Point. The weather, for once, played no great part in the mysterious events that unfolded in Brace Cove.

It started at four in the morning of December 19 when the schooner *Eliza Helen* of Hancock, Maine, Captain Dow, sprang a gusher leak passing outside the Cove, bound from Calais for Boston with a deckload of lumber. She filled faster than the pumps emptied, capsized and drifted onto Bemo Ledge, where she was pounded to pieces by the swells.

The crew of the *Eliza Helen* made it ashore. Instead of striking across toward the Niles farmhouse or the fort, being strangers they followed the shore to the lighthouse, where they were taken in, wet, freezing and exhausted, by Keeper Cross and his wife, whom they later credited with saving their lives. (Benjamin Cross, it might be noted, was the first keeper to be allowed an assistant, Osmond, probably his son. Keeper's salary $400; assistant's $250.)

Three days after *Eliza Helen* disintegrated on the ledge, the schooner *Erie* of Calais, likewise bound for Boston with a deckload from St. George, New Brunswick, cut the Point too close and crunched up on precisely the same rocks. This was ten o'clock on the night of December 22. There was not much sea running, however, and her crew got her off and anchored out a way off the Cove. The *Erie* was badly strained, though, and when the Gloucester schooner *Fairy Queen*, Captain McQuin, came up on her early in the morning she was filling, so they hove alongside and took off her crew.

That very afternoon the schooner *H. E. Bishop*, Captain Coston, returning to Portsmouth from Boston with a cargo of iron and government stores, departed Gloucester where she had put in for a few hours. She was spanking along after rounding the Point, with a fair wind and nothing to worry about, when for no apparent reason she veered in toward Brace's, struck full on Bemo and bilged. In a trice her decks were awash, but the seas remained quiet enough for her crew to make shore. Gloucester's wreckmaster, John Ayars, Jr., came out and took charge, and they set to saving some part of the cargo which was carried up the hill and stashed for the time being at the fort.

All the while, the *Erie* wallowed at her anchor off the Cove, half-sunk. The day before Christmas, looking to give himself her salvaging for a present, Captain McQuin sailed his *Fairy Queen* around and put a line on the Maine schooner. Too bad—the slightest way on was all she needed to turn turtle. Over she went. Empty-handed, McQuin returned to Gloucester for the holiday.

As if he had not played tricks enough for one week, Father Neptune had one more. *Fairy Queen* was just out of sight when *Erie*'s deckload of lumber snapped its lashings and broke loose with a mighty splash, and she popped up and righted herself like a cork, her spars rising to the upright even as a Lanesville schooner chanced by and took this bounty out of the blue in tow to Lane's Cove.

One man's poison is so often another's meat. The cargo of the *H. E. Bishop* was entirely uninsured, and the owners calculated their net loss on that at $30,000. As for their vessel, they valued her at $7,000 and had her insured for $5,000. Four days after Christmas what remained of her was knocked down at auction to Thomas Niles for $32.

Valiant General Lee surrendered his shattered army to General Grant at Appomatox Court House on April 9 in this year of 1865. The killing ended. The Union was preserved. Two days later, at noon, a victory salute of two hundred guns was fired from the fort at Eastern Point.

One week more, and President Lincoln was assassinated. Gloucester was draped in black, and every flag was half-mast high. On the day of national mourning a salute of thirteen guns roared out from the ramparts on the Point and reverberated across the harbor every thirty minutes until sundown, when thirty-six bursts of flame and smoke brought the dirge to an end.

The war was over, but animosities remained.

At midnight on the twenty-sixth of May the alarm rang out, and there it was across the water, the Point in flames again. A spectacular fire—all six of the ice houses, owned by Niles's father-in-law Benjamin F. Porter of Danvers, full to the eaves of sawdust and sawed ice—an estimated 10,000 tons of it (which sounds like a pondful). Four were brand-new, only last February.

By the time the steam pumper *Cape Ann* (which the town was induced to buy after the great fire of 1864) had hurtled over the road, joined by the East Gloucester engine, the whole works had crumpled in showers of sparks, clouds of smoke and explosions of steam, $10,000 worth, snapping timbers crashing in, flights of embers rising volcanically into the night sky.

The selectmen agreed that this was the work of firebugs and posted a reward of $300 for their conviction. There were those who persisted in wishing Thomas Niles no good.

The war was over. That first spring of peace the garrison at the Eastern Point fort chafed for their mustering-out. Dr. Charles Hildreth decided he had done his duty and resigned as post surgeon. The men liked their sawbones and one day late in May paraded into Gloucester behind the band and paid him their respects with a salute of musketry outside his front door.

The orders arrived. On the sixth of July, 1865, with Captain Dennis at their head, the Second Company of Unattached Infantry hiked for the last time down the farm road past the home of Mr. Niles and over his beach and through his gate, by Wonson's Point and up Patch's Hill, swinging briskly past Rocky Neck, and the knots of cheering citizens, past the schooners and the flake yards and the wharves, through East Gloucester Square and around the head of the harbor. There they reformed in parade order behind the band lately attached to the Second Brigade, First Division, Twentieth Corps, and stepped out smartly through the streets of the port, between the yelling, cheering, whistling crowds of Gloucester, on to the depot, and then they boarded the forenoon train for Boston, Gallups Island and their mustering-out.

The Eastern Point fort, where all was quiet now for the first time in two years, was left in charge of a regular army ordnance sergeant.

The long war was over. And now that peace had descended on the land, and everyone else had put down his arms, Thomas Niles characteristically rode out to do battle, his last.

Earliest known photo of Gloucester Harbor, probably 1870s, looks toward Eastern Point, with white Niles farm buildings and, on the heights to the right, the old Civil War fort, schooners passing off Back Shore beyond Niles Pond. (Procter Brothers photo, Steve Howard collection)

~14~
THE BATTLE OF
EASTERN POINT HEIGHTS

For a man who had spent six years in the courts establishing his right to drive trespassers off his beaches, the summary occupation of the heart of his estate by the U.S. Army for twenty-four months amounted to a full-scale foreign invasion. Worse yet, after the war was over, he couldn't get the government to get out. An ordnance sergeant retained possession of the fort, and Thomas Niles—more frustrated than ever—stumped glumly over the ruins of his farm.

But not for long. The curmudgeon of Eastern Point, the old veteran of 1812, had one good fight left in him at sixty-eight, and late in 1865 he filed a demand for the return of his property and a claim for damages with the special Claims Commission of the War Department headed by Major General E. R. S. Canby. He asked $64,980 in compensation, plus interest and taxes.

The engineers sent the now Colonel Blunt down to have a look. He put fair compensation at $7,025, based on his contention that the army had only occupied ten acres around the fort, not the fifty-three that Mr. Niles asked damages on.

His superiors seized on Colonel Blunt's report to build a down staircase under the claimant. The next April, the chief of engineers recommended to the secretary of war that authority be sought from Congress to purchase outright for $1,000 the ten acres occupied by the fort and outbuildings, obviating payment for damages.

The secretary did his engineers one better and in May proposed to the Senate Military Committee that Congress appropriate $7,000 to buy the whole fifty-three acres and right of way to them, said sum to indemnify Niles for all damages.

Just as the secretary of war counterattacked Mr. Niles on one flank, the ladies of East Gloucester moved up on the other. He held his lines against the U.S. government, but fell before the females.

They wanted to have a picnic at the fort to raise money for the East

Gloucester war memorial monument, and how could he resist them? It was held on the eighteenth of June, twenty-five cents admission for ladies, fifty for the gents. A delicious day. Procter's Full Band. Dancing, singing, games. Refreshments. And sufficient policemen, as the ladies had promised, to preserve order, so successful that permission was wheedled from Mr. Niles for an encore on the Fourth of July.

As for the War Department, Farmer Niles retained Governor Andrew to bear his standard, an able lawyer with ties in Washington who had determined to quit public life and was now serving his last term in the State House.

Job himself could not have recited a more dolorous lament than was presented by Thomas Niles before the stern-faced officers of the Canby Commission on November 8, 1866:

> For the three years succeeding [June 1863], there was a constant train of soldiers, laborers and visitors traversing every portion of my grounds. The constructors did not open up any new road to the land which they had occupied, but made use of my own farm roads which I had laid out at such care and expense, and which led directly past the door of my dwelling and through the group of my farm buildings. . . . For a year there was a continual procession over them of work people, and also of carts and wagons loaded with material for construction. My road-beds were cut all to ruin, the shrubbery and trees along their margin were greatly injured, all the privacy of my domestic life was intruded upon, enjoyment of the estate, and finally even residence on it, was made impossible to my family, and it is no exaggeration of language to say that at last we were actually driven away.
>
> Had not the workmen and those whom they attracted to the spot been sufficient, of themselves, for this purpose, the appearance of a garrison of 250 [a hyperbole by about double] raw troops there, while the work on the fort was still in progress, would have insured the result. The people of Gloucester and of the neighboring towns became naturally impressed with the belief that wherever there was a Federal fort and garrison, the public had a right to go, and consequently, during the two years and more that the garrison remained, every part of my grounds was inundated with intruders.
>
> On the land occupied by the troops stood one of my largest barns, 35 x 76 feet. This also was occupied, and was used daily for target practice, destroying all the glass, and in various other respects injuring the building. Daily there was artillery and musket-firing over my grounds, making them unsafe for my family, or even for the farm laborers. The pond was invaded, and was fished almost empty of the pickerel with which I had stocked it.
>
> My whole crop for two years was inevitably ruined. What was not necessarily cut down, was ruined by theft, and by trampling it

down, and the grounds became so common that a great part of my fruit, vegetables and cranberries were stolen; I was compelled at last to abandon all planting, and to use my land only for pasturage; and even then, I have been obliged to hire an extra farm hand for the summer months, every year, at $1 per day and his board, to keep my cattle off from that portion of my ground which had been surveyed and taken for Federal use, for no fence was built, nor other barrier of any kind erected around the 53 acres, which nominally the United States took—I say nominally, for actually it was of the use of my whole estate that I was deprived.

The garrison remained until April [actually July] 1865; and since that time no part of the property has been restored to me, but the United States have continued to hold possession of the fort and of the land included in their survey, under the charge of a keeper, have gathered the crops, have pastured cows upon it, and have mowed and sold the hay this year and the last, and use my large barn, before mentioned, for the storage of it.

In the building of the fort, the turf for sodding the embankments was cut, not alone on the district of 53 acres included in the Government survey, but from various other portions of my land; and sod with grass of closer fibre being desired for the embrasures, all the surface of about two acres of my best black grass meadow was shorn off, leaving a bog-hole in its place, and cutting off all access to the rest of the meadow, and ruining it forever. I might enlarge at greater length on all the injuries thus done to me, but I desire not to be led into any display of feeling. . . .

The continued occupation of the fort, or the possibility that once surrendered it might at some future date be reoccupied by the government was enough, Niles affirmed, to "forever deter any gentlemen from making investments in expensive residences there"—including the total area below the pond, for that lay in the line of fire of the guns.

If the United States did not wish to satisfy his $64,980 claim for damages, he would be willing to sell and relinquish the whole estate for $100,000, he stated, believing that before the earthworks were thrown up he would ultimately have been able to realize $150,000 privately, "but, after all the trouble and anxiety which I have endured, I have no longer the energy to endeavor to reconstruct my broken plans, or to frame new plans for its disposal."[1]

The monody of Farmer Niles was scored for the legal accompaniment of Governor Andrew, who explicated with eloquence his client's constitutional rights to restoration of his property and compensation; the chief executive of the Commonwealth observed that although the land had been seized without benefit of negotiation or even terms, "he was cheerful in his submission to the power set over him, trusting then, as now, in the equity by which it is governed."[2]

The Eastern Point fort (center) and outbuildings, 1864, probably looking south, hospital in right foreground, men and horses by the barracks, and mess hall at left. (William D. Hoyt)

Niles and His Excellency swelled their elegy with a chorus of twenty-six well-blended affidavits from men large on State Street who owned or had intimate knowledge of gentlemen's seaside residences along the North Shore. They were as one voice that Eastern Point, except for the presence of the U.S. government on the premises, ranked with or ahead of Nahant as the choicest resort on the coast, but that so long as it crouched under the guns of a fort it was not fit for habitation.

Joining in this cantata were such eminent soloists as Charles G. Loring, senior member of the Boston bar; Franklin Haven the banker, who was in charge of filling in the Back Bay and was the greatest landowner on the North Shore; Colonel Henry Lee, Jr., of Lee Higginson, who had been one of Governor Andrew's military aides; Robert E. Apthorp, the leading real estate agent in Boston specializing in seashore property; Samuel E. Sawyer, the Boston merchant and Gloucester native and philanthropist whose family estate was at Freshwater Cove across the harbor; George O. Hovey of Boston, eminent yachtsman and Sawyer's summer neighbor; and my great-grandfather, John Kimball Rogers, president of the Boston Type and Stereotype Foundry, one of the four major printing establishments used by the Boston publishers Ticknor & Fields, and a son-in-law of Mr. Niles, a relationship that did not prejudice him against the merits of the Point.

The counterpoint harmony was provided by two gentlemen who vouchsafed that the day the army retreated from Eastern Point they were ready to march in to the tune of $1,000 an acre.

To Lewis A. Roberts, head of the Boston publishing house of Roberts Brothers, this was the most beautiful peninsula on the entire East Coast, and

he would take five acres of it below the pond the minute the fort was abandoned. His identity as another of Mr. Niles's son-in-laws was not considered relevant enough to bother the commission with.

And finally, John B. Prince, head of the house of John B. Prince and Company of Boston. He and his family had resided on the Niles estate during parts of 1861 and 1862, he testified, and he had intended to purchase a piece of it as a permanent summer place before Major Blunt captured the heights. Instead he bought into Little Nahant, but he would still be glad to deal with Mr. Niles at $1,000 an acre as a matter of speculation—if the army ever got out.

A year passed, during which the Canby Claims Commission was dissolved, and in November 1867 the chief of engineers decided that the world outlook had improved to a point that justified the return of his land to Thomas Niles.

It was not until the following July, however, that a special board of officers was appointed to investigate ways and means of abandoning the Eastern Point fort. In August they recommended that the government level the earthworks and restore the land to its antebellum condition at a cost of $6,050. Either that or pay Mr. Niles the same to do it himself. They proposed further that he receive $8,237.50 rent for the period of occupation and be referred to Congress to pursue the balance of his claim for redress.

The War Department offered Niles the suggested payment for rent, which he refused and fired back with a petition to Congress at the end of January 1869, praying for the restoration of his property and $49,890 in damages. This plea was introduced in the upper branch by Senator Charles Sumner of Massachusetts and two months later in the House by Congressman Ben Butler, the astounding Civil War general and politician of consummate convolution who had settled at Bay View, across the Cape, in 1866.

Two could play the game, as far as Farmer Niles was concerned. He billed the government in this petition for the cost of manure and the spreading of it over the fields on which the army had roamed its horses and cows and let go to weeds and brush; for fifty tons of stone the Army quarried; for the $3,000 legal fee he had paid Governor Andrew, who had died in the interim; and for the $1.50 a day (not the $1.00 of the previous bill) that he now remembered he had paid a hand to keep his own herd off the tract occupied by the army.

This got results—this, and having friends in Congress. Within a week after Senator Sumner introduced his bill early in February, Ordnance Major James Whittemore arrived at Eastern Point to supervise the dismantling of the fort. Another fortnight and all the outbuildings and even the incredible flagstaff had been sold at public auction for $500 cash, everything to be removed within ten days. Isaac Patch bought one of the barracks, split it apart into three cottages and moved them up on Locust Lane on the rise above Niles's infamous gate where they stand today. Two more weeks and the schooner *Daniel D. Smith* was tied up at the stone wharf taking on the guns and stores for the first leg of their journey to the arsenal at Watertown.

Victory at last. On the fifteenth of April, 1869, the War Department notified Thomas Niles that the United States hereby returned to him the land it had occupied under necessity of war for nearly six years. Eastern Point was his again, whole, free and clear.

Niles was seventy-two. It's not clear whether he relented and accepted the $8,237 rent offered by the engineers. But the Treasury refused to approve payment of the $6,050 the army recommended for damages, and in spite of his friends there, Congress gave him no satisfaction in his lifetime. Niles left this claim in his will as part of his personal estate. His heirs were as stubborn as he. They lodged petition after petition with Congress, and in the end, eighteen years after his death and twenty-five after he first made his claim, Congress on September 30, 1890, passed a special act awarding his estate the $6,050 in full compensation for damages to his land by the erection of a fort thereon for the defense of Gloucester Harbor during the late Rebellion.

It didn't take Mr. Niles very long to reassert his hegemony once the United States had relinquished its. Six days after he received the glad news from Washington, he harnessed up his white horse, drove into Gloucester and inserted the following in the newspapers:

PUBLIC NOTICE

Notice is given to all persons from this date, that riding in carriages, or passing in any way over my grounds on Eastern Point, and all gunners and parties of pleasure who have theretofore landed and pitched their tents on my grass grounds, and in other ways made common my estate, that they are strictly forbidden the continuance of such liberty, under the penalties affixed by the statutes of this Commonwealth.

The fact that the United States Government owns the land where the Eastern Point Light stands, and Government officials, and persons having direct business with the Keeper, being privileged to pass to it, gives no license or right to other persons.

April 21, 1869.

THOMAS NILES

Things were back to normal on Eastern Point.

Walter Gardner photo of Eastern Point Light, probably in the 1880s. The new lighthouse was built in 1890. (From Gloucester Picturesque, *published by Charles D. Brown)*

~15~

BREAKWATER TALK

Gᴇɴᴇʀᴀʟ ʙᴇɴ ʙᴜᴛʟᴇʀ ᴡᴀs ꜰɪʀsᴛ elected to Congress, as he liked to say, "while I lived in the tent on the beach" at Bay View overlooking Ipswich Bay beyond Annisquam where his summer estate was building. This was 1866, the first year of the Reconstruction. Ben Butler officially lived in Lowell, but he had spent parts of summers between army commands since 1863 tenting on his Bay View shore and pondering the ways and means of his future.

Within a month of his election a proposition was being bruited to build a breakwater from the Eastern Point Light out over Dog Bar. Wise heads on the waterfront said that a wall of granite across the entrance would break the backs of the swells that rocked the harbor in every easterly gale. The effect would be to make the outer harbor a safe refuge in all winds and to relieve the shortage of berths around the inner waterfront by opening up the Eastern Point shore outside Rocky Neck to wharves.

So the *Cape Ann Weekly Advertiser* thought, anyway, and somebody ought to get busy circulating petitions to Congress for a breakwater, in every seaport in New England whose coastwise shipping had occasion to visit Gloucester.

This was the first talk of a breakwater since 1857 when some of the masters and owners failed to interest Washington in building one between Rocky Neck and Ten Pound Island. It's a wonder that the current proposition—far more bold and imaginative—wasn't broached after the calamitous storm of 1839 made a shambles of the harbor.

To pry a public work of this magnitude out of Congress required the application of economic weight to political leverage against a fulcrum of urgency. The lever was now at hand, or appeared to be, in the person of Congressman Ben Butler. The local economy was most certainly getting heftier, and as commerce increased, the urgency—the threat of maritime disaster always in the air—hung ever heavier over Gloucester Harbor.

No less than 360 schooners having an aggregate tonnage of 24,000 and a value of $2,144,000 hailed out of Gloucester in 1866, not to mention a number of square-rigged vessels in commerce. Forty-seven hundred were employed in the fisheries; that industry alone grossed $3,650,000. One hundred and fifty-five vessels entered from foreign ports, while 165 cleared for the world trade. By count of the Customs, 3,071 vessels boarded in the harbor for no less than a day, and the officials estimated this was no more than a third of the total that sought shelter at Gloucester during the year—at least 9,000!

Most of these transients dropped their hooks in the outer harbor, keeping on the Pancake Ground, if the masters knew what they were about. But it was a risky business.

The harbor was heaving with the undertow built up by a heavy northerly gale the night of the ninth of January, 1866, when the hermaphrodite brig *Hyperion* of New York, 306 tons burden, bound from Boston for Portland, swung in for refuge and hove to under Ten Pound Island.

At midnight her anchor broke ground and *Hyperion*, helpless under her bare poles, was carried before the wind out the harbor and onto Dog Bar. The swells were surging in on a flooding tide, and each lifted up the listing brig and then whacked it down on the rocks for the next to play with.

Captain Lewis could see nothing to do but abandon ship. They swung their boat over, hazardous as the operation was with rocks all around, and the six of them rowed in, their backs to the storm, hanging close to the Point shore, poking along in the dark until they found the lee of Niles Beach, where they landed in the light surf and pulled their boat up. They hiked along the farm road in the blackness, the wind and rain blasting down their necks all the way to the lighthouse, where they banged on the door and Keeper Tom Burgess took them in.

Drying off in front of his fire, they peered out his window at their brig, in ghostly outline a stone's throw through the storm, to all appearances beating herself to death on the bar. The tide kept coming, and the wind held from the nor'ard, and at three in the morning *Hyperion* floated off Dog Bar and disappeared to sea right before the stunned eyes of her master and crew.

The gale blew off, and next day this Flying Dutchman was spoken outside of Boston Bay by the wrecking schooner *Ophelia,* which, getting no response to her hail, sent a boat alongside, boarded, claimed her and took her in tow to Hull. The underwriters had no alternative but to settle with the salvager for $5,000. What sort of settlement occurred between the owners of the *Hyperion*, when she was returned to them, and Captain Lewis is not recorded.

Either slope of Dog Bar could be a lee shore for that matter, depending merely on the quarter of the wind. Take the strange string of events that began on the blowy first of February, 1868.

Like the *Howard* and the *Persia*, the brig *Jennie Cushman* was in the last hours of a voyage from the other side of the world. She was a new Salem vessel, built in 1865 in New Bedford, a handsome clipper brig of 280 tons, owned by Michael Shepherd and her master, bound home from

Muscat, in the Gulf of Oman, with a cargo of ivory, spices, coffee, dates and such exotics worth $120,000. The afternoon southerly had piped up to a sharp gale by evening as she beat in from the eastward off the Back Shore, and her master at an hour before midnight thought he had best put into Gloucester for shelter.

He miscalculated and cut too close, the lighthouse in his lee. Seeing he hadn't way to carry around Round Rock buoy, he ordered both bowers dropped. It was no good. In the wind and the swells and the tide, the *Cushman* dragged and bounced onto Dog Bar and bilged.

Just before they struck they got the boats over, found open water and made shore on the Point . . . fairly down to the gunwales too, for they had aboard the crew of the British schooner *Sprig,* whom they had plucked from their vessel two weeks earlier, sinking with a hold full of fish on a voyage from Halifax to Puerto Rico.

The next morning, Sunday, Wreckmaster John Ayars and the Customs Officers arrived on the Point. A tug steamed out from town, but the seas were too rough to get a line aboard the wreck. Hundreds visited the lighthouse to gawk at the stricken brig and watch the salvagers at the tricky work of lightening her cargo, a quantity of which was brought ashore and stored temporarily in Mr. Niles's large barn near the quarry.

The most valuable lading, 12,000 pounds of ivory appraised at $36,000, was not trusted to local jurisdiction in its dutyless condition but was taken in custody by the Customs men, who had it hauled to town by Hilton's teams and stashed away in their bailiwick.

For two days the gale held out of the south, holding the damaged *Cushman* on the bar, and on February 3 it was still blowing hard, when out of the thick loomed the brig *Manson* of Searsport, Maine, Captain Gilkey, from Havana for Boston by way of Holmes Hole, way off her course and trying to make Gloucester for shelter. They fell into the same trap, veered too near the Point, couldn't keep her off and hove up on Dog Bar right alongside of the *Cushman.*

The seas were still running high next day. The *Cushman* had holed, and the tides slopped through her. The *Manson* was leaking badly, but a towboat got to her, hauled her off on the flood and took her to Boston for repairs, her crew at the pumps.

Still the *Jennie Cushman* ground her bones on the rocks of Dog Bar. Her third morning of distress, February 4, the Russian barque *Windau,* Captain Pyndt, from the Gulf of Riga for Boston, came into the harbor, giving the stranded brig a wide berth. It was blowing a hundred devils out of the southwest that day—such a sea making that the steam tug *Joseph Boss* (no one aboard, as luck would have it) shipped a big one and sank like a stone at her anchors in the outer harbor. They raised her when they got to it.

It had let up enough the fourth day for the stately Russian to clear for Boston. Outside the Point she ran into snow. Off Baker's Island the snow came down thick, blinding, and the barque struck the ledges. She got off, but the blow had started a leak, and Captain Pyndt thought he had better run back to Gloucester.

This time, in the thick of the snow squall, he missed the channel—as the brigs had before him—and the *Windau* crunched up on Dog Bar in the same insecure berth alongside the poor *Cushman* only just vacated by the *Manson*.

A second time she was lucky. *Windau* was stranded there only an hour, gnashing her keel but nothing worse, when a tug steamed up through the snow and hauled her off up into the harbor. Three more days and the Russians once again resumed their voyage for Boston, behind a towboat and at their pumps.

Not until the morning of the sixth of February, her sixth day on Dog Bar, were her rescuers able to budge the *Jennie Cushman*. The tug *Clover* did it at high water and brought her in to anchor; the day after, she towed the wreck to Boston for repairs. *Jennie's* owners were not likely to forget the treacheries of Gloucester Harbor; those rocks cost them $24,000.

This rash of groundings revived calls for a breakwater, as from a Boston newspaper that it be built from shore out as far as the Dog Bar buoy, a distance of 400 feet along the spine of rocks, Dog Rocks, which shoaled to less than a fathom at low water, the idea being that it would keep vessels off the bar—hardly realistic since the buoy marked only its shoalest part; the 1,200 feet beyond was covered by depths of only two fathoms, over which the storm swells broke. The paper was sure this short mole would render the outer harbor "quiet as a mill pond" and could be laid down out of stone at hand within a quarter of a mile of the site, obviously meaning Mr Niles's unused quarry, a cue that he may have had something to do with inspiring the article.[1]

With wry clairvoyance, the *Cape Ann Weekly Advertiser* three weeks before Christmas peered into its crystal ball and predicted "it is not probable that the work of building a breakwater on Dog Bar will be commenced this year."[2]

Talk was all right, but Captain Joseph (Uncle Joe) Proctor was bred to action. He was one of the colorful old-time skippers, owner, sometime selectman and a leader of the fishermen. The year previous Uncle Joe had successfully campaigned to reopen the Cut to vessel traffic between Squam River and the harbor, and now he was bent on getting a breakwater.

More than any other man, Captain Proctor deserves to be honored as the Father of Dog Bar Breakwater. In the spring of 1869 he circulated a petition urging on Congress the need for a breakwater, which by the end of April had six hundred signatures. He planned to lay it before the Committee on Harbor and Coast Improvements which was to visit Gloucester in May, and hoped Congressman Butler would introduce it in Washington later in the year.

Enthusiastically the *Cape Ann Weekly Advertiser* foresaw wharves fingering out from the length of Eastern Point in the lee of the breakwater that was already half built in its editorial rooms, and the next week, it seems, the vision had caught the imagination of the owner of the Eastern Point farm: "We learn that Mr. Thomas Niles has agreed to furnish free of expense, all the stone required to build the breakwater on Dog Bar. This is certainly a very magnanimous offer on his part."[3]

Quarryman Niles must have done a little figuring on the quantity of stone this would commit him to and the going price of granite, for however much he may have viewed the project in his favor, he never publicly repeated his offer.

It is interesting that at just about this time Congressman Ben Butler became associated with Colonel Jonas H. French, his inspector general in the expedition against New Orleans, in organizing the Cape Ann Granite Company, with French as president. They bought the old quarry at Bay View. At the end of the year Butler introduced Captain Proctor's petition in Congress, with the request that a committee be appointed to view Gloucester Harbor and investigate the desirability of the proposal.

General Ben had been embroiled in what his detractors called conflicts of interest during the Civil War. Not that he now looked to benefit by espousing a public work that would require untold quantities of the stone he was in business to sell on the other side of the Cape or by acquiring a quarry precisely while a petition was in circulation requesting him to interest Congress in building a granite breakwater out from the shore of his hometown. Certainly not.

If Thomas Niles was not a man to bear a grudge, neither was he one to let bygones interfere with the dictates of justice. In the course of tidying up the ledger of his three score and twelve that year of 1869, he recalled that those three fishermen who had trespassed on his close, trampled his corn and committed sundry enormities some twenty years back had never come forth with the award the Court of Common Pleas had given him against them in 1849; this had amounted to $1.50 damages and $49.68 costs.

So he brought the Rowes, father and son, and Ben Brazier before the Supreme Judicial Court of the Commonwealth before the year was out and won a nice little Christmas judgment against them at twenty years' interest, bringing it up to $113.95, in addition to what it cost him to take them to court to get it, $13.27.

Whether the man from the *Advertiser* rowed across to the lighthouse because he preferred oaring over the harbor on a July day, or because Mr. Niles barred the gate to him, he didn't let on. Yet elsewhere in the same issue that he reported his excursion, he found fault with the restrictions and slyly supposed that on proper application to the proprietor people could get permission for a few hours' visit to the Point. This was the summer of 1870.

Keeper Henry P. Woodbury, successor to Thomas Burgess, was discovered busily bemoaning the lighthouse board's disinclination to give him an assistant. Between light and fog bell he had his hands full. The bell tower

Eastern Point Lighthouse keeper Charles Friend in 1875, etching by E. R. Morse. (Frank Leslie's Illustrated Newspaper)

had blown over in the hurricane of the previous September that drove a number of vessels ashore and toppled some forty of Niles's trees, but it had since been rebuilt more securely and closer to the outer ledges. The striking mechanism of the bell, which itself was on a platform outside the tower, had to be wound every two hours when it was working. The keeper had a lanyard to the hammer so he could toll it by hand in case of a mechanical failure.

This clockwork machinery of the Eastern Point bell was described thus in a contemporary periodical:

As the scape-wheel revolves, a tooth comes in contact with the pallet of one arm, giving this an upward impulse; this brings the other arm down between two teeth, and checks the scape-wheel going further, until the swing of the pendulum in the other direction carries the pallet out. This swinging of the pendulum causes the striking of the bell, the interval of blows being regulated by the arrangement of the teeth.[4]

The light was of a type known as the fountain; the flame issued from the characteristically tubular wick of an Argand burner and was focused through a Fresnel lens, a refinement in beaming for which General Totten, who had for so long urged the fortification of Eastern Point, had pushed when he was a member of the lighthouse board.

Possibly the gentle jibes in the *Advertiser* found their mark in old Niles, for a few weeks later a jolly chowder party was being got up by the "Veterans."

Chartering Russell Gill's boat on August 19, they landed their stores at the stone wharf and then sailed outside the Point to fish for an hour or so on a mysterious ground described as "the outer edge of the inner bubble," from which they hooked 200 pounds of cod and cusk. Returning, they spoke to Representative Pew and General Cogswell (later Congressman) of Salem on a similar party and invited these political gentlemen to join them ashore. All landed in high spirits at three. A fire was built on the beach and three pots set up for chowder, "properly charged" with slices of fried pork, after which the substantials were dumped in. Chowder downed, and every-thing cleaned up so as to keep in the clear with Mr. Niles, the veterans enjoyed another sail outside, helped along with song and story, and arrived back in town at 7:30 in the evening.

The vets had such a good time that they got permission for an encore in a week. It blew a gale in the forenoon, and the men were soaked and slightly queazy fishing and glad to get back to the Point. Soon, however, the chowder was sending out clouds of enticing steam, the sun broke through, wet clothing dried and cheer was restored. At five a light breeze sprang up, and once again they embarked, this time for a brisk reach up inside Kettle Island and then a fine run back to Gloucester to the strains of the seagoing Cornet Band.

In the midst of these summer pleasantries a team from the Corps of Engineers in charge of Mr. H. F. Bothfeld was cruising between Round Rock Shoal and the Point, making soundings, measuring the current and the tide, poking around on Dog Bar in a diving bell and otherwise exploring the practicalities of a breakwater; one day Congressman Butler was taken out for a look and pronounced himself heartily in favor.

> *Next, where the Sirens dwell you plough the seas;*
> *Their song is death, and makes destruction please.*
> *. . . Fly swift the dang'rous coast; let ev'ry ear*
> *Be stopp'd against the song! 'tis death to hear!*[5]

It was the evening of February 8, 1871, and the new forty-eight-ton schooner *Zephyr,* delivered just last fall to John Pew and Sons of Gloucester by her builder at Hodgdon's Mills, Maine, returning from the winter shore fishery, was trying to harbor in a blinding onshore snowstorm. And then she made that fatal turn, around the False Point, and threw herself on Bemo Ledge. The crew took to the boats and rowed into Brace Beach.

But now comes the little schooner *Ocean Bride,* twenty-seven tons. It is less than an hour later. She too is in the shore fishery, pounding along through the storm, her peering lookout pelted by the snowflakes. Suddenly he spies a masthead light, and after that the sails of a vessel, and he shouts to his helmsman that all is well, just follow that schooner in up ahead there!

Another five seconds, four seconds . . . and with a fracturing of wood against rock the *Ocean Bride* fetched up alongside of the *Zephyr,* which had been abandoned in such haste in her precarious state that her crew never bothered to douse her light or haul down canvas.

So close were the two, the *Siren* and her prey, that the men on the *Ocean Bride* merely leaped deck to deck to the *Zephyr,* for their own craft had bilged and looked a goner. Casting about them, and seeing that all was not lost, and being able men, they decided to improve the moment. In no time they had *Zephyr* free of the rocks and afloat, but she had smashed her rudder on Bemo and drifted into the beach, where her disappointed salvagers jumped over and waded ashore.

Next day a steam tug chugged cautiously into the cove, put a long hawser aboard and towed *Zephyr* around to Gloucester for repairs. The

Ocean Bride, whose crew had failed to stop their ears against the song (but saved the singer), broke to pieces on "the dang'rous coast."

A month in the wake of this sirenic happening at Brace Cove, Major General John G. Foster of the Corps of Engineers made public his report to the War Department concerning the Gloucester breakwater proposal, based on the survey of the previous summer. This was March 1871.

General Foster favored a sea wall of stone pushing 3,870 feet out from the end of the Point as far as Round Rock Shoal, which he was confident would shut out the heavy storm swells and make the outer harbor a safe anchorage. It would be 1,000 feet longer than the great Delaware Breakwater completed in 1869 after forty years, the longest in America and probably the world, jutting 60 percent of the distance across the harbor entrance from Eastern Point to Muscle Point.

The Engineers estimated that 232,994 tons of rough stone would be required for the base, at seventy-five cents a ton—this to be built out from shore and dumped from cars running on a track to quarries in the vicinity (the Niles quarry and others that might be drilled nearby). Awash at low water, this base would range in thickness from eleven to thirty-five feet according to the bottom; it would serve as the footing for the foundation blocks—24,363 tons of them at $1.25 a ton—pyramided to mean high water.

And then the breakwater itself—two parallel walls of gigantic granite blocks, dovetailed in the form of headers and stretchers, ten feet wide, eleven feet above high water and the gulf between them filled with 8,373 yards of concrete at $8.50 a yard, rammed home and all capped with granite monoliths ten by four by two-and-a-half feet. Cost: $494,148.

Congressman Butler's preoccupation this spring with an unsuccessful campaign against his conservative foes for the Republican nomination for governor may have had little or nothing to do with the failure of the barrel to produce any pork for Gloucester. Anyway, the Foster report was filed and all but forgotten.

The second daughter of Thomas Niles by his first wife, and her namesake, Sarah McClennen Niles, married for her second husband John Kimball Rogers, great-grandson of the same Daniel Rogers who bought the Eastern Point farm in 1790. Their daughter, my grandmother, was a gentle and artistic lady of beauty and calm dignity who used to visit the Niles farm. She remembered the reluctance of her Grandfather Niles to alight from his carriage and open his gate after dark for fear of attack. And though she appears to have been his favorite, she never forgot that he scared off the boy who would be her future husband, Joseph Everett Garland, from blueberrying in his pasture.

Another family tradition relates that on one occasion Grandsire Niles marched down to his beach in a great rage, waving his walking stick, and chased off a party of young people who had landed there for a picnic without his permission. That evening they returned in their boat and hove to off

his rocks, below his bedroom window, singing at the top of their lungs—
"My country tis of thee, sweet land of liber-tee . . . !"

There may have been another side to the coin. That Farmer Niles was a severe and intransigent man, uncommonly jealous of his property, angular of elbow, litigious, carrying chips on both shoulders, there can be no doubt; the record takes care of that. Still, a man who could woo, win and wed three wives in succession and beget fifteen children was conceivably endowed with some of the warmer and more affectionate ardors alongside of choler and a passion for unrelenting justice.

Many years after Niles had joined his fathers, something induced an "Old Timer" who had known him somewhat to write:

> I remember the property when it was owned by Thomas Niles Esquire, a very genial gentleman, if you used him right, but a terror to those who sought to impose upon him. He used to be greatly enraged by people trespassing upon his premises gunning and picnicking. Very many thought they had a perfect right to go there and do as they pleased; but Mr. Niles taught many of them that he owned the property and proposed to have some say in regard to managing it.
>
> I used to go there frequently with friends, landing at the wharf and spending the day, cooking a chowder and having a delightful time. But I never went there without permission. I would meet Mr. Niles at the post office or somewhere on Front Street and get his permission to come, which was always granted most courteously. I always invited him to join our party and on one or two occasions he came down when the chowder was ready. I found him, if you treated him as one gentleman should treat another, a most companionable man. When we got ready to leave, as the shades of night were falling, our party took good care to extinguish our fire and leave everything on the wharf clean and nice, and Mr. Niles was a man who appreciated such treatment.
>
> There were some men in town who tried to bully him, and they had a hard time of it. "You can catch more flies with molasses than you can with vinegar" was found to be most truthful in this case.
>
> How well I recall Mr. Niles as he drove into town with his spirited white horse. One of the old time gentlemen, he had his faults, as who of us has not? But there was much that was loyal and lovable in his make-up, and that was what I found in my acquaintance with him.[6]

The health of Thomas Niles faltered at the approach of his seventy-fifth birthday on March 6, 1872, but he recovered some of his spirits at the end of May and was seen again on the streets, showing a return of his old vigor. Then on the eighth of June the proprietor of the Eastern Point farm for twenty-eight years suffered a stroke and died at the home of his brother in Arlington, where he was visiting.

*The fate of many a sailing vessel mistaking Brace Cove for the end of the Point and ending on Bemo Ledge. (*Fishermen's Memorial and Record Book*)*

~16~

MOTHER ANN'S COW

WHEN THOMAS NILES DIED IN 1872 he left a span of thirty-one years between Tom, Jr., by his first wife, the eldest surviving of his fifteen children, who was forty-seven, and Rhoda, the youngest by his third.

Rhoda was sixteen and only five years older than her father's favorite granddaughter, Sarah McClennen Rogers, namesake of his first wife. In his will he nominated his eldest sons, Thomas and William, and his favored son-in-law John Kimball Rogers, Sarah's father, as the executors and trustees of his estate and guardians of his minor children, Rhoda and his youngest son (by his second marriage), Washington Allston Niles, named after the American painter Washington Allston (1779–1834), prominent in his time, with connections in Boston and admired in England.

The patriarch of the Eastern Point farm left instructions that it should not be sold until Sarah reached twenty-one, in October 1882. Like Charlemagne, he hoped to guide the course of empire from beyond the grave.

Furthermore, like Charlemagne, he was bound to enhance and perpetuate its holiness by proselytizing the bordering lands of the East Gloucesterites. He ordered that half an acre of ground be reserved and $20,000 set aside to erect a house of worship on it at a time deemed appropriate by his executors. This temple of a thousand seats was to be open to all without regard to creed or color. In a burst of posthumous neighborliness, not untouched with whimsy, he left to sons Thomas and William "the agreeable task of seeing that the pulpit is supplied, the services of the clergyman to be gratuitous, as it is my wish that money shall never be taken under any circumstances from the congregation."[1]

A score of years later the sons would do their darnedest to defuse this ecumenical time bomb, which the family regarded as one of the less amusing of the old martinet's eccentricities.

After their father's death William broke Allston into the management of the farm, though it fared well or ill according to the exertions of the faithful John Burke, foreman since 1868. In July 1877 William offered to lease out

the quarry, which he described as an admirable source of paving blocks. A series of stereoscope photographs of about this vintage implies that he was successful; they depict a force of about fourteen working the pit with the aid of a derrick, a couple of yoke of oxen, two-wheel stone carts, horses and a schooner alongside the wharf taking on stone, her furled mainsail, boom and gaff swung outboard as a counterweight and to free the main hatch.

"Extremely rough" and better traversed on foot, an 1879 guide to Gloucester described the lighthouse road along the beach and through the fields and pastures, "if one cares to open three or four gates," remarking that the old Civil War fort was dismantled and deserted, the barracks "fast going to ruin."

Quarrying on Eastern Point, 1870s. (From Procter Brothers' Cape Ann Scenery, Cape Ann Historical Association)

"In sailing from Cape Ann lights to Cape Ann harbour," Blunt cautioned generations of mariners in his *Coast Pilot*, "you will first open Braces Cove, before you come up with the harbour, which will, when open, bear N.N.W. which you must avoid. Cape Ann harbour lies one mile further to the westward, and when you open bears N.N.E."

The False Point—how many vessels would have to break their bones on the ledges of the Back Shore trying to sail into the harbor across Niles Pond before the government did something about it?

At five in the afternoon of the twenty-first of October, 1876, the 116-ton coasting schooner *Saxon* out of Sullivan, Maine, bound for New York with a load of stone, crashed up on the ledge west of Brace Rock, near where the *Persia* wrecked, in a thick o' fog. The crew swung the boat over and rowed ashore. At one in the morning the stricken schooner rolled over and sank. Captain Bragdon reported that during the night six other vessels, sailing blind, came near and were only warned off by his wreck.

The *Saxon* was at least the ninth vessel to be fooled by the False Point since the *Howard* and *Persia* went up in 1807 and 1829 with a loss of sixteen lives. Others unrecorded surely made the same miscalculation during the seventy years, and uncounted more certainly drove ashore there in earlier times.

This latest wreck roused the *Cape Ann Weekly Advertiser* to demand that a warning steam whistle be installed at the end of Eastern Point, more dreaded in fog and storm, as it said, than any other peninsula on the coast.

As if to drive home the point, twelve days after the *Saxon*'s premature demise the schooner *Mazeppa*, 47 tons, Captain George W. Butler of Lanesville, was returning from a shore fishing trip on the black night of November 2. She hugged the coast too close and collided with Bemo Ledge. The crew got ashore. *Mazeppa* broke up, a total loss.

Then six days before Christmas the schooner *W. H. Dean*, returning to her home port of Canning, Nova Scotia, missed stays departing the harbor—that is, simply failed to come about in a breeze—fell off the wind and drove ashore in Lighthouse Cove. The tugs *Tiger* and *William Kemp* steamed out, but it was too rough; two more days, and *Tiger* got her off and into Parkhurst's wharf.

Yet these collisions with Eastern Point were but a snack between meals for Neptune in his dark moods. Two gales swept the banks in December alone, the most terrible the oldest fishermen could remember, and hurled ten schooners and ninety-eight men to the bottom. Gloucester staggered under her losses this centennial year of independence: 27 vessels and 212 fishermen.

The years 1877 and 1878 were as the eye of the hurricane—comparatively calm—twenty-one schooners and ninety-five men lost between them. The next—1879—was the most disastrous in the annals of the fisheries; 249 Gloucestermen sailed off, and none sailed back. Some were drowned dory fishing inshore, some working their trawls on the banks; some were swept over by boarding seas, or off the plunging bowsprit, fighting thrashing headsails; some were blown out of the rigging, or bashed by a jibing boom. But most went down in the sea with twenty-nine ships.

It didn't take the smart skippers long to diagnose the primary cause of these epidemics of founderings—the dandifying of the clipper schooner beyond all reasonable considerations of safety for the sake of speed. That these extremes of design had turned Gloucester's fleet into a flotilla of streamlined coffins, underdrafted and overcanvassed, was to be the thesis of Captain Joseph W. Collins in the 1880s, and it would agitate a drawing-board revolution.

But in 1879 Captain Collins was still halibuting out of Gloucester, and from the pen of the thirty-nine-year-old veteran we have a gripping description of the anxious approach

Loading a schooner with stone from the Eastern Point quarry, 1870s. (From Procter Brothers' Cape Ann Scenery, *Cape Ann Historical Association)*

of his halibut schooner *Marion* (repeated God knows how many times) to the buoyless lee shore of Eastern Point in thick weather. Coming from the eastward, they could see Thacher's lights. It was four in the morning of January 16. Then the snow started and the glass dropped. Captain Collins was extremely uneasy:

About ten o'clock in the forenoon the wind breezed up from the southeast and increased quite fast. We ran for Eastern Point as nearly as I could judge, the various courses and distances which we had steered during the morning, in consequence of the baffling winds, rendering it somewhat uncertain in what direction the Point lay from us. Soon after the wind came, the snow cleared up so that objects could be seen about a mile distant. We saw a shore fishing vessel—a haddock catcher—coming astern, and wishing to speak with her we hauled our sheets aft and let her run up on us. She proved to be the *David F. Low,* bound to Gloucester, having run across from Cape Cod. She ran ahead of us a little way, and just before we saw the land the snow came down so thick that we lost sight of her.

Knowing that we were close in and fast approaching the shore, all hands were on deck and on the alert to do any duty which circumstances might demand. A dozen pairs of eyes peered out ahead, anxiously watching to catch a glimpse of the land or breakers. A few minutes later the thrilling cry of, "Land ho! breakers ahead!" came from half a dozen at once, and a line of white foam and the snow-covered shore above it were indistinctly seen to leeward. "Hard down! hard down the helm!" was the order shouted to the wheelsman, for so close in were we that any delay in changing the course of the vessel must have resulted in piling her up on the rocks. As the wheel was put down and the vessel came to the wind, most of the men, in obedience to orders, quickly pulled in the sheets, while the rest of us strained our eyes to make out some familiar object on the shore whereby we might be certain of our position.

We made the land a little to the westward of Bass Rocks. When we first saw it we were running in with the sails on the port side, the wind at the time blowing a smart breeze from south-southeast, and as we hauled to, just clearing the surf on the shore, we fortunately saw and recognized the summer houses which are only a short distance from the water. As soon as I was sure of our "land fall," we tacked and ran for Eastern Point, following the line of breakers along the shore as near as safety permitted. Every eye was now on the watch for well-known land-marks, and soon the spray dashing over Brace's Cove Rock was seen, and a few minutes later we went sweeping in by the Point, near enough to catch a momentary glimpse of the white tower of the lighthouse, and to hear the hoarse-toned fog-bell which rang out its notes of warning.

We could now laugh at the storm, and the broad grin which appeared on the bronzed faces of many of our crew and the shrugging and chuckling of others gave ample evidence of the general feeling of satisfaction among all hands.[2]

That was the way it was. You got home if you were cautious and skillful and lucky enough. But a year later, returning to Gloucester from Boston where she had taken out her trip of haddock, the schooner *E. L. Rowe* sailed into a wall of fog in the early hours of January 8, 1880. They could neither see the light nor hear the fog bell, clean missed the harbor and rammed her ashore near High Popples.

All that way out and back, surviving all the risks of the winter fishery, just to pile up on the backsides of the Point. One indignant old skipper wrote the *Advertiser* that a person couldn't hear the dratted fog bell at the light in an onshore breeze; why didn't they moor a whistling buoy a mile south of it? That would have saved the *Rowe* and would be an immense aid to piloting the coast.

Like a mocking echo, ten more days and the *Winifred J. King* was feeling her way back to Gloucester from shore fishing during a very heavy snowstorm on the night of February 3. Judging they were clear, they rounded and crashed into Brace Cove. The men waded ashore through the icy breakers and nigh froze finding a warm hearth. In a few hours the *King* was dead.

No one took up the old salt's suggestion except a letter writer who informed the *Cape Ann Weekly Advertiser* that a whistling buoy off Newport caused a sick gentleman there to "die raving for want of sleep," that the shore owners at Beverly had blocked one, that summer people would stay away, and improvements from Eastern Point around to Magnolia would be abandoned.

The False Point remained as false as ever. The middle of the afternoon it was, on the twenty-eighth of February, the next winter of 1881, and the wind was blowing easterly from off the sea, carrying with it, as so often it does this season of the year, a dense galloping fog. Pete Comeau and Ed Eason, two young fellows from East Gloucester, out fowling, had crossed the upland moors and were picking their way along the ledge above Grapevine Cove. A heavy sea pounded in below them; they could hardly see the swells parading in through the murk, but the spray spattered against their cheeks.

All at once both looked up and cried out. A sound out there—a sigh, a kind of rumple, a swoosh—and then in an instant the high-above sails and spars and the ghostly emerging bulk of a square-rigged vessel—all struck the senses together.

And before the two could take it in, out of the muff of fog and spindrift she came at them, easy, majestic, every thread of her canvas proudly set, straight for shore.

She broke through the thick, a grand ship from out in the sea, rising and falling in the swells, square on, no quarter given, no inkling of her fate. She threw herself to her destruction, right on it with the surge of the whole Atlantic and the whack of the gale behind her, onto the ledges of Grape Vine, tearing, splintering, crashing, rending, screaming, scraping to within a few rods of precisely where the great ship *Howard* had smashed ashore— absolutely and exactly seventy-four years before, less no more than six hours, on that night of February 28, 1807.

Those on board were as dumbfounded as the two gunners on shore. And then they rushed to the bows of her, as their ship shuddered like a dying thing in the surf, and threw a rope arching ashore. Comeau and Eason recovered their senses now and jumped to it, retrieved the lifeline and made it fast to something like a stump or a boulder, and the crew rigged a chair to it and one after the other slid to the solid ground of Eastern Point from the vessel that a few minutes before, they had supposed, was running free with the wind sixteen miles out to sea.

She was the 300-ton barque *Brothers* of New York, bound for Boston from Havana, which she had cleared three weeks ago to the day with a $50,000 cargo of 550 hogsheads of sugar. And a rough passage it had been, and a rougher ending. Imagine that!—sixteen miles to the landward of his course! Captain John Lawson couldn't get over it.

Nor could his owners.

That night with the ebb the wreck careened, and her spars and all her sails went by the board. At the next flood, the gale holding fresh and the seas mounting, the rollers tore her deck off. The hogsheads of sugar, one by one and two by two, were borne out of her and exploded on the rocks, and by morning the shore was all barrel staves.

That afternoon was a sight to be remembered. The swells built up way out to sea by the abating storm rolled in for mile after mile along the Back Shore, each glorifying its disintegration in a white blossom of spray and growl of foam. The word was out; the people came from all over to witness the death of the *Brothers*.

Each last flex of the sea muscle lifted the breaking barque a fathom up, and the muscle vanished, and the carcass whacked back down on the lathered rocks, and the grinding and splitting and gnashing of the wooden bones was horrible for the people to hear. Water against rock tore off the stern, and then the sides, and then broke the gaunt stark ribs to pieces, and that was the end of her.

The *Bunker Hill* was next. A big hundred-ton schooner, she had cleaved the winter seas and braved the arctic blasts on a long trip down to Fortune Bay, Newfoundland, after frozen herring, bait for the Gloucester fleet. Now she was coming home, and all hands glad to fetch the welcome beams of the Twin Lights on the night of February 4, 1882, the winter after the *Brothers* went up.

Snowing thick, and blowing. From Thacher's, Captain John McDonald ran for Eastern Point, and when he thought he would be opening the light (he couldn't see his bowsprit), he put his helm over. There were the breakers, and before they could make a move to keep off, the *Bunker Hill* had driven herself high on Bemo.

All the way to Fortune Bay and back, to go ashore on the Point—the harbor beckoning, and laughing at them, just across Niles Pond. Captain McDonald and crew swung their dory into the surf and rowed into Brace Beach, and floundered, soaking to the skin and near frozen, three-quarters of a mile through the driving snow and the drifts to the doorsteps of East Gloucester.

During the early morning the *Bunker Hill* capsized, and then sawed her bilges on the rocks for a day before the seas flattened enough for the steam tugs *S. B. Jones* and *S. E. Wetherell* to get around to her. On her beam ends they dragged her into the harbor, and she was righted with the boom of the big Rockport stone sloop *C. E. Trumbull*. But the hulk was beyond doing anything with, and they sold it for junk.

The sight of this wreck deposited in its front yard, this rebuke, aroused the vested interests of the waterfront at long last and a petition was passed around requesting the lighthouse board to moor a first-class whistling buoy one mile southeast of the light to guide mariners away from the fatal flirtations of the False Point.

Thus began the second battle of Bunker Hill. You might think that the anchoring of a buoy to warn vessels off from such a graveyard would be acclaimed by one and all. On the contrary. Hardly had this modest plea been advanced along the length and breadth of Front Street when a counterpetition was making the rounds on the outskirts and gathering plenty of signatures, too, at East Gloucester, Eastern Point and Magnolia. The antiwhistler people complained to the *Advertiser* that its plaintive call would ruin their properties for living purposes, that shore improvements from Eastern Point all the way around to Magnolia would have to be abandoned, and that

> though there has been an occasional loss, owing as they believe very much to the absence of due care by captains of coasting vessels, not a single life has been lost within the knowledge of the oldest inhabitant; that they believe that such a buoy would be the cause of more deaths than its absence, for its injurious character to invalids is well known, and its establishment would cause a much greater loss of property than it would ever be likely to preserve.[3]

Here in this letter signed "Benefactor" might have been discerned the fine hand of the insomniac authoress Elizabeth Stuart Phelps, who summered a hail beyond the Niles farm gate, or even of a Niles.

"Benefactor" was quite blunt about it next week: a whistling buoy will discourage sales of shore lots to summer people. (Eight months hence, incidentally, Sarah Rogers would reach the magic age of twenty-one, established by her late grandfather as the date on which the Eastern Point farm could legally be offered for summer estates.)

"Benefactor" went on to observe that in the last ten years but five

Author Elizabeth Stuart Phelps.

Gloucester vessels had gone ashore between Bass Rocks and the lighthouse, and three of these were got off; there were rumors of a lifesaving station to be built at the Point—good—forget about a whistling buoy and raise the height of the light so it can be opened over the land and install a good bell there, for what is there now is a "poor thing."[4]

"Truth" replied to "Benefactor" that twenty-one lives (a bit high) had been left on that stretch of Back Shore in the last fifty-five years, and had the Bunker Hill gone up an hour later all hands would have been drowned because the seas and tides were rising. A whistler, advised "Truth," should be moored a mile broad off Bemo so a vessel fetching it would see Eastern Point Light while well offshore.

"The absence of any guide to the entrance of Gloucester harbor in thick weather," reflected the writer, "is a source of great perplexity and wearing anxiety to mariners. The losses are many, and the number who escape almost by miracle is much larger."[5]

The last shot of the first skirmish was had by "old Georgesman" who wanted one whistler located in the shoal water on Middle Bank fifteen miles off the Point and another four miles southeast of the light. Either that or raise the light to first-order status, flashing red and white, and back it up with a fifteen-inch steam whistle, for the existing station is of hardly any use at all.[6]

That was the end of that, and the disputants went back to their corners.

Four months passed, and a large fleet of mackerel seiners—mostly from Gloucester but some from other ports—was following the spring run a few miles east of the Point, when unexpectedly it breezed up from the southeast and raised a thick fog. This was the morning of June 6, 1882.

In the fleet was the former Gloucester schooner *Catalina*, now hailing out of Boothbay, Maine, Captain William H. Johnson. He made for the harbor—incautiously it proved—for before he could fairly get his bearings he was onshore and at the mercy of the southeaster, which hove his vessel onto Bemo. There she took a hard pounding before a towboat came and hauled her into the harbor, the men at the pumps just keeping her afloat.

It turned out that stranded there, *Catalina* had served at least as an object lesson to her sisters, many of which were already close onshore, all unaware of their peril. The incident elicited a powerful letter to the newspaper from the skipper of one of those luckier ones, Captain James L. Anderson of the schooner *J. J. Clark*:

> I have noticed in your columns several times, articles in relation to an automatic buoy off Eastern Point. There is no place on this side of the Atlantic that stands more in need of a signal of some kind. Every day and night of the year there are some of our vessels and coasters running for the Point. In thick snow storms or fogs there is no guide except a small bell that cannot be heard 400 yards to windward in a whole sail breeze, not far enough if made right ahead in a gale to clear the breakers, if a vessel had to tack ship or jibe over.
>
> There have been several vessels lost in that vicinity, on account of having no guide to run for in thick weather. I came near losing my vessel last Sunday, not a quarter of a mile from the light, on the False Point. I was fishing with about 50 other vessels between Middle Bank and Eastern Point, and there came a squall from S.E., and a thick fog set in. I set my course as near as I could judge for the Point, to get in the harbor, and so did most of the fleet. I made for the breakers [Captain Anderson thought he was approaching Dog Bar] and could hear no bell, and hove my vessel head off shore. The wind died out suddenly, and a heavy swell heaved up from S.E.
>
> We were fast drifting on the rocks, and let our port anchor go with a cable; as it did not bring her up we let our other anchor go with a chain, and that brought her up, her stern almost in the breakers. We had to lay there an hour and a half, when the wind sprang up from the N.W., and we got clear. If the wind had come up from the S.E. again, blowing as hard as it usually does in a southeaster, we should have lost our vessel, as she could not have been saved where she was. When the fog lifted, there were five more of the seiners between our vessel and the Point, all close to the breakers.
>
> There ought to be something done right away to have a signal buoy placed off the Point, for the safety of our fleet of 450 vessels, and the lives of over 6000 men that go fishing from this port. I think that the few summer boarders that come here in the hot season can get used to the sound of the buoy, as can also the people that live near there . . .[7]

Under rising pressure the lighthouse board met in August and took up the vexing problem of finding some way to guide mariners into Gloucester Harbor without offending the sensibilities of the landed interests.

Well, well, they hemmed, a whistling buoy off Eastern Point might be confused with others nearby. (There were none.) But they had to do something, so they gave the fog bell a heavier hammer and ordered revolving machinery to alter the Eastern Point Light from fixed to flashing red at five-second intervals as of the first of October, this year of 1882.

It was done, and in November old George Friend, keeper for the last ten years, decided the extra chore of winding the new machinery was too much for him and was transferred to Narrows Light in Boston Harbor; the keeper there, George Bailey, came up to Eastern Point.

The *Advertiser* expressed the dissatisfaction of the Gloucester maritime community with these measures. Fixed or flashing, it felt, Eastern Point Light is hidden by the shore to the eastward of it from vessels that are too close in and is invisible in thick weather offshore. The fog bell still can't be heard upwind; as for the Board's objection to a whistler, a skipper would have to be mighty far off his course to confuse it with the nearest groaners, one marking Boon Island off the coast of Maine, way beyond the Isles of Shoals, and the other at the Graves in Boston Harbor.

Shortly before Christmas the lighthouse board let it be known that it was reconsidering the matter, but nothing happened. Winter and 1883 came on, and spring and summer, and no more wrecks. . .

Until the night of September 23. The *Isaac A. Chapman,* Captain Charles Smith, returning from mackereling, made Thacher's in a squall and then ran for the red light that the lookout and all on deck swore was Eastern Point.

But it wasn't. Next they knew the breakers were dead ahead. They put their helm hard over, jibed, broke their main boom and ran up the foresail, but quick as they moved, it was too late. The *Chapman* drove aground on Good Harbor Beach and bilged. The crew jumped over and sloshed up through the surf. They saved 40 barrels of her deckload of mackerel, and another 150 from the hold, but the rest of their fare of 505 barrels in the round washed out to sea.

The *Isaac A. Chapman* was pulled off the beach and taken around and hauled up on the railway in the harbor. But the men lost $150 share each, all because they had mistaken the light shining through a red curtain in a window for the Ruby Light of Eastern Point, and there was no whistler to whistle them in.

That did it. On the nineteenth of November, 1883, a whistling buoy was moored in sixteen-and-a-half fathoms off Eastern Point by order of the lighthouse board. Magnetic bearings: Eastern Point Light north by east one-half nautical mile, Thacher's outer lighthouse northeast by east five-and-a-half nautical miles, to emit between twenty and thirty blasts a minute.

At about the same time a relief hut was built at Brace Cove for ship-wrecked mariners. It doubtless housed a lifeboat and was surely the work of the Massachusetts Humane Society, which would keep one there for years, though the early particulars are missing.

But could you please these Gloucester fishermen? Of course not. The whistler had not been gasping out its groans and sighs for six weeks when another petition was presented to the lighthouse board wanting it to be moored where the Gloucestermen had first asked for it, a mile southeast of the Point. Where it was, they claimed, was too far inshore and actually increasing the danger of the ledges by bringing the mariner too close to them when he was running for the sound of it.

For that matter, lamented the *Advertiser,* if the buoy can't be put in the right place, let it be removed altogether, for where it is "it better serves the purpose of destruction, like its ancient prototype the Siren, than the safety of the poor mariner."[8]

Stoutly did the lighthouse inspector defend his choice of location; he had placed the buoy there, in consultation not with mere fishermen but with the masters of the Boston-Portland steamers no less, and on the basis of his personal examination of the area. That vessels can seek it out in thick weather, he reasoned with some logic, was demonstrated by the number of dents in its guard rail.

So there "Mother Ann's Cow" grazes mournfully to this day, groaning and sighing and ruminating on the fate of the mariners who still can't hear her to their leeward in a breeze.

Pen-and-ink drawing of the Eastern Point farm, probably by Frank Rogers, grandson of Thomas Niles.
(Private collection)

~17~
OCEANA

Τ HE CAPE ANN WEEKLY ADVERTISER
passed the word to its readers on September 1, 1882: "It is whispered that
the Niles property at East Gloucester is to come into the market as a seaside
resort."

When Sarah McClennen Rogers, his granddaughter, reached her
twenty-first birthday, Thomas Niles had willed, his executors could put the
Eastern Point farm up for sale if they wished. Next month my grandmother
was to be twenty-one. Hence the whisper.

Whether offered or not, the Point was not sold. The eldest son, Thomas,
Jr., the following spring sold his ninth share to William, who was managing
the farm, for $5,555.55, indicating that the family agreed the property was
worth, *en famille*, $50,000. As the real estate tax was only about $720, they
could afford to sit tight on "Ocean Farm," or "Oceana" as the old man had
called it, and wait for an offer that suited them.

The younger Thomas Niles had entered the publishing business in
Boston as a six-dollar-a-week apprentice with William D. Ticknor's Old
Corner Bookstore in 1839, thereby advancing James T. Fields to senior
clerk. Twenty-four years later he joined his brother-in-law's firm of Roberts
Brothers (absorbed by Little, Brown in 1898) and was regarded as one of
the most sagacious editors in America. Among other notable contributions
to the literary scene, the reticent, sensitive bachelor persuaded Louisa May
Alcott to write *Little Women,* published Emily Dickinson's poems after their
rejection by Houghton Mifflin and introduced the works of leading British
authors to the United States.[1]

An 1884 atlas of Cape Ann shows the executors' subdivision of Niles
farm honeycombed with roads, largely of the paper sort. One, labeled
"Niles Avenue," skirts it by shore and across the upland south of the
Cushing Wall; sea and harbor are also connected around the south side of
the pond by "Pond Street." The rest of the network is alphabetized, up to
"W Street."

This imaginary plat shows a real "boarding house" a few yards back from the south end of Wharf Beach, near Indian Spring, the freshet that then bubbled forth from a sandy oasis surrounded by willows. The house, long since gone, was known as Indian Spring Cottage, and the woods behind it as Niles Grove.

For several seasons during the early 1880s Niles Grove and Indian Spring Cottage were a favorite resort for annual picnics of a convivial nature. The Sea Side Association cooked up their clambake and chowder there every summer, and in 1882 so did sixty employees and guests of the Gloucester Steamboat Company. Captain Francis Locke's steam lighter *Abbott Coffin,* named after the line's agent, was the transportation of choice on another occasion when the Gloucester Cornet Band had its outing. The band and guests marched down to the steamboat wharf, "discoursing some fine music on the way," and continued to discourse out the harbor, one supposes, until they landed merrily at the stone wharf.

A picnic in a more rustic vein was remembered by Mrs. Frances Cunningham, an excursion from the family cottage at Bass Rocks in the summer of 1886 out to the old Civil War fort when she was a small girl:

> We planned to go at low tide so that we could drive over Niles Beach as there was no sea wall or road above the beach. There were five barred gates between the end of Niles Beach and the Lighthouse to keep the cattle in. . . . We drove in a barge, my uncle and aunt, my father and mother, with five or six children, over Mt. Pleasant Avenue and along East Main Street. . . . This Gloucester barge was not a boat, but a large wagonette with seats facing in along the sides, drawn by two horses. We went through the first gate, someone getting out to open it and close it after us, drove along Niles Beach where the horses' hoofs made a pleasant noise on the hard sand, through the second gate by the farmhouse and on along the narrow road and through the gates to the old fort, where we children climbed the grass-grown walls and picked blackberries while our elders sat by.[2]

So much for a pleasant noise on the hard sand of the Point. Others were not so pleasant.

The Newburyport schooner *Lydia A. Davis* was returning from fishing early in the morning of March 30, 1884, when she sprang a bad leak off the Back Shore—started a butt, most likely. Captain Tom Dailey put the men to pumping and ran for Brace Cove to beach her before she sank under them. But he missed the entrance channel, and the *Davis* cracked up on Bemo. The eight of them got their dories over and landed. The sea flattened at dawn, and they lightened her of 3,000 pounds of fish before she broke up. The wreck brought forty dollars.

Then there was the miraculous escape of the *Carl Schurz.* It was the afternoon of the thirty-first of that October. The schooner had ridden one of those drenching fall northeasters all the way from Georges Bank, making ten knots double reefed. Heavy seas had built up, and when the *Schurz*

The author's grandmother Sarah Rogers Garland, whose twenty-first birthday triggered the sale of the farm owned by her grandfather Thomas Niles. (Author's collection)

fetched the Point, it was some sight for all hands—and a shivery one—to mark the harbor by the smash of the swells on Dog Bar and the shoal of Round Rock, explosions of spray shooting fifty feet in the air.

Preparing to haul in by, Captain John Constance put his helm down and ordered the foresail trimmed (the mainsail was furled). At that moment a squall hit, and the miserable sail ripped from peak to foot. They lost their headway, and as the swells and tide swept them toward the fearsome breakers on Dog Bar, Captain Constance yelled to let the anchor go.

Five of his crew dashed forward. They loosed the anchor and ran out their cable, and when they bitted it, she fetched up hard just short of the rocks under her stern and reared back like a stallion brought to rein. Then she plunged her bow and took two seas of green water, one after the other, that swept every man of the five overboard. Impossible, but true, the captain and the two or three others left on deck snatched four of them back on board, all but Jim Farnsworth, a young fellow from Nova Scotia.

Desperate, between dousing seas they cut their cable and worked the *Carl Schurz*, under just her jib, away to the westward a short distance and let their other anchor go in the deep water. There they rode out the night and repaired their foresail, and sailed into the harbor next morning, flag at half mast.

And then the *Hopvine*. She was a coasting schooner, ninety-one tons, bound home to St. John, New Brunswick, on the night of January 26, 1885. It was bitterly cold, blowing hard onshore, and they must have been close-reaching under short sail, because off Thacher's their foresail blew out—as the *Schurz*'s had—and in trying to run back around the Point and into Gloucester they couldn't keep her off; *Hopvine* sagged ashore east of the lighthouse.

Captain Best and his gang got a dory over the side and into the surf which was pounding their vessel against the ledge. They landed probably with more luck than skill and made their way to the keeper's cottage, badly exposed. The next night at low water they performed the astonishing feat of taking 204 barrels of meal and flour out of their stranded schooner before the returning tide shut them off. A junk dealer bought the remains of the *Hopvine* for $40, the going rate for $5,000 schooners after the Point got through with them.

And finally, for those who never cease to see in the smallest coincidence a meaning, there were the events that came to an abrupt stop a few weeks later in or very near Grape Vine Cove, scene of the casting-up of the *Brothers* on the very seventy-fourth anniversary of the *Howard*'s wreck.

The *Four Sisters,* in ballast, was on her way home from Lynn to St. George, Maine, the evening of April 2, when she came in thick off Baker's Island. Captain Bunker had the bad luck to be so far off in his reckoning, never realizing he was so close to Cape Ann, that before they had the faintest idea of where they were the *Sisters* had informed them by driving herself high, if not quite dry, on the same shore where the *Brothers* had ended it all four years earlier.

All the rest of the night the incoming seas beat the schooner against the rocks, and then by the first light of the rosy-fingered dawn Captain Bunker and his men took to their boat and got ashore. All that day she pounded, and it was not until she had lain there beating on the ledge for two days that a brace of tugs came around and towed her, half submerged, to Boston, where she was a sensation.

The *Four Sisters* was the worst wreck ever brought into Boston Harbor and successfully docked, avowed the incredulous *Boston Advertiser*. She had one hole seven by eighteen feet in her port bilge "you could drive a span of horses through," another ten by ten feet on her starboard side where the rocks had chewed her and her keel had been torn entirely off. That she floated at all defied belief. But they repaired her—a stout vessel, to be sure.

One last living link with the Niles farm of the early 1880s survived with noble vigor to the 1970s, James C. Walen of East Gloucester—Captain Jim, as he was hailed by three generations of summer people who had absorbed from him the art of sailing and the lore of Gloucester. Going on ninety-eight, Jim was a compact, apple-cheeked veteran of the old times with bald pate, twinkling eyes, snow-white mustache and puckish humor. For many years he was a sailmaker and professional small boat sailing teacher. Every morning during the summer of 1969, as he had since retiring as its steward, he drove to the Eastern Point Yacht Club to hoist the colors and impart some kindly wisdom and sly humor to the young sailors gathering at the

"Gashouse," and then at sundown back again to lower Old Glory and fire off the cannon that concluded the day.

Jim Walen was born on Rocky Neck's Clarendon Street on June 2, 1872. When he was eight or ten he worked a couple of summers for Howard Wonson, who kept a herd of thirty cows in his large shed between the Walen home and Smith Cove. Come spring Wonson drove the herd across the bar and over to the Niles farm to a piece of pasture he rented south of the pond.

Jimmy milked seven of the cows, morning and evening, in the dairy shed by the pond and the south end of Brace Cove, then peddled the milk to his master's Rocky Neck customers. Carrying an eight-quart can over each shoulder, he trudged around the Neck, ladling it out with a one-quart measure to the women at their back stoops until his route was ended.

A dollar a week was his wage, and the lad kept a tally with a piece of chalk on the inside of the shed door. But when his first summer was done, and it came time to pay up, Mr. Wonson accused him of chalking up two extra weeks, so his Pa made him go back and put in two more. After two summers of this Jimmy had saved eighteen dollars for a suit of clothes to go to school in.

Jim remembered Allston Niles, who had charge of the farm then, as "a short, nice kind of a feller—what you'd call a dressed-up farmer." He wasn't overenthusiastic for the agricultural life; after the farm left the family, Allston turned to the city and for a while was a salesman for a manufacturer of electric vibrators that he assured his customers were guaranteed to reduce their girth.

Collecting seaweed, south end of Niles Beach, probably 1890s. (Martha Rogers Harvey photo, private collection)

Allston's next oldest brother, William, was an amateur artist and kept a studio at the bend in the road across from the homestead, beside the pond. He wanted no company but his muse when he was painting outdoors, and if Jimmy or someone would come up behind and peer over his shoulder, William would brusquely turn his easel about-face to let the kibitzer know he wasn't welcome.

"Oceana" was not extensively cultivated in these closing years of the Niles era. Most of the cleared land was pasture. The slope of Fort Hill was given over to hay and vegetables, and Allston kept maybe sixteen cows, as Captain Jim recollected, with some horses and two yoke of oxen in the big barn across from the farmhouse, a few pigs and the usual chickens underfoot. The oxen performed most of the draft work around the place. Between the road and the pond, from the barn to the end of the beach, was a sizeable orchard that produced sweet yellow apples of a locally famous variety, the honeypinks. And some scattered pear trees. The only cutting on the Point was for cordwood.

The quarry had ceased operations in Jim's youth, but he retained in his mind's eye a building about where Indian Spring Cottage was, used formerly as a smithy, where stonecutting tools and drills had been sharpened and repaired in former days; they may have been one and the same.

In the fall of the year the hands would take the wagons down to the beaches and ledges and load them up with rockweed that was spread around the fields, to be ploughed under before spring planting—Farmer Niles's "inexhaustible supply of sea manure."

Billy Rackliffe, Benny Hodgkins and Johnny Foster also leased pasture land from the Niles family. Every morning from spring to fall they drove their cows up from Rocky Neck, over Patch's Hill and along the road through the gate, raising clouds of dust, to the Niles grazing grounds, and then back again every afternoon for milking and the night, and Jimmy Walen or a chum would be there at the Niles gate to tend to that for a two-cent piece.

Farther along past the pond, where the cart tracks to the overgrown ramparts branched off from the road to the lighthouse, Jim remembered another one of the Niles stock gates; nailed to it was a weatherworn sign painted by John Warren Young of Lanesville, who worked for Allston for some years, which instructed simply enough: PLEASE SHATE THE GATE.

Isaac Patch had outlived his arch foe, and after the death of his first wife, Eliza, had remarried in his seventies. It was her deathbed hope that a second wife might present him with issue: Eliza even suggested her successor, Hattie Lyle of East Gloucester, who, as ordained, married the widower and in 1875, when he was seventy-four, bore him his first child, Isaac, Jr.. Two years later arrived a daughter, Harriet.

Old Farmer Patch had a way with the sea and the soil and the fruits thereof, and Jim Walen used to watch him get out on the south side of his barn with a yoke of oxen just before the first deep frost and plough out a deep trench. Then he would roll into it anything he wanted to keep but not to freeze, such as a barrel of cabbage, and cover it over with layers of hay and seaweed. And there it would remain in a fine state of refrigeration until he wanted it.

In his last years Mr. Patch sometimes took notions.

One day Jimmy and the gang were playing in the field up by the Patch place when old Ike came stomping up, lined them all against the side of the barn like a squad of green recruits and crackled: "I'll give any of ye ten acres if ye don't sarse me!"

Somewhere out of the rank came a giggle. Farmer Patch shook a horny fist at them and roared "Not a damn inch!" and stomped off.

He died on the Fourth of July, 1886, at the age of eighty-five.

Life on the Niles farm was even sleepier and husbandry less energetically pursued after John Burke, the faithful Niles foreman of sixteen years, suffered a fatal fall from the wagon while pitching out a load of September hay in 1884. Jim Walen quit milking to go lobstering and help with his father's fish trap off Niles Beach.

The days of shipwright Stevens and blacksmith Allen, of Dan'l Rogers, Burnham, Sayward, Plumer and John Perkins Cushing, and the Nileses, were running out.

On the twelfth of November, 1887, the executors of the estate of Thomas Niles sold his great farm to a syndicate of businessmen, the Eastern Point Associates, for $100,000.

The gate lodge built by the Eastern Point Associates. (Author's collection)

~18~
EASTERN POINT
ASSOCIATES

Dᴀᴠɪᴅ ᴀɴᴅ ᴊᴏʜɴ ᴏꜰ ᴛʜᴇ ᴊᴀᴍᴀɪᴄᴀ
Plain Greenoughs were first brought to Gloucester as boys in 1855 when the
family came to the Pavilion, Cape Ann's original summer hotel. Then only
six years old, the Pavilion gave the beach up in the harbor its name, later
The Surfside, and after that burned in 1914, The Tavern.

Eastern Point fingered like a romantic island into the sea across the harbor, beckoning the two brothers, eleven and nine, to adventure. They would
row over in their skiff, beach it up toward the lighthouse and "spy out the
land," taking care to avoid Mr. Niles. Their favorite haunt was Black Bess
Point, which David and John vowed they would some day own.

"At that time none of Eastern Point was settled except for a farmhouse
here and there," John recalled in an interview in 1928 when he was eighty-
two.[1]

> In fact, when I was grown up and married, and Mrs.
> Greenough and I came down here for a brief visit after our wed-
> ding, there were few houses even then. When we left, our boarding
> mistress put her arms around Mrs. Greenough in farewell, so you
> can see how changed it is now from those days.
>
> All the land down here was owned by a farmer named Niles.
> He was one of these fellows who hated the world and wanted to be
> by himself. When he died, my brother and I heard that the land was
> to be divided and sold. We came right down, and together bought a
> section of the Niles farm. Every rock along the harbor shore here
> was familiar to us. We knew every crack by heart. I knew about the
> little chasm here, and the rocky island just off the shore at this point
> [Black Bess Rocks and Point], and thought it the best location. And
> here I have been ever since.

The Greenough brothers were fortyish then, successful capitalists, and
had summer places elsewhere, but they moved rapidly when their boyhood

dreams suddenly materialized. Who took the lead is not known, but some American and Canadian men of affairs came together, presumably on the initiative of the Greenoughs, to acquire the rest of the Point, carve out for themselves the choicest estates and turn the dream of Thomas Niles and his faith in his property into profitable reality.

The whole farm below the Cushing Wall, with the exception of the lighthouse reservation owned by the United States and a half-acre south of the Hill of Rocks, high in back of Niles Beach, that was reserved for the late owner's house of worship, was sold by the Niles trustees for $100,000 on the twelfth of November, 1887, to the Trustees of the Eastern Point Associates, namely Cornelius G. Attwood of Boston; Walter Barwick of Toronto, a prominent Canadian lawyer; and Captain Albert Lewis of Boston, proprietor of Lewis Wharf, one-time vessel master and shipping magnate who, it was said, "has sailed the world over many times and was quick to see the many attractions of Eastern Point as soon as his attention was called to it."[2] Their clerk was A. Spalding Weld of Boston.

The syndicate was capitalized at 10,000 shares and paid $40,000 cash, giving the Niles trustees a $60,000 mortgage to be met, they had no doubt, from the sale of lots, 250 of which, averaging somewhat more than an acre, were forthwith surveyed.

Streets were laid out. Like rivers making their valleys, their course has changed in places but many of the names remain: Stewart, St. Louis, Lake, Toronto, Elm, Fort Hill and Eastern Point Boulevard, east and west, the perimetrical road linked across the peninsula by Farrington Avenue (honoring Charles F. Farrington, the Boston businessman who succeeded as a trustee when Attwood died unexpectedly in January 1888). H. H. Pomeroy of Gloucester was retained to improve the old farm roads and to clear the first building lots.

The Associates must have a porter, and they engaged Boston architects Daniel Appleton and H. M. Stephenson to design a gate lodge at the entrance by the Niles gate.

They had no intention of developing the Point as a residential summer resort exclusively. The key to their plan was to be the toniest vacation hotel on the coast for which they set aside Fort Hill—695,000 square feet of Farmer Niles's best land, right down to Wharf Beach. In February 1888 they were reported to be organizing a separate company to build it; in the meantime, however, they bought the Seaside Hotel on Niles Beach from Dederick C. Voss of Worcester (the only lot the Niles family parted with before they sold the farm), changed the name to The Beachcroft and refurbished it for opening that season under the management of Mrs. Maria H. Bray.

Somewhere out of all this activity popped a rumor that would recur for years: the New York Yacht Club was imminently preparing to designate Eastern Point a cruising station and would build a clubhouse there. And it was also said that a steam launch would soon connect the premises of the Associates with Gloucester by water. In this case the group pulled it off, for

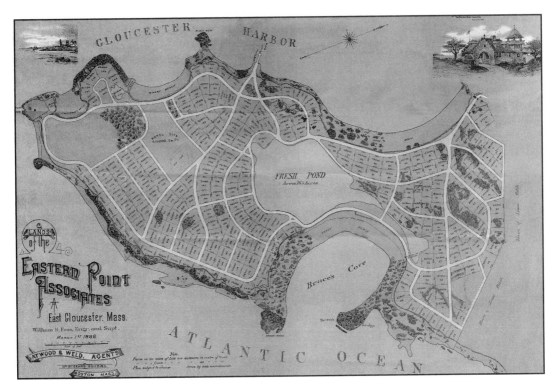

in March the harbor commissioners licensed them to construct at the foot of their projected Fort Hill Avenue on the harbor a 300-foot stone-and-wood pier, T-shaped, 100 feet across the head, not for a launch but as a summer stop for the steamers of the Boston and Gloucester Steamship Company carrying excursions, hotel visitors and freight, and for the convenience of the Associates and their families.

The pier and gate lodge were built that spring at a feverish clip. The Associates wanted both completed for their first summer season—one for a display of the Point's charms to potential buyers and developers, the other as the palpable and authoritative, yet tasteful and diplomatic, cornerstone of their foreign policy.

In July the steamers were touching at Eastern Point on their twice-daily runs between Central Wharf at Boston and the line's wharf at the foot of Duncan Street. Late in August the Associates threw a *déjeuner* for their Boston prospects.

The party of 350 ladies and gentlemen left Boston at 9:30 on the *City of Gloucester,* arriving at about noon at the new pier, where a waiting caravan of barges and barouches conveyed them to a spacious tent pitched on the hill near the romantic old fort. Here in the zephyred coolness beneath the marquee Caterer Dooling served his sumptuous *déjeuner à la fourchette* at row upon row of long tables, after which all returned to their vehicles for a guided inspection of the grounds.

Pomeroy's workmen were extending the nearly completed boulevard above Niles Beach, lacking only the side rail and electric lights and said to

The Associates'
steamship pier,
from the vantage
of "Red Roof,"
October 6, 1910.
(Andrew L. Gray)

have cost the owners $10,000 already. The sturdy Gothic lodge at the end of it was a reassuring sentinel, no doubt of that.

Returning, the visitors were informed that the freshwater pond that had been named for Mr. Niles would be dredged, cleaned and converted into a reservoir to provide a limitless supply for the future residents of the Point, the city water pipes not having advanced beyond Rocky Neck.

The Civil War earthworks, it was explained, would contain the most magnificent summer hotel on the New England coast. This would of necessity be the stopping place for all transient visitors to the Point, since deed restrictions banned all other hostelries without the written permission of the trustees. Moreover, none but one-family dwellings with outbuildings and stables (location subject to approval) could be built without the consent of the Associates, and they must cost above ground no less than $5,000, not including the stable.

Before the guests of the syndicate were returned to the pier for the trip back to Boston they learned that twenty-two lots had been sold and fourteen cellars were planned for excavation before the snow fell. Price of a square foot of Eastern Point: ten cents.

Eleven private cottages were actually completed by its members between fall of 1888 and summer of 1889, carefully designed to establish the tone of the new resort and pictured in a promotional brochure published soon after by the Associates.

First, after passing the Gate Lodge, was the large beach-stone and frame house of John J. Stanwood, Gloucester fish dealer and real estate speculator.[3] It commanded the height above Niles Beach and was among the first to be started, costing about $6,000 to build.

Proceeding along the new Eastern Point Boulevard West past the farmhouse one came upon the high-gabled frame cottage, on the right and well above the ledges, of Henry J. Scott of Toronto, retired merchant, member of the Dominion Parliament and a friend of Trustee Barwick,[4] and designed by Appleton and Stephenson, architects of the gate lodge, cost $9,000. The Scott estate was sold at auction to George Marsh in 1892 for $9,000 and acquired in 1899 by Nathaniel L. Gorton of the Gloucester fishing firm.

Continuing on toward the lighthouse, next encountered were the two houses on that dreamed-of point of land, Black Bess, built together by David Greenough. The first was a classic gambrel-roofed New England seaside cottage[5] that he put up for future occupation by brother John, who at this time was summering in Pierre Lorillard's plush private resort of Tuxedo Park, New York.

"Tanglewood" was warmed by Moorfield Storey, related to John by marriage, a prominent Boston lawyer, unsuccessful politician, espouser of unpopular causes and clean government addict, an eccentricity that led him to oppose vociferously a memorial statue to Gloucester's Ben Butler some years after that gentleman's demise. It was rented to James Murray Kay of Boston from 1891 until 1897, when David sold "Tanglewood" to his codreamer of forty years back, John.

This tall and distinguished gentleman with the flowing mustache—if not the father, certainly the rich uncle of yachting in Gloucester Harbor—was born in Boston in 1846, graduated from Harvard at nineteen in 1865 and went to London for six years. Back home, with one classmate he formed the South American shipping firm of Wilder and Greenough in New York and, with another, Poor and Greenough in Buenos Aires, making such fortunes all around in railroad financing and merging that he retired in 1898 at fifty-two and devoted himself to such philanthropies as the American Geographic Society, of which he was president for years, and to his yachting.

"Black Bess," David Greenough's own house occupying Black Bess Point, was another spacious, sprawling, airy beachstone and frame type of the period, designed by Sanford Phipps and built in 1888–89.[6] On one of his fishing trips to his vacation place at Franklin, Maine, not far from Bar Harbor, David asked his guide how the men up that way supported themselves in the winter, and got the curt reply: "Chop wood." So chop they did, and the timber was taken to the mill, and then coasted up by scow and landed at Wharf Beach for the building of "Black Bess" and "Tanglewood" on the brief strand south of the Associates' pier—a good bargain on both sides.

And when the big Niles barn behind the quarry became too crowded with the equipages of the Associates for his liking, David Greenough sent to Franklin for a third deckload of wood that was beached at Lighthouse Cove and converted into the stable and grooms' quarters across the road at the edge of the marsh that he later shared with John.[7]

David Greenough was graduated from Harvard in 1865 and married Marie Fenton Lewis in 1879. After she died in 1890 at thirty-seven, he went into retirement from his position as managing partner in the Boston firm of Abram French and Company, America's largest importer of china and glassware. Two years later he married Caroline Wendell Greenough, the widow of another younger brother, Arthur. A man of taste who took pleasure in his business travels abroad, horticulturalist, outdoorsman, equestrian, angler, sailor, hiker and swimmer, he won the 60- and 200-yard races off Niles Beach sponsored by The Beachcroft in the summer of 1898 when he was fifty-four. His daughter-in-law, Mrs. David S. Greenough. Jr., remembered him as "a very strict man, beloved by his friends and disliked by some." He revealed another side of his character in a note to my grandfather, Dr. J. Everett Garland of Gloucester, from his Boston office:

> My dear Dr. Garland:
>
> I have received your bill and feel sure you have made a mistake, for I was at your office with my bad knee at least three times, and you made several visits at the house, two surely and I think more.
>
> However, I send check to cover bill, and would ask you to apply the balance to the accounts of some of those whom you serve without payment. I know you have a lot of them on your list, and I should like to feel that I am helping a little.
>
> We have let our place for this summer so that Mrs. Greenough can have a rest from housekeeping. Next year I hope we may meet again.
>
> Yours very sincerely,
> D. S. GREENOUGH

The Greenoughs were abroad for the 1910 season and rented to Charles Stewart, the very British manager of the Cunard Line office in Boston, whose daughter Liz, a lifelong summerer on the Point, recalled his invariable preprandial habit in the early evening of fishing from Black Bess Rocks in his dinner jacket.

Across Lighthouse (or Quarry) Cove from Black Bess Point, first on Quarry Point was the commodious cottage of J. Hamilton Kane, a Toronto banker and another friend of Walter Barwick, who built next door; but Kane occupied it only briefly, if at all, and in 1897 the house was rented by J. Murray Kay and bought by him two years later.[8]

Kay was a native of Glasgow. He worked in a London bank as a young man, emigrated to the United States, married an American girl and became a citizen. By the 1880s he was treasurer of Houghton Mifflin Company, the Boston publishers, and a friend of David Greenough, who interested him in first renting, then buying, on Eastern Point.

At the end of his family's first season in the Kane cottage it occurred to Kay that fishing in the quarry would be improved if the pickerel with which it had been stocked at one time were replaced with trout, to which end he hired three local men, Charles Atwater, Alonzo Varney and Prince Nickerson.

One Indian summer day in October, Varney and Atwater embarked in a punt with dynamite bombs wired to a battery in the charge of Nickerson on shore, the object being to first get rid of the pickerel.

Reaching the middle, they dropped the charge overboard, but their signals were crossed and Nickerson fired it off prematurely. With a mighty rumble it exploded, and boat and blasters were catapulted into the air on a spout of water. So high did Varney soar that on his return he struck the bottom of the quarry, driven to his hands and knees, sixteen feet down. When he popped gasping to the surface, the boat was in splinters and Atwater was about to go down for what looked very much like the last time. An oar floated near him, and Varney shoved it at his drowning friend, shouting for him to grab it. Then he swam over to poor Atwater, who turned out to be more dazed than hurt, and helped him ashore.

The roomy verandaed house facing directly on the bold harbor beyond this scene of maladroitness was erected by Walter Barwick, the Toronto attorney who shared in initiating the Associates.[9]

Barwick was a strong swimmer whom fate had a way of putting in the way of events, happily, and in the end, tragically. For several seasons before the Associates acquired the Niles farm the Barwicks had stayed at the Seaside Hotel, later The Beachcroft. One day in August 1888 he heard cries for help from the water near the gate lodge just finished, stripped and swam out and rescued a drowning bather. It was his fourth rescue in the vicinity, and a month later he was back at it, leaping into the harbor with a rope to assist a boy who was having trouble saving another swimmer.

The Canadian remained devoted to the Point until his death, which occurred on July 1, 1906, in a train wreck that took twenty-six other lives at Salisbury, England. At the time he was a senior member of the law firm of Barwick, Aylesworth and Moss, and King's Counsel at Toronto.

Next around Quarry Point from Barwick's was the large granite and frame cottage of Major Benjamin S. Calef, a Boston insurance man who spent but a summer or two there before letting it to a succession of occupants.[10]

Major Calef was a friend of General Francis A. Walker, president of Massachusetts Institute of Technology, who climbed from private to brevet brigadier general in the Civil War and followed that with a brilliant career as an economist and statistician and educational reformer. General Walker and his family rented the Calef house for at least one summer, probably in 1896, the last vacation of his life, for he died on January 5, 1897.

Major Calef was marshal at his friend's funeral on January 8, which must have been too much for him, for the following day he died at his home on Marlboro Street. A colleague wrote of him: "He was loved and honored

by all who knew him. He was a man who thought of the right thing at the right time, and not as so many do, the day after. He was a man who didn't wait until his friend was dead to pin a flower on his coat."[11]

These three houses cost about $7,000 each to build and were all designed by Architect Arthur Hooper Dodd. Access to them was at first interrupted by the jagged surface cuttings of the quarry, which scarred the ledge nearly to the door of the Calef place; these crevasses were filled, and Aileen Terrance was created. For some years they pumped their fresh water from the quarry into storage tanks.

On the seaward side of Quarry Point opposite the lighthouse John V. Lewis of Cincinnati built his dramatically situated, dormered, bay-windowed and liberally porched mansion—now the Eastern Point Yacht Club—designed by Appleton and Stephenson and one of the most expensive homes on Cape Ann, at a cost of $12,000.[12]

Mr. Lewis was said to be "largely interested in the Standard Oil Company, and is ex-president of the Cotton Seed Oil Trust. He is so much pleased with the locality that he expects to make Eastern Point his permanent home. He has a commodious and fleet schooner yacht [the *Peerless*], and finds attractions hereabouts sufficient to induce him to locate here, and this after a thorough investigation of the entire Atlantic coast."[13]

One of J. Murray Kay's daughters, Mrs.

Winifred Kay Shepard, used to say that Lewis came by his location when the Associates drew lots after the initial survey for the choicest. He won and picked the stunning point he built on; David Greenough had the second choice and selected Black Bess Point, which he had wanted all along.

But the oil magnate's early enthusiasm seems to have flagged. The Lewises summered at Nonquitt in 1893 and rented the cottage, and in 1896 he let it to the family of Robert Garrett, the late railroad king.

Gloucester was agog with a taste of high society in the Newport style. The four Garretts arrived with a retinue of seventeen, and when they departed, the East Gloucester correspondent of the *Advertiser* had learned that the Garrett fortune lay somewhere in the uncounted realm between $18 million and $28 million and that the family planned to sojourn at their country seat in New York state before returning to Baltimore: 'Their elegant appointed turnouts, retinue of servants and baggage of 125 trunks attracted much attention."[14]

Lewis built a stable at the end of his drive next spring and rented the cottage to the married daughter of the late Governor Oliver Ames for that summer of 1897. In 1899 he leased it for a term of five years to John Clay, a wealthy Chicago stockman who had visited the Point the previous season.

If the day were mild and a sea not running, one might ride on along Eastern Point Boulevard by the lighthouse and around the outer shore just above the surf-washed ledges, the broad Atlantic laid out from horizon to horizon, to Fort Hill Avenue and then up the dirt road to the meadow almost across from the abandoned fort. Here L. P. Atwood of the Boston real estate firm of Atwood and Weld and another friend of David Greenough (no relation to the late Cornelius Attwood, an original trustee) had built a most striking cottage "in the Queen Anne style," with a long red roof that slid down over the porches,[15] and large stable and servants' quarters in the rear.[16] The view to the ocean and the harbor was elegant, for there was naught but ledge, field and scrub for acres around. Like Stanwood's, it was designed by an architect named McKay and cost about $6,000 to build.

Well up on the harbor slope of Fort Hill were the large cottages of Charles F. Farrington, who, the newspaper said, "has a palatial country

Seven of the first eleven summer cottages built by members of Eastern Point Associates in the winter of 1888–89. Clockwise from bottom of facing page: David S. Greenough, John Greenough (built by David), Walter Barwick, L. P. Atwood, John J. Stanwood, Charles F. Farrington, and Albert Lewis. The other four cottages are pictured overleaf. (From Description of the Sea-Shore Property of the Eastern Point Associates)

The first summer cottages of Eastern Point Associates, continued from previous page, left to right: Benjamin S. Calef, John V. Lewis, J. Hamilton Kane, and Henry J. Scott. (From Description of the Sea-Shore Property of the Eastern Point Associates)

home at Jamaica Plain which he abandons for Eastern Point,"[17] and Captain Albert Lewis, the owner of Lewis Wharf,[18] both amply constructed of masonry and frame a few rods above the remnant of the old road to the lighthouse called Elm Avenue.

These were the first eleven summer cottages on Eastern Point. A twelfth lot between the Farrington estate and the fort was bought by the twelfth charter Associate, John Church of Cincinnati, an organ manufacturer, but he died in 1890 and his property went to his daughter, Miss Edith Church.

Late in 1893 Miss Church began her comfortable country house,[19] and within five years she married Roswell T. Burchard of Little Compton, Rhode Island, who was voted a trustee of the Associates. During the remainder of the nineties the house was shared or occupied exclusively by her uncle and aunt, Mr. and Mrs. Edward T. Russell. Russell died in 1900.

Farrington's stable across the road from his house burned to the ground on October 16, 1895. The family had been gone for two weeks, and it looked like arson. A billiard room and a brace of carriages were destroyed. It was all over by the time the steamer *Defiance* got there from the Union Hill engine house, and the firemen ran 1,800 feet of hose from the stone wharf to throw water on the ruins, pumped up from the harbor by the steamer *N. M. Jackman*. Next year Farrington and Miss Church jointly built a stable at about the same location.[20]

The authoress Elizabeth Stuart Phelps bought a thirteenth lot to the north of the Hill of Rocks, near the Patch line, in September 1888. She put up a small camp on it, then changed her mind and had it moved, along with her cottage in Wonson's Field down by the harbor, up to Grapevine Road. Doubtless she got her money back from the Associates, for they sold the land in November 1890 to Henry Ware Eliot, a St. Louis brick manufacturer whose youngest son, Tom (the future T. S.), was then two years old.

A few other lots were picked up in 1888 but were not developed by their original purchasers. One other early owner was Parker Mann, a Boston and Washington artist; in 1896 he built a low, rambling, shingled studio-cottage in the field to the south of Sunset Rock above Niles Beach, which after a few years was moved off the Point.

Thomas E. Day was the first keeper of the gate lodge, where he and his family occupied an upstairs apartment above the office and waiting room of the Associates. The mails were delivered and picked up here, and it was the home of the Point's first electricity in May 1890 and its only telephone until the lines were extended to the cottages in 1896. Miss Lillian Day, his daughter who died in 1969 at ninety-four, told of running out as a child to open the gate for the privileged to pass through; after the first year or two, it was kept closed on Sundays only—for a while.

Tom Day was a well-known man around Ward One, and there survives a glimpse of him one April morning in 1890 "riding on a horse car with an umbrella and a lighted cigar in his hand, when the latter in some way set fire to the umbrella, which blazed up briskly, resisting all attempts to extinguish it."[21]

By convincing Lil's mother that among other things her famous fish chowder would attract a clientele from near and far, the Associates in 1891 persuaded the Days to take over the management of The Beachcroft. Lil and her sister Ethel, affianced to real estate man George Percival Chick, worked waiting on table.

So successful were the Days that the Associates gave them a three-year lease on The Beachcroft in 1893, and after toying with the idea of building another hotel back of Niles Beach nearby, they settled on an addition that presented the habitués of 1897 with more chambers, a larger dining room, hot water heat and electric lights.

For fresh milk the Days kept the smartest cow on Cape Ann: "They have a cow at the Beachcroft House, Eastern Point, who will, when she is thirsty, turn the faucet in the water tank and help herself. Unfortunately, she never learned to turn the faucet so as to stop the water and they have been obliged to tie it up, and thus the cow's propensity to turn on the water has been brought to a close."[22]

Every June, Captain John F. Bickford brought his boat livery around and moored his landings off the beach in front of The Beachcroft for the season. Skiffs and sailboats for hire.

Captain Bickford was an authentic hero. Many the shipwrecked sailor he succored while in charge of the Massachusetts Humane Society's lifeboats at Rocky Neck and Brace Cove. He was the only man in the history of Cape Ann to receive the Congressional Medal of Honor, for his courage while serving as master's mate on the *Kearsarge* in her victory over the Confederate raider *Alabama* off Cherbourg, France, on June 19, 1864.

At the end of June 1889 the steamship company posted its summer schedule. Either the *City of Gloucester* or the *George A. Chaffee* (replaced by the *Cape Ann* in 1895) would leave Gloucester at 3:00 A.M. and 2:00 P.M. and Boston at 9:30 A.M. and 2:00 P.M. daily, all trips touching at the Eastern Point pier except the early morning boat from Gloucester. Fare was fifty cents one way, ninety cents round trip (later reduced to seventy-five cents).

The *City of Gloucester,* as she was in her prime a few years later, has been affectionately recalled by Theodore S. Ireland of Dearborn, Michigan, a Gloucester boy born and raised:

> She was a homely thing, but it has been said when she didn't make the run out of Boston nothing moved. Salt fish to Boston and general merchandise and packages to Gloucester. My mother's piano came down on her. . . . The excitement and thrill of my life (10-12 years) was a 3:30 A.M. trip to Boston on the old *City.* At the wharf, bright stars, creak of lines on the bollards as the engine was idled, then the churning of water as we slid away from the dock, and later the sun coming up out of the ocean. A mug-up from the galley with coffee and donuts. . . . I doubt if any ship had a whistle like the *City.* It was single tone and I believe high C. Just after daylight on a thick foggy morning it was really something to hear the *City* leave the harbor, blowing every 20-30 seconds.[23]

The Associates hired Mr. Andrew Edmondson, an old country Swede, as caretaker, and one of his chores was to be at the pier to help the steamers tie up. As part of their program to establish the proper tone, the way Jim

Walen told it, they decked Andrew out in a handsome uniform. The first day in his new duds he was at the pier promptly as usual when the steamer inched in with a blast of her whistle amid a great maelstrom as her engine was thrown in reverse to bring her to a stop, but when a deck hand tossed him the docking line, Mr. Edmondson recoiled with the shout: "I catch no lines wid *dese* close on!"

Edmondson lived in the Niles farmhouse for a few winters, but when the big blizzard of November 1898 struck—the "Portland Breeze"—he and his family were occupying a structure near Brace Cove that shook and swayed so, windows smashing in the wind, that they fled to the gate lodge.

A year later the Associates had this place moved down the road and

Niles Beach with Stanwood cottage above it, about 1890. (Author's collection)

reestablished near The Beachcroft as a summer cottage. Then they built a new house for their loyal caretaker a few yards back from the west shore of Niles Pond.[24]

All the money spent on the fine pier notwithstanding, the steamers touched at the Point on their scheduled trips only through about 1892. Excursions were not selling house lots, a hotel had not yet materialized, and the Associates discovered that it was one thing to make their grounds available for Sunday devotions, as they did to a very upright assembly in September 1889, but something else to have their summer slumbers sundered by the bacchanalian cries of revelers deposited in alcoholic disarray on their shores. Once, they caught some naked women swimming in the quarry.

It is told of one of the Associates, who liked his "cup of tea" returning on the steamer from Boston on business when the Point was still a port of call, that on a certain evening at about dusk the child of a neighbor came running breathlessly home with the announcement that she had that minute seen Mr. ___. "And why is he lying on the ground under his rose bushes?"

"If Mr ___ wants to smell his roses in that manner, my dear," was the hasty reply, "he has a perfect right to, doesn't he?"

It was after making a delivery that a driver emerged into Pierlane to find his wagon missing. As the story goes, something had frightened the horse; the frantic creature bolted, hell-bent for the Association pier, galloped the length of it as if the devil were astride of him and dove straight into the harbor, wagon and all.

After a little less than five years the Eastern Point Associates ran out of steam.

What avails it, the *Advertiser* wondered, to develop such a beauty spot, so potentially productive of taxes, when a large part of East Main Street from Point Hill to the gate lodge of the Associates is such a preposterous bog hole? And after the watering carts had fallen victims to politics, the whole way from the depot to the Point was such a swirl that "the dust will down more summer visitors than the cars and steamboat will bring to town."

Even closer to the heart of the matter, as one prominent Eastern Pointer later put it: "The scheme was doomed to failure from the beginning. There were no water mains, no gas mains, no electric light wires, no telephones. Purchasers for such land could not be found."[25]

On the first of March, 1892, the property of the Eastern Point Associates was foreclosed by the mortgagee, the Boston Loan and Trust Company, and the approximately 350 acres of it remaining was sold at auction for $84,000 to a Boston lawyer, Walter I. Badger, acting for a smaller, reorganized syndicate.

The roads were extended and in time improved further. Eastern Point Boulevard East in 1894 was run over the causeway between Brace Cove and Niles Pond, around by the lifesaving station behind Bemo Ledge, looping through the moors near the lichened Cushing Wall before it swung back and descended, later to be known as Edgemoor Road, by Stanwood's estate into Farrington Avenue. Toronto and Bemo and St. Louis Avenues were laid out, but the rest of the grandiose web of road expired on paper.

The Gloucester Water Supply Company blasted its pipes through the ledge as far as the gate lodge, but not until the turn of the century were they pushed through toward the lighthouse. In 1896 it was rumored that the Boston people were about to sell the Eastern Point Syndicate to New York parties anxious to develop the property along the resort lines of Magnolia Point, making the land around Niles Pond an exquisitely manicured park, but nothing came of it.

Recurrently there was talk of a grand hotel in the offing in 1895 and again in 1897 when it was said that the always mysterious New Yorkers had even signed contracts for a 300-room resort the likes of which had never been seen on the North Shore. But such talk remained as premature as the ever-imminent move by the New York Yacht Club to invest the Point as its eastern station was ethereal.

Eastern Point seemed to resist all attempts to glamorize it and to exploit it, and the Associates found themselves reduced in the spring of 1896 to such futile projects as the attempt to turn what they called "Black Duck Pond" (beyond the woods before one got to the lighthouse) into an asset by draining it and planting it to cranberries. But Cape Ann is harsher than the other cape, and this project, too, bogged down.

Inaccessibility, and its unreconstructible position as a sea-surrounded appendage of a port preoccupied with fishing, and a certain air of "roughing it" in the New England style that your solid-gold Newporter sneered at—all added up to the insurance of privacy the Associates knew they wanted, but it also slowed development of their investment to a very offhand saunter, a hands-in-the-pockets kind of progress.

Yet utter seclusion eluded our summer pioneers. First it was the vandals who brought on a retaliatory shutting of the gate to the public on Sundays and holidays as early as 1891. And then the bicyclists, in a decade when the "wheel" turned with the century, everywhere, and with frightful enthusiasm.

In the midsummer of 1896 this madness drove the Associates to bar their roads to cyclists for Sunday "scorching" over them. Midway in the next summer they reinforced this ban with a police officer at the entrance, a move regarded by the summer colony on the proletarian side of the gate lodge as a provocation, an act of aggression, and they were "rife with indignation," as the newspaper spluttered. "This is an alarming state of affairs and will greatly injure the popularity of East Gloucester."[26]

T. S. Eliot's older brother Henry snapped this view from the family's veranda, looking out the harbor about 1900. (Robert F. Brown)

~19~
SEA VOICES

Suddenly at the end of our journey, hot, dusty and discouraged, toiling up what is known as Patch's Hill, we brought our tired pony to a halt, and drew the breath of unexpected and undreamed-of delight. We had discovered Eastern Point. . . .

The suddenly revived explorer was Elizabeth Stuart Phelps of Andover. The year was no later than 1875. Miss Phelps had a best-seller to her credit, *The Gates Ajar,* published in 1868 when she was twenty-four, inspired by her grief for a love lost in the Civil War.

Out of the salt dust, out of the narrow, scorching streets, by the fish-flakes and the fish-teams, past the rude roads whose boulders seemed to have been only "spatted" down by the whimsical street-commissioner, Time, we came upon the fairest face of all the New England coast—the Eastern side of Gloucester Harbor. . . .

She was the nervous, moody, rather handsome, firm-faced daughter of a nervous father, Professor Austin Phelps of the Andover Theological Seminary, and a nervous, brilliant, psychic mother—a successful authoress—who succumbed when Elizabeth was eight.

The traveling American, who has seen the world, often tells me that here is one of the most beautiful scenes upon the whole round face of it. On this point I am not authorized by experience to testify; but my private convictions are that it would not be easy to find a lovelier bit of coast survey. . . .

Miss Phelps was in search of a summer retreat. First she boarded with Clarence and Annie Wonson in their flat-roofed cottage at the north end of Niles Beach behind Island Rock, and then in 1880 she leased a bit of their field and constructed thereon "The Old Maid's Paradise."

This I built, and there I lived from May to November, or nearly

Elizabeth Stuart Phelps's "Old Maid's Paradise." (From her Chapters from a Life)

that. The waves played almost to my door; in winter the spray dashed upon the piazza. The fishermen, my neighbors, drew up their dories upon the rocks in front of me; the foreground was marked by lobsterpots, and nets spread upon the scanty grass to dry or to mend.

So it was, in the 1880s, as the much-admired female writer of tender temperament returned year after year. She got the Point with Victorian realism:

When the breeze struck from the east or southeast, then the whole length of the western shore of the harbor broke into white fire. Hours were short in watching this blaze of foam. Suddenly it shot up—call it fifty feet, call it twice that, according to the vigor of the storm—in jets and great tongues; as if it believed itself able to lick the solid cliffs away. Seen through the window of my throbbing little house, it was easy to believe that it could. [No breakwater then.]

Perhaps the wind fell, but failed to die with the day. Then came on the wonder of a stormy sunset. All Gloucester harbor tossed against it. The bows of the anchored fleet rose and sank angrily. The head-lights came out one by one, and flared, surging up and down. Ten Pound Light flashed out for the night; but her blinder was on, towards us. The little city, glorified now, forgiven of her fish, and her dust, and her bounding roads, loved and dreamed over, and sung in heart and pen, melted all through her pretty outlines against the massive colors of the west.

Then, off Eastern Point, far to the left, where the shadow fell, sprang out the red, revolving flash of Cape Ann Light.

Not many Hiawathan moons before he found his happy hunting ground in 1882, Henry Wadsworth Longfellow visited his feminist friend at "The Old Maid's Paradise," and she pointed out to him across the harbor Norman's Woe, which, "though he had wrecked the schooner *Hesperus*, and broken half our hearts upon it, he had singularly enough never seen (I think he said) before."

Another of her admirers, more avuncular than patriarchal, was the celebrated Dr. Oliver Wendell Holmes, thirty-five years her senior but enchanted enough to pay her periodic visits from his summer home in Beverly Farms. She recalled of the Autocrat of the Breakfast Table (not hers, one can be sure):

> I remember that on his first call I felt moved as one does with a new guest, to show off our attractions at Eastern Point, and that I took him, thoughtlessly enough, down into the big [fish] trap gully in front of my chalet, where the purple lava and the bronze kelp and the green seaweed brightened and faded beneath the rising and ebbing waves, whose "high-tide line" came almost to my doorstep.
>
> It was very rough walking; and when I saw that it was not easy for him—for he was even then an old man—I cannot say what I might not have done by way of atoning for my mistake. I do not think I had extended my hand; I had only extended my thought; which he read by that marvelous perception of his, needing to wait for neither word nor motion.
>
> "No, no!" he cried decidedly, "No, no, no! Don't you offer to help me! Don't you dare offer to help me! I couldn't stand that."
>
> I had nothing for it but to let him clamber about over the jagged boulders as he would, without protest or assistance; and I thanked the heavenly fates which brought him without accident back to the piazza. Here he found the breeze which blows eternally on Gloucester harbor too cool for him, and we retreated indoors, where it seemed to be tacitly understood that we should agree to dispense with any further explorations; as from that time we did.[1]

She had her own distinctive graces, this literate lady who leashed old literary lions, and among the more saving was a certain wild prudence, perhaps born of spinsterhood. Having reverted to her father's house in Andover for the winter as was her custom, Miss Phelps was awakened one night by a faint noise downstairs. From under her pillow she withdrew her revolver (might this have been the source of her chronic insomnia?), but decided not to get out of bed and investigate—as she told the newspaper reporters later—concluding that it was merely rats astir below. The next morning bonds worth $10,000 were missing.

Her literary forte, it may be safely said, was prose.

On one of her strolls down the Point road, a few steps past the Niles farmhouse and the pond she came upon an old granite gatepost near the barn. In her mind's eye it was a fisherman's gaunt wife, "stunted of nature and thin," peering forever out to sea for the return of her man. She wrote of *The Stone Woman of Eastern Point*:

> *Did she stand like that in the flesh,*
> *Vigilant, early and late?*
> *For the sake of a scanty love*
> *Bearing the blast of fate;*

Acquainted with hunger and pain;
Patient, as women are;
Work, when he is at home;
Pray, when he's over the bar;

Loving and longing and true,
Gilding her idol of clay;
Bride, when the boat comes in;
Widow, it sails away.

Waiting and watching and gray;
Growing old, poor, and alone;—
Was it worth living for? Say,
Tell us, thou woman of Stone![2]

And so on. A proper sympathy for the women who watched and waited and grayed, but it failed to save the schooner *Addie John,* eighty-eight tons, on a passage home from Lynn to Weymouth, Nova Scotia, from driving ashore on the rocks of Grape Vine Cove in a northeast gale at midnight May 27, 1887. She holed and sank. The crew climbed up and lashed themselves in the rigging, where they remained until dawn revealed how they could get ashore, which they gained at great hazard.

Captain Norman said that as they were approaching Cape Ann in the darkness they could not see the Eastern Point Light but expected to be warned by the whistling buoy. He didn't know that this aid to navigation had been removed for the summer through the influence of the impressionable eulogist of *The Stone Woman,* of whom an admirer has written:

> As few but the greatest have done she understood and expressed the sufferings of gifted and sensitive women, the depths of loneliness, the torture of jangled nerves. This last experience was hers by birthright. Like her father she was a victim of insomnia in some of its most excruciating forms.[3]

The groans of the whistler jangled the nerves of Miss Phelps, and so she had it removed and replaced according to her comings and goings. The first instance of its being taken up for the summer was in May 1885.

And then, fortunately for coastal navigation, Elizabeth fell in love with the Reverend Herbert Dickinson Ward, a cultivated young man brought up by a father and two maiden aunts who insisted that the pursuit of theology take precedence over his natural inclination toward mineralogy. On October 20, 1888, the bride, forty-four and her groom, twenty-seven, were married by her father Austin Phelps in the parlor of "The Old Maid's Paradise."

"Since her marriage," observed the *Boston Record,* "Mrs. Ward is much better, and the officer who had to remove the buoy has put it back with the assurance that next summer he will have no orders to disturb it."[4]

But that did not close the book. The *M. A. Baston* was returning from the banks with a fare of halibut on the morning of September 27, 1890, feeling her way in the thick, listening for the familiar sound of the groaner, when they heard instead the breakers and struck at Brace Cove. Captain Thompson rowed ashore in his boat, walked to the Gate Lodge and telephoned for the tug *Emma Bradford*, which came around, pulled the *Baston* off and towed her into the harbor.

The whistler was there all right, but it wasn't whistling. It had been put out of commission by some miscreant who evidently thought he was performing a public service in view of the unabated agitation to have the buoy beached for the summer.

Early next season a letter to the editor demanded the removal of this "instrument of torture placed on Bemo Ledge [actually due south of the lighthouse] by a defiant Lighthouse Board," which the writer claimed had driven from their estates some of the biggest taxpayers on the western shore of the harbor.

Such an expression of concern for the ears of capitalists moved the Deep Sea Assembly of the Knights of Labor of Gloucester to thunder forth a resolution defending the board "in these days of cringing and subserviency to the wealthy few at the expense of the poor but worthy many," namely the fishermen.

The debate waxed and waned with the tides of the summer population, and in the spring of 1892 the jangled ones for whom the moos of Mother Ann's Cow provided neither guidance nor music suddenly found themselves bedfellows with their opponents.

A letter writer had harrumphed, leave the buoy be. "Which needs protection first—those men who are keeping up the leading industry of the place, or a few nervous cranks who are safely on shore?"

Then the Gloucester Master Mariners joined the argument. The fishing skippers talked it out and agreed that the buoy was useless where it was, the sound lost on the lee shore when the wind was east, and moored too close to warn in time of the land. They requested Congressman Cogswell to have it moved seven miles south southeast of the light. However, it remained where it was.[5] Meanwhile Mrs. Elizabeth Stuart Phelps Ward discovered a fresh source of irritation, so abrasive to her equanimity that even the distant recall of it gave her pain. "The choice spot on the chosen side of the harbor became in time a Babel, in which only those 'who sleep o' nights' could rest. The tramp and the tongue of the summer army devastated Paradise."[6]

And she grew even more sensitive to the 4:00 A.M. clatter of the fishermen ("my neighbors") and lobstermen off the rocks tending their gear. She tried to persuade them to be less nocturnal in their habits. They demurred. So a month before her marriage she bought from the Eastern Point Associates that acre of high ground on what would in future be Edgemoor Road and built a cozy new Paradise for two, removed from Babel.

It proved still to be too close to tramp, tongue and thump. Whereupon Mrs. Ward returned the lot to the Associates, bought another up on the moor off Grapevine Road, summoned the house mover and had her Paradise transported to this new Eden, Mr. Ward in the bargain. Elizabeth installed an outside stair to his bedchambers, to insulate herself from his sometimes tardy homecomings.

Besides an occasional prose production and one or two collaborations with his regal mate that established him as a sort of literary Prince Albert, Herbert Ward was an ardent golfer and supervised a small and rough course that meandered over the Wonson downs, known as the Eastern Point Golf Links, in which he was assisted by Robert Forsythe, a genuine bonded Scotch semi-professional.

And he was a yachtsman. Mrs. Frances Cunningham recalled that his nervous wife would call her mother, who had the only telephone in any of the cottages at Bass Rocks, to look out and see whether she could see Mr. Ward's boat and whether he was becalmed.

The authoress, writing in 1896, couldn't get away from the feeling that after all she had done to immortalize it she remained an unappreciated outsider in Gloucester. "Her summer guests may come and go, may pay or not, may criticise or adore, but her fish bite on forever. The result of my own observation has been that Gloucester, in her heart of hearts, regards her large summer population with a certain contempt."[7]

For her part, as if in retaliation, after encountering the aftermath of a drunken murder near East Gloucester Square in 1875, she threw herself into the temperance movement briefly but intensely, lecturing the fishermen in the saloons and churches with fervent noblesse oblige on the evil consequences of their debauchery.

Twenty years later, when she published her observations on the fishing life in *McClure's Magazine*, Elizabeth felt hurt and aggrieved that a reader should grumble that her article gives strangers the impression that the fishermen of Gloucester "without exception, are indeed a depraved lot of mortals, who live in wooden huts by the sea where they are principally engaged in quenching their alcoholic thirst and beating poor defenceless women until they are black and blue."[8]

Complained John J. Pew, the fishing magnate who would build his mansion on the Point: "Oh! novelists and story writers, when you write about our fishermen give them the language they use, 'fairly good English,' and not a Kipling or Phelps lingo."[9]

One suspects that Elizabeth Stuart Phelps Ward felt herself to be more in tune with Gloucester than Gloucester was with her. Like her Stone Woman, she was an extraordinary female, destined to suffer, nervously and sleeplessly, the quite exquisite pangs of insufficiently requited love.

The high ground of the Point that Mrs. Ward relinquished in favor of an even quieter retreat on the moor was purchased in 1890, with another acre backing on it, from the Eastern Point Associates by Henry Ware Eliot, a well-to-do manufacturer of bricks in St. Louis. Eliot was two generations removed from New England, but its call was strong in him. He did not

The Eliot house on Eastern Point, where the poet summered as a boy, painted in water colors by his sister Charlotte in 1897. (Henry Ware Eliot Collection, Sawyer Free Library)

begin to build his large, handsome, breezy house, however, until five autumns had passed, and the family arrived for its first season in the summer of 1896. Neither trees nor other houses obstructed the view, which overlooked the whole peninsula.

Of the several small Eliots who were by this means returned to the edge of the ancestral sea, Charlotte was the elder sister and already an artist of talent; Henry, Jr., was two years away from entering Harvard and a keen sailor and amateur photographer of the Gloucester scene who would one day be an expert in the archeology of the Near East; and Thomas Stearns, the younger of the two boys, was but eight. Destiny would assign T. S. Eliot the Nobel Prize in literature and perhaps the greatest influence over the development of twentieth-century poetry of any writer in the English language.

Little Tom, as some of the neighbors called him, was a pupil at Smith Academy in St. Louis (shortly to transfer to Milton Academy near Boston), a greedy reader, precocious, quite withdrawn apparently, and yet full of an environment that suffused him with mixed feelings. A family snapshot shows him at age nine all scrunched up in a rocking chair on the piazza, clad in long stockings and knickers, engrossed in a book. Mrs. Jean Kay Burgess remembered that he was "interested in all that had to do with the sea life. He used to sail boats with my brother, James Murray Kay, Jr."[10]

A shame that so little has been preserved of the summers spent on the Point by young Tom Eliot between 1896 and 1909, the year he was graduated from Harvard. In 1911 he went to Europe to study, and the rest is literary history: his rejection of America or his further search for roots that caused him to take British citizenship and to embrace Anglican Catholicism.

What was the nature of this sense of alienation? He felt it at Eastern Point, as everywhere:

The family guarded jealously its connections with New England, but it was not until years of maturity that I perceived that I myself had always been a New Englander in the South West, and a South Westerner in New England; when I was sent to school in New England I lost my southern accent without ever acquiring the accent of the native Bostonian. In New England I missed the long dark river, the ailanthus trees, the flaming cardinal birds, the high limestone bluffs where we searched for fossil shell-fish; in Missouri I missed the fir trees, the bay and goldenrod, the song-sparrows, the red granite and the blue sea of Massachusetts.[11]

Three years after his death in 1965, the New York Public Library's Berg Collection accessioned the manuscripts acquired in 1922 by

Three views of young Tom Eliot: as painted by his sister Charlotte, at the piano and fogbound at Eastern Point. (Henry Ware Eliot Collection, Sawyer Free Library)

John Quinn, an American collector, and it was revealed that between 1910 and 1919 the young writer had committed probably the greater part of his poetic output to a seventy-two page notebook he had bought for twenty-five cents at Procter Brothers' Old Corner Book Store in Gloucester.

T. S. Eliot could never get rid of Gloucester; it stuck with him like the Procter's notebook he carried into his self-exile. Another manuscript in the Quinn Collection was found to contain seventy-one lines describing the outbound trip of a Gloucester schooner past the craggy reef of the Dry Salvages off Sandy Bay and her fatal collision with an iceberg, written as part of *The Waste Land* (1922) but deleted from the final version by the author and never published.

Yet some phrases from the suppressed lines (Gloucester again, always cropping up in Eliot's vivid memory) surfaced in the stream of association twenty years later in his haunting work, "The Dry Salvages," published as one of *Four Quartets* in 1943. Eastern Point in St. Louis, St. Louis in Eastern Point . . . the river within and the sea all about . . . the voices of it . . . "the wailing warning from the approaching headland . . . the heaving groaner rounded homewards . . ."

When he was seventy in the spring of 1958 the expatriate came to America with his newly wed second wife to lecture and to look in on the widow of his late elder brother, Henry Ware Eliot, Jr., of Cambridge, where in the course of their visit he expressed a desire to return after some fifty years to Eastern Point, the inspiration for much of his verse, and to inspect the family cottage there if it still stood.

This was Friday, the second of May. Accordingly, Mrs. Henry Eliot arranged with some Cambridge friends, Edward and Emma Norris, to drive

the party down to Gloucester the next day. When Eliot made no bones about his aversion to dining in a restaurant on the way, it occurred to Mrs. Norris that her old classmate at Wellesley College, Helen D. McGlade, and her housemate, Mary H. Tolman, might be agreeable to entertaining them at lunch in their ancient and charming colonial cottage at 9 Langsford Street in the Lanesville section of Gloucester, which the Norrises and Henry Eliots had visited many times when the former summered at the Folly Cove Inn. Misses McGlade and Tolman ran, respectively, the Atlantic Monthly Bookshop and the Women's Educational and Industrial Union in Boston.

Mary Tolman recalled the poet's visit that memorable third of May in an interview I published as a newspaper column fourteen years later:[12]

> They arrived, and T. S. had apparently had a very happy morning going over things at Eastern Point [he'd found and rambled through the cottage of his boyhood, then owned by Mr. and Mrs John R. Cahill, Jr., of Gloucester] and was in a very good mood.

> At that time this house had only one bathroom, upstairs, and the ladies went up first to primp. It left me, as hostess, with the two gentlemen. There is a cut-down church pew in the small front hall which came from the Church of Unity in Worcester when I was growing up there—they were changing the decor and sold off the pews—and it is a catchall for things because there's no hatrack or closet. Well, I asked the men to put their hats and coats on it, and I said to T. S. Eliot "if you don't mind using a Uni-

tarian pew." He laughed. He was brought up a Unitarian, as all the Eliots were, which I knew and which he recognized I knew, but he didn't take it amiss at all.

Later on he and his sister-in-law got into a conversation about the church he attended in London. The kneelers in that church were all very lovingly done in needlework by the ladies of the parish in memory of the more famous members after they had died. Some went back to Shakespeare's time. T. S. was teasing her and asking if she would embroider a kneeler for him, and she reminded him that she couldn't do it until after he died. Well, that was a little gentle joking between them. She was in the division of the Museum of Fine Arts that had to do with needlework and costumes and that sort of thing and was originally an artist of precise scientific illustration.

Eliot seemed immediately pleased with everything, and especially with Miss McGlade's books, which the house is full of as you can see. He looked around—and this was another thing that was quite endearing of him to my mind—because when the gentlemen came down from upstairs he was beaming; he had poked around very obviously and didn't mind admitting it, and looked at everything, and found a number of his publications which he was reporting to his wife. He just was in an awfully good mood, and as simple as could be.

I don't think we did any walking around outside at all. They'd had enough of strolling in East Gloucester when they got here. We had discreet cocktails as the company preferred. T. S. had a couple of whiskies and water. And then we went in the dining room to a very simple luncheon. Miss McGlade and I were so excited that we had stayed up practically all night cooking a turkey which was in the house because we were having guests for dinner Sunday. So for lunch we started, I believe, with a cup of soup, and then cold turkey, hot rolls and a tossed salad, rhubarb pie for dessert, and coffee. It was the fresh rhubarb season, and it had come from our garden, and Eliot was delighted with it and pointed out to his bride that it was pieplant, another name for rhubard that I hadn't heard before.

During lunch there was some conversation between him and Miss McGlade about literary pirating, especially of autographs, and the devices which certain unethical people use to secure autographs. That was *à propos* of the fact that he didn't like to sign his books for people. At that point Emma Norris said Helen was going to leave some of her books to Wellesley College, and wouldn't he sign his among them? Of course we hadn't been warned of this, but Miss McGlade had at least eight of his books or pamphlets or introductions, which he had discovered, and he rather reluctantly did sign them, and they have gone to the Wellesley College Library.

I gathered that this reluctance to autograph stemmed from some unfortunate experiences. He was most difficult to approach by worshippers. He kept himself to himself definitely, and I remember his mentioning that he didn't go to church too often because he valued his privacy, and people whom he met casually expected him to welcome them in his retreat later on.

He had spoken at some kind of academic gathering in Texas before coming to Cambridge and was highly amused because he was given an entire cowboy outfit of chaps, broad hat and the rest. After lunch we returned to this room, the parlor, and the feeder in the window over there was being visited by purple finches and goldfinches. He saw them and exclaimed—"Oh, a purple finch!"— and one of the ladies who was a city person said scornfully—"You don't mean to tell me that you're one of those birdwatchers, do you?" Well, he just ignored her, he was so excited about the purple finches.

About then the man who fixes clocks came to return a clock he'd mended, and I greeted him. He observed the goings-on and would gladly have joined the party, but he's the kind of person who takes over, and I didn't think that would be good. So I walked him out, don't you know—put him nearest the door and proceeded to walk into him, and when I finally closed the door on him and came back, Eliot said to his wife—"There, you see what I mean?"

I didn't know what he meant at the time, but afterwards an English acquaintance explained to me that he meant your attitude toward a person you were hiring to do something. In other words, he meant that this was America, a country without the kind of class feeling which in England they recognize.

Well, I have never seen a man happier than he was that day. He was obviously crazy about his wife, who was English and had been his secretary, and he was very fond of his sister-in-law. I think he felt he was with family. Certainly there was nothing here to ward off. They were with us for three hours at least, and he was such a completely happy man throughout it all that when it came time to leave, the ladies just had to pull him away.

Golf Course, East Gloucester. *Maurice Prendergast's water color of the tea garden adjoining the clubhouse above Farrington Avenue. (Addison Gallery of American Art)*

~20~
KNIGHTS OF THE BRUSH

THE SUMMER VISITOR TO EASTERN
Point in the 1890s, after the stop at the Association pier was given up, had
the option of reaching Gloucester by steamer, rail or carriage from Boston
and then continuing by electric car, ferry, buggy, bicycle, foot or any convenient combination.

The steam ferry, and a sailboat when demand warranted and weather
favored, made frequent trips under the management of Douglass Brothers
across the inner harbor and Smith Cove between Duncan Point and the
town landing by the North Shore Arts Association building down back of
East Gloucester Square, with a stop at the tip of Rocky Neck. From that
point the electric trolley car could be picked up; it would have already
passed the Methodist Episcopal and Baptist churches, which one guide
writer described as "situated within rifle shot of one another."

By the fish firms and flake yards and wharves all crowded between with
schooners, by John F. Wonson's building with the fake "sea serpent" of
leather stuffed with hay nailed to the clapboards the trolley would clatter,
skirting the sheer ledges that footed the upland and Bonfire Rock, high
above, where every Christmas Eve within memory the youngsters had set off
a grand tar barrel fire to drive Santa Claus from his hiding place.

At the head of Rocky Neck Avenue the passenger wishing to continue on
up through the dust of East Main Street toward the Point would get off, leaving the electric to rattle down over the causeway (protected from the souther-
lies by a board fence on the Wonson Cove side) and loop around the Neck,
which officially became a summer resort with the completion in 1896 of Billy
Rackliffe's Rockaway House on what Rocky Neckers nicknamed "Scandal
Hill," under the management of his son-in-law, Captain Frank Foster.

(The previous year the ingenious proposal of some hydraulically disposed local to flush out the stagnant head of Smith Cove by connecting it
with Wonson Cove via a large culvert under the causeway was cried down
by summer hoteliers on the Wonson side of the equation who envisioned the
collective results stranded on their shorefront.)

Left to his own devices, our Point-bound visitor might be conveyed the rest of the way by his host's coachman, or he might hire a hack or a wheel (bicycle) if need be, or take to his feet, off through the little whirlwinds of dust and dried horse droppings.

Just at the foot of Patch's Hill, on Wonson Cove, sprawled the Harbor View Hotel with its short beach and long pier, popular with the Washington crowd, managed by Mr. and Mrs. Walter Osborne. On the left, as one toiled up the rise, was Merrill Hall, formerly Craig Cottage, and beyond that on the crest the handsome Patch residence.

Now the traveler was in the thick of the East Gloucester summer colony. Next on the left was the Delphine, operated by Mr. and Mrs. Simpson Lyle and favored by the artistic set, including such distinguished painters as Walter L. Dean and Childe Hassam, who stayed in a small house opposite that got to be known as "Hassam Cottage." Originally this had been the ell of the Patch house and boasted the only inside bathroom in East Gloucester, so it's said; to reach this proud facility the family had to pass through Mrs. Patch's bedroom—an annoyance when her children were young, but downright awkward as they and their friends grew up. Finally she would put up with this traffic no longer, and the ell—bath and all—was detached and moved down the road.

On a ways, the great gnarled Patch Willows, and down the shady lane toward the harbor, George Stacy's famous, sprawling Hawthorne Inn, focus of the resort life of East Gloucester. The nonstop hotel man finished Old Home, the nucleus, in 1891 and enticed Mrs. Bray away from The Beachcroft (where he had worked) to manage it with him. Each year there-after he plowed part of his profits back into its greater glory, buying, moving and converting local homes, and building out of the secondhand materials that were his trademark—in the name of his favorite author—The Manse, Seven Gables, Province House, Orchard Cottage, Baldwin Cottage, Wayside, Peabody, Endicott, Felton, Cherryfield, Blythedale (Stacy was indefatigable) and the Casino, accommodating 450. Dances, entertainment, bands, concerts, sports, theater, boating, even the derelict lumber schooner *George F. Prescott* he converted into a houseboat in 1910. Name it and the host had it, and not for naught was it said that matches aren't made in heaven but in the Hawthorne Inn.

On toward the Point (glimpses of Niles Beach up ahead), an elevation on the left hand led to The Fairview, opened by Mrs. Mary Wonson in 1842, owned by her daughter and son-in-law, Mr. and Mrs. Thomas Renton. For several weeks during the seasons of 1894 and 1895, Mr. and Mrs. Rudyard Kipling and family stayed here, down from Brattleboro, Vermont, while the author (a stranger, and an Englishman at that) pursued his research and soaked up the atmosphere and the lore for *Captains Courageous*, that classic story of Gloucester fishing.

"A strange establishment," Kipling wrote therein of The Fairview, "managed apparently by the boarders, where the tableclothes were red and white checkered, and the population, who seemed to have known one another intimately for years, rose up at midnight to make Welsh Rarebits if it felt hungry."

Louisa May Alcott was registered at The Fairview in 1868 and 1871, having visited Gloucester as early as 1864 when she was thirty-two, writing in her journal that in August she stayed with a large family and "had a jolly time boating, driving, charading, dancing, and picnicking. One mild moonlight night a party of us camped out on Norman's Woe, and had a splendid time, lying on the rocks singing, talking, sleeping, and rioting up and down. . . . The moon rose and set beautifully, and the sunrise was a picture I never shall forget."[1]

Camping on Norman's Woe, the storm-crashed chunk of rock on which Longfellow wrecked his fictional *Hesperus?*

Miss Alcott's riotous visits to Gloucester may have stemmed from her close professional relationship with the junior Thomas Niles, who the same year of 1864 had joined the Boston publishing firm of Roberts Brothers and persuaded her to write *Little Women,* which appeared in 1868, when she is recorded as staying at The Fairview, a mile from the Niles homestead. Several Niles collaborations and seventeen years later she rejoiced that the combination of "an honest publisher and a lucky author" had earned her $200,000 in royalties from *Little Women* alone, which ultimately sold three million copies.

In the 1880s Stephen Parrish and his family were frequent guests at The Fairview, accompanied in 1881 by the Philadelphia artist's eventually better known son Maxfield and Maxfield's pal Charles Adams Platt, a talented young painter who would be a noted etcher and architect. That summer Platt did a large oil of Niles Beach and the farmhouse from the same vantage as an undated etching by Stephen, likely at the same time.

The future "female Sargent," Cecilia Beaux, took a room at The Fairview to paint in 1897, nine years before she built her "Green Alley" farther out on Eastern Point. In fact, she had a studio next to Parrish's in Philly but was too awed to introduce herself.

Beyond The Fairview, at the bend in the road on the left, was the hospitable old Mehlman Cottage and on the right, the gate lodge of the Eastern Point Associates. If a weekday, the gate would be open without hindrance to Niles Beach, and the promenade of the summer colony just passed through. Here The Beachcroft was the center of activity, the road before it cluttered and clomped and dust-puffed with driving parties and cyclists, and the beach itself well occupied by bathers, sunners, showoffs, baby carriages, romping and shouting children, the athletically inclined and the determined walkers. If the light afternoon easterly was floating off the Point in little flutters of cat's paws over the water, a few gaff-rigged sloops would be taking advantage of it outside Bickford's floats.

On such an afternoon in midsummer of 1896 Miss McKenna, special correspondent for the *Boston Sunday Herald* and an admitted bloomer girl, joined a party of young ladies for "A Wheel on Quaint Cape Ann"[2] that took them dashing out to the Point in the course of their outing. Past the gate lodge

*The Beachcroft
Hotel at the
northerly end of
Niles Beach,
about 1904.
(Author's
collection)*

the road remains a dusty, stonestrewn, uneven way. What a charming boulevard it would make! A noisy crowd of girls upon a float tipped us off our bikes to watch the sport and envy. They were having great fun weighting the craft at one corner til, one by one, they were dumped or dragged into the water.

There was one stunning creature, a swimmer surely, for she disdained stockings and mitts and bonnet, and wore a plain suit with short tight arm caps, softly sashed at the waist, and short and scant as to skirt. It was pretty too, of some spotted wool stuff with bands of coarse lace, and prettier than all was the way she dived and swam.

Bathing suits were not included in the luggage strapped to our wheels, and we didn't appreciate turning ourselves into guys with the affairs we knew would be offered us in the round bath house above the beach. We could only compromise with wading, so in we paddled with our bicycle trousers pushed up as high as they would go, after the example of the children about us, and our short linen skirts held high above all danger.

But even this paled after a bit, and we went on our way for new experiences. The road becomes narrow and deplorably sandy, but it is interesting as it winds about like a snake between high bushes that brush us as we whizz by. There have been built lately on this barren point of land and scrubs a half dozen or so of charming country houses that have proved it too long neglected . . .

A fresh water pond, half choked with lilies and reeds and cat-o'-nine tails, lies in the center of this neck, with only the narrow road to separate it from the ocean.

We did everything that is expected of a party who visits a light-house, including counting the steps up and throwing our hats from the top. One was irretrievably lost, but it was a girl's and she was easily consoled, for it is quite the fad to ride bareheaded, and it is so much easier to be foolish if you have to. To do the thing correctly, she took the pins out of her hair—it is that crinkly kind—and rode off happy at outdoing us all. Fortunately the sky was just overcast enough to make a hat a burden on a hot day.

When one contemplates the outpouring of art Gloucester and its harbor have inspired for so long, the more puzzling that there's nary a trace of an artist or a work (name one of either!) worth mentioning prior to the native Fitz Hugh Lane's discovery of the prize at his very feet in the 1830s. Winslow Homer surely knew Lane's work as painter and lithographer when he made his own discovery of Gloucester in 1873 at thirty-seven, awakening his interest in maritime life and the art of water colors while staying for July and August at Washington and Main Streets.

Perhaps by more than coincidence, Edward Moran, the marine painter and elder brother of Thomas and Peter—the famed trio of English-born American artists—caught the lighthouse in a brisk westerly that same summer of 1873. And at the same or almost the same time William Morris Hunt of bald pate and flowing beard, back in Boston from his Barbizonian affair with Europe's ancient muse, was roaming the North Shore for subjects for his newfound insights, sometimes in his gypsy wagon of a painting van drawn by a span of horses, sometimes accompanied by a clutch of worshipful female students, seventeen of whom invaded Annisquam in his wake to immortalize the apple blossoms of 1875.

Two years after that, Hunt bought an old barn in Magnolia and converted it with the help of his architect friend William Ralph Emerson into a studio, a giraffelike gazebo they called "The Hulk." In two more years, after creating an oil of Gloucester Harbor whose capture of light pleased him immensely, so masterfully realized that in a few strokes it ushered in the era of modern luminism, Hunt drowned at the age of fifty-five—by accident or suicide—at the Isles of Shoals off the New Hampshire coast while visiting Celia Thaxter.

The next summer of 1880, perhaps drawn back by the tragedy of Hunt's death and the auctioning of his Gloucester work in Boston, Winslow Homer returned. His New York roommate, Samuel T. Preston, was related to the wife of Octavius Merrill, keeper of the lighthouse on Ten Pound Island. Preston arranged for Homer to board at the Merrills' cottage from June through September, rowing across to town when he needed supplies. From this waterbound aerie and around the harbor, Homer perfected his technique with at least fifty water colors.[3] Homer the illustrator was as taken up with the interaction of man and the sea in all their moods as Lane the panoramist with the uneasy truce between ship and sea. And from Gloucester, her wharves, her fishing, her light and shadow of life and death and play and work, the so much wider-ranging of the two was possessed, one imagines, with the inspiration for some of his most dramatic works.

Lane and Homer were as intimate with Gloucester as Hunt was detached, perched up there in his crow's nest thirty feet above the ground. Somewhere between these extremes of impressionability was the great proselytizer, the bridge in his diffident way, the German-born Cincinnati painter-etcher-sculptor Frank Duveneck, a large, fair fellow with drooping moustache who loved good talk and projected an air of indifference and indolence while in fact levitating the creative spirits of all who came to learn from him.

Twenty-seven when he returned from studying in Munich in 1875, Duveneck made a splash with a show in Boston, getting a huge boost from Hunt's enthusiasm for his red-blooded colors. He returned to Europe for more study and teaching, mostly American students—his "boys," the "Duveneck boys"—including the unpaternal "father" of American Impressionism, John Henry Twachtman. Back from Italy, he became engaged in 1879 to a pupil, formerly Hunt's, Elizabeth Boott of Boston.

Likely that year or the previous, Duveneck appears to have discovered Gloucester as a sketching ground, perhaps via his friendship with Hunt and his presumed passion for Miss Boott. The artist-writer Lester Stevens located him renting the Niles farmhouse on the Point about then, and his local obituary in 1919 had him summering in Gloucester for more than forty years. William Niles, an elder son of the owner, ran the farm after his father's death in 1872 but was more avidly an amateur painter and seems the probable agent of Duveneck's tenancy.[4]

Frank and Elizabeth didn't marry until 1886. A son, Frank, born in December, was raised by his mother's family in Boston after Elizabeth died in two years and remembers staying with his father in a rented house on the Point as early as the summer of 1893.

Three years earlier the Association had spruced up the old farmhouse for rental to a regular relay of artists who handed it from one to another for the rest of the century, beginning in 1890 with Reginald Cleveland Coxe, an etcher and painter noted for his illustrations of the novels of William Dean Howells, and son of Arthur Cleveland Coxe, the ultraconservative Episcopal bishop of Western New York. Coxe and a fellow "knight of the brush," as George Procter called an artist, wove all around the outside corners of the new piazza a fish-twine "spider web" that would remain a curiosity for two decades, interlaced with brilliant climbing nasturtiums.

Coxe was alone there the next winter and was rejoined by colleagues for the summer of 1891. Though he told people he wanted to settle on the Point, the record doesn't indicate whether he returned. One report has the influential painter and critic Kenyon Cox among his summer guests, another the author and illustrator Palmer Cox, but this may be a confusion of Coxes. "Eisham and Faxon of New York" rented the Niles place for the summer of 1895; in all probability this was Samuel Eisham, the critic and historian who knew them all.

Duveneck was definitely in the farmhouse for the summer of 1898 with an unidentified fellow artist from Cincinnati, very possibly his close friend Twachtman, who died suddenly, estranged from his large family, in 1902 while staying at the Harbor View Hotel on Wonson's Cove. So Frank Duveneck may have fallen for Cape Ann almost as early as William Morris Hunt and more than twenty years before his biographers have dared locate him there.

This amiable artist for many years kept studios at both Bass Rocks and Rocky Neck to take advantage of the morning and evening light across sea or harbor. His canvases are evocative, warm, comfortable, and full of color and light. For the effects of the light he painted Brace Rock, off the back shore of Eastern Point, ten or twelve times at different hours, as Lane did.

Duveneck could always find an excuse not to paint. One day he was set up on a wharf when someone offered him $1,500 on the spot before the oil was dry. He turned down the offer with, "I've got to take it back with me to show my boys that I've been working." In fact, home in Cincinnati, he placed the finished canvas in the Art Club exhibition for $800 so the club would get the commission.

As an aesthetic chauvinist at a time when collectors in this country were still buying third-rate European over first-rate American, this co-rediscoverer with Hunt and Homer of Lane's Cape Ann introduced a number of painters, who would be widely influential in their own right, to its always shifting theatricality as an arena of nature, one of the world's great basins of the plein air, a nursery of American art on no less a scale than the Hudson River valley and the Southwest.

Sarah Rogers drawing of her uncle William Niles doing what he enjoyed most, as long as he was not disturbed. (Author's collection)

Among these disciples who saw something new through the eyes of Duveneck were Joseph R. De Camp, Theodore Wendell, Edward H. Potthast and Lewis H. Meakin. All studied in Cincinnati, all but Meakin with Duveneck in Munich. All followed him to Cape Ann. De Camp and Wendell settled in Boston as landscapists (the former a portraitist as well), Potthast in New York specializing in bright beach scenes, Meakin remaining in the Midwest as a locally well-known producer of landscapes and still lifes. So, too, Ross E. Turner, who trailed De Camp to Boston from Munich in 1882, taught thousands of students watercolor over a long career, settled in Salem and came early to Cape Ann to sketch, as did the flamboyant, innovative, emancipative William Merritt Chase, who studied with Duveneck and Twachtman in Venice.

Niles Beach *by Charles Adams Platt, painted in 1881, probably at the same time Stephen Parrish sketched the same scene for the etching reproduced on the endpapers. (Private collection)*

Of German parentage like Duveneck (the families were friendly in Cincinnati), Twachtman was twenty-two when the two traveled to Munich to study in 1875. He didn't return to America to settle until 1889, when he joined the coterie of painters infected with the work of Monet and the new European Impressionism and affected by the snide expatriate Whistler. That summer he was drawn to Gloucester, probably by Duveneck. Twachtman in turn is the likely culprit in Gloucester's seduction of his close friend, the even-tempered, beloved and not terribly exciting J. Alden Weir.

Frederick Childe Hassam and Twachtman developed a productive and in some respects supportive friendship. One, Maine-born, athletic, a devotee of the outdoors, was as physically dynamic as the other was ostensibly enervated, temperamental and unstable in all but what his inner eye conveyed to him. The two palled around together, drank too much together and painted the New England shore together, with a common partiality for the Connecticut coast around Greenwich and for East Gloucester where Hassam had his studio. Twachtman was much the painter's painter and was joined in the plein air and in attendance at the classes of Charles A. Winter in 1895 for the first of many summers by another rising luminist, Willard L. Metcalf out of Lowell.

"Muley" (Frederick Remington's nickname for him) Hassam often claimed the credit, though Twachtman with his scraggly beard is just as likely the moving spirit—but in 1898 they, De Camp, Weir, Metcalf and Edmund C. Tarbell, Boston portraitist and pillar of the Museum School then painting in Annisquam on occasion, broke away from the Society of American Artists, itself a splinter from the National Academy, and with four friends—Frank W. Benson, Salem portraitist and etcher of waterfowl; Thomas W. Dewing of Boston, limner of dreamy damsels; and the muralists Robert Reid of Stockbridge and Edward Simmons of Concord—organized as the "Ten American Painters," commonly "The Ten," showing more or less together for another twenty years. William Merritt Chase replaced Twachtman on the latter's death in 1902.

After the turn of the century the influx gathered such impetus that the independent folk of East Gloucester and its pendant Rocky Neck looked around one fine luminescent morning to find themselves, to their surprise and sometimes dismay (pocket-books excepted), harboring *the* art colony north of Boston, perhaps *the* summer art colony of America, as I described it in *The North Shore*:

> Here was the heart of it all, the wharves stalling the patient schooners in still waters, the helter-skelter sprawl of fishing estab-lishments and shoreside emporia and acres of flake yards of pun-gent salt codfish spread to dry, the cozy inner harbor contrasts of bustle and serenity, the comings and goings of gray canvas in the breeze, the snug clapboard houses, Five and Ten Pound Islands, lighthouses, salt ships from Sicily airing out patched squaresails in the sun, steam-puffing tugboats, lobstermen, dorymen, beach-combers and bathers, sailing yachts and naphtha launches, tall rows of trees, upland meadows, Dogtown scrub and boulder, the Back Shore in an easterly, wild as the coast of Maine, and Eastern Point, the means of it all.
>
> Above all, literally, the light over and around, enveloping, per-meating, insinuating, suffusing the Olympian amphitheatre of Gloucester Harbor and the very water itself, as if under that evanes-cent presence of airy, heaven-sent light almost as palpable—it strikes one who has dwelled within its embrace for forty years—as the hard rock shore. As well as any, John Wilmerding tried to put his finger on this famous glow "which seems always to clarify, even press against the configurations of land and sea. The contours of a

landscape, however memorable, do not alone insure their appeal to an artist; but in combination with a seemingly present quality of atmosphere they can inspire the artist to consider aesthetic problems he may never discover elsewhere."

Not infrequently this almost landlocked bowl of the damnedest light you ever experienced, in its thousand shifting nuances from day to night and night to day, scowl to smile, season to season, has been compared with the Bay of Naples alone. And many the traveler has rounded the world, only to return, gaze about him, breathe a deep sigh, and announce as if he had the tablets in hand at last that there was nowhere, anywhere, for that interplay of land and sea and sky and inhabitants to surpass the old, old fishing port of Gloucester, on the North Shore of Massachusetts Bay.

Here Prendergast was drawn back summer after summer to dip and dab on paper the dreamy colors of an open-air tea party on Eastern Point above the harbor (a *dauber*, scoffed the traditionalists of the colony). To honest Gloucester came honest yeomen of the brush, solid marinists the likes of Walter Dean who would as happily sail as paint, Frederick Mulhaupt from far-away Missouri, Swedish-born Theodore Victor Carl Valenkamph and A. W. Bühler, a well-trained painter and etcher who shifted his ground from Annisquam in 1898 because there was more to paint over at East Gloucester and the Neck, more of the fishermen and the way of life he so singularly preserved on canvas. And Leonard Craske, creator of that noble bronze colossus *The Man at the Wheel*, watchman over the harbor.

Their own veils lifted in Europe, the Impressionists had opened America's eyes inward, to dreams of life as God had wrought it to be, to Gardens of Eden populated by exquisitely kissable young women floating across mauve

meadows in the early morning haze of the American happy land. And then, along came Europe again—always Europe—crudely nude, disarticulating down an abstract tumble of stairs at the Armory Show. That bombshell of modernism exploded in mid-Manhattan in 1913 and in the back alleys of John Sloan's head, clearing his visual landscape in one clean sweep that propelled him to Gloucester, which must already have been beckoning through his friends and those he wanted to know there.

John and Dolly Sloan, and Charles Winter (Twachtman's old teacher) and his artist wife Alice, took a cottage on East Main Street above the causeway to Rocky Neck for the 1914 season. Sloan was one of The Eight, whose single show of realism amidst the Edwardian in 1908 clatteringly introduced the discordant Ashcan School to the world of art. In the summer of 1915 they were joined by the much younger Stuart Davis, even more mind-blown by the Armory Show, for the first of his many years in Gloucester with his wild brush and poster colors.

Sloan spent but five summers in Gloucester, spanning the war in which he was too old to serve, but they were the most productive of his life, the fork in a career that led him from the monotones of the big city to the full spectrum of land and sea at Cape Ann, and finally of desert and mountain in the Southwest.

In Ernesta (Child with Nurse), *1894, Cecilia Beaux, "the female Sargent," painted one of her favorite subjects, her niece. (Metropolitan Museum of Art)

But how truly was the Great War a Great Divide in time and place, separating the rightness in some things and the wrongness in others.

There is noble irony in the appearance, in the middle of it, on the East Gloucester scene of a pair of patrons dedicated to forward movement in the arts whose very intentions bore the seeds of their disappointment. These were William Atwood, a civilized Connecticut textile manufacturer and amateur artist, and his gracious wife Emmeline.

Finding the artists all roundabout trying to seduce the muse (and the custom) in waterfront warrens of "dark little lofts, old outhouses, chicken coops, stables, tiny rooms, poorly lighted and unattractive," the Atwoods took the extraordinary step of buying upland above the Sloan-Davis-Winter cottage and engaging the Boston architect Ralph Adams Cram to design and build the medieval-revival "Gallery-on-the-Moors," and nearby, their own summer home, "House-on-the-Moors." In the midwar year of 1916 the Gloucester colony's first genuine gallery opened, with high promise. A Duveneck was the centerpiece. The Atwoods would accept no commissions. All was for the artists' sake.

As so frequently is the reward for the Samaritan who pokes his nose into the business of those beside the wayside, the benefactors within a couple of seasons were being roundly, if *sotto voce,* muttered at by many and possibly most of the nose-bent colonists who found their work excluded from the new gallery by the well-intended efforts of the owners to decorate their walls according to certain standards.

It's said that Sloan had sold one painting before he came to Gloucester, and that at the Atwoods' gallery he sold none. The market was seeking its own level. East Gloucester was alive with artists—or dying from them, as one writer lamented, the new bungalows "elbowing out" the old fisherman who "clings to the olden days. These radical changes almost make him weep. He is oftentimes seen lost in contemplation of the 'curse' that has overtaken Rocky Neck." For the solitary painter there was hardly anywhere left to be alone. Gone were the days when my great-granduncle Will Niles would disagreeably turn his easel around at the approach of an innocent kibitzer, when William Morris Hunt draped himself with sandwich boards advising I CAN'T TALK and I CAN'T HEAR. Even gregarious Lester Stevens was wont to pine for his boyhood when he and his art teacher "would wander all day through the fields, or along the shore, and never meet another painter."

Sloan gave up painting in the streets of Gloucester after a disagreeable encounter with a drunken fisherman (no more ashcans for him!) and fared no better with his peers, complaining to his friend Van Wyck Brooks that he had no use for art colonies (though he could not stay long away from them), that "there was an artist's shadow beside every cow in Gloucester, and the cows themselves were dying from eating paint-rags," that he could see why the natives called the summer people "summer vermin."

There was, of course, another side to the matter, expressed with some asperity during the summer of 1912 by Cecilia Beaux in an interview in the *Boston Post* and still resonating eight-five years later.[5]

> Each year, like many others in my profession, I look forward to my annual vacation at Eastern Point with pleasant anticipation, for to me there is no place in the world like this little spot. The natural beauty of Gloucester, of its particular kind, is unsurpassed. Its harbor, the shores and the quaint old fishing industry with its ships and characteristic skippers, lend every inspiration to an artist for his or her best work. There is a subject for a painting at every glance, and

And ladies of the brush ... An unidentified female painter captures Gloucester Harbor from Niles Beach, about 1890. (Procter Brothers photo, Steve Howard collection)

that is the chief reason why we have such a large colony of artists at this resort.

The summer artists' colony will move away from these parts if a few over-ambitious and unthinking real estate men persist in destroying the natural beauty of this famous shore. By erecting large and unsightly sign boards in conspicuous places, allowing people who buy land from them to put up small and crude-looking cottages and dumping dirt at many points along the shore, they are ruthlessly defacing that which has been admired by the artists from all sections of the country.

Each advertising sign that is put up in the endeavor to sell valuable property, especially in the vicinity of East Gloucester, Eastern Point and Lanesville, causes a groan of indignation from the many artists. The painters of landscape have talked among themselves and questioned if anything could be done to prevent the destroying of the landscape and marine views which they have studied and painted for years, but they feel that it would be useless to appeal to the offender.

One suspects that the redoubtable portraitist's immediate concern was less for the landscape of the brethren than for her own, suffering as she had through the overwhelming presence almost next door of George Stacy's Colonial Arms (see Chapter 25), only to observe with alarm, a mere four seasons after its fortunate destruction, the rising that summer of 1912 of the startling, multichambered superstructure that Stacy called "Bramble Ledge," kitty-corner across the road from her jealously guarded "Green Alley" at the corner of Eastern Point Boulevard and Toronto Avenue.[6]

Beaux had been well-established in her field for twenty-five years by then, having already overcome the obstacle of being a female painter in a day when that was not done, especially in portraiture where her uncle forbad her to study at the Pennsylvania Academy of the Fine Arts that painted

the male nude, as related by the novelist Mary Gordon (who incorporated aspects of her life in "Men and Angels") in an assessment of a 1995 exhibition at the National Portrtait Gallery in *The New York Times*.[7]

It would be difficult to imagine a painter whose work seems more distant from the press and stress of contemporary life. . . . We seem to be hungry for the Gilded Age. . . .

Beaux's determination to combine principles of classical portraiture with her love of paint and painting results in a series of portraits that are simultaneously rigorous and rich. Her brushwork is free and sensuous, particularly in her renderings of the opulent garments of her female subjects, who often wore their husbands' wealth on their backs. . . .

Her portraits absorb us because of their dramatic narrative power. She has a particular gift for portraying children unsentimentally; her children of privilege often look at us as if they thought we weren't good enough to be in the room with them. . . . Beaux's men meet the gaze of the viewer, but her women, unless they are professional, most often avert their eyes and convey the inwardness of some of Eakins's dreamier Philadelphians—her sense that men live in the world and domestic women live apart from it; their lives are lived in private, interiorly.

By the summer of 1919 the war was over. John and Dolly Sloan abandoned Gloucester forever for Santa Fe. Stuart Davis took off for Cuba. Frank Duveneck died, and so did Alden Weir, the third of The Ten to pass away, The Ten who were by now almost passé.

And the Atwoods surrendered. The show that season was hung by a jury selected by the colony and dominated by landscapes executed, according to one caustic critic, "to catch the eye of the wealthy tourist." For three more seasons the Atwoods compromised their tastes.

There would be lonely exceptions wandering across the landscape— Edward Hopper, Marsden Hartley and a few others. But Gloucester was overrun, now that the war was over, with the Pharisees of the familiar, of the endless surf upon an endless shore, of the seagull and the saccharin, of blue canvas and green paper.

In 1922 the artists organized the North Shore Arts Association, bought a hulking old warehouse on Reed's Wharf with acres of walls. The "Gallery-on-the-Moors" tiptoed out with a last small show. Deftly, the victors installed the Samaritan as their first president.

So let us return to that pioneer knight of the brush Cleveland Coxe, who drew with words a picture of Eastern Point and the harbor and the sea and the weather and the vessels of Gloucester a hundred years and more ago, while he was in residence in the Niles farmhouse and before the protecting Dog Bar Breakwater was built, that no artist could have painted. "In Gloucester Harbor," illustrated with his etchings, appeared in the August, 1892, number of *The Century Magazine*:

> The arm of land called Eastern Point, stretching out from the town of Gloucester and forming its harbor, possesses more attractions for one fond of the sea than does any other place on the coast that I know. Its shore toward the sea is protected by an armor of granite that breaks the force of storms, and within its shelter ride safely at anchor great barks from Italy and Spain, the fishing fleet,

and picturesque coasters, with their deckloads of hay and timber. In the background rise the foreign-looking towers of the city, and at its extreme point is the old Eastern Point Lighthouse. Opposite, guarding the other side, is the rock of Norman's Woe, and stretching back toward the city are the dark Manchester Hills.

It was this intimacy with the sea that led me to make the Point my home. I moved into a farmhouse, a comfortable building of the American country type, surrounded by great birch trees, a row of which stretched along the seawall across the lawn at its back, and beneath which I have the whole harbor spread out before me. In front of the house lies the lake, bordered by old willows and covered with lily pads. Beyond the lake are Brace's Rock, the cliffs, and the sea.

Although life on the Point is lovely enough in summer—I know of no place in the North where there are more songbirds—its real interest and beauty begin in the autumn. In spite of its bleak exposure, it is warmer than Boston or Gloucester itself; the air is bracing, of course—and such color! The trees around the farmhouse are of all colors, from the dark green of the willows in shadow to the silver of the birches in sunlight; farther away, tall elms line the old fort road. Grass meadows stretch up toward the hills, and gray rocks jut from the green. Over the meadow thence to the sea are blueberry bushes and rich furze, changing with different seasons, making a brilliant carpet in pleasant weather, or softly toned into grays when clouds hide the sun. Then comes the delicate fringe of pale-green sea grass, changing at another season into a golden yellow. All the gamut of color exists in rich profusion, from the deepest to the highest tones, tempered generally by the blues of the atmosphere. It is a place in which to live and study, like some of the old towns of France. My dog and cat take walks with me, and we enjoy them together; for Nature tempers us brutes into reasonable beings, and we find content in her society.

From the high land on the middle of the Point the shore stretches off to Thacher's Island, with its two needle-like lighthouses, and down the coast on a fair day the eye can make out Plymouth: one of real New England faith and enthusiasm can almost see the Rock. You take in the whole sweep of ocean, horizon, and sky. The vessels lie anchored at your feet in still waters, and the town nestles comfortably in the distance. One afternoon I was watching the schooners sailing out on their mackerel trips. All sail was set, even to the great staysails high up between the masts, the wind being fair from the northeast. Two or three coasters were at anchor, with mainsails up to keep their noses pointed toward the wind; the sun was shining, but far down toward Marblehead the sky was black. One or two schooners anchored near shore were taking in their canvas, a sure sign that the barometer was falling.

Another, pointing out under full sail, came about. The sky and water in the west had turned so dark a purple that the usually brown seaweed showed a golden yellow. A lull came in the wind, allowing a dull rumble of thunder to roll from Manchester; a vivid fork of lightning shot across the sky with a splitting shock, and a low-lying yellow cloud of dust rose from Magnolia. The wind was starting from the west with a rush; all the ships were brought up to meet it; and sails were coming down with a run, a brilliant, uncanny white against the intense black sky. The schooners were almost human in their panic as the fierce squall broke and the rain came down as though the heavens had been ripped open.

Such storms seldom touch the Point; tearing in from the sea, they pass over the harbor toward Annisquam, and in as short a time as it takes them to come up, they have swept out again. Then the sun shines out against the clouds piled up in the east; the vessels pluck up fresh courage, and are again on their courses, or have come quietly to anchor. The great arch of a rainbow stretches from north to south, and the day dies in a glowing mass of splendor. As the stars appear faintly through the deep blue, the riding lights dot the harbor, the green of a new arrival creeping slowly to her berth; then comes the splash of an anchor, the rattle of a cable; and night is here.

Some evenings, when the wind has died away, leaving the air damp with heavy dew, the quiet of the harbor is often intensified by a chance noise. The cry of a man on shore hailing a schooner to send a boat for him will only make the quiet doubly still. One has an instinctive desire to go out and tell him to hush. The road along the beach was my regular evening walk, to get the letters and New York paper. Generally it was a pleasant one, and even in bad weather, when I was rigged in oilskins and carried a lantern, it served only as an appetizer to a snug evening before the fire. One night in February I had gone as usual for the mail. The air was heavy with moisture; the night very dark and still. The glare from the town made the atmosphere brilliant in that direction, and the yellow lights of the vessels were reflected in the calm water almost to my feet. The only sound came from the booming foghorn on Thacher's Island. A gentle wind sprang up, ruffling the reflections, and brought across the water the sound of a band playing in Gloucester.

That was the only time I remember when loneliness became oppressive. The music was not of the classic order, nor of the quieter kind dreamy and soft, but of the real city German-band sort. I smelt New York, heard the abominable streetcars, saw the carriages driving fast to a dinner or the opera with a bit of white something inside, and I felt homesick. The hoarse whistle of a steamer offshore interrupted the music and my memories. Then the fog bell sounded

at the Point, and a white cloud of steaming vapor poured in from the sea and rushed past me over the harbor, blotting out the lights, the water, and everything but loneliness. My wretched lantern kept company with me on one side, and my ghostly shadow clung to me against the mist on the other. The trees dripped big drops that seemed to crawl in under my souwester and down my neck, and the salt air was fishy. That bad music had upset my contentment.

A winter's gale is always good and entertaining company, and a walk to the lighthouse sure to be exciting. The harbor is crowded with craft, coasters tugging at their anchors, burying their noses in the heavy southwest sea that rolls across the harbor. The more graceful fishermen curtsy to the black lighthouse tender and to the high, white steamers bound to Portland and Nova Scotia. Far out, many another craft under reefed foresail and jib is making for safety, sinking half-mast deep between the heavy seas. Seaward the cliffs are pouring cataracts of salt water inland, the very waves seeming glad to get ashore. A great angry, gray-green wall gathers together, and, as the back-wash runs out, piles up, and then hurls itself onward with dull thunder—to rise in a cutting mass of spray as it tears over the rocks. As darkness comes on, you climb over the slippery stone to a safe place, watching the ocean getting blacker and the rising columns of spray more ghostly; the shrieking wind and the noise of the waters sound like the cries of men cast away. I can almost see the wreckage to which they must be clinging, and it becomes too real to enjoy. I turn to go home, almost pitching head-long in my haste. I know absolutely that it is all imagination, yet as a great souse of spray comes pounding on my back I do not linger. That last dash seems almost an evidence of contempt on the part of the ocean, and as I scramble into the furze and bushes inland I have very little breath with which to give a sigh of relief. The farmhouse looks wonderfully cheerful as I pass the stone woman of Eastern Point standing grim in the gathering darkness, and as I take a last look at the rising and falling lights of the harbor my dog welcomes me into cozy comfort. The wind has risen and brought driving sleet, that dread of sailors. The house trembles with the shock of the blast as it beats against the windowpane, and my thoughts and sympathies turn toward the man at the wheel, the fishermen in their dories on the Banks, or the helpless schooner, broken from her moorings on the Georges, going to destruction, and carrying death in her path to another.

Sunshine gladdens the earth when I wake; the wind is fresh from the west, and a clear blue sky reflects itself in the water. Already those transient guests, the steamers, are crossing the Dog Bar, pitching in the brilliant seas, and rising with a white mantle of foam. The rattle of the pawls, the creaking of blocks, the clank, clank of the windlass, and the slowly rising white sails, tell that soon all will be tearing on their courses with a bone in their teeth. It is a very forlorn old hooker that cannot shine as a beauty on such a morning. High up in the heavens white clouds throw down again the brilliant sunshine. It is a day when darkest life seems good. . . .

I have sat under the trees on a morning when returning spring softens and lights up everything, and the birds have come, and the leaves are just breaking from their winter sheathing. Slowly a schooner rounds the Point, with her flag at half-mast. It is impossible to be careless in thought for that day; no matter what joy may be in your heart, you feel with the skipper and his crew, and the dread that must be theirs of telling who it is that is missing. Once I used to see an old man and a young woman on the rocks where I was painting. They came regularly every morning and afternoon, and carried an ancient telescope with which they searched the horizon. But the sea kept its secret from them and the overdue schooner never came. She had been out for four months, a long time for a voyage, but they could not give up that hope which was then their sole interest in life.

But a schooner's homecoming is generally of a brighter cast, and you find yourself quite as much in sympathy with the fishermen's joys as with their sorrows. Usually they sweep in from the northeast over a blue sea, and, passing the red buoy on the Dog Bar, turn the tiller for a straight and fair course up the harbor past Ten Pound Island. But they may come with a heavy fog. Then there is a screeching tug that seems to go out to patrol the coast, warning vessels off the rocks. She really hopes to find one so near danger that her assistance will be grateful to a wearied crew; or if the wind is light, as it generally is in a fog, she counts on the crew's impatience to get ashore. The fee is made up by the tired-out fishermen, and they pass up the harbor in luxurious ease.

In September 1900, the coaster Ellenora Van Dusen, *carrying 23,100 paving stones and 82 tons of granite, ran aground on the breakwater. (E. L. Blatchford photo, courtesy of Gordon W. Thomas)*

~21~
THE REEF OF
GLOUCESTER'S WOE

One might suppose that the raising of a public work as patently good for the port of Gloucester and the seafaring world at large as a breakwater off Eastern Point would have been a cut-and-dried affair. But it wasn't. There weren't very many votes in Gloucester in the 1880s and 1890s, as now; the voice of the fishing interests was barely audible in Washington, then as now; and Congress was as partial to the meretricious fat in the pork barrel as to its meritorious lean, then as now.

Besides, Washington had already dumped several hundreds of thousands of dollars worth of granite into Sandy Bay for a breakwater on the other side of Cape Ann, and neither end was in sight yet, never mind the middle.

The idea that a mole from the end of the Point out over the shoal of Dog Bar would render the harbor as calm as a mill pond when the easterlies raged was first advanced by George H. Procter in his *Cape Ann Weekly Advertiser* in 1866. Three years later Captain Joe Proctor got up a petition to Congress, and in 1871 the project looked alive when the Corps of Engineers' General John G. Foster proposed a 3,870-foot breakwater clear out to Round Rock Shoal, to be the longest in America and doubtless the world, to cost $494,000.

Instead Congress authorized a survey of Sandy Bay as a possible harbor of refuge in 1882, and in 1885 work on that breakwater began. Gloucester was investigated again in 1884. Again the engineers urged a breakwater over Dog Bar to Round Rock Shoal, to cost $752,000, and another to run easterly from Norman's Woe Rock at an estimated $607,000 (the first and the last ever heard of it). Each succeeding year they resubmitted their Dog Bar recommendation, to deaf ears. Federal funds were poured into Sandy Bay, where there was almost no commerce and no potential for it, while the outer harbor of the busiest fishing port in the world just around the corner lay at the mercy of the great onshore storms.

The government tore down the old lighthouse on the Point in the summer of 1890 and built a new one—which stands there today—out of a vessel-load of bricks delivered one day on the beach. But still no breakwater.

On the first of March, 1892, Keeper George G. Bailey lay on his deathbed in his cottage. Outside, a violent gale from the northeast belted the station with squalls of snow, and the mounting seas crashed in on Flat Point and over Dog Bar and splatted with spray the windows high up in the light.

It had come in thick and gustier than ever as the schooner *M. M. Chase,* from Eastport, Maine, bound for New York with a cargo of sardines and herring, made Thacher's Light, and her master decided wisely to run for Gloucester. She tore in around the Point full tilt, smacking through the swells, surged by the Dog Bar buoy and came about on the port tack to get in the lee. Just as they were hauling to and trimming their sheets hard aft, both the foresail and the jib blew out.

There she was, home but helpless, Dog Bar snarling to her leeward. Quick as thought, they let go both anchors and raised their signal in the rigging for a tug.

Their anchors held them off the bar all that night, and in the morning two towboats steamed out from town, but the tide was out, and a heavy sea coming in made it too risky. At the next high water the tug *Emma Bradford* returned, got a line aboard the *M. M. Chase* and towed her in to a safe anchorage. Foot by foot the schooner had been dragging toward the rocks and was saved with only a few hours to spare.

While the *Chase* was hanging on for dear life, the twenty-five-ton schooner *Fannie E. Thresher* was in trouble. She had left Portland in ballast in the morning, bound for the tarpon fishery at Pensacola, Florida, when a squall struck her as she was crossing Ipswich Bay and carried away her maintopmast and her springstay.

The *Thresher* limped around the lighthouse in the afternoon, but it was so rough and the visibility so poor that they dared not try for the harbor, crippled as they were with a spar whacking around overhead and rigging in a tangle, and anchored just outside Dog Bar. In an hour their cable parted and the little schooner was drifting seaward. They let go their other anchor.

William Hart and Peter Olsen jumped into the dory and rowed through the turbulent seas for shore to get a towboat out. They made it inside Dog Bar but couldn't land through the surf on Wharf Beach and had just started out again in search of a quieter spot when Olsen lost an oar. Last seen, they were being carried faster than one man could pull upwind, toward the immense swell thundering up on the Magnolia ledges. Then they disappeared.

At 2:00 A.M. the *Thresher* started to drag, but the anchor hit up again. At daybreak the frightened crew set their flag in the rigging and it was spotted. At noon a Gloucester crew volunteered to go after them in the lifeboat. The storm was at its height. Life preservers and a ten-gallon cask of oil were hove aboard the tug *Startle,* which crossed to Smith Cove, transferred this gear and the volunteers to the lifeboat and took it in tow. At three she was churning out by Ten Pound Island when they were spoken by the *Emma Bradford* steaming in with the *M. M. Chase* at the end of her towline and were given more details on the *Thresher*.

When they reached the *Thresher* she had dragged three-quarters of a mile beyond Round Rock. Dog Bar, behind them, was in a white fury. The waves tossed her about violently and swept her decks. The broken main-topmast swung and banged crazily in the snarl of rigging aloft. With every pitch, she reared back on her slender lifeline like a scared mare.

While the *Startle* ranged ahead of the schooner, the tug's deckhands bent one end of a light line to her hawser and the other to the lifeboat and paid it out, letting the bouncing lifesavers downwind toward the *Thresher*, some at the oars, guiding the rest bailing like fury for they had discovered to their dismay that they were leaking like a basket.

Once alongside, the line was tossed to eager hands at the rail of the schooner, and the well-soaked rescuers half climbed and were half pulled aboard the little vessel that shot up and down past their noses in a most precarious manner. In spun the small line, then the hawser, made fast to the bitt. While the *Startle* steamed slowly ahead, the hawser took the strain off the anchor cable; the men on the schooner walked in the slack, fell to at the windlass and broke out the anchor. She was free, and under tow.

When they got the *Fannie E. Thresher* into the inner harbor, flag half-mast high for Hart and Olsen, they found that the holding fluke of that anchor was bent back almost straight from the strain; a few more jerks on the cable and she would have been adrift at sea. As for the leaky lifeboat, they'd forgotten to put the plug in the drainhole; it was found under the pile of life preservers.

Keeper Bailey died in two weeks: Civil War veteran, sixteen years with the lighthouse service, assistant keeper at Boston Light before Eastern Point. In a few days his son, George E. Bailey, was sent up from the same post at Boston Light to replace his father. Like father, like son—$600 a year and no assistant.

The army's chief of engineers reiterated his annual plea in Gloucester's behalf in 1893 (the price tag on the breakwater was now up to $752,000), observing that the previous year the harbor had been used by all classes of vessels up to 1,500 tons and that 3,312 of them had boarded there, not including fishermen; most were coasters, with a sprinkling of salt barques. This time around, the secretary of the treasury was persuaded to recommend that $250,000 be provided in the Rivers and Harbors Bill to get the project going.

Urged on by George Procter, the Gloucester Business Men's Association put him in charge of a committee to pressure Congressman William Cogswell into nudging the bill and the money for it through Congress.

That summer of 1894, twenty-five years after Uncle Joe Proctor's first petition for it, Congress appropriated $40,000 to start a breakwater from the Eastern Point Light out to Round Rock Shoal, designed pretty much along the lines engineered by General Foster in 1871. In September the engineers asked for bids for the laying of the rubblestone base, thirty-one feet wide at bottom, to be of granite quarry grout preferably, averaging two tons but not less than half a ton, dumped to a height of mean low water and as far out as $40,000 would carry it. Low bidder was the Rockport Granite Company at eighty-seven cents a ton.

The stone sloop *West End* sailed around the Point from Rockport and dumped the first load of granite for Dog Bar Breakwater on November 28, 1894. All winter they kept it up under the supervision of the Corps of Engineers, the sloops and barges skirting the Point every day the weather afforded with their cargoes of rough granite from the north cape quarries.

By mid-September 1895 the substructure was out to about 400 feet from shore, visible only at low water, and the engineers moored a red barrel buoy to mark the end of it, a warning that did not suffice for the Lunenberg brig *Ethel,* bound home from Boston with a partial cargo of sugar. A late November storm was making up on the twenty-ninth, and being unacquainted with the coast the Nova Scotians made the mistake of following a shoaler draft schooner into the harbor, right in her wake, and came to unexpected grief on the submerged rocks Uncle Sam had been putting there. Her crew rowed out with an anchor and kedged her off, little damaged on the rising tide, with the help of the new and wondrously energetic Keeper Bailey.

That mean low line of low mean rocks had crept 1,000 feet from the Point by early summer, and Congress dribbled out another $40,000 so that work could resume just before Christmas 1896.

If granite were molasses the job couldn't have moved more sluggishly, and the lighthouse board was made aware enough of the creeping hazard to install at the lighthouse in January what was said to be the only two-ton, steam-tolled fog bell in the world. This magnificent instrument of percussion was struck a double blow every twenty seconds by two hundred-pound hammers operated by a steam engine and cocked by eight large steel springs. A second engine was held in reserve, and so was the old hand-wound clockwork bell.

At the end of that fiscal year, June 30, 1897, the engineers were able to report that 74,467 tons of stone had been deposited for a distance of 1,100 feet by the Rockport, Pigeon Hill and Cape Ann (Ben Butler's—but he had been dead four years) granite companies, which were under contract to dump another 34,000 tons by the following spring.

Thrust a few hundred feet farther into the entrance to the harbor by each Rivers and Harbors Bill, the man-made reef had nipped four vessels in its first three years of construction. The latest was the three-masted schooner *Tena A. Cotton,* from Philadelphia with 580 tons of coal, trying to enter the harbor on September 12; the *Startle* got her off on the flood.

A lucky thing, commented the *Advertiser,* that all so far had grazed the rocks in light weather, and it called for a lighted buoy or fixed light to mark the end of the foundation. No sooner suggested than during the calm and quiet night of the third of January, 1898, a big unidentified three-stick schooner sagged up on the rubblestone, then slid off as easily and went her way on the coming tide.

Ninety-eight was going to be the year that Gloucester and the whole coast would talk about for generations.

A tempest of thick, blinding snow struck the seaboard from the northeast on the first of February. It drove twenty-five vessels and boats ashore in Gloucester Harbor, three of them pounded to pieces. At least twenty lives were believed lost. Some of the wrecks had dragged anchor, others had torn loose from their wharves; several had collided and fouled their cables, so that they were dashed up on the shore separately or in a jumble. The debris was everywhere, and over everything lay a stifling, immobilizing blanket of snow. The master of the steamer *City of Gloucester* ran her aground on the beach at Lovell's Island in Boston Harbor to save her. The Eastern Point whistling buoy was uprooted and swept, screaming, clear across the bay almost to Provincetown.

At the worst of the storm the 101-ton schooner *Lizzie Griffin* broke away from William Bennett's wharf up in town. As she left, she snapped off four spiles and the corner of the building that Bennett's office was in. Captain Albert Gosbee of the lifesavers spied her from Rocky Neck, bearing down hell-bent for Black Bess. He rounded up his son Alonzo, Archie Fenton, Hiram Varney, George Wheeler, Erastus Elwell, Charles Brown and Officer Jack Mehlman, and they put out in the lifeboat from Oakes Cove in pursuit.

Even in the harbor the seas were mountainous, and when the surfboat caught up with the runaway she had lurched up on the shoal inside Black Bess, and they discovered to their disgust that there was no one aboard to rescue. They could make no headway at all against the storm, rowing back, so they beached their boat on the Point and pushed through the drifts on foot to the Humane Society shack at Brace Cove. But the snow was coming down so thick that they couldn't have seen a ship if it were in trouble, so they waded back through the blizzard to their homes—a long way, too.

As for the *Lizzie Griffin,* she remained where she was, pounding against Black Bess on the flood, left high and dry on the ebb. When the wind fell off, her crew came and took out the ballast and stripped her trying to float her, to no avail. Tugs put lines on her and thrashed at the water, but she wouldn't start. Broadside to the seas she lay, the rocks nibbling at her bottom.

Four days later, on February 5, the tugs *Startle, Joe Call* and *Eveleth* and the lighter *Abbott Coffin* with all their combined might and main hauled her off her bed of pain and beached her on the Rocky Neck flats. Three more days and the *Lizzie Griffin* was on Parkhurst's railways for doctoring. Her keel from forefoot to skeg had been ground off, her bottom planking was in shreds and she had a ragged hole in her port side. But her heart was stout.

The schooner Lizzie Griffin, aground on Black Bess Point, February 1, 1898. (E. L. Blatchford photo)

The notion that society might mount an organized effort to assist mariners shipwrecked on our coast was transplanted to America from Europe by the Massachusetts Humane Society, founded after the Revolution initially for the purpose of advancing techniques for the rescue of the drowning. Broadening its objectives, the Society built and provisioned shelters for castaways at remote and disaster-prone locations. Then in the 1840s it took active steps to effect actual rescues from wrecks with lifeboats and associated lifesaving apparatus at a growing number of strategic points on the Massachusetts coast. These were manned by crews of local volunteers whose services the trustees recognized with certificates, small cash awards, or medals, according to the valor involved.

Various stations were established around the rocky rim of Cape Ann by the Society during the latter nineteenth century—at Annisquam, Lanesville, Bearskin Neck, Gap Head, Rocky Neck, Stage Head and Magnolia, and at Brace Cove on Eastern Point. The first notice of the last appeared in the *Cape Ann Weekly Advertiser* on November 23, 1883: "A relief house has been built near Brace's Cove for the benefit of mariners shipwrecked in the vicinity." It was probably a bonus of the same agitation that finally resulted in a whistling buoy after all those pileups on Bemo Ledge, and the hut was put just to the west of where the Ledge makes out into the Cove.

Soon the station was given a surfboat; mortar and breeches buoy were added, and it was placed under the command of Captain John F. Bickford, the Civil War hero and boat livery-man who had charge also of one at Rocky Neck.

Brace Cove was remote and wild, headquarters in mid-summer for the gatherers of Irish moss, who barreled their season's stock for shipment right above the beach. One corre-spondent of the newspaper reported that "I recently saw a picnic party at the place, going in and out and finding pasture for all they were worth. To what base uses are surfboat houses put!"[1]

The trustees having indicated in their usual tactful manner that periodic drills might enhance the efficiency of their sta-tions, Captain Gosbee at 9:30 on an October morning of 1897 mustered his East Gloucester stalwarts at Station Six, Brace Cove.

On his signal, they ran the gun cart out of the shelter and along the beach (the tide was out) to an elevation above the ledge about 800 feet from Brace Rock. Four of the crew raced over to the Rock, to act the part of the shipwrecked. The rest, under Captain Gosbee's direction, quickly swung the gun cart into position and readied the mortar, known as the Hunt gun after the man who invented it in 1879, Edward S. Hunt of Weymouth.

Hawser, whip lines and the rest of the gear were overhauled, the gun cart was firmly chocked, the gun was loaded and the projectile with its attached whip line was dropped down the muzzle. Captain Gosbee sighted it carefully, fastened the lanyard in the touch hole and yanked. With a tremendous roar the projectile flew out like a rocket, the line streaming in a whipping arc behind it, clear over the heads of the men on Brace Rock—a 1,000-foot shot, right on the mark.

The boys out on the rock hauled in the light whip and then the hawser tied to it, which they made fast to an iron bar jammed in a crevice. On shore the rescuers hauled their end taut and inserted the crutch under the line to raise it above the imaginary surf. The breeches buoy was swung up and sent

Massachusetts Humane Society lifeboat crew launches another mission from Gloucester's Dolliver Neck station, by A. W. Bühler.

on its pulley along the hawser to the gang on the rock, but they preferred to return on foot and sent it back empty.

Captain Gosbee fired another projectile with as good effect, and after the gear had been packed up and the gun cart returned, the crew wheeled out the surfboat, launched it in the gentle breakers and took a row around the cove before securing it and breaking for lunch.

Back at Rocky Neck in the afternoon, they launched the boat from Station Eight (no Hunt gun there) and rowed across the harbor to Station Seven on the south shore of Stage Head, where another mortar shot was fired from Fishermen's Field under the command of Captain Isaac P. Morse, the veteran chief of that station which rarely used a boat, relying on the breeches buoy to reach the wrecks that were cast up there, close under the bold ledges. (It wasn't until 1900 that the government's fully manned station at Dolliver's Neck was built by the Treasury, which had jurisdiction over the U.S. Lifesaving Service, on land at Old House Cove donated by Henry Hovey.)

One never knew when fate might push time too hard to get the lifesavers to the scene. So it was, one cold day in the late fall, around 1907. Lobsterman George Jacobs had gone round to Brace Cove by water to raise for the winter the mooring he kept there for his extra boat. At low water earlier he had slung a heavy timber across the gunwales of a pair of dories and bent the mooring pennant to it in between, figuring to let the moon and their buoyancy do his work for him.

John Dedcovich happened to be approaching the beach in his dump cart behind two horses, after ballast stone, when he saw something go wrong with George's rig. There was a mighty crack and a splash; the dories capsized, and then Jacobs rose to the surface, spouting and thrashing, weighed down in his oilskins, hanging onto the bottom of one of the dories. And that water was like ice.

Dedcovich, as Douglas Parker recalls the incident, veered around, put the whip to his team and rattlywhacked that dump cart clear across the Point to the house of Joe Douglass, Parker's grandfather, up above the gate lodge. Joe and brothers Orrin and Fred answered John's shouts on the run, and the four of them picked up a beached dory, shoved it in the cart and lashed the horses back to Brace's, right down to the water's edge, launched the boat, jumped to the oars and pulled George Jacobs out of the drink, stiff as a stick and blue as a lobster, but still alive.

Returning to that wreck-ridden year of 1898, we find that work appears to have been suspended on the breakwater at the end of spring; Congressman William H. Moody, elected in 1895 to succeed General Cogswell, who had died, told Gloucester there would be no Rivers and Harbors Bill that year. A total of $154,000 had been appropriated to date.

On the eighteenth of April the schooner *David K. Allen* of Dennisport, bound from Hyannis for Gloucester, struck the substructure and stove her bow planks. The crew kept her jib and foresail in the wind to hold her from sliding off and sinking, but in a while she fell on her beam ends and they had to crawl up over the side to get in their boat. The *Startle* and *Eveleth* steamed out and towed the capsized *Allen* into the inner harbor, where she was righted by the *Abbott Coffin* and hauled out on Parkhurst's railway.

A month passed and a gas buoy was moored to mark the incompleted end of the breakwater.

The night of the third of September, thick fog, the yacht *Sea Gull* of Quincy, feeling her way in, felt Uncle Sam's rocks first and sank. The yachters, including a lady, got into their skiff and rowed to the lighthouse, where they were put up by the Baileys. In the morning the *Abbott Coffin* raised the sloop and beached her at East Gloucester for repairs.

Ninety-eight, remembered also for a disagreement with Spain, wound up with one of the worst blizzards of the century—the "Portland Breeze" that set in on November 26 and was so named after the Portland-to-Boston steamer that sank in the fullest fury of it somewhere off Cape Ann, taking all 157 aboard down with her. Congressman Lawrence told the House later the *Portland* could have saved herself behind the breakwater—if it had been completed.

Cape Ann was buried, paralyzed under mammoth snowdrifts. Trees, wires, chimneys down, roofs caved in everywhere. Gloucester Harbor was in a worse state, if that can be imagined, than after the February storm.

Twenty-seven vessels broke loose and hove ashore from Freshwater Cove to Eastern Point. At least forty small yachts were sunk or driven on the ledges. Yet not a life was lost.

The morning of the second day the thirty-four-ton schooner *Anna H. Mason*, in the Gloucester shore fishery, went adrift from the anchorage, careened out of control down the harbor and crashed up on Black Bess. Her crew waded ashore with as many of their belongings as they could save and took refuge in one of the summer homes, where they watched their vessel pound to pieces. A half mile further in, the schooner *Rienzi* snapped loose from Willam H. Jordan's wharf and struck so hard at the south end of Niles Beach that she drove broadside nearly into the trees in the farmyard. They had to build ways and launch her side-on back into the harbor.

Keeper Bailey said his lighthouse was marooned at the worst of the storm by enormous seas that broke through the adjoining coves and merged over the road.

The breakwater inched out. By January 1899, most of it was awash at low water, and the vessels rode noticeably easier while at anchor in the outer harbor. The base of the superstructure was now being laid—two walls of heavy split stone stepped up from the rubble foundation, the space between to be filled with rubble and capped by a top course of massive stone blocks ten feet wide.

Unavoidably, every new hunk of granite increased the menace to navigation. The British coaster *G. H. Perry*, bound from St. John, New Brunswick, for Quincy with lumber, struck on the rising tide August 11 and then floated off but had to be towed to Boston, leaking badly.

Running through heavy seas for the harbor on the night of November 27, the coasting schooner *Mentora* of Bucksport, Maine, bound home from Boston with a general cargo, struck full on. The *Eveleth* tugged her off next morning and towed her into Bennett's wharf with a serious leak. Exactly a month later the schooner *Twilight* of Jonesport, Maine, bound for Boston with lumber, grounded. Two tugs came out and floated her in an hour, only slightly damaged.

The state of the tide could make all the difference. Only four days after *Twilight*'s accident—it was the final day of 1899, ten in the morning—the 147-ton coasting schooner *Carrie L. Hix* sought shelter in the harbor on her trip from Rockland, Maine, for New York with a thousand barrels of lime. It was blowing hard, and so cold that the morning temperature gradient had raised up a vapor that obscured the friendly flash of the gas buoy at the end of the submerged government work. She struck with a shuddering blow and drove up high. The tide was on the half ebb, unfortunately, and as it dropped the jagged rocks punched through her bottom and she sank. Captain Hatch and his crew of five launched their dory and spent the night aboard a three-master anchored inside. By next morning the *Carrie L. Hix* was gone beyond saving, and they stripped her for salvage.

The *Advertiser* calculated that the *Hix* was the twenty-first vessel to strike the unfinished breakwater in the five years since the first stone was deposited in November 1894. Ten days after this last grounding the Gloucester Master Mariners' Association met to discuss the manmade mischief to the shipping it was supposed to protect, all the more exasperating as again this fiscal year work had been suspended because there was no Rivers and Harbors Bill, hence no money.

The least that should be done for the time being, the skippers agreed, was to build up the end of the works as far as it had gone and plant a fixed light there. Most of them now were convinced the engineers ought to have left a 200-foot gap between the lighthouse and the start of it to keep a channel for the current to carry the pack ice away from the Point shore and out to sea, a maneuver they thought would keep the Pancake Ground anchorage clear in the dead of winter.

Too late for that now, but still time to affect the length of it. How long should it really be? Harbormaster John C. Foster explained that the engineers planned to carry the construction over Dog Bar as far as Cat Ledge, then swing it 23 degrees due west to Round Rock, the theory being that this angle would carom the storm swells up along the Magnolia shore, away from the outer harbor where they caused such a troublesome undertow—for it was this surge that carried vessels at anchor ahead, and then with each recession sucked them back with a snap that broke out their hooks or parted their cables.

On the other hand, harbor pilot Robert N. Miller spoke for many of the experienced men when he advocated cutting the breakwater short at Cat Ledge, arguing that its extension to Round Rock, by constricting the mile-wide entrance of the harbor to a mere 750 yards, would make hard work for a vessel beating in by the end of it against a stiff northeast breeze and would create a strong race current where the tide funneled through the narrows. The Master Mariners decided to give the matter more study.

Except for a few small nudgings, the breakwater left 1900 in peace until the evening of September 12. The glass was dropping, and Captain H. W. Godfrey of the 309-ton coaster *Ellenora Van Dusen* of Sommers Point, New Jersey, thought he had best harbor at Gloucester until the foul weather passed—a sensible discretion since they had just cleared Bay View, logy with 23,100 paving stones and 82 tons of rough granite for New York.

But Captain Godfrey mistook the channel. Groaning onward with her burden of stone, the *Van Dusen* cut inside the warning buoy and struck the submerged breakwater with relentless momentum that carried her high on the rocks. They blew their horn and burned a torch for ninety minutes but were neither heard nor seen. The captain and his crew of six lowered their boat with some difficulty in the sodden southerly sea that smacked into the sinking schooner, and they rowed into Pavilion Beach. That was the end of the *Ellenora Van Dusen*, the twenty-seventh to thus make the acquaintance of the unfinished Dog Bar Breakwater, and she added her cargo to it as her monument.

"Go to bat for Gloucester and get this thing finished!" cried a citizens'

committee, and Congressman Moody responded that he would if the people would simply get together and decide what they wanted. The Master Mariners had by now made up their minds that the breakwater should be carried 2250 feet to Cat Ledge from shore, then hook to the west for 500 feet, 1,100 short of its original destination on Round Rock, which they wanted removed by blasting. So the citizens committee voted on November 8, 1900, to endorse this plan and so notified Moody.

Another month, and on December 12 up on the rocks crashed the schooner *Mansur B. Oakes,* bound from Calais, Maine, for Boston with a deckload of lumber. She'd been making three knots with all sail flying in a light southwest breeze. They kept her on it with jib and foresail spread before the wind while Captain George Beam rowed into the Cut for help. But the tide was only an hour on the ebb, and the wreck was left sprawled on the rocks, pointing her bowsprit in silent appeal to the heavens. The *Startle* started her on the midnight flood, but she only fell on her starboard bilge.

Captain Beam was pretty upset. He said he hadn't been to sea for three years and nobody ever told him about any breakwater there. Next day they took off most of the *Oakes*'s sails and running rigging, and the day after that the lighter *Eagle* relieved her of her deckload and anchors and chain. Thus lightened, the swells banged her over the rocks and up on the beach in Lighthouse Cove. There the hulk lay, spars askew and jibs in tatters, until it was floated and sold for $110, the thirty-first victim of the stinginess of Congress.

The thirty-second was the 210-ton, three-masted coasting schooner *Carlotta* of St. John, New Brunswick. She was on a passage from Hillsborough, New Brunswick, for New York with limestone, and had left Salem in the morning, intending to round Cape Cod, but the head wind pushed her back to Gloucester.

Near the breakwater she misstayed, and they dropped their anchor. It was about 1:30 P.M. The *Eveleth* had just towed a schooner out to get sea room and ran up and offered to give them a line but was refused. At that moment the *Carlotta*, heaving in the swells, dragged sternways and then swung broadside against the rocks.

Wreckmaster Tom Reed happened to be in the area with another tug; he jumped in a skiff, boarded the *Carlotta* and tried to persuade the mate, who looked to be in command, to accept help, but the man seemed in a panic. After valuable time had been wasted, Captain J. C. Rogers made an appearance and gave Reed charge of his vessel. Reed rowed off in his boat to arrange for hawsers.

All the while the swells had been jumping the Canadian along the breakwater, and when she reached the end of it her stern swung around by the rocks into the deep water and she started to sink, stern first. The six crewmen lowered the boat and rowed clear. But Captain Rogers had gone below for something and found himself trapped as the sea poured into his cabin. He groped to the companionway; the water was over his head; he lunged on deck, his chest bursting, swam to the backstay, climbed high as he could and hung on for dear life halfway up to the crosstrees until he was rescued.

"The Sable Island of Gloucester Harbor!" trumpeted George Procter, outraged:

> No spot on this Atlantic coast is as dangerous as this jagged pile of rocks at the entrance of one of the best harbors on the coast . . . a menace to the lives of every man on vessels sailing these waters, a source of danger to every vessel and worriment to their owners. . . . Somebody surely is responsible for the dilatory work and should be made to see the importance of early completion and enormity of the crime of further delay. As the work now stands, this long, black line of threatening jagged rocks is as bad as the most dangerous reef or sand bar along the coast.[2]

The work jerked forward, as Congress tossed the dribs and drabs. Six years of it when the century turned, and the superstructure had only just broken the surface at high water. That finishing block still lay somewhere in a vein of Rockport granite.

Of course, the breakwater wasn't always to blame; now and again the Point got in the way, as during the dark and rainy evening of November 22, 1902.

The schooner *Beta*, 152 tons, had dropped Boston Harbor astern and was under way for Portland with five hundred barrels of cement when her steering rope blocks jammed, passing the Eastern Point Light. While Captain N. C. Danforth and his crew sweated to free the lines to their rudder, the impotent coaster drifted toward the Point on the southerly breeze and swell. Even as they got them fixed, the *Beta* struck the ledges at Flat Cove, a short way east of the lighthouse. Apparently they left no watch on deck and were all so preoccupied below that no one had thought of anchoring.

Lucky for them that Keeper Bailey was more attentive to their plight than they. He saw the *Beta* sag ashore and wigwagged with his torch across the harbor to the new station at Dolliver's Neck. (The lighthouse was connected by telephone to the city in January 1902, though not quite yet, it seems, to Dolliver's Neck. Previously the keeper had to race all the way to the gate lodge, where the nearest phone was, to report vessels in distress.)

The signal was seen, and Captain Nelson King and crew soon had crossed over in the surfboat and landed by the lighthouse.

The seas swept the wreck, making it impossible to reach her. So, from the *Beta* they floated a light line on a buoy to the lifesavers on shore, who tied it to a hawser that was thus hauled back to the wreck. Captain King rigged a bosn's chair with a block; they drove the hawser through it and he pulled himself aboard the schooner. When all was secured, Captain Danforth and his four men were brought ashore via this makeshift breeches buoy, but not ahead of his wife and daughter, who had retired and were barefoot and stockingless in the classic tradition of rescued womanhood.

The last of the crew had barely touched land when both masts went by the board in an avalanche of sails and rigging, and the unfortunate *Beta* began breaking up.

The thirty-seventh vessel by the newspaper's count to have a run-in with the breakwater was the schooner *William M. Walker* of Provincetown. Making harbor at midnight on September 28, 1903, she struck. Captain King and the lifesavers rowed to her rescue and ninety minutes later pulled her off. She was beached at Smith Cove for repairs, two ugly holes in her bottom.

And next spring, again the question, what good was the whistler where it was? The *Olivia Domingoes* was returning from shore fishing. It was one in the morning of April 9, 1904, rain squalls and very thick and not a whisper of a whistle to be heard—no Ruby Light to be seen behind the obscuring edge of the Back Shore. They were just too close in. They cut around the False Point and struck Bemo. Every wave lifted the schooner and dumped it back on the ledge. Captain Manuel Domingoes and his crew made the beach and hastened for help. At daybreak Captain Heberle came around to Brace's in the tug *Priscilla,* but it was no use. The *Domingoes* was going to pieces.

Finally, the end was in sight. In his annual report late in 1904 the chief of engineers asked for a last appropriation of $67,083 to finish off the Dog Bar

Breakwater. And two weeks shy of the tenth anniversary of its beginning, it had one more victim to finish off itself before it settled permanently into the seascape.

Captain E. A. Tolman of the 135-ton schooner *Nautilus* had regarded the dipping of his glass with some perturbation. It was the thirteenth of November, and the uncertainties of winter were at hand. He and his three men were bound home to Rockland, Maine, with a hold full of coal from Perth Amboy, New Jersey. Tolman decided to drive her for Gloucester. With a hard northeast gale setting in, the barometer had been correct.

At five in the afternoon the *Nautilus* lunged through the swells half-breaking over Round Rock Shoal and rounded the low mass of ragged rock marking the unfinished end of the breakwater. And then, just as the sardine schooner *M. M. Chase* had in 1892, she filled away on the port tack and before she could fairly get under way, a squall hit. Jib halyards parted with a crack, down the sails flapped, spilling the wind, her head sagged and *Nautilus* was in real trouble, drifting, with no way on, toward the break-water.

They let both anchors go on short cable, not knowing just where the rocks were. That was their mistake. They hadn't scope enough to let their flukes bite in, and the mounting downharbor gale pressed the schooner with agonizing slowness toward the breakwater, now just visible through the gathering dusk.

The moment before she struck they lit torches and fired off rockets. Keeper Bailey saw them and telephoned the Dolliver's Neck station. Then he put on his oilskins and fought his way against the wind and spray over the superstructure of the breakwater, but the *Nautilus* was too far from the completed section to reach, and there was nothing more he could have done for them than he had already.

Captain King and his seven men launched the surfboat and pulled into the tossing harbor. Three times the storm and the tide swept them past the breakwater into the raging Atlantic, and three times they bent to the oars and crawled back. Upwind of the *Nautilus* they gained one of the dolphin buoys that had been moored inside the work to warn vessels away from the incompleted section. Tying to it, they paid the lifeboat downwind toward the schooner, which now was shattering herself on the fierce rocks that seemed to reach out for the rescue boat with each receding wave.

It took skillful seamanship and all their flagging strength at the oars to hover under the schooner's quarter while her four stranded crew swung out from the yawl boat davits and dropped into the laps of their saviors.

Hand over hand they hauled their loaded surfboat back to the mark buoy and cast off. Again they were in the grip of the storm, and even with two of the rescued giving a hand with the oars they could no more than hold their own against the full force of the gale that seemed bound to sweep them out to sea.

As fate would have it, the tug *Nellie* was in the harbor, and somebody on board caught the frenetic arm-waving through the scud. She steamed down and threw them a line and towed the lifeboat far enough up to windward for a fair pull back to Dolliver's Neck.

The lights of the *Nautilus* were seen in the rigging until an hour before midnight, when they disappeared as she passed out over the foundation blocks and sank.

Dog Bar Breakwater was officially completed at sundown on the fifteenth of December, 1905, eleven years in the building. Keeper Bailey walked the length of it, climbed the ladder up the wooden tripod on the rubble round and lit the white oil lamp that would from that time on, until it was changed to red and electrified, provide him with his daily constitutional and lead mariners to a haven that had been sought for thirty-six more or less disastrous years.

Sarah Rogers drawing of the Eastern Point fort. (Author's collection)

~22~
CAMP WOLCOTT: BASTION AGAINST THE SPANIARD

The coast was enjoying a most titillating case of the jitters. Tension had been building since the *Maine* blew up in Havana Harbor on February 15, 1898. War with Spain was surely imminent, and the enemy fleet was said to be terribly formidable. (Everyone knew how cruel and vengeful Spaniards were.) Reports flew about that their gunboats might any day, any hour, materialize off the coast and bombard summer residences to smithereens out of sheer Spanish spite.

Dame Rumor, attended by her handmaiden, Panic, bustled from seaport to seaport so busily that the *Cape Ann Weekly Advertiser* (a little less jingo than Hearst) felt compelled to quiet the public pulse:

> A Spanish admiral, even if he could get a fleet over to this part of the Atlantic coast, would not waste his time and impoverish the Spanish treasury by firing off $25,000 worth of ammunition in an attempt to hit a $2500 cottage on the seashore. Even a Spanish admiral has some regard for the fitness of things . . .[1]

Without a bit of doubt, the Gloucester paper added by way of further comfort, the scare that had so agitated the proprietors of shore property was "set afloat by owners of mountain resorts in order to gain patronage at the expense of the seaside."

Still, mused George Procter, "forearmed is forewarned," and Gloucester is in an "utterly defenceless condition." So he proposed editorially that "we need a good battery on Eastern Point, with guns of sufficient calibre to sink any craft which would seek to damage the city, and the proper authorities should take immediate action."[2]

Admiral Cervera's squadron was at this moment hovering indecisively off the African coast.

Two days later Spain did indeed declare war on fair America, and compliment was returned by a righteous Congress on the twenty-fifth—retroactive, for good measure, to the day before it was tendered. Spain's Atlantic warships sailed for the Caribbean on the twenty-ninth, and Commodore George Dewey sunk their Pacific sisters in Manila Bay on May 1.

The spectacular defeat of the Spanish sea power by the Hero of Manila brought to mind that twenty years or so earlier, in the dull interbellum days, he had served as lighthouse inspector on the New England coast. His duties certainly would have called him to the Eastern Point station regularly.

On one of his trips to Baker's Island, Inspector Dewey had hardly stepped ashore when he was charged by the bull of Thomas Gilbert, who had the only farm on the island. Dewey was not so intrepid then; he raced back, leaped into his skiff and pulled away from shore shouting to Keeper Rogers, who had run to the rescue: "Mr. Rogers, kill that bull. I'd rather go into an engagement any day than face that beast!"[3]

Five days after Admiral Dewey's decisive sea victory, Gloucester Mayor Frank E. Davis and two officers on Governor Roger Wolcott's Massachusetts coastal defense board inspected the rusticated earthworks of the old Civil War fort on Eastern Point.

The brass felt that guns sent for Gloucester's defense should be placed there; His Honor thought the city could spare enough highway tools to restore the works, which had fallen into peaceful desuetude, to warlike trim. Consideration was given to the possibility that some of the cottages might have to be torn down if they stood in the line of fire of the guns; this prospect was alarming enough to induce the owners of the Atwood estate across the road to sell it posthaste on terms advantageous to my grandfather, Dr. Joseph E. Garland, in midsummer 1898.

To make doubly sure Gloucester and her influential and wealthy summer residents understood that President McKinley intended they should suffer no harm at the hands of the Spaniards, the Civil War monitor *Catskill*, with a hundred Massachusetts naval reservist aboard, was towed up by the tug *Argus* and anchored in the inner harbor. She was armed with two fifteen-inch turret guns and two rapid-firing one-pounders fore and aft. It was promised she would guard Gloucester until peace was restored.

Gloucester's own Company G paraded to the depot amid paroxysms of patriotism and entrained into the unknown. There were rumors that the harbor had been mined by the navy (the steamer *Cape Ann* had been observed to deviate from its usual course while passing out one day), but they appear to have been unfounded.

Some of the members of the Myopia Hunt Club in Hamilton let it be known that they were organizing a crack Myopia cavalry troop of Rough Riders whose services they would offer the government.

Congressman Moody notified Mayor Davis that the navy had bought J. Pierpont Morgan's 204-foot steam yacht *Corsair* for $200,000 and planned to honor the city by renaming it the USS *Gloucester*. The mayor wired back a vehement protest: his city deserved more, in view of her services and sacrifices—at the least a permanently commissioned cruiser. But the navy changed *Corsair* to *Gloucester* anyway and sent her off against the Spanish.

Camp Wolcott it was called, after the governor, and the Eastern Point Associates gave the Fifth Regiment, Massachusetts Volunteer Militia, thirty days' use of the Fort Hill tract from the Back Shore to the harbor, to keep Admiral Cervera at bay—until the first of June, at least.

Infantry Companies D and K of the Second Battalion landed amphibiously in Gloucester at noon on the ninth of May, feeling somewhat unsettled at their stomachs after a choppy trip from Boston on the *Cape Ann*. Company I arrived by train, and since all three made their appearance unexpectedly, there was not much of a reception for the 185 men and officers. They boarded the electrics and then marched out to their bivouac in the field across the road from the fort, where they slept that night in the open.

No such easy travel for Battery C of the First Battalion of Light Artillery. They departed their hometown of Lawrence at 8:30 that morning—ninety-seven men and officers, four fieldpieces and sixty-eight horses. They halted twice on the march to rest, eat, and feed their horses—at Boxford and by Lovett's barn in West Gloucester. The word had gone ahead, and crowds were gathered along Main Street and at the Cut when the column arrived at 7:15 p.m., mighty tired after their forty-mile hike and a way to go yet.

"About a half an hour after the passage of the main body," a reporter sympathized, "a lone artilleryman leading his tired horse by the bridle came walking over the Cut, and a more forlorn looking picture it has seldom been our lot to view."[4]

An advance detail was already making camp between the quarry and the beach, and when Battery C finally rumbled and rattled in, the horses were rubbed down in the Niles barn and a large tent adjoining, and the men took a break.

Next day Camp Wolcott got down to business under the command of Colonel Jophanus H. Whitney, former chief of police of Medford. His Fifth was a prideful regiment and one of the oldest in the militia, dating back to 1805, mostly Middlesex County men. From early morning until dark, supply wagons clanked steadily past the gate lodge, where three militiamen with rifles (with the help of Caretaker Edmondson, breveted as a constable) were under orders to let no one through without a pass. Sentries were posted along the Back Shore to raise the alarm if Spanish warships should appear over the horizon. Guards were stationed at the summer residences lest they succumb to the friends at home defending them from the foe abroad.

The officers were quartered in the Niles farmhouse. The infantry boys pitched their tents in neat company streets on Fort Hill, the national and state colors flapping before the headquarters tent. Battery C's tents were arranged in an "A," with headquarters at the apex.

Where the sandy road wound across the marsh just before the lighthouse the artillerymen went to work with picks, shovels, rakes and hoes and dug in two of their fieldpieces to sweep the harbor clear of Cervera's armada (any, that is, lucky enough to make it past the submerged breakwater). The

roadway was about three feet above the marsh, and twenty feet wide. Fill was shoveled in to support the carriages, and earthworks were thrown up around the two, banked up to the road.

That evening they began the daily ritual of shooting the sun down with a blank charge behind the western hills across the harbor. The crew of a small sailboat reaching across the cove in the line of fire thought it was a signal to heave to, and they jumped to their halyards and doused their sails. But when they perceived that no notice was being taken of them, they got up sail again and resumed their spin.

Since the Fifth was also manning batteries at Marblehead and Plum Island, headquarters must have its own naval transport service, and the forty-foot steam launch *Hattie* was commandeered. *Hattie* struck the sandbar in Squam River with a cargo of officers returning from an early inspection trip to Plum Island, however, and there she remained for some days. After her chagrined passengers were taken ashore they replaced her with the Ipswich-Plum Island steamer *Carlotta*, and the command communications between the batteries—so vital to the defense of the red, white and blue—were resumed.

Most of the dash, spit, polish and derring-do about Camp Wolcott were concentrated at Major Duchesney's "Battery Park" down by the harbor on Quarry Point. Drills were stirring sights and sounds, the guns and caissons thumping and bouncing into line, wheeled about by the horses on the dead gallop, half hidden in swirls of dust. Most of the men were able equestrians and proficient with the saber; a favorite maneuver consisted of galloping full tilt at a potato hung from a limb on a string, the rider taking a wide, back-handed, whistling cut at it as he thundered by. Fresh potatoes were much in demand.

Two of the battery tents were occupied by the "Sherman Guards" of Lawrence who sealed their bonds of camaraderie by growing goatees and flying the lone-star flag of Cuba behind their quarters on "Goat Avenue." They tried their luck at fishing off the wharf with meager results, namely one small flounder. Every morning at four they rose from their cots and dashed jubilantly to the beach for a dip and a three-mile run.

From some local patriot the militiamen wheedled an upright piano, and when they weren't harmonizing around it, they were fishing, swimming, running, beachcombing, skylarking, playing baseball and football with the

Brace Cove, with Bemo Ledge extending from left, probably by William Niles, the author's great-great-uncle, about 1860. During the Spanish-American War, Gloucester feared that Spanish ships lurked over the horizon. (Private collection)

infantry up on the hill, drilling, to be sure, and figuring ways to sneak by the guards. Their officers batted the ball around in interservice matches with their opposite numbers from the *Catskill*.

A great war. Must it end?

The first Sunday of the encampment the gates were opened and hundreds of the public, ignoring the showers, streamed down to the Point on the electrics and by foot and wheel and buggy. Chaplain House conducted open-air services with the help of an ample delegation of Christian Endeavor members who were in good voice but were cut short by the rain. Teachers brought their classes to see how smartly Gloucester was being protected from the horrid Spaniards, and the children had the workings of the Gatling gun explained to them by the foot soldiers.

Such a lark, in truth, that extra guards had to be assigned to the Niles farmhouse gate and the road by Brace Cove; some of the men were making it into Gloucester rather too frequently for even the most easygoing officer of the day and "on one occasion had more fun than the law allows,"[5] which for Gloucester was plenty.

A wigwagging squad practiced its signals near the lighthouse to the mystification of visitors, "Russian stoves" arrived to drive the night chill out of the tents and add an air of permanence to the camp, the infantry and battery drills grew snappier with each new day of practice, and on the second Sunday in the life of Camp Wolcott, May 22 and a glorious day, five thousand visitors poured past the gate lodge and swarmed over the Point. The camera craze was on, Kodaks were everywhere, and the flutter of shutters was heard from shore to shining shore.

"At the infantry camp," observed the *Advertiser*, "are three colored servants who rejoice in the appellations of Sunshine, Snowball and Cloudy Day. The former is the shadiest while the latter is the lightest."[6]

A particular point of pride with the Fifth for thirty-five years, incidentally, had been its part in freeing the black man.

All good things, even home guard duty at a seaside resort during a fashionable war in springtime, must come to an end. The American Navy bottled and corked the Spanish fleet in Santiago de Cuba Harbor on the twenty-second of May, much to the relief of the hotel men of East Gloucester and the summer residents of Eastern Point. Their nervous embrace of the defending troops now gave way to anxious impatience over this continued reciprocation of it, for the Fifth seemed happily entrenched and showed no signs of breaking camp. The prospect of an indefinite occupation (shades of Farmer Niles) was a real and present threat to the profits and privacy of the impending season, a hundredfold more unspeakable than the fantasy of destruction by Spanish warships.

Certain private conversations were had with the adjutant general of the Commonwealth, and it was announced that when the tour of duty of the Fifth was completed on June 1, the defense of Gloucester would be shifted across the harbor to Stage Fort, which had recently been acquired by the city for a park.

The militia were liable for only eight days of active duty in this war of wars, and so the Second Battalion of infantry had been replaced at Camp Wolcott by the Third, and the Third currently by the First. Battery C continued to serve beyond the expiration of its term, perhaps by common consent along the canvassed mansions of Goat Avenue, where the tinkling of the piano and the crack of the bat mingled with the splunk of the split potato; but they, too, must return to reality and were scheduled to be relieved when they reached Stage Fort by the heavy artillery battery of the First Regiment, which had been ordered to Gloucester.

News of these decisions up to Boston provoked some grumbling in Camp Wolcott and around town. A general feeling was detected among the militiamen that Eastern Point was much to be preferred as the annual training ground for the Fifth to their regular inland camp at Framingham, and rumor had it that the top brass were cogitating how they might seize what time was running out on for a permanent fortification. In Gloucester a petition circulated requesting Governor Wolcott to retain Battery C at Eastern Point until the war was over.

The Eastern Point Associates, however, were unmoved. The Fifth's tour, and by agreement the loan of the land, expired on the first of June, and that, as far as the residents who were looking to the fast approaching summer season were concerned, was that.

Visitors thronged Camp Wolcott over the Memorial Day weekend. It was perhaps not quite as military and exciting as the two previous in the history of the post, for it was marked by the somewhat long-faced departure of the last of the infantry companies and the band.

The holiday was saved by Battery C. They staged a handsomely executed gun drill and played an ebullient game of baseball for the spectators, and a horse ran away with a buggy, upsetting the lady passengers in a welter of screams, petticoats, neighing, spinning wheels and rescuers.

On the eve of their evacuation the boys in the remaining platoon of Battery C put on a banquet as testimony of their affection for Keeper Bailey and his family and presented him with an Odd Fellows watch charm and his daughter with a pretty gold ring.

Next morning being the first of June, the tents were struck, the area was policed up, the horses were hitched to the field pieces that had done such sunset service for twenty-four days in the defense of Gloucester, and the last unit of Battery C of the Fifth Regiment, M.V.M., clomped and clattered along Eastern Point Boulevard and out past the gate lodge.

"With their departure," reflected the *Advertiser*, "Camp Wolcott and its pleasant memories becomes a thing of the past [the cooking especially was enjoyed by all] and the officers and men are congratulating themselves that their temporary abode was free from liquors of any kind during their stay."[7]

Henry Clark Rouse, by Wilhelm Funk, 1904. (Madeleine Williams)

~23~
THE RAMPARTS

Nᴏᴛ ᴛʜᴇ ʟᴇᴀsᴛ ᴏꜰ ᴛʜᴇ ꜰᴏʀᴄᴇs that precipitated the reluctant evacuation of the commanding ground of Eastern Point by the Fifth Regiment, M.V.M., that first of June in 1898 was the impatience of a bachelor railroad tycoon and yachtsman with a dashing handlebar mustachio, Henry Clark Rouse of Cleveland and New York, to occupy it himself.

Barely three weeks after the rear guard of Battery C tramped out past the gate lodge, with many a longing look aback, Rouse announced that he had purchased twenty-five acres from the Associates, from the Back Shore to Gloucester Harbor, including what he fancied calling "Fort Independence," whose bastions he planned to restore for the containment of a $75,000 mansion.

It was the syndicate's biggest deal and had been in the works for some time. Boston architect H. B. Ball had plans drawn, and Mott Cannon, a civil engineer, was already surveying the old earthworks from the original blueprint that Rouse had obtained from the Corps of Engineers.

By the Fourth of July Cannon had a crew restoring the redoubt and trenching a dry moat around it. Two more weeks and Henry Rouse was in deed as well as word the owner of the largest estate on the Point. His neighbors slept easier o' nights, now that this robust newcomer had removed the specter of a summer hotel from their midst.

Another week, and the masons were at work on the foundation. Rouse decided he would call it "The Ramparts." Once launched on a project, he was not a man to waste time.

He did not build "The Ramparts" as a showplace, according to Mrs. Hilda Raymond Williamson, but simply as a pleasant summer cottage for himself and his old and close Cleveland friends, Hilda's father and mother, Mr. and Mrs. Samuel Atwater Raymond and their family; in fact, he would not have assayed it without their agreement to share it with him. He had made his home in Cleveland with his mother, and after her death with his Grandmother Miller. When she died, being entirely alone, he

Henry Rouse's ninety-six-foot schooner Iroquois. *(Peabody Essex Museum)*

invited the Raymonds to bring their six children and live with him at 1030 Euclid Avenue. The two households under Emma Raymond, who played hostess for "Uncle Henry's" frequent business entertaining, became as one.

At forty-five, Commodore Rouse, as he desired to be addressed, was at the peak of his career. He was born in Cleveland on March 15, 1853, son of Edwin Coolidge and Mary Miller Rouse. He is said to have been one of John D. Rockefeller's early Cleveland associates in organizing the oil industry (though fourteen years John D.'s junior), and this connection gains credence from the fact that on several of his trips of investigation to Eastern Point Rouse was accompanied by Rockefeller's closest partner in Standard Oil, Henry M. Flagler, an old Cleveland neighbor.

As Rockefeller sought to polish tarnished coin with the cloth of philanthropy, so Flagler proposed to convert the swamps and sands of Florida into the nation's playground. Rockefeller reminisced of him:

> For years and years this early partner and I worked shoulder to shoulder; our desks were in the same room. We both lived on Euclid Avenue a few rods apart. We met and walked to the office together, walked home to luncheon, back again after luncheon, and

home again at night. On these walks, when we were away from the office interruptions, we did our thinking, talking and planning together.[1]

Flagler was reported to be so enthralled with Eastern Point as the result of his visits with Rouse that he wanted to purchase a similar tract. But whatever the reason, he didn't.

Since 1891, when he was thirty-eight, Rouse had been president and chairman of the board of the Missouri, Kansas and Texas Railway, and since 1892 president of the Boonville Railroad Bridge Company. When the immensely land-rich, repeatedly plundered Northern Pacific Railroad went into bankruptcy in 1893 Rouse was appointed one of the receivers who imposed two drastic wage cuts and then, when a strike was threatened, secured a court injunction which the House Judiciary Committee castigated as oppressive and unconstitutional.

During the last three years of his Northern Pacific receivership, from 1894 to 1896, Rouse became president of twelve more railroads in addition to the M, K & T: the Northern Pacific & Manitoba; Northern Pacific & Cascade; Central Washington; Washington Shore Line; Rocky Fork & Cooke City; Sanborn Cooperstown & Turtle Mountain; Tacoma; Ortin & Southeastern Dakota; Winnipeg Trans-County; Fargo & Southwestern; Southeastern Dakota; and Coeur d'Alene Railway & Navigation Company. He was a director of twenty-seven other transportation companies and one of the largest landowners in Cleveland.

As it was with others of his peers, a summertime avocation of the Commodore was yachting in the Edwardian style, and like many another Midwestern magnate, he yearned to reestablish roots in the rich soil of an Eastern resort. He kept an apartment at Sherry's in New York and since 1896 had been Commodore of the Seawanhaka Corinthian Yacht Club, from whose basin at Oyster Bay he sailed forth in his flagship, the beautiful ninety-six-foot schooner *Iroquois*, on leisurely cruises to the eastward, sometimes with a Raymond sprout or two in tow, coming to anchor each afternoon at about five, as was his custom, so that he might be rowed ashore for a stretch of the legs on good old Mother Earth. The Commodore was very particular about yachting etiquette, and in this ritual of going to and from ship, being the owner, he was the last to enter his launch and on the return the first to board the gangway.

Iroquois was a lovely, white clipper-bow schooner with a long pole bowsprit, designed by A. Cary Smith and launched in 1886. Ed, one of Mrs. Raymond's boys, took his first cruise with Uncle Henry aboard of her in 1897 when he was six: "When the command 'Ready About' was given, I was to run to the companionway, in order not to be trampled upon by the crew."[2]

It was on one of his early cruises that the balding bachelor who carried off a Teddy Roosevelt mix of dash and derring-do, lost his heart to the heart of Eastern Point. The eventuality of a safe anchorage behind the beginning

breakwater certainly conjured in him the vision of the Point as the eastern station of the Seawanhaka.

Rouse had traveled with General Nelson A. Miles, when, in 1895, as commander-in-chief of the army the famous Indian fighter represented the United States at Queen Victoria's Jubilee and visited the theater of war between Turkey and Greece. They were acquainted through the Shermans of Cleveland, Mrs. Miles's family, and this tour may be the inspiration for the perhaps apocryphal version of James Nugent, a later employee at "The Ramparts," of how Rouse closed the deal on his estate:

While taking his ease in the men's bar of the Shepard Hotel in Cairo the Commodore fell into conversation with a fellow American who proved to be Roswell Burchard. Further exploration uncovered that he was a trustee of the Eastern Point Associates and that a substantial acreage of their prime land was for sale to the right party. The property—if coincidence will stand the stretch—was the very land that he had had his eye on, and Rouse forthwith satisfied his chance companion that he was indeed the man they had been waiting for. They cabled their respective stateside agents to consummate the deal, shook hands heartily over a round of Shepard's special and resumed their separate travels.

Or so Jimmy Nugent's story goes.

Equally as credible in the management of this bargain would be the fine hand of John Greenough of the walrus mustaches, for he was a specialist in the merging of railroads and a close friend of Henry Rouse whom he twitted jocularly with building his castle inside a fort to protect himself from the unmarried ladies of Massachusetts.

"The Ramparts" was manorial, nay, baronial in conception, a fitting country seat for a Baron of the Rails, set inside a reconstructed U.S. Army fort, commanding a peninsula, guarding a great harbor.

The twenty-seven-room castle (for it was no less), with its masonry first-floor walls, timber and stucco gables and dormers, and spiking chimneys, rose in sturdy, if stolid, majesty behind the enormous earthwork on Fort Hill. The whole pivoted on a massive stone tower about forty feet high, just right for sending forth showers of arrows and torrents of boiling oil. In actual fact, this battlement supported a 5,000-gallon wooden water tank that could just be seen through the crenels; it was kept filled by a steam pump from a twenty-five-foot dug well that gave way after a couple of years to one that was drilled precisely 294 feet, 4 inches, through what the driller claimed was solid granite and yielded, allegedly, 18,000 gallons an hour.

The floor of the battlement around the tank was drained of rain and snow through the sneering lips of four monsterish copper seahorses that clung to its stone walls. The crest was spiked with a high flagpole. When the Commodore was at the Point, and a good breeze was blowing, his quartermaster had his hands full managing the vast United States ensign that flew therefrom.

Entrance to the three inside stories of the tower was through the corresponding floors of the house (the smaller servants' wing jogged out from it, roughly parallel to the northeast ramparts). The circular rooms were seventeen feet across. At the summit was the Commodore's observation and flag room where he kept his charts, ensigns, pennants, burgees, maritime hooks and a sixty-power spotting scope. Below was the Indian Room, his bedroom that, with the adjoining Japanese Room, he furnished with the souvenirs of

Henry C. Rouse (right) with his friend John Greenough before "The Ramparts," on the edge of the future Fort Hill Avenue. (Hilda Raymond Williamson)

a Far Eastern Trip. On the ground floor was the Breakfast Room with a small round table that could be expanded with a large round top.

A stone watchtower in the Germanic style, rather smaller, was erected freestanding a few feet off the service wing. It collapsed during construction and was rebuilt with iron cross braces. Its battlement was reached by an outside spiral stair that the Commodore installed for the convenience of Bobby Miller, the harbor pilot who for years had been accustomed to climbing up on the old earthworks with his spyglass to watch for the incoming salt barques. But Captain Miller rarely, if ever, made use of the courtesy; perhaps he felt displaced and awkward in such grandeur.

In the basement of the main house Henry Clark Rouse installed a bowling alley. On the first floor, a twenty-seven-by-thirty-foot dining room finished in stained cypress paneling formed the corner between the butler's pantry in the service wing, the circular Breakfast Room and the great hall, twenty-six by thirty-five, paneled in sycamore.

This hall was dominated by an ornate fireplace, across from the entry, which was tiered with fancy, trophy-laden mantels brooded over by the somber head of a moose. The Commodore himself maintained perpetual, jaunty, unflinching watch over affairs from one wall in Wilhelm Funk's five-foot portrait of him in sporting dress with his broad-brimmed grousing hat, loose jacket, necktie tucked in his shirt, hand casually thrust in his knickers pocket. At either side were hung antique shields and crossed sabers, examples of his extensive collection of exotic weaponry.

A broad billiard table squatted in the middle of this squirearchial

moraine, as if it had been left there by an absent-minded glacier. Just outside the porch door swung a bronze Japanese gong, four feet across; when whacked robustly with its leather-nobbed hammer, it resounded beyond the gate lodge in a southerly breeze.

One might pass from the great hall through either the adjoining music room or the Commodore's private office to the social room, twenty-five feet by thirty-one feet, and thence to the screened porch at the south end of the mansion.

Eight bedrooms and three baths were on the second floor, while the third—besides its four guest rooms, bath and storerooms—contained a gymnasium fully equipped with mat, parallel bars, rings, weightlifting apparatus and the rest of the paraphernalia of the doggedly healthy.

The numerous Raymonds occupied the bulk of the house. "We all respected the Commodore's quarters," affirmed Ed Raymond, "and he always respected ours. It was an ideal arrangement."

The service wing had the usual pantry, dining room, kitchen with walk-in icebox, laundry, mending room and chambers.

From somewhere Rouse armed himself with five ancient Spanish mortars and field guns (one report had it that they came from Moro Castle in Havana—by courtesy of General Miles's foray into Cuba during the Spanish War perhaps?). The largest of the mortars, which he especially prized, was said to be a relic of Philip's sixteenth-century differences with Elizabeth. He emplaced them in the embrasures through which had peeped the thirty-two-pounders of the Eleventh Unattached Company of Heavy Artillery thirty-five years earlier, and there they reclined on their haunches, muzzles uplifted like so many toothless bulldogs. Twin bronze dogs from Korea warned the unwanted from the driveway through the earthworks, reinforced by a brace of awesome terra cotta lions who crouched at the main entrance.

In the field across Fort Hill Avenue from the Garland cottage he laid out a tennis court. He considered a small golf links but decided against it. From his entrance he cut a road that first winter that curved down the slope to join the old way to the lighthouse for a short distance, then departed and emerged at Eastern Point Boulevard behind Wharf Beach, near Indian Spring.

At the southern end of the beach toward the Stone Wharf, which in 1902 he leased for ninety-nine years from the Eastern Point Company, the Commodore put up the boat and bath house which he designated Eastern Station of Seawanhaka Corinthian Yacht Club; but his fellow Seawanhakans seldom turned up to take advantage of it.

Down the grade along his private road from "The Ramparts" toward the beach he originally planned to build his stable, sixty feet square; the location was shifted to lower ground when he found it would obstruct his view over the harbor.

Construction of "The Ramparts" was well along when one day in the middle of September 1898, the New York millionaire Howard Gould put in and brought his fast steam yacht *Niagara* to anchor in the lee of the substructure of the breakwater. The financier was conveyed ashore and driven all around Eastern Point, probably at the invitation of Commodore Rouse, who was staying at the Hawthorne Inn.

Jimmy Nugent. (Madeleine Williams)

Over the next few days all sorts of rumors flew, and it was reported that the famous yachtsman, like Henry Flagler earlier in the season, was enthusiastic about the Point and wanted to purchase a tract—if he could be assured of better facilities for reaching the property and greater privacy than was evident to him on his tour. If a deal were made, it was said, the Point would most assuredly be the eastern rendezvous of the New York Yacht Club and the finish of an annual Newport-Gloucester cup race.

Likewise, other wealthy

parties were said to be interested in buying the remaining open land of the Associates (much of which Rouse soon added to his), but they were put off by its isolation. Rouse seems to have concerned himself with this problem. He reportedly investigated short-cutting the long, dusty, crowded, twisted land route with a ferry between the Association pier and Magnolia, a scheme obviated by the advent of the automobile before it got anywhere.

It was proposed that autumn to connect Eastern Point by way of the Back Shore and a $12,000 road back of Good Harbor Beach to the Joppa Road and thence to a projected summer stop on the Boston and Maine Railroad at Beaver Dam. Rouse surely pushed the new way station, for it came to pass in 1905—a slight favor, probably, from the management of the B & M for the president and chairman of the M, K & T.

President Rouse arrived with the Raymonds and selected servants each season after he was settled, first in his private car

Captain Howard Jensen, quartermaster. (Josie Boyer)

Number 36, later in Number 99. The B & M left the car at the Gloucester depot, where the travelers would be met by his carriage (he shipped his horses separately) which the Commodore kept in a rented stable at Freshwater Cove. Number 36 got around; one winter when he was down with the whooping cough Ed Raymond was taken in her by Uncle Henry way down to Tarpon Island, Texas, outside Corpus Christi.

Commodore Rouse had instructed his architect and builder that he expected "The Ramparts" to be ready for occupancy by May 1, 1899. That his domicile, like his railroads, proceeded on schedule is suggested by an item concerning his quartermaster, Captain Howard Jensen, that found its way some years later into *The Setting Sun*, a news sheet got up by the youngsters on the Point:

> Captain Jensen says that before he came to Eastern Point he was first mate on a Norwegian square rigger. He went through the Straits of Magellan. He also traded with the Indians in southern South America. He says that the Indians' canoes were made out of a single strip of bark, sewed together with rushes. They wore skins of animals. After Captain Jensen rounded the Horn, he went back to New York. The trip was very rough. He came to Eastern Point on a Yacht on May 7th, 1899.

That yacht was the auxiliary brigantine *Satanella*, which Rouse chartered in 1899 after selling *Iroquois*. He had decided to retain only one of the two quartermasters he employed, and he asked the young Raymonds to make the choice; they elected Captain Jensen.

The manner of her father's arrival in America was recounted in some more detail a lifetime later by Jensen's daughter Jenny, a very definite retired schoolmarm living in East Gloucester:

> In the late 1800s my father, Halvar Strandmyr, who had been working with the U.S. Navy in a geodetic survey of the northern Pacific coasts of Washington and Oregon, took passage in a brig, sailed around Cape Horn, and landed in New York harbor.
>
> When he applied for a landing visa, carrying his records with him, the officer asked for his name.
>
> "Strandmyr," answered Father.
>
> "What's that?" said the official.
>
> "S-T-R-A-N-D-M-Y-R, from Kragero, Norway. I am a Norwegian," said Father.
>
> "Who could spell that! We'll call you Jensen," and so the landing visa was made out to a Norwegian named Jensen. Fru Strandmyr, who sent home knitted woolen things for her grandchildren in cold New England, wondered why her son's family were called Jensen.
>
> In 1906 the Navy records were translated into citizenship papers and Strandmyr Jensen became an American citizen. His four children born in East Gloucester had claimed that right from birth.[3]

Gardening at "The Ramparts." (Madeleine Williams)

With the rolling, slightly bowlegged gait of the lifelong sailor, Howard (Halvar) Jensen was a master mariner, a true salt and the great favorite with all ages. The Rouse sloops *Olita* and *Edjako,* the launch *Mistral*, and others of his fleet that came and went were among the QM's special cares.

The master of "The Ramparts" was obsessed with flag protocol, another domain of Jensen's. Most important of all, of course, the huge U.S. ensign must be flying from the house staff on the water tower when the Commodore was in residence. Then, as Ed Raymond recalled, "he would hoist the private signal, near the boathouse. Then go to the end of the pier to hoist the Seawanhaka burgee on the main flag staff. Then the U.S. yacht ensign (thirteen stars around a fouled anchor) at the gaff. Then there was still another burgee to be hoisted aboard *Edjako*. At sunset the entire process had to be reversed.

Colors were supposed to be at 8 A.M. and at sunset. It kept Howard pretty busy, just taking care of the colors."[4]

Whenever he was on *Mistral,* naturally, the Commodore's private signal must be at the jack staff. And aboard the big yacht, well, Captain Jensen was as busy as a one-man band with the flag halyards.

(In later years the climb to the tower got to be too much for him, and Henry Williams, the Williams family chauffeur, took over the house flag. "One morning I carelessly pulled the wrong halyard and up it went with the union down. I had no sooner got down to the breakfast room when the waitress dashed in to tell me that the Coast Guard called up to know if 'The Ramparts' was sinking and needed assistance. So up we go again and pull the right halyard, and a left-handed blessing to the bosun's mate.")

Fresh produce daily from the garden of "The Ramparts." (Madeleine Williams)

When he wasn't tending the colors, teaching the young Raymonds how to tie knots, managing the Rouse fleet, taking care of "The Ramparts" and doing odd favors for the neighbors, Howard could be found polishing the ten-foot shiny brass stack of the naphtha launch. *Mistral* really ran on hot air, and at such ambling gait that it could be made to go ahead or astern simply by grabbing the wooden flywheel in midrevolution and flipping it in the desired direction.

Late in August of his first season on the Point, 1899, Rouse tried to promote another Gloucester fishermen's race. The most recent and celebrated had come off seven years earlier as the climax of the city's 250th anniversary celebration; it was sailed by the fastest vessels in the fleet at the whistling height of a northeast gale and was engraved in the annals of the sea as "The Race that Blew."

The Commodore proposed to revive the race as an annual event, to be sailed over the same course outside the Point. He offered a first prize of $250, and a second of $100, on the condition that at least ten schooners cross the starting line. Date: Saturday, September 9. And he would charter a steamer for the spectators.

The proposal fell flat. No takers, no race, and nothing more heard of it. Maybe the prize money was insufficient incentive to stay home from fishing, or the notice was too short, or too many starters were required. Or it could be that the fishermen took their usual jaundiced view of any suggestion that was not native born.

Nothing daunted in his determination to extend the hand of friendship to the population of his adopted summer seat, the squire of "The

Ramparts" donated $100 to the Fishermen's and Seamen's Widows' and Orphans' Aid Society and $25 to the Fishermen's Institute, as deferentially reported in the *Advertiser*. He then departed on Car Number 36 for Cleveland.

But he would have his race. Next season, 1900, Commodore Rouse chartered from her British owners the magnificent snow-white auxiliary brigantine *Lady Godiva*. Even as the clipper ships, she carried studdingsail booms rigged on her main yard, and she was a thrilling sight before the wind. Ed Raymond, age nine, was aboard that summer for a cruise from Eastern Point to Oyster Bay, where Uncle Henry arranged a match race with Arthur Curtiss James, then S.C.Y.C. commodore and owner of the equally stunning black brigantine *Aloha*, built the previous year. Sixty-nine years later Ed recalled it:

> You can imagine the sight when they tacked ship in this race, hauling the yards around. Instead of a spinnaker, we had a studdingsail (stuns'l). It was made of silk. My first experience at yacht racing, we actually set a studdingsail. To make a long story short, *Lady Godiva* was the winner.[5]

Something was always doing around the estate. Rouse cut bridle paths, "the galloping roads," through the woods toward the lighthouse, and his gardeners tended two vegetable plots, one on the high ground and another in the boggy area below the woods as reserve during the dry spells. Sometimes deer were seen in the forest; it was thought they swam across the harbor from the main in the spring and back again before winter.

He kept ponies and carts for the Raymond children and their friends, a couple of Western horses for riding, a team for the farm work, and a carriage horse and two carriages (open and closed, as the weather dictated) and a buggy. And each spring his men bought two or three cows "in the milk" and disposed of them in the fall.

Toward the end of 1905 he made various improvements at "The Ramparts," including a bathroom that the newspaper, beside itself with wonderment, reported had cost $10,000. And as Pilot Miller had chosen not to take his stand atop the watchtower with the spiral ramp, Rouse built for him that winter a snug cottage on the ledge hard by the lighthouse, intending to make it available to Bobby and his family as long as he had his license. The pilot could watch for the vessels from his bedroom window and moor his sloop inside the nearly finished breakwater.

They called this aerie "Mother Ann Cottage" after the familiar stone profile of the old lady reclining in the ledge that Captain William Thompson, a retired Salem shipmaster, claimed to have discovered and certainly named while he was staying at East Gloucester in September 1891, a find disputed by John V. Lewis, across the cove, who had known the old girl since he came to the Point, and by Freeman Hodsdon, the East Gloucester grocer, who claimed a twenty years' acquaintance.

Ah, but the spiritual essence of Mother Ann—"carved of God's

angels"—awaited her discovery by Alex Tupper in the *North Shore Breeze* a generation later. "The old woman creates deep, poetic feeling, peering as she does to seaward, as if searching for the sails and the brave men who have departed never to return. Such perfect features, even to eyelashes, are outlined. The sea beats its melodies at her feet and the spray rests like tears upon her wrinkled cheek."[6]

"The Ramparts," with stables beyond. (Edward Williams)

Commodore Rouse spent four days at Eastern Point inspecting the progress of his projects in February 1906. On the thirtieth of April Uncle Henry died at his home in Cleveland, after a losing battle with pneumonia. He was fifty-three.

Commodore Rouse welcomes guests in the entrance hall of "The Ramparts."
(Madeleine Williams)

~24~

MRS. RAYMOND'S REGIME

COMMODORE (UNCLE HENRY) ROUSE left "The Ramparts" to the old friend who had managed his bachelor households for him in Cleveland and Gloucester, Mrs. Emma Raymond. Beyond her lifetime, the estate was left to two of her sons, Edward and Jonathan.

Besides Ed and Jack there were four more Raymond children—Henry, Hilda, Mary and Julia—and from Miss Julia comes a memorandum of the days when these youngsters and their summer friends on Eastern Point were rampant in and out of "The Ramparts" within the omniscient purview of its mistress, their mother:

> The Kay and Barwick girls swam from the float off the beach, where I was introduced to them. They jumped into the water, and I shut my eyes and followed. That splash was the beginning of years of friendship.
>
> Sailing, picnicking on the rocks, swimming, walking around the Point after tea, exploring the woods, fields and rocks—eating wild cherries and sugar plums—we longed for something to happen to prevent our going back to school in the autumn. Many friends coming and going at "The Ramparts" and always that friendly window seat, and plenty of girls in the Kay house.
>
> At that time there was no electricity on the Point. We used kerosene lamps, and every night each one took a candle from the stair landing to light the bedroom. Of course, there were no automobiles, and a day's shopping in the city required great planning for the use of the horses. When automobiles were first seen in Gloucester, they were required to stop at the gate lodge, where a telephone was installed, and we could be notified and send down a horse-drawn vehicle to bring the visitors to the house. [In the early days nonresident autos were banned entirely from the Point,

then later from beyond the second gate lodge at the corner of Eastern Point Boulevard and Toronto Avenue.]

Gymnastics, tennis tournaments, softball, baseball at "The Ramparts." On rainy days long walks to Bass Rocks and return to a hot fire and tea. Charades in the Kay house. I remember once the dining room table turned into a stage coach, Henry Raymond and numerous girls sitting in chairs on top of it. Edward and Jack Raymond, little boys, were the only children playing on the beach in those days.

Miss Beaux [Cecilia Beaux, the portraitist, who built "Green Alley" on the harbor in 1906] rented the Calef house. She swam with one foot on the bottom, but after instructions by the Kay girls barely took her foot off and began to swim.

The Ramparts family began to expand. Hilda, Madeleine, Teddy and Mollie Williams came to spend their summers with their grandmother. A pony and pony cart were added to the stable where Uncle Ed's Winton frightened the horses but made pleasant driving for the elders [this was Ed Stone, one of Mrs. Raymond's two bachelor brothers whom she persistently but unsuccessfully tried to maneuver into marriage].

Midge and Emmy Raymond with Carlo on the lawn in front of the "Ramparts" stable. (Madeleine Williams)

There was a big stable not far from the Kay house where their horses were kept. However, Mr. and Mrs. John Greenough walked, carrying a lantern, when they came to dinner at "The Ramparts." Mr. Greenough knew about boats ("don't cher know") and was the first Commodore of the Eastern Point Yacht Club [tall and distinguished, with his great mustaches, described as invariably clad in a blue serge suit and red necktie], and Mrs. Johnnie knew the art of conversing when she had nothing to say—

"Anyone can talk about a subject, few can chatter intelligently."

Captain Bailey seemed to delight to have us climb the lighthouse stairs to see the beautiful light, with its prisms shining with all the colors of the rainbow. Mother Ann, the wonderful rock shaped like a woman near the lighthouse, was shown to all our visitors.[1]

Julia's sister Mary married Edward Williams of Cleveland, son of a founder of the Sherwin-Williams Paint Company, and their son Edward and daughter Madeleine had very decided memories of childhood summers whose character and course were guided in no uncertain terms by her maternal grandmother.

But first their grandfather, Samuel Atwater Raymond, of a Connecticut family that went west to Ohio, acquired land in Cleveland and throve on rising values, as recalled by Edward P. Williams in his memoir, *A Varied Career:*

Mrs. Raymond patrolling for dandelions. (Edward Williams)

The story is told that Grandfather's middle name should have been Augustine or maybe Augustus but the minister at the time of the christening who was hard of hearing thought the family said Atwater. Thus the chance to weave a very distinguished name into the family ancestry, which might have led some to pursue lineage from Caesar Augustus himself, failed.

Grandfather was short and rotund with a prominent mustache. He was frequently taken for William Howard Taft. He was a successful manager of a wholesale dry goods business in Cleveland. Grandfather loved to drive horses. The Ramparts stable contained all sorts of carriages, station wagons, buck boards, phaetons, etc. The horses were "Texas Ponies." These were small horses which had been tralned for polo, but for one reason or another had not made the grade, or had become too old to continue polo. So they were retrained for regular driving or riding and sold at reduced prices. Grandfather had them hitched as a team or, on rare occasions, in tandem.

It was a real treat to be invited to accompany him on one of his driving expeditions. When I was ten or twelve, he asked me to go driving with him. I sat beside him in the two-wheeled buckboard. When we came to a hill, he would always churrp and touch them lightly with a whip whereupon they would break into a gallop. I

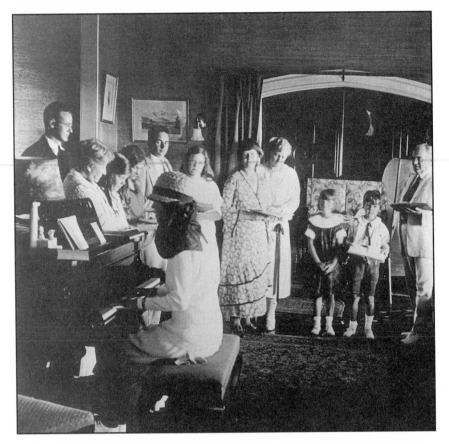

The music room at "The Ramparts" with Pauline Pollard Raymond veiled at the piano and (left to right) her husband Jack Raymond, Mrs. Raymond, Sr., Midge Raymond, Molly and Ted Williams, Emmy Raymond, Mrs. Mary Raymond Williams, "Aunt Bertha" Stockwell (a family friend), Pauline and Jock Raymond, and Edward Williams, Sr. (Madeleine Williams)

remember him saying "you may gallop a horse up hill but always walk them down hill because it is bad for their knees to run them down hill."

When he presided at The Ramparts, I can remember only one conversation. We were sitting around the breakfast table one sunny morning when news came of the outbreak of war in Europe. "Without any question, we'll be in it sooner or later," he said. Since he died in February 1915, this conversation must have taken place at the very beginning of World War I—July 1914. I consider this to be a very prophetic statement. There was very little enthusiasm for America's entrance into the war until the *Lusitania* was sunk in 1915 after Grandfather had died."[2]

The matron of "The Ramparts" for nearly half a century was a person of simple tastes, a Philadelphian who moved to Cleveland when she was sixteen. Her maiden name was Emma Eugenie Stone. Her parents died when she was quite young. It was Mrs. Raymond's unvarying routine each June to send her car ahead and to travel to Boston with available members of her family by train (no more private cars after Uncle Henry's death). There was invariably an upper berth for Teddy Williams in a stateroom shared with his sisters. Continuing from his *A Varied Life:*

After some disastrous experiences, Grandmother insisted that all children remain in bed until we had traversed the Berkshires. Some of us had acquired the habit of becoming actively ill as the train wound its way over the curvaceous tracks climbing and descending the Berkshires. Grandmother had given me a Saint Bernard which made the trip all the more exciting, because Carlo had to be chained to a post in the baggage car amidst dozens of trunks. When I became old enough, I was allowed to get off at Buffalo, Utica, Albany or wherever the train stopped in order to take Carlo for a walk. People stood back in awe as Carlo lifted his leg to relieve himself against the side of the dining car window

Upon arriving at the South Station in Boston we would be met by Goodale, Grandmother's chauffeur, who would whisk us to the Copley Plaza in the Winton limousine for luncheon. As a youngster, I could not understand why Goodale was called by his last name. I discovered that his first name was Herman. I called him Herman one day while riding to town with Grandmother. She didn't like that.

Then followed the two-hour trip to Gloucester through the winding shore road (now route 127), crossing and recrossing the Boston and Maine tracks as we passed through Lynn, Salem, Beverly, Prides Crossing, Beverly Farms, Manchester, Magnolia and finally Gloucester. Excitement all the way. Who could see the first white horse? Who would first smell the sea air? Who would first smell fish? Then finally the first glimpse of "The Ramparts" with Howard Jensen standing at the entrance patiently waiting to greet us.

The dawn of each new day at "The Ramparts" was proclaimed by Mrs. Raymond herself with a ringing whack on the great Japanese gong at precisely eight, the prescribed time of rising; in case this was not sufficient to rouse the denizens of the third-floor bedrooms, it was reinforced with the clatter of a lesser bell up there, palpitated by remote control; this alarm catapulted the younger generations from their beds into an impatient pile-up before the bathroom door.

At 8:30 the gong was struck again for breakfast, at one for lunch, and at five sharp for tea. The tea gong was the most peremptory summons of all, gathering the clan from the far corners of the Point in the dress and condition of the moment. One was expected to drop what one was doing (unless becalmed, racing, in the middle of the harbor) and arrive on the fly—sweaty from tennis, windswept from sailing, horsey from riding or sandy and adrip from the beach.

Mrs. Raymond reigned with commanding equanimity from her throne-like chair in the great hall. Before her ample form was parked the tea wagon from which she dispensed cakes, cookies and a variety of other goodies with fine impartiality from three tiers of shelves—and tea, of course, from the

Inside the redoubt, his Grandmother Raymond maintains an appraising stance as Teddy Williams goes for the stake on the croquet field trod sixty years earlier by feet less genteel. (Madeleine Williams)

upper deck. Since this was suppertime for the nursemaids, babes and fry unto the fourth generation were let free, and a few could always be sensed crawling around under the vastness of the billiard table, banging their heads, all intermingled with their begging St. Bernard, Carlo.

Seven was the moment of the dinner gong, precise and on the hour with but two exceptions: when the regular post-teatime croquet game for which Mrs. Raymond had a fondness was running overtime, and when she felt moved to listen to her favorite radio program, "Amos 'n Andy." If the races had been hard fought that afternoon (she sometimes watched them from an upper window), the participants might sail them over again after the table had been cleared, penciling their tacking duels on the sea of cloth and arguing the matter hotly, to her amusement.

The male ritual of the evening dictated pool at the billiard table, now and then joined in by the ladies, who more often favored a few hands of Russian Bank; or perhaps Mrs. Raymond would remove with her daughters to the screen porch to contemplate the sawing of the crickets and the whoosh of the distant surf and the sparking of the fireflies in the darkness of the old redoubt.

In her younger days Grandmother Raymond taught her grandchildren tennis. And running: she mandated "RRR" (Run Round "The Ramparts"), everyone's time posted. But she loved good food and grew so heavy in her old age as to make hard work of it keeping all that active herself.

Emma Raymond was not given to emotional profusion. She ran her manor with benign firmness. Her command post was in the hall, where cook conferred with her each morning and whence were implemented through the domestic hierarchy her decisions concerning the internal and external operations of the estate. She entertained in a dignified and restrained manner; regularly the summer weekly *Cape Ann Shore* informed the world that "sixteen covers were laid" (or however many) for a luncheon or dinner party at "The Ramparts."

Her success in buttressing "The Ramparts" as a sanctum sanctorum is illustrated in one incident recalled by her daughter, Mrs. Hilda Williamson. A fishing boat missed the whistler one night and went up on the ledges west of Brace Cove. One of the Italian crew, who could speak almost no English, managed to gain shore, came running up Fort Hill Avenue, and pounded on the door of "The Ramparts," yelling "Help! Help!" A maid answered, and not understanding the exact nature of the trouble, called the Gloucester fire department. After more words and gestures, the fisherman was able to get his plight across to her: he wanted to call for help on the telephone.

Just then the maid heard the approaching sirens. In a panic, the poor thing rushed out the door, through the earthworks entrance, along the drive and down Fort Hill Avenue to intercept the engines, waving her arms and screaming breathlessly: "Stop! Stop! Go back! Turn around! You'll wake up Mrs. Raymond!"

Religiously correct in the old-fashioned way, Emma Raymond conducted prayers every Sunday morning for twenty minutes, and attendance

Archie the pony poised to take Ted Williams and the faithful Carlo for a ride. (Edward Williams)

was mandatory before an assumption of the pursuits and pleasures of the day. As grandson Ted Williams well remembers:

> Each person attending would choose a hymn followed by a biblical passage such as the 13th Chapter of Corinthians, Lord's Prayer, Beatitudes, 19th psalm, or whatever. Sunday services were fun. In the evening we would gather again, each choosing a hymn but this time more appropriately attuned to the setting sun, like "Now the Day is Over" or "Crossing the Bar," a hymn that is seldom sung today except at funerals.

If she did not by intention direct the raising of her grandchildren and great-grandchildren, the firmness of her presence as the wellspring of this large family all gathered under one roof each summer (large as that roof was) had a certain inescapable impact on their lifestyles. Before the grudging acceptance of the automobile on the Point provided the means of ducking out from under now and then, a paper was left on the billiard table and the young ones were expected to sign in when they had been out after hours.

South view of
"The Ramparts."
(Madeleine
Williams)

Grandmother Raymond's door was ajar, to keep track of these nocturnal returns.

Henry Williams, the Williams family chauffeur, first came to "The Ramparts" in 1906, the spring of Commodore Rouse's death, when he was twenty-two. He had been employed as a machinist, building and road-testing vehicles in a Cleveland automobile factory, and when Edward Williams, Mrs. Raymond's son-in-law, bought a Stearnes Knight, Henry was loaned to him by the company for a week to teach him how to drive it, then for another week to accustom the ladies to riding in it, and he just never went back to the factory. The trip that spring from Ohio to Gloucester was like the trek of the covered wagons in reverse. Changing a tire was torture, oft repeated, and so abysmal were the mudholes it took chains, ropes, pulley and all the ingenuity and strength of man, and sometimes beast, to get out of them.

Henry Williams, the Williams family chauffeur, man of all work and confidant. (Edward Williams)

That November the Rouse stable burned to the ground in what was believed to be arson, as a man was seen hurrying from the scene before the flames burst out. There always lingered some question in the mind of Henry Williams about how adequately "The Ramparts" was equipped to cope with fire, considering the distance of the East Gloucester station. On the face of it well enough, perhaps, for a very large chemical extinguisher on wheels was kept up by the house in the summer; but the only time after the stable fire that it was ever needed, when a small blaze broke out in the woods, it was discovered to be out of chemical. Henry cogitated that it wouldn't have been much help anyway, since it took four strong men to haul it. They put out the brush fire with a bucket brigade.

Mrs. Raymond was remembered by Henry Williams as a large, efficient, very positive dowager. Mr. Raymond might proclaim, but his spouse ever prevailed. Her summer menage numbered close to thirty servants whose disputes she adjudicated with Portian justice and whose far-flung activities (and lapses) were immediately and intimately known to her, apparently by some extrasensory means that baffled them all. Ted Williams in his memoir ticks off her executive routine:

> Every morning at precisely 9 o'clock, Nugent the superintendent would appear to review the day's work. Nugent was in charge of a work force of 6 or 8 to care for two vegetable gardens, milk the cows, care for the farm horses, the riding horses, and pony.
>
> Then came Howard Jensen in charge of boats, followed by Goodale the chauffeur.
>
> Every Wednesday she would vary shopping routine by having Howard transport her to downtown Gloucester in the launch *Mistral*. Beside her sat Carlo our St. Bernard towering over her. On

the way home Carlo would be given an ice cream cone which he would consume without demolishing the cone itself.

Besides Captain Jensen, caretaker, and Jimmy Nugent, superintendent, Henry and another chauffeur and Jensen's assistant and Ed Marble, the houseman, all lived in quarters over the rebuilt stable. Then there was a crew of men working around the grounds from spring through fall, many of them Irishmen who lived in Gloucester; Nugent would pick up and return the older ones daily in the buggy. In the domestic service were cook and helper, resident laundress and four maids, most of these courtesy of Miss Liddell's Agency in Boston.

It had long been whispered among her staff that Mrs. Raymond rose at the crack of dawn, hours before her gong had set the sleepyheads afoot, puled on her bathing suit and tramped down the path to the beach for a dip and a chat about matters of mutual interest with her close friend from Quarry Point, Mrs. James Murray Kay. Yet none had witnessed this sunrise meeting of the matriarchs, and so Henry Williams determined to check it out.

Setting his alarm clock, he awoke one morning at 5 A.M., peered up the road from his window over the stable, and, scarcely believing his eyes, here comes Mrs. Raymond in her swimsuit and bathrobe. After allowing her time to pass, he followed at a safe distance.

And there, sure enough, as he parted the beach briers and squinted through, were Mesdames Raymond and Kay in animated conversation, heads and shoulders bobbing in the glacial water of the cove, for they were both well fixed for flotation.

Did, in fact, Mrs. Raymond "swim"? Her grandson Ted thinks otherwise.

Mrs. J. Murray Kay heads for the water at Raymond's Landing, 1907. (Lila Leonard Swift)

Grandmother taught me how to swim though she could not swim herself. One morning as she was, I thought, swimming in water just over my head, I noticed she had one foot on the ground while she pretended to teach the breaststroke to me. Her favorite bathing companion was a neighbor, Mrs. Kay. They were both quite corpulent. Although they couldn't swim they could float. One day engaging in serious discussion, while floating, the wind and tide blew them to waters way over their head. Howard, ever on the alert, manned the rowboat, and gently towed them back to the beach.

Late each August her staff was given a fortnight's notice of her departure date, and all was expected to be in readiness by then, because Mrs. Raymond invariably returned to Ohio early in September.

Her daughters tried every device to persuade her to remain at the Point just a little longer, but tears and pleas were of no avail. Her personal servants left by auto in advance to reopen the Cleveland house, and the mistress of "The Ramparts" and her entourage motored to Boston and departed for winter quarters, as they had arrived in June, on the Pullman.

"Auntie Em" Harvy, Mrs. Raymond, "Auntie May" Bainbridge, and four friends. (Edward Williams)

George Stacy's Colonial Arms — 300 feet, 300 rooms, and impressive from every vantage.
(E. L. Blatchford photo, Gordon Thomas collection)

~25~
THE COLONIAL ARMS

WHEN GENIAL GEORGE STACY TOOK a notion to make a move in the hotel line, he thought BIG. No string of boarding houses for him. He and Ed Parsons had built the bold Moorland Hotel challenging the Atlantic at Bass Rocks, and the ponderous Magnolia Hotel, and his proliferative Hawthorne Inn sprawled over the East Gloucester shore. From there Stacy could gaze across Niles Beach toward a broad brow of ledge beyond the tree-shaded Niles farmhouse on Eastern Point, and he coveted it.

The Eastern Point Associates had by no means abandoned the belief that a resort hotel was just what they needed to round out their colony and relieve them of some of their unsold land, notwithstanding that Henry Clark Rouse had bought their original choice for its site and built "The Ramparts" on it.

In October 1901 Stacy bought Lot 101 from Joseph Brannon of Cincinnati, one of the original purchasers of land from the Associates; it was next toward Gloucester from Henry Scott's cottage, then owned by Nathaniel Gorton. This generated some more dickering, and on January 2, 1902, the hotel man acquired the remaining three lots between Gorton's and the Niles farmhouse, subject to the usual prohibitions against commercial building until May 1, 1917, unless the Associates granted exceptions.

This they obviously did, for Stacy kept on accumulating land—several more acres across the road from Niles Pond and a lengthy stretch of Niles Beach on the other side of the farmhouse. At the end of July in 1903 he announced that work would soon commence on the "Colonial Hotel" practically at the water's edge a spit beyond the farmhouse; deckloads of lumber were already arriving at the Association pier.

Stacy conceived that this greatest of the great would be three and a half stories in the shape of an angular crescent, with 175 rooms, three to a bath, a dining room opening out on both sides and a roof garden. A variety of guest houses à la Hawthorne would be clustered about, with a casino, tea house, bathing pavilion on Niles Beach with hot and cold running water,

and a spacious stable. There would be regular automobile transportation from the street railway stop at Rocky Neck, and a ferry to town, touching at the Hawthorne.

As usual with Stacy, it was all he touted and more—in this case quite a lot more. The Colonial Arms, as its proprietor ended up calling it, opened to an awed clientele on Saturday the twenty-fifth of June, 1904. Instead of a mere 175 rooms, the total had swollen to around 300, and the three and a half stories first planned to four and a half, or five, depending on whether you counted the top floor under the mansard roofs of the wings, or six, if you included the observation deck on the main section with its breathtaking views.

As usual, he was carried away by his enthusiasm, doubtless causing contractor John W. Day of Gloucester to throw down his blueprints (to the extent that George ever used any) in despair.

Architecturally this extraordinary structure was a mishmash with a colonial facade of sorts, 300 feet long, 60 feet deep, doglegged in approximate conformity with the shoreline and more or less symmetrical except for the flat-roofed service wing, which halted 100 feet short of the Niles farmhouse and contained the kitchen, laundry, storerooms and living quarters for employees, 125 of whom were on hand. The roofs were studded with dormers, surely 75 of them, and a double-decked veranda girt most of the periphery of the first and second floors.

The main entrance was undeniably striking. A truly imposing portico rose to the fourth floor, supported by four immense Doric columns at least thirty-five feet in height and flanked by tiers of balconies; out from under projected a nicely arched and colonnaded one-story porte cochere. An oddly gratuitous mate to this portico was appended for no apparent reason, esthetic or functional, to the end of the west wing.

Passing through the carriage entrance, the guests found themselves in the grand lobby with a view out over the harbor that was a knockout. This great hall was decorated in "antique and modern design"—that is, well endowed with rockers, tables, sofas, "set-in Colonial seats," a piano, Stacy's collection of choice antiques, capacious fireplaces and the other appurtenances of a New England ark of the period, all done up in a green and white color scheme, white muslin draperies, walls papered with dark burlap and adorned with paintings loaned by the well-known Gloucester artist A. W. Bühler.

The dining room and grill in the east wing continued the green theme. To get to the ballroom in the west wing (two shades of green), one walked through the morning room, papered in grey-blue burlap with pale yellow furnishings and muslin drapes. And there were reading, writing and reference rooms, a newsstand and "toilet parlors."

Seventy-five shared bathrooms (each suite with its own bath, toilet, sleeping and sitting rooms), a telephone in nearly every room, and every one with a view of either the harbor or across Niles Pond to the ocean. It cost the owner $159,000 to build, and with fittings and furnishings he had $230,000 tied up in his latest investment.

George Stacy put a chap named Wing, his assistant at the Moorland, in charge, hired a six-piece orchestra to give three concerts a day and apologized that the elevator wasn't running yet due to a strike of the installers. His first gala was the next Tuesday, when the Essex Republican Club assembled from every corner of the county for its annual outing and to heed the bidding of Senator Henry Cabot Lodge.

Commencing the Fourth of July, Captain Johnnie Foster had his steam ferry *Columbia* on a regular summer circuit of the Association pier, the Hawthorne Inn wharf and the East Gloucester ferry landing from which it embarked beginning at 7:30 A.M. every hour on the half hour through the evening. Sundays Stacy rented the *Colonial,* a 30-foot gasoline launch, to transport the overflow, and Jim Walen, whom he hired to run it, was busy taking guests back and forth to church over town.

Stacy's original intention had been to own his newest hotel solo, but his need for capital (perhaps overextended by his weakness for escalation) forced him to incorporate. To all appearances, the Colonial Arms was a smashing success from the day it opened. He had already made his reputation at forty-four, and this was the heyday of the spa when entire families traveled great distances to return year after year to spend their vacations at their favorite summer hotels. His location was superb, and his guests had absolute privacy, from the public if not from each other.

After overseeing the first season's operation himself, Stacy leased the hotel to H. W. Priest and Company for five years from 1905, reportedly for $15,000 a year. Priest was also manager of the Beach Bluff Hotel at Swampscott, and he installed Joseph A. Sherrard of Medford, who ran a winter inn in South Carolina, as manager of the Colonial Arms.

Eastern Point's hotel was recognized as the largest and most sumptuous on the North Shore behind the overwhelming Oceanside in Magnolia, and it was solidly booked from the start. With the automobile rage sweeping the countryside it quickly became such a mecca for motoring parties on Sundays and holidays that Stacy gladly built a large garage complex at the fork in the road across from Niles Pond, and the Associates in some irritation put up a second, small gate lodge of stone in the opposite fork of Eastern Point Boulevard and Toronto Avenue and posted a keeper there to draw tighter the *cordon sanitaire* around the innermost sancti of the inner sanctum.

It lasted four seasons.

A few minutes after six in the evening of New Year's Day, 1908, young Eva Douglass rushed into one of the barrack houses on Locust Lane screaming at the top of her lungs that the Colonial Arms was on fire.

Dr. Herbert Morrow picked up the cry and ran to the gate lodge, where caretaker Ernest Dean phoned the East Gloucester engine house, and then he raced off and pulled Box 5. Minutes later the steamers *N. M. Jackman* and *Defiance* were hurtling down the road to the Point.

It had started in the extreme end of the west wing and was going blazes when the steamers arrived. In the absence of hydrants the *Jackman* took a position on the shore of Niles Pond; *Defiance* pumped from the curve in the road by the Niles farmhouse; and when the steamer *W. H. T. Jameson* arrived in response to the second alarm it was berthed alongside the *Jackman* at the pond.

Chief Engineer Charley Crowe was in such a rush to make the scene that he just grabbed at the nearest helmet handy, which happened to be his derby hat; he wore it through the night directing his men in what all could see from the start would be a futile effort. The chief called for the fireboat *Philip*, which soon churned up to the hotel landing and pumped in two streams from the harbor.

By seven the wind had shifted fatally full on from the southwest; from this quarter it raked the length of the cavernous frame building, pushing the fire before it as if it had been planned that way—as some thought it had. A squad of firemen gained the roof but were driven off.

When the flames broke through the west roof, the suddenly released updraft carried a shower of sparks eastward to settle in the dry grass over several acres, flecking the meadows as far as the lifesaving station at Brace Cove with brush fires like "an army camp field with its numerous bivouacs."[1] A few of the row of bathhouses at the edge of Brace Beach were in this way destroyed.

Now the whole town knew the Colonial Arms was uncontrollably on fire. It lit the sky. Eastern Point seemed a mass of flames, and the harbor

The Colonial Arms from the harbor. (E. L. Blatchford photo, Gordon Thomas collection, Cape Ann Historical Association)

shimmered red. People could feel the heat clear across on Pavilion Beach and declared they could read the fine print in the newspaper by the light of it. Thousands left their homes on the run and clogged the road to the Point by foot, bike, buggy and auto. Hundreds more jumped in their boats and rowed and chugged over, and the landing from which the *Philip* was belching clouds of smoke and steam was soon surrounded by a fleet of dories and small boats.

A silent multitude gathered on the rise to the windward of the burning behemoth, held back, hypnotized, by the heat. Thousands more lined the harbor shore and took to the heights above it. The bay was a colossal stadium, made to order for George Stacy's greatest spectacular.

One of the two west chimneys collapsed in a barrage of bricks. The upper floors buckled and disgorged bathtubs into the ruins. Flights of sparks and gobs of smoke soared up and off. The flames raced through the elevator and stairwells, pushed by the wind, and the more they ate the bigger they grew.

"A magnificent sight," wrote a shaken reporter—"awful, inspiring and appalling in its supreme grandeur and destructiveness."[2]

For a time it threatened to ignite the handsome house that Dr. James H. Knowles of East Gloucester had built in 1904, the year of his marriage,[3] 300 yards to the leeward above Niles Beach; but his townsmen and their steamer soaked and saved it, and doused the brush fires by the dozen.

It was a wonder to all that the Niles farmhouse (recently purchased by Manager Sherrard), only 100 feet from the blazing east wing, didn't catch. The pumpers kept it drenched, but it was the shift of the wind and the flames that saved it.

At 8:45 the west fire wall caved in, and in fifteen more minutes the east one. Then the main portico fell apart with a thundering crash when the spectacular columns toppled from under it. A succession of dull explosions erupted from the interior of the inferno. The dining room and grill wing crumpled. A gang of boys slipped by the firemen into the laundry, all burning above them, and raced out with cartons of soap, which they gave out in the crowd for souvenirs.

At 9:30, three and a half hours after the first alarm was raised, the service wing fell in, and the 15,000 square feet occupied for four bright seasons by the grandest hotel on the North Shore was a snapping, smoking ruin.

George Stacy had been in Boston for the day, and when he returned on the 7:10 train and heard the news he grabbed a team and scorched over. The Arms and all connected with it were insured for $120,500, and he talked bravely, if dazedly, of rebuilding as he watched his monument disintegrate before his eyes. Every room booked for next season, too, he sighed.

For several days the electrics made heavy traffic dropping scavengers off to hike to the smoldering remains, where they concentrated on where the kitchen had been, sifting out quantities of tableware for mementos of the fabulous Colonial Arms.

But for the fire inspectors the ruins yielded nothing. The hotel had been locked and boarded up, and caretaker Dean had not had occasion to enter it for several days. At first they thought that sparks from the chimney of the cottage Henry Sleeper was building close to the west wing had been carried by the wind to the roof, for fires were said to have been going there, drying plaster. But Sleeper's mason said only small space heaters had been used. Still, it looked mighty suspicious.

Ruefully wrote a Boston columnist the next day:

> It was a most imposing structure overlooking the bay, with which only the Bay of Naples is to be compared in natural beauty. Standing alone, with ample space for its foreground and back setting, its myriad lights at night reflected in the placid water of the bay made a most picturesque sight, and the sounds of music across the water lent it a peculiar value and charm in the human interest of the place. It was also a night mark for the eastern steamers that push their way in the early evening across Boston Bay.[4]

Yes indeed, the Colonial Arms should be rebuilt, declared the president of the Eastern Point Associates. The loss of the dining room grill and ball-

room in particular would be a severe blow to the Point, for after all, Stacy's hotel was the congenial center of the colony and really quite necessary to its social and material development.

Later in the year, as a park commissioner Stacy threw himself into the rehabilitation of Pavilion Beach and the making of the esplanade that would be a far more lasting monument than any of his hotels.

Ever the builder, George Stacy in March 1909 was projecting a four-story "Venetian" hotel on the ruin of the Colonial Arms, of cement and fire-proof, to extend partly out over the harbor on piers, with a satellite colony of twenty or thirty "dainty and attractive" cottages. It all might be ready for the 1911 season once a few details had been worked out.

But although Mr. Stacy was associated with "several well known business men and financiers who can be depended upon to carry the plan to a successful issue," it never was. Nor was yet another scheme two years later.[5]

By hook or by crook, Eastern Point had reverted to its pre-Colonial era.

The Colonial Arms buggy, probably, above Niles Beach en route to the hotel. (Private collection)

John Clay, a big man in every way. (Lila Leonard Swift)

~26~
SOME MEN OF
THE OLD SCHOOL

Fifteen months after the apocalyptical destruction of the Colonial Arms, the Niles farmhouse burned down under equally perplexing circumstances. One in the morning. The end of March 1909. The old place was shuttered and locked. Yet the fire started in the interior of the second floor and was beyond doing much about when the East Gloucester steamers made the scene.

They had it out by dawn's early light. Parts of the walls and ell were all that remained of the homestead that had for generations been the only habitation on Eastern Point. Two nights later a second fire, apparently unconnected with the first, left it gutted.

Spooks maybe.

> The old farmhouse surroundings always possessed a spirit of romanticism. Many a couple has made its vows of Jove and sat under the honeysuckle vine that clung above its old paneled doorway. In many an autumn night, the hoot owl has perched in the stout boughs of the tall, old beech trees and to the happy couple in the old-fashioned moonlit garden below, let his presence be known. Then again, many an intruder has been frightened away by the ghost in the old farmhouse, so the older folks say. Every time an owl would hoot, there would be curious knockings within the closed house.[1]

After renting it out for a number of years, the Associates had sold the remodeled farmhouse and 74,000 feet of land early in 1906 to Marshall Spring Perry Pollard of Boston, wealthy partner in the firm of Wood, Pollard and Company, grocers and liquor importers, who had spent a few weeks on the Point the previous season and was impressed. He talked of renovating the place and bringing down several of his fine horses and foreign motor cars. Then he changed his mind and, before 1907 was done, sold out to Joseph Sherrard, the Colonial Arms manager. Pollard shifted to Marblehead for his summers

But his son, Alonzo Wilder Pollard of Brookline was the father of five daughters and a son, and they had all fallen for the Point. So for the following season, and until 1916 when he bought the neighboring Farrington estate on Fort Hill Avenue from Colonel Sidney W. Hedges, ex-commander of the Ancient and Honorable Artillery Company of Boston, the younger Pollard rented the Church-Russell-Burchard cottage between it and "The Ramparts."

Wilder Pollard's class of 1883 at Harvard held its twenty-fifth reunion in June 1908, and he invited a couple of hundred of his classmates down to the Point for a party, for the supplying of which the family business was happily adapted. Mrs. Elise Pollard Carson of Beverly Farms recalls that the affair was placed in the hands of one of her father's most trusted men, while for transportation he chartered the *City of Gloucester* for the day. He also hired a band.

The steamer made its usual brisk run down from Boston, docked at the Association pier and deposited the Harvardians, who trooped amidst mirth and jollity up Fort Hill Avenue to the estate of their expansive classmate, where were spread long tables groaning with the refreshment of the day which featured a seafood luncheon, endless cases of well-iced champagne, an unfathomable bar, and this and that ancillary entertainment, all proffered by a gracious and immaculate staff. Neither did the crew of the *City of Gloucester* and the band escape the ever-replenishing hospitality of Mr. Pollard.

The predictable consequence was that by the hour set for departure that afternoon, or perhaps some time in the evening, all involved, including the crew of the *City of Gloucester,* were so plastered that volunteers had to be enlisted from the Gloucester waterfront to coax the bacchant alumni back aboard the steamer and sail her back to Boston, an assignment verging on the impossible, which they carried off, true to the traditions of the old fishing port, without incident.

When Pollard bought the Farrington estate which extended down across the field to Wharf Beach from Colonel Hedges early in 1916, he set about enlarging "Barlovento" with a 40-by-30-foot addition that made it 140 feet long. But he was never granted the chance to live in it; the following February 3 he died suddenly of pneumonia at his Boston home, age fifty-four. Wilder Pollard was a leader in the Eastern Point community, and he often said that though he had circled the world, East Gloucester and the Point remained the most beautiful spot on earth.

Although my grandfather, Dr. Joseph Everett Garland, had bought the Atwood cottage with the sweeping red roof across from the fort at a bargain during the Spanish War scare that summer of 1898, he got little use of it. He had an extensive medical practice all over Cape Ann when transportation was not the easiest, and the place was isolated and without a telephone. He could be there weekends and overnight only, remaining at his town house and office on Pleasant Street and installing his family for the month of June and perhaps into July at the Point, renting it for the rest of the season.

In order to finish school in the spring, my father and his older brother Kimball and sister Alice rode their bicycles every weekday to the corner of Rocky Neck Avenue, left them at Davis's grocery and took the electric trolley the rest of the way to town.

Grandfather kept two horses, Mayflower and Topsy, for morning and afternoon rounds, at the stable of Pat Finnegan, a short man with a bushy beard and a derby hat all green with age. Finnegan's was in the alley off Main Street between Pleasant and Hancock. Dr. Garland afterwards bought the first Stephens Duryea on Cape Ann from a musician in the Boston Symphony. It cranked up from inside somewhere and was steered with a tiller and had rawhide gears. A seat could be let down in front of the driver for extra passengers, and my father would sometimes go on grandfather's rounds with him, occasionally waiting in the car outside the Addison Gilbert Hospital, where he was just able to make out his father's head and shoulders above the whitewashed lower window of the operating room as he moved about the table.

My father was six years old their first season on the Point:

> I remember, nostalgically, the quails whistling in the fields behind the house, across which a narrow cart track led, then entered the high bushes, going past the swamp where the blue flags

Alonzo Wilder Pollard and Elise Welsh Pollard with their children (from left) Elise, Anna, Katharine, Wilder, Priscilla, and Pauline. (Caroline Stride)

Dr. Joseph Everett Garland and son Joseph, the author's grandfather and father.

grew, to the southerly side of Niles Pond, abutting the gravel road that separated it from Brace Cove. Here, in the pond we sailed our toy boats.

The move from Gloucester to the Point entailed an express wagon load of trunks and such gear, the trip being shared by one or more of the children and being punctuated by a stop somewhere on the way, while the driver partook of liquid refreshment.

Not infrequently we had the opportunity of watching the trial runs made by newly built torpedo boats coming from the direction of Boston and disappearing towards Portsmouth. It seems to me that the metamorphosis of this naval craft and its name went from "torpedo boat," in my early childhood, to "torpedo boat destroyer," to "destroyer." [The Fore River Engine Company of Quincy had a government contract to build "torpedo boat destroyers" which required that they attain a speed of at least 30 miles an hour over a one-mile course off the Back Shore of Eastern Point. The Lawrence was the first to be time-trialed, early in 1901.]

An almost daily walk, weather permitting, was through the path that led around the north end of "The Ramparts" through the fields and bushes, past Indian Spring, a few steps off the beach on the right and about midway in the total distance, to your beach for wading and such recreational activities. An interesting mechanical phenomenon that forebodingly illustrated the relentless advance of civilization was a hot air pump in the shed behind the kitchen, fired by charcoal, whose piston kerchunked with extraordinary deliberation when it was finally coaxed into action. It filled the gravity cistern with about a day's ration of water, from whence I knew not, but probably from a hidden well.[2]

Around 1902 Dr. Everett, as his patients knew my grandfather, gave up entirely on the attempt to manage his practice from the Point and bought a cottage at Riverview on the Annisquam River. He rented out the Point house until his death in December 1907.

For the 1908 season my grandmother let the place to Jean Clemens, Mark Twain's youngest daughter, an epileptic for many years, with four lady friends from New York. The *North Shore Breeze* reported that she was a familiar sight driving in East Gloucester and along the North Shore, quietly and simply gowned, of scholarly appearance, and was visited by her famous father.

Mrs. Lila Leonard Swift recalled from her early childhood that Miss Clemens had a manservant and a St. Bernard and that in spite of her fear of drowning, she insisted on going swimming and wore a little hat that her man carried for her while she was in the water. Jim Walen remembered her father, his long, wild, snow-white hair and flowing cape, driving a white horse and team.

Jean Clemens died in an epileptic seizure the next year, in December 1909, five years after her mother. Samuel Clemens, sick and brokenhearted, followed her to the grave in April. In 1911 my grandmother sold the Garland summer cottage with the flowing porches atop Fort Hill Avenue to Mr. and Mrs. W. Jay Little, relinquishing her foothold on her Grandfather Niles's 448 acres.

John Clay discovered Eastern Point through his Canadian friend Walter Barwick, so it is said, and in May 1899 the Chicago stockman leased for five years the John V. Lewis cottage (now the Eastern Point Yacht Club) across the little cove from the lighthouse; he bought "Finisterre" outright in the fall of 1903.

The rugged coast and the laureled uplands of Cape Ann must have reminded the doughty Scot of where he came from between the Firth of Forth and the River Tweed that bounds England's Northumberland. It was on his father's 523-acre farm in the How of the Merse, only a league or so from the North Sea, near a wee place called Lady Kirk, where John Clay was born in 1851.

When John was but a bairn his sire leased a 3,000-acre farm on the southern slopes of the Lammermuir Hills, where Sir Walter Scott laid the scene of *The Bride of Lammermoor*. It was a profitable operation, this being prime sheep country, and the Clays raised the finest stock. The young man grew up with his feet in the soil, on intimate terms with the manager, the plow," man and the herdsman. He rode a pony or a cob until he was seventeen, when his father gave him his first horse.

Hunting, fishing, riding, shooting were the pastimes of the Clays—after hard labor. John never forgot one glorious day, as a young fellow, crossing paths with the Duke of Buccleuch's hunt: "Never before nor since that hour have I realized so vividly the fact of having been born a sport and yet having to work for a living."[3] So, after he had made his fortune, he maintained an estate in Kelso near his birthplace, and he rode to the hunt as Master of the North Northumberland Foxhounds as long as he could find a horse strong enough to carry his 225 pounds and had the strength to mount.

John Clay was a big man in every way. Rankling under the burrs of caste and conservatism in his native hills, he emigrated first to Canada in 1879 and then to the United States "with an eye to the main chance" as

agent for Scotch stock interests. He soon proved a match for the roughest operators on the range and in the stockyard. Rugged and tough, canny, energetic, honest and blunt and realistic to the verge of ruthlessness, imaginative, absolutely dependable, a born leader, a sentimentalist where sentiment could be afforded, surprisingly sensitive with streaks of compassion, the man seemed to drive everyone he encountered to the extremes of loyalty or hate.

In short order he came riding out of the prairie as a central figure amongst the cattlemen of Montana and Wyoming, and though he denied any responsibility in the infamous Johnson County War—the abortive lynching bee organized against Wyoming cattle thieves by frustrated stockmen in 1892 (he was in Europe at the time)—he took their part publicly in the aftermath, lamented the incursions of the settlers on the open range and made no secret of his opinion that the only good rustler was the one hanging from the nearest cottonwood tree.

Clay's hard-riding days were astern of him when he settled for his summers on Eastern Point, a foil to Chicago where he ran with an iron fist John Clay and Company, his far-flung livestock commission and financing business. Here was a man who could write of the rustling that provoked the Johnson County invasion: "At that time like many other cowmen I had thrown discretion to the winds, and was quite willing to draw a rope on a cattle thief if necessary,"[4] and of "Finisterre":

> I was sitting down in my garden, which lies under the shelter of Gloucester Breakwater. It was a clear, brilliant day in June. A strong southeast breeze was blowing outside, and big waves with white caps were rolling up from Cape Cod way. Wreaths of silver spray

broke on the granite rocks of the wild New England shore, as the
big combers spent their energy. Across the little bay that lay quies-
cent, just enough motion to make it shimmer in the sunshine, a
lighthouse, its tower and buildings painted white, was silhouetted
against the blue sea and sky, some two hundred yards away.
Seaward there was the sound of breaking billows. Inside the bay little wavelets made music that charmed your ear. At their mooring
boats swung slowly to and fro . . .[5]

The Clay equippage before "Finisterre," Mrs. Clay at right, 1906. (Lila Leonard Swift)

Mrs. Clay, the former Euphemia Forrest, was a Canadian. She busied
herself for two decades with the enlargement and beautification of
"Finisterre," directing a large staff and entertaining frequently and diversely.
Her daughter-in-law, Mrs. John Clay VI, recalls "the many gay parties and
benefits the Clays gave when I first came to Eastern Point in 1917. There
were big formal dinners several nights a week with champagne and so forth,
and many celebrities such as H. B. Warner the actor."[6]

In September, as the 1914 season drew to a close that first year of the
war, Mrs. Clay put on an International Red Cross benefit at "Finisterre"
with the neighboring ladies of Eastern Point. There was an auction of goods
from Gloucester stores, tables about the grounds with tea, punch, ice cream
and cake, a fortune teller, card games on the verandah, strolls through the
gardens, dancing on the tennis court to the strains of the Imperial Orchestra
and harbor cruises aboard three motor yachts provided by sponsors.

Most charmingly, as the *Gloucester Daily Times* reported on
September 17, 1914, "little Miss Hilda Williams took patrons on a drive in
her attractive pony cart around to the lighthouse and then other points
along the shore." And most compellingly, "City Marshal Marchant was at

the entrance of the estate and had charge of the admittance fees."

As for the laird of "Finisterre," John Clay was accustomed to presiding at his dinner table in his pink hunting coat, and if a guest had the misfortune to be late, the host didn't wait but sat down at the appointed time. The Clays frequently took their tea on the ledge by Mother Ann, served by their butler, and they enjoyed harbor cruises in their launch *Euphemia*, a top-heavy looking craft shaded

The cast of "The Royal Family," Hilda Williams's August 1909 production, includes King Arthur Leonard, Princess Madeleine Williams, Queen Katherine and Princess Priscilla Pollard, and an unidentified knight. (Lila Leonard Swift)

with an awning.

Still, John yearned for the old days, and perhaps Euphemia did too. Besides making "Finisterre" available for numerous worthy benefits, she was concerned with the good spirits of her staff:

Of an eminently social nature and imbued with many old country ideas, she organized barn dances and festivals for the mechanics and working people about the place, and these were occasions of the highest enjoyment, the fiddler being an old Yankee stone mason from Riverdale, Joseph Brown, who played the old time dancing tunes that came down from the olden times, to the delight of all.[7]

His wife's death in the winter of 1923–24 was a severe blow to John Clay. He resolved to sell "Finisterre" and published an illustrated brochure. Since its purchase in 1903,

My late wife devoted her whole summers to adding on to the place, by building, by purchase of adjoining lands, by pushing gardens, a lawn tennis court, a conservatory into the sea. Farquhar and other florists helped her to beautify it, but the germ of floral display of blending color was a natural gift within herself. There are betwixt four and five acres now in the estate. The house and buildings are commodious, cozy and artistic. The "shore" oaks as per illustration are unique. The flower-decked lawns, the rock gardens, the Japanese iris bed, the piece of natural forest, the vivid colors of the gladioli and other flowers make it a dream in summer days. . . . But the guiding spirit is gone, so I have determined to sell the property.

But the auld Scot could not bring himself to take leave of "Finisterre."

That summer he entertained seventy members of the Border Club of Boston, men from the auld country whence sprang the Clays and the Armours and the Allisons who built the American beef industry. The next winter he remarried. A good friend of John Clay was Arthur G. Leonard, general manager of the Union Stock Yard and Transit Company of Chicago, who visited him at the Point during the summer of 1905. His family was captivated. The next season and for fourteen years thereafter, until he built his stone mansion at the ocean end of Fort Hill Avenue, Leonard leased the Calef cottage, "The Boulders," next to "Finisterre."

Warm as the summers were, the Leonards at first found the atmosphere at Quarry Point a trifle frigid. Mrs. Raymond and her bosom companion, Mrs. Kay—those ample matrons who took dawn dips at the beach—had a loose pact that neither would offer to call on newcomers to Eastern Point until they had been settled for at least three seasons. But the newcomers just across the way were a large family and appeared to Mrs. Kay from that distance to be reasonably acceptable, so she permitted them to draw water from her well during their probation period.

Arthur Leonard was the self-made man supreme of Eastern Point. Mrs. Swift wrote of him:

> He was born in New York City about 1865. His grandparents were emigrants from North Ireland at the time of the great potato famine of 1845. They were Irish and English stock, Church of England. His own parents had been born in "the old country," came from the same town, lived in the same area in New York. I suppose Father went to public school, then he went to a school that Trinity Church, way down in Wall Street, ran.
>
> His father died before Father was 17, and he went to work when he was 17. He got a job as office boy in the New York Central Railroad, and he worked his way, one might say, *around* and *up*. He was out in the railroad yards, telegraph operator, supervised cutting ice in northern New York (for all that ice water on the Pullmans). He studied law under the company lawyer, and he invented some important

Mrs. Clay (all in white) leads the way into the briny. (Lila Leonard Swift)

Bob Sanders of Big Springs, Texas, shows how it's done in Texas. (Lila Leonard Swift)

gadget when they got sued for copying something the Pullman Company had a patent on.

In 1899 he went to Chicago as general manager of the Union Stock Yard and Transit Company, which owned a little railroad that switched the cattle cars into the stock yards proper. He had charge of unloading the cattle, hogs and sheep, feeding and watering them, maintaining the pens to which the buyers came. And he drove them to Packingtown which adjoined, or reshipped them.

A diversified business, a scope for a variety of talents and imagination, and that is what Father had. Lots of energy, too.[8]

Leonard was a prime mover behind the creation of the largest cattle market in the world; he promoted the industrial complex that sprang up on the surrounding land, organized the International Stock Show and encouraged the 4-H clubs in their early days. In his fifty years with the stockyard, it never passed a dividend.

His daughter continued:

You could ask each of his children what kind of a man he was, and we each would have a different answer. He loved a good bargain; he was inventive; he loved all kinds of hand work from that of a good blacksmith through lacemaking, painting, sculpture, the fishermen setting their trawl lines. His reading was constant and covered a wide range of subjects. He loved to possess books, not only for what was in them, but for the type and the paper and the bindings. He was a good carpenter, plumber, electrician—but no gardener at all; he wanted a garden around his house . . . he would build the wall around it, but not touch a plant.

What appealed to him about Eastern Point, I think, was its ruggedness and its picturesqueness. The combination makes it a dramatic spot. It's the view from your house: the sun goes down in a beautiful red ball; the whitecaps roll over the breakwater; the moonlight is serene and calm.

Father first visited Mr. Clay and fell in love with Eastern Point. That spot is dramatic, and both Father and Mr. Clay were Victorians and were sentimental over scenery. Every evening until he was over 80 he took a walk after dinner, to Niles Beach to see the steeples of the town against the evening sky, around the pond, out to the lighthouse. We used to walk to Rocky Neck to hear the carillons over the water.

When Father was young he loved to go on motorboating picnics up the Annisquam and out to the Essex River. The social life never interested him, or my mother either. When he was older he looked at the water instead of going on it. Viewing the sea and the sky by day, watching the lights come out at night down the coast, he said it gave him peace and rest, so he had energy for the winter.[9]

The year after Henry Rouse died Arthur Leonard bought his naphtha launch, and then replaced it with his own *Dorothy* built down East. The family took *Dorothy* to town from the stone wharf on marketing expeditions, docking at the coal company wharf for ten cents; the children were warned not to venture east on Rogers Street lest they meet up with a

drunken fisherman. When they were older they were allowed to take the electric at the head of Rocky Neck Avenue and go in to Fred Barker's drugstore at the northeast corner of Main and Hancock Streets and climb up on his stools to partake of his specialty, the best strawberry and fudge college ices on Cape Ann.

And there was the time Lila Leonard's Grandfather Ashley traveled the whole distance to the Point from New York by way of Springfield on a succession of electric trolley lines, being a thrifty man who cared naught for pushing life to the limit but would rather enjoy the sights along the way, 285 miles of it for $2.85.

The library at "Red Roof." (Andrew L. Gray)

~27~

A DAB OF DABSVILLE

ONCE UPON A TIME THERE WAS A place called Dabsville, a dab on the beautiful western shore of the Eastern Point that hung out into the Atlantic from the smelly old fishing port of Gloucester. Though hardly more than six acres, it shone as brightly as a star of the first magnitude. And although it was there all right, the name of Dabsville appeared on no maps, and it was entirely unincorporated. The cartographers of the National Geographic Society had never heard of it, yet it was known to presidents and kings.

A very small ville indeed was Dabsville, having but five inhabitants, not counting household retinues and mothers.

It was not founded like some colonies, or carved out like others. Neither was it conceived in the image of Sir Thomas More's, or born as Brook Farm, or weaned in the manner of Edward MacDowell's, or even imposed after the example of the *Isles du Diable*.

Dabsville sprang into being; the time was ripe, the tide was right, the wind was from the west, and it crystallized, all sparkling on the shore, from the catalytic mix of a magnetic young man and two magnetized maiden ladies.

The exact time and place of spontaneous generation is unrecorded and unimportant. But in June 1900, Abram Piatt Andrew, Jr., received his doctorate in economics from Harvard and was joined for the season by his parents and his sister Helen, from La Porte, Indiana, in the rented Claflin cottage in Wonson's field beyond Niles Beach. Nearby, the illustrious and very positive Philadelphia portraitist, Miss Cecilia Beaux, had taken up her summer residence at the Fairview Inn; while somewhere in the vicinity were Miss Joanna Davidge, charming mistress of Miss Davidge's Classes in New York, and her maternal chaperone, of Virginia aristocracy.

Young Piatt Andrew's father, Abram Piatt Andrew, Sr., was the son of Abraham Piatt Andrew, a founder of La Porte who ran a store and the first steam sawmill in his county. After Abram mustered out of the Civil War he and his father founded a successful bank. The rather bizarre educational career of young Piatt (he disliked Abram; he and his brother-in-law-to-be, Isaac Patch, Jr., were refused admission to a White Mountains summer hotel on account of their surnames) is traced in his nephew Isaac the Third's memoir *Closing the Circle:*

In 1883 a progressive Methodist became the new school superintendent in La Porte. One of his first acts was to initiate a method of teaching music according to a system of tones. The strict Presbyterian values of my grandparents conflicted with whatever they considered "faddish," and their disapproval was heightened by the music curriculum espoused by the Methodist reformer since it embraced free-singing, folk songs and other nontraditional modes of musical expression. They wanted Piatt excused from music classes; the superintendent's only concession was to allow him to pretend to sing by moving his lips. My grandparents refused to have their son participate in such a sham, and, since Piatt was already enrolled in private music lessons, they demanded that he be excused from school singing altogether.

In the end, Piatt was expelled as a truant, and when a lawsuit brought by his parents failed to reinstate him, he was enrolled at Lawrenceville, an elite New Jersey prep school. While his grades were above average, his report card showed an excessive number of bad marks, mostly for disobedience. After several warnings, he was suspended. Although Piatt's father traveled east to plead with Lawrenceville's dour headmaster to reinstate him, it was to no avail since there was not one house master who wanted Piatt in his dormitory.

Piatt continued his education privately at home until he enrolled at Wabash College in Indiana, but he soon left after a quarrel with his landlady. His next scholastic attempt was at Princeton where he was accepted because of his good grades and family money. Piatt continued to make trouble for the authorities at Princeton, but by his junior year he had settled down to excel as a student.[1]

Well, he was a debater, and ivy orator when he graduated in 1893 at twenty, and years later Professor Andrew was elected a Princeton trustee.

The Andrew family had for some years been summer visitors to Gloucester, and Helen, who graduated from Smith College in 1899, was a good friend of Harriet Patch, an 1897 graduate. Harriet's only brother, Isaac, Jr. (both of them were born when Farmer Ike Patch was in his seventies and had remarried on the instructions of his first wife) had graduated from Amherst College in 1897, taken up business in Gloucester and fallen in love with Helen. This June of 1900 the Andrews were East most likely to applaud Piatt at Commencement in Cambridge, where he had been a graduate student at Harvard since departing Princeton, with an appointment as an instructor in economics since 1899 when he returned from three years of study in Halle and Berlin in Germany and at the Sorbonne in Paris.

And so now he was "Doc" Andrew, one of Professor Frank Taussig's bright young economists (though Taussig flunked him in his first doctoral effort, and it took Piatt another year to satisfy this exacting pioneer in the field). With a modest share of the family wealth, he was on the prowl for a seaside seat that summer, roaming east as far as Maine's Mt. Desert. But something ever drew him back to Gloucester, where he briefly considered buying Salt Island, the chunk of rock and brush connected to Good Harbor Beach's Briar Neck by a sandbar at low tide. He succumbed finally to the fascination of Eastern Point's wild ground that looked to the westward over the harbor, above the rusty red ledge north of the Association pier.

In 1901 Piatt Andrew paid the Associates $2,500 for the narrow strip of

land south of the Gorton cottage Henry Scott had built. In December his sister Helen and Ike Patch were married at La Porte. Next spring he broke ground for his bachelor's castle, and at about the same time Miss Davidge bought the lot between his place and Pierlane, the right-of-way extension of Toronto Avenue to the pier. Not for nearly sixty years was it discovered that he had violated the lady's lot by about one foot.

"Today they really began to work on my house," he wrote in his diary June 26, 1902. "My interest intense."

Thus was catalyzed the colony that would spring up around this brilliant, creative, handsome man of twenty-nine whose deep-set eyes and full, sensuous mouth contrasted so strikingly with his high forehead and aquiline nose. His grace, his intellect, his sensitivity, his overpowering ego and his mesmeric charm captivated men and women alike and drew from those he admitted behind the gate of his urbanity an often passionate devotion.

Was he the magnet that pulled Miss Davidge and Miss Beaux, both years his senior, to Eastern Point?

On September 6 he entered in the diary: "This evening occurred the laying of the cornerstone of Miss Davidge's house. After this my house was occupied for the first time by Mrs. Davidge (blue room), Miss Davidge (yellow room), Miss Cecilia Beaux (red room)."

And next day: "First meal in the new house on the verandah during a rain storm. After this Miss Beaux and I created a writing table staining it with ink and other improvised ingredients. Log fire in the evening and a talk

Harvard stag party at "Red Roof," May 2, 1903, in order of ascendance: Professor A. Piatt Andrew and students Leverett Bradley, Franklin D. Roosevelt, and Thomas Beal, Jr. (Andrew L. Gray)

on the roof." Literally. He had a small garden area on the roof, long since boarded over.

On the ledge rising above high tide to his house Andrew built a labyrinth of stone passages and portals, gates, seats, stairs, nooks, terraced walks, balconies, unexpected gardens and aeries to which he added year after year, sprinkling it with statuary, terra cotta, bas-relief and odd artifacts until it covered entirely the slope of granite up to the house, to the delight of the local masons and dealers in distant art.

His house, like his grounds, was essentially his own design, a comfortable, tasteful, shingled and shuttered three-story villa under a steep roof, flared distinctively at the eaves, bearing the imprint of the Francophile. Inside all was white stucco, rich dark beams and panels, floors of hardwood or tile, mitered windows, and at every turn a continuance of the exterior labyrinth: tucked-away window seats, more nooks, steps and stairs, mirrors in bizarre places, cloisters, clever closets, doors both trap and hidden, sliding panels, obscure passages and at least four secret rooms. And it was one of the very few houses on Eastern Point built for year-round living.

Here the owner sank the complexity of his roots. For lack of a properly inappropriate name in the expected seashore style, he called his home "my wife" or "my shanty," as when he brought Harvard's philosopher-psychologist William James down for a Sunday visit the first November he lived in it. But next summer he had his roof painted red, and with a simplicity that made the gate signs of a few of his neighbors seem contrived, Piatt Andrew christened the place "Red Roof."

William James and his disciple John Grier Hibben, who would become president of Princeton in 1912, help dedicate "Red Roof," November 2, 1902. (Andrew L. Gray)

*"Red Roof"
during its first
winter, 1902–03.
(Andrew L. Gray)*

Next over, rising out of the brush and catbrier behind the pier that winter of 1902–03, was the smaller house of the Davidges, daughter and mother. Mrs. Davidge was the great-granddaughter of George Mason, author of Virginia's Constitution and Declaration of Rights, the core of Thomas Jefferson's Bill of Rights. Her late husband was William Hathorn Davidge, grandson of Dr. John Beale Davidge, the founder of the College of Medicine of Maryland around which the University of Maryland was chartered in 1813.

Joanna was born in Paris, where her father had taken his family for his health shortly before the Civil War. Father's health may have dictated the move in more ways than one. In 1860 he had testified before a congressional committee investigating the business practices of Cornelius Vanderbilt that the Pacific Mail Steamship Company, of which he (Davidge) was president, had been paying Vanderbilt $30,000 a month of its government mail subsidy (for which Vanderbilt had lobbied) for several years as blackmail under threat of competition. The Davidges returned to New York after the war, when feelings had cooled off, and he resumed his shipping business but died soon after.

Privately educated, fluent in French and German, widely read and brimming with enthusiasm for sharing her love affair with culture, Joanna first taught in a private school and then around 1890 opened her own select *école* in New York, where she and her mother occupied an apartment near Madison Square. Literature and poetry were the main courses at Miss Davidge's classes, consumed with such genteel *bon appétit* by the young ladies that she added painting and sculpture and more instructors and

Joanna Davidge poses in white at her garden gate. (Paul M. Jacobs)

before she knew it she was, as they said, "beginning to be much spoken of in New York."

Rather tall and graced with a pleasing figure, firm and frank of face, fair complexion, deep and intriguing eyes that flashed with smiles under dark brows and a mass of curls, Joanna was fortyish and unaccountably confirmed in spinsterhood (or so it appeared) under the protective chaperonage of her mother when she built her cottage on Eastern Point next to the frightfully handsome Dr. Andrew. The Lochinvar who would scale her ramparts at last, the eminent David Randall-MacIver, had this to say of her:

The brilliant and wonderful Joanna Davidge was sought after by all the most interesting and intellectual people in the many circles in which she moved. Her social life during these years was no less full and active than her professional career as an educationist. Her vitality seemed inexhaustible and her interests were innumerable. Mere social prominence did not greatly interest her, though she was willing to give it due value in its own sphere. Her mother's universally recognized distinction as a *grande dame* of Old Virginia gave Joanna the place in society which was her right, but she found her friends as readily and naturally among artists, poets and literary men. And each of them recognized her value. St. Gaudens and Rodin were interested in her impressions of sculpture; leading poets and painters welcomed her appreciation of their work. For indeed she combined intellect and artistic sensibility in an almost unique degree. Her eye for beauty was a gift from heaven; her love for music was so intense that with more leisure she probably would have become a musician rather than anything else. And her quick perception, and loving sympathy in all human relations, were the qualities that endeared her to many simpler people who might not realize all the other riches of her nature . . .[2]

Escaping the summer doldrums of New York, the Davidges found Gloucester, and Eastern Point.

Overgrown with the sweet-scented clethra shrub and bay bushes, with a tiny copse of storm-harassed trees . . . On this little plot she built a charming little villa in Italianate Style, nestling low down amongst the trees and bushes of which not one was unnecessarily disturbed. Here she came summer after summer with her mother, tended her own garden, watered, planted and delighted in the marvelous lights, the play of colour on the water and the distant view of Gloucester, sometimes clear but much more beautiful when half-hidden in a magic haze. There is a marvelous witchery about the spot, and on many a morning one could believe that the sea was the Aegean or that the narrowing waters were those of the

Bosphorus. It was a place for dreams and poetry and all Joanna's heart responded to it. This was the true home of her spirit.

A merry party of the neighbors and other friends celebrated the completion of the house. Henry McCarter of Philadelphia had painted one of his best pictures to go over the mantelpiece in the dining room. Poems were extemporized for the occasion, one by Professor Gildersleeve the famous Greek scholar,[3] who at the last moment when he saw his sonnet apparently going into the sacrificial flames cried out, "Child, save it for me, I can never do another one as good!" One might wish now that some one had preserved not only the sonnet but all the other records of that memorable evening.[4]

Stephen Parrish was already a painter of national reputation when the young aspirant Cecilia Beaux took the neighboring studio in Philadelphia, and although her awe of him precluded acquaintance, she found his mere presence inspirational. Parrish is known to have summered at the Fairview Inn, so it may be more than coincidence that Miss Beaux as early as 1897 should be found at this well-known spa where gathered each season that singular East Gloucester colony of artists and writers.

Cecilia, or Beaux, or just Bo, was born in Philadelphia on May 1, 1855, which complicates the chronology of this distinguished, ever youthful it seemed, portraitist's life because she insisted—perhaps after she met the much younger and so fascinating Doc Andrew—on awarding herself an eight-year bonus by resolutely fibbing about her age in high places like the *Encyclopedia Britannica* and *Funk & Wagnalls,* where she got away with 1863, only to be overtaken by the truth at last, posthumously it must be admitted, in the *Dictionary of American Biography.*

Bo's mother, Cecilia Leavitt, of Puritan stock, died when the child was an infant, and she and her older sister, Aimée Ernesta, were turned over to their Grandmother Leavitt by their French father, Jean Adolphe Beaux, a Huguenot émigré, who hastened back to France. The girls were brought up in Philadelphia by their grandmother and their uncle Will Biddle and the other two Leavitt sisters, one of whom he had married. They recognized and nourished Cecilia's precocious fascination with art and music. She was educated at home until she was fourteen, then at Miss Lyman's School. At seventeen she began her art studies with Van der Whelen and William Sartain, for she had by now been initiated in the studio of the adventurous painter and authoress Catherine Ann Drinker, wife of Thomas Allibone Janvier, the writer.

Catherine ("Kate") Drinker's niece and namesake, the biographer and Eastern Point summer resident (and Bo's niece) Catherine Drinker Bowen wrote in her memoir *Family Portrait* that while her grandfather, Captain Sandwith Drinker, was in China with his children (her father, Henry, and her Aunt Kate) the great merchant "Mr. Hukwa" proposed a match between his son and Kate when she reached fifteen; the offer was politely declined. Houqua was Captain Drinker's good friend and young Henry's godfather and will be remembered as the closest Chinese business associate of John Perkins Cushing, who briefly aspired to make of Eastern Point America's seaside estate par excellence.

Cecilia's sister Aimée married Kate Drinker Janvier's brother, Henry S. Drinker, who would become president of Lehigh University, while Cecilia went to Paris to study with Joseph Nicolas Robert-Fleury, Adolphe William Bouguereau and Pascal Adolphe Jean Dagnan-Bouveret. She met and admired St. Gaudens and Monet, exhibited at the Paris Exhibition in 1890, returned to America and won the gold medal of the Philadelphia Art Club three years later. Soon Miss Beaux was the leading lady portrait artist in Philadelphia, with commissions for oils, pastels and drawings, sketches for the *Century* magazine, and teaching at the Philadelphia Academy of Fine Arts.

While Piatt Andrew's "Red Roof" was rising in 1902, Beaux was between Philadelphia, Gloucester and Washington, where she had taken over the Red Room of the White House to paint Mrs. Theodore Roosevelt and her daughter Ethel. She sketched TR and was taken sufficiently into the family's bully bosom to be amused by his gusto at the dinner table and to visit with them at Sagamore Hill.

Beaux and Andrew met probably in the autumn of 1902 as he was finishing "Red Roof." On the seventh of the following April she invited him for tea in her studio (he had found her a cottage to rent on the Point) and to meet Richard Watson Gilder, editor of the *Century*, who was sitting for a portrait by one of his leading contributing artists.

A week later, on the fifteenth of April, 1903, Doc wrote his parents elatedly (he had turned thirty two months before):

> Today has been a gala day for me! Today the Board of Overseers confirmed the votes of President and Fellows and I was made assistant professor of economics for five years. I think I am about the youngest professor in the University [Harvard]!
>
> Today I had another delightful experience. Through Miss Beaux's ingenious machinations, I was invited by Mrs. Jack Gardner to visit her new Fenway Court with Miss Beaux and Miss Irwin and Harry Drinker [Agnes Irwin, dean of Radcliffe, with whom Miss Beaux was wintering, and the artist's nephew, Henry S. Drinker, Jr., a student at Harvard Law School]. We drove out there and were received at the entrance by Mrs. Gardner herself who showed us the wonderful place from top to bottom.

The freshly elevated professor was astonished at the beauty of the Isabella Stewart Gardner Museum his ever-astonishing hostess had so recently created in her own name, and little did he imagine that in time he and Boston's enfante terrible would have as close to an understanding as decorum and the difference in their ages (which was thirty-three years) would permit. On their tour, he informed La Porte,

We saw Sargent there also, as he is living with Mrs. Gardner and painting portraits in one of her palatial rooms. He is a very businesslike, unaesthetic-looking person—very large and burly— and with a florid face.

John Singer Sargent, born in Florence, was the son of Dr. FitzWilliam Sargent, who came from Gloucester. They were direct descendants of William Sargent, the early settler who owned land bordering Niles Pond and Brace Cove. Sargent had followed Beaux to the White House, to portray the president that February. Critics would most often compare her style with his. All in all, an amusing little cycle of circumstance.

Meanwhile, Cecilia Beaux was land hunting on Eastern Point.

Piatt Andrew's mentor at Harvard, Professor Taussig, sailed for Europe in 1901 to recover from a nervous breakdown, leaving Doc in charge of his introductory course, Economics 1, which met Mondays, Wednesdays and Fridays at nine. Among his students was a cousin of the man who had just succeeded the assassinated McKinley to the presidency, an aristocratic Grotty from Hyde Park entering his sophomore year named Franklin Delano Roosevelt.

Andrew was middle-of-the-road but more liberal than Taussig. In his study of the influences on Roosevelt's economic thought, Daniel R. Fusfeld credits him with "a critical, reforming bent within the framework of his traditional economic theory," and this is what emerged out of Ec 1 that year.

The man who introduced the thirty-second president of the United States to the principles of economics presented views that were antitariff, critical of the flaws in the banking system, opposed to the trusts and

monopoly, moderate on the labor issue that was exciting the country, and favorably inclined toward the progressive welfare legislation that was then under debate. He covered the subject of socialism, Fusfeld notes wryly, in one lecture, the last of the course.[5]

The teacher was only nine years older than his prominent student and took a friendly interest in him. Nearly at the end of his sophomore year, on May 27, 1902, Franklin Roosevelt wrote "Dearest Mama" from his rooms in Westmorley Court, Harvard's Gold Coast and later part of Adams House: "I rode Saturday a.m. with Mr. Andrew, saw Harvard defeat Yale in the afternoon in the track games and went to Groton in the evening. . . ." Both were excellent horsemen.[6]

Their friendship developed, and eleven months later, on April 27, 1903 (a little less than two weeks after Piatt's introduction to Mrs. Jack and her museum and artist-in-residence), Franklin wrote his mother from the offices of the *Harvard Crimson*, of which he was now managing editor, that "next Sunday I may go to Gloucester to stay with Mr. Andrew, one of the professors. If I don't go there it will be Groton. . . ."[7]

But he did come to Eastern Point as planned, though he was not studying with Professor Andrew his junior year, and reported from Cambridge on the sixth of May:

Dearest Mama—Just a scrap to say that I am alive and well. I had a most delightful all night dance last Friday, a subscription affair & went to Gloucester Saturday to Monday to stay with Dr. Andrew, Professor of Political Economy. T Beal & Leverett Bradley also there & we had a wonderful rest by the sad sea waves . . .[8]

Leverett Bradley was a classmate at Groton and Harvard. Thomas Beal, also a college classmate, would be an usher at Franklin's wedding to his remote cousin, Eleanor Roosevelt, on March 17, 1905.

Piatt's version of the weekend was committed to his diary on the second and third of May:

Tom Beal and I went down early to Gloucester—worked all day making gardens and paths. In the evening were joined by Leverett Bradley and Franklin Roosevelt. . . . [Next day] A lovely gray day. Spent most of the morning on horseback and doing stunts, having battles with wet seaweed, building fires, etc. Miss Beaux and Miss Blake came to dinner. Toward evening we all took naps around the fire.

Gay days at Eastern Point, and nights. The fifth of August the J. Murray Kays staged a costume party and Doc mentioned to his diary that he "went as the lately deceased Pope Leo XIV, gorgeous in a robe of turkey red curtains." (He meant Leo XIII, who had just died.) A month later "Red Roof" had its first birthday party. Francis Ward entertained the company with legerdemain, mind reading and other occult accomplishments, and there was a bonfire and supper in the attic room attended by the Davidges and Beaux, among others, and young Henry Eliot, Harvard class of 1902, Tom's brother.

One day in October a seventy-foot whale, rather the worse for his passage from wherever he departed this life, drifted ashore at Brace Cove, a whiff east of the lifesaving station. People came from all over to view this vast curiosity, and later that autumn, or perhaps by early in the spring, he had earned a place as one of the wonders of the Point Doc took pleasure in displaying hospitably to his guests.

During one such visitation the professor clambered aboard the ripening bulk of the colossus, pulling the members of his distinguished party up behind him, when without any warning they sank in to their knees, a blubberish plight from which they extricated themselves with some difficulty. It was a test of aplomb all around.

By spring the old whale had so worn out his welcome that dynamite was attempted to send him on his way by order of the Board of Health, but to no avail. So two cords of wood and two barrels of kerosene were trundled out to Brace's for what was represented as a "whale and black-headed fly barbecue."

Cecilia Beaux.
(From her
Background with
Figures)

Franklin Roosevelt was finishing his senior year at Harvard in 1904 and had decided to major in economics. For the second time he chose to study with Professor Andrew, electing Economics 8-A, a half-course entitled "Survey in Currency Legislation, Experience and Theory in Recent Times."

Professor Andrew had become a specialist in money, and Fusfeld points out in his study that this course was delivered against a growing dissatisfaction around the country with the banking system and business fluctuations. He lectured on the history of money and the relation of gold to general price levels. Students were assigned to write theses on the quantity theory of money, and FDR struggled with his. Piatt's philosophy was based on sound money, stable prices and adherence to the gold standard.

The extent of Harvard's, and Andrew's, influence on the loosely knit economic creed President Roosevelt brought to the White House in 1932 is difficult to judge accurately. At least his professors agreed, as Fusfeld observes, on the pressing need for economic reform when he was an undergraduate, by the route of governmental regulation to curb the worst abuses of the system.[9]

In any event, Roosevelt's thinking continued to be shaped by his teacher until graduation parted them. He wrote "Dearest Marmer" from Cambridge on March 29, 1904, for example: ". . . This p.m. I had a long ride of nearly three hours with Prof. Andrew & C. Bigelow & it was a perfect day for it. . . ."[10]

Five more weeks, and Franklin was on the eve of his graduation. Ever the faithful son, he wrote Sara Delano Roosevelt on May 3: "I have jumped into a den of wild animals on my return, beginning with a dinner at the Club last Saturday, two private performances of the Pudding show & a crowd of 1903 men here for Herbert Burgess' ushers dinner & tomorrow we go to his wedding in Brookline . . . "[11]

Herbert Burgess recalled that "I married Jean Kay on May 4th, 1904. The undergraduates, members of our club in Cambridge, came in a body, so to speak, and when they reached the receiving line each one was introduced by Franklin to Mrs. Kay. There was nothing prearranged about this. . . . Mrs. Kay was much impressed by his savoir-faire. His charm and ease of manner were apparent in those early days."[12]

The Kays, of course, summered at Eastern Point. A young man who could charm Mrs. Kay had a bright future ahead of him.

In mid-November Cecilia Beaux bought from the Associates the large piece of wild shore front to the south of the pier between the Davidges and John Greenough, and during 1905 Simon Garland, a Gloucester builder, broke the ground of the pied-à-terre for which she had pined so long.

Her niece Ernesta sat for Cecilia Beaux once again in 1914, twenty-one years after the portrait on page 192. (Metropolitan Museum of Art)

> Partway between the lighthouse and the town of Gloucester, I began to notice a thickly wooded space on the harbor side of the road. So solid was the tangle of catbrier, primeval blueberry, ilex, bay, and sassafras that entrance upon it was impossible. Over all rose tall wild-cherry trees. Two great maples stood with only a gate's-width between them on what was then the narrow graveled road to the Point. There were many high-flat-branched trees showing above also, and which I found later to be tupelo, and to be to the number of forty on the triangle of rock and twining, branching shrubs, whose stems were thick and gnarled with age, and as if drawn and composed by a master artist. It was a "*bosquet.*" No other name quite described it so well.[13]

The artist no sooner found her setting than very definite ideas took form in her eye, though, as she wrote, "it would be difficult for a robin to describe her nest—or a tortoise its shell. The latter would have certainly to depend on hearsay in regard to the exterior, although very well conscious of the fit." Neither early American nor French manor house, however modest, suited her in spite of her genetic background, and she lit on "tropical Colonial," entailing a separate studio almost as large as the house, removed from it for seclusion, "the whole pretty much achieving what it was intended for—work and friendship—the two main divisions of its owner's interest."[14]

Beaux saw her house of a piece, as on canvas. A Philadelphia friend of many years, Thornton Oakley, an etcher who illustrated the travel books of his wife Amy, was struck that "color, texture, size, minute details of every room, of every cranny the management of light effects in the separate building of the studio, were already vividly conceived. She had visualized the allées through the tupelos, the schemes of paths across the rocks, the mirror of the pool and its reflecting herma."[15]

"Green Alley" she called the house when it was done. "On the evening of August 7, 1906, the first fire was kindled on the hearth at Green Alley, and I made a feint of sleeping there that night."[16]

Miss Beaux approached her *bosquet* with the precision of a plastic surgeon:

> I had managed—starting between the great maples on the road—to cut a way in through the thicket, without leveling a tree or even the old giant blueberry, and ilex. The bay was always sacred. For some of the paths I penetrated alone, with a small pair of scissors, clipping my way—fascinating pioneering. I never planted anything in the wood save the mountain rhododendron, and then only beside a pool at the innermost point of seclusion. I contrived, with the aid of my incomparable Italian servant, Natale Gavagnin, to give the pool the appearance of a spring, or well, confined by an oval of mossy stones. Tall tupelos arched above it, and a great fern now hangs over and sometimes dips its fronds into the dark water where the rhododendron reflects its long heavy leaves and shy, pink-tinged flowers.[17]

Natale. Who could think of "Green Alley" and Bo without calling up the image of Natale?, mused Thornton Oakley:

> Skin tinged with olive, darkly mustached, clad in spotless white, noiseless, devoted, cognizant of every need, he was personification of perfect service. [Cecilia's] eye was on every article in studio and house. Each object was required to be in its appointed place. Every branch, every leaf of every tupelo that composed not with her desires, obstructed views, was, with minute directions to the adroit Natale, ordered cut away. Every morning, with swift stride, she was now here, now there, issuing commands Then with the arrival of her sitter, Cecilia disappeared. Natale falling to, once more, upon his endless pruning."[18]

Her beautiful niece and occasional sitter, Ernesta Drinker Barlow, remembered that brook though its secret was lost:

> "Natali," I can remember Beaux's clear voice calling to her gardener, "guests are arriving. Please turn on the brook." This phenomenon seemed so natural that unhappily none of us thought to inquire how it came about, so we can no longer command the little stream to flow.[19]

Many the tale of Bo's Natale, whom Ernesta recalled was originally a Venetian gondolier. For thirty years he devoted himself to her aunt, always clad in a white sailor suit and colored sash, and in the winter he slept on a pallet behind a screen in her New York studio. Mrs. Jack Gardner tried to entice him away, but Natale was the slave of his mistress.

Cecilia didn't drive, and Natale did so with an abandon that may account for Jim Nugent's memory of her passage to a Point dinner, preceded by her servant, walking ahead with a lantern, white sash thrown over his shoulder to show him up in the dark. She would not own an automobile, Nugent declared, nor have screens in her windows, "for the hum of the mosquitoes was music to her ears." And she was of course delighted when the telephone directory her first year listed "Decilia Beans"; her friends knew her number anyway.[20]

The incomparable Natale, manservant to Cecilia Beaux. (From Background with Figures)

"It is a lovely after-fog morning," the mistress of "Green Alley" wrote Oakley. "Down on the end of the pier Natale, in his yellow sash, is fishing, a Sunday morning treat for him." And another time, "his perfection is most apparent when he has entire charge of me."[21] Natale may have had entire charge of her—but on her terms.

Beaux resisted romance with stern self-discipline. On her first trip abroad at the age of thirty-two she wrote her uncle that it was all over with a man who would never know how much he had meant to her, but that she had grown too much to fit the place he would have required of her. And so it was with a painter friend. Her painting priorities simply left no room for the demands (or challenges) of a relationship. [22]

"Green Alley" and its lady haunted Thornton Oakley. Its entrance for him was

> to a domain enchanted. The latticed door, the winding path amidst translucent leaves, the rill it crossed, the lanterns gleaming in the shadows, the allées mysteriously receding, seemed of a fairy realm, remote from the world of men. . . . The soft swards; the flowers at the foot of the rocks; the sunlight streaming through the arches of

the loggia; the steps, already worn, leading to her place of work; Dr. Gufo, the great horned owl, who behind the barriers of his retreat, stared and blinked at the astonished visitor; the studio itself, its lofty window, its everpresent fragrance of paint and canvas—all spoke of her.[23]

Bo wrote Oakley:

Here we work still at cutting, cutting. The trees are making walls of leaves and choking out air and sun. But there is the Harbor, big and empty, and I have developed things I wish you could see. One is a precipice you never knew existed, and there is now a steep descent. I call it the "Smugglers' Trail." But no brandy and cigars have yet been carried out or been brought in.[24]

Long after she and her husband, the composer Samuel L. M. Barlow, succeeded to its summers,[25] niece Ernesta evoked the lingering nuances of "Green Alley":

Each year when Beaux moved up from New York in June, she found it was still early spring on Eastern Point, the tupelos just beginning to bud. She delighted in the fanlike branches with their lacquered green leaves. Some she trimmed to grow low, umbrella-shaped; in the fall the grove turns so red that every room in the house glows from the reflection. The immense maples towering at the front gate, through the woods, and the swampy land across the road, become Chinese yellow in October.

Aunt Cecilia disliked the untidiness left by low tide and permitted the native shrubs to grow high enough to screen the debris from her sight.

In early May shadbush covers the Point as with a pale low-lying mist; next come the viburnums and elderberry, and in August every bush seems to have become a clethra. Our fishermen used to say they could tell on a foggy night when they were off the harbor, so sweet and strong came the scent of the candle-like blossoms.

Beaux was not keen on formal gardens (her chief concession to horti-culture was friendly hollyhocks, smiling in at the window), but in her niece's view she guarded the *au naturel* state of her *bosquet* beyond the allées as jealously as if she were, especially the sylvan ferns.

Hay-scented fern fills holes and crevices in the rocks, polypoly lies like a quilt over flat surfaces; there is lady fern, Christmas and evergreen fern, brake, tall ostrich, and uneven ferns. Beaux's special pride was the ancient, graceful regalis which droops three-foot fronds along the paths. Owing to violent weeding, on my part, of persistent crawling buttercup and wood aster, and the raking away of a too-heavy matting of maple leaves, our ground cover runs a lovely cycle. First come the trout lilies, soon replaced by wild lily of the valley and big white violets. Finest of all is a solid drift of dusty pink geranium. Wild vines we have too, clematis, sweetbriar, honeysuckle and one bitter enemy, catbriar—a smotherer, strangler, and killer.[26]

Cecilia Beaux saw herself as the inhabiting servant of "Green Alley," its mistress and its lover:

> How I rejoiced in submission, in the morning, awakening near my big eastern window, to which I could creep in the early mornings of late June and see Venus flashing in a primrose sky, among the moving fringes of the treetops. And the nights when great patches of moonlight lay on the living-room floor, and, mounting to the upper terrace, one could find long rays upon the little columns and glittering vine leaves of the terrace house; the even rhythm of small waves crashing upon the pebbles of the harbor beach, and to seaward the sense of the Ocean's presence and distant organ tones. . . .
>
> And do not forget, O Recorder, the midday meal on the terrace, in the shade of the great birch, looking down by the cedars to the harbor. Do not forget what it was, after a morning of fierce effort, to sink, silent and exhausted, at the little table, and be restored in every sense. Perhaps it was an echo from the remote "Provençal way" that gave such zest to these *déjeuners* under the boughs, lightened by the birds who partook with us: the catbird's plea, sweet and raucous, the silent and timid little redstart, the song-sparrow trilling at safe distance; the robin going her own way, not needing our assistance in her housekeeping.
>
> Do not forget the pine's perfume in the sun, the deep caves of shadow, and in the season's later days the orange and scarlet tupelo leaves afloat upon the dark pool in the wood. Do not forget. . . .[27]

Cecilia Beaux walks her "dogs" (Jack Mabbett and Piatt Andrew) while Henry Sleeper watches from on high (above Beaux's hat). (Andrew L. Gray)

Isabella Stewart Gardner, Henry Sleeper (middle), and probably Caroline Sinkler (seated) with unidentified friends in Sinkler's enchanted garden. (Society for the Preservation of New England Antiquities)

~28~

MORE DABS OF DABSVILLE

Eastern point cast a special spell over Caroline Sidney Sinkler, a midsummer dream to which the Enchantress of Philadelphia, as Piatt Andrew called his neighbor, added a potion no one drawn within her Titanian realm could resist. Beaux performed her magic with her art, Carrie with the lavender bewitchment of her person.

"Today the harbour is full of mysts," she sighed in one of her lilac letters to Andrew. "Don't you think it ought to be spelt with a y for Gloucester where they mean mystery and dreams and loveliness?"[1]

Caroline swept in with a swish of lavendah, tall, regal, to the manor and the manner born, cadenced with the most languid largo nawth of the wide Santee River and possessed (as if possessed) of mysts of mystery and dreams and loveliness that captivated men and incapacitated women.

Och, ma bonnie lassie she was to John Clay, the great Scot, and her whim was his command. Every season Arthur Leonard, a man whose head was not easily turned, sent her a side of beef from his stockyards decorated with the blue ribbon the steer had won in the show.

Carrie, or Cadsie, was born in the dying days of antebellum South Carolina in 1860 on "Belvidere," the plantation seat of the Sinklers granted by George III to her great-grandfather. It lay between the cypress-hung mirror of Eutaw Creek and the flowing Santee, midway from Charleston to Columbia.

The Civil War merely interrupted for a time the serene life of "Belvidere," which resumed its gentle pace after Emancipation and Reconstruction, remote and strangely untouched. The family continued to raise and race famous horseflesh under the proprietorship of Cadsie's brother, Charles St. George Sinkler, and the blacks who supported "Belvidere's" way of life continued under freedom the same easy and symbiotic relationships that had regulated the hours of their years under servitude. The black population of the plantation still numbered 185 when the Santee-Cooper Hydroelectric

Project flooded the lowlands, routed both races from "Belvidere" and broke up the old ways of 140 years of Old South.

When her older sister Elizabeth married Charles Coxe of Philadelphia, she shared with Carrie her share of the enormous income from the Coxe family's Pennsylvania anthracite holdings, an annuity that maintained Caroline in comfort and style with houses, servants, the means to entertain and travel, and enough left over on her own account to distribute largess to nieces and protégés.

In Philadelphia she met John Stewardson, a tall, thin, strikingly handsome young Harvard graduate trained in architecture in Paris who, with his partner Walter Cope, was bringing taste and poise to the Victorian mishmash of American architecture in such venues as Princeton's Blair Hall and Bryn Mawr College. A watercolorist of sensitivity, horseman, dog lover, yachtsman and skater—competent, romantic, charming and passionate for the outdoors.

John and Carrie fell gloriously in love, he thirty-seven, she thirty-five. The wedding would be at "Belvidere." Their happiness was famous. It was January 1896. The trousseau was gathered. The event was at hand.

On the afternoon of the sixth, John Stewardson "went skating

Mrs. Jack strolls through Caroline Sinkler's garden. (Society for the Preservation of New England Antiquities)

on the Schuylkill with some friends. In the late dusk he was separated from them; and there was heard the sound of breaking ice, and a cry, then silence."[2]

Carrie went into mourning after the funeral, first in black, then in lavender and lilac. And so she remained for the rest of her long and joyful life, for she would not marry after the death of her man, and she would not allow herself to forget him. Her weeds, in time, she absorbed into her joie de vivre; she made of unforgetfulness her mark, her style—a festive mourning, one friend called it.

Festive it was indeed. Vast broad-brimmed, flower-decked hats, shawls, swaths of gown and lace, gloves, drapes, linen, upholstery, decor, perfume, notepaper, ink, the words themselves—all shades of lavender, tinted and scented with lilac.

Lavender and magnolia, with a bursting, sybaritish (a favorite word of hers), sensuous love affair with life—this was the way Cadsie Sinkler carried the torch for John Stewardson for fifty-three years, until she joined him in 1949.

How Eastern Point came to be blest with this beautiful person is lost in the mysts of tyme. Quite possibly through co-southerner Joanna Davidge, whose cottage she rented in 1905, or by way of Cecilia Beaux, a fellow Philadelphian. One season was enough to bring her back for life; that October she bought the rambling, gabled Scott house north of Professor Andrew's "Red Roof," and in the spring of 1906 she was thanking him profusely for his advice about wiring it for electricity.

Miss Sinkler was irresistable.

"You were good enough to say I could plant a couple of trees or so on your side to help screen us from you," she wrote her distinguished neighbor. "I told Southworth to plant them but to consult you first. So please be candid and tell him not to if you would rather not, or if they would be in your way among yours. . . ."[3] And on another occasion, "My shingles look as flagrant as ever. I will have them painted, as time won't wither them. Do you prefer what—? Let me know so I can spare your vision this summer."[4]

Immediately her house was full of guests and relatives, among them her favored nieces: Emily, who married Nicholas Roosevelt; Anne, the wife of Dr. W. K. Fishburne; and her namesake, Caroline Sidney, Mrs. Dunbar Lockwood of Topsfield. She loved everyone, especially the young, and surrounded herself with them, and if they were from the South particularly, and gifted, she encouraged and advanced them through her wide acquaintance in the world of culture.

"Aunt Cad, with her extraordinary charm, her enormous appetite for life, would put up with absolutely anybody if they entertained her," recalled Caroline Lockwood, "including some of the most awful characters. She had no formal education, but she could pick up a book just out, thumb through a few pages beforehand and then flatter the author to pieces. She was invariably late for engagements and always blamed it on the Cut Bridge being open for a fishing boat if she had to cross the Squam River to get there; but no matter how late she was, no one could remain irritated with her. Cadsie had charisma."[5]

Guests at the famous Sinkler luncheons worked every trick to obtain her unique and delectable recipe for Russian pancakes, more than once trying to wheedle it from her cook by the back way. Few, if any, were successful. But she baited them and teased them on.

For Piatt Andrew's grandnephew, Andrew Gray,

> it was invariably my job to fetch her for luncheons at Red Roof, a function I performed from age ten onwards. She always kept me waiting, made a dramatic entrance sweeping down her staircase, did an approximation of a curtsey, and in general pretended she was younger than I [she was about seventy years older] and needed a strong arm to conduct her into a social adventure. She had a habit of prolonging the enunciation of all vowels, and the word *so*, for example, might take her several seconds to pronounce. Her voice was very beautiful.[6]

As was everything else (arranged so carefully and with such flair, "auspiciously, almost precariously," as she liked to drawl) about the Lavender Lady of Eastern Point.

"I had such a nice day yesterday," his recently met bachelor friend wrote Piatt Andrew from the apartment at 336 Beacon Street in Boston which he shared with his mother. "I was quite fascinated by your house and place, as you doubtless noticed from my comments thereon! . . ."[7]

Thus did Henry Davis Sleeper come upon Eastern Point and double up Caroline Sinkler's *S*, completing the cryptogram *Dabsville*—for Davidge, Andrew, Beaux, Sinkler and Sleeper.

Henry Sleeper was twenty-eight when Doc Andrew, five years his senior, invited the tall, slightly built young Bostonian out to "Red Roof" that eighteenth of April, 1906. Harry's large, soft eyes gazed out from his smooth, round, pale face above an incredibly high starched collar. Impeccably tailored, slope-shouldered, soft-spoken and gentle in appearance, penetrating intelligence, devastating wit, passionately loyal, a connoisseur gifted with a creative taste that he was on the threshhold of sublimating with a virtuosity wholly unpredictable.

A month after his introduction to it Sleeper was back again as a guest at "Red Roof." Through that summer the friendship of the two developed under the umbrella personality of the professor. On August 13, 1907, Sleeper succumbed to the Point and bought from George Stacy a narrow rectangle of ground and ledge between Caroline Sinkler's acquisition (which she had laughingly dubbed "Wrong Roof" and latched onto him to decorate for her) and the looming Colonial Arms. Then he contemplated the kind of house he would build in the shadow of the hotel, an impossible dream, one should think, on the face of it.

Harry Sleeper came from a family of independent means. His father was Major J. Henry Sleeper, commander of "Sleeper's Battery" in the Civil War. His Maine-born grandfather, Jacob Sleeper, made a fortune in Boston manufacturing clothing and speculating in real estate and was one of the three founders of Boston University, to which he gave over half a million dollars.

Doc and friends horse around the rigging of the schooner Nautilus, wrecked on Raymond's Beach, April 19, 1905. (Andrew L. Gray)

The late J. Henry Sleeper II stated emphatically that his Uncle Harry was a "blue baby," that "they didn't expect him to live very long at all, so he never went to school as far as I know. If he had any formal education, I never heard about it. Every year they expected the worst. He was always ill, never too healthy. They were surprised, both his brothers [Jacob and Stephen], that he lived so long."

"Blue baby" was the common designation for patent ductus arteriosus, a congenital anomaly whereby the ductus arteriosus, an extra blood vessel in the fetal heart, fails to close at birth so that an excess of arterial blood flows through the lungs, causing impaired circulation and cyanosis, blueness of the skin due to insufficient oxygen. The prognosis in the days before modern surgical correction was poor, although my physician-father survived without it until the age of eighty through a combination of rigid self-discipline, an otherwise robust constitution and fifty years under the care of the pioneer cardiologist Paul Dudley White.

So far as is known, the vulnerable young Harry Sleeper was educated entirely at home by private tutors. "Somebody bought him a dollhouse when he was a young boy, if I'm correct," recalled his nephew. "He went on decorating this dollhouse, and he got bigger and better dollhouses as presents because he was bedridden. And he used to get little pieces of furniture to put in them and make them more attractive."[8]

His father died when Harry was thirteen. He was devoted to his mother, Marie, with whom he lived in Boston and summered in the 1888 shingle-style family cottage on Marblehead Neck designed by Arthur Little, where on the billiard table he once created a memorably fantastic Japanese garden in miniature. When he came to the Point, he had studied architecture in Paris and worked for a Boston publishing house and dabbled in interior decorating, and was on the verge of something.

Toward the end of the summer of 1907 Andrew and Sleeper were motoring through the village of Essex when they happened upon an ancient, two-chimney, gambrel-roofed house, windows

broken, partly caved in. Poking around, they found that the interior was salvageable. They learned that this was the "Choate House," built in 1728 by William Cogswell out of the second of two cargoes of material transported from England, the ship which carried the first having come to grief on Hog, or Choate, Island and everything lost but the crew.

Isabella Stewart Gardner (hiding from camera), Joanna Davidge and Henry Sleeper, probably photographed by A. Piatt Andrew on the day they drove to Essex to view the "Choate House." (Society for the Preservation of New England Antiquities)

Here, they decided on the spot, was the beginning of Sleeper's Eastern Point cottage.

Presumably it was the excitement of their find and the desire to get her opinion of it that led Andrew to invite Mrs. Jack Gardner down to "Red Roof" for what appears to have been the first time.

September 7, 1907
Green Hill, Brookline, Mass.

Fancy, dear Mr. Andrew! I have this moment got your kind letter. It was dated Sept 1st & has been making a little round of visits, just after me! At last it has caught up! You say, any day before Friday the 13th! (What a day, will anyone dare to do anything that day?) Does your delightful invitation still hold out? If so, can I go to you for the night on Tuesday the 10th or Wednesday the 11th (Tuesday is best) of next week—whichever suits you best—and may I send my maid & small portmanteau down by some train, & will you motor me down? I shall be here at Green Hill, Warren Street, but if that is too far for your motor I will be at the door of Fenway Court (the front Fenway door) at any time you say. What fun all this will be for me! My love to the colony. I don't mind rain. So let us say rain or shine, unless you have changed your mind.

Yours,
I.S. GARDNER

The two men drove Mrs. Gardner and Joanna Davidge to Essex to view what they called the "Cogswell House." Harry planned to buy the entire interior, and Piatt took a snapshot of the old place before the dismantling.

That night, on her return to Brookline, Boston's *femme fantastique* rushed off a note to her host: "In a few hours, what a change! The land change does not make one into something rich & strange—alas! Your village is Fogland with the sea's white arms about you all. Don't let outsiders crawl in—only me! For I care. I love its rich, strange people, so far away. . . ."9

Overnight one of America's great houses was conceived and Isabella Stewart Gardner adopted Eastern Point as her favorite resort.

Sleeper had the dismantled innards of his Essex house carted to the Point—doors, wood carving, windows, the extensive panels and all the furniture obtainable. That fall he absorbed them in the cottage of his conception that, with the assistance of Halfdan M. Hanson, a young architect-craftsman of Gloucester, was rising up from the foundation blasted out of the ledge. Or, more accurately, they created his house around them, building from the inside out, a technique that would be one of his numerous trademarks. The Essex transplants returned to life as Cogswell Hall, Central Hall and the Green Dining Room in the stupendous complex they would inspire.

For the next twenty-seven years Hanson would work the increasingly challenging miracle of enclosing Sleeper's increasingly extravagent interior conceptions within the realities of space and building material, both for the boss and for increasingly demanding clients as the word of the Master's magic spread across the land.

The "Choate House" in Essex, the interior of which provided the nucleus of Henry Sleeper's "Beauport." Photo taken by Piatt Andrew September 12, 1907, his touring car at left. (Society for the Preservation of New England Antiquities)

Harry's workmen were hard at the plastering when the Colonial Arms next over was removed from the landscape in the awesome fire that New Year's Night of 1908; it could not have been otherwise than to his immense relief. Was he ever tempted to mutter, to paraphrase Henry II, "will no one rid me of this troublesome neighbor?"

In the spring the owner and his mother moved into the small cottage paneled from England by way of Essex. He called it "Little Beauport" after the name Samuel de Champlain had given the bay in 1606, the beautiful harbor he and the Frenchman had discovered exactly three hundred years apart.

Not without reason, Harry would soon drop the diminutive.

Doc Andrew played tennis vigorously with his neighbors up the hill on the Ramparts court. One of them anonymously committed their athletics to doggerel not long after the great clinician Sir William Osler had facetiously proposed in his 1905 valedictory at Johns Hopkins University that men generally are useless beyond the age of sixty and might as well be put away quietly by chloroform:

ANDREW'S TENNIS CLUB

I

When making application
To our association
For membership in Andrew's Tennis Club
The only stipulation, we
Require of a member, he
Must prove beyond a question
That his candidate's a dub.

II

"Doc" Andrew is our President—
Altho sometimes non-resident—
His duties often take him to the "Hub."
He reached this position
Without any opposition
Receiving all the votes for "High Grand Dub."

Professor Andrew
(in the Harvard
sweater) and
tennis chums.
(Andrew L. Gray)

III

Wilder Pollard is our Treasurer
An office filled with pleasure, for
There's nothing much to treasure except balls.
But according to our members, he
Succeeded with avidity
In purloining a collection fit for any nation's halls.

IV

The other resident "dubbers"
In the club called "plain flubbers"
Without comment from the writer are passed by.
Burgess, Williams and P. Corning
May be seen on any morning
Making smashes to the back nets—
Or a lob up in the sky.

V

Our game is rough and ready
But all of us are heady,
Especially our President when just returned from town.
Swift strokes are met with smashes
Or, more often, sharp tongue clashes,
But an oath is always silenced by a frown.

VI

The question of supremacy
Was decided without clemency
Each member trimming all the rest in turn.
Making all of us top-notchers—
Perhaps not to the watchers—
But a satisfactory thing to those concerned.

VII

While speaking of the gallery
"Doc" says that in a rally, he
Is sometimes undecided what to do.
For the smiles of all the ladies—
Not to mention dolls and babies—
Give antagonists a chance to slip one through.

VIII

This point is now decided,
But by the "Doc" derided—
The only way to keep him in the game
Is a pair of blinders, mocking
All those glances that are shocking
And are causing all our members so much pain.

IX
Our club is filled with sorrow
For there must be a "tomorrow"—
When we part and lay our tennis things aside.
We hope each passing year
Finds all our members here—
And time will prove that Dr. Osler lied.

Dabsville in 1908
from the harbor,
left to right:
"Beauport,"
"Wrong Roof,"
and "Red Roof."
(Society for the
Preservation of
New England
Antiquities)

On the terrace at "Red Roof," October 6, 1910, left to right: host Piatt Andrew, Japanese artist-scholar Okakura-Kakuzo, Isabella Gardner, Caroline Sinkler and Henry Davis Sleeper. (Andrew L. Gray)

~29~
DRAMATIS PERSONAE
DABSVILLEA

ТHE PANIC OF 1907 CONVINCED even the bankers that free enterprise, left entirely to itself, runs to anarchy, and Nelson W. Aldrich of Rhode Island, the Republican boss of the Senate, pushed through an emergency measure, the Aldrich-Vreeland Act, which created the National Monetary Commission to suggest some acceptable restraints. Having helped nominate William Howard Taft as Theodore Roosevelt's heir apparent in the summer of 1908, Aldrich was appointed chairman.

The senator needed experts to conduct a scholarly study of monetary systems in Europe. President Charles W. Eliot of Harvard was asked for the loan of a specialist in the field, and he selected Professor A. Piatt Andrew, who had been lecturing and writing on money, banking and commercial crises. Doc was thirty-five when he was named expert assistant and director of publications for the commission, with a two-year leave from Cambridge. He sailed for Europe early in August 1908, after inviting Isabella Gardner (they were intimately "A" and "Y" to each other now) to use "Red Roof" as often and as long as she pleased during his absence.

In the week or so before his departure on this high mission, Dabsville threw a round of farewell dinners that culminated in "the great fete at Miss Beaux's studio," as "Abe" recounted to his parents. Eighteen sat down for dinner, elaborately costumed: "I was made to wear a robe of a Roman emperor, with jewelled filet and placed on a kind of throne of red velvet, Mrs. Gardner sat opposite . . . on a less imposing throne of purple with a large 'Y' in gold. The air of the studio was heavy with incense and tuberoses; the table was gorgeous with old rose damask and wreathes of fruit."

They couldn't stay at "Red Roof" next month, he informed his father and mother, as Isabella would be there. "She has become a very good friend and I care a great deal about her."

Andrew left Sleeper in charge of his place and departed for New York. Harry wrote:

"Beauport" from Harry Sleeper's gatehouse. (Society for the Preservation of New England Antiquities)

Now that the hour of your sailing has come, I have a keen longing to be there, on the pier, among the multitude. Yet I'm glad I haven't got to watch the steamer slip silently away, down the harbor, toward the open sea. The train was enough, yesterday. After you had disappeared I stood looking at the cars growing smaller in perspective, until a curve swallowed them up. . . .[1]

More cheerful in a couple of days, Sleeper wrote the traveler again. He had taken friends to call at "Wrong Roof," where he found a ladies' dinner in full swing under the orchestration of Miss Sinkler, who,

with her usual skill and cleverness was "managing" the groups so they were all having a great time. Mr. Le Gendre soon put in an appearance, which made 13, so the party promptly broke up. . . . Mr. Wonson says "Madame" is much worried about the fog we are having here, and constantly asks if it is "probably foggy on the ocean where Mr. Andrew is"!!! I have caught four mice at Red Roof, and a few "brown-tails"—and have sent your "jumpers" to the laundry and your flannel trousers to Lewandos (so they won't shrink). That's all the household news just now. . . .[2]

"Mr. Wonson" was Austin Wonson, third of the seven sons of the East

Gloucester patriarch George Marble Wonson; he was "Red Roof's" care-taker and husband of "Madame," née Virginia Marie Gerrior, Doc's French cook and housekeeper. "Mrs. Wonson an excellent cook," her employer remarked in his diary as early as March 1903, and it was his regular practice to conduct guests to her kitchen to be introduced with the greatest deference to "Madame." After Austin's death in 1910 their son, George Marble Wonson II, succeeded as caretaker for nearly fifty years, and his wife Mary took charge of "Beauport's" hospitality and maintenance for Sleeper—an institution in her own right. George's younger brother Roland (Roley) was signed on as Andrew's personal chauffeur and remained with the Andrew-Patch family for many years. Muriel Wonson, wife of the youngest of the brothers, Myles (Myley), had to do with "Beauport" for years, too.

Mrs. Gardner swept into "Red Roof" with her usual swish, having invited Morris Carter, the librarian of the Boston Museum of Fine Arts, for the weekend. Like Andrew, he was a good thirty years her junior, and she made a courtier of him, putting him in charge of her own museum finally, and he did her biography. When he arrived at "Red Roof," he found her with her head in a bandage. She wrote Andrew on Sunday, August 9:

East façade of "Beauport." (Society for the Preservation of New England Antiquities)

> My dear A—
>
> So; good morning from this wonderful place! When you want "references" as a friend, send to me. I will give you one, A no. 1

The library at "Beauport." (Society for the Preservation of New England Antiquities)

kind. You have always been that to me, & this is the "comble"— For, I have not been tip top—& I came a cropper at the Hays Hammonds' last Monday, fell on my head—& so, this is such a wonderful cure. A man from the Art Museum, who is overworked & tired, is here for Sunday. He thinks it is Paradise. His name is Carter. Honest, you have no idea how wonderful it is. But there is an A no. 1 blank; that is A.P.A. And no matter where you are, it is not 1/2 as good as this! Such weather, such sunsets, such moon— The neighbors have been, one & all, devoted to me, as guest of Red Roof. Miss Davidge spent an hour here with M. Le Gendre and asked me to dinner. I lunched with Cecilia, & that enchanting Miss Sinkler comes and goes. Another hour with her yesterday. And Harry Sleeper, well, there are no words! Ella & Bridget, my two henchmen, are buzzing about like the bees about the bee balm. Ella says "Mr. Andrew ought not to lose the pleasure of being here—he is too good"—And, when you hear everything you will envy us. I came down on Friday & brought Mr. and Mrs. Sam Abbott of Rome & Henry Swift. On the way over (we were in Frick's motor) we went to Bay View by Annisquam where His Grace Archbishop O'Connell has got a place. He is a great friend of the Abbotts from Roman days. I made him come over here too! So, how you would have liked it! Everyone of those four guests were as crazy about this place as I. We had a picnic supper in the porch. Windows all open & all of us facing the water, with a sunset made on purpose. Then, as they were leaving at 9 p.m. out came the moon! We all thanked you. And the Archbishop is coming again, & if he and you are here for Thanksgiving, he has promised to come! But he will probably be in Rome, as he has been bidden. Gibbons is getting well, otherwise O'Connell might be made Cardinal. . . .

I have been writing this, dressing, & watching the bears. They were so infatuated with everything this morning that they didn't fight—but made love and were darlings. They stood up, side by side, looking up at me as I talked from the Boudoir window. And the birds! Do come back soon to see it all.

With eternal gratitude,

Yours

Y

Mrs. Jack was an occasional guest of the Hammonds in their stone castle across the harbor at Freshwater Cove, and young John Hays Hammond, the electrifying electronic engineer and inventor, and his sister Natalie were frequently entertained at Dabsville. Henry Swift was a Boston bachelor lawyer she had scooped up as her financial adviser. Though Cardinal Gibbons reigned for another thirteen years, Boston's Archbishop William H. O'Connell would soon be elevated, in 1911. As for the bears, Doc kept this pair—gifts from Sleeper—in an outdoor cage for the amusement of the house.

Isabella was in a dither over the Archbishop's visit and asked Sleeper to fetch her some lobsters for dinner and tidy up her porch. Preferring his own "ponderous carriage" to an auto, as Harry described the event, the prelate arrived an hour late and stopped to inquire the way at Miss Sinkler's, whose Protestant maid told Carrie there was "some kind of a priest at the door asking for a lost

The China Trade Room at "Beauport." Watercolor by W. E. B. Rankin, 1928. (Society for the Preservation of New England Antiquities)

gardener." The Archbishop missed "Red Roof" and turned up at Miss Davidge's, which caused Beaux to snipe that Isabella doubtless misdirected him to impress the uninvited.[3]

Y departed Gloucester but was back the next weekend and reported to the absent host that "every one & all their guests made a Tea, at Little Beauport yesterday. 100 Sinklers, 50 Davidges, & a few Beaux! I wish we could have turned the bears loose on them. *They* are a joy. I dress by the hour, watching them, in the morning."[4]

Even more eagerly she would have enjoyed loosing the bears on the U.S. Customs. A friend, thinking she was doing Mrs. Gardner a favor, brought home with her $80,000 worth of art objects Isabella had ordered in Europe, declaring them at $8,000. There were a few raised eyebrows when the inspectors opened the crates of "personal effects," and Y had to pay $30,000 in duties, and a $40,000 fine.

Beaux was amused. Joanna Davidge professed to be distressed. "Poor *dear* Mrs. Gardner, I am so sorry for her. Mr. Sleeper, the thing has a *very* ugly look about it, don't you think? Mamma says . . . "[5]

Piatt wrote home that he would "like to shoot somebody." Harry confessed to him on August 20 that he was "somewhat thrilled" when he read the *Boston Transcript*'s defense of their friend. And

Red Roof is well. Only one more mouse caught, though the traps are kept set. The one that was caught ran across Mrs. Gardner's face, in the night, before he found the trap which proved his tomb. . . . Mrs. Clay is having a function this p.m. . . . I told Miss Sinkler that the hostess little realized the danger of a "stampede" she was running when she included the guests at "Wrong Roof."

Ever gossipy, a week later Sleeper informed Piatt that a female house guest at "Green Alley" told Helen Patch "she always enjoyed a cigarette after dinner. I wonder if Miss Beaux knows what sort of a person she is harboring!"[6]

And the next day the faithful Harry gave APA an atmospheric report on the state of "Red Roof," where he said he was spending nearly half his time:

Let me tell you just how it would all look if you should come back this afternoon: The two oak trees are more green and flourishing than ever. The clematis has climbed high into the willow by the garage, and is so thick and laden with blossoms over the gate that you might have to stoop a little to pass under it. Inside, before you come to the herb garden are the shrubs with brilliant red berries, and then the herbs, all thick and pungent. The balsam still blossoming, and some of the geraniums 3 feet high. The two evergreens at the beginning of the lantern path have grown tremendously, and all along the path the wild seeds you planted have done their utmost to make it gay. The hopvines are achieving greatness, and the geraniums under the umbrella are flaming away. Next you would hear the bears (fat and fascinating) climbing up their cage to

see who was approaching. As for the geraniums by the piazza door, the vines on the outside of the porch, and the twin pines in front, they look like pictures in a florists catalogue.

Inside the house you will find green branches and bay where they always are, the latest illustration on the table, and the casements open. Upstairs, in your room, 6 fine, clean pairs of white trousers, and a row of shining shoes sticking out from under the sofa. And finally (if you had telephoned ahead that you were coming), a bowl of thyme on your writing table, and a lilac note of welcome from "Wrong Roof," another from "Green Alley," some salted peanuts, and even the thermos bottle! Down in the kitchen "Madame" busy and contented, Bessie voluble, and Susie speechless. Something good roasting in the oven, and many other familiar details. Last, and best, every one happier than you could possibly be, just because you had come home.[7]

Actually it was "Beauport" now, more than "Red Roof," creating the sensation. Arthur D. Little, partner in the Boston architectural firm of Little and Browne, who had designed the J. Henry Sleeper cottage on Marblehead Neck where Harry summered as a boy, visited "Beauport" for a day that same week and was so impressed that he offered his host the services of his organization, should he build a house for anyone else.

The magic Sleeper touch was putting "Beauport" on the map, and his blossoming creation was returning the favor. Harry was on the edge of fame

Dabsville's "Tiffany Ball," March 1913. Doc Andrew, Cecilia Beaux, Harry Sleeper, Mrs. H. P. Davison and Dallas McGrew stand behind the kneeling Dorothea and Rosamond Gilder, daughters of the editor Richard Watson Gilder. (Helen Patch Gray)

Cecilia Beaux,
Henry Sleeper,
and Piatt
Andrew's mother,
Mrs. A. P.
Andrew, at
"Beauport,"
November 1912.
(Helen Patch
Gray)

as an interior (and exterior) decorator, in the vanguard of the craze for early Americana. Even now a couple of people were after him to do a house for them. Little's offer, he confided to Andrew, "was flattering, and I haven't mentioned it to anyone (even to mother, yet). The only reason I speak of it now is because I've been thinking that I should never have taken the pains I did, nor would Beauport have existed, but for you."[8]

As for Y, she wrote A that "taking people to see Little Beauport seems to be my mission in life."[9]

Harry wasn't at home to everyone, and he delighted in recounting to Andrew:

The other day I had a letter from two snobs I know in Philadelphia. They were in Newport—had been for two months—but as the season was really over, and they had heard my place was delightful, they wanted to stop over a Sunday with me, on their way to Bar Harbor. I didn't feel up to it, so I wrote them a cordial note saying I would be delighted to see them at any time, that I had no automobile, no motor boat, no horses, and a poor cook, that my neighbors were all middle-aged unmarried women, and that I saw in the morning paper that a northeasterly storm was due here and for them to be sure to let me know when to expect them. This morning came the information that they had been obliged to go to New York unexpectedly.[10]

The sixth anniversary of the "settlement" of "Red Roof" was the second of September this summer of 1908, and Beaux and Sleeper slipped over in the early evening under a new moon and a sky full of stars, two or three coasters out there ghosting into the harbor, and they hung Cecilia's annual offering of a heliotrope wreath around the neck of the statue of St. Marie in their neighbor's garden.

The mistress of "Green Alley" was not to have Piatt to herself for long, however, even in absentia, and the sequel was related to him by Sleeper on the fifteenth:

> Mrs. Gardner came Sunday. Just before she arrived I had a note saying she wanted to do something I had asked her to a while ago:—Take a small wreath of thyme to the Archbishop and have it blessed, for Red Roof. So I made it Sunday evening, and Miss Sinkler and I met her, in the auto, at the station, and went directly to Msgr. O'Connell's. He received us in his purple, and he not only blessed the wreath, but took it into his chapel, laid it on the altar, and consecrated it. Later, after an hour at Wrong Roof, where there were guests staying, "Y" and I went over and hung it below St. Marie. . . .

> Miss Davidge, whom I saw yesterday, looked staggered upon being told that a premeditated "progress" had been made by the queen. She said that she "and mama were not at home Sunday afternoon" and were so sorry to have missed her"—(They were not visited at all, you know!). And she added, on learning the hour of

Bon voyage *to Piatt Andrew in Cecilia Beaux's studio, July 30, 1908. (Andrew L. Gray)*

Y's departure, that "it must be so convenient to be able to travel alone at night without fear of being spoken to." Miss Beaux has a slight attack of distemper, caused probably by the trinity of Mrs. Gardner, the Archbishop and the wreath. Time will heal, I trust. "Fanny" [a visiting relative of Miss Sinkler on the Wharton side] is 365 times as affected as she was a year ago. Every evening she goes out to your fence ("dressed for dinner") and gathers a *garland* of clematis, and then drifts back to Wrong Roof singing, and *lies* upon the couch in the living room, quite unable to move, reading de Musset, and occasionally requesting that a door or window be opened or closed. Tonight I am going to pay Albert extra to stay and insult her, if she goes for the clematis. . . .

The denizens of Dabsville delighted in dramatizing Doc's absence and vying for his correspondence, none with more savor than his neighbor to the north, the Lavender Lady:

> Your place looks most lovely, all blossoming fragrance and brooding solitude enveloping the whole atmosphere with the subtle knowledge that the heart of it is away. Did Mr. Sleeper write you he had been sick? I am sure not—he was wretched for a day or two, I am afraid, and looked very badly but you know how selfless he is and he made nothing of it. To us he looks much better. He has a wonderful nature hasn't he, and I am glad to say is as witty as ever and doubtless I have been slaughtered by him for your amusement. Dabsville has been quite active lately and lovers lurk lingeringly to the south of us but the 8 mile speed limit still guards some of us. . . .[11]

Carrie must have been introducing to the Dabsville stage the protagonists in Eastern Point's most Browningesque romance, for which the credit was hers. Among her house guests was an intriguing, sensitive, handsome young archeologist, Dr. David Randall-MacIver, a Scot. He was thirty-four, and he no sooner met Joanna Davidge (still very attractive, though she had thirteen years on him) than he fell (quite literally) in love with her and vowed to end the spinsterhood to which all Dabsville had supposed she, and Mamma, were quite dedicated. ("David was paddling his canoe," according to Caroline Lockwood, "and Joanna was swimming and said come on in, so he did, uniform and all.")

Overflowing with charm and wit and zest, the bearded Oxonian was of one of the founding families of the Cunard Line, and after his father died he hyphenated the name of his stepfather, for whom he had great affection, to his own. He had been Laycock Scholar in Egyptology at Worcester College, Oxford, and dug some in Egypt where he applied his anthropology to measuring skulls. He excavated in Rhodesia in 1905 under the auspices of the British Association and Rhodes Trustees, and out of that expedition published *Medieval Rhodesia* in 1906. Then in 1907 he ran a dig in Nubia for the University of Pennsylvania and was appointed Curator of Egyptology at the University Museum in Philadelphia, where he made a close friend of one of the museum's founders and financial backers, Eckley Coxe, the only child of Carrie Sinkler's rich sister Elizabeth.

Earlier in the year Caroline had written Doc from Windy Hill that "a rather interesting Scotchman" had been a house guest—"a fellow from Oxford in Rhodesia and Egypt and I assure you by the sixth day I began to feel dug up myself. . . . If Mr. MacIver goes to Harvard I want you to meet him. He is really interesting and has delightful sides. One of them is like one of yours—and you'll see it too."[12]

This quite unexpected romance—David's dashing advance against Joanna's discreet but not precipitous retreat—amazed and amused Dabsville, which tended to pay rather more homage to Puck than to Cupid. Harry gossiped to Piatt on September 19:

> Dr. McKeever went from Wrong Roof, to stay at Miss Davidge's. He is the third man she has "invited away" from Miss Sinkler, so when Miss Caroline Lewis saw her she remarked "Joanna, I hear you have become a robber of hen roosts!" Miss Davidge also asked Miss Lewis what she did when a man proposed to her on a two days acquaintance. The answer was "Nothing"— because she had "never known the situation." All the women of Dabsville are "guessing" however! Later Miss Davidge said, pensively, that she was wondering if it was wise to take any jewelry from a man. I said only a plain gold ring, that anything else would be indiscreet, without that. Miss Beaux is going to Miss Tyson's this week. She leaves two "sitters" (who are boarding at Gloucester, to be painted) and just whisks her tail and goes off like a colt for two

days. Miss Sinkler says she had better take care that all her eggs don't get cold. . . .

With Piatt about to return from his European mission, Sleeper got up a packet of Dabsville letters for him, led off by his own amusing billet of September 27:

> I caught a mouse by your living room fireplace yesterday, and just showed it to the bears, whereupon they became frantic, leaped about their cage, showing their teeth, snarling, and behaving as though they were thoroughly frightened! So I decided not to give it to them, but to wait until you got home, and could enjoy the proceeding. . . . Miss Davidge confided to me this morning that he (Old Brown, working at Wrong Roof again) was "impertinent to Miss Sinkler sometimes, without her seeming to realize it." That he was "too fond of women"!!! I lunched Thursday at "Tanglefoot," ["Tanglewood," the John Greenough cottage] to meet Mr. Justice Holmes, who was paying his autumn visit there. [Like his father before him, U.S. Supreme Court Justice Oliver Wendell Holmes, Jr., was a sometime visitor at the Point from the family summer seat at Beverly Farms.] Miss Sinkler was invited at 11 a.m., and couldn't go of course.
>
> Yesterday Dabsville had a picnic. We went by trolley to Ipswich, where on our haunches, in a field occupied only by a pregnant horse and ourselves, we ate our poor lunch. There was Miss Davidge and her visiting Frenchman, whose long repulsive mustache turned our stomachs, particularly as we were obliged to drink after him—for having forgotten tumblers, we all had to share the top of a thermos bottle. Then there was Miss Sinkler, and Miss Julia Sinkler and a man who is staying at the Greenoughs. We wandered far from the cars, and, after walking some further distance in search of an "antique shop" of which I had heard, got lost. Then followed much more walking, before we came upon a car track. Miss Sinkler never lost her gaiety during the ordeal, but "Johanna," after some premonitory murmurings of her incapacity for further pilgrimage, sat down, and put on her "immaculate conception" look—and was only ultimately moved by false promises of a livery stable in the offing. We arrived home after dark, in the fog—somewhat soggy—but still ribald. . . .

Isabella's dart from this quiver, dispatched from her Brookline estate, was sharp with anticipation:

> The Archbishop is coming to the Thanksgiving dinner, and everything will be as medieval as we can make it—Falernian wines and Eels! Only not the latter please! But we will have a poison-ring! & wind up with a Gregorian Chant. Perhaps we might (we, you & I) make the Thanksgiving Dinner a sort of Sleeper Fete—A house

warming in his big room! But the Widow C is the word—Mum I mean—Say nothing to nobody & never think of it again, if you don't like the idea. . . . [13]

When word of Y's outlandish project reached Carrie Sinkler in Philadelphia she wanted Piatt to know that "when I heard you were going to have an uncommon or Gardner Thanksgiving I wrote to Charleston to send you a basket of pomegranates and magnolia and only heard the other day that they had not been sent as the pomegranates were just over." [14]

President Taft was inaugurated that next March, 1909, and in June appointed Piatt Andrew director of the U.S. Mint with the understanding that he would continue to completion both his massive task of editing and publishing the forty-volume report of the National Monetary Commission and his collaboration with Senator Aldrich on the Aldrich Plan of fiscal reform, which had emerged from the study. (Woodrow Wilson and the Democrats adopted the plan, in somewhat altered form, as the Federal Reserve Act of 1914. Andrew was said to have been the chief architect of the draft that, had it been implemented by the Republicans, would have placed control of the system chiefly with the bankers, rather than with the government, as eventuated in the Democratic version.)

Andrew's boss was Taft's Treasury Secretary, Franklin MacVeagh. Y was agog: "Did you go with MacVeagh to see Taft on the way to Red Roof? I think you did, & I already fancy the paper dollars cut into shapes to please the powers that be, T-MacV-&A. " [15]

Senator Aldrich was said to regard Professor Andrew as the top monetary expert in the country, and he harbored a fatherly affection for him. The Rhode Island strong man had phoned Miss Sinkler when he found they were at the same hotel in London, as she relayed it to APA: "And he came in

Piatt Andrew and Mrs. Gardner at "Red Roof," December 29, 1913, flanked by Mary Berenson and her husband Bernard Berenson, the great art collector who influenced Gardner's own collection. (Isabella Stewart Gardner Museum)

and we had such a nice talk sauced mostly with you. How fond and proud he is of you! I became quite fond of him in consequence. . . .[16]

President Taft and his family were so taken with Piatt that they put out feelers in this first spring of his administration for a summer White House on Eastern Point.

"Are the Tafts really coming to The Ramparts," Carrie wanted to know from Philadelphia, "and is it for your sake?"[17]

But Mrs. Raymond, whose husband was a dead ringer for the president, stated through a local real estate agent that she had no intention of leasing or selling her estate to anyone.

"Beauport," its eclectic curiosities now expanded to twenty-six chambers of delightfully odd sizes and shapes under Harry Sleeper's compulsions, was also considered by the emissaries of the 354-pound chief executive. However, as the newspaper reflected, "it would be difficult to imagine the massive frame of the President passing through one of the small doors of ancient make."[18]

Piatt's protracted absences in Washington left a hole in the life of Dabsville. The mistress of "Wrong Roof" sighed:

> Dear Director but Dearer Doc—Why weren't you here this afternoon when I went down your path of fragrance thro' all the mystery and perfume of the winding way. I had such a nice talk with your mother while the sunset deepened and glowed over the harbour and the crescent moon hung over Red Roof like a symbol of some beautiful thing for you. . . . I know you are having a wonderful time and doing great things too for the future and for the country but you will come back soon won't you to Red Roof. We all miss you so much—and I miss talking to you dreadfully but I am hoping for us all to have some firelit talks in October if you are not lured away too long—and for music and all the wonderful things you bring into our Dabsville lives. . . .[19]

Lavender might sigh, but Y took matters in hand. Recalling that Doc had mentioned in a letter meeting the tantalizingly beautiful and eligible young heiress Dorothy Whitney in Washington in February, and having known her late father, William, Mrs. Gardner wrote her prey early in April to accompany her to Gloucester for an Easter weekend that included a beach picnic at Coffin's Beach, culminating in a party at "Red Roof" described thusly by the host:

> On Saturday Harry Sleeper and I went to Boston and got Mrs. Gardner and met Miss Whitney, followed the Harvard-Columbia boat race, and got down to Gloucester just about sundown. There were six fellows and two ladies for dinner, which was served on a foot-high table in the new library. We all sat on the floor, and in the center of the table was a little fenced-in yard with two baby rabbits and eighteen small chickens. The walls and ceiling of the room were

hung with Turkey red made up like a tent, in the top of which hung two flaming Roman lamps. On the sides of the tent were tiger and bear and leopard skins, which Harry had rented for the occasion, and other skins and skulls lay about on the stone floor. It was a dreamlike scene for us all, but especially for those who saw it for the first time when they were escorted in to dinner.[20]

Not a word of Miss Whitney. About to be appointed Director of the Mint and preoccupied with monetary matters, Doc failed to follow up. The lady took off on a trip around the world and in Peking met Willard Straight, a cordial friend of Andrew who was in the process of exchanging a career in diplomacy for international banking and grabbed the stick as if in a relay race, neither realizing they were in competition.

In a year's time Doc had done a sterling job of retooling the Mint to the tune of a $320,000 annual saving in its budget. He approached the task with a certain unconventionality that appalled the bureaucrats. Once some question arose as to the integrity of the sacred troy pound, the official standard of measure at the Philadelphia Mint. Director Andrew offhandedly lifted this holy object from its sepulcher, dropped it in his suitcase and took it with him to Washington to have it tested at the Bureau of Standards.

Secretary MacVeagh's first choice for assistant secretary in charge of fiscal affairs, probably the most significant post in the department, had been Charles D. Norton, who resigned in the spring of 1910 to be the president's personal secretary. Piatt was named by Taft in June to succeed Norton as assistant secretary of the Treasury. So high was his stock at the White House that about a year later, when Norton resigned as his aide, Mr. Taft wanted

Doc feeds a cherry to Louise Crowninshield, June 9, 1909. (Andrew L. Gray)

Andrew to take the job, an honor that he declined. Yet, though the president beamed, the clouds were gathering at the Treasury.

The clouds had already gathered behind the schooner *Minerva* of Plymouth, 56 tons gross, making for Gloucester from a fishing trip the night of February 11, 1910. All was apparently well with this retired Boston pilot boat, jogging along under her four lowers, and although they had been overtaken by a thick northeaster making heavy seas and a wall of swirling snow that blotted out beyond their bowsprit, Captain Simon Landry and his two-man watch felt assured of their offshore position.

And then she struck, full on shore with a crash that threw the rest of the crew out of their bunks. All eight rushed on deck. They couldn't see a thing through the snow, but they could unmistakably feel her grinding on the rocks, and hear the breakers all around.

They got four dories over and rowed to the westward, keeping clear of the surf. When they glimpsed Eastern Point Light they knew where they were and made it around the breakwater to safety.

When they walked back over the Point next day they found *Minerva* had run full onto the lower ledge of Brace Rock, and soon nothing was left of her but wood for the hearths of East Gloucester.

Meanwhile, rather more successfully, David Randall-MacIver, M.A., D.Sc., F.R.G.S., had been pursuing *his* course and the not hopelessly reluctant Joanna with such fancies as the following, printed on a series of cards with watercolored illustrations (surely by the swain), the whole bound in a silken folder bearing a watercolor lily-of-the-valley on the cover, nineteen verses in all:

1

Should you ask me, should you question,
Why life's song is yet unsung;
Why so late to learn the lesson
Others learn when they are young?

2

I should answer, questions dreading,
Should reply in manner savage;
My youth was lost, my life was ebbing
E're I met *** **. . . .

9

Did our staid old world, upheaving,
Cast its gems to Hoxanna's skies,

Which heaven's couriers, deeply grieving,
Had to keep for * * * eyes. . . .

                        19

I love you madly, end my strife,
And bid me live alone for thee
Take, take my hand, my heart, my life,
And P.D.Q., R.S.V.P.

Well, what could you do with a man like this, when your own life was even farther on the ebb, and he returned two summers in a row to rent the "Mother Ann Cottage" just to be near and fling about such sweet nothings?

The mistress of Miss Davidge's classes could learn as well as teach, after all—even lessons "others learn when they are young"—and she surrendered to David's most persistent expedition and married him, to the delight of their numerous friends, in the chantry of Grace Church in New York on March 21, 1911. The Randall-MacIvers honeymooned that summer in Joanna's house at the Point; Mama was surely on the scene and perhaps regarded the cessation of her protracted chaperonage, and the agent responsible, with a mixture of emotions.

Perhaps, too, the Randall-MacIver contagion that spring affected even Mrs. Jack, who nudged her Doc, "When does your time come?" He acquiesced, and a cruise in the Treasury yacht *Apache* on the Potomac and James Rivers was arranged for Piatt and Dorothy Whitney, chaperoned by Isabella (who fell ill and was replaced by a Whitney friend) and Harry in mid-April 1911. On the third day of the cruise the diffident suitor proposed. Willard Straight by now owned the inside track, and Doc was predictably refused.

Upon their return to Washington on April 25, the assistant secretary made a last try, this time by letter, "with S [Harry Sleeper] at my elbow as I write":

> I long for the chance to be with you—to tell you the things that come into my life, to share the things you care for—to work for you and care for you,—and to live for you and love you always. Can it not be?

"No, it couldn't," comments his grandnephew Andrew Gray somewhat wistfully, "and the admitted presence of 'S' during this missive's composition could not have augmented its impact. This time, at all events, the refusal stuck." And Dorothy Whitney and Willard Straight were married that autumn.[21]

Piatt Andrew's old friend Dr. William James, the psychologist who wrote like a novelist, had died the previous August, and that spring of 1911 his brother Henry, the novelist who wrote like a psychologist, traveled to Cambridge from England in connection with his estate. The author visited Isabella Gardner, whom he had known for many years, at "Fenway Court" in May, and a few weeks later she took him down to Eastern Point for lunch at "Green Alley" with Cecilia Beaux. He shuddered slightly at the recollection:

> It was even much of a reprieve from death to go with you that summer's day to lunch with the all-but-deadly Cecilia; under the mere ghostly echo of the *énervement* of whose tongue I kind of wriggle and thresh about still—till rescued by the bounty of the dear young man, the Newfoundland dog, the great St. Bernard nosing-in-the-snow neighbor, of whose conveyance of me to his miraculous house, inanimate even though exasperated, I retain, please tell him, the liveliest, literally the fondest, appreciation. . . .[22]

Harry to the rescue. More brilliant than charming, one who knew her has said of Bo, "with a face of stone." And so the expatriate seems to have found her. Cecilia, for her part, dismissed the occasion as a "day of wet fog, which he persisted in admiring, having found everything in America too hard and noisy . . . unendurable, in fact."[23] But each relented, and later she sketched him in New York.

Following the annual spring custom he began in 1910, Assistant Treasury Secretary Andrew entertained the hoary-handed, salt-encrusted members of the Gloucester Master Mariners Association at "Red Roof" on April 17, 1912—three days before the launching from the Tarr and James yard in Essex of the 105-foot fishing schooner *A. Piatt Andrew*, built for Captain John Chisholm and her master, Captain Wallace Bruce.

The *Andrew* was a handsome, spoon-bowed vessel carrying a short bowsprit and plenty of sail, after lines drawn by Boston designer Tom McManus. In three weeks she was fitted out and ready for her maiden voyage under Captain Bruce to Cape North. Harry Sleeper conveyed the excitement of the departure in a letter dated May 9 to her namesake, who was in Washington:

> The "A. Piatt Andrew" went out "to the Banks" this morning—looking glorious! Capt. Chisholm only gave me about 25 minutes notice, but I rushed over to Red Roof, with my *enormous* American flag (inherited, but never used by *me* before!) and, with help from George, spread it over your west roof where it was vastly effective. Then I *raked* out your smaller American flags, and quantities of Turkey red, and summoning the Tarr family and George Wonson, managed to make a fine showing of enthusiasm! So that they towed over toward us, and gave us several salutes!!! Of course they knew you were in Washington, but, I fancy, suspected that the attention was due to your orders (as it *was*, for you asked me to take notice!) and so they were especially responsive. . . .

Piatt proudly took Isabella Gardner and Caroline Sinkler aboard the *Andrew* on a tour of inspection that October. She had already made her mark as a highliner and would set records as one of the top money-makers

in the history of the Gloucester fleet before she was sent to the bottom, with two other Gloucester fishermen, by a Canadian steam trawler off the Nova Scotian coast in August 1918. Her crew took to their dories before she was sunk and were picked up later. The trawler was an enemy prize, a decoy for the German submarine *U-156* lurking nearby. Two more months, and this famous U-boat struck a mine in the North Sea and went down with all hands.

Doc would have the last word, though. On May 15, 1922—to show what Gloucester thought of him—a second *A. Piatt Andrew* was launched at Essex by Arthur D. Story—schooner-rigged at first, then altered to a dragger, and years later sold down to New Bedford.

Meeting of the Gloucester Master Mariners Association at "Red Roof," April 6, 1912. Front row from left: Linda Thomas (in white), Mrs. Cole Porter-to-be; Mrs. Ethel Roosevelt (TR's daughter); Doc Andrew (fourth); Mrs. Jack (sixth). (Helen Patch Gray)

Henry Sleeper, Louis Allard, Piatt Andrew, and Edgar Carter Rust, about 1909.
(Society for the Preservation of New England Antiquities)

~30~
OF POLITICS AND PRATFALLS

A HABITUÉ OF THE "SHESHORE," AS some sharp tongue dubbed Dabsville, was the stage and screen actor H. B. Warner, who had starred in *Alias Jimmy Valentine* on Broadway and then in Boston. Stumbling onto Bass Rocks in 1910, he built a cottage there in 1912 that he and his wife called "Alwysyn," which sounds Gaelic but isn't. The actor was a favorite on the Point, especially at "Red Roof."

Bright if not early one summer morning Harry Warner and Doc Andrew bounded up Fort Hill in their pajamas to roust out a couple of the vivacious and athletic Pollard girls for doubles at tennis, and how uproariously they laughed when Mrs. Pollard informed them tartly that she was sorry but Elise, anyway, couldn't join them just then as her nightdress was in the wash.

A more usual costume for tennis (now sweeping the precincts of the privileged) consisted of white ducks and shirts for the men, and for the more daring (and younger) ladies, skirts that split the difference twixt ankle and knee, and middy blouses. The females had invaded and indeed routed "Andrew's Tennis Club," and the twang of ball against catgut and the skid of sneaker on clay had turned "The Ramparts" court into an arena of more or less amiable intersexual rivalry by the summer of 1910.

The end of that August Edward Williams of Sherwin-Williams, one of Mrs. Raymond's sons-in-law, surveyed these scamperings (in which he took a leading part) and announced in a circular letter "To the Tennis Players of Eastern Point" that the day had arrived to perpetuate good times and the tournaments in which they had culminated in recent years by the award of a trophy. And who better than Uncle Henry to memorialize? For "the name is one which has always represented to me what is best in clean, fair, outdoor sports of all kinds. And I hope you will all enjoy competing for the ROUSE CUP."

Thus was offered what has been said by Point chauvinists to be among the oldest, if not the oldest, American tennis cup in active competition until its retirement eighty years later in 1990. Rules were promulgated, a committee was gathered and a more governed-than-ordinary tournament was held. And the donor himself, immortalized in that peculiar doggerel of an earlier chapter as one of the "plain flubbers," discovered himself to be the first winner of the Henry C. Rouse Tennis Cup.

This was the Point's most Olympic period. Besides the yachting and the golf tourneys at the links and the tennis, baseball "matches" were played two seasons running in 1911 and 1912 between the "Beets" and the "Cabbages" (the Beets beat, four to three), the "Mother Ann Tennis Tournament" in 1911 (for ladies in the fullness of their maturity, won by one of the Mrs. Greenoughs), a yapping good dog show the same year (Mr. Clay's sheepdog did not account himself well), preceded by three weeks by the one and only Eastern Point gymkhana of record, an amalgam of tennis, ping-pong, bowls, three-legged race, thread-and-needle race, potato race, bowling and pool; this test of versatility and endurance was won by the boundlessly kinetic boy-and-girl team of Pauline Pollard and Jack Raymond, who would in a few years conquer all by uniting as husband and wife.

Indoor sports, on the Dabsville shore in any case, were possibly more bizarre yet. One evening Harry Sleeper threw a Roman feast. The guests were instructed to arrive in the garb of the ancients. At the banquet they found that they had been consigned to couches on which they were supposed to recline while partaking from tables only a foot off the floor, much to the annoyance of the less adept, who complained bitterly that they couldn't keep their togas out of their food.

Some trifling unconventionalities of libidinous expression as well have been attributed to one or another subdivision of Dabsville. But we are well advised to let delicacy prevail; nothing is so helpless before hearsay, or so private where public offense is neither meant nor made.

After all, Dabsville was no less discreet than debonair. Its principals made of it a principality, and the years of their ascendance—in the studied view of Piatt Andrew's grandnephew Andrew Gray—were *La Belle Epoque* of Eastern Point, indeed, not to make too fine a point of it, perhaps of *La Belle Epoque* itself:

> Sleeper, Beaux and Andrew ran the show, I think, though I must say the documents show Andrew to have been the king pin. The nucleus they formed on the Point appears to have expanded to absorb people according to their wit, good looks, vivacity and capacity for self-dramatization. . . . They all drank very little—most worked rather hard, even when playing—and took great pleasure in each others' success. Those still living who attended their frequent costume parties and ceremonial dinners recall them in detail to this day. They were very hospitable to outsiders—Leslie Buswell and Jack Hammond among others—but surely rather snobbish toward people less verbally adept than they. They were very private people. . . .

Dabsville south to Black Bess, December 1971. (David B. Arnold III)

Senator Nelson W. Aldrich (seated left) and his family at "Red Roof," August 12, 1910. The party includes John D. Rockefeller, Jr. (standing right), Richard Aldrich (chatting with Henry Sleeper, center), and Piatt Andrew's parents. (Andrew L. Gray)

The key was the absence of children. No sailing, no nonsense, no preoccupation with childish things. Sinkler, Davidge, Beaux et al. were completely free to carry out the elaborate social functions which Andrew and Sleeper devised for them. (Of course Beaux was very much a queen in her own right.) They collaborated very well. . . . They were quite snooty toward newcomers to the Point: by that time Beaux and Andrew were in the great world and were more interested in attracting guests than courting new neighbors.[1]

Out in that great world on the twenty-second of June, 1912, the Republican steamroller renominated President Taft and shoved his onetime patron Teddy Roosevelt over the edge into enmity and the third-party candidacy that ended both their political careers; it also flattened Piatt Andrew's as a sub-Cabinet member.

The assistant secretary of the Treasury's relations with his superior, Secretary MacVeagh (whom he regarded as an incompetent obstructionist), had fallen apart. They were barely on speaking terms when Andrew, against MacVeagh's explicit instructions, traveled from Washington to Chicago to attend the Republican national convention.

A few days after his return, on July 2, Piatt wrote the president and the secretary letters of resignation. He said he spoke for most of the key officials in the Treasury Department, whom he cited by name, when he charged that its work was being impossibly hindered at every turn by MacVeagh's "idiosyncrasies and incapacity for decision."[2]

As it turned out, there was some question whether the initiative here was Dr. Andrew's, for in reply the White House issued a brief statement that the president had requested his resignation "in view of his failure to obey orders given him by the Secretary."[3] The president was having a miserable time of it anyway, and here was one more hair added to his shirt.

Secretary MacVeagh deplored his former assistant's "inefficiency" as an administrator (which brought an immediate defense from Senator Henry Cabot Lodge); in the course of insisting on going to Chicago against his wishes, MacVeagh contended, Andrew had admitted he planned to enter politics and regarded the convention as a good opportunity to make some useful contacts.[4] (Several years afterwards APA said the real quarrel was over the Aldrich Plan, that MacVeagh was jealous and resented his mission to Chicago, which was actually undertaken at the request of several Republican senators who urged him to lobby for its adoption in the Republican platform, in which he was successful). Piatt told the press he held no grudge against Mr. Taft and intended to work for his reelection in the fall.

Three months after this parting of the ways, President and Mrs. Taft motored unexpectedly from Beverly, where they were staying, to Gloucester to hear Mr. Taft's old friend from Yale, the Reverend Samuel Bushnell, preach at Trinity Congregational Church. After the service they were greeted by the nieces of the president's late advisor, as reported in the press:

> As President and Mrs. Taft descended the outside steps, Helen A. and Paula L. Patch, the former nine years and the latter three and one-half years, daughters of Mayor and Mrs. Isaac Patch, presented the President and his wife with bouquets of flowers. Mrs. Taft kissed little Paula affectionately, while the President also thanked Miss Helen for her kind remembrance and entered the auto which was in waiting.[5]

"And so Wilson is victor and what a dismal petering out for Taft," Carrie Sinkler wrote Piatt in November. "But I do rejoice in thinking of that jealous and spiteful and small-brained MacVeagh returning without honor to his grocery or whatever they called it." (He was one of the biggest wholesalers in the Midwest.)

It is time to cast up on the shores of our narrative another wreck.

The coasting schooner *Clara Jane* of Calais, Maine, 124 tons gross, had been making hard weather of it, bound from Portland for Boston with 140,000 feet of lumber. It was early in the morning of the tenth of January, 1913, and she had taken a pounding from heavy seas scuffed up by a northwest gale, and she was leaking.

Off the Point in the darkness they tried to come about and work offshore but misstayed; in irons, the *Clara Jane* drifted stern first toward the rocks about 200 feet east of Mother Ann. Captain F. A. Kilton ordered the anchor hove, but too late, and she struck. The four of them put their dory over and rowed to Flat Rock, waded ashore and found shelter at the lighthouse.

The schooner Clara Jane pounds ashore at Eastern Point Light, January 10, 1913. (H. Spooner photo, courtesy Gordon W. Thomas)

For three hours next day the tugs *Eveleth* and *Nellie* from Gloucester tried to pull the burdensome schooner off. The day following, while the lifeboat from Dolliver's Neck was running her hawser out to the wreck, it caught in the *Eveleth*'s propeller.

Now the disabled tug was on her way to join the *Clara Jane*. They let both anchors go, when a sudden squall came up, giving her added way toward shore, and they broke out. Just as the tug was on the point of striking the rocks, a bight in the hawser fouled a jagged jut of ledge and she fetched up.

This gave breather enough to send for the tug *Mariner*, which steamed out the harbor and towed the *Eveleth* in. They stripped *Clara Jane* and abandoned her, and she pounded to pieces, but not before Chester Walen went out with his camera and recorded the scene.

It was two years after his departure from the Taft administration before Piatt Andrew entered elective politics. With Europe brought almost to war by the assassination of Archduke Ferdinand on June 28, 1914, internationalist Andrew hankered to get in the action and made up his mind to go after the sixth congressional seat of the deeply entrenched Augustus P. Gardner of Hamilton. Besides being Senator Lodge's son-in-law and the dashing darling of the North Shore oligarchy, Gussie Gardner happened to be a favorite nephew of Mrs. Jack Gardner. The job was to win the Republican primary in September, which amounted to election in this district.

Piatt was of course a Hoosier, an outsider, which was made much of; and the rumor was set afoot that he was a Jew. Neither the fact nor the fiction was a political asset in the parochial precincts of Essex County. He campaigned vigorously while Congressman Gardner remained nearly all summer in London, whence he sent word to his constituents that the ailing health of his distinguished father-in-law the senator (who was the Republican boss of the North Shore) required his loyal presence.

Few climbs are more uphill in politics than trying to unseat a congressman, and Doc made time as fast and high as his own energy and the new technology of aerodynamics would carry him. In fact, he was one of the first,

A few hours later, Clara Jane was being stripped of her lumber. (Paul C. Morris)

if not the first, of the flying candidates: he chartered the prototype Burgess-Dunne hydro-aeroplane, a thoroughly air-conditioned framework of wire, struts and fabric with radically swept-back wings, three pontoons and pusher propeller fashioned at Marblehead by the pioneer aircraft manufacturer and yacht designer W. Starling Burgess. On June 24, with Clifford L. Webster at the controls, he flew up the coast, buzzed Haverhill and landed on the Merrimack River near the yacht club before a crowd of five thousand. Flying over Cape Ann, Piatt leaned over, aimed his camera at his hometown and snapped the first air photo ever taken of Gloucester. Proudly he mailed a picture postcard to Carrie Sinkler, whose European sojourn was soon to be cut short by the war, and she replied from Venice:

Fancy dear AP my perplexed and excited interest over your postcard. After close scrutiny I even soaked it in water thinking something would develop on it! When suddenly I realized that the tiny ink mark was you aloft. . . . How I wish I had been there to see you soaring over us. How like you to have done such a dashing thing, but it must be a terrible and thrilling feeling. How goes the campaign? Mr. Gardner couldn't fly I feel sure. . . . The Pages were very nice to us in Rome and we went to a beautiful dinner given in honour of your old friend Cardinal O'Connell. He was in full regalia and enjoying unctuously the Roman Princesses kneeling and kissing his ring. So I gave it a nice cozy shake, and we had a fine talk about Gloucester. He rumours he is coming down to see us. Will that hurt or help your case?

But when Doc prepared to take off in the seaplane on a last-minute tour of the sixth congressional district, it had disappeared, sold out from under him. He was furious and accused the Republican machine of sabotaging him. (Actually, at the outbreak of war in August, a Canadian Aviation Corps officer came to Marblehead and bought the Burgess-Dunne, his country's first military plane, for $5,000.) Starling Burgess offered to reassemble a dismantled Wright contraption that hadn't been flown for three months, and the candidate reluctantly agreed. Worse luck, the Wright job had only half the horsepower of the newer Burgess-Dunne model and was nearly upset by the wind on the attempted takeoff from Marblehead Harbor; the tour was called off.

Doc wound up his campaign in the prescribed style with a rally, and a motorcade through Gloucester, which attracted more than usual notice for its sprinkling of such Eastern Point divas from Dabsville as the Misses Beaux and Sinkler, granting the multitudes a glimpse of their persons.

Professor Andrew failed miserably in the September primary to carry off the coalition of Republicans and Progressives he had hoped to achieve in the district (he won the Progressive nomination, but so few voted that he withdrew). He lost to Gus Gardner by four to one and carried only two wards in Gloucester, his own political base.

So that was enough of politics for a while. There was a war on.

As wars go, America was not taking this one too seriously. A month after the primary election Germany and the Allies were locked in the Battle of Flanders; as this was none of its concern, the United States was strictly neutral.

Of much more interest around Gloucester the autumn of 1914 were the antics of a motion picture company that had moved into the Harbor View on Wonson's Cove—actors, actresses, director, cameramen and the rest, equipped with the simple tools for extracting a classic from the local scene.

The Peerless Feature Producing Company of New York, six months old, had picked Gloucester to shoot most of a five-reel silent picture to be called *As Ye Sow*. All was such a rushing to and fro of these peerless pioneers of the celluloid over the next two weeks that the plot, as far as the local archives are concerned, got lost in the shuffle. Only fleeting, subliminal vignettes have survived.

One day the cameraman was seen in a boat off Magnolia, cranking away at two grappling figures posed on the brink of Rafe's Chasm. Silhouetted against the sky, the villain got his due and was cast down into the boiling sea. And the company popped up at Freshwater Cove and Annisquam and Bass Rocks and along the Back Shore of Eastern Point.

And there was the day it was being talked all over town that Peerless would pay $500 to the man bold or crazy enough to drive an automobile off the end of the breakwater ($600 if he'd furnish his own car).

A few takers showed up, but Director Frank Crane laughed it off as somebody's hoax. A wonder he didn't work it in.

The lead in *As Ye Sow* was Alice Brady, who had been starring on Broadway in *What Is Love?* Some of the others in the company were John Hines, Emma Trentinni, Walter MacLean, Beverly West, Lydia Knott and Otto F. Hoffman. And of course every heart was captured by the darling three-year-old actress Jane Lee, "her fat little cheeks encircled with golden curls," as the newspaper gurgled.

Early in November the Peerless people left to shoot in New York and wait for the easterly gale Crane wanted for his spectacular climax, a shipwreck he had scheduled for Brace Cove.

They had bought the decrepit schooner *Island Home* from Thomas Reed, and she was lying at the Reed & Gamage wharf in East Gloucester, fixed up enough to fool the average moviegoer of 1915, who was not very sophisticated about shipwrecks.

The weather remained on the mild side, and so Peerless returned to Gloucester, prepared to go ahead anyway at the first sign of a breeze.

Early morning shore check on the twenty-third of November showed not much sea running, but the wind was brisk from southwest, and local opinion thought it might make up by noontime. Go ahead, ordered director Crane, and at 11:00 a.m. Captain Andy Jacobs took the wheel of the *Eveleth*, gave a blast on the whistle and moved away from the wharf with *Island Home* in tow.

At the helm of the creaking old thing for her final, glorious voyage was Captain Charles S. Martin, Jr., with William Sawyer, Cornelius Linnehan and Salvatore Puglise for crew. Bringing up the rear of this odd flotilla was the Humane Society surfboat under the command of Captain Forrest ("Bunch") Bickford of Rocky Neck (Captain John's son now in charge of the stations at the neck and Brace Cove), with a crew of Henry Bickford, Charles Osier, Jr., Everett Osier, Albert Bates and Orrin Douglass.

Island Home made hard work of it out the harbor, steadied somewhat by double-reefed main and foresails and a jumbo. But being unballasted, she was so hard to manage that for a while, slatting out there in the beam seas off the Point, she looked to Tom Reed from where he was watching near the lighthouse as if she mightn't make it. The Portland steamer passing offshore thought likewise and stood by, as did two Gloucester fishing steamers in the area.

The plan was to have *Eveleth* drop her tow outside Brace Cove. Captain Martin and his men would then shape her sails and lash their helm on a course for Bemo Ledge, abandon ship in their dory and be rescued by the lifeboat while the cameras caught it all.

Around they came. Beyond Brace Rock the hawser was dropped and the tug steamed off camera. *Island Home* was on her own. Director Crane and his cameras and hundreds of spectators were waiting on the beach. A lively sea was coming in.

But when Captain Martin tried to get her to steer herself for Bemo she balked like a wise old mule at the glue factory door. The schooner just wouldn't hold a course, and so the four of them, being true Gloucestermen, stuck with her.

They got her on target, rolling in toward the ledge, breakers ahead—and now, before she lifts on the next rising swell, now is the moment of parting!

Sal Puglise jumped for the dory. Bunch Bickford's crew bent to their oars and swept alongside, and he scrambled over. Linnehan was next into the dory. Again the lifeboat darted in between the rocks.

But this time a wave raised the dory up and whacked it down on the ledge. The bottom exploded and the sea poured in. Hands reached out and grabbed Linnehan, and where he had been in the sinking dory a split second before, there was naught but white water.

Island Home struck Bemo bows on and ground up on her forefoot and poised there, pointing the finger of her bowsprit at the sky. She settled back on her stern as if this last unwilling voyage had tuckered her out (she was launched before the Civil War), and she lay there while the waves

smacked her tail, and flapped her clipped wings in the wind like a crippled bird.

Martin and Sawyer, the two left aboard, sat down on the cabin house to wait for Bickford to figure how to take them off without getting their feet wet.

To those watching on the beach it seemed that *Island Home* was coming to something less than the stupendous and colossal end Peerless had plotted for her, when an extra high swell raised her off her resting place. It sucked her back into the deep water and she floated, and then another rolled in, spun her slowly around, flung her on high and dashed her broadside onto the ledge with a crackling of arthritic timbers that resounded across the cove to the appalled delight of the throng on shore.

Now, at last, *Island Home* was a genuine wreck, like untold before her in this very boneyard. She was filling rapidly, settling at the stern, and the wild surf broke over her rail and swept her afterdeck.

Martin and Sawyer picked their way up to the high-pitched bows of her. They were in real-life trouble. Henry Bickford waded out on the rocks with a lifeline but couldn't get near. Time after time the surfboat men worked toward the wreck, only to be thrust at the rocks by a surge and have to pull back for dear life.

A granddaddy sea foamed in and threw *Island Home* on her side. The sudden lurch snapped her main shrouds and her mainmast toppled by the board, carrying gaff, sail and a skein of rigging with it. She settled, and the boarding seas drenched the two figures that clung to the headstays.

The schooner Island Home heads for her moment in movie history, November 22, 1914. (Eben Parsons photo)

Another big bad sea, and she shifted on her bier. With a great crack, her foremast broke above the deck and pitched over—gaff, canvas, shrouds, halyards, boom, sheets, forestay, jib and all with it. The two men gripped her upraised bow like life itself.

Police Officer Jack Mehlman of Rocky Neck, one of the smartest amateur sailors on the coast, raced up the beach to the Humane Society boathouse, shouting for his crew to follow, and they did—Archie Fenton, Warren and Charles Brown, Mel Trefry, Alex Lyle, Jack Riley and Jack MacMillan. They rolled out the lifeboat into the surf, dug in their oars and were on their way.

After an exchange of shouts between the two rescue boats, Bickford steered for the *Eveleth* where she was lying, helpless to do anything, at the mouth of the cove. He got a line from her, and while his crew pulled back into the cove he tied an end to his stern. Alongside Mehlman, he threw him the line and the policemen's bow man bent the other end to his thwart.

Bickford's men pulled upwind until the line came taut. Then they eased off and drifted, letting the wind and waves sweep the other boat down toward the breakers and the bow of the wreck.

Like rappelling mountaineers, one hanging from the other, the surfboats let themselves downwind. Now Mehlman was so close to the wreck's bow he could have touched it with an oar. The rocks were a fathom away. Each sea bore his boat nearly to the bulwarks of the *Island Home,* then dumped it in the trough.

Martin and Sawyer had one chance. They crawled out on the shambles of the foremast that hung over the rail, draped with the sopping sail. They balanced there on the spar, doused by every sea.

Up soared the lifeboat, brushing their white faces. The rowers played their oars, holding it fixed in its vertical track like an elevator. Down it plummeted.

Up it bounced again, poised on the crest, and down once more, and the rowers yelled. The two flung themselves in a heap on top of them.

And at that other end of the line Bickford's crew dug their blades into the foaming seas, and their muscles cracked and they buckled their backs. The rope came tight, and it was done.

Ashore, the rescued were taken to the warmth of their homes. Two hours more, and the schooner *Island Home* was driftwood on the beach.

The Peerless Feature Producing Company packed up and left for New York, the filming of *As Ye Sow* finished to their satisfaction.

Of course, their two cameramen had failed to record the actual rescue of Martin and Sawyer. Perhaps they had been told not to waste film on anything that wasn't in the script.

Owing probably to ill health, David Greenough rented "Black Bess" in 1915 for the first of several seasons to Harry Sleeper's recently married younger brother Stephen, a Boston real estate broker who, though evidently not much of a sailor himself, had resigned as regatta chairman of the

Eastern Yacht Club in Marblehead and was about to be elevated to treasurer for seventeen years.

Early in the afternoon of the tenth of November, 1916, while carpenters and painters were working on the harbor side of the cottage, fire started from a gasoline torch being used to burn off interior paint on the second floor, as the *Gloucester Daily Times* reported. The wind was brisk from the northwest. The first fire apparatus to respond mistakenly drove all around the Back Shore, the flames got away from a bucket brigade of the workmen, and, according to the *Times,* "the place was virtually totally destroyed and what was not burned was practically ruined, causing a loss of about $10,000."

David Greenough engaged Halfdan Hanson, Henry Sleeper's architectural collaborator at "Beauport," writing him from his Jamaica Plain winter home on November 14 that "considering my helpless condition you take entire control of all matters connected with rebuilding my house at Eastern Point," including insurance settlement. He insisted on doubling Hanson's 5 percent commission, "and at that I think I shall owe you a lot of thanks besides."

Hanson wrote Greenough the next day that the damage was confined to the exterior walls of the west-facing living room alcove and bedroom above, that everything including furnishings could be restored equal to or better than its previous condition and "that if found out that torches were used and cause of the fire, that we could not collect any insurance."

Harry Sleeper's "Beauport" architect concluded with this astonishing revelation: "I have signed off after a very hard fight to avoid arbitration, as that would mean the discovery of the cause of the fire and that of course would result in no insurance at all"—adding that in fact Mr. Greenough would come out of it with a balance unexpended of $415, "which will remain at your pleasure to dispose of as you may deem fit."

How on earth did Halfdan Hanson keep the insurance adjuster away from the workmen, the fire chief and that telltale copy of the *Gloucester Daily Times?* David Greenough did indeed owe him a lot of thanks besides.

Stephen Sleeper, race committee member, Eastern Yacht Club of Marblehead, August 1910. (Eastern Yacht Club)

End of an American Field Service ambulance. (From Friends of France)

~31~
THE AMERICAN FIELD SERVICE

W̲HILE WE WERE CONVINCING ourselves with seeming logic that Europe's war was Europe's business that ominous fall of 1914, the American colony in Paris was engaged in the first relief work of the conflict, with headquarters in the small hospital it supported at Neuilly-sur-Seine.

Piatt Andrew had been treasurer of the American Red Cross from 1910 to 1912, and as soon as the fighting started, his friends in Paris enlisted his support. Doc was ardently pro-France and believed everything possible should be done to bring his country into this war against German militarism.

American friends of the French were told that the most effective assistance they could render the French Army consistent with neutrality would be to evacuate casualties from the front lines. Bouncing back from his election defeat, Doc threw himself into the cause. On December 3 he wrote his parents in Indiana that "I have been turning things over in my mind lately and have about decided that I must go over to France for a few months."

Once in Paris, he volunteered at the American Hospital in Neuilly and was quickly in the thick of it, organizing a group that under his leadership early in 1915 gained French approval to create a volunteer corps called at first the American Ambulance Field Service, which he headed with the semiofficial rank of inspector general.

Before a public support campaign could be mounted in the States, it was necessary to reassure the French that this service wouldn't be subverted into an unwitting Trojan horse for spies and saboteurs masquerading as neutrals. After lengthy negotiations, Inspector General Andrew signed an agreement with the French Army in April 1915 guaranteeing satisfactory screening and minimum tours of duty for volunteers and at least their nominal submission to French military authority.

The inspector general's Eastern Point neighbor, Henry Davis Sleeper, was in on the planning from the beginning and was made the American representative of what was soon abbreviated to the American Field Service, with organizational headquarters in Boston. He took on the unfamiliar challenge of getting up committees all over the United States, sending around lecturers and propaganda films, recruiting volunteers (largely from colleges) and raising money for ambulances—the whole the more remarkable, considering his retiring nature.

It was decided to organize the AFS along the lines of the French ambulance corps, in sections of twenty-five to thirty men, each such unit assigned to an infantry division in the field, equipped to maintain itself and incorporated for administrative purposes into the French Army's automobile service.

After much study and debate Andrew concluded that a lighter and more maneuverable model than the French ambulance was called for, namely the car produced by Mr. Henry Ford. The first ten to arrive had bodies made out of packing boxes. By the end of the war, some 1,200 Ford chassis were sent to France, assembled by the AFS and finished off with bodies custom-built by the French to Andrew's specifications. Not even wholesale rates could be obtained for their purchase, he wrote later with bitterness: "We received no favor or assistance from their manufacturer, who with his peculiar ideas of philanthropy, was averse to giving any assistance to war activities, even to the relief of suffering entailed by war."[1]

By spring of 1915 the first Yank college boys were driving their flivvers in the first cranking-up of a shuttle that in high gear would transport tens of thousands of wounded *poilus* from the *postes de secours* just behind the trenches to the *postes de triage* for assignment, according to the severity of their wounds, to the field and evacuation and base hospitals.

Early in 1916 the headquarters was moved from the cramped hospital in Neuilly to a spacious estate loaned by the owner at 21 rue Raynouard on the banks of the Seine. Here Doc put to work the administrative talent so begrudged by Secretary MacVeagh and somehow found time and energy back in Boston that August to arrange publication of *Friends of France: The Field Service of the American Ambulance described by its members*, a moving, 300-page volume illustrated with graphic photographs from the front whose purpose was eloquently and frankly put forth by the founder:

> The little group of Americans told of in this book who, during the past two years, have dedicated valiant effort and, not infrequently, risked their lives in the service of France, can best be thought of as only a symbol of millions of other Americans, men and women, who would gladly have welcomed an opportunity to do what these men have done—or more. For, notwithstanding official silence and the injunctions of presidential prudence, the majority of Americans have come to appreciate the meaning, not only to France, but to all the world, of the issues that are today so desperately at stake, and their hearts and hopes are all with France in her gigantic struggle . . . in defending the ideals for which, as they feel,

A Field Service inspection trip in Alsace, Piatt Andrew second from left. (From Friends of France)

America has always stood, and for which France is now making such vast, such gallant, and such unflinching sacrifice.

The service to France of Americans, whether ambulance drivers, surgeons, nurses, donors and distributors of relief, aviators, or foreign *legionnaires* . . . when measured by the prodigious tasks with which France has had to cope during the past two years, has indeed been infinitesimally small; but their service to America itself has been important. They have rendered this inestimable benefit to their country. They have helped to keep alive in France the old feeling of friendship and respect for us which has existed there since our earliest days and which, otherwise, would probably have ceased to exist. They have helped to demonstrate to the chivalrous people of France that Americans, without hesitating to balance the personal profit and loss, still respond to the great ideals that inspired the founders of our Republic. They have helped France to penetrate official reticence and rediscover America's surviving soul.

Simultaneously with *Friends of France* in August 1916 was published a shorter volume by AFS driver Leslie Buswell of West Gloucester. *Ambulance No. 10: Personal Letters from the Front* was prefaced and introduced by the English expatriate actor's friends Sleeper, to whom one infers they were directed, and Andrew. Like *Friends* it was intended as a recruitment both for dollars and drivers, though much of the descriptive detail can hardly have had the desired effect on potential volunteers.

A particular friend of Jack Hammond, the handsome and charming Buswell had been swept up by Sleeper and Andrew and the rest of the Dabsville circle who of course wrote him at the front. His letter to Sleeper of August 6, 1915, is especially poignant. Doc had dropped by earlier in the day, when Leslie recounted to him a recent ghastly experience with the evac-

Inspector General A. Piatt Andrew of the American Field Service (right) in France with ambulance driver Leslie Buswell. (Andrew L. Gray)

uation of the wounded under shellfire; a few hours later he endured a repeat of it and was now back in his quarters near the field hospital.

> Here I am writing to you, safe and sound, on the little table by my bedside, with a half-burnt candle stuck in a Muratti cigarette box. Outside the night is silent—my window is open and in the draught the wax has trickled down on to the box and then to the table—unheeded—for my thoughts have sped far. To Gloucester days, and winter evenings spent in the old brown-panelled, raftered room, with its pewter lustrous in the candlelight; and the big, cheerful fire that played with our shadows on the wall while we talked or read—and were content. Well—that peace has gone for a while, but these days will likewise pass, and we are young. It has been good to be here in the presence of high courage and to have learned a little in our youth of the values of life and death.

A week later Buswell was bucked up to get a packet of letters from Sleeper, Hammond, Beaux and Sinkler. Two months later France awarded him the *Croix de Guerre* for valor.

By America's entry into the war in April 1917 Doc was directing 1,200 volunteers and a fleet of 1,000 ambulances assigned among 33 sections to as many French divisions committed to the entire Western Front, including two sections in the Balkans.

At rue Raynouard he had a singular effect on the newly arrived volunteer. One of them remembered being brought to headquarters and introduced first to "Doc," "who greeted you cordially, told you how glad he was to welcome you to the Service, warned you of the—ahem—evils of Paris, made you feel you were the one man in all America he had been hoping would come over."[2]

The AFS nerve center in Paris had the appearance of an army base, with its reception and construction and repair parks, supply depot, training camps, hospital and quarters for men on furlough.

The skeptical French were sold. They asked Andrew to organize a transport adjunct along similar lines, and by October 1917, 1,800 additional volunteers were manning 14 camion sections recruited by Harry Sleeper's stateside workers, driving ammunition and military supplies to the lines backing up the Battle of the Chemin des Dames.

As the result of Marshal Joffre's appeal during his trip to the United States in 1917, the ambulance sections of the American Field Service were incorporated in the U.S. Army Ambulance Service assigned to the French Army, while the camions became the "American Mission with the French Army" of the U.S. Motor Transport Corps. Most of the volunteers enlisted as army ambulance drivers or in other branches, while the officers were regularly commissioned.

Inspector General Andrew was commissioned a major, then lieutenant colonel in the Army Ambulance Service, and had been joined by Harry Sleeper as director of the headquarters in Paris by October 1918, when on the fourth he wrote Isabella Gardner of his pleasure in being able to help the AFS boys in any way, hoping "I shall keep as well as I am now, so that things may go on properly."

But it was not to be. Ever in fragile health, within a few days Harry was down with what he must have been fearful was the influenza then raging worldwide, for he wrote Mrs. Jack a month later on November 7, just after being awarded the Legion of Honor by the French government and four days before the Armistice, that it "has left me with a wretched cough and feeling very below par." Another three weeks and on the twenty-seventh Sleeper wrote her again:

> Don't worry about me! I am really all right—just that devilish bronchial thing which the grippe left me. I did think I was going to have pneumonia. For a while I felt pretty sick, and had a nasty cough, but I escaped that, and having had my lesson, I am as foxy as possible when the dampness tries to catch me. I am just like Tweedledum and Tweedledee when I go out to the front. You would have been amused last night at my preparations for the evening. The lights and engine of our automobile gave out in a wild, wet, strange road, near the little town of Nanteuil. We had to wander around from house to house, to find a building which had not been vacated by its owners. We finally got a place over a bar-room, where there was of course no heat and no hot drinks, and no food, and a very sick looking bed. I took the blankets out of my automobile and spread one under me and one over me, besides all the rest of the bed clothing, and got out my hot Thermos bottle, and was roasting to death ten minutes after I got into bed. I have to take such precautions secretly, as of course it

would be considered very effete if it were discovered by the people I am with.[3]

At home and abroad the Field Service was a valiant effort for one of Harry Sleeper's lifelong vulnerability, and a valiant, fading gasp—there on a rainy night over the barroom under the automobile blankets near the little town of Nanteuil—of *La Belle Epoque*.

Meanwhile, the war effort was being pursued on the fields of Eastern Point, specifically the Pollard field, where Priscilla and her friend Liz Stewart, pupils at the May School for girls in Boston's Back Bay, were literally bent in the summer of 1918 on a school-wide project of "some kind of War Work connected with the production or conservation of food." Any proceeds were to be invested in War Savings Stamps. Priscilla, who continued the effort on her own in 1919, preserved a detailed notebook illustrated with faded snapshots of the harvest, a precise map of a prodigious vegetable garden 159 feet by 72 feet, and a log of practically every pea picked and "raddish" wrenched from the soil.

The young patriots' remarkable efforts were recognized by Helen Andrew Patch, the inspector general's sister, who wrote them on August 16, as the war's end approached: "It is a pleasure to write to you to acknowledge your generous contribution to our work for the American Fund for French Wounded. How splendid to increase the food supply at the same time! If you have extra vegetables to sell at any time, I wish you would telephone to me and they could be left at the Red Roof garage with the chauffeur."

Except for a brief visit or two home, Colonel Andrew remained in France until December 1919. Then he was back at "Red Roof" writing his parents in La Porte of the history of the AFS on which he was already hard at work while the steel of experience and memory was still red-hot:

> It is surprising how busy I am. I had hoped that the book might be ready by the end of this month, but I doubt now whether it will be out before March. There are so many gaps to fill, so many people to push and urge to finish material promised, and I keep thinking of new matter the introduction of which would add to the story. In the end, however, there will be two fine volumes, each larger than "Friends of France"—and I am anxious to make the work as fine a memorial as possible to our little service and of the great days in France—a book which will have an interest fifty or a hundred years hence when all of us are gone and otherwise forgotten. . . .
>
> Meanwhile, although it is rather extravagant, I have been making little improvements in the house, improvements which can easily be made at this time of year, and can be looked after by me in the making, which might not be possible at another time. I have had gas put in the house and a gas stove with hot water attachment installed in the kitchen, also a little gas fireplace in the small dining room

(where the pewter is) and I am going to have a little gas fireplace, of a new model which does not vitiate the air, installed in your blue bedroom so that you can easily heat the room in the morning when you are getting dressed—or in the afternoon when you want to lie down, without waiting for a fire in the fireplace or furnace. . . .

It is sunny and cold, but no wind—and everything is lovely—at night almost magical in the still white light of the moon.

Priscilla Pollard and the ubiquitous Carlo deliver vegetables for the war effort, with proceeds to benefit the Red Cross. (Elizabeth Baldwin)

The two volumes emerged in 1920 as the three-volume *History of the American Field Service in France: "Friends of France" 1914–1917. Told by Its Members*. It was followed in 1921 by a memorial volume of profiles of the 127 who were killed or died overseas.

From the retrospect of three wars later, what a terribly sad picture of this game that fascinates the race so. What a commentary, what an accusation from the superb letters and reminiscences and personal histories and reflections and art of these educated, idealistic young men whom John Masefield called "the very pick and flower of American youth." What an indictment. What irony.

Observing that two-thirds of the 3,000 AFS volunteers came from 100 American campuses, Colonel Andrew thought:

> It was in fact because of this that the organization was able to render what was probably its most important service to France and the allied cause. For during the long years when the American Government was hesitating, and those in authority were proclaiming the necessity of speaking and even thinking in neutral terms, and while the American people were slowly accumulating the information that was to lead to the Great Decision, these hundreds of American youths already in France were busily writing and agitating in terms that were not neutral, and were sending to their families and friends throughout the Union, to their home papers, to their college publications, and to American weeklies and magazines the great story of France and her prodigious sacrifice. . . . They were developing a deeper and more active interest in American participation. This was the aspect of the Field Service which in the thought of those of us who were privileged to direct it seemed heavily to outweigh all others. Herein lay by all counts the greatest con-

tribution which the men of the Field Service could make and did make to France.[5]

Andrew felt a mystical affinity with the French. These four years of involvement were the climax of his life:

> When all is said and done, the Field Service volunteers themselves gained far more than the wounded *poilus,* far more than the armies of France, far more than any one else, from the work which they performed. . . . The epic and heroic quality of France's whole history, and especially of that chapter of which we were eye-witnesses, the quenchless spirit and unfaltering will of her people, the democracy, the comradeship, and above all, the calm, unboasting, matter-of-fact courage of her troops, kindled something akin to veneration in all of us. The Field Service motto was "*Tous et tout pour la France.*" We all felt it. We all meant it. It is forever ours.[6]

Walker Hancock bust of Inspector General A. Piatt Andrew at American Field Service memorial in France. Six bas reliefs on stele show men of the AFS in action. (Walker Hancock)

Doc expressed particular appreciation to his co-founder, Henry Sleeper, "who during these years with unflagging energy organized the committees and spread from one end of America to the other the information which resulted so successfully in providing men and money for the work in France."[7]

Sensitive Harry, in his part of the introduction, reviewed the experience with conflicting emotions and addressed the thousands he had recruited with a not altogether happy alternation of wistfulness and wishfulness:

> Through the burdens which we have been privileged to assume in their support, most of us have probably reached as high a mark of satisfied effort as we shall know. Remembering that, and realizing how much they have passed through that was worth while, we may have sympathy with their problem of the future. If for us there

is some poignance in having finished an era of unselfish labor, even less stimulating it must be for younger men to suspect, as some of these doubtless do, that they have reached their zenith. . . .

The spirit which led them to France by inclination, before the time of obligation, is the same that in considering the future makes them hesitate to dedicate themselves permanently to a purpose with little human interest. In the maze of possibilities they have come home to face, some may be fortunate in finding their desire, but very many will have to be content with small monotony, unless those of us whose lives are more established can serve them to finer purpose. That they are unconscious of the debt we owe makes the obligation doubly ours. . . . If we can put many such men forward with the knowledge of our reliance on their strength and resource in meeting new problems in their own country, as they have met the greater crisis, we shall have done something for them, more for ourselves, and much for posterity. . . .

In going first to France we took what seemed our best, but now returning we have brought a finer thing than ever we were able to put upon the altar of our good intention.[8]

Sleeper was awarded the Legion of Honor for his service to the cause of the Allies. Andrew was burdened with decorations that included the Legion of Honor, the Croix de Guerre, and from his own nation, the Distinguished Service Medal.

For exceptionally meritorious and distinguished services. Coming to France at the beginning of the war, he showed remarkable ability in organizing the American Field Service, a volunteer service for the transportation of the wounded of the French Armies at the front. Upon the entry of the United States into the war, he turned over to the U.S Army Ambulance Service the efficient organization he had built up, and by his sound judgment and expert advice, rendered invaluable aid in the development of that organization. To him is due, in large measure, the credit for the increasingly valuable work done by the light ambulances at the front.[9]

Six hundred veterans of the American Field Service met in reunion in New York in May 1920, and Colonel Andrew announced that their corps was to live on, to carry forth through peacetime the fraternity of France and the United States. There were to be established fellowships for advanced study by Americans in the universities of France, in memory of the 127 men of the AFS who gave their lives there.

It continues this work today, eighty years and three wars later—a memorial to the hopes of Piatt Andrew and Henry Sleeper, and a remembrance of the part Eastern Point played in their lives, and beyond.

The Eastern Point quarry, before "Villa Latomia" was built on the edge.
(Cape Ann Historical Association)

~32~
MASONRY TEMPLES

THE MAN POKED A REVOLVER through the teller's window at young Henry Davison and presented a check for a million dollars made out to "The Almighty."

"A million dollars for The Almighty," said Henry coolly, in a loud voice. "How will you have it?"—and he began counting out small bills while the alerted guard of the Astor Place Bank in New York slipped up behind The Almighty's self-appointed surrogate and disarmed him.

The afternoon papers carried the story to the boardroom of the Liberty National Bank downtown even as the directors were looking for a new assistant cashier, and one of them who was acquainted with Davison convinced the rest to hire a man of such sangfroid.

Within five years Henry, at thirty-two, was president of the bank. Within a few more he was working for Pierpont Morgan, whose ear he had during the bank crisis of 1907, which led to the National Monetary Commission and Davison's membership thereon, and a close friendship with Piatt Andrew.

Henry and Kate and their four children visited "Red Roof" in the summer of 1909 and were enchanted. Next January he bought from the Eastern Point Company the tract around the water-filled quarry and the stone wharf, which bordered on the J. Murray Kay estate, the beach and the road to the lighthouse.

Whatever caused his change of plans (he was by now a Morgan partner), he sold this land in August 1912 to his sister Mary of New York. Miss Davison was a short, red-haired woman whose inseparable companion, said to be a person of exquisite taste, was Theodosia de R. Hawley. They designed and furnished the striking Italianate villa that rose from the sheer north wall of the woodland quarry on one side, facing its stuccoed balconies and belfry to the harbor on the other. They called it "Villa Latomia," Quarry House.

The friends hadn't spent more than a few seasons on the quarry's verge when Mary was swept off her feet by Anatole Le Braz, a writer some years her elder. She gave him hand and house, and he carried her away to Port Blanc in his native Brittany. Exit, one infers, Miss Hawley.

The Le Brazes sold "Villa Latomia" in 1921 to Eliot Wadsworth of Boston, President Harding's assistant secretary of the Treasury and a retired partner in Stone and Webster who had been prominent in the International Red Cross and a member of the Rockefeller Foundation's European Relief Commission in 1915. So he was probably well acquainted with Doc Andrew. In the summer of 1922 (Henry Davison died that May) Secretary Wadsworth married the widow of an old friend, Mrs. Guy Scull, and they honeymooned at "Villa Latomia."

Next spring Wadsworth represented the United States at Paris in negotiations for reparation of the cost of maintaining the American Army of Occupation on the Rhine. He remained with the Treasury until 1925, and among numerous other positions was Chairman of the Overseers of Harvard College in 1929.

In the meantime, however, the attention of the Wadsworths shifted to Bar Harbor, and for several years his sister, Mrs. T. Russell Sullivan of Boston, and her family summered in the unique missionesque creation that bridged the fresh and the salt.[1]

On upper Eastern Point, north of Farrington Avenue and the Hill of Rocks, the Henry Eliots of St. Louis had for years occupied the heights almost exclusively, undisturbed except for the stray ball lofted from the nine-hole golf course on the moors that stretched off toward the Back Shore.

Their solitude was not to last. After Nathaniel Gorton, the treasurer of Gorton-Pew Fisheries, vacated the Henry Scott cottage on the harbor (to be taken up by Caroline Sinkler), he bought land from the Associates in 1905 on the north corner of Bemo Avenue and Eastern Point Boulevard, on Niles Beach, and built a house since destroyed by fire. Not to be upstaged by his partner, president John J. Pew of Gorton-Pew acquired from the syndicate in 1906 a tract bounded by Farrington and Stewart Avenues and the last loop of Eastern Point Boulevard (east), which was later cut off and renamed Edgemoor Road; eight years later he put up a large, Spanish mission-style mansion, now part of St. Mel's School.

Pew's seizure of the brow below Eliot opened up this section to development. In 1907 the Reverend William Beach Olmstead, headmaster of the Pomfret School in Connecticut, bought and built at the west corner of Stewart and Niles Beach. Two years later Miss Edith Weld of Boston and Waterman A. Taft of Arlington bought lots near the Eliots and built "Nest on Ridge" and "Balmaha," respectively.

South of Miss Weld, on the Hill of Rocks, about 1912, Laura Wheeler of Sharon, Connecticut, and Julia Gavit of New York built a large stucco villa looking across the "Seine Field" to the Atlantic. (The field was named for the seine nets the owners allowed the fishermen to spread to dry there.) North of the Eliot cottage W. Jay Little, a Boston artist, put up a Tudor house and studio at around the same time.

Down across from Niles Beach, at the south corner of Farrington Avenue above Sunset Rock, the well-mortared home of Seth K. Ames of Melrose, head of the butter-and-egg chain of stores, was finished in 1914. East of "Sunset Rock" rose another stuccoed villa in 1912 on land purchased in 1909 by Annie, Florence and Lela Weeks of Boston, sisters of Congressman John Wingate Weeks of Newton, partner in Hornblower and Weeks, later a U.S. senator and Harding's secretary of war.

At the dead end of what was to be Edgemoor Road, against the Cushing Wall, a rather large tract was acquired in the fall of 1909 by General Anson Mills of Washington, a unique old warrior who had been taking the summer salt air at Bass Rocks since 1902 or so. Here he built a great house for his family that he called "Bayberry Ledge."

General Mills was an Indiana farm boy who flunked out of West Point, worked as a surveyor in Texas and laid out the limits and named the city of El Paso. With the Civil War, he returned north and was commissioned in the infantry. He fought in the West, from Shiloh on, and spent most of the rest of his military career until 1893 on the frontier, much of it fighting Indians.

Yet it was as an inventor that Anson Mills made his fame and fortune. He patented an improved cartridge belt as far back as 1866 and then put in years of spare time perfecting a method of weaving it in one piece. The general wrote a little sheepishly of the trials of an army wife doubly burdened as an inventor's:

> I purchased foot-power lathes, drills, etc., to develop models of my various patents in belts and equipment. I installed them in one of her best rooms in each succeeding one of perhaps twenty posts, soiling the carpets with grease, filings and shavings, which would have driven most wives mad.[2]

Finally success. The belt was adopted by the U.S. Army. But by the time his factory had geared up for the Spanish War, it was over, and Mills and his associates had a hundred thousand on hand, with big payables and no market.

Then along came the Boer War, and the British bought his belts by the thousands. Soon all kinds of military and outdoor equipment were being manufactured under his patents. In 1905, at seventy-one, General Mills sold out and retired from business a rich man. He transferred "Bayberry Ledge" to his daughter, Mrs. Constance Overton, in 1920, and died in 1924 at the age of ninety.

The last and the biggest of the big builders on Farmer Niles's north forty was George E. Tener of Sewickley, Pennsylvania. In 1914 he bought the height between the Pew and Eliot houses and two years later completed a thirty-room brick mansion, now part of St. Mel's School, where he summered until his death in the late 1920s and which his widow occupied for almost twenty-five years thereafter. Tener was the brother of John K. Tener of Pittsburgh, a major league baseball player in the 1880s, member of

Congress from 1909 to 1911, governor of Pennsylvania from 1911 until 1915 and president of the National League until 1918.

While all this estate-making was adding hauteur to the uplands and taxes to the city treasury, another of Eastern Point's famous romances was approaching sublimation on the other side of Niles Pond.

Everyone had assumed that those summer sweethearts from childhood, Jonathan Raymond and Pauline Pollard—beautiful Pauline of the mischievous wit, her lithe, athletic figure swathed against the sun to keep white by candlelight—would marry one day, and they did, in the early spring of 1917 as America was entering the war and a few weeks after the death of the bride's father, Alonzo Wilder Pollard.

If Mrs. Raymond expected her son to move her daughter-in-law into "The Ramparts," she was disappointed. Secretly in April they bought the Amos Story house at the corner of Highland Street and Highland Place above East Gloucester Square. It had stood there in the shade of its ancient elms since before the Revolution.

Henry Parsons, the building mover, jacked it up, rolled it down Highland Street through the Square and launched all ten rooms of it aboard a barge at the town landing, towed it out the harbor to the Point, and grounded on Wharf Beach. Then it was back on rollers, up the beach and across the road and through the sloping field behind the straining oxen to come to rest finally at the bend of the old cart track that once skirted the fort and joined the first road to the lighthouse.

"Whatever is Pauline doing to Jake?" Mrs. John Greenough is said to have expostulated when she looked out and saw their new home sailing sedately by her porch—"bringing a house full of bugs across the harbor on a barge!"

They called their road "Chicken Lane," and Pauline recalled with amusement that to overcome the absence of plumbing "we had to carve bathrooms out of closets and under stairs, with tubs you had to scrunch up to get into."

She was one of the rare younger women to whom Isabella Gardner took a liking. The summer of 1918 Mrs. Jack, then seventy-eight, rented "Wrong Roof" briefly from Carrie Sinkler for what proved to be the last *vacation*, as she would put it, of her life; she came to tea one afternoon with Jack and Pauline at the end of Chicken Lane on the fringe of, if not entirely out from under, the domain of Mrs. Raymond, Sr.

Y had a word of typical Gardnerian advice:

"Oh," she told the young couple, "you really ought to have a snake here, you know . . . that's the best luck you can possibly have in a house!"[3]

With the Great War fast approaching its denouement this summer of 1918, President Wilson snatched a respite from the cares of it to visit his "silent partner," Colonel Edward M. House, at Coolidge Point, Magnolia. On the morning of August 17 President and Mrs. Wilson, Colonel House and Dr.

T. M. Grayson motored around to Eastern Point, pausing frequently to
enjoy the scenery. The President wore an "outing suit of white flannels and
a cap." They went almost unrecognized, doubtless to their relief, and
returned to Magnolia for lunch.

If Miss Davison could put her house beside a quarry already there, others
could do her one better: they would blast their own out of the ledge and
build their stately mansions over the hole with the excavated granite, doubling the usefulness of their cellars. Thus did Edith Notman of Brooklyn,
New York, cause hers to rise like a very solid phoenix on the ashes of the
Niles farmhouse.

Miss Notman had been a summer visitor at George Stacy's Hawthorne
Inn since girlhood. About 1916 she and her bachelor brothers, Charles and
Grant Notman, Wall Street brokers, rented "Beachend" cottage, the handsome frame colonial that Stacy built for a summer place on a quadrant of
land he filled in behind a retaining wall at the south extremity of Niles
Beach. The house is of uncertain vintage but was erected after the Niles
homestead burned in 1909.[4] As was his custom, Stacy used secondhand
material said to have included some parts of the antique Sargent house in
town, and stair risers (according to Jim Walen) from fish boxes, and about
this time put up a similar house across the road by Niles Pond.[5]

Charles Notman saw his chance and in October 1917 purchased from
Joseph Sherrard, who had been Stacy's manager of the Colonial Arms, the
lot the Niles place had occupied at the bend in the road between
"Beachend" and the grass-grown remnants of the burned hotel.

Both Charles and Grant Notman died during the first influenza epidemic of 1918, and the estate fell to their sister, who went ahead with construction of the English lodge-style mansion designed by Walter Chambers

of New York as the war was ending. "Three Waters" rose, rock by blasted rock, through 1919 and into the summer of 1920, when it was all but finished.

Edith Notman died in 1932. Her striking home on the Point's longest occupied ground remained in her family for several years and was sold to Raymond O'Connell of Gloucester in 1943.[6]

Even as one gang of masons was shaping the Notman mansion, another labored up the road on a manor palatial in its proportions, an enormous "North Easton" Gothic quarried from the ledge and set down on it so close to the harbor's edge that high tide slapped against the foundation.

This was the summer cottage of Mr. and Mrs. Frederick Garrison Hall, built on the westerly portion of the tract where once the Colonial Arms had dominated the shore, and sold to them in 1912 by George Stacy when he was trying to recoup his losses from the fire.

Ground (rock) was broken that summer by the well-known North Shore "cottage" builder J. T. Wilson of Nahant for "Stone Acre"[7] designed by Bellows and Aldrich of Boston and estimated to cost $100,000. One report had the owners in the spring of 1915 occupying at least a portion of the structure, whose cost was by then more than $150,000. Construction must have been suspended for the duration of the war since in April 1919 a local news item again had the house under way for $500,000. Fifteen months passed, and the *Cape Ann Shore* noted that the Hall house of granite was being excavated for its foundation!

Some time in the summer of 1920 the Halls moved into their enormous L-shaped domestic institution occupying the central harbor frontage, formerly dominated by the Colonial Arms, to the tune of well over half a million dollars. There were courtyards and loggias and porticos arched with intricate carvings, a semicircular driveway of massive granite blocks, sculpture everywhere, stone walls embracing stone walls, fountains and pools, exotic landscaping with pines and other flora rarely seen on the Point, and a stone studio for the master on the west line by "Beauport."

The whole was highly striking, hardly intimate in aspect, reminiscent of the grandiose architectural monuments created by Henry Hobson Richardson for his patrons, the Ames family, to bestow upon North Easton, the seat of the Ames shovel works and the dynastic fortune it piled up.

North Easton was the home of Mrs. Hall, the former Evelyn Ames, eldest daughter of Governor Oliver Ames, politician, capitalist and, in his retirement, patron of the Boston arts. The interest of the Halls in Eastern Point may have been aroused via various routes, including the Ames Estate at Bay View. Evelyn was related, coincidentally, through the marriage of her brother, Oakes Ames the Harvard botanist, to Blanche Ames, granddaughter of General Adelbert Ames and great-granddaughter of that estate's first proprietor, Ben Butler.

Evelyn and Frederick Hall were among Eastern Point's most interesting personalities for nearly twenty-five years. Evelyn was said to be one of the

finest amateur pianists in Boston, probably accomplished enough but much too shy to appear professionally.

Freddy was an artist of some distinction and range, a portraitist and etcher who had been so unexpectedly successful as a pen-and-ink designer of book plates at Harvard that he quit his architectural courses after two years for Paris and art. He painted meticulous still lifes and porcelain figurines but was best known for his etchings of French city scenes. He collected jade and oriental art and was a devotee of carved wood, which adorns "Stone Acre" (now "Shoal Water") at every turn. He was also a keen sailor.

Hall contributed works to the National Academy in New York and the Pennsylvania Academy in Philadelphia and exhibited summers at Gallery-on-the-Moors in East Gloucester. At the request of his neighbor Piatt Andrew, who at the time was serving as the first commander of the American Legion in Gloucester, he designed the base for the 1921 statue of Joan of Arc by the Annisquam sculptress Anna Vaughn Hyatt that honors the dead of World War I in Legion Square.

Not long after they moved into "Stone Acre" the Halls gave a dance for their niece Pauline, Oakes Ames's daughter, the future Mrs. T. P. Plimpton of New York, mother of the superenergetic author George Plimpton. She recalled how her aunt's spacious music room, said to be an acoustic tour de force, was the romantic setting for her party, opening onto the terrace that broods over the harbor like a castle on the Rhine.

That concert room resounded to many the memorable musicale. The Halls frequently invited more than a hundred guests. Evelyn had a wide acquaintance in the music world, and a diverse one; she and Freddy were devoted, for instance, to that mad genius of pantomime who happened to be one of the world's great harpists, Harpo of the Marx Brothers. He was a

A coaster ghosts past Mother Ann. (Chester N. Walen photo, from Gordon W. Thomas)

close friend and often a house guest, and so was the actor Roland Young of the classic motion picture comedies *Ruggles of Red Gap* and *Topper*.

A staple of these soirées was lobster in heavy cream, washed down with champagne and topped off with the astounding harpistry of the ever mute Harpo, accompanied at the piano (if he had not already reduced that to a naked, plucked sounding board) by his hostess. Communicating in the bedlam style that endeared the unkempt little man in the crazy wig to millions through the screen, Mr. Marx would not break his silence until the very end of the evening.

To Mrs. Plimpton her aunt was "an extraordinary musician, extremely shy about her playing, so that she never did play professionally, but when the mood to play came to her, there was no one to equal the romantic bravura of her touch."[8]

The mood might come at any hour—in the middle of the night perhaps, when Evelyn, suddenly overcome by a desire to play, would pick up the telephone and summon a few close neighbors. Helen Patch Gray remembered her Uncle Piatt Andrew hurrying over to "Stone Acre" in his pajamas: "Doors were opened to the harbor and the music poured out. He always treasured those memories."[9]

Another memory Doc surely relished was of the evening Evelyn brought an alarm clock to dinner at "Red Roof" and stuffed it under a pillow to remind her when to leave.

As a lover of animals, Evelyn Hall was in a class by herself.

"I remember once walking along the street with her in Boston when she saw a large white dray horse being whipped by its driver," wrote her niece. "To my embarrassment, Mrs. Hall stepped right into the street and berated the driver. She was one of those extraordinary Boston women with no self-consciousness whatever in a situation of that kind."[10]

Helen Gray recalled a similar experience:

> One day driving through the center of Gloucester in the days when we [the Patches] had a chauffeur, Mrs. Hall, in our car, ordered him to stop. "Do you see that old horse? He looks tired and very hungry. Here is money to get him some carrots at the grocery store there. Do feed him." Our chauffeur, a proud Wonson, did just that. Her flair was sometimes irresistible.[11]

Cats were her *bêtes blanches*. A stray was rarely passed by; cats preempted the five Georgian chairs in her drawing room, and she brought them scraps from her restaurant plate.

This preoccupation was shared with Miss Carolyn Morrill, known locally as the "Cat Lady of Rockport," who kept dozens of cats and is alleged to have conversed in something resembling Shakespearean English. Mrs. Hall felt a kindred, if proprietary, interest and wrote Piatt Andrew's sister, Mrs. Isaac Patch, from Beacon Street:

Dear Mrs. Patch:

The books of sea tales you so kindly let me have, for Roland Young to read, are in my linen closet here. Much to my humiliation my maid brought them here by mistake instead of leaving them at your door on her way to Boston. You shall have them very soon! I found them only yesterday.

And now I am going to ask a great favor, hoping you will be able to grant it. Miss Carolyn Morrill now has her family of cats, waifs and strays in a little house with a porch and plenty of surrounding land. Therefore conditions are very much better, and I have yielded at last to the situation and am carrying her through the winter. After all, I have acquaintances here who are self-indulgent in more selfish and distasteful ways—people I disapprove of more highly—and here I must add, most humbly, "and what am I, to disapprove!"

Her little house has thin walls. She says she is strong but she looks very delicate, and she is alone. Today in my Christmas letter I have enclosed a page for her to tack on her wall. It asks neighbors in case of her illness to telephone to me at Back Bay 0581, and should I be away to call you, Gloucester 250. I would not ask you to go there, but I hope you would be able to suggest proper action at my expense, and see that her cats were given a kindly end. I will learn from her the name of an experienced Gloucester Swede who has kindly advanced methods in such emergencies. Is this too much to ask? Do let me know; I should completely understand and make another arrangement, while not losing my conviction that you are generous and kind-hearted. One has so much—too much—to do anyway. . . .

In the fall of 1928 Mrs. Hall expressed concern to Mrs. Patch that the Cat Lady have warm clothing for the approaching winter, charged to her, and a good snow shovel, for "my one fear is that if a bill is not sent to me, or a list of things and prices so I can scud the money, she will divert the amount for other things for her 'family's' benefit."

"A stimulating pair," wrote Pauline Plimpton of her Aunt Evelyn and Uncle Freddy Hall, "both highly artistic and excitable. The by-play between them was amusing and delightful—they were both strong, colorful personalities in the tradition of some of the other Eastern Point residents of their time, their like not to be seen in the next generations."[12]

Salt Island, November 18, 1919, before and after. (Gordon Thomas collection)

~33~

MORE PRATFALLS AND POLITICS

AUXILIARY ENGINES WERE THE saboteurs of the Gloucester sailing fleet. First steam and then diesel drove the fishing schooners out to the grounds and back to market faster and safer. Ironically, the engine proved to be the ecological tyrant whose instrument of disaster, the power-hauled otter trawl, would sweep the deep clean of the salt bankers and dory trawlers, decimate the fishermen, eradicate the fish, and in the process turn the cruel romance of man with hook and line against the sea into bittersweet nostalgia. Inexorably sail would go down before the philistines of fishing, the squat and stinking draggers.

The engine and radio and, ultimately, radar would all but eliminate the hazard of such lee shores as Eastern Point, and after the turn of the century the rate of Back Shore casualties declined until by the First World War they were a rarity.

All the same, some few of the fishermen and many of the old coasters stuck to their canvas, more from necessity than choice, no doubt, and occasionally—as it always had been—it was their undoing.

Less than three weeks after the Armistice, on the black Thanksgiving night of November 28, 1918, the three-masted schooner *Harold B. Cousens* of Portland, 379 tons gross, out of St. Johns, New Brunswick, for New York with 371,000 feet of lumber, was wallowing off the back of the Point in a southeast gale and battering seas.

The coaster had taken a beating the whole trip. To top it off, during the night she started a leak. Captain Thomas Carey put the men at the pumps, but the water in the hold kept ahead of them. The slowly filling *Cousens* grew unmanageable, settled in her stern, lost her headway and at around two in the morning carried up onto Bemo Ledge. She slid off, and then was hove by a mountainous wave fast on the rocks, breakers all around.

The seas ripped away her yawl boat, the only means of getting ashore. By daybreak her stern was awash and her decks were swept; Captain Carey

Schooner Helen W. Martin, *281 feet, built by Percy and Small at Bath, Maine, in 1900—aground in Brace Cove, September 25, 1911. (Helen Patch Gray)*

and his wife, who was cook, and the six crew took shelter in the forward deckhouse.

They were spotted, luckily, and Captain King and the motor lifeboat lurched around the Point through the dying gale and took them off. They had suffered severely from exposure. The big schooner's mainmast had gone by the board, the other two were wobbling, and she was beginning to break up—as she did entirely in a few days, scattering her deckload and her bones up and down her last shore.

Monsterlike, Bemo lurked in its lair.

Had there been a more immediate sequel to *As Ye Sow,* that 1914 flick that nearly terminated in real-life disaster on Bemo Ledge, it might have been called *Ye Are Like to Reap.* As it was, the next attempt at moviemaking on Eastern Point was as foreboding in title, *Bride 13,* and if anything, the assembly of this wild and watery fifteen-part silent serial by Fox Films was even more perilous.

These cliffhangers were contrived to lure the audience back to the local movie palace each week, panting for the next episode, and were shown as come-ons for the main feature. *Bride 13* was directed by Richard Stanton and starred Jack O'Brien, Marguerite Clayton, Edward Roseman and Greta Hartmann, with a company of fifty-five. A number of installments were shot on Cape Ann.

The plot had something to do with twelve rich and beautiful brides kidnapped from their various altars in New York by a gang of Moroccan pirates and whisked to a castle to await ransoming by their fathers, all tycoons. Miss Clayton was the thirteenth bride, the decoy set out to trap the baddies and effect the rescue of the other maidens in distress.

The filming of *Bride 13* was thirteen times as exciting as the viewing. It was a case of anything that can go wrong will, and did.

It was August 1919, and while the company was shooting at Newport, Rhode Island, workmen nailed together a very impressive wooden castle on Salt Island, off Good Harbor Beach. On September 8 an 85-mile-an-hour tornado whipped across Cape Ann and blew the whole works down and out to sea. A month more, and it had been rebuilt and the company was in town, staying at the Harbor View. Among other props, they brought with them a submarine on loan from the navy and a steam yacht.

Filming started. First, the chief cameraman was swept into the sea from a ledge off Salt Island, but he was rescued by Forrest ("Bunch") Bickford in a launch. (Bunch, you will recall, was involved in the making of *As Ye Sow*.) Then two extras up on the parapet of the castle, playing pirates repelling the submarine, stuffed too much powder into their cannon; it broke loose on the recoil and crashed through the floor, thirty feet down to the ledge, knocking one unconscious and carrying the other through the hole with it. They were revived and dusted off and sent back into action.

Three thousand spectators were on the beach to see the great balloon rescue and getaway from the castle. The bag ripped twice while the men were filling it with hot air. The third try it got away from them and soared out over the Atlantic, where Bickford recovered it.

When the balloon finally took off properly, instead of dipping down and letting the two occupants unload themselves gently from the wicker basket into the water, a breeze came along, wafted it on high, then dropped it in a thicket of Brier Neck catbrier. The unhappy passengers had no choice but to get out. Relieved of its burden, the bag drifted all the way to the Rockport depot, where it was pinned down after a frantic chase up the Nugent Stretch.

The climax that all of Cape Ann had been waiting for was to be the blowing-up of the castle by the pirate chief just before he and his band escaped in the submarine, which must have defected or been captured. It was all set up with an arsenal of dynamite and gunpowder planted around the structure and six cameras trained on the scene. Thousands watched, a thousand breaths were held, but when director Stanton barked out the order to blast off, nothing happened. Something was wrong with the wiring.

So while the experts gingerly inspected their circuitry, the filming moved on to the shipwreck scene. It was now the middle of November.

Fox Films had bought the antique coasting schooner *Mineola*, launched in 1860, rotting in the dock at Davis's Wharf. Director Stanton had her floated and fitted out for fakery with old sails and rigging. He put Bunch and Henry Bickford, Mort Mayo and Westover Brazier aboard for a crew, along with the actors, and hired the tug *Eveleth* to drag her around to Brace Cove. Shades of *Island Home*.

Up sail, and bring her in on the southeasterly. The cameramen cranked away as the pirates bludgeoned the crew, and right on cue Billy Carr, a Gloucester boy, and George Birdsong, who appears to have been a stunt man, broke loose from the melee, jumped for the sheer poles and scrambled up the ratlines to the main crosstrees, sixty feet above deck.

They poised dramatically and leaped. But the impact of the dive and the stunning effects of the frigid water had not been anticipated. They surfaced, numbed and bruised, and Carr went under again. The old schooner surged slowly on by them, bound for destruction.

Useless lines were thrown from deck. Bunch Bickford sprang into the dory and rowed after them, while four of the pirates plunged overboard to the rescue. Carr rose and sank for the third time. Les Francis, a Gloucester extra, dove and came up with him, coughing and limp. The others reached Birdsong where he was floating, unconscious. One of his rescuers went down sputtering. They reached and grabbed him, unconscious too.

Somehow or other, rescuers and rescued clambered or were hauled aboard the *Mineola* just before she struck the shore near Brace Rock with such a jolt that her mainmast snapped (*that* was in the script) and crashed into the sea, missing Bickford in the dory by a few inches (*that* wasn't).

The waterlogged were taken ashore and hustled away for drying off. The rest waded in through the surf to be ambushed on schedule by a gang of Arabs who dragged their captives disdainfully over the rocks above the beach.

In the windup, they dynamited *Mineola* and burned her carcass to the water's edge. A glorious end, and she had earned it.

The Emperor of Salt Island, as they called director Dick Stanton, had meanwhile been assured by his demolition experts that all was ready. As dusk approached on the nineteenth of November, the countdown began before a goodly crowd of Gloucester folk.

KER-POW! BARR-UMP! Up went castle and all. A roar, an echo, a thunderous, pluming cloud of smoke and dust, a blossom of plaster. Splinters, planks, sand and stone, a splashing all about as it rained down on the water.

The dust settled, the smoke drifted out to sea, and Salt Island was once again Salt Island. The magician of the silver screen had waved his wand from the porch of a summer cottage, and the movieman's castle in the air had simply evaporated, at exactly 4:20 P.M.

Within two hours, all thirteen of the brides, the heroes and the pirates, the cameramen and the set men and stunt men, makeup artists, director and all the rest of Fox Film's touted million-dollar movie company had moved out, leaving nothing but the memory. They were off for the New Hampshire woods to shoot the lumber camp scenes, the next spine-tingling episode of *Bride 13*.

Ten months later it opened at the Strand Theater in Gloucester, and they had to run an extra show for the crowds that couldn't jam in by the box office.

A kid of ten, Joe Oliver was down at the beach every day after school (though he missed the castle explosion because he had to stay after) and recalled the filming of another silent, *Down to the Sea in Ships,* starring Clara Bow.

> Half of a steamer ship was built on Good Harbor Beach; the filming was done from the front with the ocean as background. It was two-decker, and on cue the planes on the beach would rev their motors, men would stand in front with hoses, and as the water emerged the propellers would swish it across the deck while men underneath cranked the boat to make it roll from side to side.
>
> The stunt man would run from the top deck to the lower deck and when he reached it, a huge tank of water on the side (not seen by the camera) opened up and a huge wave came over the ship, sweeping the stunt man into a net. When the wave hit the deck, the masts and barrels came tumbling down, and when they had to redo the scene, they automatically returned to position.[1]

In that fleeting moment when All Was Quiet and the Western world hung between a won war and a lost peace, a group of enthusiasts in America commissioned a gallery of portraits of the victorious Allied leaders. Cecilia Beaux was one of five artists selected by the American Committee on War Portraits in the spring of 1919 to execute a total of fifteen to be given to the U.S. Government.

Bo's assignments were Cardinal Mercier, Archbishop of Malines, defier of the Kaiser, hero of Belgium; Georges Clemenceau, Tiger of France, Her premier in the darkest hour; and Admiral Lord Beatty, tactician of Jutland and commander of the British Grand Fleet.

Arriving in Paris, the portraitist was taken in hand for a brief tour by Harry Sleeper, who was running the American Field Service headquarters, and then on to Belgium for sitting with Cardinal Mercier. Clemenceau was less accessible, and the painting of *Le Tigre* was delayed a year. These two continentals intrigued her with their wit and warmth; but Lord Beatty she found just too British, unbending, tradition-bound and all in all, an unsympathetic sitter.

In July 1924, as she was on the point of returning to the States, Bo fell and broke her hip. Less than a fortnight later, her old friend Isabella Stewart Gardner, honorary citizen of Dabsville, died in Boston at the age of eighty-four.

For the next eighteen years Beaux hobbled with a crutch.

When war broke out in August 1914 the Randall-MacIvers were at Eastern Point. David sailed immediately for his native England. He was commissioned a captain of intelligence, served on the Western Front and later in Macedonia and was discharged in February 1919. He and Joanna rediscovered each other at the Point that summer.

Joanna's mother, Mrs. Davidge, died in New York in December, going on ninety. These two events, the long war absence and the passing of his mother-in-law, rather starched up David: "I was fully decided that Joanna had worked long and hard enough; and, though she felt that it was a great loss to give up all the teaching that she loved, yet she also thought that it was only fair to my life as an archeologist to set me free to go abroad. So after very careful consideration I decided that in future we would spend half the year in Italy, returning for the summer to America, or sometimes spending the summer in England."[2]

A new phase indeed. By 1925 they were settled in a large apartment in Rome in the Corso d'Italia, and David was well into the studies of the Etruscan civilization that his peers regarded as the largest contribution of his career. In England their favored goal was Oxford, where he kept up with many friends of long ago.

"Italy and Oxford, Gloucester and Virginia," he reflected, "these are our ideal memories."[3]

Congressman Augustus Peabody Gardner, who shellacked Piatt Andrew so thoroughly in the 1914 primary, had gone to war as an infantry major and died of pneumonia in 1918. He was succeeded by his secretary, Wilfred W. Lufkin of Essex. When Lufkin was appointed collector of customs for Massachusetts in early 1921, Colonel Andrew, now a returned hero, was urged to run for the Republican nomination for Congress, which was wide open, in the special primary that fall.

The prospect was tempting. He was well known for his organization and leadership of the American Field Service; he had been a delegate to the preliminary conference at Paris in March 1919 from which the American Legion emerged; and he was the first commander of the Legion's Gloucester post.

Moreover, Doc had spoken around the state at the request of the Republican Party during the presidential campaign the previous fall; he argued strongly against American entry into the League of Nations, contending that Article X of the Covenant, intended to guarantee the territorial integrity of members (on which the Senate, Henry Cabot Lodge taking the lead, had based its refusal to ratify the treaty), would jeopardize the future of the United States and the peace of the world.

The freshly elected vice president, Governor Calvin Coolidge, and his wife had spent the night of November 8 as guests of Doc at "Red Roof" after attending a dinner in Gloucester celebrating another victory—that of the Gloucester schooner *Esperanto* over the Canadian *Delawana* at Halifax in the first of the international fishermen's races.

With Warren Harding's inauguration Piatt had hoped for a diplomatic appointment. It never came, and when he finally decided to go after the nomination for Congress and announced his intentions publicly, the Republicans, and specifically the remnant of the Gardner machine, had already taken their blessings to Haverhill and Ransom C. Pingree, an estimable man of no special distinction.

It was a runaway from the start. Piatt got the women's vote favoring rights for females and Prohibition enforcement ("like it or not, it's the law of the land"); he turned to his own credit Pingree's horror at his opposition to a literacy test for immigrants (Candidate Andrew had seen plenty of Yanks in the trenches who couldn't pass one); and the old rumors that he was a Portuguese Catholic or a Polish Jew, he concluded, probably helped him with the ethnic vote.

In fact, he had the sixth district ticking like a clock for him. The *Gloucester Daily Times* froze Pingree out and ran on its front page a stentorian command from Mayor Percy Wheeler:

A PROCLAMATION
I hereby proclaim it the duty of every citizen of Gloucester to vote for Colonel Andrew for Congress. Gloucester's future and Gloucester's welfare demands this action. I request those who have in charge the ringing of bells and blowing of whistles, to give ten minutes of their time Tuesday at 10 o'clock to start things going with all the noise possible.[4]

The result on September 14 was Andrew 19,419, Pingree 10,401. Gloucester went overboard for Doc 4,753 to 267—some turnabout from 1914 when he could carry only two wards of his hometown against Gus Gardner.

Judge Charles I. Pettingell of Amesbury was unopposed for the Democratic nomination in this traditionally Republican district. Doc became Congressman A. Piatt Andrew on September 27, 1921—22,545 to 6,792 over the judge.

The veteran political writer for the *Boston Globe,* M. E. Hennessy, came down to Eastern Point to size up the new Congressman.

Col. Andrew is in his 48th year. He is a rich bachelor, who enjoys his books and his friends, his pictures and his curiosities, his music and his rare and extensive collection of Roman war relics. His house and grounds are after a design of his own. There is nothing gaudy about the furnishings of the house. It was built for comfort and contains many unique cubby holes, secret panels, trap doors, nooks and corners cozily furnished.

His trophy room, containing his war relics, one of the largest and finest collections in the country, is carefully guarded and locked. His collection of old china and glass occupies one room and overflows into another. His library is filled with fine books. . . .

Personally Col. Andrew is a man of medium height, spare, with gray eyes and hair, worn pompadour. His nose is aquiline, his features sharp, although as he nears the half century mark, he is filling out and there is just a trace of the double chin.

He takes great delight in showing callers over his house and grounds [that] remind one of some old French chateau. There are fountains, sequestered nooks, shady dells, tables and seats, where one may rest and read or study the landscape and breathe in the ozone of the salt air.

A large marble figure of Buddha looms up in the garden on the harbor side of the house. "No," answers the colonel. "I'm not a Buddhist. It is about the only thing my opponents did not accuse me of being in the campaign. They overlooked this. It was once the property of Lord Minto, Governor General of Canada, and before that of India. I bought it at an auction of his effects."[5]

Inviting Piatt to dinner one evening with Mrs. Gardner and herself, Carrie Sinkler directed the card "To him who Sleeps near Buddha" and signed another invitation "Yrs with the peace of Buddha between us."

A year later a rather more impressionable writer than the hardboiled Hennessey was given the first-class tour by Doc and wrote it up, wide-eyed and revealing, in the *North Shore Breeze*.

"This is not a house; it is a passion!" In some such phrase as this a visitor at "Red Roof" exclaimed when once going through the home of Congressman A. Piatt Andrew. The phrase does aptly fit the place, for everywhere you may turn there is a surprise; but the surprise always is one that adds to the interest and to the comfort of the place. Instinctively anyone would sense that "Red Roof" is a man's home, and that a man's hand guided its course, for everywhere there is the souvenir or the trophy or the memento that to man's heart carries infinite appeal. And there are ingenious creature comforts, too.

This unusual house has been written of more than once, yet there is ever something which appears new to the visitor—something that strikes so forcibly on the mind that the place once seen is

not forgotten. Therein one may say that "Red Roof" is unique. There it stands, a thicket of the Eastern Point woods between its hospitable door and the avenue, its old mill-stone set as a lawn table beside the entrance door with its small ship's bell and its lantern. That door which enters upon a tiny hallway makes the visitor sure he is going into a house of the Colonial day, but that is only an impression created by Colonel Andrew, for the house has been built under his own direction—he has been his own architect.

The big living room, extending across the house from front to rear, is so comfortable in appearance that anyone would enjoy just to sit there before the open fire on cool fall days and read volume after volume from the library, not so far away. Then, sitting there in the comfort of the deep chair, the guest could study the tile used in the fireplace and extending up the side of the room. This tile is unusual, most unusual in fact. It was made especially for the house by Harry Mercer of Doylestown, Pa., and shows again something distinctive in this North Shore house.

Perhaps the Congressman will ask the visitor to see his library, and in going to it he starts for what looks like a portion of panelled wall with a cushioned wall seat along it. Up comes the seat, and the door is opened from the paneling, low, but with steps leading to a lower level. There, automatically, you will stop, for at the right is a small pocket-like place filled with trophies of the Titan struggle in Europe, where Mr. Andrew earned his title of lieutenant-colonel through his work with the Red Cross [American Field Service]. But at the left there is a blue light, a light rightly toning the little alcove wherein stands the organ and pictures, originals, made at the front in France. This spot is called by your host his "temple of memories of war experiences," the blue light lending a solemnity, almost an atmosphere of reverence. A Napoleon death mask adds to this feeling. And then there peals forth stately measures from the instrument behind you, for quietly this most unusual man who is showing you his home has slipped to the stool and has set the organ pealing through the space and over the house through some special passages and openings. With a sense of sympathetic feeling he makes the music live. There, too, is rightly placed the original of the figure now surmounting the Church of Our Lady of Good Voyage in Gloucester, given by Mr. Andrew some time ago.

Across the passage, in that little spot where you first stopped, are souvenirs, each of which sets the average imagination going at feverish speed. For instance—the life buoy from the *Lusitania;* the sign from the frontier post bounding France and Alsace; ambulance panels from France; a photograph of Viviani, one time French premier, and the man whom Americans particularly remember as the wonderful orator accompanying Marshal Joffre in his wartime visit.

You hesitate, but the library has an attraction, and the room, when entered, carries out the knowledge that you already have that this Massachusetts Congressman is a student. Books, books everywhere from floor to ceiling. Here on the long side is the large globe, and also a flat, desk-like table; there may be seen one of the treasures of the place—a gift from the Master Mariners Association of Gloucester and inscribed "Greetings," on which one sentence in particular stands out: "They have found, hold and proclaim him their friend; a friend among friends,—a man among men." Is it any wonder that Congressman Andrew treasures this souvenir of esteem?

In another place, over in a corner on the shore side, is a smaller stand, and there is a visorless cap of a German soldier. It is hanging on something, but before it leans a photograph, one of Ambassador Jusserand, cordially inscribed and given to his friend, Mr. Andrew. Then you will be told that the cap came from the first dead soldier he saw in France. With a whimsical smile, accompanied by a subdued twinkle, the Jusserand photo will be moved, the cap will be raised from its resting place, and the features of former Ambassador von Bernstoff, smug and self-satisfied, pop up. Irony of fate—that, too, was inscribed by the donor, back in pre-war days.

Doc's pet bears, Gold and Silver, grew so fast they had to be given to a circus in the fall of 1908. (Andrew L. Gray)

Again to the opposite end of the library your eyes may then wander, past books, leopard skins and tapestries; past the little high fireplace to the cases beneath the windows. Hundreds, probably over 1500, war posters are here assembled in one of the large private collections. Just how many there are Mr. Andrew cannot tell you. But to read some of those sheets posted by the one-time foe is to make the blood surge again, try as one will to remember that hostilities are over and that peace has been declared.

Back across the living room you will undoubtedly be invited, and a room lined with mugs of various types, pewter, old silver, with plates and such interesting things, suggests a small dining room; but, pointing to the left, Mr. Andrew will mention that an outer, porch-like room is where he dines, and out there you go. Two small tables are fastened to the outer wall, and over them arched screened openings, hung with a profusion of vines, frame one of the enviable views of Gloucester harbor and the Magnolia shore. By an ingenious arrangement these two tables may be joined into one to accommodate some dozen or more guests in an unusual setting along one side. Dutch tiles add charm to this most interesting niche.

Many, many other things of interest there are on this floor, but there are the rooms above where guests find comfort and pleasure. Up there is the collection of samplers, a rare one, too, and there may the guest be surprised by hearing the full-toned organ pealing forth as though in his own room. On, to the third floor; there are

the quarters of Congressman Andrew, for what would have been an attic has been fitted into an attractive study open to the peak of the roof, with a suite of rooms for his private occupancy. The huge, flat-topped desk, set near the middle of the room, shows that it is a business affair, and by it the Representative from this Fifth Essex district may be imagined studying and weighing carefully the momentous matters of state ever before our national government. Here, also, is a second of the tiled fireplaces from the hand of Mercer.

By this time you have had your hasty glance at this home and are curious to see what the grounds offer, assured that it will be something out of the ordinary. It is. At one spot toward the outer harbor end rise the serene features of Buddha, far from his native clime, but resting comfortably there among the greenery of this North Shore place. At the opposite end of the house there is a seat against a wall, and beside it a rough, worn door of plank. A second look, and wear and grinding from the waves shows the door to have been made from planks washed ashore whence no man knows.

The natural bushes and shrubs are all along the shore, seemingly as nature made them, but beside the walk to the Venetian post at the head of the private pier there opens surprisingly what seems a yawning cavern, for it is not visible from above. This is Colonel Andrew's bathhouse, built of concrete in among rough, low cliffs of the shore, roofed of the same material, on which grass and shrubbery grow. Figureheads of one-time ships decorate this spot here and there, while a guard rail makes a finishing touch along the outer side, close by the lapping of the waters. Here you can imagine luncheon on a hot day as having advantages of coolness and comfort far away from the rush of life, yet near enough to jump into that life at a few moments notice.

That is the atmosphere of the entire place—restfulness, comfort, the unusual, with here and there a delightful whimsy. This is then "Red Roof," the place where Congressman Andrew rests, plays and works. It is indeed "not a house"; it is more than that—"it is a passion." [6]

Was there anyone to whom Piatt Andrew was not a deepening riddle, as mysterious as the Lavender Lady's mysts, a marbled mix of the very private and the very public? A man of convolutions, with his taste for the odd and the bizarre, his Buddha and his caged bears, his bowl of heliotrope, his brilliant, probing intellect, his sunbathing in the nude and physical culturism and fear of growing old (he kept gymnastic equipment in his attic quarters, and a steel-spring hand exerciser on his desk), his full-length portrait of himself on the wall of his secret mirrored bedchamber and his practical jokes.

Well, and his acoustic battles with Jack Hammond across a mile of harbor when they directed the loudspeakers of their phonographs full blast at each other's bizarre bachelor quarters on calm evenings in a curious quiz of musical sophistication. An over-the-water *bash*, one might say—meaning, as it originated with the British, a jolly good time—as expropriated, some claim, in Dabsville, the same, but from the acronym of Buswell Andrew Sleeper Hammond.

Isaac Patch has come as close as anyone to outing Doc, yet maintained in *Closing the Circle* the circumspection appropriate to his uncle's, and perhaps anyone's, era, when he wrote:

> Some of Piatt's friends were homosexuals, giving rise to speculation that he was as well. Although he never married, in 1911 he proposed to the very wealthy Dorothy Whitney, who turned him down. My uncle's closest confidant was Harry Sleeper, but much of the correspondence between them has been lost. Piatt was very reticent about himself, and, though he and my mother [Piatt's sister] adored each other, he revealed nothing of his inner life to her or to others in the family.

Mysterious, marbled, magnetic, magnificent—restless and unfulfilled—what on earth, people wondered, made Piatt tick?

Hooch and Booze—or Gin and Whiskey? (Milton H. Clifford, MD)

~34~
THE TEETERING TWENTIES

DESOLATE AND UNFIT FOR MAN, the surf-pounded back that Eastern Point turned against the ocean seemed as remote in 1920 as any stretch of rock and scrub on the Atlantic. Open to the easterlies that gathered energy from a thousand miles away to explode on its sea-smoothed ledges, wind-swept, sun-caressed, storm-battered, this bleak, brief, unyielding coast a few leagues from Boston looked as wild as it ever had across the heaving swells to the curious eyes of the discoverers, and before that into time.

A mere quarter of a mile inland, the smack of ball on gut, the chig-a-chug of the cocktail shaker, the hum of well-bred voices modulated on the breeze—at Brace Cove, Persia Head and Flat Point, only the scream of the lonely gull, the conch-shell hiss of surf, the endless wind rattling the dry brush. No sight, no sound of human life.

If the time had come to gain a foothold here, it deserved to be done with style, with strength, with grandeur.

Two men had the boldness and the flair for it, John Wing Prentiss, senior partner in the investment banking house of Hornblower and Weeks, and Arthur Leonard, president of the Chicago Stock Yards.

Prentiss was born in Bangor, Maine, on August 15, 1875. His father's family had made money lumbering. When he was about seven they moved to California for ten years, and on their return he was enrolled at Phillips Andover Academy and was graduated from Harvard in June 1898.

That fall he started at the bottom as a messenger boy at $3 a week for the Boston Stock Exchange House. Leaving Horatio Alger far behind, he soon talked himself into a job with Hornblower and Weeks.

"When can you open up an office in New York for us?" Jack was asked one day in 1904 by partner John Wingate Weeks.

"Right now," was the ready reply. When he got there someone had to show him the way to Wall Street. Two more years, and he was admitted into partnership. From three bucks a week to partner in eight years. His advice,

An impressive spread, "Blighty." (Milton H. Clifford, MD)

from the top of the pile, to ambitious young men: "Get the job you like and work like hell."[1]

Colonel Prentiss (in World War I he was a lieutenant colonel with the General Staff, and enjoyed the address) attracted national attention with the financial deals he managed for General Motors, Hudson Motors, Chevrolet and Timken Roller Bearing. He astounded Wall Street with his testimony at a tax hearing in Washington in February 1927 that in 1924, 1925 and for the third time within the previous thirty days he had offered Henry Ford a cool billion dollars cash on the line for the Ford Motor Company on behalf of interests he represented. He was of course turned down, but in spite of Ford's antipathy for The Street, they had enjoyed a friendly luncheon together.

His cousin, the late Mrs. Winifred Kay Shepard, remembered how Jack came to visit the Kays at Quarry Point:

> He was the son of my mother's youngest brother. We Kays lived in Brookline and of course our cousin came constantly to his aunt's house. My mother was my father's second wife, and I had a stepsister, Marie Gordon Kay, something more than two years my senior. My sister was very beautiful and before either of them was old enough to be thinking of that sort of thing they were in love. Of course the family never said anything about that youthful affair, but in 1904 they were married and lived happily ever afterward. John used to visit us at Eastern Point once or twice every summer, and he and Marie always said that when he made his pile they would buy a big piece of Eastern Point and build a house.[2]

Jack made his fortune, and in February 1917 he bought that big piece

from the Associates, about twenty acres on the Back Shore, Brace Cove and Niles Pond. Arthur Leonard had amassed his pile too, and the next May he followed suit with the purchase from them of the acreage west from Prentiss along the shore up to the Raymond land, with access from Fort Hill Avenue.

Prentiss planned to build astride the primitive shore road where it curved around behind Brace Rock. To do this, and to insure his privacy, he proposed to shut it off and lay legal claim to it. In midsummer of 1918 he made his move; he had a ditch dug and a stone wall built and barbed wire strung across the road at Brace Cove.

To the people of East Gloucester this looked like a declaration of trench warfare. Mine host George Stacy, the Bass Rocks Improvement Association and residents who for as long as they could remember had been used to passing this way for a view of the sea were enraged. Many recalled that as recently as 1909, when the Associates completed the last 500-yard section between the Patch land and Brace's, they announced that Gloucester citizens were welcome to drive right around from Good Harbor Beach along the Back Shore to the lighthouse and return to East Gloucester by the harbor.

Mayor Stoddart and the city council demanded that Prentiss remove his barrier within forty-eight hours, and when he didn't, a highway crew went out and did.

Prentiss petitioned the land court to register his purchase and the conveyance to him by the Associates of the section of road that bisected it.

At the hearing in Salem in June 1919 a parade of oldsters was trundled in by the opposition to testify to the existence of a cart track on the ocean shore and their unhindered use of it as far back as their memories served them. But they were outnumbered and outtalked by witnesses summoned for the petitioner (with evident resentment, sometimes) and stating that access to the Point had been restricted as far back as *their* memories served and that for years the public had been stopped at the gate lodge.

One witness minded the day Constable Simms halted two men trying to get out past the gate lodge. He hadn't let them in; where did they come from? They had to admit they had scaled the old boundary wall and knew it was private property. Well, said Simms, he wouldn't arrest 'em for trespass, but they could darn well leave the same way.

Perhaps the climax of the hearing came when Colonel Prentiss testified that he too had been challenged at the gate more than once and found it very annoying.

The land court concluded that the shore road between Brace Cove and Mother Ann was private and granted the Prentiss petition to register his land. The city appealed to the Massachusetts Supreme Court, that familiar arbiter of Eastern Point affairs. The high bench denied the city's exceptions in the spring of 1920, once again affirming the inviolability of Thomas Niles's privacy.

Jack Prentiss now relaxed, and as he prepared to build, he cut a way through the moors, inland of the site, and made it known that Gloucester people were welcome to take this road around Niles Pond to visit the rocks known as Persia Head.

Persia Head is actually somewhat east of that haunted ledge where the *Persia* met her doom, and it was only about 200 feet to the west of the brig's grave where Arthur Leonard, as soon as Prentiss won his case, started his rock mansion in the early spring of 1920. It was set bluff and bold against the crashing surf, steep-roofed and stubborn. Like the Notman and Hall manses on the quiet harbor, the granite was quarried from the enormous, descending ledge it stood on. The Leonards called their fortress against the

Laying the foundation for "Druimteac," May 12, 1920. (Lila Swift Monell)

sea "Druimteac," Gaelic for "House Back of the Ledge." They instructed one and all in the proper pronunciation ("Drum-hack") and moved in for the 1921 season.

The stockyard king was not one to give ground before such a puddle as the Atlantic Ocean, and if he did not propose as Canute did to teach his retinue an object lesson in futility by commanding the tide to halt, neither would he have Neptune encroaching one fathom beyond his own

Raising "Druimteac." (Lila Swift Monell)

domain. "Druimteac" stood so daringly close that winter storms sometimes broke the windows and covered the floors with tons of sand and stones, and more than once rocks as big as suitcases were hurled by Poseidon in his frustration, clear through the high gallery window. Leonard nonchalantly repaired the damage.

Mr. Leonard was a determined man. Years later, in May 1934, when the Chicago Stock Yard was destroyed by an $8 million fire, he wired the news to Frederick Henry Prince, its Boston owner who was bound for Europe. From mid-Atlantic Prince wired back one word: *Rebuild.*

Leonard did. One who knew him called him "a genius of construction and a sentimentalist in things architectural."[3] He built the Stock Yard Inn in Tudor style; the Saddle and Sirloin Club, copied in part after a dining hall at Cambridge University; the Live Stock National Bank Building after Independence Hall in Philadelphia; and the original structure of the International Amphitheater in Chicago, with its balconies seating 8,000.

The Canute of Chicago wanted no pillars to obstruct the view of the arena and decreed that the balconies be hung from the walls. The architects are said to have protested that it couldn't be done. But it was, bent to the same will that planted "Druimteac" in the teeth of the sea—and they've been hanging balconies the Leonard way ever since.

Once his road had been cleared by the courts Colonel Prentiss called in the quarrymen, and the rasp of drill and crump of dynamite again rocked the Point in the fall of 1920. He, too, carved from the giant ledge a sprawling citadel of granite, with a fortress of a servants' wing and an equally imposing garage, approached by a majestic drive around the south shore of Niles Pond and up across the moor.

During the summer of 1921 it was still under construction, and the Prentisses rented a cottage Dr. James Knowles had built between his house

Arthur Leonard
(left, in hat)
surveys work on
his mighty
"Druimteac."
(Lila Swift
Monell)

on the harbor and the pond. Prentiss was an active Harvardian and at one time president of the Associated Harvard Alumni. Late that summer he persuaded the Harvard football squad to travel en masse to Eastern Point for the privilege of laboring on his place by way of a preseason conditioning workout. Sweating it up the ladders and along the staging with hods of cement, scabbing the job, the panting athletes were soon butts for the friendly scorn of the regular workmen.

Colonel and Mrs. Prentiss moved in for their first season in 1922, lord and lady of almost all they surveyed, commanding a breathtaking view out to sea over Brace Rock, massive and strangely out of place, and across the pond to the harbor. Marie named her cottage "Blighty"—as the English say, "One's Home Place." It cost upwards of a quarter of a million dollars, how far upwards was anyone's guess.

If the Prentisses had one quality more than another in common, their friends agreed that it was hospitality. Childless, they shared a compulsion for having people around, especially young, athletic Eastern Point people and their friends. Their largesse is legend; it throve through the Roaring Twenties, survived the Crash (thanks to his inheritance) and coasted into the thirties. The script might have been written by Scott Fitzgerald.

Jack's passion, after making money, was tennis, and he built two courts in the field adjoining "Blighty." He also enjoyed a round of golf; to attract foursomes, and possibly to put down a twinge of guilt, he laid out a six-hole pitch-and-putt course behind the garage, the longest hole being 85 yards.

The guilt, if this was a motive, would have arisen from his having spoiled the pleasure of his neighbors by buying and closing down the nine-hole course that had served their convenience since the turn of the century, all for the protection of his estate and what he took to be the interests of the Point.

Persisting in the illusion that they might yet make of the Point the Newport of the North Shore, the Eastern Point Associates in the autumn of 1899 had engaged Mott Cannon, who had engineered Henry Rouse's "The Ramparts," to create for them a nine-hole link on their forty acres of undeveloped land lying from the Cushing Wall almost to the sea, Brace Cove, the pond, St. Louis Avenue and Edgemoor Road. It would cost $10,000 and be open to the Point and the East Gloucester summer colony.

By winter's end Cannon's crew had cleared and plowed the downs and moors, dumped the movable rocks in the ocean, burned the brush and drained two swamps, and the next May 1900 they harrowed and manured. In August they seeded, and there were the first golfers striding briskly around that September, the whole under the supervision of Mrs. Phelps's Reverend Herbert Ward. All was done but the tees, which were promised for the following spring. The clubhouse was erected in due course at the east margin of the links, and the teagarden created, looking down over the harbor, enchantingly preserved forever by the brush of Maurice Prendergast. When the clubhouse had been deprived of its purpose by Colonel Prentiss, it was purchased by Mrs. Frances Carter, moved a few hundred yards into the rough on Stewart Avenue and christened "Harbor Lights."

Actually the golfing craze produced two other East Gloucester courses, the short-lived Delphine Golf Links on the Patch farm and a rough nine-holer bushwhacked on his father's estate at Bass Rocks by Henry Souther, Jr., much to the annoyance of that gentleman, who chided his son that the hay from the fields he was ruining was worth $500 a year to them. In 1904 a group purchased this layout from Souther; they called themselves the Bass Rocks Golf Club, improved it and eventually added the second nine that makes the modern course.

Perched on the tide's edge, "Druimteac" dares Neptune. (Lila Swift Monell)

So beyond Bass Rocks the Colonel's microcosmic course was the sole heir of the sport. Although considerably less challenging, it offered certain unusual attractions. Once established in "Blighty" the Prentisses inaugurated two institutions now indelibly of the lore: the July 4 and Labor Day all-day buffet, golf and tennis tournaments, which by general consensus opened and closed the season at Eastern Point for the sixteen years of the Prentiss primacy.

All the Point was invited. The luncheons were sumptuous. As for the tennis and the golf (and bowling on the green for those so inclined), everything was provided, including liquid fuel. The courts and the links were maintained as if with whisk broom and manicure scissors, and if one had arrived unequipped, racquets, clubs and plenty of balls were available in the hall closet.

Andrew Volstead, by his Act the father of Prohibition, might as well have saved himself the trouble, for the Prentissdom of "Blighty" recognized no twelve-mile limits. After the buffet and during the afternoon's play the popping of corks mingled with the crackle of distant firecrackers, and every spirit lifted on the flooding tide of champagne.

Helen Patch Gray, who played in the National Doubles at Longwood in 1940 and credited Jack Prentiss with teaching her the strategy that carried her that far, wrote that "finals of the tennis tournament were held on Labor Day morning and the buffet party was not over until the end of the golf tournament in late afternoon when many of us, champagne in hand, watched the last golf foursome play—usually Colonel Prentiss himself, Charles Stewart, my father Isaac Patch, and I forget who else. There was always a bottle of champagne presented for a hole in one."[4]

For years the Rouse Singles Tournament, confined to Eastern Pointers of both sexes, was held on the "Blighty" courts. Mixed doubles, open to off-Pointers, competed for the Prentiss trophy, and juniors for the Clay cup. (The tradition was continued after World War II on the court of Mr. and Mrs. David L. Richardson at "Indian Spring.")

All summer the courts and the links were crowded, and on weekends from noon until suppertime the Nineteenth Hole was open, a terrace room at the end of "Blighty" with Teachers Highland Cream, soda, ginger, ice and glasses on the table. Every afternoon during the week Marie Prentiss presided at tea, warm and gracious, everyone invited.

It has been said that children were frowned on at "Blighty," and perhaps this was the case with the smallest, for the childless master and mistress had things their own way and expected a certain deportment from their guests.

Yet Mrs. Isabella Wigglesworth of Cambridge remembered "Blighty" as the center of gaiety during her family's five summers at the Point in the mid-twenties: "The Prentisses actually seemed to enjoy hordes of children invading their tennis courts at all hours and used to send out buckets of iced ginger ale for their benefit. . . . Tea there was an institution—you never knew who or how many would come, but I never left without something of

interest to take away, the latest book or current art show at East Gloucester."[5]

Jack Prentiss's cousin, Edward R. Godfrey, Jr., of Huntington, Long Island, first visited "Blighty" in 1923. He was fifteen and the ink on his driver's license was still wet:

Tennis at "Blighty," summer 1922, Marie and John Prentiss at left and right. (Milton H. Clifford, MD)

> My parents permitted me to drive them from Bangor to Gloucester. The drive was nothing compared to my drilled-in fears, for Cousin John was a Colonel and Cousin Marie was the perfection of manners and neither understood children. So not to let my parents down I must outdo myself. Of course I could not like the Prentisses as they (so I understood) did not like children. I looked forward to a difficult and miserable visit.
>
> All went well. Cousin John boasted about his house, stating it was solid enough to support a railroad train on the second floor. Fanning, the chauffeur, was more impressive. He cared for a Chandler sports car, a Locomobile touring car and a dull Packard limousine, plus several minor vehicles.
>
> Fanning was a semigod during the early period of Blighty. He was more or less general manager of the servants—could control the straying butler who liked the maid better than his wife, the cook, could manage the cars, the work about the grounds and give general sage advice. Cousin Marie leaned heavily on Fanning to manage the problems of her some fourteen servants.
>
> At one visit Fanning took me fishing off the Point. A sea was running and we were lost from sight in the troughs. I got seasick, which for some reason didn't bother me, and we caught a number of cod. I was impressed with the dory, which was decked in and a mighty sturdy vessel.

Later I learned that this sturdy dory constituted a means of extracurricular activity on the part of Fanning—bootlegging.

As a freshman at M.I.T. I found myself with nothing to do on a rainy fall weekend. It occurred to me that Blighty existed. So by train I went on a Sunday visit. No warmer welcome could have been possible. The summer was over, but my cousins were there to welcome me. Such was that welcome and many others that to some extent Blighty was my home during my college career. Whenever I had the blues they would console with me, and when cheery they would add to my cheer. In the spring I'd drive (in my Model T given to me by Jack's mother, my Auntie Wye) down with a friend or two, male or female, and the welcome mat was a wonder to behold.

Jack didn't get along with his mother, who had given me my first car. After her death her Buick was in the Blighty garage. So one day he took me to the garage and ordered me to drive my Model T into the sea and drive back to college in the Buick. I turned him down, and I think he liked me for it.

Yet my deep recollection and real closeness with Blighty came in the 30's when, just married, my wife and I paid a visit. This generated into annual visits, usually on the Fourth of July which was tournament and party time. The family was there—Kays and ourselves—and with many visitors on the Point we'd whack the golf ball over the little course. Between holes the butler, followed by the maid, would sally forth to the course with trays of champagne—a wonderful sight to behold, but not a means to improve one's golf. It was gala and at times almost unreal. . . It was a party land during the Depression yet withal there was much in family ties and sympathy and fondness.[6]

The famous Fanning (always Fanning, never Pat) lived in the memory of another Prentiss cousin, Dr. Milton Henry Clifford of Bedford, who visited "Blighty" the summer it was opened and remembered the chauffeur as quite a dashing, undisciplined soul. One of his exploits, related with some skepticism by Dr. Clifford, concerned his mode of transport to "Blighty" with the two Prentiss dogs one winter. "Driving out of New York there was a blizzard, and from Springfield east the roads were closed. So Fanning checked train schedules and somehow drove the auto onto the Boston and Albany tracks and came on through over the railroad ties between trains!"[7]

The Prentiss dogs were Hooch and Booze (according to Dr. Clifford) or Gin and Whiskey (as Henry Williams, the Raymonds' chauffeur, remembered it). No matter. Fanning's dory was moored in Brace Cove, and to finance his voyages to the well-laden schooners lying beyond the twelve-mile limit on Rum Row, his employer would provide him with three $1,000 bills. Henry didn't think Fanning had to make many trips out to Rum Row to raise "Blighty's" spirits because so many of them were landed in the darkness of the night at Brace Beach during those dry years, the bootleggers having found that the Pollard stable near Niles Pond made a handy off-season warehouse, as the owners discovered one day unexpectedly and delightedly.

The coast of Eastern Point and all of Cape Ann with its myriad coves, rivers, inlets, marshes, secret places, wharves and maritime sophistication came alive between sundown and sunup during Prohibition, and all this activity was spiced with bursts of melodrama, Coast Guard chases, gun battles, rammings, burnings, mysterious explosions, scuttlings, highjackings and piracy. Pointers occasionally witnessed a hot pursuit off some landmark of topical renown such as Whiskey Ledge, but in general events beyond the gate lodge were cloaked in a discretion appropriate to the character of an upper-level summer colony, and a fair share of the contraband that reached Eastern Point by land or sea didn't find a ready route to the outside lest its effects merely accelerate the already deplorable relaxation of law and order.

At the James Murray Kay house, 1922, from left: Jim Kay, Winifred Kay Shepard, Beatrice Clifford, and May Murray Kay. (Milton H. Clifford, MD)

There was, of course, the rare exception to seemliness within the Point, though "The Ramparts" was the last place you'd expect to find evidence of anything short of the utmost decorum. Ted Williams recalls "The Kick of a Mule" with something bordering on unseemly gusto in *A Varied Career*:

> One summer in Gloucester around the time I entered Yale, a family named MacKinnon rented the Mother Ann Cottage, a small home next to the lighthouse. Tris and Bud MacKinnon were about my age. It was no time at all before we developed what turned out to be a deep but transitory friendship. . . .
>
> Grandmother Raymond had outlawed alcoholic beverages in The Ramparts in conformance with the law. Jim Nugent, the superintendent of the work force, knew how to make homemade beer. He said he would help us boys make a batch if we could obtain Grandmother's consent. Grandmother, thinking that homemade beer would be much like root beer, readily consented. Nugent obtained the ingredients—malt, hops, yeast, rice, sugar and some other portions that I cannot recall. Nugent insisted on an extra large portion of rice. "That will give it the kick of a mule," he said.

*John Wing
Prentiss, 1920.
(Edward R.
Godfrey)*

We bottled the brew into pint size bottles after it had fermented and stocked them on a shelf in the basement to age. A week or so later we were all awakened by the sound of bangs below. Grandmother called the police, thinking that members of the Coast Guard were shooting at bootleggers, an event which had occurred previously at the home of one of our neighbors.

We cleaned up the mess and examined the remaining bottles which had not yet exploded. What shall we do with these, we wondered. They seemed to have a layer of silt in the bottom of each. The evening was still young. We decided to test them. We consumed enough to become very venturesome. What to do? "Let's go down to the Rockaway Inn and serenade Jack Mehlman." Jack was a retired policeman who had taught us all how to sail and how to race.

So we journeyed to the Rockaway where we sang such ballads as "Show Me the Way to Go Home" and "Blow Ye Winds Hi Ho." Soon Jack stuck his head out the window and shouted that one of the tenants had called the police.

We hit the road, and when we saw the blinking lights of the police car we dove for the bushes. All would have ended peaceably had I not sneezed. It was the height of the hay fever season.

The cops put me in the slammer. The MacKinnons escaped. Why they locked me up for the night I'll never know. I was willing to recant but had no bail. The next morning the *Gloucester Times* was ablaze with a front page article about "son of prominent Eastern Point family jailed for disturbing the peace."

Mother was so upset that she hid the newspaper and messed up my bed so that the maids would think I'd spent the night at home.

Evidence of bootlegging was more often than not as circumspect as it was circumstantial. Like the night of June 9, 1926. The Coast Guard patrol boat chased a suspicious launch off the Back Shore that jettisoned its cargo and escaped. Or so it was supposed, for some claimed it struck a rock off Brace's and sank.

Anyway, incoming fishermen reported the waters outside the Cove littered with floating cases of booze, and a lobsterman told the police that while he was hauling at daybreak he watched case after case being taken out of the Humane Society boathouse and loaded into a truck.

Then a young fellow who had been delivering fresh fish to summer homes on the Point revealed that as he innocently approached the boathouse that afternoon two men emerged, stuck a gun in his belly and suggested he move on, which he did without delay. When the marshal and the Prohibition agent raided the old boat shed, they found 25 gallons of alcohol in cases and fresh signs of recent doings, but no culprits.

Early in the morning of October 7, 1922—the day of Caroline Sinkler's scheduled departure from "Wrong Roof" for Philadelphia for the winter with her domestic staff—her chauffeur and one of her maids were found prostrate on her kitchen floor by her housekeeper, who after throwing water on their faces and otherwise trying to revive them for forty-five minutes called the houseman, who assisted her for some further time, when they at last notified their mistress, who called the doctor, who arrived and pronounced them dead.

Headlines in the *Gloucester Daily Times*. The district attorney filed a John Doe complaint of murder, and the Lavender Lady appeared in court to put up $300 in bail for the release of her three staff on her recognizance as material witnesses. It developed that the deceased and a couple of other servants had gone into Gloucester that evening to do errands and take in a picture show, and on the way home the chauffeur had stopped the car, slipped down an alleyway for fifteen minutes and returned with a package, obviously of hooch.

Back in the kitchen a couple of the women complained of colds, and the chauffeur spiked their hot lemonade, hot water and sugar, and ginger ale. The evening wore on, and all retired but the soon-to-be-departed.

Though in shock and under the care of her doctor, Miss Sinkler met with police and reporters and made arrangements with the undertaker. A week passed, and the medical examiner announced, after autopsies, that the two had died accidentally of carbon monoxide poisoning from a gas heater.[8]

Old Jack O'Donnell was John Greenough's coachman and the dean and father confessor of the Irish help on the Point who came to him with their troubles. He lived above the Greenough stable that was toward the lighthouse and tended a beautiful Irish garden, and he set wire noose snares, as they did in the old country, for pheasant and rabbit.

One black night Jack thought he heard something around the stone pier at the end of Wharf Beach. He pulled on his breeches and his boots, as Henry Williams told it, and crossed the road to investigate.

Sure enough, a launch was alongside, making a transfer.

"Hi thire, you fillas, wat th' hell's goin' on thire?"

John was a big man with a high piping voice you could hear to East Gloucester Square against the wind.

One of the figures separated from the rest and came running up to him and tucked a pistol in his ribs.

"Shaddup, shaddup," he hissed, "and if yer know what's good fer yer, old man, get t'hell outa here an' go back to beddy-by."

"Ah, put that ting away, me lad. This is pry-vit propity here, dawn't ye know that? Say, wat if I go an' put in a jingle to th' cops now?"

And so on, old John kept at it in that voice of his, the guy shushing and trying to put the quietus on him.

They wised up after a while and stopped Jack's talk with a bottle, and he rolled back to the stable for the rest of his night's sleep, content that he had done his best to sound the alarm.

(That Greenough stable. The field beyond it—now part of the Audubon Sanctuary—served as a sand lot for some time where, as Henry Williams recalled, "quite a few men working around the Point and some of the faithful from Rocky Neck would get together for baseball. Jimmy Walen did not play but would jump around and holler.")

As for Fanning, after Colonel Prentiss's death in 1938 the hand of easy restraint was gone, and problems and the bottle took its place. Increasingly he was a trial for Marie, and when at long last she had acquired her heart's desire, a Rolls Royce—and Fanning (just Fanning) drove it one night into Niles Pond—she could bear him no longer and their ways parted.

Try as he might, Jack Prentiss never really succeeded in overcoming the resentment that his perhaps ill-considered barricade across the Brace Cove road touched off in 1918. It was a public relations disaster, and for years local politicians made hay of it and its consequences. His success in closing off the Back Shore was regarded widely in Gloucester as an arbitrary denial by the rich and powerful out-of-towners who had taken over Eastern Point of an age-old right of local people to visit the coast—private property, private roads and what the courts had to say about it notwithstanding. And in spite of assurances that Gloucester residents were welcome to use the roads, the continued presence of "the cop at the gate" and his scrutiny were considered by many an affront.

It was even bruited about that Colonel Prentiss had installed an outlet from Niles Pond to Brace Cove and was bent on draining it by imperceptibly slow degrees until its area had shrunk from 36 acres to below 20, thus removing it from the category of "great ponds" to which, under Massachusetts law, citizens have certain rights of access. This would have been quite a trick.

He strove to improve his image. He cultivated city officials and was made finance chairman of the city's three hundredth anniversary celebration in 1923, to which he gave $5,000. And the Prentisses entertained the anniversary committees at "Blighty" throughout the summers of 1922 and 1923.

Yet the very next winter the administration of Mayor William J. MacInnis proposed to build a public highway around Brace Cove, through the Prentiss and Leonard estates and on to the light. The Prentisses agreed in writing to leave their roads open to the public, subject to their regulation, and the matter was dropped. Two years later, in another effort to soothe ruffled feelings in town, Prentiss offered the city a piece of the Point—seventeen acres for a park on the site of the former golf course—but the city council turned him down, under pressure from his objecting neighbors, as reported July 29 in the *North Shore Breeze:*

> The summer folk at Eastern Point have a delightful time among themselves, like one large family, with their gay little times here and there, motoring, walking and yachting. They take a decided interest in the welfare of Gloucester as a community despite the fact that they are here for but a portion of the year. They are anxious to help the city in a municipal way, but with the advantages of Stage Fort Park which meets the city's need of a public park, it seemed inadvisable to make any more public than now the lovely natural section at Eastern Point. Needless to state, the Prentiss offer is widely appreciated by both factions.

Marie Kay Prentiss at Blighty, 1922. (Milton H. Clifford, MD)

But Jack Prentiss would not be put off. The next year he built a connection through from the end of Atlantic Road to the dead end of Farrington Avenue, permitting public use of it—the purpose being to divert shore-viewing traffic from the outer Point.

Nevertheless, in his inaugural address in 1930 Mayor John E. Parker proposed to seize Prentiss's road around Brace Cove and Niles Pond as far as the harbor. Jack and Marie gave $50,000 for a wing at the Addison Gilbert Hospital. Talk of condemnation persisted, and in May 1931 Prentiss published *A Memorandum on Eastern Point,* tracing the history of its privacy and suggesting that to take the roads to which they already had free access would cost the taxpayers of Gloucester about $230,000.

Meanwhile the Associates went ahead with plans to put a third gate lodge at Farrington Avenue and Eastern Point Boulevard by Niles Beach. They held off at the request of Mayor Parker, but in July he brought his old inaugural proposition before the city council.

At the hearing, Eastern Point spokesmen reiterated the position advanced in the Prentiss white paper, namely that they wanted "simply a reasonable protection of their privacy. To get this the residents on the harbor side of the Point station an officer at the inner gate lodge for only three months of the year. His duty is not to exclude Gloucester people—Gloucester people are always welcome—but foreign tourists, picnic parties, petting parties, speeding youngsters in high powered cars are not welcome."[9]

Just as an uneasy truce was being consummated with the city, Prentiss and the Associates made his road around the pond and the cove one way going east and stationed a constable at its intersection with his extension of Atlantic Road to Farrington Avenue. City Hall retaliated by getting Representative Harold Webber to file a bill with the legislature authorizing all of Niles Beach and Eastern Point Boulevard all the way to the lighthouse to be taken by eminent domain. This scheme was rejected by the General Court that winter.

"Blighty" was literally the Prentisses' "home place" on Eastern Point. Here, little involved in the social do beyond their own borders, they sublimated their summers and created their own atmosphere of the youth and sport and white flannels and elegant, insouciant pleasure of the Tinseled Twenties. And if their aura was swept by habit and its own momentum into the Threatening Thirties, when all about them the glitter had faded and gone, the echo only sharpened the bittersweetness of their American Dreamlike lives.

As Rawson Godfrey saw them:

> Cousin John could be sociable or moodily disagreeable. He liked his liquor. He was abrupt at times and we were always a little stiff in conversation. Cousin Marie, on the other hand, was so easy to talk to and seemed to have exceptional understanding of the other person. Looking back, I suspect both attitudes were in part due to a lack of children. In a way they were lonely people with no real objectives. Thus, I remember after one visit with my parents my mother coming away with some explosive remarks about all that Marie could talk about were the problems of the servants—she seemed obsessed with their management.
>
> Withal, I fear that Jack and Marie Prentiss did not have a particularly happy and fruitful life—though goodness knows they were wonderful to me.[10]

"It was a Castle in the Air," said Marie's sister Winifred, "that had a foundation put under it."

Over on the harbor side, before you got to all that private Niles country "down the Point," the namesake son of the namesake banker-son of old farmer Ike Patch grabbed every chance to slip away from the modest family mansion on the crest of the namesake hill overlooking the beautiful port. His father was a bank president and former mayor, and they had a chauffeur, a Pierce Arrow and three servants. Young Ike wrote about it in *Closing the Circle* when he, too, was Old Ike seventy years later.

> When I entered first grade, my parents hired a nurse to accompany me on the twenty-minute walk to Point Grammar School, causing me to be ridiculed by my classmates. When I begged my mother to let me go it alone, her idea of a compromise was to have the chauffeur drive me. In the very first act of defiance that I can

remember, I ran out the door and all the way to school. The subject never came up again at home, but it was too late to change how I was perceived by my peers. I was labeled "the rich kid," a barrier that caused me pain for some time to come. . . .

I must have clambered over most every rock on the edge of the harbor. My summer days were spent playing in tide pools, collecting starfish, and smashing periwinkles for bait to catch crabs and tasty cunners. One day in our early youth [Ike was born in 1912], Hasty Gamage and I discovered a little island—25 by 75 feet—just off the Hawthorne Inn. Known as "Bedbug Island," it was a thriving home for bugs and insects in the summer. We considered it our territory, and it was a big day when we rowed our punt out to have a picnic, fish and swim on Bedbug Island. We never told anyone else about our special place.

One of the happiest memories of my youth, together with my best friend, Bill (DuDu) Little (at that time I was called Duzzie), was the building of a hundred-foot pier out into Gloucester Harbor from the edge of the Patch property. I was sixteen years old; Bill was fifteen. Peter and Hasty Gamage, close neighborhood friends, managed to scare up a few pieces of lumber from whence I know not. When the tide was out, we dug post holes in the mucky and stony bottom. We then built cribs to hold the heavy rocks which anchored the pier. One-by-four boards were nailed in crosscross fashion to strengthen the cribs. We built a gangway attached to a small dock made buoyant by four empty, watertight steel drums. We used the dock to tie our skiff which ferried us to our Sonder racing sloop, the *Shamrock*. To our dismay, winters later the harbor ice froze around the posts and carried our pier away.

My young friends and I raced small sailboats made of broken shingles with twigs for masts and paper for sails. We sucked the saltwater from seaweed bulbs, rolled barrel hoops along Niles Beach, basked in the rain of electric storms, and thrilled to the thunder and the lightning flashes that lit up the Magnolia shore. We ran out into the blast of autumn hurricanes, and the northeast storms of winter sent us trudging through snowdrifts for a glimpse of the sea's fury towards the land. I was a restless child, gone from the house from morning til night, causing my mother to wonder what I disliked about home. But it was just that I preferred the exciting world of East Gloucester over listening to adult conversations.

"Tower of Four Winds," the home of Lucy Taggart, with uncollected rubble from the foundation hole. (Mrs. Thomas Mumford)

~35~

COMINGS AND GOINGS

As IF THEY HAD BEEN SENT TO
pierce with beams of piety, propriety and sobriety the spirituous fogs raised
over land and sea by the Eighteenth Amendment, three spiritual lighthouses
were raised on Eastern Point during the Naughty Twenties.

Perhaps Philip Mercer Rhinelander, Seventh Bishop of the Episcopal
Diocese of Pennsylvania, first knew the Point through the Enchantress of
Philadelphia, since he and his family occupied Caroline Sinkler's cottage
during the summer of 1921.

That winter he bought the Barwick house on the outside tip of Quarry
Point from John H. Procter, and the adjoining Calef cottage, "The
Boulders," which had only just been vacated by the removal of the Leonards
across the Point to "Druimteac."

Born in 1869, the bishop was the youngest of the nine children of
Frederic and Frances Rhinelander. His father shared in the family fortune,
divided his seasons between New York and Newport and was of a philan-
thropic and religious bent. After St. Paul's School, Philip was graduated
from Harvard in 1891 and took his degree in theology at Oxford in 1896.
Thereafter he ascended rapidly in the hierarchy. He taught at the Berkeley
Divinity School in Connecticut and for four years at the Episcopal
Theological School in Cambridge. In 1911 he was elected bishop coadjutor
of Pennsylvania, and bishop a few months later.

Bishop Rhinelander resigned in 1923 and was appointed first warden of
the College of Preachers in the cathedral close in Washington, where he
remained until his retirement in 1937.

When he was thirty-five Philip married Helen ("Daisy") Hamilton, a
descendent of Alexander Hamilton. As his close friend and biographer,
Professor Henry Bradford Washburn, put it:

> The spirit of noblesse oblige was there to reinforce Philip's con-
> ception of social and religious responsibility. . . . Philip was proud
> of his wife. His attitude toward her was invariably chivalrous.

Neither husband nor wife trespassed on the freedom of the other. Although of dissimilar disposition and temperament she understood her husband well. She was thoroughly alive, not only to his normal frame of mind, but also to his moods and occasional eccentricities, and with her exquisite sense of humor she could, at the right time, and invariably without offence, bring him back to normalcy.[1]

The bishop was much involved in the lives of his sons, Frederic, Philip and Laurens, who entered medicine, education and the law. Though limited physically by a cardiac condition, he was devoted to professional baseball and a close observer of his boys' sailing progress from his vantage on the veranda of "Dog Bar."

As a dinner table wit and storyteller, he was full of fun and riddles. He loved light music and was a lively pianist, and he added rather a flair to his religious services in the home, pumping away at the little parlor organ. Though his well-worn pipes were ever at his elbow, the bishop used beer and wine temperately "though needless to say," as one of his sons wrote, "during the days of Prohibition no alcoholic drinks of any kind were seen in our house."[2]

Bishop Rhinelander was astute in financial matters, and he inherited a sizeable estate late in life from his brother-in-law. It troubled him; "his conscience was not at rest; his sense of stewardship intensified; his realization of the economic differences in modern society became more vivid."[3]

He was an orderly man; everything had its place and must make its own inner sense with him. One afternoon the constable at the second gate lodge telephoned to inform him that a man was there wanting to get by to see him: "But Bishop, I don't think you want to see him."

"Well," responded the bishop with his usual calm, "if you don't think so, constable, then I'm sure I don't."[4]

Harry Sleeper decorated their great, rambling place for them before they moved in, but the garden was Bishop Rhinelander's own, his joy, and as well arranged and kept as his life.

It was a fairly spacious plot on a well-walled terrace facing the harbor. His fondness for it was the deeper because it was his especial care and responsibility. Within it he found rest—complete physical and mental relaxation. It was a well-ordered garden with a wide variety of shrubs and flowers with paths picturesquely winding among them. The Bishop was somewhat of a horticulturalist. He knew his garden intimately. He was familiar with genus and species; he knew the Latin as well as the English names. . . . Furthermore, he was not willing to leave to his gardener the exclusive cultivation of the garden. As long as his strength lasted he would work in it with spade, rake, and trowel. . . . Occasionally he had to be called into the house for fear that his love of his garden would carry him beyond his strength. . . . And when he was confined to the house, there were his flowers beautifully arranged by loving hands.[5]

Their daughter-in-law Constance, who married Frederic, wrote a charming reminiscence of her husband's family.

Perhaps it is the sea and the tides and the sunsets. There is a sense of the continuity of life there. It is not a matter of historic interest or a great monument—but of life—renewed in tranquillity.

I first went there as the guest of the eldest son, to a purple Episcopal "cottage." It was a hot summer afternoon, and all the blinds had been drawn. I was politely invited to "rest until tea time." I raised the blind in my room, slightly, half expecting to find a bathing machine and an old white horse (such as I remembered from my great-aunt's house), waiting patiently on the sand.

I was a brash intruder into that twilight household.

"And are you going to the tennis courts in that?"

"This is the trophy I won in the tournament at New Port—and this is a photograph."

And there it was—the beautiful grass court at the Casino, underhand Service, and an "appropriate costume"—long sleeves and skirts trailing on the ground. Champion form.

And the Bishop was concerned for the well-being of a young female guest in his house. On a rainy day I offered to wax the bindings of a collection of early volumes he had inherited. He hesitated and only when I promised not to look inside Ovid, etc., was I allowed to get on with it.

Conversation at dinner one night turned to God Fathers—a reasonably safe subject I had assumed. But there was a dreadful silence when I asked about one person. I assumed he had committed an especially gory murder and could hardly wait to walk in the garden and get the details.

"He went over to Rome," I was told.

Later, as a daughter-in-law, I was taken on the slow afternoon drives in an almost closed car, when visiting cards were genteelly distributed—never beyond a certain railway bridge in a northerly direction and almost never in Bass Rocks. And the Bishop sat in front with the sympathetic chauffeur, the glass divider screwed up all the way, and the baseball game going full blast.

The gentle Bishop liked to work in his garden and always wore a blue shirt. It was the only place he allowed himself to discard the collar of his profession. I enjoyed being there with him and to pick and prune and pull out an occasional weed, and put it in a pile in the middle of a path. It was then the gardener's job to remove them.

The wonderful little brown children played on the beach while their devoted nurses watched every move. They made endless sand castles and tunnels and collections of shells and bits of beautiful

Bishop and Mrs.
Rhinelander with
their grandsons
John, Frederic
and David.
(Constance
Templeton
Rhinelander)

blue Magnesia bottles for mermaids' necklaces. And they took off
in tippy boats and then something larger—to be taken on the tow
to Marblehead. They would return, their long legs covered with
scratches and goose-pimples, struggling with wet sails.

The weekly "treasure hunt" designed by some fiend at the
yacht club, which sent children flying in all directions to borrow
appropriate booty—a gold tooth pick or false eye-lashes (when
only an actress could own them).

The Bishop came to the Point for a respite from his Episcopal
duties but "Dough Sunday" arrived once in every August, when
funds for the local church had to be solicited. And he was prevailed
upon to call on possible donors. A lady whose large fortune had
been derived from biscuits [Mrs. Jacob Loose] proved very generous, and the church flourished. But when the Depression hit, she
explained she could not continue.

"I understand," he said sympathetically, "and anything you
can manage will be gratefully received."

And they arrived steadily for the next two years—an endless
supply of biscuits.

Constance Rhinelander continues:

Beautiful summer days in bright sun, and every year, some bitterly cold ones when the sun seemed to have got lost in heavy fog.
But always a promise of more sun to come—to the Point. Storms
and hurricanes and death and human misunderstandings took their
toll—but the sea and the tides remained constant.

After watching the Eisenhower inauguration on television, Mrs. Rhinelander announced she needed a "Mrs. Eisenhower hat." It was a tiny collection of veils and velvet, and word had got around that such confections were only to be found in Filene's Basement. I had spent hours with her at a milliner's in Robbers' Row, and the idea of The Basement seemed preposterous. But she insisted—and we went. I explained it would be hot and crowded and odoriferous. We stood at the top of the staircase, the Episcopal relict and I—she in a purple dress and cape and an enormous purple hat.

And the crowd parted as the Red Sea had done. We were ushered to the hat bar and found the "Mamies." She bought four— one for herself and one for each daughter-in-law, from a charming little sales girl who said "Yes, Madam" and "No, Madam." And we were escorted out by a polite young man who thanked her for having come. And she turned to me, baffled, and asked why I had lied?

And now the purple memories remain. The houses have changed hands. But the sun and the wind and the tides fascinate the little brown children on the beach while bemused parents and grandparents watch them.

"You're out too far, little Freddy."

"But I am not afraid."

"No. You were never afraid."

Constance Rhinelander with sons Freddie, Johnny, and David, "Dog Bar," about 1940. (David Rhinelander)

And "little Johnny, you're turning a deep Yale blue. Please stay out of the water."

"But I'm emptying the ocean, and keeping score."

"Poor Mary Frederica, you have cut your hand on the glass!"

"It's nothing. I need it for a mermaid."

"Helen Maria Hamilton—what a beautiful bikini!"

And what an appropriate costume.[6]

The second Episcopal luminary of this era was the Reverend George C. F. Bratenahl, Dean of the National Cathedral in Washington. He and Mrs. Bratenahl in September 1923 bought from the Associates the bluff at the eastern head of Brace Cove where the dark and surf-smashed rocks of Bemo make out.

By the 1924 season their brown-stained, rambling reproduction of a seventeenth-century country home was ready for them. Again, Henry Sleeper was in charge of the interior design. Much of the material had been gathered from early American houses—some of the doorways from Ipswich, Salem and Newburyport. The pine-paneled kitchen was designed around a deep old fireplace, and George Sibley of Rocky Neck, a master boat carpenter, was called in to give the ceiling beams a hand-hewn look with his adz.

> There was a small chapel, and an herb-drying room; Mrs. Bratenahl was an herbalist and raised funds to plant shrubbery around the Washington Cathedral by raising herbs at the Point and selling them.[7]

(While Sleeper was supervising the Bratenahl interiors in 1923 he was host to Henry Francis du Pont, who had become fascinated, in 1910 and on subsequent visits, with what he had created with "Beauport." The super-rich heir to the chemical fortune and collector commissioned Sleeper to decorate "Chestertown," his new summer home in Southampton, Long Island.)

The third episode in this theological trilogy involves St. Anthony's-by-the-Sea, a fieldstone Roman Catholic chapel at the east corner of Farrington and St. Louis Avenues consecrated by Cardinal William O'Connell on August 23, 1925.

The 500-seat church and its land were donated to the Archdiocese of Boston by Mrs. Margaret Brady Farrell of Albany in memory of her father, Anthony Brady; she was the widow of James C. Farrell, who bought the estate of J. Sloat Fassett on Grapevine Cove, a large part of the old Patch farm, for a reported $225,000 in 1916. The Farrell place adjoined that of Jacob L. Loose of Kansas City, senior member of the Loose Wiles Biscuit Company, which had been built on the Back Shore in 1916 on land also bought from Isaac Patch.

St. Anthony's was designed by Edward T. P. Graham of Boston after "English Parish Gothic." It nestled on a knoll of the Hill of Rocks, with a broad view of the ocean and harbor from an observation deck on its tower. Nearby, Mrs. Farrell erected a summer convent for the Sisters of Mercy who conduct St. Ann's School in Gloucester. The chapel was designated by the cardinal as a summer mission for the priests of St. Peter's parish in East Gloucester.

St. Anthony's was put directly across St. Louis Avenue from the site selected by Thomas Niles for a $20,000 nondenominational house of worship; after a probate battle his legacy landed in the coffers of the newly founded Gloucester Fishermen's Institute in 1896.

Eighteen months after St. Anthony's-by-the-Sea was dedicated a sign calling the attention of the public (and the abutters) to "Capt. Joe's Clambake" sprouted in the spring of 1927 from the lot east of the church on Farrington Avenue. The parcel was owned by Arthur and Herbert Smith. Joseph B. Ruth, a retired fisherman, had obtained from the city council a victualler's license for a peanut, popcorn, ice cream and soda pop stand in this oasis surrounded by some $500,000 worth of religious and residential real estate.

After the expected explosive reaction, the council (which was having a little fun with the Point) revoked Captain Joe's license. But what was put down here erupted there in a form the more dire—a dance hall.

More uproar, and in the end "Spite Hall" was torn down. Meanwhile, however, Homer Marchant, the fire chief and building inspector, approved the application of the Smiths to erect forty-six one-room camps on their property, the nearest to be twenty feet from the chapel.

At another public hearing, lawyers for the neighbors called this chain of harassments a studied campaign to extort from them an exorbitant price for the land. "A blackmail contrivance" to sell lots, the *North Shore Breeeze* called it. "Cheap, small-visioned, low-down politics." Construction on the camps started and then stopped when the diocese and co-complainants took this thorn in their side to court. The honky-tonk affair went through several more choruses and a couple of legal encores before the curtain finally rang down.

Years back, with little more than oxen, horses, carrying timbers, rollers, block and tackle, human brawn and ingenuity they moved buildings around Gloucester frequently and thought nothing about it. Jim Nugent claimed that when Henry Parsons, the building mover and the most colorful mayor in the city's history, was engaged to levitate the Parker Mann house from back of Niles Beach to a lot on Grapevine Road, he jacked it up and eased it over a rather high hedge onto the road without breaking a twig.

Then there was the Civil War barrack that was split three ways, moved from the fort and reconstituted as three small frame houses on Locust Lane above the Gate Lodge. One wintry night Douglas Parker of East Gloucester was visiting his grandmother in one of them when he was petrified by the sudden apparition at her window of three dark and bearded faces that turned out to belong to sailors from an Italian salt barque just come to anchor on the Pancake Ground; they had rowed into Niles Beach, seen the light and walked up to inquire in their broken English the way into town.

As we have seen, when it came to housemoving the Point was in the import as well as the export trade. First there was the harbor ride of the young Raymonds' "house full of bugs." Then in 1924 a very small and aged "salt box" was recreated by a wholly different technique on a little plot almost on the site of the big Niles barn.

This ancient import was built around 1720 by Samuel Strowbridge who, with son and grandson, was a minuteman of the town of Canton during the Revolution. At the time of moving it was known as the "Tucker House," after a branch of his descendants, and it stood some three hundred yards toward Boston from the Ponkapoag general store in Canton.

Samuel Temple of the Tucker strain bought a plot on the Point in the brush across the road from the Hall chateau, with a right of way, and moved the house in 1924.

> The entire work was done under my supervision. I had two carpenters go from Gloucester every day to take the house down and mark the timbers, to make reassembling easier. Their names were Stevens (brothers). Even the chimney bricks were saved; there were seven large truck-loads of material which made it expensive—the round trip being about 68 miles. Total cost to me, exclusive of my own work, was $7,200. At the time of original purchase I was offered $4,000 for the two rooms of paneling alone.[8]

The Halls regarded this vintage old newcomer as an affront and put up a high masonry spite wall along the right of way and around the two sides of their thicket that Temple's land abutted.

For the third on-Point housemoving, Priscilla Pollard and her husband of two years, Joseph Woods, reverted to the water route taken by her older sister Pauline and her brother-in-law Jack Raymond when they transported the Story house to Chicken Lane in 1917. Mr. and Mrs. Woods got hold of the antique Coffin house behind the North Shore Arts Association at East Gloucester Square in 1927, rolled it down to the town wharf and onto a barge, out the harbor to Wharf Beach, across the road and into the Pollard field. Priscilla died less than two years later, within a week after the birth of her son. She was only twenty-five.[9]

Keeper George E. Bailey died on February 23, 1926, at sixty-seven, after thirty-four years at the Eastern Point Light. He had succeeded his father, George G., in 1892, and the elder Bailey had tended the light since 1882; so father and son between them kept the vigil for forty-three years.

There was no count of the vessels Bailey the younger had warned off or of the men and women he had been instrumental in rescuing or that his wife had put up and fed and loaned a change of dry clothing for the night at their storm-beaten cottage. He had been commended by the lighthouse service for risking his life to keep the lamp at the end of the breakwater going during storms that sent the swells exploding across the top of it. (One regular and occasionally fanciful contributor to the *North Shore Breeze* claimed Keeper Bailey would crawl on his hands and knees over the icy breakwater on stormy nights to light the beacon.) He had clanged the fog bell and shouted good luck through his megaphone at Howard Blackburn each time the lone voyager rounded out by the lighthouse on one of his singlehanded Atlantic crossings. The warm hospitality of two generations of Baileys had made the light a friendly one indeed.

Keeper Bailey had been in ill health for several years, and in 1921 Gilbert M. Hay was transferred from Chatham Light, where he was assistant keeper, to carry the heft of the job. Hay was a Shetland Islander, first mate on Atlantic freighters before he swallowed the anchor at Chatham in 1912, and he succeeded George Bailey as keeper in 1926.

The guns were still warm from World War I when Arthur D. Story, the most productive of all the Essex shipbuilders, thought he would get in on the resumption of unfettered coastal trade. On April 30, 1919, he launched one of the biggest he ever built, the *Lincoln,* a three-masted tern schooner of 405 tons.

Hailing from Gloucester, the *Lincoln* was a successful carrier of coal and lumber mostly, between the Maritimes and Boston or New York until the night of September 10, 1928, when she was struck down by the Boston collier *Sewall's Point* in the fog off Chatham. The collision broke her back, fractured her starboard side from rail to bilge and dislocated her mainmast five feet out of line.

The hull of the wrecked schooner Lincoln *serves the Leonard family as a playhouse at "Druimteac." (Dana Story)*

Archimedes to the rescue. The 388,000 feet of lumber the *Lincoln* was carrying from Selmah, Nova Scotia, to New York kept her afloat, and the Coast Guard patrol boat *Active* towed her across the Bay to Gloucester. She was irreparably damaged. The lumber was discharged, and the wreck was stripped. In April 1929 Story transplanted her rigging to her sister, the three-masted *Adams,* which the loss of the *Lincoln* had stirred him into launching after eight years on the ways at Essex, incomplete and buyerless. (The postwar building boom had collapsed, and he had built her on speculation.) Rarely does a vessel become a landmark, but the *Adams* did, her famous bowsprit overhanging the Essex causeway.

However, all was not lost with the *Lincoln.* Story was on the point of scuttling her when Arthur Leonard, for whom he had built a yacht or two, heard about it. The rest of the tale comes from Lila Leonard Swift.

> Father thought it would make a good playhouse for the grand-children. So instead of towing the stern out to sea and sinking it, it was towed to a little gravelly beach that used to be in front of the playhouse. The land went out flat, and then there was a drop of two feet or more to this little beach. Shortly after she was beached there was a storm; she was taken out and landed in front of the terrace steps, the first of many journeys. She was propelled somehow to the rocks almost in front of the dining room, and there is still a cement block that was put under her there. She was moved several times from this foundation—up against the terrace, hauled back and anchored again, and finally she moved down in front of the studio. By that time all the grandchildren were big. Nothing was done about her for several years. Then during the last war Father amused himself one summer directing two men who crowbarred her apart and sawed her up and we had oak firewood for a long time.[10]

It may have been the continental air of the house, or the look of the harbor, or the Adriatic blue of the ocean that reminded her of the dear gone days in Venice. Whatever it was that attracted her, the daughter-in-law of the English poets Elizabeth Barrett and Robert Browning moved to Eastern Point for the first of several summers in August 1926.

Fannie Coddington Browning of Washington, widow of Robert Wiedemann Barrett Browning—"Pen"—the sole offspring of the immortal lovers, bought the Italianate cottage built by Miss Edith Weld on Edgemoor Road and named it "Villino Browning." It was directly across the road from the house where Tom Eliot daydreamt away his boyhood vacations.

The Coddingtons were wealthy New Yorkers, and Fannie spent much time in England as a girl. It was in London in 1866, when she was twelve, that she first caught a glimpse of the famous Robert Browning; Elizabeth Barrett had been dead five years. Fannie's father, a widower, died in 1886, leaving her a fortune. She was already acquainted with the Brownings from her Kensington days then, and within a few months she and Pen were engaged. Pen was an indifferently successful artist, at thirty-eight still financially dependent on his father, burdened by the fame of his forebears, weighed down by the poet's aspirations for him.

The old bard was understandably relieved at the prospect of this liaison, writing Pen of his high approval of Fannie, who "has spoken to me with the greatest frankness and generosity of the means she will have of contributing to your support."[11] For the son the marriage meant independence and freedom from his father for the first time in his life; but some hint that the match was not made altogether in heaven is conveyed by the bride's evident pique that Pen should assign her to break the news to the poet that he had decided they would get out from under and live in Venice.

Still, there was much visiting between London and Venice in the two years before the poet's death. Once deprived of the cementing presence of Browning, the two separated and Fannie, according to one biographer, resolved to take the vows as an Anglican nun. Apparently she didn't follow through; Pen died shortly before the First World War (had there been a reconciliation?), and Fannie returned to America.

Fannie Browning was about seventy-two when she came to Eastern Point. She had been urged by friends and Browning clubs for years to write a reminiscence of her father-in-law, and her eventual decision to do this appears to have led her to Gloucester, one supposes for seclusion and atmosphere. She also had some connection with Wellesley College, to which she gave a collection of Browning memorabilia.

Some Memories of Robert Browning was a slim affair published in Boston in 1928. The authoress signed her Introduction at "Villino Browning," June 1928, but ventured no word of her life in Gloucester, or how she came to be there.

The little volume is not so sentimental as one might suppose (she helped care for Browning in his last illness and assisted the nurse to lay him into his coffin at Venice, where he died). One cannot help suspecting that Fannie Coddington was at least as much in love with the Barrett and the Browning as with the son all along.

Fannie Barrett Browning sold "Villino Browning" to Dr. Robert P. Cummins of Germantown, Pennsylvania, in November 1930 and departed Eastern Point as quietly as she had arrived.

When Mrs. J. Murray Kay died in the spring of 1928, her cottage on Quarry Point was bought by Myra Tutt of New York, a friend of Caroline Sinkler who had summered at Bass Rocks as early as 1920 and leased Carrie's "Wrong Roof" for several seasons, including the previous one. While redoing the house that summer Miss Tutt rented "Villa Latomia." Her sister had married lawyer George Fraser of Morristown, New Jersey, and Mrs. Fraser's daughter, Mrs. Sarah Fraser Robbins, inherited the house on her aunt's death.

In 1928 Mrs. Edwin Bradley Currier of New York, who with her late husband had vacationed at Bass Rocks since 1903, bought the Russell-Church cottage on Fort Hill Avenue. Mrs. Currier replaced the gas lights with electric and cleared the brush and planted a striking garden behind the house. Their water was supplied from a wooden gravity tank in the attic pumped up from a well behind this garden; after city water was piped in, the tank had to be taken apart to get rid of it. Mrs. Currier moved the old outhouse from down back to Wharf Beach, where it became a bathhouse, with running water, fireplace and awning, until it was carried away one year by a storm.

Commodore John Greenough, the grand old man of Eastern Point and its yacht club, rather summed it all up in a piece he wrote for a profile of himself in the *North Shore Breeze* in August 1928 as everything in America was going great guns. His brother David, with whom he had founded the summer colony, had died in 1924, and the heirs in March had completed the sale of "Black Bess" next door to Stephen Sleeper, who had been renting since 1915.

Probably many frequenters of the North Shore have a very vague idea of what and where is Eastern Point, for in order to reach it, one has to pass more than three miles through the city of Gloucester, along the harbor of which the Point forms the eastern boundary. The little colony of some twenty-five to thirty cottages has come to feel that nature has endowed the Point with some exceptional charms for summer habitation. In the first place it faces the broad waters of Massachusetts Bay to the southwest and thus receives the prevailing southern breezes cooled by contact with the sea. The western sunsets as the golden orb descends behind the wooded hills illumine sky and sea with glorious colors. Two remarkable bodies of fresh water are located in pond and quarry but without visible source of supply, thus indicating a subterranean conduit from the interior of Essex County. The geologist would find this phenomenon worthy of investigation.

The beauty of the wild flowers and shrubbery which cover the Point is a continuous joy and the roads traverse the natural tangle sufficiently to afford access to all dwellings. These roads are all owned and maintained by their residents and their legal right has been adjudged by the highest court, but a liberal policy has been adopted for the admission of all foot travellers and of motor vehicles belonging to any known townspeople or to acquaintances of resident cottagers. A guardian is maintained at the lodge entrance to exclude joy riders and strangers whose inroads would menace the safety of women and children in the narrow highway. The multitude of such trespassers is shown by the fact that 9,200 were turned back during the three months of last summer.

The personnel of Eastern Point residents includes prominent families from ten large cities, Washington, Baltimore, Philadelphia, New York, Boston, Cleveland, Indianapolis, Chicago, Kansas City and St. Louis, thus creating quite a cosmopolitan social atmosphere and agreeable variety. All of them share in appreciation of the simple and wholesome life during the summer which restores them to their serious occupations with renewed health and spirits.

In the early summer of 1919 Cecilia Beaux invited her friend and student, the talented Indianapolis painter Lucy Martha Taggart, to accompany her and Harry Sleeper, who was in Paris tending to postwar Field Service matters, on a drive through France to Belgium, where Beaux had been commissioned to paint Cardinal Mercier.[12]

Lucy had moved to New York in 1899 when she was nineteen to study with the Indiana artist William Merritt Chase, and with her talent for portraiture it was practically inevitable that she should seek out Cecilia, presumably in Philadelphia. She also painted landscapes and still lifes, with occasional sculptures, notably busts. No telling when she was introduced to Dabsville, except that in 1922 she rented "Green Alley" from Beaux. She did so again in 1924, when she purchased the easterly half of the harbor tract once occupied by the Colonial Arms.

Lucy Taggart. (Mrs. Thomas Mumford)

Dabsville must have thought Lucy Taggart as intriguing as she evidently found the colony within the art colony. She was the second of the six children of Thomas Taggart, son of Irish immigrants who worked and politicked his way up from dining hall clerk to hotelier (notably the international spa French Lick Springs in southern Indiana), Democratic boss of the state, thrice mayor of Indianapolis, chairman of the Democratic National Committee and U.S. Senator.

As adept politically as artistically, Lucy—who never married—was the pride of her large clan and maintained studios in the Taggart home in Indianapolis and, by a curious Celtic coincidence, in the family summer home, "Amyvale," built in 1916 in Hyannisport down on Cape Cod, next to which in 1928 Joseph P. Kennedy bought the core property of another notable political compound.

Lucy Taggart, Woman Reading a Book. (Private collection)

So in 1924, with her father's financial support, Miss Taggart set out to build a house all her own. She engaged the noted architect Ralph Adams Cram to design for her a turreted and steep-roofed stone mansion after the French farmhouse style (or so it was represented—some farmhouse!). "Tower of Four Winds" was started in 1928 (even as Arthur Leonard on the opposite shore of the Point broke ledge for a stone companion to "Druimteac" for *his* daughter, Mrs. Groverman C. Ellis, 200 yards to the northeast and about as tauntingly close to the Atlantic). The Taggart place was finished at an estimated cost of $125,000.[13]

Henry Sleeper decorated the Taggart "farmhouse." "Lucy's studio at

Four Winds was a superb space," wrote Indiana historian James Philip Fadely, "a two-story room with a wood-beamed ceiling that gave it a cathedral effect. Perhaps the room that best reflected both Lucy's and Sleeper's aesthetic tastes, though, was the octagonal dining room on the lower level, the showcase room: French doors draped with green silk and vermillion fringe faced the harbor. The walls displayed hand-painted Chinese wallpaper that featured birds, trees, and flowers on a cobalt-blue background. The ceiling was silver leaf with bamboo moulding. The custom-made table had faux bamboo legs and trim painted silver and flecked with vermillion.

Schooner Alice and Wilson *on Bemo Ledge, November 15, 1929. (C. W. Sibley)*

Made-to-order chairs were a simple Chinese design and painted green."[14] The music room, with a collection of ship models, was in the Italian style, while the bed chambers were early American.

Besides the Dabsvillians, Lucy Taggart's close Gloucester friends included the artist brothers Gifford and Reynolds Beal and the sculptors Walker Hancock and Paul Manship. Hancock considered her "an extremely attractive woman, with a quick wit and sense of humor, an excellent painter, and much too modest about her own work." Close to lifelong was her friendship with the Hoosier writer Booth Tarkington and both his wives; she traveled with them abroad, and they visited between "Tower of Four Winds" and the Tarkington summer cottage in Kennebunkport, Maine.

On October 29, 1929, the stock market collapsed.

A fortnight later, as if to punctuate the point, the fishing schooner *Alice and Wilson* drove up on Bemo Ledge, and after giving her chagrined crew a chance to get off, gave up the ghost and sank, leaving only her mastheads showing above the treacherous waters of Brace Cove.

Black Cloud, *queen of the Cape Ann Yacht Club, clips by the mark boat on June 25, 1887, probably in Boston Harbor. (H. G. Peabody photo, Peabody Essex Museum)*

~36~
OLD REGATTA DAYS AND THE CAPE ANN YACHT CLUB

EASTERN POINT FOR EIGHTY YEARS has been the sole legatee and custodian of organized yachting in Gloucester Harbor, as distinct from the joyous and proletarian pastime of messing about with boats that's been happily wasting time around here since the Sieur de Champlain caulked his shallop in 1606.

And while the Eastern Point Yacht Club is the junior on Cape Ann in point of continuous existence, it draws the deepest water, being the direct descendent of the first at this end of Massachusetts Bay, the Gloucester Yacht Club.

The original GYC, let it be said, lived and died, ad hoc, all in the month of September 1878, yet it served its purpose, and though but a wave in the sea of corinth, it shall be perpetuated. It was Cape Ann's first.

Her fame is built on three centuries of working sail, and Gloucester has never exerted herself unduly to encourage the sneakered race in her midst, organized or otherwise. Yet the yachtsman, tolerated if he kept the hell out of the fisherman's way, has always found his niche, some backwash on the waterfront whence he could tack forth with all his cotton flying in the fulsome years and to which he could retreat and winter through the lean.

Yachting out of Gloucester has always had its special flavor, and a strong one, at the same time providing an abundant source of new life, for the old port ever has exerted a mysterious, magnetic effect on compasses the seven seas over.

The first duly recorded American yacht race, as remarked in an earlier chapter, was won (to the westward of Gloucester, to be sure) one August day of 1835 by the schooner *Sylph,* until that very moment owned by John Perkins Cushing, Esq., consolidator of all the lands of Eastern Point behind his famous wall.

Ten years passed, and the first yacht regatta east of Cape Cod was sailed off Nahant on July 19, 1845.

Three years and thirteen miles farther on, Gloucester got around to having its first on the twentieth of May, 1848, reported in the *Gloucester Telegraph* four days later as the largest regatta ever sailed in America (one wonders how they knew), with sixteen "clippers" from ports between Boston and Portsmouth. The starting line was off Fort Point on a course of about eight miles out the harbor. The winner was the sixteen-tonner *Globe* of Newburyport, Captain Lunt, rig unrecorded, in three hours and seventeen minutes. First prize a spyglass. Needless to say, much griping over handicapping.

The second Gloucester regatta on June 21 in light air attracted eighteen entries, another twenty sail-alongs, thousands watching from shore, cannons and flags. *Excelsior* of Salem won a new pilot's "canoe" as first prize for her skipper.

Not for another seven years was another Gloucester regatta reported in the press, briefly noted in August 1855. Three more years, however, and in 1858 they *really* got organized.

It came off on the third of September, fine sailing day, smart breeze from the southwest, a swell running outside the Point but smooth in the harbor. The start was from the judges' boat to the buoy marking Babson Ledge, which is between Ten Pound Island and the Fort. The courses all took the boats well outside the harbor and back; the shortest was eight miles.

Four classes had been created for the occasion, presumably based on waterline length: Class 1, from thirty to forty feet; Class 2, from eighteen to thirty feet; Class 3, centerboarders under thirty feet; and Class 4, less than eighteen feet. Time allowances of forty seconds a foot over the whole distance for Class 1 and sixty for the rest were established in an effort to even up the odd lot of boats, for rarely were any two small yachts alike in those days. It was a sweepstakes, the winners to divide up the entrance fees.

This first Gloucester regatta of any note attracted eighteen boats, most of them local, including a surprising number of small schooners among the predominant field of sloops. The Gloucester schooner *Neptune's Favorite* flew away with Class 1 without much difficulty, and, as someone commented, she would have won if it had taken her a month to get around the course, for there were no time limits and she was the only entry. The sloop *Comet* of Gloucester beat off four little schooners in Class 2. Class 4 was won by the sloop *Spray* against a field that included the sloop *Dutchman* with the extraordinary hail of Surinam.

The biggest thrills of the day were in Class 3, the centerboarders, and the eight dollars prize money was carried back to Manchester by the twenty-four-and-a-half-foot sloop *Grace Darling*, sailed by our colorful old friend Captain Robert Bennet Forbes, Jack Cushing's cousin. Black Ben was going on fifty-four, had bought his Manchester summer estate two years earlier, and had not lost his tiller touch; *Grace Darling* "won the commendations of all by her very superior performance."[1]

Two years later there was an informal sweepstakes race in August 1860, but these early regattas were at best catch-as-catch-can affairs in the absence of institutional sponsorship, and they were much too informal and irregu-

lar to suit the American compulsion to organize everything within reach. And then came the War of Secession.

But with the Union preserved and peace restored (and the waters of the bay free of mines and Reb raiders), the Boston Yacht Club was founded in 1865. Others followed, such as Eastern in 1871 and Beverly the next year (Manchester not until 1892).

Of course, yachting was for those with the means and leisure to pursue it, mainly the summer residents whose discovery of the delights of the North Shore tended eastward only slowly. Cape Ann was a long way from Boston, and Gloucester was for the fishermen, who preferred whiling away their summers racing their hookers after mackerel in the Bay St. Lawrence and home to market.

Still, Cape Ann abounded with first-rate small boat sailors cradled in a trawl tub and raised in a dory. Sooner or later the yachting fever that was spiking in the late 1870s must quicken even Gloucester's stolid pulse. With the exception of a centennial race got up more out of patriotic than yachting fervor on the Fourth of July, 1876, the first serious revival after a lapse of twenty years must be credited to the summer pioneers of Annisquam.

The date was Saturday, August 24, 1878, and it came off in Ipswich Bay. They raised a purse for two classes, over and under nineteen-foot waterline. Seventeen boats entered each. The wind held, and it was such a crashing success that Rockporters took up the idea and two weeks later, on September 10, had their first Sandy Bay regatta with the same division of entries, plus sailing dories. All were becalmed, and it was sailed over again a few days later.

As a daredevil young fisherman, Alfred Johnson sailed his dory Centennial *to* Gloucester, England, *in 1876 in the first singlehanded crossing of the Atlantic, a feat he commemorated on a Gloucester, Massachusetts, wharf in old age. (Author's collection)*

The contagion had struck, and it raced around the Cape; on Thursday, September 26, what was described as the first regatta of the Gloucester Yacht Club was sailed in the harbor. No further reference to this fleeting, and apparently fleetless, fraternity has been found—and no one around today remembers it—so one is left with the conclusion that it sprang full-blown into being for the occasion and disappeared back into the murk, like the features of the Cheshire Cat, when it was all over, leaving behind nothing but the smile.

The committee of this apparitional progenitor of Cape Ann yacht clubs that arranged the regatta were Samuel Elwell, Jr., a block maker; Aaron Brown, a sail maker who ran a Main Street billiards parlor with his brother; and Lewis Merchant, box manufacturer. The judges were Captain Charles Babson, Bennett Griffin and Councilman William Thompson.

The starting line was off Pavilion Beach. The course for the nineteen-to-twenty-five-foot waterline boats was eleven miles—out to a flag boat two miles off Eastern Point Light to another off Kettle Island and back to the start. The under-nineteen class sailed about six miles around the Point Ledge buoy to a flag boat off Norman's Woe and return.

Wind fresh out of the sou'west, harbor crowded with spectator craft, the shores thronged. After the first results were published, the judges thought they should divide the twelve entries in the large class and the eight in the smaller according to keel and centerboard. The ten-dollar first prizes went to Captain Pigeon's *Judith*, a 21'8" centerboarder that covered the eleven miles in 2:20:23; *Gleaner*, Captain Bakeman, keel, 23'9" in 2:29:42. Over the six miles it was *Zip*, Captain Howard Elwell, centerboard, 18'6" in 1:25:10; and *Hard Times*, Captain Samuel Elwell, Jr., keel, 17'9" in 1:26:07.

This marker in the history of Cape Ann yachting was not repeated in the harbor in 1879; instead, an informal August union regatta was sailed in Ipswich Bay.

For a few days in midsummer of 1880 Gloucester Harbor was adorned by the magnificent *Ambassadress* in the anchorage, the schooner yacht of William Astor, old John Jacob's grandson. Launched in 1877, "The Astor House," as the wags called her, was, at 146 feet 2 inches overall, nearly the largest yacht in the world. She was a centerboarder, later converted to keel, furnished luxuriously, for cruising only. From his vantage on Five Pound Island, where he was boarding with the lighthouse keeper, Winslow Homer dashed off a dreamlike drawing of *Ambassadress* dated August 25, now in the collection of the Cape Ann Historical Association.

Probably *Ambassadress* was headed east. Mr. Astor told some of the local Sunday sailors that if they ever got around to organizing a yacht club, he would join. The Astors were worth a hundred million or so at about this time, and whether this fact had anything to do with it or not, forty Cape Ann yachtsmen had signed up by the end of July. At a get-together in the

/440

Gloucester police station, several locals were designated to propose a slate of officers and bylaws. The committee included William N. McKenzie, a store clerk; self-described laborer John Bickford, a Civil War Medal of Honor winner; and fisherman Eben Elwell.

On August 5, 1880, the Cape Ann Yacht Club was organized to carry on the tradition started two years earlier by the transient Gloucester Yacht Club. Bennett Griffin, the lumber and hardware dealer who judged the 1878 regatta, was elected commodore; Frank H. Gaffney, a caulker, vice commodore; John Bickford, fleet captain; H. Frank Sanford, "guano manu- facturer" (thought the gulls did that), secretary; William F. Parsons, trea- surer; and Joseph M. Cook, a boat carpenter, measurer.

If William Astor was admitted to membership (a point on which the record is silent), he gave the club no more than its due, for although it was their first intention to hire Hicks Hall on Western Avenue as a clubhouse, the members for some years had to be content with the room of the Gloucester Cornet Band in the Sawyer Block on Main Street.

The Cape Ann Yacht Club did not sponsor a regatta its opening season.

Winslow Homer used pencil and chalk for the visit of the Astor yacht Ambassadress *to Gloucester Harbor, August 25, 1880. (Cape Ann Historical Association)*

Not until September 1881 did they hold their first meet, an open in Ipswich Bay that was beset by calms, postponements and recriminations over handicapping. The following year all was retrieved. Their union regatta was back in the harbor, starting off Pavilion Beach one day early in August. Thirty-one entries in four classes sailed over essentially the same courses that served the 1878 races, and in spite of the light air the event was pronounced the most successful in Cape Ann waters to date.

That wordful reporter and historian of the Gloucester scene, James R. Pringle, recalled some years later in the *Boston Globe* that for several seasons after it was founded, the regattas of the Cape Ann Yacht Club were unequaled attractions on the North Shore. Pringle gave a large share of the credit to two rule-of-thumb designers and builders, Samuel Elwell (who helped arrange the 1878 regatta and sailed his *Hard Times* in it) and George Wheeler of Wheeler's Point on the Annisquam River.

Elwell, according to Pringle, was the first builder on the North Shore to recognize how much speed can be gained by reducing wetted surface, by designing hulls to sail over instead of through the water. The centerboarder *Zip,* which took a first in her class in that regatta, was after his design—high freeboard and flat floors.

In the winter of 1883–84 George Wheeler built *Black Cloud* for Charles E. Cunningham and Aaron Brown of Gloucester, twenty-six feet overall and twenty-two feet on the waterline. She was a centerboard skimming dish conjured up to sail in the sweat off a mug of beer and was no doubt influenced by the success of Sam Elwell, whose *Hard Times* was said to have won more prizes than any other yacht ever built up to her time in Gloucester before she was sold up to Chelsea in 1882 for $225.

Black Cloud, hailing from the Cape Ann Yacht Club, was a phenomenal flyer. She won the first regatta she entered, off Nahant, and went on to clean up the coast to Boston and back, coming home with everything in her class. In July 1887 she won the race from Squam Light around the Isles of Shoals and return, 9:00 in the morning to 9:24 that night, bringing her record to twenty-two prizes totaling $511.

Aaron Brown, *Black Cloud*'s sole owner in 1887, then stuck out his chest and flung an open challenge to all boats on the coast under twenty-five-foot waterline for a sweepstakes race from Pavilion Beach around Halfway Rock and back. He got not a taker. *Black Cloud* won the Cape Ann Yacht Club's first Tappan Cup race in 1888, swept several regattas up and down the line in 1889, and was still taking prizes as late as 1894.

The Cape Ann Yacht Club, all the while, was having fat years and lean ones. Eighteen eighty-three was a busy season in the harbor. Ben Butler's pride, the old schooner *America,* first winner of the America's Cup, was at anchor off and on, and so was *Ambassadress.* Fifty-three yachts entered the September regatta.

The next season, 1884, the harbor fleet numbered fifty-four, the Squam River contingent forty-four. William Astor was again a visitor, this summer with his new *Nourmahal,* 227 feet, the first yacht built of steel in America and the largest steam yacht ever, barque-rigged, and a romantic sight at night with her Edison lights twinkling through the cabin ports.

Newspaper reports imply that the more energetic sailing in the mid-eighties had shifted to Squam River and Ipswich Bay. Mention of the Sandy Bay Yacht Club at Rockport is found as early as 1887. Then Herman Tappan's trophy revived interest down in the harbor in 1888, but again it subsided. The Cape Ann Yacht Club held its last successful open harbor regatta in July 1893, and the next one—run by an ad hoc committee in 1895—reminded the reporter a little sadly of the club's "palmy days."

The Golden Age of Yachting.
(Al Swanson collection)

The Presidential yacht Mayflower *and the coasting schooner* Catherine *in Gloucester Harbor, July 9, 1910. President Taft was in the summer White House in Beverly after being denied "The Ramparts" by Mrs. Raymond. (Eben Parsons photo, private collection)*

~37~

THE BELLE EPOQUE
OF YACHTING

For some reason or other the Cape Ann Yacht Club had faded away by 1894. But not the fever. The same year a nub of enthusiasts started up the Nahant Dory Club—which one may assume inspired the creation of the Squam Dory Club in May 1896, which crystallized into the Annisquam Yacht Club in 1898—to race Swampscott dories.

This, and the prospect of the "mill pond" supposedly assured by the commencement of the Dog Bar Breakwater late in 1894, was all the encouragement the harbor lads needed for a revival. On the fifth of June, 1896, a gang of them met in Percy Wheeler's blacksmith and wheelwright shop off Parker Street at the head of the harbor and organized themselves into the East Gloucester Yacht Club.

Wheeler, boat builder and motor mechanic, was elected the first commodore. Captain Albert Gosbee of Rocky Neck, carpenter and the Humane Society's intrepid local lifesaving chief, was acclaimed vice commodore. Archibald Fenton, a Nova Scotian boatbuilder and designer who had shifted over from Essex to Rocky Neck, was decided on for fleet captain, and sparmaker Scott Call for secretary. Other founders included Alex McCurdy, the carriage maker and shipsmith; Police Officer John G. Mehlman; Freeman H. Brown, a fish skinner; Melvin Haskell; Joseph Merchant, woodworker; Sidney Pomeroy, a mason; Deputy Collector of Customs J. Warren Wonson; and carpenter Horace Sargent.

Headquarters for the new club (or the reincarnation of the old) were found in an old fish house on the Wonson Wharf at Smoky Point, up the head of the harbor. The place was repaired and painted, and a float and moorings were put out. The names of that early fleet reflected the easy temper of the times: *Eulalie, Ariel, June, Hoodoo, Cymbria, Hustler, Anemone, Luna, Brownie, Skedaddle, Coot, Bird, Doris, Voma, Torment* and others.

Their first cruise in mid-July took them through the Cut to Annisquam, then across Ipswich Bay to Plum Island for a clambake.

Swampscott dory sailing off the Hawthorne Inn, July 8, 1911. (Eben Parsons photo, author's collection)

The East Gloucester Yacht Club crowned its maiden season in the expansive mood of the 1890s with its First Annual Fete Night and Illuminated Tender Parade, on September 8, 1896. All the windows and balconies of the clubhouse out on the wharf were lit with candles and Japanese lanterns, and the weather-beaten exterior was all decked out with flags and bunting. Fireworks were torched off, introducing the climactic event of the evening, when the whole flotilla of club tenders rowed all around the inner harbor, lighting up the waterfront in dancing glow and shadow with lanterns, red fire and more fireworks, while the members raised a clamor blowing horns and shooting revolvers into the night sky. The show wound up with three cheers and a tiger.

This burst of élan carried them through the chill of the first winter, when the clubhouse was kept open for dances, whist parties and sundry entertainments while the members resailed their races "around the stove."

Those early years they raced to Marblehead and Plum Island, with evening sails from the anchorage behind Five Pound Island out into the harbor. Their cruises lasted from three days to two weeks, and all agreed the best were down Maine; twelve boats and ninety sailors made the first run to Boothbay. The initiation fee for a new member in 1898 was one dollar; the annual dues were two dollars.

From the beginning, or near to it, each season of competition closed with the open Chowder Race. This Cape Ann yachting ritual was provended by Officer Jack Mehlman, a man of many parts, and not the least of them was his artistry as a cooker of fish chowder and steamer of clams.

Officer Mehlman came on the force as a rookie of twenty-eight in 1890.

An admirer once wrote of him that "his outstanding mental characteristic was unfailing good nature even under the most trying circumstances. Cast in stalwart frame, of great strength, and slow to wrath even if occasion should occasionally tend to bring such to the surface . . . Early connected with the police force, never aggressive, always considerate of the offender under his ken, he suffered bodily injury before resorting to that reprisal to which the law entitled him."[1]

The summer previous to his joining in the founding of the yacht club the *Advertiser* observed that "Bass Rocks people want police protection extended to them, and it will be, thanks to the fact that Officer Mehlman is an expert with the wheel." He could row as well as pedal and for years commuted by skiff from near his home on Rocky Neck to muster at the station across the harbor over town.

As if proficiency as cook, cop, cyclist and oarsman weren't enough for one man, Jack Mehlman was considered by those who knew what they were talking about in the first rank of amateur sailors on the coast, if not Number One—a helmsman whose brilliance gave rise to a school of waterfront opinion that if he had been at the wheel of the challengers during the International Fishermen's Races, the *Halifax Herald* cup would never have left Gloucester after Marty Welch brought it back in the *Esperanto* in 1920, a safe enough conjecture. Mehlman hadn't.

A small boat sailor of a different stripe and by all odds the most famous member of the club was Howard Blackburn, the fisherman-turned-saloon-keeper-yachtsman who had been a sort of living legend since he rowed his dory sixty miles into the coast of Newfoundland from Burgeo Bank with his hands frozen to the oars and his dead mate in the stern. That was back in January 1883, and Blackburn lost all of his fingers and most of each thumb. Now, at the end of the century, he was back in Gloucester after quarreling with the Klondike gold expedition he organized and led around the Horn in 1897 and 1898, and restless as ever ashore.

On the sixth of June, 1899, Hugh Bishop launched the thirty-foot sloop *Great Western* for Blackburn. That evening the East Gloucester Yacht Club voted the Fingerless Mariner a member. On the eighteenth, to the cheers of a vast concourse of well-wishers ashore and afloat, Captain Blackburn sailed alone out the harbor, flying the EGYC burgee and accompanied around the Point and into the open ocean by five of his fellow members in their sloops. His destination was Gloucester, England, where he arrived after sixty-two days at sea.

Summer people provided the yacht club with another brand of sailor yet, and the one who led all the rest was John Greenough, the financier just retired, the old lover of Gloucester who had first visited her with his brother David in 1855, now settled summers in his cottage at Eastern Point. For Greenough the sport of small boat sailing as pursued by his professional crew, the good company of it, high or low, rich or poor, on the Point or beyond the gate—this was what counted.

During the infancy of the East Gloucester Yacht Club, when he had just begun to come to Tanglewood for his summers, John Greenough unobtrusively joined, attended the meetings and supported and encouraged it and added his crack sloop *Onda* to the fleet. And when within four years the club had incorporated (on July 30, 1900) and grown to fifty members and was bulging the poor sides of its fish house at Smoky Point, he offered to advance the funds to build a new one.

A lot was purchased off Wiley Street on Rocky Neck, facing across to Ten Pound Island and beyond, and in the fall of 1900 the new commodore, sail maker Benjamin H. Colby, appointed a building committee; on it was Percy Wheeler (who had been succeeded by Alex McCurdy, Colby's predecessor); grocer Freeman Hodsdon; Mott Cannon, the landscape engineer; Jack Mehlman; and Captain Bobby Miller, the harbor pilot. Scott Webber, a local architect, designed the clubhouse.

The new quarters were dedicated on January 10, 1901, with panoply, refreshments, dancing and music by Sawyer's Orchestra. It cost about $3,100 without the furnishings. A broad veranda was stilted on spiles over the flats. There were spacious assembly and reading rooms, a billiards and pool room, kitchen and basement mug-up room for the ladling-out of Mehlman's chowders. The place was heated after a fashion, and it was in the hot-air shaft that the fire was thought to have started that caused some damage one day that next December, bringing the steam pumpers *N. M. Jackman* and *Defiance* on the whistle. The hook and ladder from town got stuck trying to surmount Point Hill and had to put out a call for more horses.

Having returned triumphantly from England but restless as ever, Captain Blackburn on New Year's Day, 1901, challenged the world to a single-handed race to Lisbon, Portugal, and posted half of his stake of $100 (to be matched by the taker) with Commodore Colby. As for himself, he would make this second projected crossing in his 25-footer *Great Republic,* which he had commissioned his fellow EGYC member Archie Fenton to design and build at his shop up at the head of Smith Cove.

No one would seriously take him up. Captain Gosbee offered to race in his sloop *Ariel,* proposing to leave from the new clubhouse and take his dog along for company if someone would make it really worth his while with a purse of, say, $1,000. But no one did, and on the ninth of June, after attending a reception in his honor at the club, Blackburn strode down to the landing and was conveyed to his sloop, raised sail and started off to the cheers of the thousands.

He did it. He crossed the Atlantic, again alone and in spite of his famous disability, in thirty-nine days. Home once more, the club threw a smashing smoker for the lone voyager, attended by two hundred, replete with chowder, speeches, spirituous aids and the congratulatory clamors of Clark's Military Band.

The whole gala scene was repeated more festively than ever for the third and final time on June 7, 1903, when Howard Blackburn embarked from the Rocky Neck clubhouse in his sailing dory *America* for Le Havre, France. Fortunately, probably, foul weather and ill health forced him to turn back off the coast of Nova Scotia. For the succeeding three decades he contented himself with day sailing and short cruises.

In his decked-over Swampscott dory America *Howard Blackburn sails off for France, June 7, 1903. (Author's collection)*

Pollard's Privateer II ghosting past Raymond's landing (top) and the family's stately Shur *(below). All aboard for Clay's* Euphemia *(top right). (Lila Leonard Swift)*

Facing page: Skirts for all occasions. (Lila Leonard Swift)

Marking its tenth anniversary, the members of the East Gloucester Yacht Club voted in March 1906 to drop the *East* and raise the dues to ten dollars on January 1, 1907. The club had spread its umbrella, and the shorter name was more urbane. By now most of the Eastern Pointers who enjoyed getting their tails wet were members. Class boats, if not yet one-designs, were tending toward fairly uniform ratings and playing a more dominant role in racing.

For several seasons an open "Eastern Point Regatta" was sailed out of Lighthouse, or Quarry, Cove under the sponsorship of some of the summer residents; in early August 1911, for instance, it was arranged by Wilder Pollard and Edward and Jonathan Raymond. A large, crisp crowd of the elect watched from shore; others followed in boats.

Sloops sailing in the first handicap class this day included John Greenough's *Onda II*, Ben Colby's *Elizabeth*, L. E. Andrews's *Jingo*, Archie Fenton's *Urchin* and the Raymond family's *Edjako;* among the second handicaps were the Leonard family's *Tid II* and Pollard's *Privateer II.*

Swelling the fleet was a batch of Annisquam fifteen-footers from up the river and a class of so-called Gloucester fifteen-footers that included Jonathan Raymond's *Olita* and Frederick Hall's *Kiddo.*

The powerboat race around Baker's Island and back was won by William Sheafe's *Magpie* (the Sheafes had bought the Lewis cottage at the corner of Fort Hill and Elm avenues), with John Greenough's *Camaranda*, Clay's *Euphemia*, Pollard's *Shur* and Raymond's *Mistral* close in his wake.

Ben Colby, a master with the light sails, decided not to stand for reelection as commodore of the Gloucester Yacht Club in 1913 and was followed after thirteen years of it by Austin H. Perry, a Haverhill shoe manufacturer who stayed at the Hawthorne Inn. To suitably mark the occasion of his elevation, Perry had Archie Fenton build him a fifty-foot cruising sloop, *Saracen,* for his flagship. Irving Trefry of Rocky Neck was a paid hand with

Commodore Perry before and after the First World War; after a while his boss tired of *Saracen* and turned her in for a seventy-foot baldheaded schooner from Maine.

The yacht club was at its zenith, with 150 members. They voted to start races in 1913 off the Hawthorne, obviating the often difficult and frustrating light air hitches to get out from under the lee of Ten Pound Island. John Greenough, "the right bower of the club and prince of yachtsmen," was anxious to try out his brand new Class P boat; Jack Raymond had sold *Olita* down to New Bedford and was racing *Edjako;* and the anchorage was graced with several pretty sloops from the shop of Archie Fenton. The racing fleet had settled down to four distinct classes: the fifteen- and eighteen-footers, the P boats and the Bar Harbor 30s.

The half-dozen 15s remembered by Irving Trefry were hand-me-downs of 1911 or so from the Hull Yacht Club flotilla, fin keel, decked-over forward, well built and smart sailers, likely the first one—designs in Gloucester Harbor. The 18s appeared right after them, probably in the same way via Marblehead, also fin-keeled and with a little more deck.

John Greenough's *Onda II* was one of the P boats. Their vogue peaked about 1912. They were thirty feet on the water or close to it, built to the Universal Rule with long overhangs. There were very few in the fleet, and, at that, they hardly outnumbered the Bar Harbor 30s of roughly the same size, designed by Nathanael Herreshoff in 1904, clustering at Marblehead.

Iceboating on Niles Pond, around 1913. Knowles estate on shore; beyond that, the harbor. (Chester N. Walen photo)

The roster of the Gloucester Yacht Club in these serene prewar years excluded only those who had no interest in yachting. The Eastern Pointers, especially the younger generation, raced stem and stay with and against the natives, and many a clever sailor from the Inner Sanctum learned his ropes and a cutthroat tactic or two from such rough-and-tumble, hard-sailing and hard-betting East Gloucestermen and Rocky Neckers as John Bickford, Archie Fenton, Ben Colby, Scott Parker and Jack Mehlman.

All sorts of people. Nai Choate, for instance.

The Siamese legation in Washington had somehow discovered Gloucester back in the 1890s and kept returning, year after year, usually to the Thorwald Hotel or some other location at Bass Rocks. For some thirty years the Siamese were represented by Edward Loftus of the British East Indian diplomatic staff. After a brief flirtation with the Adirondacks in the mid-1930s they returned, this time to the Back Shore cottage of the Frederick Holdsworths, "The Sumacs," their nation now being represented under its new autonomy by Ambassador and Madame Phya Abhibal Rajamaitri.

In the earlier days before the First War the young attachés to the Siamese embassy were generally Oxonians, polished and properly Anglicized for the Western taste, and superb tennis players. Nai Choate was among the most popular, always in demand on the courts and at the dinner table, and one of the better helmsmen of the Gloucester Yacht Club. His surname, originating in the mysterious East, never failed to amaze the Yankees of Essex County.

And there were others, such as John Greenough's hearties under the command of his sailing master, Captain Charles Ahlquist, a Swede who went to sea when he was eleven, mastered the full-rigged ships and rounded the Horn six times and the Cape of Good Hope four before he settled down to yachting.

One of Greenough's professionals was Jim Walen of East Gloucester, who at ninety-seven in 1969 was still motoring to the yacht club, running the flags up and down and firing off the sunset gun.

Captain Jim started yachting when he was around eighteen and working as a sail maker, and he and his chums would get out sailing Sundays and evenings, sometimes drifting around the harbor til dawn. He began spare-time crewing for Captain Charley Ahlquist around 1897 when he was about twenty-five. The East Gloucester Yacht Club had just got going. Greenough was not too particular about the subtleties of corinthianism and paid three dollars a day when they were racing. Jack Mehlman generally had the helm, Ben Colby with an assist from Ahlquist on the sheets and Jim at the light sails, having the job of setting the ballooner off the wind.

In Captain Jim's view, Jack Mehlman and another police officer, Ben Stanley, were the crackerjack small boat sailors on Cape Ann.

Mehlman 'specially. He was a master at the tiller or the wheel, and it didn't make a bit o' difference whose boat he had—just give him a good hand on the sheets and he'd win.

One day we was racin' up to Marblehead. Somebody protested that Mr. Greenough had a professional crew on board. He never sailed himself, y'know, just sat in the cockpit or stood there in the companionway and looked hard at ya and didn't say nawthin.

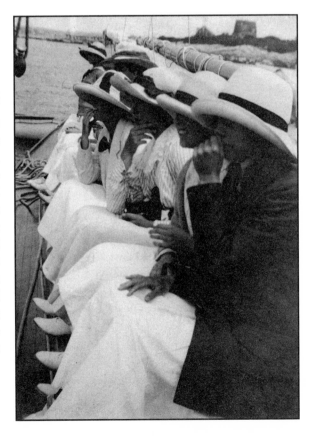

A sunburnproof line of Point beauties is intent on something— races? (Lila Leonard Swift)

Well, the committee up there called him on the mat. In them days they sailed for cash, not cups much. So he told 'em we warn't pros but was racin' for the prize money!

We had some times, I guess. I 'member we was racin' one of Greenough's boats off of Hull one day, and I went forrad, just as we was comin' up to the buoy, y'know, to set the ballooner so's we'd be ready for the run on the next leg. I got her up all right, but just as we rounded I thought that sheet trimmed some quick. Wal, I looked back, and there was Ahlquist in the water, draggin' along like a sea anchor. He'd got the sheet wrapped round his hand, y'know, to haul it back good'n hard, and fell overboard. But he wouldn't let go. We fished him out.[2]

Schooners off Mother Ann, 1906. (Lila Leonard Swift)

No account of yachting in the waters off Eastern Point before World War I would be complete without a mention of the sport as it was pursued at breakneck speed over the waters on the Point in their frozen state.

Around 1905 a crowd of high school boys from East Gloucester organized the Gloucester Iceboat Club and got permission from George Stacy to use as their clubhouse one of the ramshackle frame garages he had thrown up for the Colonial Arms in the field across the road from Niles Pond.[3] Every winter until the war put an end to such eye-watering sport they lugged their heavy, homemade, gaff-rigged iceboats down the road from East Gloucester on their backs, piece by piece, or brought them sometimes around by dory.

When the ice was firm and the northwest wind was sharp as aces they raced up and down the brief span of the pond until each crew could stand the piercing cold no longer and stumbled ashore to stamp life back into their feet and course the blood through their bodies again before the roaring blaze of driftwood from the beach.

The records are incomplete, but the *Gloucester Times* of November 4, 1914, reported that the boys had just opened their tenth season with a "banquet" at their Eastern Point clubhouse. The officers that year were Ernest S. Davis, commodore; Leonard E. Wilson, vice commodore; Everett O. Swinson, rear commodore; David H. Swinson, fleet captain; Clayton Stockbridge, secretary; Herbert Joyce, treasurer; Ledgewood Swinson, measurer; and Irving Trefry, Carl Peterson and Max Parsons, regatta committee.

It was said that six new iceboats were under construction in 1914, bringing the fleet up to ten. The first race was set for Thanksgiving, weather favoring, with matches every Sunday thereafter (ice holding out) for cups donated by summer residents.

And after each race, it was solemnly compacted, the losers were honorbound to cook the banquet for the winners in the clubhouse.

The war ended it all, and organized yachting was suspended. After the Armistice, returning to pick up their lives again, the members found that the Gloucester Yacht Club was no more. The impetus had been lost, and the once festive clubhouse on Rocky Neck was sold.

Commodore John Greenough
by Cecilia Beaux. (Private collection)

~38~

THE EASTERN POINT
YACHT CLUB

Archie Fenton was a long, lank Novie from along toward Canso on the south coast of Nova Scotia, all bone and muscle, who came up to Essex boat-carpentering as a young fellow. Then he set up shop near the ferry landing at East Gloucester Square, then to Rocky Neck where he built his first yacht in about 1897, then to his shop and yard above the East Main Street flats at the head of Smith Cove.

An exacting craftsman. Irving Trefry worked for him for a time and hardly dared pick up a tool when the boss was at his elbow lest he find fault. Let the men fasten a plank with a grain he didn't like, or try to slip one knot by him, and Fenton would growl and rip the whole strake off the frames. Once he sent a wagonload of lumber that didn't suit him straight back to Boston.

The finished product was his vindication: Captain Blackburn's *Great Republic*, for example, was still under sail in Long Island Sound at the age of sixty-five and is preserved in the Cape Ann Historical Association museum.

Gruff and hard to please around his shop, Archie waxed affable in the office with cronies and a bottle during the slack season, and he was an elegant sailor and the best of shipmates. He designed and built tenders and sailboats and launches, and workboats such as the small one-man line trawlers he made for the Rocky Neck shore fishermen, and he laid down the lines for a number of fishing vessels that were built in Florida.

When the boys came marching home after the First World War to find the Gloucester Yacht Club defunct, its roster at sixes and sevens, its fleet aged and scattered on the beach, Archie Fenton was the man to turn to. And that is what Frederick G. Hall, the artist and master of "Stone Acre," did. A good sailor himself, Freddy asked Fenton in the summer of 1920 to design a prototype and build a fleet of little sailboats, if half a dozen buyers could be rounded up.

It was a deal. That winter, when he was sixty-six, Fenton built three

one-designs. The prototype was for Freddy Hall, who christened her *Midget,* hence the name of the class—the Gloucester, or Fenton, Midgets. The "mosquito fleet," as it was nicknamed, buzzed the harbor for the first time in June 1921 to the delight of Gloucester. *Midget*'s sisters were *Gatina* (Italian for "Little Cat"), which Edward Williams bought for his son Ted, and *Philetas,* young Phil Tucker's.

Fenton never liked working to another's design; the Midgets, the only class of sailboats ever built for Gloucester Harbor, came from his own early life. He often molded his small craft on vessel lines—deep hulls with full bilges and sloping floors, with a long run of keel—and the Midgets were midget adaptations of a familiar Novie design that originated in Mahone Bay; this was the Tancook whaler, a double-ended fishing boat, schooner- or sloop-rigged, with clipper bow, fine run, long keel and quarters drifting back to merge at the extreme, raking stempost from which hung a narrow outside rudder.

The Fenton Midgets were sixteen feet, or a hair less, on deck. Unlike the whalers, they had no centerboard and were proportionately deeper, drawing about thirty inches. They had the same Tancook lines—clipper bow, high freeboard forward (another Fenton and Nova Scotian characteristic), fine entrance, full bilges, long sloping keel, lifting sheer and raking stern. Steamed oak frames, pine (or perhaps cedar) planking and copper fastened, a rather light bar of lead in the keel, mostly inside ballast.

"The fitting together of those little craft," admired Henry Williams, "would have made Chippendale, the furniture man, happy."

For some curious reason, Fenton gave his miniature vessels a cat rig with a marconi sail on a tall and willowy mast that was stayed only at the stem. The cockpit simply faired with the line of the gunwale; it was pointed at the ends and only thirty inches wide amidships, leaving extra broad decks out of a beam of fifty-six inches.

The following winter Archie Fenton built at least two more Midgets, *Wanderer* for Melancthon Jacobus, Jr.,[1] and another, probably for Russell Hinchran, a summer resident of Grapevine Road, which was sold in early 1924 to Bishop Rhinelander for the use of his sons and named *Wind.* In the winter of 1922-23 Fenton built his last Midget of record, launched in the spring for sculptor Leonard Craske.

Ted Williams mastered the Midgets as a boy, and his *Gatina* won several prizes. He writes:

The boats were fairly fast, very poor on maneuverability because of the long shallow keel, and surprisingly, turned out to be quite tender. In addition to the keel we had quite a bit of rock ballast in the cockpit which became a problem and nobody seemed to know whether a light boat or a heavy boat would come up with the best all around record. We never had jibs or spinnakers although a small jib could have been provided if a bowsprit had been added. Although the boats were tender, the narrow cockpit helped to make them fairly seaworthy. I think I only swamped mine once.[2]

The mosquito fleet's inside course usually was from Quarry Cove to Ten Pound Island and back. The Midgets were in the yacht races celebrating the three hundredth anniversary of the town in 1923, and in 1925, 1926 and 1927 they sailed at Marblehead during Race Week. In 1925 the winning Midget covered a 4 1/2-mile course in 1:12, not quite as swift as the Annisquam Bird Boats, but two minutes faster than the Squam Cats and four better than the winning Manchester 15.

They were memorable and unique, the only sailing class ever designed, built and raced in Gloucester Harbor. The Gloucester Midgets revived yacht racing after World War I, and they were the very first class of the Eastern Point Yacht Club.

Archibald Fenton died on August 6, 1923. But his boats live on,

The Gloucester Midgets run for it off Black Bess rocks. (Edward Williams)

Blackburn's *Great Republic* for one. And *Wind*, the last known survivor of the Midgets. The master was the model for Finley Archer, the Smith Cove boatbuilder in *Gus Harvey—The Boy Skipper of Cape Ann,* by Captain Charlton Lyman Smith. Some of the scenes in this rare and authentic 1920 gem of small boat sailing in Gloucester Harbor are laid on Eastern Point. In forty years of owners *Wind* picked up a bowsprit, had her cockpit widened and her mast shortened and moved somewhat aft, and her rig lowered to gaff and jib. I bought her in 1966, repaired her with Captain Bill Sibley, and relaunched her from Rocky Neck at the age of forty-four, sound as ever.

During that interim after the first of the wars of modern civilization, when yachting in Gloucester Harbor was clubless, there occurred the most celebrated and Achillean case of sulk in the acrimonious annals of that clas-

The Henry Ford. *(Adolph Kupsinel photo, author's collection)*

sic of obstinacy, the International Fishermen's Races. The day was saved at "The Ramparts," and this is how it came about.

Gloucester's rivalry with Lunenberg, Nova Scotia, had commenced in 1920 when Captain Marty Welch and the schooner *Esperanto*, responding to the challenge of the *Halifax Herald*, sailed down and beat *Delawana* at Halifax and sailed back with the cup. With blood in their eyes, the Canadians built their matchless *Bluenose* next spring, and she recaptured the trophy from Gloucester's gallant little *Elsie* (*Esperanto* in the meanwhile was wrecked off Sable Island).

Come 1922, and the Yanks were hot for it. *Mayflower* had been ruled out of the competition as too yachty. The Burgess-designed *Puritan* was launched at Essex in March and, right after her, Captain Clayton Morrissey's *Henry Ford*. In June *Puritan* was wrecked off Sable before she ever had a chance to show her stuff.

The second week in October the *Henry Ford* eliminated Captain Ben Pine's *Elizabeth Howard,* and the *Yankee* and *L. A. Dunton* of Boston, in the American trials, and *Bluenose* arrived. The tension was high already, and the match so widely touted that even Secretary of the Navy Edwin Denby was on deck.

On the very eve of the first race, scheduled for Saturday, October 21,

Captain Clayton Morrissey at the helm of the Henry Ford. (Adolph Kupsinel photo, author's collection)

the committee decided the *Ford*'s canvas exceeded the allowable limits specified in the trophy's deed of gift by 380 square feet, and Clayt had to round up a sail maker to work through the night cutting two cloths out of the leach of the mainsail and two and a half out of the foregafftopsail.

They raced the next day in light airs. After a false start that both Morrissey and Captain Angus Walters of *Bluenose* agreed to ignore, they sailed the course and the *Henry Ford* won. The international committee, however, had tried but failed to halt the boats after the start and deemed it no race. And then the committee had second thoughts, and instructed Morrissey to reduce his sail for a second time, by fifty-seven feet, which required doubling the seam of the main leach, making a sad piece of rag out of it in the opinion of his crew.

By Monday morning the *Ford*'s gang had worked up a good mad over the committee's fancy yacht rulings and refused to go on board and race. They wouldn't budge from the dock, and Morrissey wasn't pushing them, either.

Here was a fine how-do, when who should come tripping down to the wharf but Mrs. Jack Raymond, one of the Eastern Point swells, whose husband was a part-owner and a member of the American race committee. Pauline was a pretty well-known lady sailor by now, and she pleaded with the men to get aboard that vessel and take it out there and race it if only for the sake of sportsmanship and the good name of Gloucester.

Nothing doing. Secretary Denby harangued but was no more able to talk the men into sailing than he would be two years later trying to convince Congress that the oil leases he had signed with Doheny and Sinclair were legal. So Pauline had another go at it, and this time she really gave it to them.

No one spoke. No one moved. Then Captain Clayt muttered tersely: "Come on, boys, let's go. Get that mainsail on and let's get started."

They raced, and the *Henry Ford* won again, this time officially. Captain Walters was reported to have said he'd go along with two out of three, counting the first, and this made two for the Ford. So good and early Tuesday morning Morrissey had the lumpers loading the ballast back. To hell with the committee. His was a moral victory, and Angus agreed, and he was going fishing. Fishermen's races should be run by fishermen and not by a bunch of yachtsmen.

Faced with an international incident in the making, the committee was up against it. Somehow Clayt and the boys had to be sweet-talked into sticking with it. But how? Certainly not in the atmosphere of agitation and partisanship that pervaded the streets and wharves and bars of Gloucester.

Then Jack Raymond put in a phone call to "The Ramparts," where his mother and sister Hilda were staying later than usual for the time of year. Could he bring a bunch to dinner? The crew of the *Ford?* Oh, a coupla dozen or so.

This took Mrs. Raymond somewhat aback, as most of the servants had departed. But she consented, and they went at it, the dowager in the kitchen

and her daughter in the dining room, and when Jack and Pauline brought in Captain Morrissey and his crew of fishermen, "The Ramparts" was ready.

Hilda waited on table, and as her brother had instructed, poured each guest two fingers of Prohibition whisky to start off with. Each in turn threw his head back and downed it neat, much to her wonderment. The reporter from The Associated Press turned up at the door in the middle of dinner, and Mrs. Raymond imprisoned him in the kitchen under her matriarchal gaze lest he upset the apple cart.

After dinner Jack and Clayt Morrissey and the crew of the American challenger sat before the fire in the big room for some time, and Hilda did not hear what transpired; her mother convoyed the AP man to a distant part of the mansion, under house detention.

About an hour before midnight, it was later reported, Clayt put it to them: "Well boys, what do you say?" And they voted to a man to stand by him and the *Ford*, and then they were driven back to Gloucester where the anxious crowds were still knotted in the streets as if awaiting news of war or the outcome of a royal lying-in.

The exact nature of what had transpired that evening at "The Ramparts" was not disclosed, but the news that the *Ford* would race again drove the excitement to a higher pitch than ever. Several of the men who'd been out to the Point talked knowingly of "the money that was bet" on the

Gloucester's three-hundredth anniversary race, August 31, 1923. Schooner Henry Ford, *center, won over* Elizabeth Howard, *right.* USS Shawmut *is between the two. Stern at right margin belongs to* USS Langley, *the Navy's first aircraft carrier, a converted collier. (Henry Williams photo, private collection)*

race, and two of them told one street corner gathering that "everything was explained to us at the dinner. Now we're going out and fight and win!" Another, Captain John Matheson, told people the men had decided to go on with the game to satisfy the public desire for more races until a winner had been officially declared.

And that was the way it finished. Next morning, early, the lumpers hove the ballast back on shore, and the *Henry Ford* sailed again. But the breeze was strong from the southwest, to the liking of the heavy-weather *Bluenose,* and she won easily. How much the *Ford*'s cut-down sails crippled her it was hard to say. The day after, the *Bluenose* won again and took the series, two out of three officially.

Gloucester went down, but her colors were flying. Credit the Raymonds and "The Ramparts," and perhaps a few fingers of stuff that got by the Coast Guard.[3]

The sharp-prowed mosquito fleet of Midgets rewarmed the racing blood around Gloucester Harbor, and the races Jack Raymond arranged in late August 1923 for the city's three hundredth anniversary celebration brought it to a boil.

The Raymond launch Mistral, *Captain Jensen at the helm, 1925. (Madeleine Williams)*

Riding a wave of enthusiasm, a group of Eastern Pointers met on September 9 with the aim of reviving organized yachting: John Greenough, Mr. and Mrs. Jonathan S. Raymond, Frederic W. Rhinelander II, Philip M. Tucker and Edward M. Williams, joined later by William V. MacDonald.

This was the nascent Eastern Point Yacht Club. They looked over the field of one-designs and settled on a boat that originated in Germany in 1905, the Sonder—somewhat past its vogue, but readily available by reason of that, and a very fast racing machine.

Jack Raymond, Ben Colby and Jack Mehlman (who had retired from the police force in 1922 after being badly knifed by a drunk he was collaring) were delegated to find boats. Next spring (1924) the nucleus of the fleet began building around the purchase of *Panther* by Bishop Rhinelander; *Bandit,* an ex-Manchester Sonder of vintage circa 1908, by Edward Williams; *Olita II* by Jonathan Raymond; *Hevella,* German-built, by Philip

Tucker; *Shamrock* by Isaac Patch; and *Vim*, a Marblehead boat that was one of the three American winners of the races with Germany at Marblehead in 1906, by John Greenough.

The design of these craft was guided most liberally by the Sonder Rule, which when it broke on the yachting world "caused almost as much excitement as a new girl in a mining camp,"[4] and was essentially as follows: the sum of waterline length, beam and draft should not exceed 32 feet, nor mast height 45 feet, nor sail area 550 square feet, and displacement shall be no less than 4,035 pounds.

Most of the Sonders were skimmers—scows flat and furiously fast. The rule allowed a wide range of design, obviously, and rigs varied from cat to sloop and gaff to marconi. Some were much swifter than others, but skill could prevail nonetheless.

Mrs. Emma Raymond loaned her bathhouse at the end of Wharf Beach and her landing

The Williams's Sonder class Bandit, 1925, runs off Black Bess Point. (Madeleine Williams)

at the stone wharf for the first activities in June 1924, and on the twenty-eighth the newly organized Eastern Point Yacht Club, refashioned from the fragments of the Gloucester, and before that East Gloucester, and before that Cape Ann yacht clubs, held its maiden race.

The course that inaugural day was from Quarry Cove to the Norman's Woe bell buoy to the whistler, back around the bell buoy and home. The breeze was light from the southeast. *Olita*, Jack Mehlman at the helm, led all the way and won in 1:30:03, *Hevella, Vim* and *Bandit* at his heels.

Bandit, confesses Ted Williams in *A Varied Life*, fared badly under any weather conditions.

> We struggled through two seasons, ending up last each time. Father was not to be denied. He got in touch with Starling Burgess and asked him to build a Sonder boat suitable for Gloucester and Marblehead waters. Burgess was at first reluctant. "Any boat I

A Sonder rounds the mark, 1925. (Madeleine Williams)

build for you," he said, "will be so much faster than the rest of this aged fleet that it will be no fun for you."

This did not deter Father one whit. "Build it," he said, and build it Burgess did, ordering the construction at Abeking and Rasmussen in Germany. The boat arrived and we sailed off in a burst of glory, only to finish last in her maiden race. The poor performances continued in ensuing races. We tried different jib leads, different crews, and even different skippers.

Finally a friend suggested we get in touch with George Owen, well-known yacht designer and professor at M.I.T. Owen came down, sailed the boat and finished with a very poor performance. He said the kindest thing he could say about Starling Burgess was that he had never seen the design and that he had probably turned it over to some draftsman. It had a stern designed for light weather performance and a bow for heavy weather.

Burgess had originally promised to come to Eastern Point to help us tune up the boat. Since he never showed up (he had just signed a contract to build the cup defender *Enterprise*), Father withheld the last payment of the bill, whereupon Burgess without notification sent the sheriff out to attach the boat each race day.

Fortunately, the sheriff was assigned by mistake to our old boat, the *Bandit,* which was just lying at anchor anyway. So he sat there during races every Wednesday and Saturday smoking a big black cigar while we sailed off in the new boat *Buccaneer* hoping somehow to win a race. The dispute was finally adjudicated by Burgess agreeing to cancel the disputed bill provided Father purchased a new suit of Ratsey sails.

Competitively, Pauline Pollard Raymond was of the lore. One Marblehead Race Week Henry Williams was drafted to crew for her in the Raymond Sonder *Hevella.*

> Just the two of us aboard when Charley Ahlquist comes about on a port tack with Mr. Greenough's Sonder. We were on a starboard tack, it was close, and I says to Mrs. Jack, "We are on a collision course." Says she, "I know it, and I will show you how to fix that squarehead!" Fifteen seconds later the *Hevella* was on Charley's foredeck, his starboard shrouds and jib sheet snapped. Charley, who thought he could bluff her and make her bear off, and who would normally curse and roar like a lion, never peeped. He and his son run down the mainsail and made ready to rope down the wire shrouds, and headed for the harbor.
>
> "That, Henry," quoth Mrs. Jack, "is how it is done.[5]

Indeed, during one final series when Pauline's sister Elise went forward to help her male crew set the spinnaker and tumbled overboard, Pauline sailed on by in *Olita* and went on to win but was disqualified for failing to pluck her sibling from the briny.

Young Ike Patch, on the other hand, took it all with a grain of salt, as he recalled in *Closing the Circle:*

> The crackerjack skipper of that whole bunch was probably Jack Mehlman, a crotchety and ornery man when I met him. "Money has spoiled you," he used to tell me. "Learning to race is no picnic." Ben Colby, a rigger and sailmaker by trade, taught me the finer points of racing. Seated behind me as I handled

The master hand himself, Officer Jack Mehlman, in flop hat. (Dorothy Mehlman DeCoste)

the tiller of the *Shamrock,* Ben would advise me to "Keep her up! Keep her off! Take advantage of the puffs!" Ben used to say as we sailed along, "only a plank between us and eternity." Ever the optimist, Ben's attempt to run a boat business met with failure, and Jim Walen never let me forget the "three-minute bow" Ben added to the *Shamrock.* The Sonder's new bow, which ended up costing my father $800, was supposed to speed up the boat by three minutes; instead, it cost us a couple of minutes. At age sixty-five, Ben (using his hands and feet) could walk up the wire shrouds of our racing boat.

And the tobacco-chewing Waldo Brazier, who drank his whiskey straight. In the summer of 1932 Waldo was with me aboard the *Shamrock* when a thunderstorm came up in the middle of a race. "Don't take down the sails!" he boomed, whiskey bottle in hand. "Let 'er go!" With a gale behind us, we jibed around the last mark, tore along in a following sea, and passed the other boats which had taken down their sails.

Lieutenant Leonard Melka had embarked from the ramp of the Coast Guard Air Station at Ten Pound Island and was taxiing his amphibian down the harbor into the southwesterly. It was a routine flight, a beautiful twelfth of September in 1928, and all his controls checked out. Just abreast of the breakwater he gave her the gas and they were "on the step"—aloft, but with not speed enough yet to climb.

The engine sputtered. Melka shouted to mechanic Wesley Saunders, behind him in the cockpit, to take over while he checked his instruments. They were now skimming a few feet above the sea.

The pilot found that one of his twelve cylinders was misfiring; later it proved to be due to a broken rocker arm. When he looked up, he saw to his consternation that they were headed straight for a sailboat.

It was *Tid III,* one of six Sonders that had just got under way for the start of the EPYC ladies' series on the windward leg toward the mark off Manchester. Paula Patch had taken the place of Mrs. Groverman Ellis, who usually had the helm of the Leonard boat, and for crew she had her brother, Isaac, Jr., and two other boys, Townsend and Franklin Hill. The fleet was about a quarter of a mile off the breakwater.

The astonished pilot jerked back on his stick, throttled and banked hard to starboard. The crippled amphibian roared down on *Tid,* struggling valiantly to climb, and as it banked, the port wing tip snapped the sloop's gaff near the peak, parted the halyard and ripped the head of the mainsail to shreds.

"We gazed speechless at one another," recalls Ike Patch. "If we had had the wit, we would have jumped overboard, but there was no time to think!"

The seaplane roared on and almost stalled, but Lieutenant Melka, unaware he had even flicked the boat, was able to swing back into the harbor and touch down. The shaking crew of *Tid* brought their winged craft about and ran under their jib for the mooring in Lighthouse Cove.

Paula's Uncle Piatt Andrew fired off an angry congressional wire to the Coast Guard commandant in Washington demanding reparations and firm steps to prevent a recurrence of such an outrage. They all made the headlines next day.

"The daring of the girl captain and her remarkable skill as a sailor," reported the *Boston Globe,* "saved the boat from being capsized."

It goes almost without saying that the first commodore of the nascent Eastern Point Yacht Club, by acclamation, was the venerable John Greenough, whose energy and appearance belied his seventy-eight years. Commodore Greenough presided benignly at those early bathhouse meetings, the members on the benches or sprawled on the floor. His vice commodore was William V. MacDonald, who added *Lady,* the seventh Sonder, to the fleet that July. Captain Jensen, caretaker of "The Ramparts," fired the start and finish guns from *Ichthus*—the *Itch*—the committee launch donated by Mrs. Margaret Brady Farrell.[6]

An eighteen-foot centerboard sloop produced by the Cape Cod Shipbuilding Company in the early 1920s, the Cape Cod Baby Knockabout, had established itself as a racing class by 1935 and was an apt boat for youngsters, with the small jib and weather helm that brought it head to every puff. The Gloucester Midgets had served their purpose by 1926, having revived yachting in the harbor; no more were built after Archibald Fenton's death, and for all their charm, they were tender and slow to answer the helm. That year five Cape Cod Knockabouts were added to the squadron, largely for the benefit of the neophytes.

Wide variations in performance under the Sonder Rule, the advancing age of the boats and the desirability of further diversifying the fleet had the leaders of the club on the lookout for a new class of true one-designs. Their search ended at the drawing board of the superlative Boston designer John G. Alden, whose *Malabars,* small sisters of the Gloucester schooners, were famous already.

They found the Triangle, one of the loveliest marconi sloops ever to grace the waters of New England. The Triangles were conceived by Alden in 1925 and built by James E. Graves at Marblehead, where the class shared its origin with Annisquam. In 1927 five new Triangles were raced at Squam, and that summer EPYC made the decision to adopt the class. Eight were on order for Eastern Point at the beginning of the 1928 season, and it was concluded that the day had arrived at last to officially retire the Midgets from racing.

Rigid specifications governed the Triangles. Dimensions were 28'5" overall, 18'5" waterline, 7'6" beam and 49" depth. They were required to be built from Graves's original molds; unfortunately these were destroyed in a fire, and Triangles from the new molds were said to be somewhat inferior. Graves licensed some to be built at Jamestown, Rhode Island. Sails had to be cut at a designated loft, only one suit per season, and every effort was made to prevent boats from being sold outside the racing clubs.

The late Laurence A. Brown, Jr., a master at the helm himself, told the story of one young Eastern Point lady who just couldn't persuade her Triangle to get going and at her wit's end talked Ben Colby into taking a diagnostic spin with her. Colby took the helm, and she the sheets. In a jiffy the boat was speeding through the water as if hexed, and he allowed as how he was getting about all the boat had to give. Whereupon fair lady, ecstatic, prepared to mark the exact positions of the sheets in the cleats with bits of colored thread.

"Well, you could," said Ben. "The condition of your bottom and the cut of your sails and the way they're sheeted all have something to do with it — but young lady, it's who you got hangin' onto the end of your tiller that counts.'"

Indeed the Triangles were the ultimate test in their time of helmsmanship—nicely shaped to Gloucester conditions, as able on the outside course as inside, in heavy weather or the featheriest of harbor airs. The fleet grew to sixteen in the 1930s. C. Hastings Gamage, in *Injun,* was acknowledged the champion "Point-grown" Triangle sailor, followed closely by Robert W. Sides. Skill flowed from East Gloucester and Rocky Neck to the Point, from the weathered mitts of Mehlman and Colby and that crowd of hard-sailing Gloucestermen to the eager young hands of the Pointers. And the exciting high mark in the heyday of the Triangles, as it had been with the Sonders, was the annual Professional Skippers Race "for those who have been instrumental in instructing the less experienced members." Contestants drew their boats by lot an hour before the starting gun, and winners included such masters at the tiller as Al Bates, Russell Young, father and son Scott and Doug Parker, Carl Sampson, and brothers Jim and Kirk Walen.

Graves discontinued building Triangles as the depression wore on. One
after another the aging beauties were retired from the postwar scene. By
1970 racing of these handsome antiques had ceased. For three years in the
early 1970s I had *Goblin,* the sweetest boat I ever owned and the last of the
Triangles in Gloucester Harbor.

*Triangles!
(Edward
Williams)*

For five years the Eastern Point Yacht Club had sailed out of Mrs.
Raymond's bathhouse at Lighthouse Cove, but Commodore Greenough
and his older cohorts were watching the membership grow and the stock
market rise, and they pined for the halcyon days of their prewar establishment at Rocky Neck. And so it was decreed in this better-than-ever year of
1929 that conditions couldn't be more propitious for the club to have its
own house. Philip Tucker took on the job.

Commodore Greenough, tall and erect, with his flowing white mustache, was the epitome of all that was good and true and of the old values,
and with such affection was he regarded in his eighty-fourth year that the
starting line was shifted to broad off Niles Beach so he could get a clear view
from his veranda of the jockeying for position.

At the end of August the club purchased the Beachcroft Hotel at the
north end of Niles Beach, and the affected residents advanced the funds to
acquire the balance of the beach and rights to it for $37,500.

The yacht club announced that a $50,000 clubhouse would be built on
the site of the hotel's old circular bathhouse—a spacious, three-deck, half-

timbered English manor type designed by Woodbury and Stuart, architects of Boston. Out from this edifice would be thrust a 200-foot pier on Stone caissons, terminating in a "gunhouse" surmounted by a Norman Gothic tower that the architects said harked back to the castle in Spain from which Vasco do Gama took his departure in 1497 (he left from Lisbon). From this formidable jump-off it was planned to extend floats another 110 feet into the harbor.

Precisely two months to the day after this announcement the stock market collapsed. But prosperity died hard on Eastern Point. Philip Tucker pursued his plans (rather scaled down), and that winter the money was found to purchase almost the entire Wonson Field between the gate lodge and the Hawthorne Inn from Mrs. Marion Wonson Walen. The Claflin cottage situated therein, "Rockmere," was adapted for the clubhouse, a landing was put out in the spring, and on Saturday the twenty-first of June, 1930, it was dedicated.

Overhead fluttered the new burgee. Inside, Commodore Greenough confided to a packed house his satisfaction at the club's growth to 130 members and a flotilla of 43 boats. And like old times, Steward Jack Mehlman dished out the chowder.

Yes, prosperity, or the appearance of it, or the belief in its return, or its momentum, hung on at Eastern Point. Unlike old times, the club was exclusive now, the possession of the rich. The fleet at the opening of the 1931 season dressed up the down-and-out old fishing port with sixteen Triangles, fourteen Sonders, twelve Cape Cod Knockabouts, eleven power boats, six miscellaneous sailboats, and a new class of three R boats, rated between seventeen and twenty feet on the water, long and sleek with all sorts of allowable variations.

John Wing Prentiss, for one, was not the man to lose confidence in the resiliency of the system, and it struck him and some of his New York associates this summer of 1931 that The Beachcroft could be turned to good account when its lease expired (now that the club owned it) by converting it

WOODBURY & STUART ARCHIT
COPLEY SQ BOSTON

into a private hotel-club for yachtsmen, its doors invitingly open in the direction of the New York Yacht Club.

Thus Colonel Prentiss picked up the standard first raised by Commodore Rouse in his efforts to get the NYYC to establish a cruising station at Gloucester, and fifteen years later by the same William Astor of the great schooner yacht *Ambassadress* who had vainly sought to buy Stage Fort for the same purpose. Prentiss was just as unsuccessful.

By 1932 even the most optimistic were playing it close to the belt with their venture money, and the newspaper lamented with an almost audible sigh that the Eastern Point Yacht Club's grand plans were on ice until "the return of the happy days."[7]

President Roosevelt jovially accepts painting from artist Emile Gruppe with delegation of Gloucester skippers aboard schooner yacht Amberjack II *at anchor inside Eastern Point breakwater, June 21, 1933, en route down east on vacation cruise. (Author's collection)*

~39~
THESE PARLOUS TIMES

THAT THE GREAT DEPRESSION WAS having its effects on the habits even of Gloucester's gold coast was hinted by the Eastern Point correspondent for the *Cape Ann Shore* on July 16, 1932:

> We note the growth of the morning marketing practice "in person" along the main street—long a practice of the southern woman. "She looketh well to the welfare of her household," perhaps not the exact quotation but its essence. Particularly applicable in these parlous times.

The times were parlous indeed when Point dowagers preempted Elsie and the chauffeur on the forenoon errands over town—watching the pennies and trusting, one supposes, that the dollars would continue taking care of themselves.

Three thousand unemployed drifted through those same streets that winter, and Howard Blackburn—seventy-three and ailing—started a relief fund with $100 to the Fishermen's Institute for 250 meal tickets.

A resentful, defensive consciousness of class was abroad in the land. Eastern Point looked to its welfare behind the ramparts of wealth, social antisepsis, the gate and the law. Neither charity nor noblesse oblige nor the democratizing influence of the morning marketing could bridge the deepening chasm.

In the hundred days since his inauguration, the one man who was having some success straddling the extremes—and enjoying it—had come to be viewed with a crescendo of horror by his class, though he hadn't yet been cast out entirely. It had been an exhausting, exhilarating honeymoon with Congress, cranking up the New Deal and deploying the forces of the unexpected that so frightened the Haves of America, and *That Man* deserved to rest on the 101st day.

An easterly cruise to the family watering place at Campobello was in order, and in the third week of June, 1933, Franklin D. Roosevelt embarked from Marion, Massachusetts, with son James and a crew of two in *Amberjack II,* an able forty-six-foot schooner that had crossed the Atlantic and returned the year she was built, 1931, chartered from Paul D. Rust, Jr. For company they had the destroyers *Comanche* and *Ellis.* The commander-in-chief of the armed forces had planned to put in at Provincetown for the night of the twentieth, but he had a fair wind and abruptly decided to bypass it, to the disappointment of the local politicians.

Amberjack reached across the bay to Gloucester and dropped her hook inside the breakwater at ten minutes to midnight, almost incognito. (Captain Ben Pine had gone out to greet the presidential convoy in the schooner *Gertrude L. Thebaud* fourteen miles off the Point but kept a discreet distance away in the dark for fear one of the escorts might get jumpy in the blackness and take a pot shot at him). The destroyers anchored farther in on the Pancake Ground.

Congressman A. Piatt Andrew next morning from "Red Roof" could see *Amberjack* in the lee of the breakwater, and when he judged his student from Harvard days had breakfasted, he had himself rowed out and gave a hail to see if he was welcome aboard.

He certainly was, and later the congressman confided to newsreporters that down below he found the president in his bunk, still wearing pajamas, reading the paper, with son Jimmy lounging about in the same attire. "Hello Piatt!" FDR sang out with his usual jauntiness, and the greeting was immortalized in the local headlines that afternoon.[1]

They had a mug-up, and whether teacher took student to task for what he considered the utter folly of his playful manipulations with the currency was not revealed by the judicious legislator. The friendly foes enjoyed a gam over old times, though, and a good chuckle over the snapshot Doc brought along, taken at "Red Roof" that day of May in 1903, showing young FDR third man up on his prof's human totem pole.

After twenty minutes Congressman Andrew returned ashore to Eastern Point. Ben Pine sailed out with a deckload of dignitaries aboard the *Thebaud,* and a delegation was rowed over to *Amberjack* to return the courtesy to the president that he and British Prime Minister Ramsay MacDonald had paid the racing schooner when they greeted her in Washington after she had sailed up the Potomac in April to play up the hard times of the fishing industry.

At noon Skipper Roosevelt upped anchor and, to his delight and the high alarm of his naval escort that had to steam around the outside of Cape Ann, steered *Amberjack* through the Annisquam River to the eastward on the next leg of his vacation.

The peninsula whose lee had sheltered the chief executive for the night was as well buffered as any geographical or social unit in the country against the economic buffets that brought him to power. The fortunes of the summer residents of Eastern Point suffered but in the main survived the shrinkage, and enough remained after the exigencies of the morning marketing to maintain the simple leisures of the afternoon and evening such as sailing, bathing, tennis, a bit of golf, a round of croquet, tea (for "benefit" or no), the garden party, and by the end of 1933, the legal cocktail blast. A minimum of real estate was mortified by foreclosure, although new construction was stopped almost dead, but not quite.

Like a crocus in the snow (or the last rose of summer), an elegant shape took form amidst the shambles of the economy during the spring of 1930 on the ground above Niles Beach. It was a brick porticoed mansion conceived on a splendid scale in what might be described as "White House revival"—an undoubted monument to sound money and such a testimonial to the faith and fortune of its creator as to revive in the eye and mind of the passerby some momentary feeling, at least, of confidence in the system.

This cheerful seashore seat was said to have cost $200,000 in depression money. And when it was completed in midsummer of 1931, the measured landscaping of the grounds and the promise of the gardens that were beginning to float down to the harbor left the impression that the owner desired to share his optimism with all who saw, on land and wave.[2]

Clarence ("Bob") Birdseye in June 1929 had received about $1 million for his patents for the quick-freeze process he had developed in Gloucester that was turning the food industry upside down. One of his future executives was asked to lunch at Gloucester's Hotel Savoy the next February by the newly wealthy inventor.

Clarence Birdseye, 1955. (Barbara Erkkila)

> He drove us to the hotel in a Model A Ford coupe and then phoned his wife to bring down the Packard 8. After lunch Mr. Birdseye drove us along the shoreline and pointed out a beautiful home lot on the ocean. He remarked: "All my life I have desired a Packard 8 car and that property. Now I have them."[3]

Bob Birdseye meant it. Another associate wrote that "one of the first things Bob did when his wealth was assured was to build a beautiful new home and to buy, not one, but three cars for his family. *He* drove his old Ford!"[4]

An unpredictable mixture. Though born in Brooklyn in 1886,

Mrs. Post's 316-foot four-masted barque Sea Cloud, *flying 36,000 square feet of sail, at anchor off Ten Pound Island (under her bowsprit).* Sea Cloud *today is in the luxury cruise trade. (Author's collection)*

he was almost the stereotypical Yankee, a graduate of Amherst College, field naturalist with the U.S. Biological Survey from 1908 to 1912, adventurer, tinkerer, outdoorsman and fur trader in Labrador. In 1915 he married Eleanor Gannett, daughter of a founder of the National Geographic Society, who throve on roughing it, and a good thing, for he carried her off to the frozen north for a fling as a trapper, traveling that hard coast by dog team and buying furs from the natives in competition with the Hudson's Bay Company while she tended their winter trap line.

Birdseye found he could preserve cabbage indefinitely by putting it up in brine and exposing the barrels to the freezing winds. In like manner they froze up a winter's supply of duck, rabbit and caribou meat.

In 1917 they returned from the tundra and he was hired as assistant purchasing agent for Stone & Webster in Washington and in 1918 as purchasing agent for the U.S. Housing Corporation.

His next job as an investigator for the U.S. Fisheries Association from 1919 to 1923 so disgusted him with the inefficiency and filth involved in the distribution of iced fish that he got the idea of combining what he had learned so pragmatically in Labrador with existing quick-freeze techniques for bulk-processing fish. The Birdseyes pooled their insurance and savings, moved to Gloucester in 1924 and formed the General Seafoods Corporation in 1925 in W. T. Gamage's Fort Wharf building.

Not long after, Marjorie Merriweather Post, the already rich daughter of the founder of Postum Cereals and then in her late thirties, steamed into

Gloucester on one of her yachts for provisioning and was served with a goose for dinner that was so consummately tasty and tender that she sought out her chef in the ship's galley to determine its provenance.

He told her he'd bought the bird from a small plant on shore where the owner had the novel idea of freezing food quickly to preserve it. The goose had been frozen for several months.

Mrs. Post immediately urged her second husband, Edward F. Hutton, to go ashore with her and interview the owner of the plant. The owner's name was Clarence Birdseye. She was impressed with the Birdseye method, but her husband was not.

At that time—1926—Birdseye and his frozen foods were on the verge of bankruptcy and the venture could have been picked up for a bargain $2 million. But it was three years before Mrs. Post could persuade her board of directors, which included her husband, to invest in Birdseye. By that time, Birdseye had weathered his financial problems, and the Postum Cereal Company had to pay ten times what Birdseye had originally asked to buy him out.

After the addition of Birdseye Frozen Foods, the name of the Postum Cereal Company was changed to General Foods Corporation.

It took another seven years before Mrs. Post's faith in the future of frozen foods was justified. . . . But eventually her judgment was vindicated, and General Foods [a name Birdseye invented in anticipation of dominating his industry as GE and GM did theirs] became a multimillion dollar enterprise.[5]

In spite of his meager technological background, Clarence Birdseye was granted more than a hundred patents. An associate saw him as "a combination of a superb restless mind, an insatiable curiosity, enormous persistence, and the total lack of mental blocks. He was an impatient man and had little interest in the routine affairs involved in running the business. Once a problem was solved, he was eager to turn to something new."[6]

This archetype of the American native genius once received a $120,000 option on a dehydrated food process. He developed and then sold outright a store-window spotlight. He invented and for a while marketed a long-life light bulb, and an infrared heat lamp, and a harpoon for marking whales in their migration. And it was while he was in Peru looking for a way to make paper out of the native agave plant that he first suffered the angina that restricted his outdoor activity in later life.

A keen sportsman, he loved hunting so much (he was a good cook, too) that he built a shooting gallery in his Eastern Point basement, and he deep-sea fished from his cruiser *Sealoafer.*

Poor health forced Birdseye in his last years (he died in 1956) to squeeze the outdoors into manageable proportions—and into a gem of a little book that he and his wife drew from the mutuality of their experience, *Growing Woodland Plants.* From the preface:

The 85-foot drag-
ger Red Skin, for-
merly the
Governor
Saltonstall and a
World War II
minesweeper,
broke loose from
her wharf in a
northeast storm
on January 3,
1948, and fetched
up on Black Bess
Point. An ocean
tug finally got her
off after three
days, seven
pumps going.
(Gloucester Daily
Times)

We moved to Gloucester, Massachusetts, and Eleanor joined a garden club. Soon she began identifying wildflowers and ferns of which I knew nothing. That was bad for family discipline—for I was supposed to be the naturalist of the clan. About that time, too, a gale wrecked my 40-foot offshore fishing boat and abruptly ended my hobby of placing migration markers in 60-foot, 50-ton finback wales. Simultaneously, a developing case of angina pectoris imperiously suggested a less strenuous form of outdoors recreation.

So suddenly and completely, I ceased to be a horny-handed harpooner and became a babysitter for the gentle maidenhair and dainty ladyslipper. . . . More important, while seasickness had kept Eleanor from joining me in whaling, we have been able to pursue our wildflower hobby together for a score of years.

Their special pride beyond the pale of their formal gardens was their wildflower retreat near the road, with twenty-eight varieties of wild fern, a cameo lily pond with goldfish, and a Visitors Welcome sign. For nearly fourteen years Andrea Barletta was their gardener, raising all the plants from seedlings, one season putting out forty dozen petunias, 402 begonias, 200 dahlias and a great variety of marigolds, zinnias, roses and others.

Mrs. Birdseye, who was president of the Gloucester Garden Club, used to have members come over, and one day someone asked Mr. Birdseye to identify a fern. He didn't know the name, so he studied wild plants and learned the names and characteristics. We had twenty kinds of ferns, Dutchmans breeches, Mayapple and lady's slipper. I used to go into the Southern Woods and find plants like the cowslip and wild aster.[7]

How Clarence Birdseye loved Gloucester! Whenever and wherever he was away, to savor his food he carried with him a vial of healthful salt dehydrated from his own harbor.

The tide was ebbing, and the little sunbrowned grandchildren built their ramparts of sand on the glistening beach behind it.

Joanna Davidge Randall-MacIver died at their home in Rome on May 15, 1931. She and David had spent their last summer at the Point in 1929. Her husband buried her in the Roman cemetery thirty yards from the grave of her favorite poet, Shelley.

When my Joanna left me it did not seem a moment for grief. Rather all sense of personal loss, and all recollection of small details, seemed to fade before the impression of heroic greatness. It was a great soul that I had known, and I had been privileged to study its very essence. . . .

Of all the things that Joanna taught us I think one lesson stands out clear beyond any others. Life is very beautiful, and it was given us by God to enjoy; sorrow must come and it must be faced, and the sorrow of others demands our deepest sympathy. But with this, and above all, it is the beauty everywhere around us that we must recognize and that it is a sin against our very being to ignore it. Such a glorious creed and such a noble soul cannot be forgotten; to have known her is to be convinced of immortality.[8]

The archeologist buried himself in his work in the prehistoric cultures of Scandinavia so deep that he read everything extant in Old Norse. In 1936 Dr. Randall-MacIver married Mrs. George M. Tuttle of New York. They moved from Florence to New York at the outbreak of World War II, when he assisted the War Department in selecting Italian monuments to be preserved from destruction. The gentle scholar died on April 30, 1945, at the age of seventy-one, and the Eastern Point cottage his Joanna had built in the hamlet of Dabsville was sold.[9]

Jack Mehlman, steward of the yacht club, the old cop, the chowder maker, the master hand at the tiller, died at seventy-one on January 21, 1934. And then it was dominoes.

On St. Patrick's Day the great stockman John Clay passed on, eighty-two, Master of the North Northumberland Foxhounds, Legend of the West

The Gloucester seiner Uncle Sam, *a 104-foot converted World War I subchaser, meets her end in the night fog south of "Blighty," July 24, 1938. (Author's collection)*

Laird of Finisterre. Then in April his neighbor across the cove, Keeper Gilbert Hay died in April, and the lantern he kept lit for thirteen years was passed to Carl Hill, up from Highland Light. Captain Charles Ahlquist, the ancient commodore's sailing master going on thirty-five years, died the next day.

Deeply affected, John Greenough from New York wrote a tribute to his shipmate for the Gloucester newspaper and the week after, on May 4, 1934, breathed his last himself. He was eighty-eight. Wished the paper: "May the commodore find friendly haven in the Fortunate Isles in the Ultimate Harbor."

In 1928, three years after Harry Sleeper had finished the interior decoration of "Chestertown," Henry du Pont's summer home on Long Island, du Pont commissioned him to do the new wing of his family home, "Winterthur," in Winterthur, Delaware. The job seemed to be proceeding well enough until Sleeper got the ultimate call, to California, in 1930 with a commission to do the Hollywood house of the popular film star John Mack Brown. No doubt, with the Depression on, he needed every new dollar for his constantly shifting schemes to invent and reinvent "Beauport."

The attempt to juggle his West Coast work, and other commissions in the East, with his commitment to "Winterthur" nettled du Pont, who proposed to penalize Sleeper financially. Harry got his back up. In August 1931 they parted company, and a briefly productive early chapter in American interior decorating came to an end. Some onus for this unnecessary breach can probably be laid to Sleeper's failing health, in and out of the hospital in Boston, New York and Baltimore with recurrent complaints of digestive problems and weakness.

In 1932 he was able to take on some commissions in Pennsylvania, then again in 1934 when he began work on R. T. Vanderbilt's "Green Farms" in Connecticut. He was in California that summer, probably doing the home of motion picture actor Frederic March and his wife in Beverly Hills, when he was taken ill and rushed home to the Massachusetts General Hospital in Boston, from which he wrote Morris Carter, director of the Gardner Museum, on August 21:

> Since we saw each other, I have been very near to the edge of the world, as you know, but at last I am on the upward turn. They will not let me see anyone, but as soon as they do, I want to see and hear you.[10]

A month later, on September 22, 1934, Henry Davis Sleeper died of leukemia. He was fifty-six. Eulogized Piatt Andrew:

> His fund of technical information, together with his impeccable taste, and his ingenuity in color and design, which was distinctly creative, brought him a countrywide reputation as an interior decorator, the evidences of whose skill remain today in many important homes from Maine to California.

Whether the American Field Service was the monument on which Harry would have preferred his epitaph or not, Doc praised it as the achievement that exceeded even his life work, which, "frail in body, and without any experience as an organizer, he undertook almost singlehanded at first. . . . What he lacked in experience in organization work was more than offset by his crusading spirit, his intuitive ingenuity and his tireless energy."[11]

Long before, Harry had reacted to Assistant Secretary Andrew's remonstrance that he did him too many favors.

> You have never asked very much of me, but, as I have always been fonder of you than of any other friend I've had, such few things as you have accepted from me have been a very potent factor in my happiness. In a world where each man is really so solitary, and inwardly on the defensive, by lack of faith in those about him, it would compensate for many disappointments if I knew you believed in my stability. I have no less an admiration now, for your fineness than I ever had, and am as eager now as I have ever been for your approval and affection. . . . [12]

"Little Beauport," forty haunting rooms of it at his death, and the gentle effects of this laboratory of taste on the aesthetics of his times—these are Sleeper's monuments. "Beauport's" guest book holds the testimony: a glitter of ambassadors, statesmen, senators, governors and capitalists, socialites, prima donnas, authors, artists, poets, musicians and sculptors, biographers, novelists and playwrights, idols of the matinee, stars of the stage and screen, dilettantes, aficionados, entrepreneurs, critics, climbers, connoisseurs, and doubtless a rascal or two.

"Beauport" brought its creator trusteeships of the Boston Museum of Fine Arts and the Isabella Stewart Gardner Museum, and it inspired Henry Francis du Pont to begin the collection of American antiques and interiors at Southampton, Long Island, in 1919 that was incomparably fulfilled in his Winterthur Museum in Delaware.

After Henry Sleeper's death his executors were besieged by collectors who wanted to buy everything from a single objet d'art to an entire room. Fortunately for those who regard him as the high priest of Americana and "Beauport" its temple, his house was discovered by Mr. and Mrs. Charles F. F. McCann of Oyster Bay while they were cruising in their 247-foot yacht *Chalena*. On October 21, 1935, Mrs. McCann, who was one of the daughters of F. W. "Woolworth," purchased "Beauport" substantially intact from the Sleeper estate for approximately $41,000, and the next running entry in the guest book was:

October 22, 1935
Helena W. McCann
Charles F. F. McCann
Chez nous "Beau Port" premier fois!

Helena McCann owned 565,000 shares of Woolworth common stock and was able to persuade the company to build an extra-special five-and-ten store on the site of the old post office at Main and Pleasant Streets in Gloucester. The heiress occasionally shopped there when she was staying at "Beauport," and one can imagine the flutter this raised with the manager and his sales clerks.

Less than three years after she bought "Beauport" Mrs. McCann died in New York on March 15, 1938. In 1942, her children, Constance, Frasier and Helena, presented "Beauport" to the Society for the Preservation of New England Antiquities, with an annual maintenance grant from the family's Winfield Foundation, as a memorial to their mother for the benefit and education of the public.

Eighteen months after Harry died, Doc returned to "Red Roof" from Washington to recover from influenza complicated by arteriosclerosis, in a state approaching collapse. On the third of June, 1936, at sixty-three, he suffered a fatal cerebral thrombosis. His nephew, Ike Patch, held his hand as he lay dying in the garden room at "Red Roof."

For fifteen years, since his first election to Congress and so easily after that he hardly bothered to campaign, Piatt Andrew had been in the thick of it. At first he was concerned with tariffs and the reduction of the Allies' war debts and the rights of veterans and the problems of the postwar immigration. He was conservative in his Republicanism, but independent. A strong supporter of a big navy, which made points with that former student now in the White House, and ardent for the repeal of Prohibition, he was at the same time a states' rightist, a sound money man and a fervent opponent of most of the New Deal domestic measures aimed at involving government in human welfare.

As he wanted it, the service was conducted by a minister, a priest and a rabbi, and his ashes were scattered over "Red Roof" from an airplane.[13]

Two years had not gone by when John Wing Prentiss died of a heart attack on the eighteenth of March, 1938, at sixty-two.

The tide was on the ebb.

The Gloucester seiner *Uncle Sam,* a 104-foot converted World War I sub chaser, was feeling her way through the fog near midnight on the twenty-fourth of July, 1938, bound home with 40,000 pounds of mackerel. Her diesel throbbed steadily, and most of the crew of thirteen were below.

And then, *crash,* and men and everything in a heap on the forecastle floor. She rose up on her bow in a splintering of plank and timber, and the sea poured in.

Mrs. Groverman Ellis heard the first crack against the ledge between her house and "Blighty," and the muffled beating of the engine going nowhere, and called the Coast Guard.

They came by land and sea, and the rest of that night Captain Sam Scola tried to save his vessel. The tide was going. He put some of the men at the pumps and the rest dumping the mackerel overboard. But after the tide turned, it was useless. The *Uncle Sam* broke up and filled with the flood, and the men abandoned ship for the shore by the light of the dawn coming up across the ocean.

Adolf Hitler invaded Austria, the Allies betrayed Czechoslovakia, Spain lay at the feet

Helena and Charles McCann. (Society for the Preservation of New England Antiquities)

of Franco, Germany and Russia signed a nonaggression treaty and on September 8, 1939, President Roosevelt proclaimed a limited national emergency.

Nine days after this anomalous state of the nation was declared, the 3,200-ton Norwegian freighter *Rio Branco,* in camouflage gray with her national colors painted on each side, was steaming along the coast, keeping close to avoid German U-boats. She was bound from Para, Brazil, for Boston under the command of Captain Thor Orvig with twenty-nine crew, five American passengers and 4,700 tons of cocoa beans, wheat bran, hides and rubber worth $300,000.

The Rio Branco, *all 3,200 tons of her, stuck fast off "Druimteac," September 1939. (John Adams photo, Gordon Thomas collection)*

The night was clear that Sunday the seventeenth of September, and the tide was high. A few minutes before 3:00 A.M. the watch spotted a light. Thinking it must be the entrance to Boston Harbor, the helmsman swung her in toward it, and before another order could be given, there was an appalling crunch of plates against rock and screech of wounded steel and clanging of bells and Norwegian oaths and American curses. The *Rio Branco* was hard and fast upon the ledge, 300 feet in front of Arthur Leonard's "Druimteac."

The light the watch had seen, of course, was Eastern Point; the freighter was twenty miles off the beam.

A late-staying resident heard the frantic toots of distress piercing the early morning darkness and phoned the Coast Guard. Patrol boats came

around and took the passengers off, and Sunday morning they were joined by six tugs from Boston. All eight strained at the *Rio Branco* from astern, but she wouldn't budge.

The crowds from near and far caused such a traffic jam and threat to property that the police had to ban autos from the Point.

The ebbing tide had impaled the freighter on the rock, which might have done more damage save for her double bottom. But still the pumps couldn't keep up with it, and by the second day the first three holds were filling. A mounting swell from the northeast ground the vessel against the ledge with every surge. Merritt, Chapman and Scott, the salvagers, put in an SOS for lighters from New York.

The Lavender Lady, Caroline Sinkler, eighty-six. (Caroline Sidney Lockwood)

On the morning of the twentieth, her fourth day of impalement, with nine feet of water in her burst forward compartment, they started lightening her. The men hoisted up 3,000 bags of cocoa beans and bran, slit them open and jettisoned the contents—225 tons of cocoa and bran that mushed into a brown blanket on the sea, oozing and undulating up and down the shore.

At high water that day the tugs carried four anchors out a distance from her stern and dropped them, and *Rio Branco* tried to kedge herself off with her winches, but it was no good.

The New York lighters arrived alongside. Over the next three days, and by floodlight at night, they took off another 3,000 tons of cargo. The curious kept coming, leaving their cars before the gate and hiking a mile over the roads and through the brush to observe the plight of the gray freighter and the toils of its rescuers.

By evening of Saturday the twenty-third, her seventh day on the rocks, the salvagers were ready. Suction pumps, twelve and six inches in diameter, were started up in the ruptured holds and were able to keep ahead of the inrushing sea. Four kedge anchors were carried off her stern as before, and the big salvage tug *Peacock* put a hawser aboard.

At 7:30 p.m. on the high tide, pumps, kedges, winches and tug all strained together, and *Rio Branco* slid off the ledge and floated. Her pumps disgorging torrents of water, she steamed around the Point under her own power and anchored 200 yards off Niles Beach over sandy bottom (just in case.) Three more days, and the greatest ship ever to go ashore on Cape Ann proceeded to Boston for drydocking.

The last link to the Niles Farm, James C. Walen, on his ninety-eighth birthday, June 2, 1970. Cap'n Jim died on August 8. (Author photo)

The last links to the Associates— the sisters Winifred Kay Shepard and Jean Kay Burgess, 1960. (Sarah Fraser Robbins)

It was the eve of autumn, 1939. In the rambling house with the garden that looked out over the breakwater and across to the horizon of the sea, Bishop Rhinelander died. He was seventy. The twenty-first of September.

Captain Howard Jensen hoisted his last flag over "The Ramparts" in 1940.

And then the war. Some went off, and some remained and did their bit their way, among them Mrs. Helen Patch, Doc's redoubtable sister and a considerable organizer in her own right, as Constance Rhinelander told it:

> Mrs. Patch got up a women's defense corps to defend Gloucester when the Germans should come to blow up the Cut Bridge. She got Mrs. Sargent of Manchester in with her on it and Ann Robinson and others, and they worked up a sort of "taxicab army," inventorying the cars of summer people that were put up on blocks during the winter, so as to be on hand to evacuate Cape Ann in case of attack.
>
> Ann braced Bamma [the Bishop's wife] to have the Rhinelander car left on its wheels with gas in the tank, but her chauffeur scotched the idea—said it would ruin the tires.

Still painting, Cecilia Beaux died in her "Green Alley" on September 17, 1942. She was seventy-nine.

Mrs. Samuel Atwater Raymond, the mistress of "The Ramparts," died in 1943. She was eighty-nine.

World War II fought itself out. Some of the men, and the boys, returned; some didn't. Young Jonathan ("Jock") Raymond, born just before the end of World War I, was killed in action on May 8, 1944, while commanding a torpedo boat squadron off Bougainville in the Pacific.

To the senses, the Point had hardly changed; but behind its serene, timeless, seabound aspect the inner style was fading out.

Arthur Leonard, defier of the Atlantic, died in Chicago on February 4, 1949. He was eighty-six.

Caroline Sinkler, dear Carrie, antebellum and lavender to the last, followed on the fifth of May, just turned eighty-nine.

Marie Kay Prentiss, the last arbiter, with no one to leave "Blighty" to who could afford to own it, died on the first of December.

After the death of their mother, Jack and Ed Raymond leased out "The Ramparts" for a time as a tutoring school with indifferent results.

During the summer of 1950 somebody stole one of Commodore Rouse's stone lions that had guarded the earthworks for half a century and decapitated the other.

The taxes on the empty mansion, growing seedy behind its embrasures, begged the question. Mrs. Raymond's children, and their children, had their own homes within earshot—when the breeze was right—of Uncle Henry's Japanese gong. But there was no one to whack it.

So the Gloucester Building and Wrecking Company was summoned and in the last week of September 1950 began to tear "The Ramparts" down.

All but the Commodore's watchtowers, which were left standing.

The last rampart. (Lila Swift Monell)

Niles Pond, Brace Cove and beyond, from the tower of "The Ramparts."
(Henry Williams photo)

FORTY YEARS ON,
1950–1990

March Hare *rides out Hurricane Bob, August 19, 1991,* Zeus *a mile offshore.*
The catamaran didn't quite flip. (Author photo)

NAUTICAL

THE DAY I FIRST SET FOOT ON THE ancestral soil in the mid-1930s I was twelve or fourteen. For no particular reason I remember it quite well. We were taking our vacation turn in Grandmother Garland's old cottage in Riverview on the Squam River when my father, then a pediatrician in Brookline, took a notion to pile us in the Model A Ford for a tour of Eastern Point, where he had vacationed as a boy in his late father's summer cottage on the top of Fort Hill Avenue across from "The Ramparts."

By golly, Pa was going to show us around what had once been his Great-grandfather Niles's farm!

But when we pulled up at the gate lodge, or perhaps the stone markers at the foot of Farrington Avenue, the summer constable politely but firmly barred our way. No amount of remonstrance would do. Seething, my Old Man drove us back over town, hell-bent for the police station. He presented his credentials to the chief in no uncertain terms, acquired a temporary visa to this damned enclave of snobs, drove back, waved it at the surprised constable and was waved on in.

A magical, mysterious sort of island, I remember—the old cottage with its slouch hat of a red roof, Niles Pond, the lighthouse, the breakwater at low tide, where enormous, nightmarishly ugly skates were beached out or in the shallows, dead, dying or laying eggs, for all I knew. Yuk.

A mere but momentous twenty-five years passed. Becky and I were living with our daughters Peggy and Susie in the old town of Sudbury in an old farmhouse I'd rehabilitated while evolving from reporting in Boston to newspaper union organizing and now free-lance writing. An upturn in family fortunes made it possible to think about a modest, vine-entwined vacation spot on the shore in the summer of 1959. Thoughts turned idly and somewhat dismissively to Gloucester, the Riverview family cottage having been sold.

First I must see again "The Captain's House" on Pleasant Street where Pa had been born and grew up, now owned by the adjoining Brown's Department Store, where we introduced ourselves to Bob Brown, a grandson of the founder. And what brought us to Gloucester? "Ah! I've just the place for you: 'Black Bess' out on Eastern Point, right on the harbor and begging on the market for months. Ask Mrs. Chick, the realtor."

We did, and looked high and low on the coast but were always drawn back to shingle-style, shuttered "Black Bess" with its ivied beach-stone front walls and overgrown grounds, practically presiding over the outer harbor. Three times as big as we had in mind, but there were the two acres of shore frontage, another across the road, and it was fully furnished and begging on the market, and the young owner was anxious to sell and get his Air Force duty behind him before embarking on an architectural career, and the price was astonishingly right.

My first night in "Black Bess" that October going on forty years back, I lay in bed, bewitched by the gentle clang of the Norman's Woe bell buoy wafted over the harbor until, with a slight shift in the breeze, I sat bolt upright at the sound of distant traffic. My God, this idyll, this undreamed dream come true—shattered by the roar of trucks hurtling along Route 128! A nightmare! I rushed to the window in a cold sweat.

'Twas but the swish of the wavelets upon the pebbles of Raymond's Beach not a hundred yards away.

The winter was taken up with winterizing, and by the spring of 1960 this upstart heir to Niles curmudgeonry had succeeded in uprooting his family from a country town on the verge of suburbanization and moving them to a private enclave that eighty years earlier had been his ancestral farm— ironically on the right side (or was it still the wrong?), by secondary intention, to be sure, of the guardian constable.

Six years elapsed while I wrote five books, tried my hand at sailing after thirty years of lubbering, rose and fell from governor of the Eastern Point Yacht Club to rear commodore in charge of housekeeping to ex-member (having my own mooring within a long stone's throw of my piazza); the club had only recently sold its Wonson's Point home in order to buy the Clays' "Finisterre" opposite the lighthouse. And a jolly time it was getting to know my neighbors during that last fling of partying in the old style that expired with the settling in upon the land of the war in Vietnam, even as I got to know some of the neighbors on the townie side of what *they* sardonically derided as "The Inner Sanctum."

It seems to me sometimes, ensconced up here on a ledge forty paces from the sea in a landmark that for 110 years has withstood everything nature could hurl at it, as if I inhaled and exhaled with the tides. Thousands upon thousands of vessels—missile carriers, square-riggers, junks, J-boats, presidential yachts and "Old Ironsides" and a hostile British sloop-of-war, fishing vessels of today and great schooners of long ago, skiffs, sailboats and canoes back 394 years to Champlain's queer-looking rig—have passed by, from or to the Atlantic just beyond the Point, or on some mission or other in the harbor, or on none, and we've seen our share.

With the gradual displacement by steel of the old wooden fishing drag-

High but not dry, Ohio dies on the ledges of "Druimteac," April 7, 1964. (Author photo)

gers (some of them converted minesweepers from the world wars); with the general adoption of the war-born depth sounder, radar and Loran, the radio direction-finder and high-frequency radio; and with the application of war lessons in search and rescue—the safety and efficiency of the fishing effort out of Gloucester, as elsewhere, improved rapidly after 1950, even as there were early signs that fishermen were achieving the overkill that would endanger their livelihood.

Among the last of the old-timers still hanging on were the 104-foot mackerel seiner *Beatrice & Rose* and the whiting dragger *Santo Antonino*, 110 feet—both 1918 wooden subchasers adapted to fishing that joined so many before them in the graveyard of Brace Cove. When the former caught fire while fishing off Thacher's Island on November 4, 1949, another seiner tried to save her with a tow to the cove. Once there, the fire was doused, and the crew of ten got off, but a towboat couldn't pull her free, and she broke up. Six years later the *Santo Antonino* was returning from fishing on the tenth of September when her steering gear jammed in churning seas and she hove up on Bemo Ledge. Captain Frank Sinagra sent his crew of four ashore in the dory and climbed into the rigging. But they were unable to make it back to him through the surf. There he remained aloft until Coast Guardsmen arrived in a patrol boat, tossed him a life ring, and he leaped into the sea and was hauled aboard. His weary vessel broke up on Bemo Ledge.

Well do I mind the fate of the homebound ninety-foot steel dragger *Ohio* that strayed in a thick o' fog and piled up on "Druimteac's" ledges at two in the morning of April 7, 1964, back in the days when you could hail into Gloucester with 110,000 pounds of haddock. Up back on the high ground the Monell family heard the eerie scream of her whistle in distress and the crunch of her steel on the rocks, and called the Coast Guard. Two of the crew jumped overboard and were rescued by the forty-four-footer; the other six came hand-over-hand on a line thrown ashore. *Ohio*'s rusty bones are down there, off in the deep water somewhere today.

Only four months previously, on the last day of that fateful November of 1963, giant seas driven by a freak sixty-mile gale from the southwest came smashing full on the breakwater with such force, unprecedented from that quarter, that the air compressed by each wave in the spaces between the rocks blew a forty-foot section apart about 130 feet from shore, and eight of the twelve-ton blocks were toppled into the deep water on the harbor side like so many loose bricks.

For two more years our breeched breakwater crept up the wish list of the Corps of Engineers until the end of 1965, when a temporary road was built from the Audubon parking lot below the lighthouse just above high water to the beginning of the mighty structure. A hundred-ton, seventy-five-foot crane lumbered along Eastern Point Boulevard, out over the fill and out along the breakwater to the gap, soon followed by great flatbed trucks vibrating our house as they rumbled by with twelve-ton replacement blocks from a Rockport quarry.

The operator was in the habit of moving his crane back to the security of the shore when a storm was predicted, as I recall, except that at the end of work on Friday, January 21, 1966, he left it out there.

A no'theaster made up that weekend, and when I glanced out my bathroom window at the breakwater as I was about to shave early Tuesday morning, horrendous swells were exploding over the top and around the crane, and when I finished and glanced again, it was gone, all 175 feet of it somewhere in the calm depths off the lee side.

Somebody told the *Gloucester Daily Times* it happened at two that morning, but it didn't. It was while I was shaving. They rounded up two more cranes that hoisted their half-drowned brother back up where he belonged.

Some time subsequently the Engineers riprapped the stepped seaward side to enable waves to slide over instead of smashing against the breakwater, and it was an awesome sight—drivers with nerves of steel backing their big rigs, laden with huge boulders and chunks of granite, a half mile out that narrow highway of rock, a few inches to spare on either edge. Or did they back back?

A word about our lighthouse. In June 1937, a 125-foot steel antenna was erected on the grounds with a twenty-mile radio beacon sending signals for the new navigational aid, the radio direction-finder (RDF) with which vessels were being equipped. In February 1960 the classic rotating fourth-order Fresnel lens was replaced with a rotating airport beam.

Then in April 1969, the most radical change for the worse: the great bronze bells at the lighthouse and out in the tower on the end of the breakwater were taken down and replaced with electronic hooters. Ah, that solemn, inexorable tolling signaling the arrival of a thick o' fog, the great clappers—once swung by weights cranked up every few hours by the weary keeper, then wound by electric motor—still so measuredly sonorous, so reassuring that the big lighthouse and its sidekick with the blinking red light

a half mile out in the harbor were there yet, even if you couldn't see 'em, guardians to be steered clear of at all costs.

For ten years I had arisen from sleep, conscious that the fog had either crept in or lifted, and the bells should be turned on or off, and phoned the lighthouse and rousted out the always grateful keeper on duty, and in a minute or so, Old Reliables would be pealing from across the cove, or silent.

On September 13, 1985, the final degradation of the noble and long-defunct U.S. Lighthouse Service, the final degradation of the human touch, of the watchfulness over those at sea. The blatant horns on that day became activated and deactivated by an electronic fog sensor. Fourteen years later it remains so unreliable that these soulless hooters sometimes hoot for sunny days and starry nights on end and sometimes not in the thickest of weather.

A week later the revolving flash of the high-powered light was turned on twenty-four hours a day, the keeper was assigned elsewhere, and the Coast Guard's time-honored lighthouse service at Eastern Point, Gloucester, was put on automatic as part of the dehumanizing of government for the sake of false economy.

One of the bells has been mounted down on the lighthouse lawn, clapper immobilized, as a memorial to beacons of humanity. Toss a stone at it and listen to the echo.

To seal the past, in 1987 the Eastern Point Lighthouse was placed on the National Register of Historic Places.

From the day of our arrival Eastern Point endeared itself to me as my home place, as this magical peninsula and all the rest of Cape Ann have to so many for so many generations. And it begged so seductively to be written about that we had been in residence only since June 25, 1960, when, on September 2, I had already jotted in my journal, "Trouble developing a

Donald Monell at Raymond's Landing. (Author photo)

'point of view' as the basis for a book about Eastern Point."

I should think so. Becalmed again in the writer's horse latitudes seven years later, a slight history occurred to me, say of forty or fifty mimeographed pages. The idea grew, and the germ of a point of view, as such do, and it soon took on a life of its own with the urging and help of Donald Monell, an early friend here, and with the offer of neighbors to guarantee any deficit if a modest book should eventuate.

"No palpable hurdles, therefore, remain in the way of the author," I wrote in an open letter to everyone I could think of as a source on November 20, almost forty years ago, requesting information:

All his alibis have been swept aside, and the time for doing has come.

Largely as a by-product of other research, I have collected some material on the early days of the Point until its sale by the Niles heirs in the eighties. I have sketchy data on the Associates and the families that came here later. Of course the old days when this was one big, discretely bounded farm are easier to trace than the era of the growing summer colony, the past eighty years when the land was divided into estates and occupied by more and more families, many of whom resided in several houses in succession, most of whom, perhaps, were interrelated and all of whom, it seems, have ranged from the intriguingly individualistic to the astonishingly bizarre.

Eastern Point, all 424 pages bound in white sailcloth, was published in 1971 by Bill Bauhan's Noone House in Peterborough, New Hampshire. Reissued in a second, bluebound edition two years later under Bauhan's own name from nearby Dublin, it sold 2,200 copies before going out of print, which was about 2,000 more than we had expected of such a big book about such a small place.

A series of the worst blizzards within the memory of most of us before and since struck the coast in 1969 between the last day of February and the fourth of March. Buried under layer upon layer of drifted snow, Gloucester was at a standstill. Pipes and even mains froze, lines were down, a general state of emergency was declared, the Army and National Guard brought in heavy plowing and dumping equipment and were supplying residents with fresh water. For three or four days Eastern Point was isolated except by foot, for not an automobile could move, and we had to trudge through the drifts to the Railroad Avenue Market beyond Rocky Neck Avenue for supplies.

Not until two or three weeks later was the ghoulish tragedy of the Great Blizzard discovered by the local police. For some years a plain, foursquare building on the Atlantic shore about a quarter of a mile east of the light-house, a coastal radar station during World War II, had been owned and occupied off and on by the Merola family, principally the elderly Mrs. Merola and her daughter. The site was exposed and isolated until a few of the Raymond lots were developed in the area, and the Merolas made it plain, with backup from a pair of German shepherds, that they wished to be left alone.

And so they were during the marathon blizzards, when nothing was seen or heard of them, only the occasional barking of the dogs, until some days after the weather had cleared, and the police were alerted to the now-frenzied clamor inside. Arriving and getting no response, the officers broke down the door. The dogs rushed out as if gone mad. One was shot.

Inside, both women were long dead, Mrs. Merola seated in a chair, her daughter in bed and partially consumed by the starving animals.

Three years passed, and in February 1972 the coast and perhaps most particularly this same bold southeast Atlantic shore of Eastern Point was struck by what qualified as a tidal wave, although no one except perhaps a few oceanographers and meteorologists quite viewed it as such. Bold stone

The radar station. (Sherman Morss, Jr.)

Raymond's Beach from the upper deck of "Black Bess," March 4, 1969. (Author photo)

"Druimteac," completed by the defiant Arthur Leonard on the crest of the ledge in 1921 and broken into by winter storms as often as not ever since, and a new summer home erected just to the southwest almost as daringly by Laurence Brown and his sister Dorothy, stood in the way, as I wrote in a column ten days later.[1]

It was certainly a tidal wave that engulfed two of my neighbors on the backside of Eastern Point that afternoon. Back in the fifties they built a compact modern house with sliding glass walls that presented a stunning view of the North Atlantic lapping pleasantly at the ledge a hundred feet down from them. It was chancy and they knew it, except that in all those years they have watched storm upon storm pile the white breakers just short of their patio, with nothing worse than coatings of salt and strewings of Irish moss to show for it.

Not so this time. With increasing awe they saw the surf advance to the retaining wall. Then it carried away the heavy slate wallcaps and flooded into the patio. On it came. The raucous waves smashed the cellar window and poured in. In no time six feet of sandy water was slopping around in the basement, hurling flotable goods against the furnace and playfully wielding a five-foot log that forced entry as a double-ended battering ram.

Still rising, the tidal wave crashed the lower-level glass wall and streamed into bath and bedroom. Up the ledge to the land and over, white water flinging flotsam against the window wall of the main living room until it shattered with an explosion of glass shrapnel around the stunned heads of my friends.

So there, after a decade and a half of deceptive docility, was the Atlantic Ocean sloshing about in the parlor, making itself at home with the furniture and soaking up the good reading on the shelves. Needless to say, the inquisitive waters liked what they found and wanted more; they seethed inland, rearranged the landscaping, checked over the driveway and moved the car 25 feet up toward the road.

UnArklike, the house was well designed and solidly built and did not float away. The waters have relented, the heater is back working, the rugs are back from the cleaner, the chickadees are back at the feeding stations and Father Neptune is back where he belongs.

But I think there was a fleeting moment in the shambles of that night, as they huddled powerless before their miserable hearth, an anonymous bottle of Bordeaux [all the labels of a well-rounded stock in the wine cellar had gone with the tide] their sole defense against the next onslaught (which never came, praise be), a moment of doubt, when they wondered if they might have calculated their chances a mite on the close side, after all.

And what yon vengeful tidal wave did to "Druimteac" next along the Point's rusty ledge, that massive mansion not merely built on rock but quarried from it by the stubborn Stock Yard King—ah, hell hath no fury like a woman or an ocean scorned. Gaelic for "House Back of the Ledge," "Drum-hack" is still back of the ledge

"Druimteac" ninety minutes after high tide, February 19, 1972. (Lila Swift Monell)

after fifty years of pounding, but the scars of defiance have deepened. It has the look of a beachhead after the battle.

Whatever the great storm did to the tender balance of midlife between sea and land, nature will redress as it always has. It may require another Ice Age to undo what man has done.

On the other hand, to be born with the bravado to build your pad an inch from the teeth of the sea, to risk wipeout for the beauty and the glory of it—there is a broke worth going for . . . the more piquant if the Bordeaux holds out.

That summer of '72 Mrs. Lila Leonard Swift, who had inherited her father's great stone fist in Father Neptune's face and annually supervised the cleanup of winter's almost annual invasion of the sea in response, arrived from California, surveyed the worst ever, and in September "Druimteac" was dismantled and returned to the ledge from which it was extracted by a very bold man indeed, fifty-one years before.

Six years passed, when a storm of even greater violence struck the coast on the sixth and seventh of February 1978—"The Great Storm of '78" that peaked with high-course tides, crashed head-on into Rockport, flooded Bearskin Neck, toppled Motif No. 1 (the town's icon for artists from everywhere and nowhere) into the harbor, knocked down the major portion of the Lane's Cove breakwater in Gloucester, smashed and gnashed the Back Shore of East Gloucester and the Point, hurling rocks ashore like cannonballs and sucking buildings, wharves and boats back to sea, and dumping thirty-two inches of snow as if offering to gloss over the mess it had made.

So violent was the surge of waves refracted across the tossing harbor to the normally protected Eastern Point shore from the big ones smashing on the West Gloucester shore that a boulder four feet across was tossed like a pebble or rolled like a marble forty feet up on our lawn, where it remains immovable to this day.

As the storm was building late in the first afternoon, I watched the Gloucester pilot boat *Can Do* bucking out the harbor past Black Bess until she plunged into the great seas building ever steeper beyond the breakwater, and I wondered where in hell those crazy guys were going out there and why.

They were off to save the crew of the tanker *Global Hope* which had sent out an SOS as it knocked about in Salem Harbor. *Can Do* got no farther than Magnolia that night before the raging storm overcame her. She capsized and sank, and five brave men drowned. The Coast Guard rescued the tanker's crew.

In the first ten years, learning and never fully satisfied, I ran through a succession of seven wooden sailboats including *Great Republic,* a little old plumb-stem gaff-rig sloop of eighteen feet that resonated with its namesake in my Blackburn book underway at the time, and the thirty-five-foot old-time gaff schooner *Bandit.* In varying degrees I fixed 'em up under the supervision of my late good friend, the well-known East Gloucester fisherman and boat builder Bill Sibley, who coined "Inner Sanctum" for Eastern

Bandit *romps past Dog Bar Breakwater, October 8, 1967. (Charles A. Lowe photo)*

*Capt. Bill Sibley
inspects the haul
aboard his one-
man dragger*
Peggybell,
*June 27, 1961.
(Author photo)*

Point and whose daughter Ann—off to a
birthday party there one afternoon—instructed him to drop her off at the stone
posts, preferring to appear on foot than in
their ancient beat-up station wagon for
which *she* had coined the name, on behalf of
her "siblings" and herself, "Our Shame."

It was Bill who in 1961 put down my
mooring in the cove off Black Bess Point
from *Peggybell,* his one-man dragger named
for his indomitably British spouse. It consisted of the engine bed from the ancient
steam tug *Charlie,* with thirty-five feet of
three-quarter-inch chain once the bobstay of
the famous stone sloop *Albert Baldwin,* both
salvaged from these noble relics of another
age while they were beached at the head of
Smith Cove for dismantling by WPA workers in the 1930s. You can have your mush-
room anchors; Sib's mooring's been pulled
once for inspection in thirty-eight years and
serves me today.

My most memorable sail in snug little *Great Republic* was with my
summer neighbor in "Green Alley's" shoreside cottage, the distinguished
biographer Catherine Drinker Bowen, Cecilia Beaux's niece. A tall, rangy,
forceful personality and a sort of seasonal mentor of mine, Kitty hadn't
sailed for years and was dying to get out. So one afternoon I rowed her to
the mooring, and off we took in a freshening westerly—so freshening that
as we close-reached off "Green Alley" I found myself to my consternation
trying as nonchalantly as I could to keep from dumping us both in the tide
on her doorstep in the puffs, while we heatedly debated my attempt to talk
her into doing a sequel to her famed *John Adams and the American
Revolution.* My gung-ho passenger, nearly of an age to be my mother,
seemed wholly oblivious to her peril, which merely added to my anxiety.
Good old *GR.* We made it, of course, scarcely a drop taken aboard.[2]

Bandit was a good, old-fashioned, spoon-bow schooner built at
Mahone Bay, Nova Scotia, in 1938. I rerigged her for singlehanded sailing,
enlarged the cockpit, rebuilt the cabin while she was hauled out on Sibley's
marine railway over on Rocky Neck causeway, and enjoyed many the brisk
day sail, a couple of down East cruises and a few close ones in her.

Fickle owners, rarely fickle boats. As these things happen, I sold *Bandit* in
1970 and acquired my eighth wooden one, my loveliest, slipperiest,
sailingest, my very own awesome, long-legged and long longed-for Triangle
sloop, all twenty-eight feet and five inches of her—formerly *Puma, Tid VI*
and *Goblin*—from the late, generous-to-a-fault Groveland ("Grovey")

Cook. I renamed her *Sylph* and put her on Sib's mooring and had the happiest sailing in her I ever had or would.

Among the last, devoted Triangle sailors on the Point then were Gloucester dentist Carroll ("Bud") Wonson, direct descendent of the first keeper of the lighthouse, and the late Laurence Brown, he of the Bordeaux labels astray in the tidal wave. The only bothersome feature of the Triangle was its pair of running backstays to hold the lofty mast and hence the jib taut on either tack in the absence of a standing backstay, the boom extending way aft of the transom. You had to shift lively to slack off the weather backstay and haul in the leeward when coming about, and never ever get caught in a jibe when running, which Doctor Bud did one gusty day in his beloved *Carelcilla*. Her boom whipped around, snapped the weather backstay, and down came mast, sails and all.

Laurence Brown, summer 1981. (Dorothy A. Brown)

Someone came along and towed chagrined *Carelcilla* back to her mooring off the Wonson house above the Raymond's Beach bathhouse. Bud's one thousand dollars in insurance just covered the new mast, and the company promptly cancelled his policy.

Lawyer, naturalist and puckishly humorous raconteur, it was said of Dorothy Brown's encyclopedic brother Laurence (always Laurence, never Larry, which he couldn't abide) that he and Elliott Richardson were the brightest students in the annals of Milton Academy. Laurence could remember when the Yacht Club fleet inside the breakwater included fifteen Triangles, and he yearned for those days of beauty on the blue and classy racing and did his utmost to keep them going with the passing years, even buying up two or three that he kept in dry storage at Burnham and Thomas's yacht yard in East Gloucester, just in case.

Just in case. Returning from an outside race one afternoon, he told me, old *Aix* or *Cix*, or whichever one he was sailing that day, suddenly and unaccountably refused to respond to the helm. So Laurence dropped the sails and got a tow to his mooring, where someone dove under and found *Aix* or *Cix* or whichever headed on one course and her 2,500 pounds of lead keel on another—hanging underneath by only one of the six long keel bolts that were supposed to secure keel to hull, the next to the last having just corroded adrift like the rest.

My *Sylph*, later restored to her original color (red) and name (*Goblin*), was the last Triangle in Gloucester Harbor when I hastily sold her in 1976 to a lubber who let her go to hell—hastily, because Charlie Freyer sailed his 1929, Gloucester-built, gaff-rigged, thirty-two-foot cruising sloop *Seascape* up from Florida with the intention of hooking me. And I had to have *Seascape* because I had written the book about her first owner, Howard Blackburn. He had named her *Cruising Club* back in 1929 when Marion

Cooney built her on the Gloucester waterfront for the aging lone voyager. Why? Because the Cruising Club of America had elected him one of only eight honorary life members and planned a rendezvous in Gloucester that summer in his particular honor, and he was going to reciprocate in his own way as he raised sail to greet them.

Fifty-one years later, four years of restoration, joyous day sailing around Gloucester and deeply satisfying cruising the coast of Maine came to an end on October 26, 1980, when *Cruising Club* broke loose from her mooring in an early morning southwest gale in a rising tide and broke up on my rocks at the north end of Raymond's Beach.

The late Charlie Lowe, veteran ace photographer for the *Gloucester Daily Times,* was driving by on the lookout for just such a disaster. He ran up to the house to alert me, then back to the beach to film the heartbreak of it as I phoned my boatbuilder buddy from Rocky Neck, Larry Dahlmer, who rushed over and tried to help me save her. It was hopeless in the pounding surf, and within an hour Blackburn's last boat had been smashed to pieces on his biographer's rocks.

What had gone wrong? *Cruising Club*'s broken mooring pennant was still shackled to the chain to *Charlie*'s steam engine block, and the bight was secure on the forward deck cleat. But the three-quarter-inch polypropylene pennant, so carefully protected within a length of reinforced nylon fire hose, had stretched under the plunging yanks of the oncoming waves and had pulled this chafing gear out of the bow chock. The unprotected section of pennant simply wore through and snapped.

Eighteen months passed.

It was the sixteenth of March, 1982. Married five months, Helen and I were preparing to have lunch on our porch at "Black Bess" when we noticed the Fulford boys, Frank and Bruce, young fishermen tending their nets about a hundred yards upwind of the Stone Wharf at the south end of the beach where I had lost *Cruising Club*. It was brisk out of the northwest, but they knew what they were doing, and I joined Helen on the settee, our backs to the window.

Perhaps thirty, perhaps forty-five minutes later a screeching siren drew my attention to the window, and I saw the flashing red light of the Fire Department Rescue squad speeding past our house down the road and out onto the Stone Wharf, and rushed out after it. If something, anything, had caused me to turn to the window again perhaps thirty minutes earlier, I might, just might, have been able to get my dinghy in the water and row out and save Bruce. Haunted, I felt compelled to express something in the *Gloucester Daily Times*.[3]

Although I have seen death and faced it many times, I have not been able to overcome my depression over last week's drowning of Bruce Fulford, a young fisherman of eighteen, though only a waving acquaintance, or my grief for his family and friends.

Partly it is because it happened only a couple of hundred yards out in Gloucester Harbor from my house on Eastern Point a few minutes after I'd noticed Bruce and his older brother Frank out there hauling their nets.

I've kept half an eye cocked on the harbor for years, but I paid

The author and Larry Dahlmer try futilely to save Cruising Club, *October 26, 1980. (Charles A. Lowe photo)*

Bruce Fulford.
(Lisa Fulford
Aptt)

the Fulfords no mind, confident that they knew what they were doing, as they always have, even though it was blowing quite hard.

But while my back was turned they capsized, by a complete fluke, and it was all over by the time I heard the rescue squad sirens go by and saw the Coast Guard patrol boat trying to grapple. Frank had made it, with some heroic help from shore. Bruce had not.

My memory retains so starkly all that I witnessed that early afternoon down at the other end of the beach, all of the valiant efforts to find Bruce's body, and then to save him, and so poignantly that awful walk back above the beach to their car with Bob and Mary, the boy's parents. Minutes after they headed for the hospital to be with one son, the body of the other was dragged from the water.

The youth of that boy is burned in my mind as I contemplate how the sea has demanded its price again, before my very eyes. What a cruel partnership this has been, for so long, with our forever stoic, forever heartbroken old town! How many thousands of souls have been traded in the bargain! Why? we ask ourselves once again. What does it mean? What has it ever meant? For what? Why this boy?

Well, we see how life goes on, on land and sea, and how all affected carry on somehow in spite of this loss which is not his family's alone, or his friends', but the whole city's, as it always has been. And I am inspired and experience some kind of renewal of faith as I recall how everyone who was involved in this tragedy tried in his or her way to reach out, desperately, to another human being: the passing nun who gave the alarm, the man who leaped in to the rescue at the risk of his own life, the intrepid divers, the Coast Guardsmen, the Fire Department rescue squad, the police, the people at the hospital, family, friends, neighbors in the area, passersby.

Everything that fate would allow to be done was done.

That sudden, spontaneous outpouring of caring—of the community coming together—magnified a few million times will be, must be, the salvation of humanity. There is no other way.

But what of Bruce Fulford! What of this young life taken, so it would seem, just as it had fairly gotten under way!

The Fulfords are a close Gloucester family. Bob is an expert fisherman. He brought up all five boys on the water, taught them how to fish for themselves, how to respect the sea and what it can do, and boats and what they can't, even the best of them.

Fishing is very much the Fulford family way of life, as it has been around this town for 360 years. Everyone knew the risks, not least Mary Fulford and her daughters. But the act of living is a risk.

The boys loved their parents, and each other, and the water, and dipping their nets therein. They are surely even closer together now in their anguish as a family, in their love and in their privacy.

No doubt a strong family. An example, without the least self-consciousness, to their community.

The boys worked hard, fished hard, wore out one outboard motor after another, wresting their living from the sea with unbounded optimism as hundreds of thousands have before them in the Gloucester tradition. Probably played hard. They had their self-respect and the respect of their friends. They had earned it.

Bruce Fulford had earned his self-respect and his young manhood at the age of 18. Some boys and men never do, let them live to 80.

The eternal thing about youth, like spring, is that it has a life of its own, a completeness. Youth is what the young do with it.

Young people in Gloucester, and everywhere today, should be commanded to live their youth as if there were no tomorrow, as if with each day their lives come to completion, to completeness.

When old men, on whom youth has been wasted, say what a shame it is to waste youth on the young, it is up to the young to fling the gauntlet back at them, isn't it! Ah, what a shame to waste war on youth! Yes, youth belongs to the young, and it is eternal.

Does all this have anything to do with the meaning of the young life of Bruce Fulford, and of the many, many young men who have gone down to the sea before him over the centuries from this place?

Who knows? But it seems to me that what happened out there in our harbor was an end, and a beginning. Let that short life be an example to all young lives. Its completion, its completeness, is a challenge to every one of us, young and old, to look to the future as if we would live forever, to act as if we might die tomorrow.

And so, I believe, this young fisherman lived a life that was complete and full of meaning for us all.

At about this time George Carter, a successful entrepreneur of thirty-three from Ohio who had sailed small boats on Lake Erie as a boy, discovered and fell for Gloucester and its deep-sea traditions, bought Lucy Taggart's "Tower of Four Winds" and moved in with his wife Judith and twin sons. In 1986, after sailing his forty-two-foot sloop *Retrac* in the singlehanded race from Provincetown to Monhegan Island in Maine the previous summer, this "tall, thin 37-year-old man with icy blue eyes, tanned skin, mustache and a short, gray-speckled beard,"[4] slipped out the harbor past his house in *Retrac,* alone and bound across the Atlantic for Faro, Portugal.

Having merely taken *Cruising Club* home alone from Portland in an explosively blinding thunder-and-lightning storm that left five inches of water in my dinghy, I read with alarm and relief (for George had told hardly a soul of his plans) that eight days out he was wrecked by a hurricane and, perforce abandoning *Retrac,* plucked from the Gulf Stream by a passing tanker bound for Houston.

Another damn fool, I thought. (Myself, I volunteered as a foot soldier in World War II.) What the hell was big George trying to prove? Well, he told the *Times* reporter, during the worst of the hurricane, while curled up on the cabin floor under the table and a cushion for twelve hours to protect himself from flying objects, he simply thought, just thought,

. . . the purest form of thinking I have ever done, just a pure sense of what's really important to me and what isn't. Priorities. And as opposite as it may sound for a person who likes solitude—the only real purpose for life is other people. The problem with our day-to-day lives is that we lose sight of that, can't feel it or focus on it properly, and slowly but surely replace that single purpose of living for other people with a million and one other pressing priorities, goals and purposes.

How can one practically live today, set goals and keep involved with activities which lead to success, contribution and making a practical living, and yet still keep the sense of priority of life without going through what I had to, is probably the most important question today for mankind and the future survival of the race.

I know now that I do not fear death for the loss of myself to me, but for the loss of the people I love to me.[5]

And then again, George Carter had dedicated his first transatlantic try to his recently deceased father, a Marine veteran of World War II, who had pounded into him since he was a child, "You never fail until you quit trying. Persevere, persevere, persevere. Climb back on the horse and go for it."

So he did, four years later. Admittedly driven by the example of Blackburn's indomitability at sea a hundred years ago and by the admonitions of his father, Carter pressed his reluctant Judy, who said he should risk it if it meant that much to him, and prepared to set out again for Portugal in what he hoped might be a Blackburn memorial crossing by several singlehanders. It finally dwindled to himself in his forty-foot, 1972 yawl *Windswept* and Peter Way of Cataumet in his thirty-eight-foot cutter *Rosanna.*

He was now forty-two and the owner of Carter's Yacht Yard on the

Gloucester waterfront, from which the two sailed forth into the North Atlantic on June 26, 1990. They were soon separated but maintained contact by radio.

A week out Carter ran into a gale, followed three days later by a near-hurricane that kicked up monstrous waves about halfway from Bermuda to the Azores, not far from where he got hit in *Retrac* four years earlier. As the wind was subsiding, a rogue wave rose up behind *Windswept*, broke over her stern, swept away the mizzenmast, steering wind vane and some stanchions, and knocked out his long-range radio and electronic navigation.

Strapping himself to his pitching stern and continually dunked, he repaired his self-steering gear and knew then that he would make it. When Peter Way couldn't reach Carter, he had radioed the Canadian Coast Guard, which sent a plane to establish contact with him via his still-functioning VHF radio. Pausing four days in the Azores, George sailed on, met up with his figurative dorymate, and the two converged on Vilamoura, Portugal, thirty days out of Gloucester.

Thus did George Carter of Eastern Point join the pantheon of Gloucester's transatlantic soloists: "Centennial" Johnson, the first ever, 114 years before; Howard Blackburn in 1899 and 1901; and Philip S. Weld, our late newspaper publisher, journalist and one of Merrill's fabled Marauders in Burma during World War II. Phil won the London Observer Singlehanded Transatlantic Race from England to Newport in 1980 in his big trimaran *Moxie*, at sixty-five the oldest contestant ever and the first Yank, in the fastest lone crossing to that date.

And like Weld, and more metaphorically Blackburn, Carter had climbed back on with a new boat after having to abandon ship in a mid-Atlantic storm and be rescued by a passing freighter.

Captain Carter's forty-foot yawl Windswept *(in foreground) at the end of his singlehanded voyage to Portugal from Gloucester, July 1990. (George Carter)*

Helen's grandchildren
Raymond's Beach

RUSTICAL, AND MORE OR LESS SOCIABLE

An unexpected bonus in my introduction to this captivating enclave was the creation in the fall of 1961 of the Massachusetts Audubon Society's Eastern Point Sanctuary. With some limited residential subdivision of "The Ramparts" estate eastward to the ocean in the works, the possibility of acquiring such a permanent protective preserve of woods, the only true forest on the Point, and both fresh- and salt-water marsh extending south from Dr. Carroll Wonson's new house at the southerly end of Raymond's Beach and west of Raymond's field had been informally considered early that year by architect Donald Monell, Sarah Fraser Robbins, and Laurence Brown and his sister Dorothy.

Brothers Jonathan and Edward Raymond agreed to give twenty-eight acres of the family estate to the Audubon Society, provided nearby residents raised a minimum maintenance endowment of $15,000. This was achieved, and the sanctuary has since been enlarged to about forty acres by a gift of upland from Jonathan's daughter Elise ("Butch") Raymond, wife of Neil Wallace. The sanctuary's principal objectives are to provide food and shelter for the migrant birds for which the Point is a major stopover on the Atlantic flyway, protection for indigenous flora and fauna, and shelter for the adjacent area from wind and storm.

Under the supervision of Sarah Robbins, my neighbor across the cove, a path was broken through from the road to the lighthouse that meandered along the northern rim of the former "Ramparts" vegetable garden, then amongst the great oaks on the high ground and across a couple of brooks via felled tree trunks back to the start.

Somewhere in this primeval forest, as seemingly anomalous to the Point as its sylvan freshwater pond, stands the "Monarch Tree" in which thousands of the great amber butterflies mysteriously congregate for a night or two's rest, year after year, on their wondrous autumnal migration from Canada to Mexico. In forty years I've never found the tree, and I live just up the road. How on earth do they?

We had not been long on the old sod when I encountered Mrs. Robbins's redoubtable credentials as naturalist, ornithologist, marine biologist, geologist, ecologist and tireless field mentor of young and old, pioneering the education program she would officially direct in 1971 at the Peabody Museum in Salem. Hundreds of fellow travelers treasure memories of Sarah's field trips from the tidal pools in front of her home to inspect and instruct on anything and everything else in nature from pole to pole and around the world. Almost invariably she is accompanied by her constant companion, Dottie Brown, who before her retirement was the first female vice president in the annals of the Boston Safe Deposit and Trust Company. Most frequently their expeditions are under the flag of the Peabody, or just out of shared curiosity and excitement about the planet the rest of us tend to take for granted.

Sarah's *The Sea Is All About Us: A guidebook to the marine environments of northern New England waters* (with Clarice M. Yentsch, marine scientist at the Bigelow Laboratory in West Boothbay, Maine) remains a high-water mark in popularizing appreciation of the tidal zones.

Spotting an unfamiliar (to me) shore bird down inside Black Bass rocks at midtide one day early in my tenancy, I rashly supposed I might get one up on this formidable neighbor and let her in on my find with a studiedly offhand phone call. "Oh yes," said she, with barely a hint of amusement. "It's a _____." (I had never heard of it). "We've been keeping track of a flock of them out there all week."

After a couple more desultory tries at one-upmanship I withdrew with relief, content to provide Sarah with specimens of migratory songbirds that immolated themselves against the deceptive reflections of the great outdoors in the picture windows of our sun room. "Just put the poor thing in a bag in your freezer," she'd suggest, "and I'll stop by for it on my way to the Peabody."

And then came the sixth day of October 1971. Abed with the flu, I was jolted into full consciousness by the three-point landing of what proved to be a juvenile bald eagle in the old rum cherry tree forty feet beyond the bedroom window. I managed to slip out of bed, cross to the door on my hands and knees, get

Dottie Brown and Sarah Robbins about to lift off over the Jungfrau from Hurran, Switzerland, July 1974. (Dorothy A. Brown)

downstairs, find the movie camera, crawl to a half-hidden vantage point on the sun porch, snatch about a dozen frames of him through a window before he flapped away, pull myself upstairs and collapse back into bed.

The certainty of his eagleship, I might add, was proposed to me by my neighbor Laurence Brown, who identified him subsequently on sight and who forgot more about such things than I will ever know, except that he never forgot.

Fourteen months later my birdwatching career achieved the height of its inadvertency. November 25th was perhaps a little late in the season for such a vicarious coup, but never mind.[1]

His eagleship flaps away, caught on the wing by the author.

The uncommon is getting to be so common around our place here on Eastern Point that I was not especially surprised by a booming voice that seemed to be unconnected to any corporeal presence that I was aware of:

"Hey Joe! You've got a rare bird there!"

I was chainsawing a fishing dragger's derelict that had washed up on our harbor rocks three or four years ago, wondering how they got separated. It was a fine straight stick of pine about three fathoms long, painted the bright orange usual to such sailless spars, with a stub topmast for the radio antenna, and a masthead light. Snapped off at the deck, I should say.

Then that extra high tide of the infamous storm of last February 19 left it high and dry in our thicket of poison ivy and cat brier, and there it rested until this particular afternoon when I got around to making firewood of it.

Looking around for the source of the resonant announcement, I spotted not one but four rare birds perched on the weathered old stockade fence that lurches along our stone wall by the road, held up more by the jungle of shrubbery against it than the posts whose footings rotted out a generation or two ago, and they are cedar. It must be a very old fence.

These birds looked like human heads arrayed on the pickets all in a row as an Elizabethan (I, not II) reminder that offenses against Queen and Parliament shall not go unpunished.

But then one of them moved in such a way as to convince me it must be attached to a body that was perhaps out of sight, possibly the case with all four. This hypothesis was strengthened when the jolly visage on the left called forth in the same stentorian tones substantially the same hearty news about a rare bird being present, and when I put down the hunk of mast and put on my glasses, I discovered that the voice came from none other (I mean no disrespect to

Joe Garland reports the sighting of an Ash-throated Flycatcher

John Gibson's cover cartoon, North Shore '72. December 9, 1972.

the bench) than H. Lawrence Jodrey, Justice of the Eastern Essex District Court.

I was trying to think up an alibi when I remembered that the good judge, in his moonlighting phase, is an amateur ornithologist of note. Mayhap he is not jesting with me after all, I thought to myself. The quip about there certainly being some rare birds around died on my lips.

So I approached this gallery of heads gazing on me from above my fence and invited them in by the gate. They came, perfectly reunited with their bodies and accompanied by all the paraphernalia and armamentaria, namely binoculars and tripodal spotting scopes, which told me I had correctly guessed their business and their pleasure.

"You have an ash-throated flycatcher here," Larry Jodrey explained calmly, setting down his tripod. "We first saw him down toward the beach. He's a western bird, and as far as I can tell this is the first time he's ever been recognized in New England. There he is, up in the yew there by your door. Here, take my glasses."

And there he was, a small, slate-backed flycatcher with wing bars, whitish breast, yellowish belly and rufousish tail, flitting about the premises quite contentedly, uttering infrequent laconic chirps and occasionally soaring off on a steep climb that culminated presumably in the capture of some tasty bug that had escaped the recent frosts.

I could see it was a flycatcher, but otherwise you wouldn't have been able to prove a thing by me, and I could have cut wood all day for a month of Mondays alongside of him without ever an inkling that the little fellow was that rarest of the rare, an "accidental," and apparaently a first, at that.

The judge's amiable jury assured me that this was an historic moment, not alone for Gloucester and the Commonwealth of Massachusetts, but for any birdwatcher fortunate enough to glimpse my guest, the kind of sighting that almost never occurs in the lifetime of the most devoted birder.

After a while they moved on but were back in 15 minutes with a dozen more of their subspecies who trooped excitedly through the grounds in pursuit of our confused friend and who turned out to be members of the Brookline Bird Club, of which the judge is a past president and which he explained to me is 60 years old, still holds its dues to a dollar a year and has members from all over.

Our Peterson's *Field Guide to the Birds* halts at the Rockies, so the ashthroated flycatcher is not picture. But he is briefly described in the appendix of accidentals as similar to but quite smaller than the crested and belonging to Florida and Louisiana. Another source extends the range of *Myiarchus cinerascens cinerascens* to the western United States and northern Mexico.

He's a long way from home, and in the wrong direction, and I wonder how he'll manage as winter comes on. It's unsettling to read Peterson's comment about the verification of accidentals (he defines them as birds that have occurred less than twenty times in eastern North America), that "the tradition amongst ornithologists has been to accept sight records only if a specimen has previously been taken in the state." What a cruel irony that the only sure way to prove the pioneer visit of such a hardy stranger is to shoot him.

This all happened the afternoon of Saturday, November 25. The word went out, and the next day our shore of Eastern Point was visited by some scores of friendly human accidentals with their scopes and field glasses. Ash throat and all, our flycatcher obligingly fluttered about for a couple of hours, and all of them spotted him, I believe.

"Thanks for letting us see your distinguished guest," smiled one pleasant watcher.

"Not at all," said I. "He is not mine, but humanity's. Indeed, he is for the ages."

As I write this two days later, I've just glanced out my study window and spotted another spotter lurking in my honeysuckle. I hailed him: "Seen the bird?"

"Not yet, but there was a yellow-breasted chat in your yew up there!"

That's the same tall yew our ash-throat was hopping around in (a red berry bearer) no more than ten feet from my typewriter.

I think sometimes I should pay more attention to what's going on under my nose.

When Bill Morris kept the Yacht Club going from snowing to mooring to mowing time (as he had for years as their caretaker when the property was the Clays'), in the off-season he trapped foxes all over the Point and told me how they seesawed with the rabbit population out here. No more. Way back, I observed a thin and mangy specimen lope forelornly along the harbor ledge below the house, but I haven't seen a fox since, except last winter when one crossing the ice on Niles Pond paused to look back at me on my early morning walk. So a few must be around.

And otters purposefully swimming along behind their flat, furry heads, trailing delicate Vs of wakes as transient as a ripple.

Worst ice in decades, or none at all. Bill and half a dozen East Gloucester fellers would be out there fishing through it for perch and pickerel, stamping their feet waiting for the red flag to pop up telling 'em the bait's gone. Right thick it was then, like the old times when Grandsir Niles harvested the blocks for the market schooners. The older folks would be skating sedately around the shore—iceboats whizzing across midpond with the hiss of escaping steam if the breeze was right, runners spewing ice flakes, fellers playing pick-up hockey with boots for goals, kids learning how to do it on their ankles. No more.

It's swans now, the mute aristocrats of our pond, except in flight when a compact squadron mounts aloft, necks straight ahead, wingtips flicking the surface as they pick up speed, then with majestic, measured swoosh-swoosh-swooshes gaining altitude as stately and steady as 747s rising into the sky from Logan Airport. First a pair from Manchester, cygnets soon, more pairs, and the word was out: Niles is the place unless it's frozen, in which case the meeting is adjourned to Wonson's Cove in the harbor, where in a recent winter I counted a quorum of thirty, or off the rocks down front, swooshing by our big windows to splash feet-first into the tide.

Niles Pond and the North Atlantic, fresh and salt, cozying up to each other one brilliant late summer day when my imagination strolled over that way.[2]

Back into namelessness, I suppose, the pond's shore has been afire this time of the year with the purple loosestrife, as it is today, hedged around by the pungent sweet pepper bush salted with golden nuggets of jewelweed. So dense is the clethra it has kept even the rugged rugosa at bay. Here and there in the neutral territory between them have settled the yellow squatters' colonies of tight tansy, goldenrod, and I don't know what all else . . . an aviary of wildflowers, a bower of birds, a busyness of bees.

I have heard it advanced that the underground spring that refreshes Niles Pond originates in the White Mountains of New Hampshire, and I imagine that one less skeptical and more energetic than I might test the proposition by dumping a vial of safranine dye on the summit of Mount Washington in a rainstorm and then rushing back to see if the pond has turned red.

Wherever its wellspring, Grandsir's pond has retained its relative purity. To the uneducated senses it seems to have escaped, so far, civilization's outpouring of the nitrates and phosphates that are strangling our waters, fresh and salt, on a supereutrophic gag of aquatic growth.

The only noticeable source of pollution beyond a few broken hockey sticks is the year-round gathering of gulls, and since this gaggle of white-jacketed croakers and mewers and their forebears has been assembling there from the pond's birth, its outlets into the ocean must be keeping it well flushed.

Big snapping turtles lurk in the Loch Ness of Niles, biding their time to grab yon fowl by the feet and pull them to their watery lairs for devouring at leisure, of which snappers have plenty.

Water lily and pickerel weed float amicably along the shallow coves of Niles Pond, visited in their aimless way by the scoot bugs and the water beetles and presided over by darting dragonflies.

Blue flags and peepers and warblers in the spring . . . the southward fluttering monarch, and the thistle, more warblers and a ring of dying color in the fall.

Half embraced by its parent sea, and half by a spit of land, here is a pond for all seasons, and of them.

Bill Morris ice-fishing on Niles Pond. (Private collection)

When I came upon it and for generations before that, Champlain's Beauport was a tidal cesspool and community dump. The city in 1960 had two routes for the disposal of its collective waste. One was overland along Western Avenue to the Magnolia dump, where accumulations swarmed over by our gulls of eclectic taste were torched as often as required, adding Disneylike hues to the natural inadequacy of our sunsets. The other route accepted both solid and liquid matter, was more convenient (being right at hand), and offered the advantage of short-term cost effectiveness combined with regular, if superficial, twice-daily flushing at no apparent expense.

Add to this gurry and guano, waste from fish processing plants, vessels and boats of all sizes and types, from commercial to pleasure, pumping their bilges and dumping their waste overboard as a matter of course, old tires, broken-down wharves, tons of indestructible plastic, and the disposal into the middle of the harbor, directly across from "Black Bess," of the entire sewage of a city of 25,000 (nigh double in summer) through a large pipe known familiarly if not affectionately (save by those who fished there for lobster bait and occasionally even for the market, as I can attest) as "The Bubbler." The litter abandoned on Raymond's Beach and the shore of Black Bess Point by wind and tide was as profusely varied as the habits of the inhabitants of Gloucester and their visitors.

Add to this fish processors dumping spent cooking oil down the drain and reefers (refrigerator ships carrying foreign frozen fish blocks) and other vessels large and small emptying their bilges of leaked bunker oil and other noxious mixtures in the outer harbor—and a fresh westerly on an outgoing tide would leave masses of yellow, putrid, gluelike gunk on the harbor shore of the Point, covering the ledges and seaweed, and a nigh-ineradicable band two inches wide and a half inch thick around the waterline of every pleasure boat moored inside the breakwater.

And finally, the collective contribution of Inner Sanctum harborfront homes set above the ledge, lacking cesspools or septic systems on this sewerless enclave of privilege and relying on outfall pipes, that is, adding our bit to The Bubbler for the delectation of our neighbors bathing (between oil and grease spills) at Niles and Raymond's beaches. Indeed, an East Gloucester friend was particular about setting his pots just beyond our outfall for what he proudly called "Garland-fed lobsters."

In those days of summer homes, plumber Larry Peterson's men, a pair of genial Sicilians, came around each spring to "lead" together the cast iron pipe sections down to below the low-tide mark, then at the season's close to melt the lead and pile the pipes again up beyond reach of winter's waves. Breaking for lunch, they'd gather a few mussels to boil in a pail over their plumber's torch, or perhaps raw sea urchins, with a few swigs of a locally favored red wine labelled "Vino Fino."

Having "winterized" Black Bess, I stuck it out with the outfall with which I had an invariable falling-out every February, almost invariably during a northwest gale, wind-chill thirty below, when of course it froze solid before I had got around to loosening the joint where it emerged from under the lawn. If a driftwood fire failed I must rent a heavy-duty propane burner and industrial-strength wallpaper steamer, thrusting a length of hose up the outfall, inch by slowly melting inch, foot by foot—stamping mine for a couple of hours with the cold—until at last a portentous, enemaic roaring foretold success, and if I jumped quick I could get out of the way of the hydraulics in time, but not always.

The creation by Congress of the Environmental Protection Agency in 1970 may be said to have marked the dawning of the green movement in America and of the renewal of Gloucester Harbor. The city was given until 1972 to get a primary sewage treatment plant into operation with the aim of cleaning up not only the harbor but the polluted shellfish beds therein and those in the Annisquam River. Dramatic local impetus was given on two fronts: inauguration of the popular annual summer "Clean Harbor Swimming Race" by Sarah Robbins and daughter Sarah from Raymond's to Niles Beach, and the funding by environmental actvist Phil Weld across the water on Dolliver's Neck (who shared with me the closest proximity to The Bubbler) of a harbor cleanup research and action program under the auspices of the Massachusetts Audubon Society.

Aside from the new solid waste treatment plant's probably unavoidable siting just above the harbor on a portion of the salt marsh it was supposed to be protecting to the southwest of Essex Avenue, the results were astonishing and inspiring. Waters so murky that one could rarely see more than a few inches below the surface gradually cleared to a depth of a fathom or two for

the first time, probably, in generations, and swimming returned, especially under the impetus of the gift to the city of the sandy portion of Niles Beach by insurance man and Pointer extraordinaire, the late Mervyn Piper.

The Bubbler, however, continued to disgorge the population's raw effluent until, again largely with the aid of government funding, the city was compelled to extend the outfall pipe a mile out to sea beyond the breakwater. This tricky underwater engineering job was undertaken in 1989 with great difficulty, until the contractor purchased an oil drilling platform the size of a city block to provide a base steady enough to lay the huge pipe over an uneven bottom as directed by a laser beam from shore.

Running into a blow while under tow off Cape Hatteras, the clumsy rig capsized and of course sank irretrievably. The tug was ordered back to the Gulf, and another platform humorously named *Zeus* was bought and brought. It dominated the harbor like a giant dog in the manger for months, continually pulling up the gaunt legs that secured it to the bottom and crawling along with the outfall's periwinkle-like progress, until at last the end was reached a mile off the breakwater, where it was parked. On December 15, 1990, it caught fire mysteriously, at great length was repaired and yet remained—the object of thousands of logical questions and illogical answers—until September 30, 1993 (my birthday! what a cake!) when a tug appeared and took old *Zeus* in tow over the horizon, ne'er to be seen again.

By then even the old Magnolia open-burning dump had been closed down for a landfill operation. No more flamboyantly enhanced sunsets over Ravenwood Park, no more *parfum de pneu brûlant* drifting through the open bedroom windows of a summer eve.

Zeus burns a mile off the breakwater, December 15, 1990. (Author photo)

And by then our outfall had been replaced by a garden upon a leeching field that yields foxglove seven feet high.

The razing of "The Ramparts" up there on the pinnacle of the Point exactly at mid-century and a mere sixty years after the appearance of the first summer cottages in 1890 placed an emphatic period on a history written twenty years later when nearly all the leading players of the era had departed the stage.

That was 1970, and we were in the worst of the Vietnam War, with Watergate on the way. There was a growing sense of siege. Further pause for a spirit more mordant than mine might have been provided by an amusing letter, from someone who may or may not have been pulling our leg, that appeared in the *Gloucester Daily Times* not long after the initial publication of Eastern Point:

> As a visitor to your city, I have been greatly disturbed by the many signs having the words "Eastern Point."
>
> Just as creeping socialism found its way into school systems when some subversives decided to change Citizenship Education to "Social Studies," so now does communism seem to have infiltrated your town.
>
> As a refugee from communism, I have had enough of Eastern Ways. What makes the situation even worse is hearing people refer to "Eastern Point" as "The Point"—as though there is no other point but the Eastern Point of view.

Of course I am not suggesting that you change the name to Western Point. That would not make sense. But I should think there are enough good American names without having to resort to such leftist terms as "Eastern Point."

I should like to say I have enjoyed your fair city, but I am afraid I will not be able to return until Gloucester realizes that we are living in the West.

T.T. YUREK, New York City

Notwithstanding, three more decades have elapsed. We still hole up and hold out behind our dachas, the threat of the Eastern Point of view has evaporated, and now the world around us balances on the verge of the millenium. None of the original families occupies its ancestral cottage in our dot upon the map, yet all eleven stand well kept, and Raymonds, Pollards, Patches, Leonards and Garlands still cling to the old turf or have returned to it.[3]

In his foreword to my brief *Eastern Point Revisited: Then and Now 1889-1989*, my late good neighbor William F. A. Stride, Jr., then president of the Association of Eastern Point Residents, recalled his own family rootedness back to his grandfather, Alonzo Wilder Pollard. He and his wife Caroline occupied and enlarged with great taste that other old saltbox house floated to the Point from East Gloucester by his Aunt Timmy, inherited after her untimely death by his mother, Katherine Pollard, and his namesake father, the ramrod-straight, British-born Episcopalian divine and grower in his retirement of the most glorious gladiolas on Cape Ann in Stride Field above Raymond's Beach. Bill Stride wrote:

Katherine and the Rev. William F. A. Stride at Robbins-Stebbins wedding, August 27, 1960. (Sarah Fraser Robbins)

The Raymonds—
Edward, Jonathan
and Henry, and
Julia, Hilda and
Mary. (Edward
Williams)

    Providentially, the old guard has been reinforced by its heirs and by a new guard of energetic families bringing a fresh commitment to the Point and its old values. . . .

    The City, which in early days regarded the Point with considerable awe, now seems to look at us with a sense of proud tolerance, wanting us to preserve it as we always have, but unwilling to let us get away with anything while so doing. While the City Council and the Association of Eastern Point Residents do not always agree, our mutual relationship is healthy and respectful, which bodes well for the future.[4]

Of course life styles—certain internal and external disciplines and indulgences—have changed, if not forever, at least until the pendulum swings back, as indeed it may be poised to. You may have noticed that raucousness is occasionally frowned upon again, if not with quite the finality of Grandmother Raymond's dinner gong.

    The genus *chauffeur* (except for the admiral of the stretch limousine) has exited, and with him (save for the rarest of holdover households), the maid, cook, laundress, house man and yard man, and with them the deliveries of a frock by Grande Maison de Blanc of Magnolia's Robber's Row, packaged laundry by Lewandos, capers and caviar by S. S. Pierce, cupcakes by Cushman's, a prime roast of beef by the Murphys of Railroad Avenue Market on East Main Street, and a haddock by old John Alexander of Beacon Marine.

    Long gone is the ineffably accomodating Egyptian, I think he was, whose gentle knock on the door presaged a seasonal spread of the most exquisite imported linens and laces, irresistible to milady; the ancient scissors grinder in his hot-weather shorts, plodding up the road, bell vigorously in hand; the honey-and-jelly man all the way from somewhere west of Boston; and the weekend-constable-at-the-gate/sometime-salesman (or vice versa), minus pith helmet, dumping fireplace ashes on the rug to demonstrate the latest wonder of the vacuumed world.

Still . . . Mrs. Jack and Beaux, Harry and Doc and the Lavender Lady, Joanna and David, the Freddie Halls and the Misses Taggart and Notman, Bishop and Bamma Rhinelander, dreamy Tom Eliot, Cap'n Jim and all the rest who were or weren't of Dabsville could reappear on our insular stage and know in an instant that they were back, back "in Fogland with the sea's white arms about you all," as Y exulted to A.

Caroline and Bill Stride. (Caroline Stride)

Ike Patch and Luba—and his sister, Helen Patch Gray. (Semi-private collection)

Even mine host George Stacy, Grandfather Leonard, Grandmother Raymond, Commodore Rouse and the Prentisses would rejoice in Fogland's magic, notwithstanding the curse of fire, salt water, the tax collector, and in the case of "Blighty" (which since 1954 has served as an admirable memorial as the Jesuit retreat house "Gonzaga"), childlessness.

The descendants of farmers Niles and Patch, who carried their quarrel to the highest court in the Commonwealth, are today the best of friends and neighbors. Sixty-five years on, "Red Roof" and "Beauport" remain as instantly redolent of their creators as if those two distinctive gents of taste and wit had stepped out for an early evening stroll down the boulevard to the lighthouse with their amusing and probably distinguished guests—and are expected back momentarily, won't you come in and make yourselves comfortable?[5]

Nor can anyone quite match the reigning presence of David and Jane Richardson ("Mr. and Mrs. R" to us), presiding with such implicit assurance of stability above the intimate old tennis court they made ours, with its familar tarred cracks, and the stateliest copper beech on Cape Ann. Always with us who remember are their hosting of the Rouse Tourney marking another season's end, and the *al fresco* luncheon for all the Point on their spacious verenda, and the evenings of Christmas carols with Mister R at the piano, and their unwavering faith in a system of values handed down to them and by them to us.[6]

The Yacht Club's graceful Triangles are Flying Dutchmen on the seas of memory, and so, for the present anyway, is its raison d'être, racing. The moment of truth was faced in the early 1960s when it became apparent that Pointers alone could no longer bear the expense of the noble Clay establishment in such contrast to the modest old quarters above the other end of

Linda and Ted Williams (three days short of his ninety-first birthday), celebrating their fiftieth wedding anniversary with Tim and Lindy, December 30, 1997. (Linda Williams)

Niles Beach. To attract new members from beyond the pearly gates, the decision was made to install a swimming pool in place of the Clays' abandoned sunken tennis court. No longer is the club the resort almost exclusively of the Point, nor racing its rationale, and outer harbor moorings that for generations were taken for granted are coveted by members from afar. It remains the most dramatic yacht club location on the coast.

There is less and less seacoast left for more and more who want to live by it, and even the gulls are on short rations. For thirty years the fishing has been in a freefall, and Gloucester gurry is on the endangered list. The more resolute, fish-catching cormorant, on the other hand, thrives. The southern cardinal, crimson and cocky, is now ubiquitous on the Point all year. Mockingbirds too, coming and going, summer and winter. But where are the pheasants, squawking in our brush, emerging so cautiously to inspect the grounds, even down to the tide?

Mr. and Mrs. R— Jane and David Richardson at Robbins-Stebbins wedding, August 27, 1960. (Sarah Fraser Robbins)

When we came, poison ivy suffocated rum cherry trees clear to the top from a trunk so thick you had to cut it with an ax. Thirty years after I cleared it out the catbrier pokes back up through the lawn. As for the oriental bittersweet with its golden autumn berries, it was so admired in some far-off place by a lady of the Point, so they say, that she had one planted on her grounds—bittersweet indeed; the birds digest the berries and broadcast the seeds from shore to shore, and now this apparently unstoppable pest climbs utility poles, chokes transformers and slithers underground to embrace everything in its way.

But what of it? With us, of us still somehow, are the first impatient drifts of snowdrops, followed by those brave clumps of purple peeping croci and then the yellower-than-yellow nodding cumuli of daffodils, the shimmery shad of May, the dogtooth violets and the wild geraniums, the wilder honeysuckle, the clethra and the beach rose, the summer seaside gardens, the loosestrife and the laurel down around the pond, the goldenrod, the tansy, the bitter sweet of the bittersweet, the autumn asters and, with them and on them, the monarchs on wings lighter than the zephyr that wafts them from afar, and the mums glowing with quiet finality.

That enticing, exciting whiff of low-tide iodine, the mewing gulls, our groaner off our lighthouse sighing on the southeasterly, the sea smoke blowing ashore so ghostly through the branches in the February dawn . . . while "under the oppression of the silent fog," Tom Eliot's gently tolling bell buoy "measures time not our time rung by the unhurried ground swell."

Sea smoke on a snowy morning from the south piazza of "Black Bess," February 1993. (Author photo)

It's September of 1971. The book on Eastern Point is about to appear:[7]

Here on the coast this has been a pretty good summer for fog. For a while at the beginning of August it looked as if we were going to get stuck in one of those queer lows, like the one that hung around stray-cat fashion four years ago (little feet everywhere), but it was only a short spell of thick that moved by and left us alone.

So the fog never got oppressive, just enough of it to be interesting. Plenty of sun, plenty of westerly breeze, rain when we needed it bad, a couple of theatrical thunderstorms and I guess some of the clearest nights for starwatching in years. One evening we were checking up on the moons of Jupiter when the brightest meteor I ever saw zapped across, searing a white scar in the firmament from the North Star clear through the Big Dipper.

Dramatic, but untouchable. Most of the natural phenomena in our citified civilization are for spectators, but we coastal people know that fog is for participating. It meets you more than half way. It forces human reaction. It embraces you, befuddles you, stifles you, enchants you, but it is there compelling your attention until it tires of the game and takes its leave.

So fog is my favorite weather . . . as long as it doesn't break a leg on my doorstep and stay for the season.

Why, there are New Englanders who live twenty miles from the coast and have never been fogged in, literally at least, and never will; something important is missing from their lives, though they don't know it in their inland ignorance.

They will never know the sense of possession and of being possessed, the intimacy, the closing-in of the world and the transfor-

mation of it . . . all without imprisonment, for the privacy that descends and envelops doesn't instill claustrophobia. Fog does not strangle at the shore, it enfolds.

Of course I am talking about the land side of the sea. Fog on the ocean is something else, and I want no part of it.

At sea fog is no friend unless you are up to no good, pulling the other fellow's lobster pots, or sneaking out to Rum Row under cover of it, as they did in the twenties, after a load of hooch in your launch, your old one-lung Lothrop turning so steadily . . . putt, putt, putt . . . putt, putt . . . putt, putt, putt, putt . . . putt . . .

Offshore in a thick o' fog nothing is where it ought to be. Big noises sound small, and small big, and a man's voice can be heard a half a mile for no reason at all. Cruising by the compass, a red bobbing lobster buoy suddenly looms up like the number-six nun you've been trying to pick up, and on every quarter, beyond your bowsprit and the stern of your dinghy, lurks menace.

I don't like driving in the fog either, when it always seems to come at night, and all you can do is follow those twin, mindless, mesmerizing shafts of your headlights wherever they may lead, which is like following your nose with your eyes shut.

Nevertheless, and for all its obfuscations, fog in the right doses is one of the joys of coastal life, and as a writer I like to work in it. This penchant begs the obvious question which I prefer to answer by protesting that really nothing can match a good, solid, galloping fog for mooring a worker to his machine—a typewriter to windward, you might say—and leaving him alone for that most difficult of confrontations, the one with his brain. It's not the fog outside the head that bothers, anyway; it's the other one.

Nothing feline about these gallopers. They sweep in and around and through, and in the old days they left your best gut-strung tennis racket in a limp state of twangy uselessness. This kind of writing fog swirls and shoves in from the Atlantic, leaves the trees dripping into pools of condensate. Through the open windows it pours, a summer fog, abandoning beads of moisture on the screen, casualties of its progress. Against a dark background you can watch it spill over the sill and billow into the room as if it were smoke or steam.

Clothes left overnight on a bedroom chair can almost be wrung out before breakfast, and the inside of your sneaker is sticky and stubborn to sneak into. Wallpaper goes soggy and wants to wearily fall away from the damp plaster, and infinitives split out of pure humidity. Salt won't pour, bread moulds, and a piece of deathless prose left in a typewriter emerges with a permanent warp.

Outside, what discovery in all creation can compare with the fog-caressed snare, the watchful spider swaying tall amongst the weeping branches of the spruce, each proud maneuver of its maker, each gossamer knot, every cable of concentric cunning, spun off in silver droplets for the world to wonder at, meaning only me, as if the fog were real, the web a mere fancy left over from some magic of the night.

Ah, the sounds of it, of it and through it. The unseen surf out there, gentled by it. The forlorn shriek of the sightless gull. The whump of the distant diaphone. The electronic blats of the twin horns at the lighthouse and the breakwater, disharmonious and dispassionate. The wail of the whistler, rising, falling, sighing under the burden of the deep. The haphazard clang of the bell buoy, far off, unsure, feminine, fickle and alone.

And through it a brontosaurus blast from a big one poking out the harbor with its radar, so piercing you might think it would overpower the fog and shatter a tunnel for itself to steer through. Then an answering WHAP from a dragger rounding in by the Point. And a raucous beep from a lobsterman. And a vigorous jabbering of her bell from the soaking cockpit of some cruising yawl, on her way down East, socked in off Black Bess until it lifts.

With the rising sun, the night-made fog scales up from the top down. Then, the illusions. From the Back Shore, brilliant blue overhead, I've gazed out to sea over a cotton cloud of ground fog as if from the window of an airplane; and thrust up through this coverlet, perhaps no more than fifteen or twenty feet thick, the twin light towers of Thacher's Island, as irrelevant to the strange scene as London Bridge to the desert.

And some mornings, all unexpectedly it will burn off just enough in Gloucester Harbor to reveal Ten Pound Island, a disconnected mirage in a gray waste of fog, ashine in the sun, ten thousand miles from nowhere.

Or the fog will hang wistfully along the western shore across from Eastern Point as if unwilling to disperse, enshrouding the whole rusty ledge from the gull-streaked lump of Norman's Woe to the Cut, while above it the modest and intimate but disembodied ridges of Bond Hill and Ravenwood Park loom as high and mighty and remote as the presidential peaks.

An hour ago that fog of mine broke up and departed on the wings of the westerly. The sun is bright. The clouds scud off to sea, and the world is out there, just as it is, if not as it ought to be.

But the spell of it stuck with me, and my work is done.

ACKNOWLEDGMENTS
FIRST EDITION

THE WRITING OF LIVELY LOCAL history requires the lively cooperation of living people, some near, some afar, all with a bit of earth (and in our case, sea) in common; hence I am eager to express my gratitude for the contributions of so many who have responded so generously to my calls for assistance in the preparation of this work.

Especially am I indebted to Robert F. Brown, who painstakingly provided invaluable sources and leads from his Cape Ann bibliography and personal library; to Miss Dorothy Buhler, for a wealth of matter and memories about the upper Point and its personages; to Mrs. Jean Kay Burgess, Mrs. Frances Cunningham, James P. Nugent, Douglas E. Parker, Irving Trefry and James C. Walen for vivid personal recollections of the Point and East Gloucester; to Paul H. Sherman for making available to me his extensive compilation of Cape Ann shipwrecks; and to Richard W. Updike, for important information about the history of the Eastern Point Lighthouse from his lighthouse researches, and Gordon W. Thomas, Jane of the fishing fleet, for coming through as always with vintage photos and facts.

To a large extent this has been a chronicle of distinctive families and individuals. I am deeply indebted to Mrs. Helen Patch Gray and Andrew L. Gray for permission to examine and publish letters of Isabella Stewart Gardner, Henry Davis Sleeper and Caroline Sinkler to A. Piatt Andrew and from Evelyn Ames Hall to Mrs. Isaac Patch, and for their many anecdotes and insights and the loan of pictorial material; to Mrs. Paula Patch Newell for permission to publish portions of letters from Sleeper to Andrew and from Andrew to his parents; to Mrs. Hilda Raymond Williamson, Miss Julia Raymond, Mrs. Pauline Pollard Raymond, Samuel Edward Raymond, Henry A. Raymond, Miss Madeleine Williams Edward P. Williams and Henry Williams for their colorful additions to the story of The Ramparts; to Edward R. Godfrey and Milton Henry Clifford, M.D., for lively memories of the Prentisses and Blighty; to Mrs. Constance Templeton Rhinelander for her delightful vignette of the Rhinelander family; for their family material and recollections, to Mrs. Lila Leonard Swift and Mrs. Lila Swift Monell (Leonard), Mrs. Elise Pollard Carson (Pollard), Mrs. David S. Greenough, Jr., (Greenough), Mrs. Caroline Sidney Lockwood (Sinkler), Mrs. Francis T P. Plimpton (Hall), Mrs. Virginia Parsons Burns (Hillier), Mrs. Dorothy Eastman Clay (Clay), Mrs. Jane Currier Richardson (Currier) and Mrs. Elizabeth Garland Lewis, Mrs. Alice Garland Walen and Dr. and Mrs. Joseph Garland (Rogers, Niles and Garland); and to Mrs. Frederick Sayford Bacon, particularly for her information and material relating to Joanna Davidge and David Randall-MacIver

Further, I am grateful to Llewellyn Howland III for reviewing the manuscript and introducing it to its publisher; to William L. Bauhan for the energy and imagination (and fortitude) with which he has graced and braced its publication; to Mervyn F. Piper and David L. Richardson for joining with Donald Monell in assuring the financial back-up which encouraged me to begin the work;

Others who have assisted in a variety of ways include E. Parker Hayden, Jr., Mrs. Maritje Jacobus Saling, James L. Kercher, Theodore S. Ireland, Isaac Patch, Jr., Mrs. John R. Cahill, Jr., Miss Alice E. Babson, Thomas E. Babson, Mrs. James B. Benham, Arthur E. Jensen, Charles W. Sibley, William D. Hoyt, Laurence A. Brown, Jr., Miss Dorothy A. Brown, Mrs. William Morris, Jr., Harold J. Warnecke, Mr. and Mrs. William B. Blanford, Mrs. Frank Wigglesworth, F. J. Torrance Baker, Mrs. Sarah Fraser Robbins, the late Miss Lillian Day, Leland G. Davis, D.D.S., Mrs. William G. Brown III, Mrs. Barbara Erkkila, Dana A. Story, Mrs. Ralph Hamilton and Julian deF. Hills.

And to the following and their staffs, my thanks for innumerable facts and favors: Cape Ann Historical Association, Gloucester; Gloucester City Clerk and Board of Assessors; Sawyer Free Library, Gloucester; Essex County Registries of Deeds and Probate, Salem; Supreme Judicial Court of Massachusetts and records of the Court of Common Pleas, Salem; Essex Institute, Salem; Peabody Museum, Salem; Legislative Records Branch, Military Records Division and Diplomatic, Legal and Fiscal Records Division, National Archives and Records Service, Washington; Addison Gallery of American Art, Phillips Academy, Andover; Boston Museum of Fine Arts; Isabella Stewart Gardner Museum, Boston.

J. E. G. 1971

BIBLIOGRAPHY

Atlas of Cape Ann. G. M. Hopkins, 1884.

Babson, John J.: *History of the Town of Gloucester*. Gloucester, 1860. *Notes and Additions to the History of Gloucester*, 1st and 2nd Series, Gloucester, 1876 & 1891.

Barlow, Ernesta Drinker: "Cradle Song of My Youth," *Yankee,* October, 1963.

Beaux, Cecilia: *Background with Figures*. Boston, 1930.

Bentley, William: *The Diary of William Bentley, D.D.* Salem, 1905.

Birdseye, Clarence & Eleanor C.: *Growing Woodland Plants*. New York, 1951.

Blanford, William B. & Elizabeth C.: *Beauport Impressions*. Boston, 1965.

Blunt, Edward M. *The American Coast Pilot*. New York, 1817 & 1847.

Bowen, Catherine Drinker: *Family Portrait*. Boston, 1970.

Briggs, L. Vernon: *History and Genealogy of the Cabot Family*. Boston, 1927.

Browning, Fannie Barrett: *Some Memories of Robert Browning*. Boston, 1928.

Chamberlain, Allen: *Pigeon Cove—Its Early Settlers and Their Farms: 1702-1840*. Rockport, Mass., 1940.

Chamberlain, Samuel & Hollister, Paul: *Beauport at Gloucester*. New York, 1951.

Champlain, Samuel de: "Account of visit to Le Beauport in 1606," translated from French edition of 1613, with map, *Cape Ann Advertiser,* Gloucester, May 3, 1878.

Clay, John: *My Life on the Range*. Norman, Oklahoma, 1962 (first published privately in 1924).

Old Days Recalled. Chicago, 1915.

Copeland, Melvin T. & Rogers, Elliott C.: *The Saga of Cape Ann*. Freeport, Me., 1960.

Coxe, R. Cleveland: "In Gloucester Harbor," *Century Magazine,* August, 1892.

Cunningham, Frances F.: "Memories of Cape Ann" (unpublished).

Curtis, Nancy and Richard C. Nylander: *Beauport: The Sleeper-McCann House*. Boston, 1990.

Description of the Sea-shore Property of the Eastern Point Associates, located on Cape Ann, Gloucester, Mass. Boston, ca. 1890.

Dictionary of American Biography. New York, 1961.

Eastern Point Yacht Club: Yearbooks.

Eastman, Ralph M.: *Pilots and Pilot Boats of Boston Harbor.* Boston, 1956.

Eliot, T.S.: *Four Quartets.* New York, 1943.

———— "Introduction to This American World" (Edgar A. Mowrer, London, 1928) in *Oxford Anthology of American Literature.* New York, 1945.

Ellery, Harrison: "Letters," *Cape Ann Advertiser.* Gloucester, 1878.

Ellery, James B.: *Records of Ellery-Dennison-Parsons Families.* 1956.

Encyclopedia Americana. New York, 1969.

Encyclopedia Britannica. New York, 1968.

Fishburne, Anne Sinkler: *Belvidere—A Plantation Memory.* Columbia, S.C., 1949.

Forbes, Robert Bennet: *Personal Reminiscences.* Boston, 1882.

Fusfeld, Daniel R.: *The Economic Thought of Franklin D. Roosevelt and the Origins of the New Deal.* New York, 1956.

Garland, Joseph E.: *Eastern Point Revisited. Then and Now: 1889-1989.* Gloucester, MA., 1989.

———— *Lone Voyager.* Boston, 1963.

———— *That Great Pattillo.* Boston, 1966.

———— *The North Shore: A Social History of Summers among the Noteworthy, Fashionable, Rich, Eccentric and Ordinary on Boston's Gold Coast, 1823-1929.* Beverly, MA 1998.

Garrett, Edmund H.: *Romance and Reality of the Puritan Coast.* Boston, 1897.

Gloucester City Directories.

Goode, G. Brown et al: *The Fisheries and Fishery Industries of the United States.* Washington, 1887.

Gould, Bartlett: "Burgess of Marblehead," Essex Institute Historical Collections, January, 1970.

Greenbie, Sydney & Marjorie: "Around the Horn to China—via 'Oregon,'" *Asia,* June, 1925.

Guinane, J. E., Rice, I. L., & Seyler, P. G.: Articles on Clarence Birdseye, *Quick Frozen Foods,* March, 1960.

Hennessy, M. E.: Article on A. Piatt Andrew, *Boston Globe,* Sept.18, 1921.

Herreshoff, L. Francis: *The Common Sense of Yacht Design.* Jamaica, N.Y., 1966.

Higginson, Francis: "Journal," in *Founding of Massachusetts.* Boston, 1930.

History of the American Field Service in France. Boston, 1920.

Howe, Henry F.: *Salt Rivers of the Massachusetts Shore.* New York, 1951.

Hunt, Freeman: *Lives of American Merchants.* New York, 1856.

Josselyn, John: *Two Voyages to New England.* Boston, 1865.

Junger, Sebastian: *The Perfect Storm.* New York, 1997.

Letters from Isabella Stewart Gardner to Abram Piatt Andrew. New York, 1967.

Memorandum on Eastern Point Gloucester, May 12, 1931.

Memorial of the Two Hundred and Ftfiieth Anniversary of Gloucester, 1892. Boston, 1901.

Miller, Betty: *Robert Browning—A Portrait.* New York, 1952.

Mills, Ruth E.: *George Marble Wonson—His Forebears and Descendants.* Gloucester, 1958.

Morison, Samuel Eliot: *The Maritime History of Massachusetts, 1783-1860.* Boston, 1921.

Myers, Gustavus: *History of the Great American Fortunes.* New York, 1937.

Niles, Thomas: Statement to the Canby Claims Commission of the War Department, November 8, 1866. National Archives., Washington, D.C.

———— re the claim of. Reports and correspondence of the Canby Claims Commission. National Archives. Washington, D.C.

———— Petition to Congress, January 30, 1869. National Archives., Washington, D.C.

———— deceased. Report Number 884, Committee on War Claims, House of Representatives, 51st Congress, Session l. March 19, 1890. National Archives, Washington, D.C.

———— deceased, An Act for the relief of the estate of. Chapter 1232. 51st Congress, Session I, September 30, 1890. National Archives, Washington, D.C.

North Shore Blue Book and Social Register, Boston 1920 ed.

Oakley, Thornton: *Cecilia Beaux.* Philadelphia, 1943.

Ogilvie, W. E.: Lecture on Union Stock Yard delivered before Chicago Historical Society, April 14, 1965.

Patch, Isaac: *Closing the Circle: A Buckalino Journey Around Our Time.* Wellesley, MA 1996.

Phelps, Elizabeth Stuart: *Chapters from a Life.* Boston, 1896.

Pleasure Drives around Cape Ann. Gloucester, 1896.

Pringle, James R.: *History of the Town and City of Gloucester.* Gloucester, 1892.

Procter, George H.: *The Fishermen's Memorial and Record Book.* Gloucester, 1873.

The Fishermen's Own Book. Gloucester, 1882.

Randall-Maclver, David: *Joanna Randall-MacIver—A Memoir.* Oxford, 1932.

Randall-MacIver, David, obituary of, *American Journal of Archaeology,* July-September, 1945, 359-360.

Robbins, Sarah Fraser, and Clarice M. Yentsch: *The Sea Is All About Us.* The Peabody Museum, Salem, Mass., 1973.

Roosevelt, Elliott, ed.: F.D.R. *His Personal Letters.* New York, 1947.

Sewall, Samuel: "Diary of Samuel Sewall," *Massachusetts Historical Collections* VI.

Shaler, Nathaniel S.: *The Geology of Cape Ann, Massachusetts.* Washington, 1888.

Smith, Charlton L.: *Gus Harvey, The Boy Skipper of Cape Ann.* Boston, 1920.

State Street Trust Company: *Some Merchants and Sea Captains of Old Boston.* Boston, 1918.

———— *Other Merchants and Sea Captains of Old Boston.* Boston, 1919.

Stephens, William P.: *Traditions and Memories of American Yachting.* New York, 1945.

Story, Dana: *Frame-up!* Barre, Mass., 1964.

Tharp, Louise Hall: *Mrs. Jack.* Boston, 1965.

Thomas, Gordon W.: *Fast and Able.* Gloucester, 1968.

Trial of Marshall and Ross for Barn-Burning. A Brief Exposure of a Systematic Attempt to Mislead the Public Mind, and to Create a False Sympathy in Behalf of Convicted Incendiaries. By "A Looker-on in Vienna." 1859.

Tryon, W.S.: *Parnassus Corner: A Life of James T. Fields, Publisher to the Victorians.* Boston, 1963

Updike, Richard W.: "Winslow Lewis and the Lighthouses," *The American Neptune,* January, 1968.

Warren, Edward: *The Life of John Warren, MD.* Boston, 1874.

Washburn, Henry Bradford: *Philip Mercer Rhinelander.* New York, 1950.

Webber, John S., Jr.: *In and Around Cape Ann.* Gloucester, 1896.

Williams, Edward P.: *A Varied Career: Recollections and Anecdotes.* Essex, Conn., 1988.

Winsor, Justin, ed.: *The Memorial History of Boston.* Boston, 1880.

Winwar, Frances: *The Immortal Lovers.* New York, 1950.

Zobel, Hiller B.: *The Boston Massacre.* New York, 1970.

PUBLICATIONS CONSULTED

Boston Globe; Boston Herald; Cape Ann Advertiser; Cape Ann Light; Cape Ann Shore; Frank Leslie's Illustrated Newspaper; Gloucester Daily Times; Gloucester News; Gloucester Telegraph; North Shore Breeze; Salem Advocate; Salem Courier; Salem Gazette; Salem Register.

CHAPTER NOTES

1. DISCOVERED
    1. Higginson, *Journal,* 72.
    2. Champlain, in *Cape Ann Advertiser,* May 3, 1878.
    3. Josselyn, *Two Voyages,* 22.
    4. Garrett, *Romance and Reality,* 193.
    5. Josselyn, 23.

2. GRANTED
    1. Babson, *History of Gloucester,* 203.
    2. Ibid., 205.

3. SETTLED
    1. Clark to Cushing, Essex Deeds, 274–75, Oct. 31, 1833.
    2. Ellery, in *Cape Ann Advertiser,* Nov. 8, 1878.

4. A VERY ROUGH FARM
    1. Babson, *History of Gloucester,* 477.
    2. Chandler, *Diary,* in Babson, *Notes & Additions, 2nd Series,* 48.
    3. Ellery, in *Cape Ann Advertiser,* Nov. 8, 1878.
    4. Bentley, *Diary,* I, 265-7.
    5. Ibid., II, 8.
    6. Copeland and Rogers, *Saga,* 46.
    7. Bentley, II, 327.

5. SHIPWRECK SHORE
    1. *Cape Ann Light,* Sept. 12, 1857, from *Salem Register.*
    2. Bentley, III, 279.
    3. *Cape Ann Advertiser,* Feb. 11, 1859.
    4. Bentley, III, 280.
    5. *Cape Ann Advertiser,* Feb. 11, 1859.
    6. Babson, *History of Gloucester,* 512.
    7. *Cape Ann Advertiser,* Aug. 5, 1870. "Webfoot" was identified to the author
as Captain Phelps by his descendant, Warren Poland, MD, of Gloucester.
    8. Thomas to Daniel Hillier, May 8, 1826.
    9. Gorham Burnham to U.S.A., Essex Deeds, 253-256, July 24, 1829.
    10. *Gloucester Telegraph,* Mar. 14, 1829.
    11. Ibid.
    12. Ibid.

6. LIGHTHOUSE

1. Babson, *History of Gloucester*, 279.
2. Addison Plumer to Thomas Hillier, Essex Deeds, May 19, 1830.

7. KU-SHING

1. Hunt, *Lives*, 64.
2. Briggs, *History*, 529.
3. Forbes, *Personal Reminiscences*, 338.
4. Niles, *Statement*.
5. Eastman, *Pilots and Pilot Boats*, 29-31.
6. Ibid.
7. *Gloucester Telegraph*, Mar. 9, 1859.
8. Niles, *Statement*.
9. State Street Trust Co., *Other Merchants*, 18.
10. *Gloucester Telegraph*, Jan. 5, 1839.
11. Procter, *Fishermen's Memorial & Record Book*, 10-11.

8. THE COMING OF THOMAS NILES

1. *Niles, Re the claim of,* from argument of John A. Andrew.
2. Warren, *The Life of John Warren, MD,* 302ff.
3. Winsor, *Memorial History,* 111, 602.
4. Henry F. Jenks, "Old School Street," *The New England Magazine,* Nov. 1895.
5. Niles, *Statement*.
6. *Gloucester Daily Times,* Aug. 9, 1911.
7. Niles, *Statement*.
8. Thomas to Daniel Hillier, Aug. 7, 1845.
9. Niles, *Statement*.
10. Ibid.
11. Ibid.
12. *Gloucester Telegraph,* Sept. 23, 1848.
13. *Gloucester News,* Nov. 4, 1848.

9. AN OPEN AND SHUT CASE

1. *Niles v. Rowe et al.,* Massachusetts Supreme Judicial Court, December 1847, term.
2. Ibid.
3. *Cape Ann Advertiser,* Mar. 23, 1883.
4. Related by Miss Alice Babson.
5. *Gloucester Daily Times,* Aug. 4, 1911.
6. *Gloucester Telegraph,* Aug. 13 & 17, 1853.
7. *Gloucester Telegraph,* Mar. 9, 1859.

10. THE FOUR-CENT FERRY

1. *Cape Ann Advertiser,* June 10, 1868.

11. I DID NOT LIKE HIS CONDUC

1. Trial of Marshall and Ross, 13.
2. *Gloucester Telegraph,* Feb. 13, 1858.
3. Account from *Gloucester Telegraph,* Mar. 3 & Apr. 28, 1858.
4. Account from *Gloucester Telegraph,* March 17, 20 & 24, 1858.
5. Account from *Gloucester Telegraph,* March 9, 1859.

12. FARMER NILES BELEAGUERED

1. *Cape Ann Advertiser,* Mar. 11, 1859.

2. Ibid.

3. *Cape Ann Advertiser,* Mar. 18, 1859.

4. *Cape Ann Advertiser,* Apr. 8, 1859, from the *Boston Herald.*

5. "The tongue is an unruly member . . ." Commonly misquoted from "The tongue can no man tame; it is an unruly evil." James 3:8.

6. *Gloucester Daily Times,* undated.

7. *Gloucester Daily Times,* undated, probably 1900.

8. *Gloucester Telegraph,* Oct. 25, 1862.

13. FORT NO-NAME

1. *Gloucester Telegraph,* Nov. 18, 1863.

2. *Gloucester Telegraph,* Nov. 28, 1863.

3. *Gloucester Telegraph,* Feb. 13, 1864.

4. John Milton, "On His Blindness."

5. *Gloucester Telegraph,* Feb. 1, 1865.

14. THE BATTLE OF EASTERN POINT HEIGHTS

1. Niles, *Statement.*

2. *Niles, Re the claim of.*

15. BREAKWATER TALK

1. *Gloucester Telegraph,* May 23, 1868, from the *Boston Advertiser.*

2. *Cape Ann Advertiser,* Dec. 4, 1868.

3. *Cape Ann Advertiser,* May 7, 1869

4. *Frank Leslie's Illustrated Newspaper,* Mar. 27, 1875.

5. Alexander Pope, *Odyssey,* Book XII.

6. *Cape Ann Advertiser,* Aug. 26, 1898.

16. MOTHER ANN'S COW

1. *Gloucester Daily Times,* Sept. 15, 1891.

2. Procter, *Fishermen's Own Book,* 199–200.

3. *Cape Ann Advertiser,* Feb. 17, 1882.

4. *Cape Ann Advertiser,* Feb. 24, 1882.

5. Ibid.

6. *Cape Ann Advertiser,* Mar. 24, 1882.

7. *Cape Ann Advertiser,* June 9, 1882.

8. *Cape Ann Advertiser,* Mar. 14, 1882.

17. OCEANA

1. Tryon, *Parnassus Corner,* 230–232.

2. Cunningham, *Memories.*

18. THE EASTERN POINT ASSOCIATES

1. *North Shore Breeze,* Aug. 3, 1928.

2. *Cape Ann Advertiser,* July 19, 1889.

3–10. These homes today are owned by: (3) Doctors Jan Koch Weser and Diane Chen; (4) Mr. and Mrs. Virgilijus Martinonis; (5) Mrs. Louise Loud; (6) Mr. and Mrs. Joseph E. Garland; (7) Mr. and Mrs. Eben Knowlton; (8) Mrs. Sarah Fraser Robbins; (9) Mr. and Mrs. Edward Kaloust; (10) Mr. and Mrs. Adair Miller.

11. *Cape Ann Advertiser,* Jan. 15, 1897.

12. Purchased by the Eastern Point Yacht Club in 1951.

13. *Cape Ann Advertiser,* July 19, 1889

14. *Cape Ann Advertiser,* Oct. 2, 1896.

15–20. These homes today are owned by: (15) Mr. and Mrs. John Sueuss; (16) Duncan B. Cox, Jr.; (17) John Haley; (18) Ever Curtis, M.D.; (19) David Brown; (20) Mrs. Roger Saunders

21. *Cape Ann Advertiser,* April 11, 1890.

22. *Cape Ann Advertiser,* June 15, 1894.

23. Personal communication.

24. This home today is owned by Donald Saunders.

25. *Memorandum on Eastern Point.*

26. *Cape Ann Advertiser,* July 23, 1897.

19. SEA VOICES

1. Phelps quotations from *Chapters From a Life,* 193–6, 157, 167–8.

2. *Memorial of the 250th Anniversary,* 336–7.

3. *Dictionary of American Biography,* X, Part 1, 418.

4. Copeland and Rogers, *Saga,* 70.

5. These exchanges appeared in the *Gloucester Daily Times,* June 22 & 30, 1891; May 13 & June 10, 1892.

6. Phelps, *Chapters,* 273

7. Phelps, *Chapters,* 199.

8. *Cape Ann Advertiser,* Oct. 16, 1896.

9. *Gloucester Daily Times,* Jan. 1, 1901.

10. Personal communication.

11. Eliot, Introduction to *This American World.*

12. *North Shore '72,* May 27, 1972.

20. KNIGHTS OF THE BRUSH

For the account of the rise of the East Gloucester art colony, this chapter relies materially on the chapter entitled "Painted Place and Painted Face" in the author's *The North Shore* (Beverly, MA, 1998.)

1. *Louisa May Alcott: Her Life, Letters and Journals.* Boston, 1899.

2. *Cape Ann Advertiser,* Aug. 14, 1896, from the Boston Sunday Herald.

3. *Gloucester Daily Times,* July 26, 1912, from *The Boston Post.*

4. After ten years in California as a young man, William Niles was a London representative of the Boston publishing house of Roberts Brothers, of which his brother, Thomas, Jr., was a partner. On his return to Boston he devoted himself to painting, ultimately retiring to Bedford, where he died in 1905 at seventy-eight.

5. *Gloucester Daily Times,* July 26, 1912, from the *Boston Post.*

6. This house today is owned by Donald Saunders. Although registered as built in 1912, it is possible "Bramble Ledge" was erected by George Stacy as housing for employees of the Colonial Arms, as tradition has it. Some real estate in Gloucester improved prior to 1912, it is said, is listed as built in 1912, owing to loss or destruction of some records prior to that date.

7. Mary Gordon, "Recording the Good News of the Gilded Age," *New York Times,* Oct. 29, 1995.

21. THE REEF OF GLOUCESTER'S WOE

1. *Cape Ann Advertiser,* Sept. 28, 1894.

2. *Gloucester Daily Times,* Dec. 20, 1900.

22. CAMP WOLCOTT: BASTION AGAINST THE SPANIARD

1. *Cape Ann Advertiser,* April 22.
2. Ibid.
3. *Cape Ann Advertiser,* May 13, 1898.
4. *Cape Ann Advertiser,* May 20, 1898.
5. *Cape Ann Advertiser,* May 21, 1898.
6. *Cape Ann Advertiser,* May 23, 1898.
7. *Gloucester Daily Times,* June 1, 1898.

23. THE RAMPARTS

1. *Dictionary of American Biography,* III, Part 2, 451.
2. S. Edward Raymond, personal communications.
3. *Gloucester Daily Times,* Aug. 3, 1976.
4. Raymond.
5. Ibid.
6. "The Eastern Point Colony," *North Shore Breeze,* Aug. 17, 1923.

24. MRS. RAYMOND'S REGIME

1. Personal communication.
2. Williams, *A Varied Career.*

25. THE COLONIAL ARMS

1. *Gloucester Daily Times,* Jan. 2,1908.
2. Ibid.
3. This house today is owned by Mrs. Ute Gräfin Haller von Hallerstein.
4. *Boston Globe,* Jan. 2, 1908.
5. *Cape Ann Advertiser,* Mar. 9, 1909; *North Shore Breeze,* Apr. 7, 1911.

26. SOME MEN OF THE OLD SCHOOL

1. *Gloucester Daily Times,* April 12, 1919.
2. Personal communication.
3. Clay, *My Life on the Range,* 4. This vigorous and colorful memoir is a classic in the documentary literature of the West.
4. Ibid., 268.
5. Ibid., 12-13.
6. Personal communication.
7. *Cape Ann Shore,* undated.
8. Personal communication.
9. Personal communication.

27. A DAB OF DABSVILLE

1. Patch, *Closing the Circle.*
2. Randall-MacIver, *Joanna Randall-MacIver—A Memoir.*
3. Basil Lanneau Gildersleeve, University Professor of Greek at Johns Hopkins University.
4. Randall-MacIver.
5. Fusfeld, *Economic Thought of FDR,* 23–25.
6. Roosevelt, *F.D.R. His Personal Letters,* I, 474.
7. Ibid., 486.
8. Ibid., 487.
9. Fusfeld, 30–33.
10. Roosevelt, 529.

11. Ibid., 531.

12. Ibid., 531n.

13. Beaux, *Background,* 339.

14. Ibid., 340–1.

15. Oakley, *Cecilia Beaux,* 3.

16. Beaux, 340

17. Ibid., 341.

18. Oakley, 9.

19. Barlow, *Cradle Song.*

20. Frederick Platt, *A Portrait of Cecilia Beaux,* L'Officiel/USA, Oct. 1978, 156–161.

21. Oakley, 10.

22. Ibid., 6–8

23. Ibid., 10.

24. Platt.

25. On her death in 1942 Cecilia Beaux left "Green Alley" to her nephew, the late Henry S. Drinker, Jr., who shared summer occupancy with his sisters, Ernesta Barlow and Catherine Bowen. It is now owned by Roger Saunders, whose late wife Nina conceived and supervised a superb restoration of the house and estate.

26. Barlow.

27. Ibid.

28. MORE DABS OF DABSVILLE

1. Caroline Sinkler to A. Piatt Andrew, probably spring of 1910. (Most of her letters are undated.)

2. *Dictionary of American Biography,* IX, Parts 2, 3.

3. Caroline Sinkler to A. Piatt Andrew, probably early in 1908.

4. Ibid.

5. Personal interview.

6. Personal communication.

7. Henry Davis Sleeper to A. Piatt Andrew, Apr. 19, 1906.

8. Interview with J. Henry Sleeper II by Philip Hayden, Aug. 11, 1991, in *Beauport Quotes,* 2 & 3. Unpublished.

9. Isabella Stewart Gardner to A. Piatt Andrew, Sept. 12, 1907.

29. DRAMATIS PERSONAE DABSVILLEA

1. Henry Davis Sleeper to A. Piatt Andrew, Aug. 4, 1908.

2. Ibid., Aug. 6, 1908.

3. Ibid., date unclear, 1908.

4. Isabella Stewart Gardner to A. Piatt Andrew, Aug. 16, 1908.

5. Henry Davis Sleeper to A. Piatt Andrew, Aug. 20, 1908.

6. Ibid., Aug. 27, 1908.

7. Ibid., Aug. 28, 1908.

8. Ibid., Sept. 3, 1908.

9. Isabella Stewart Gardner to A. Piatt Andrew, Sept. 5, 1908.

10. Henry Davis Sleeper to A. Piatt Andrew, Sept. 7, 1908.

11. Caroline Sinkler to A. Piatt Andrew, mid-Sept., 1908

12. Ibid., probably early 1908.

13. Isabella Stewart Gardner to A. Piatt Andrew, Sept. 26, 1908.

14. Caroline Sinkler to A. Piatt Andrew, autumn 1908.

15. Isabella Stewart Gardner to A. Piatt Andrew, Aug. 10, 1909.

16. Caroline Sinkler to A. Piatt Andrew, undated.

17. Ibid.

18. *Gloucester Daily Times,* Dec. 11, 1909.

19. Caroline Sinkler to A. Piatt Andrew, possibly spring of 1910.

20. Andrew Gray, "A New England Bloomsbury," *Fenway Court,* Isabella Stewart Gardner Museum 1975 Annual Report, 3.

21. Andrew Gray, "Mrs. Gardner as Matchmaker," *Fenway Court,* Isabella Stewart Gardner Museum 1982 Annual Report, 48–53.

22. Henry James to Isabella Stewart Gardner, October 1911 (from Archives of Isabella Stewart Gardner Museum).

23. Beaux, *Background,* 233.

30. OF POLITICS AND PRATFALLS

1. Personal communication.

2. *Gloucester Daily Times,* July 5, 1912.

3. *Gloucester Daily Times,* July 6, 1912.

4. Ibid.

5. *Gloucester Daily Times,* Sept. 29, 1912.

31. THE AMERICAN FIELD SERVICE

1. *History of the AFS in France,* I, 32-33.

2. Ibid., II, 491.

3. Henry Davis Sleeper to Isabella Stewart Gardner, *Beauport Quotes* 3. Unpublished.

4. "Garden Book" courtesy of Priscilla Woods McCoy.

5. *History of the AFS in France,* I, 8–9.

6. Ibid., I, 15-16.

7. Ibid., I, 12.

8. Ibid., I, 56-59.

9. Ibid., I, 16.

32. MASONRY TEMPLES

1. Owned for many years by Mr. and Mrs. James O. Welch and purchased in 1994, after two more owners, by Mr. and Mrs. Robert L. Crandall, who regretfully razed "Villa Latomia" as beyond repair and built a new home there.

2. *Dictionary of American Biography,* VII, Part 1, 1, from General Mills's autobiography, *My Story,* privately printed in 1918.

3. Mrs. Pauline Raymond, personal interview. Today the house on Chicken Lane is owned by her grandson and his wife, Mr. and Mrs. Gordon P. Baird.

4–7. These homes today are owned by (4) Mr. and Mrs. Richard Bell; (5) G. Anthony (Tony) Bryan; (6) Mr. and Mrs. Bradford D. Whitten; (7) Patrick D. Brady.

8–12. Personal communications.

33. MORE PRATFALLS AND POLITICS

1. *Gloucester Daily Times,* September 27, 1989.

2. Randall-MacIver, *Joanna Randall-MacIver—A Memoir.*

3. Ibid.

4. *Gloucester Daily Times,* Sept. 12, 1921.

5. *Boston Sunday Globe,* Sept. 18, 1921.

6. *North Shore Breeze,* Oct. 6, 1922.

34. THE TEETERING TWENTIES

1. *Gloucester Daily Times*, Feb. 3 & 4, 1927.
2. Personal communication.
3. Ogilvie, *Union Stock Yard*.
4–7. Personal communications.
8. *Gloucester Daily Times*, October 9 & 16, 1922.
9. *Memorandum on Eastern Point*.
10. Personal communication.

35. COMINGS AND GOINGS

1. Washburn, *Philip Mercer Rhinelander*, 7-8. To the author's distress, Mrs. Rhinelander severely blue-pencilled Dean Washburn's authorized biography before publication.
2. Ibid., 10.
3. Ibid., 12.
4. Related by David Rhinelander, a grandson.
5. Washburn, 14–15.
6. Personal communication, Constance Templeton Rhinelander.
7. "Culbuoy" was rented in 1935 and sold in 1938 to Judge and Mrs. Horace Forbes Baker of Sewickley, Pennsylvania, and remains in their family.
8. Samuel Temple to E. Parker Hayden, M.D., Dec. 8, 1944. The house was inherited on Dr. Hayden's death by his son, E. Parker Hayden, Jr., and on his death in 1992 by his son Philip.
9. Owned for many years thereafter by Mrs. Woods's late sister, Katherine, and her husband, the Reverend William F. A. Stride. On his death in 1970 the house passed to his son, William F. A. Stride, Jr., who died unexpectedly in 1997. The house remains in the Stride family.
10. Personal communication.
11. Winwar, *The Immortal Lovers*, 318.
12. Notation in Taggart's copy of 1913 Normandy guidebook, author's collection.
13. Sold after Lucy Taggart's death to her old friend Kathleen, widow of Paul V. McNutt, who later married Roy Garrett Watson, publisher of the *Houston Post* and treasurer of the Christian Science Church. Mrs. Watson predeceased her husband, and on his death "Tower of Four Winds" was sold to Mr. and Mrs. George Carter, who sold it to its present owners, Mr. and Mrs. Theodore E. Charles.
14. James P. Fadely, "Subtle Grace, Radiant Color: The Life of Hoosier Artist Lucy Taggart." *Traces of Indiana and Midwestern History*. Publication of the Indiana Historical Society. Indianapolis. Summer 1997.

36. OLD REGATTA DAYS AND THE CAPE ANN YACHT CLUB

1. *Gloucester Telegraph*, Sept. 4, 1858.

37. YACHTIN' AT EAST GLOUCESTER

1. *Cape Ann Shore*, July 7, 1934.
2. Personal interview.
3. T. Chittenden Hill of Boston acquired this lot in the fork of the road in 1926 and built a house there, now owned by Arthur E. Stickney.

38. THE EASTERN POINT YACHT CLUB

l. Professor Melancthon Williams Jacobus, Jr. (1855–1937), Dean of Faculty at

Hartford Theological Seminary from 1903 to 1927, acquired "Cragmoor" at the east corner of Farrington Avenue and Edgemoor Road in 1920 from Misses Wheeler and Gavit.

2. Personal communication.

3. *Gloucester Daily Times,* issues of October 1922; Mrs. Hilda Raymond Williamson, personal interview.

4. Herreshoff, *Common Sense,* II, 44.

5. Henry Williams, letter, Nov. 6, 1972.

6. The *Itch* was finally scratched in 1970.

7. *Cape Ann Shore,* July 9, 1932.

39. THESE PARLOUS TIMES

1. *Gloucester Daily Times,* June 21, 1933.

2. Concurrently, Epes Merchant of Gloucester was moving into the well-tailored brick Tudor house he had snuck under the wire between Niles Pond and the Harbor before the full force of the Crash descended. He lived only two years to enjoy it. The house is owned now by Mr. and Mrs. William Copeland.

3. Guinane et al., in *Quick Frozen Foods,* 326.

4. Ibid., 320.

5. Post obituary in *Boston Globe,* Sept. 13, 1983.

6. Guinane, 319.

7. *Gloucester Daily Times,* Jan. 27, 1976; Mar. 5, 1977.

8. Randall-MacIver, *Joanna Randall-MacIver—A Memoir.*

9. "Pierlane" was sold to Mr. and Mrs. Frederick S. Bacon and is now owned by Mrs. Paul M. Jacobs.

10. *Beauport Quotes,* 5.

11. *Gloucester Daily Times,* Sept. 24, 1934.

12. Henry Davis Sleeper to A. Piatt Andrew, May 5, 1912.

13. "Red Roof" is owned by Andrew's niece Mrs. Paula Patch Newell, his grandnephew Andrew L. Gray, and his grandniece Mrs. Patty Critchlow. In 1956 the new Route 128 bridge spanning the Annisquam River was named for the late Congressman Andrew.

FORTY YEARS ON, 1950–1990
NAUTICAL

1. *North Shore '72,* April 1, 1972.

2. Four or five years after our maritime adventure, Mrs. Bowen wrote me on May 22, 1970: "I am touched and complimented that you asked me to write an introduction to your history of Eastern Point. But I have settled on a subject for a new book and started work. And at this stage I simply daren't stop; it takes so long to get back on the track. I just have a long vacant road ahead and follow it selfishly. . . . P.S. You don't need an introduction, Joe. You are a darn good writer and anything you say about Gloucester will be well received. But I know how you feel. I wanted to have somebody write an introduction to *Family Portrait,* but Ted Weeks dissuaded me."

Family Portrait was just that and was published the day of her note, as she wrote, by Little, Brown and the Atlantic Monthly Press, of which Edward Weeks was editor.

3. *Gloucester Daily Times,* March 22, 1982.

4. *Gloucester Daily Times,* June 28, 1986.

5. Ibid.

RUSTICAL, AND MORE OR LESS SOCIABLE

1. *North Shore '72,* December 9, 1972.

2. *North Shore '71,* August 28, 1971.

3. A generation after the razing of "The Ramparts" the vitality that raised it a hundred years ago resurged with the reoccupation of the remaining tower in 1971 by Mrs. Raymond's great-grandsons, Jonathan (Jock) and Gordon (Gordo) Baird. As their Aunt Elise (Butch) Raymond Wallace prepared to donate more land to the Audubon Sanctuary, their mother, Ann Raymond Baird, turned over to them her share of the estate surrounding the old fort within which "The Ramparts" was erected and the antique house down "Chicken Lane" moved from East Gloucester Square by their late grandparents, Jonathan and Pauline (Bubby) Raymond.

Jock and his wife Linda clustered a modern solar house around the commodore's watchtower, while Gordo and his wife Joe Ann Hart moved into the "house full of bugs" Mrs. Greenough had spied sailing by her porch on a barge. Long ere the return of these natives they had been ushered onto the fields of popular music by that debonair maestro of the amateur jazz pianoforte, Frederick (Ted) Holdsworth, Jr., boyhood summer resident with his sister Nancy of the extreme northeast corner of the Point near Grapevine Cove, and long and happily married to Harriet Swift, one of Canute Leonard's granddaughters.

Ted encouraged Gordo and Jock with drums and guitar, and soon they formed the nucleus under his guidance of "Teddy and the Juniors," playing the oldies at functions social and charitable, yet inevitably surrendering to the rockous temptations of the day, to their mentor's benign dismay.

As these things go, Gordon and Sam, the Holdsworths' eldest son (who during the years of Protest fell into the habit of showing up at the annual Rouse Tourney at the last minute from somewhere in a torn shirt with a broken tennis racquet and sauntering away with the cup), founded *Musician* magazine, based in Gloucester, and in due course further astounded everyone by selling it to Billboard Publications to mutual advantage.

4. The Association of Eastern Point Residents was incorporated for charitable and other purposes on March 16, 1954, with the principal objects of maintaining and plowing the private roads, directing a security program, overseeing its Brace Cove beach for the benefit of the residents, protecting the one-acre/single-family zoning status of the Point, and representing its interests in relations with the City and the Commonwealth.

In 1960 the dues were five dollars a household plus a sixty-dollar assessment for the road fund. Merged with the dues twenty years ago, the assessment has increased tenfold.

For many years Donald Monell concentrated on zoning and environmental integrity and, with Adair Miller, on road maintenance, while William Copeland inaugurated and oversaw effective security measures, and Dr. Robert Ackerman a significant updated wetlands inventory.

The Association and subsequently the Directors individually were sued for alleged negligence in the July 1984 death of a boy who ran his motorbike against a chain posted at the north end of St. Louis Avenue and in the injury of a companion seated behind him. After lengthy litigation, the suit was dismissed in 1992.

From 1970 until his resignation in 1993, William Francis Adair Stride, Jr., presided over the Association with patience, persuasiveness and tireless attentiveness to the interests of the Eastern Point of his ancestors and contemporaries, and in so doing affirmed the essence of its character. He was succeeded by his cousin, Gordon

Baird. Bill Stride's unexpected death following surgery on September 3, 1997, at the age of sixty-six, left an emptiness in our midst.

5. Thanks to their steadfast appreciation of both the enduring and more ephemeral qualities of "Uncle Piatt" and his cottage on the harbor, his Patch nephews and nieces unto the third generation have reaped sixty-five years of summer pleasure from "Red Roof" for both family and a panoply of friends from Eastern Point and the world over while preserving it as a nigh-mesmerizing evocation of the man, his circle, his taste and his works, most particularly the American Field Service and the years in France.

Many are our memorable moments at "Red Roof." The author always pauses en route to Doc's famous terrace to reassure himself that the framed photograph of Grandsir Niles presented to the heirs of Isaac Patch so long ago still glares from the desktop.

All along, the reputation of Harry Sleeper's "Little Beauport" has both broadened and deepened as the curatorship of the Society for the Preservation of New England Antiquities has attracted increasingly wider interest and attendance, and with them fascination, during an extended season while probing ever more thoroughly the ever-broader spectrum of the setting, the extraordinarily agile architecture, the expansive variety of the rooms, the collection and its provenance and arrangement, the brilliance of the decor and the genius of the collector.

Piatt Andrew's grandnephew, Andrew Gray of "Red Roof," and the late E. Parker Hayden and his son Philip, summer neighbors in the Temple house across the boulevard, have made material contributions to further understanding of the "Beauport" and Dabsville mystique, as the late Nancy Holdsworth Scheerer did to restoration of the Sleeper decor.

Of great assistance in this resurgence has been the Beauport Advisory Committee, including interested neighbors, organized about 1982 by Caroline and Bill Stride. This group, increasing in size over the years, has worked to strengthen appreciation and support by the neighbors of the Point's most extraordinary "cottage" and has raised substantial funds for maintenance, restoration and endowment, an area in which Bill and Susan Copeland have played a sustaining and exemplary role.

6. The "Ramparts" tower was still encumbered with vines and the old fort's moat with trash when in November 1969 Don Monell, who played the game like a chessmaster, wrote his neighbors that the time had arrived for more tennis facilities on Eastern Point. The Richardson court was overburdened. Mrs. R was willing to sell about an acre of field directly across Fort Hill Avenue from "The Ramparts" for the creation of two courts if fifteen to twenty families would chip in.

Twenty-one by the following April had pledged $1,500 each, the land was bought for $10,000, Connolly Brothers laid in two cork-asphalt courts for another $21,000, and in June 1970 the first smacks and whacks and shouts and groans rose up from the precincts of the Fort Hill Tennis Club, Donald Monell its founding president.

Twenty years passed, and Ted Williams, then eighty-three and playing almost as vigorously as ever, circulated his own letter to the neighbors, beginning:

> Four score years ago my father brought forth on Eastern Point a tennis trophy known as the Rouse Cup, conceived in the idea of stimulating interest in tennis and dedicated to the proposition that all Eastern Pointers, young or old, tall or small, male or female, were created to compete in the

game of tennis. Now we are engaged in a new era, with new types of rackets, new types of balls, new types of court surfaces and new styles of living, wherein it is no longer practical to run a tournament over an extended period of time.

With that, what has been said to be among the earliest local tournaments in the American game was terminated in 1990 at the age of eighty. Ted and Linda Williams, and Bill (champion eight-time winner of the Rouse Cup) and Caroline Stride, who had been running it for several years, agreed to retire the Rouse, Prentiss and Richardson trophies for singles, mixed and father-and-son doubles to the families with the winningest members.

Edward P. Williams died suddenly in his hometown of Essex, Connecticut, on February 1, 1999, at the age of ninety-two.

7. *North Shore '71*, September 11, 1971.

INDEX

Marblehead Neck, 297, 311
Marchant, City Marshal, 269–270
Marchant, Homer, 397
Marsh, George, 157
Marshall, Lucy Allen (Mrs. Thomas), 18
Marshall, Robert, 87, 88–90, 91–92, 99
Marshall, Col. Thomas, 18
Martin, Capt. Charles S., Jr., 334, 335
Martinonis, Mrs. and Mrs. Virgilijus, 509
Marx, Harpo, 356
Masefield, John, 345
Mason, George, 279
Mason, John, 50, 53
Massachusetts Audubon Society, 483, 490, 516
Massachusetts General Hospital, 52, 61
Massachusetts Humane Society, 52, 142, 163–164, 208–211, 334, 335–336
Massachusetts Volunteer Militia Fifth Regiment, 223, 224
Massachusset Indians, 5
Matchett, Capt. John, 18, 21, 23
Matheson, Capt. John, 434
Mathews, Percy, 43–44, 46–47
Mayo, Mort, 361
McCann, Charles F. F., 454, 455
McCann, Helena (Mrs. Charles F. F.), 454, 455
McClure's, 174
McCurdy, Alex, 415, 418
McDonald, Capt. John, 138–139
McDougall, Daniel, xiv
McDougall, Jenifer, xiv
McGlade, Helen D., 177, 178, 179
McGrew, Dallas, 311
McKenzie, William N., 411
McManus, Tom, 322
McNeill, Capt. Hector, 22
McNutt, Kathleen, 514
McQuinn, Capt., 111
Meakin, Lewis H., 188
Mehlman, John G. ("Jack"), 207, 336, 384, 415, 416–417; death, 451; as sailor, 418, 422, 423, 434, 442
Mehlman Cottage, 183
Melka, Lieut. Leonard, 438–439
Mercer, Harry, 367, 370
Merchant, Epes, 515
Merchant, Joseph, 415
Merchant, Lewis, 410
Merola family, 469
Merrill, Octavius, 185

Merrill Hall, 182
Metcalf, Willard L., 190
Methodist Church ("Old Sloop"), 34
Midgets, boats, 428–429, 430, 434, 439
Miles, Gen. Nelson A., 232
Miller, Mr. and Mrs. Adair, 509, 516
Miller, Capt. Robert N. (Bobby), 213, 234, 240, 418
Millet, Capt. Tom, 32
Mills, Gen. Anson, 351
Milton Academy, 475
Minot's Ledge, 104
Monell, Donald F., xii, 468, 483, 516, 517
Montgomery, Nancy, 85
Moody, Congressman William H., 211, 214, 222
Moorland Hotel, 255
Moran, Edward, 185
Morgan, Pierpont, 349
Moriarty, Dr. John, 45
Morison, Samuel Eliot, 53, 63
Morrill, Carolyn (Cat Lady of Rockport), 356–357
Morris, Bill, 487–488, 489
Morrissey, Capt. Clayton, 431–434
Morrow, Dr. Herbert, 258–260
Morse, E.R., 38, 46, 47, 82, 128
Morse, Capt. Isaac P., 210
"Mother Ann Cottage," 240, 321
Mother Ann (rock), 240–241, 245, 270, 329–330, 355, 376
Mother Ann's Cow, 134–142, 172–174
Motif No. 1, 472
motion pictures at Eastern Point, 332–336, 360–363
Mount Pleasant Hill, 73
Mud, Peter, 7
Mulhaupt, Frederick, 191
Murray, Judith. See Stevens, Judith Sargent (Mrs. John Jr.)
Murray, Rev., 26
Murray, Rev. John, 19
Musician magazine, 516
Myopia Hunt Club, 222

N. M. Jackman, fire engine, 162, 258, 418
Nahant Dory Club, 415
Natale (Gavagnin), 288–289
National Register of Historic Places, 467
Native Americans, 4–6
Naumkeag (Salem), 7
"Nest on Ridge," 350

INDEX OF VESSELS